Lecture Notes in Computer Science 6156

Commenced Publication in 1973
Founding and Former Series Editors:
Gerhard Goos, Juris Hartmanis, and Jan van Leeuwen

AF731398

Editorial Board

David Hutchison
Lancaster University, UK

Takeo Kanade
Carnegie Mellon University, Pittsburgh, PA, USA

Josef Kittler
University of Surrey, Guildford, UK

Jon M. Kleinberg
Cornell University, Ithaca, NY, USA

Alfred Kobsa
University of California, Irvine, CA, USA

Friedemann Mattern
ETH Zurich, Switzerland

John C. Mitchell
Stanford University, CA, USA

Moni Naor
Weizmann Institute of Science, Rehovot, Israel

Oscar Nierstrasz
University of Bern, Switzerland

C. Pandu Rangan
Indian Institute of Technology, Madras, India

Bernhard Steffen
TU Dortmund University, Germany

Madhu Sudan
Microsoft Research, Cambridge, MA, USA

Demetri Terzopoulos
University of California, Los Angeles, CA, USA

Doug Tygar
University of California, Berkeley, CA, USA

Gerhard Weikum
Max-Planck Institute of Computer Science, Saarbruecken, Germany

M. Ali Babar   Matias Vierimaa
Markku Oivo (Eds.)

Product-Focused Software Process Improvement

11th International Conference, PROFES 2010
Limerick, Ireland, June 21-23, 2010
Proceedings

Springer

Volume Editors

M. Ali Babar
IT University of Copenhagen, Software Development Group
Rued Langgaards Vej 7, 2300 Copenhagen, Denmark
E-mail: maba@itu.dk

Matias Vierimaa
VTT Technical Research Centre of Finland
Kaitoväylä 1, 90571 Oulu, Finland
E-mail: matias.vierimaa@vtt.fi

Markku Oivo
University of Oulu, Department of Information Processing Science
P.O. Box 3000, 90014 Oulu, Finland
E-mail: markku.oivo@oulu.fi

Library of Congress Control Number: 2010928476

CR Subject Classification (1998): D.2, K.6, J.1, H.3, H.4, C.2.4

LNCS Sublibrary: SL 2 – Programming and Software Engineering

ISSN 0302-9743
ISBN-10 3-642-13791-1 Springer Berlin Heidelberg New York
ISBN-13 978-3-642-13791-4 Springer Berlin Heidelberg New York

This work is subject to copyright. All rights are reserved, whether the whole or part of the material is concerned, specifically the rights of translation, reprinting, re-use of illustrations, recitation, broadcasting, reproduction on microfilms or in any other way, and storage in data banks. Duplication of this publication or parts thereof is permitted only under the provisions of the German Copyright Law of September 9, 1965, in its current version, and permission for use must always be obtained from Springer. Violations are liable to prosecution under the German Copyright Law.

springer.com

© Springer-Verlag Berlin Heidelberg 2010
Printed in Germany

Typesetting: Camera-ready by author, data conversion by Scientific Publishing Services, Chennai, India
Printed on acid-free paper 06/3180

Preface

On behalf of the PROFES Organizing Committee we are proud to present the proceedings of the 11th International Conference on Product-Focused Software Process Improvement (PROFES 2010), held in Limerick, Ireland. Since the first conference in 1999 the conference has established its place in the software engineering community as a respected conference that brings together participants from academia and industry.

The roots of PROFES are in professional software process improvement motivated by product and service quality needs. The conference addresses both the solutions found in practice as well as relevant research results from academia. To ensure that PROFES retains its high quality and focus on the most relevant research issues, the conference has actively maintained close collaboration with industry and subsequently widened its scope to the research areas of collaborative and agile software development. The main themes of this year's conference were "Agile and Lean Processes" and "Engineering Service-Oriented Systems."

These two main themes enabled us to cover the contemporary software development demands and trends in a comprehensive manner and to tackle the most important current challenges identified by the software industry and software research community—namely, the shift of focus from "products" to "services."

The technical program featured invited talks, research papers, and experience reports on the most relevant topics related to processes for developing software-intensive services and products. In addition, a number of workshops and tutorials were hosted.

PROFES conferences have continuously attracted attendees from industry, research, and academia. This confirms that the conference covers topics which are up-to-date, important, and interesting. PROFES 2010 offered a unique forum for industry and academic professionals to discuss their needs and ideas, especially from the perspective of software as a business

The conference included two top keynote speakers: (1) Bashar Nuseibeh, Chief Scientist at Lero—The Irish Software Engineering Research Centre and (2) Christof Ebert, Managing Director at Vector Consulting Services.

PROFES 2010 also featured three workshops, four tutorials, a Doctoral Symposium, and panel discussions.

We wish to thank the University of Limerick, the IT University of Copenhagen, VTT Technical Research Center of Finland, the University of Oulu, and Fraunhofer IESE for supporting the conference. We are also grateful to the authors for their high-quality papers, the Program Committee for their hard work in reviewing the papers, the Organizing Committee for making the event possible, and we would especially like to thank Irja Kontio and Kaarina Karppinen from VTT for their valuable help in the proceedings finalization.

April 2010

M. Ali Babar
Matias Vierimaa

Organization

Profes 2010 was organized by the University of Limerick, VTT Technical Research Centre of Finland, University of Oulu, Fraunhofer IESE, and IT University of Copenhagen.

Organizing Committee

General Chair	Markku Oivo	University of Oulu, Finland
Program Chairs	M. Ali Babar	IT University of Copenhagen, Denmark
	Matias Vierimaa	VTT, Finland
Organizing Chair	Lorraine Morgan	Lero, University of Limerick, Ireland
Publicity Chair	Andreas Jedlitschka	Fraunhofer IESE, Germany
Publicity Co-chairs	Raimund Feldmann	Fraunhofer Center Maryland, USA
	Guilherme H. Travassos	COPPE/UFRJ, Brazil
	Katsuro Inoue	Osaka University, Japan
	Jacky Keung	NICTA, Australia
	Timo Koivumaki	VTT, Finland
	Xiaofeng Wang	Lero, Ireland
Short Papers and Poster Chairs	Tracy Hall	Brunel University, UK
	Jason Zhang	NICTA, Australia
Tutorial Chairs	Ken Power	Cisco, Ireland
	Rory O'Connor	DCU, Ireland
Doctoral Symposium Chairs	Martin Höst	Lund University, Sweden
	Mahmood Niazi	Keele University, UK
Panel Chair	Silvia Abrahão	Technical University of Valencia, Spain

Workshop Chairs	Davide Falessi	University of Rome "TorVergata", Italy
	Alok Mishra	Atilim University, Turkey
Webmaster	Klaas-Jan Stol	Lero, University of Limerick, Ireland

Program Committee

Zeiad Abdelnai	Garyounis University, IT College, Libya
Pekka Abrahamsson	University of Helsinki, Finland
Silvia Abrahão	Universidad Politécnica de Valencia, Spain
Teresa Baldassarre	University of Bari, Italy
Stefan Biffl	Technical University of Vienna, Austria
Andreas Birk	SWPM - Software.Process.Management, Germany
Luigi Buglione	ETS / Nexen Engineering Group, Italy
Danilo Caivano	University of Bari, Italy
Gerardo Canfora	University of Sannio, Italy
Jeff Carver	Alabama University, USA
Marcus Ciolkowski	Fraunhofer Institute for Experimental Software Engineering, Germany
Reidar Conradi	Norwegian University of Science and Technology, Norway
Beniamino Di Martino	Second University of Naples, Italy
Torgeir Dingsøyr	SINTEF, Norway
Marlon Dumas	University of Tartu, Estonia
Tore Dybå	SINTEF, Norway
Raimund Feldmann	Fraunhofer Center Maryland, USA
Paul Grunbacher	Johannes Kepler University Linz, Austria
Jens Heidrich	Fraunhofer Institute for Experimental Software Engineering, Germany
Frank Houdek	Daimler AG, Germany
Hajimu Iida	NAIST, Japan
Katsuro Inoue	Osaka University, Japan
Letizia Jaccheri	Norwegian University of Science and Technology, Norway
Michel Jaring	Fluxica, Finland
Erik Johansson	Ericsson Mobile Platforms, Sweden
Natalia Juristo	Universidad Politécnica de Madrid, Spain
Janne Järvinen	F-Secure, Finland
Pasi Kuvaja	University of Oulu, Finland
Kari Känsälä	Nokia, Finland
Casper Lassenius	Alto University, Finland
Marek Leszak	Alcatel-Lucent, Germany
Jingyue Li	Norwegian University of Science and Technology, Norway

Lech Madeyski	Wroclaw University of Technology, Poland
Kenichi Matsumoto	Nara Institute of Science and Technology, Japan
Makoto Matsushita	Osaka University, Japan
Maurizio Morisio	Politecnico di Torino, Italy
Mark Müller	Robert Bosch GmbH, Germany
Jürgen Münch	Fraunhofer IESE, Germany
Haruka Nakao	Japan Manned Space Systems Corporation, Japan
Makoto Nonaka	Toyo University, Tokyo, Japan
Paolo Panaroni	INTECS, Italy
Dietmar Pfahl	University of Oslo, Norway
Minna Pikkarainen	VTT, Finland
Teade Punter	Embedded Systems Institute (ESI), The Netherlands
Austen Rainer	University of Hertfordshire, UK
Ita Richardson	Lero, University of Limerick, Ireland
Daniel Rodriguez	University of Alcalá, Spain
Barbara Russo	Free University of Bolzano-Bozen, Italy
Outi Salo	Nokia, Finland
Klaus Schmid	University of Hildesheim, Germany
Kurt Schneider	Leibniz Universität Hannover, Germany
Michael Stupperich	Daimler AG, Germany
Guilherme Travassos	COPPE/UFRJ, Brazil
Markku Tukiainen	University of Joensuu, Finland
Mark van den Brand	Eindhoven University of Technology, The Netherlands
Rini van Solingen	Delft University of Technology, The Netherlands
Sira Vegas	Universidad de Politecnica de Madrid, Spain
Hironori Washizaki	National Institute of Informatics, Japan
Claes Wohlin	Blekinge Institute of Technology, Sweden

Table of Contents

Keynote Addresses

Software Quality Assurance I

Agile Software Development

Software Quality Assurance II

Software Business

Software Systems

Process Quality I

Software Measurement

Process Quality II

Software Process Improvement

Mobile Privacy Requirements on Demand

Bashar Nuseibeh

Lero - The Irish Software Engineering Research Centre

Process and product improvements are noble goals. Structured, document-driven processes have played an important part in the development of some mission critical systems. Likewise, agile and lean development processes are showing increasing promise in competitive, changing environments. The 'software as a service' paradigm is adding a further challenging dimension to the mix, and is redefining the notion of a software product.

However, in this talk, I argue that an increasingly important kind of development needs our attention - one that focuses on the quality of the software (product) experience. As mobile and ubiquitous computing technology becomes a reality in everyday life, such technology is able to offer individual users a very personal and personalised set of services and experiences, with their own set of concerns and requirements. In our quest to ensure that the required service functionality is delivered, we risk neglecting how best to achieve the desired quality of service and user experience. This is an area that raises many difficult research questions and challenges. In my talk I will focus on some issues drawn from my own experience in requirements engineering and ubiquitous computing. In particular, I examine the socially and technically challenging topic of privacy in a mobile computing, and suggest that we need new development processes and methods to enable the elicitation and development of privacy requirements. I will present a number of qualitative empirical studies that explore how "requirements engineering in the wild" may be better suited to eliciting mobile privacy requirements than traditional requirements elicitation processes - agile, lean or otherwise...

M. Ali Babar, M. Vierimaa, and M. Oivo (Eds.): PROFES 2010, LNCS 6156, p. 1, 2010.

Lean Development - Potentials, Principles and Practices

Christof Ebert

Vector Consulting Services

To survive in a fast changing environment, we need to continuously improve productivity, reduce rework, and optimize product strategies. Lean development and lean management offers the right ingredients: Eliminating waste, empowering teams, delivering as fast as possible, seeing the whole. But there is a dark side, as recent industry experiences show. Too lean is mean. Lean often fails due to lack of vision, misalignment and insufficient execution. It is thus crucial for companies to successfully manage change towards lean development. This keynote will introduce to lean principles and practices. It will draw upon experiences from a variety of industries with topics such as lean transition, introducing new tools, improving engineering processes, and setting up a global software organization. A change check is provided so that participantscan address their specific challenges.

M. Ali Babar, M. Vierimaa, and M. Oivo (Eds.): PROFES 2010, LNCS 6156, p. 2, 2010.

A Qualitative Survey of Regression Testing Practices

Emelie Engström and Per Runeson

Department of Computer Science, Lund University, SE-221 00 LUND, Sweden
{Emelie.Engstrom,Per.Runeson}@cs.lth.se

Abstract. *Aim*: Regression testing practices in industry have to be better understood, both for the industry itself and for the research community. *Method*: We conducted a qualitative industry survey by i) running a focus group meeting with 15 industry participants and ii) validating the outcome in an on line questionnaire with 32 respondents. *Results*: Regression testing needs and practices vary greatly between and within organizations and at different stages of a project. The importance and challenges of automation is clear from the survey. *Conclusions*: Most of the findings are general testing issues and are not specific to regression testing. Challenges and good practices relate to test automation and testability issues.

Keywords: Regression testing, Survey, Industry practice.

1 Introduction

Regression testing is retesting of previously working software after a change to ensure that unchanged software is still functioning as before the change. According to IEEE, regression testing is *Selective retesting of a system or component to verify that modifications have not caused unintended effects and that the system or components still complies with its specified requirements* [1]. The need for effective strategies for regression testing increases with the increasing use of iterative development strategies and systematic reuse in software projects. Studies indicate that 80% of testing cost is regression testing and more than 50% of software maintenance cost is related to testing [2].

There is a gap between research and practices of regression testing. Research on regression testing mainly focuses on selection and prioritization of test cases. Several techniques for regression test selection are proposed and evaluated. Engström *et al.* reviewed the literature in the field recently [3] and highlights the importance of the test context to the outcome of regression testing techniques. Only few empirical evaluations of regression test selection techniques are carried out in a real industrial context [4], [5], [6].

However industry practice on regression testing is mostly based on experience alone, and not on systematic approaches. There is a need for researchers to better understand the needs and practices in industry. Rooksby *et al.* [7] argue for the need for investigation and characterization of real world work. They conclude

M. Ali Babar, M. Vierimaa, and M. Oivo (Eds.): PROFES 2010, LNCS 6156, pp. 3–16, 2010.
© Springer-Verlag Berlin Heidelberg 2010

that improvements of current testing practices are meaningful in its specific local context and "cannot be brought about purely through technically driven innovation". In their paper they highlight, based on experiences from testing in four real projects, that improvements in industry are not always sophisticated and accurate as is often pursued in research.

In order to retrieve a better understanding of real world needs and practices, a qualitative survey [8, p. 61-78] of industry practice of regression testing is conducted, by means of focus group discussions in a software process improvement network (SPIN) and a questionnaire to validate the results. Issues discussed in the focus group were definitions and practices of regression testing in industry as well as challenges and improvement suggestions. A total of 46 software engineers from 38 different organizations participated in the focus group and questionnaire survey. Results are qualitative and of great value in that they highlight relevant and possible directions for future research.

To the extent of our knowledge no industrial surveys on regression testing practices have been reported on. However experience reports on regression testing in industrial software development projects can be found [9]. Onoma *et al.* conclude that regression testing is used extensively and that several companies develop in-house regression testing tools to automate the process. Re-test all is a common approach and the selection of test cases is not a critical issue.

When it comes to testing practices in general a couple of industrial surveys have been undertaken [10], [11], [12], [13], concluding that test automation is a key improvement issue [13] and that test case selection for continuous regression testing is a hard task. No systematic approach for test case selection was used by the companies but instead they relied on the developers expertise and judgment [12].

This paper is organized as follows: Section 2 describes how the survey is conducted and discusses validity issues. In section 3 results are presented and analyzed. Finally conclusions are provided in section 4.

2 Method Description

The study's overall goal is to characterize current regression testing practices in industry for the sake of research. It also aims at identifying good practices for spreading across different companies as well as areas in need for improvement within the companies and possibly identification of future research topics. Hence, a qualitative survey is found appropriate [8, p. 61-78]. The research questions for the survey are:

RQ1 What is meant by *regression testing* in industry?
RQ2 Which *problems* or *challenges* related to regression testing exist?
RQ3 Which *good practices* on regression testing exist?

The survey is conducted using two different research methods, one focus group discussion [14, p. 284-289] in a SPIN group, and one questionnaire in a testing interest network. The focus group was used to identify concepts and issues related to regression testing, while the questionnaire was used to validate the findings in a different setting. A similar approach was used for a unit testing survey in 2006 [12].

2.1 Focus Group

The focus group meeting was arranged at one of the monthly meetings of SPIN-syd, a software process improvement network in Southern Sweden [15]. The members of the network were invited to a 2.5 hour session on regression testing in May 2009. 15 industry participants accepted the invitation, which is about the normal size for a SPIN-syd monthly meeting, and the same as for our previous unit testing survey [12]. The focus group meeting was moderated by two academics and one industry participant, and observed by a third academic. An overview of the focus group participants is shown in Table 1.

Table 1. Participants in focus group meeting. Number of developers in the surveyed company: extra small is 1, small is 2 – 19, medium is 20 – 99, and large 100 – 999.

Company	Domain	Size	Role
A	Automation	Medium	Participant
A	Automation	Medium	Participant
A	Automation	Medium	Participant
G	Medical devices	Medium	Participant
G	Medical devices	Medium	Participant
I	Information systems	Large	Moderator
I	Information systems	Large	Participant
S	Telecom	Large	Participant
S	Telecom	Large	Participant
E	Telecom	Large	Participant
X	Consultant	Extra small	Participant
C	Consultant	Extra small	Participant
Q	Consultant	Medium	Participant
K	Consultant	Medium	Participant
O	Consultant	Large	Participant
L	Academics	N/A	Researcher
L	Academics	N/A	Researcher
L	Academics	N/A	Observer

The industry participants represented automation, medical devices, information systems (IS), and telecom domains. Consultants also participated which were working with testing for their clients. The product companies all produce embedded software and were both of medium and large size, while consultancy firms of all sizes were represented.

The session was organized around five questions:

- What is regression testing?
- When do the participants regression test?
- How do the participants regression test?

- What are the participants' problems regarding regression testing?
- What are the participants' strengths regarding regression testing?

For each of the questions, the moderator asked the participants to write their answers on post-it charts. Then each participant presented his or her view of the question and the responses were documented on white boards.

After the session, key findings were identified using qualitative analysis methods. Statements were grouped into themes, primarily structured by the five questions, and secondary according to keywords in the statements. Further, the results were restructured and turned into questions for use in the questionnaire.

2.2 Questionnaire

The resulting questionnaire consists of 45 questions on what regression testing is, with five-level Likert-scale response alternatives: *Strongly disagree, Disagree, Neutral, Agree, Strongly Agree* and an additional *Not Applicable* option (see Fig 1). One question on automation vs manual used five scale alternatives from *Automated* to *Manual* (see Fig 2). Further, 29 questions on satisfaction with regression testing practices in the respondents' organizations had the response alternatives *Very Satisfied, Satisfied, Neutral, Dissatisfied, Very Dissatisfied* and *Not Applicable* (see Fig 3). The questionnaire was defined in the SurveyGizmo questionnaire tool for on line data collection [16].

Respondents were invited through the SAST network (Swedish Association for Software Testing) through their quarterly newsletter, which is distributed to some 2.000 testers in Sweden, representing a wide range of company sizes and application domains. Respondents were promised an individual benchmarking report if more than three participants from one company responded, and a chance for everybody to win a half-day seminar on testing given by the second author. Thirty-two respondents answered the complete questionnaire, which are presented in Table 2.

The respondents cover the range of company sizes and domains. Out of the 32 respondents, 9 were developing embedded systems in particular within the telecom domain, 12 developed information systems in particular within the domains of business intelligence and finance, and 11 were consultants. Out of 21 product companies, 3 represent small development organizations, 9 represent medium sized organizations and 8 represent large organizations. The size of the consultancy organizations are not specifically relevant, but is reported to indicate the variation.

2.3 Threats to Validity

The study does not aim at providing a statistically valid view of a certain population of companies, as intended with general surveys [8]. The research questions are focused on existence and not on frequencies of responses. Hence, we consider the survey having more character of multiple case studies on a certain aspect of several cases and consequently we discuss threats to validity from a case study perspective [17].

Question	Item	Strongly disagree	Disagree	Neutral	Agree	Strongly agree
What is regression testing?	1. Repetitive tests	0	3	3	14	11
	2. Retest of functionality	0	0	1	8	22
	3. Reexecution of testcases	0	1	7	12	11
	4. Same as system testing	11	12	4	2	1
Why is regression testing applied?	5. To assess if the system has the desired properties	1	12	6	8	5
	6. To find defects	0	4	4	15	9
	7. To ensure that nothing has been affected or destroyec	0	0	0	2	30
	8. To guide further priorities in the project	1	9	9	11	0
What kinds of changes generate regression testing?	9. New versions	0	0	3	11	18
	10. New configurations	0	1	7	11	12
	11. Fixes	0	0	6	9	16
	12. Changed solutions	0	1	3	8	18
	13. New hardware	1	5	5	8	11
	14. New platforms	1	3	4	6	17
	15. New designs	0	1	7	9	15
	16. New interfaces	0	2	4	10	15
	17. RT is applied regardless of changes	3	12	6	5	5
At which levels are RT carried out?	18. Single components	3	4	7	11	4
	19. Single modules	1	3	5	15	5
	20. Whole system	0	0	1	9	22
When in the development process is RT applied?	21. As early as possible	3	6	6	7	7
	22. Continuosly during the whole process	1	4	5	11	9
	23. At the end	3	1	3	9	16
	24. Daily	8	11	6	2	1
	25. At each software integration	3	4	9	9	5
	26. At each milestone	1	6	6	9	6
	27. Before each release	0	0	1	9	22
	28. As often as we have resources	6	9	5	6	3
What determines the amount and frequency of RT?	29. The assessed risk	0	0	3	14	13
	30. The amount of new functionality	0	2	2	15	12
	31. The amount of fixes	0	2	3	16	9
	32. The amount of available resources	4	6	6	8	6
Which tests are used in regression testing?	33. A selection of developer's tests	5	10	6	6	2
	34. A selection of tester's tests	0	2	1	21	8
	35.A selection from a specific regression test suite	0	4	1	8	18
	36. New test cases are designed	1	9	8	12	2
How are regression test cases selected?	37. The same tests are run each time	1	4	13	8	6
	38. Selection depends on the situation	0	4	6	13	9
	39. We do a complete retest each time	2	8	12	3	6
	40. We do a complete retest of safety critical parts	0	2	9	10	8
	41. Test cases on changes and possible side effects	1	2	5	14	10
	42. A selection is made ad hoc	9	12	7	3	0
	43. Run as many as possible from a prioritized list	4	9	7	6	4
	44. We focus on functional test cases	0	2	8	14	8
	45. We execute smoke test	1	4	11	10	5

Fig. 1. Number of responses for each questionnaire alternative on regression test practices

Construct validity concerns the underlying constructs of the research, i.e. terms and concepts under study. We mitigated construct validity threats by having the first question of the focus group related to terminology and concepts. Thereby, we ensured a common understanding for the rest of the group meeting. In the

Question	Manual		Equal		Automated
46. How do you execute regression tests?	8	2	15	4	3

Fig. 2. Number of responses for each questionnaire alternative on automated vs. manual regression testing

Question	Item	Very dissatisfied	Dissatisfied	Neutral	Satisfied	Very satisfied
How satisfied are you with following in your organization?	47. Processes/practices for change impact analysis	4	7	9	10	1
	48. Assessment of the extent of test coverage	2	6	12	8	2
	49. Assessment of the amount of required tests	1	4	11	14	1
	50. Prioritization of test cases wrt product risks	1	3	9	16	3
	51. Prioritization of test cases wrt fault detection ability	0	4	13	10	2
	52. Time to design good test cases	4	6	9	10	1
	53. Methods/tool support to design good test cases	3	12	9	4	4
	54. Assessment of cost/benifit of automating RT	3	11	12	2	4
	55. Time to RT	3	12	7	7	2
	56. Balance between manual and automated RT	3	14	4	4	4
	57. Execution of automated RT	2	12	8	2	3
	58. Environment for automated RT	2	14	7	3	2
	59. Execution of manual RT	0	2	9	19	0
	60. RT in real target environment	0	4	8	15	4
	61. RT in simulated target environment	0	5	9	13	3
	62. RT of GUI	2	5	7	15	2
	63. RT of data base applications	1	4	10	13	0
	64. RT of third party products	1	5	15	6	0
	65. Consistentcy of verdict reporting	0	3	14	11	1
	66. Time to analyze results	1	3	15	12	1
	67. Processes/practices for analyzing results	1	5	14	10	1
	68. Presentation of results from automated tests	2	8	6	5	4
	69. Maintenance of tests in case of changes in products	3	7	13	8	1
	70. Methods/tool for traceability between TC and reqs	6	9	6	7	3
	71. Minimization of redundant tests (wrt test coverage)	2	10	8	11	0
	72. Coordination between designers and testers	1	1	8	21	1
	73. Minimization of dependencies in the system	1	12	12	6	0
	74. Modularization of the system	0	9	15	7	0
	75. Testability issues in design guidelines	2	9	14	5	0

Fig. 3. Number of responses for each questionnaire alternative on satisfaction with regression test practices

survey, however, the terms may be interpreted differently and this is out of control of the researchers.

Internal validity relates to identification of casual relationships. We do not study any casual relationships in the study, and we just briefly touch upon correlations between factors. Patterns in the data that might indicate correlations are interpreted conservatively in order not to over interpret the data.

Table 2. Respondents to the questionnaire. Number of developers in the surveyed company: extra small is 1, small is 2 – 19, medium is 20 – 99, and large 100 – 999.

Company	Size	Domain
Me	Small	Automation
Te	Medium	Automation
V	Large	Automotive
Tc	Small	Business intelligence
Ql	Medium	Business intelligence
Ti	Medium	Business intelligence
C	Large	Consultant
Ha	Large	Consultant
H	Large	Consultant
H	Large	Consultant
Q	Medium	Consultant
R	Small	Consultant
K	Medium	Consultant
Si	Large	Consultant
So	Large	Consultant
T	Small	Consultant
Tp	Medium	Consultant
Eu	Medium	Finance
Sk	Large	Finance
A	Medium	Finance
U	Medium	Information systems
Sm	Medium	Information systems
W	Small	Information systems
B	Large	Information systems
L	Large	Insurance
Mu	Large	Insurance
Ma	Large	Medical devices
E	Large	Telecom
Hi	Medium	Telecom
M	Medium	Telecom
S	Large	Telecom
S	Large	Telecom

External validity relates to generalization from the findings. We do not attempt to generalize in a statistical sense; any generalization possible is analytical generalization [17]. In order to help such generalization, we report characteristics of the focus group members and questionnaire respondents in Tables 1 and 2.

3 Analysis of the Results

The focus group and survey results were analyzed using the Zachman framework, which originally was presented for analysis of information systems architectures [18]. The framework has six categories, *what, how, where, who, when* and *why,* although these terms were not originally used. For each category, questions are defined and tailored to the domain under investigation. Originally intended for IS development, Zachman proposed that it might be used for developing new approaches to system development [18]. We use it similar to Runeson [12], i.e. to structure the outcome of the focus group meetings and to define the validation questionnaire, although we primarily focus on *what, how* and *when.*

An overview of the questionnaire results is shown in Figures 1, 2 and 3. Questions are referred to in the text as [Qx] for question x. The analysis is then presented according to the framework questions and identified strengths and weaknesses in subsections 3.1 to 3.4.

3.1 What?

There is good agreement in the focus group and among the survey respondents regarding what regression testing is. Regression testing involves repetitive tests and aims to verify that previously working software still works after changes to other parts. Focus can be either re-execution of test cases or retest of functionality. As for testing in general the goal of the regression testing may differ between different organizations or parts of an organization. The goal may be either to find defects or to obtain a measure of its quality. Regression testing shall ensure that nothing has been affected or destroyed, and give an answer to whether the software has achieved the desired functionality, quality and stability etc. In the focus group discussion, an additional goal of regression testing was mentioned as well; to obtain a guide for further priorities in the project. Regression testing offers a menu of what can be prioritized in the project, such as bug fixes. This additional goal was only confirmed to some extent by 35% of the respondents [Q8].

Different kinds of changes to the system generate regression testing. Mentioned in the focus group discussion and confirmed by the majority of the respondents were: new versions, new configurations, fixes, changed solutions, new hardware, new platforms, new designs and new interfaces [Q9-16]. One third of the respondents, mostly small and medium sized organizations, indicated that regression testing is applied regardless of changes, while in larger organizations, regression testing was tighter connected to changes [Q17]. The amount and frequency of regression testing is determined by the assessed risk, the amount of new functionality, the amount of fixes and the amount of available resources. The first three factors are confirmed by the majority of the respondents [Q29-31] while the agreement on the dependency on resources availability varies to a greater extent among the respondents [Q32].

3.2 When?

Regression testing is carried out at different levels (e.g. module level, component level and system level [Q18-20]) and at different stages of the development process. From focus group discussions it was found that that some organizations regression test as early as possible while other regression test as late as possible in the process, and some claimed that regression testing is continuously carried out throughout the whole development process. The purpose may be slightly different for the three options; early regression test to enable early detection of defects, and late regression testing for certification or type approval purposes.

How often regression testing is carried out differed as well; some organizations regression test daily while others regression test at each software integration, at each milestone, or before releases [Q24-26]. In some cases the availability of resources is determinant. Among the questionnaire responses, there were large variations on how often regression testing is applied. The most common approach is to regression test before releases (indicated by 95% of the respondents) [Q27]. Only 10% of the respondents regression test daily [Q24].

3.3 How?

From the focus group discussions it was identified that tests used for regression testing may be a selection of developer's tests, a selection of tester's tests, a selection of tests from a specific regression test suite, or new test cases are designed. According to questionnaire responses, the most common is to reuse test cases designed by testers. Strategies for regression test selection mentioned in the focus group were: complete retest, combine static and dynamic selection, complete retest of safety critical parts, select test cases concentrating on changes and possible side effects, ad-hoc selection, smoke test, prioritize and run as many as possible, and focus on functional test cases. Questionnaire results confirm that it is common to run a set of specified regression test cases every time, together with a set of situation dependent test cases. Ad-hoc selection seems not to be a common approach; only 10% of the respondents indicate that approach [Q42]. 70% of the respondents confirm the focus on functional test cases [Q44] and 50% confirm the usage of smoke tests [Q45].

A project may include several different regression testing activities. Both manual and automatic regression testing are applied. 50% of the respondents indicate an equal amount of manual and automatic regression testing while 30% perform regression testing exclusively manually [Q46].

3.4 Weaknesses and Strengths

The focus group had an open discussion about both weaknesses and strengths in their regression testing practices, and it showed that in several cases representatives from one organization had solution proposals where others had problems. Some problems were common to most of the participants (e.g. lack of time and resources to regression test and insufficient tool support) while others were more specific. The outcome of the discussion was a list of 29 possible problem areas which were validated in the questionnaire.

Test case selection. Several problems related to test case selection were discussed in the focus group. It was mentioned that it is hard to assess the impact of changes on existing code and to make a good selection. It is hard to prioritize test cases with respect to product risks and fault detection ability, and to be confident in not missing safety critical faults. Determining the required amount of tests was also considered a problem, and it is hard to assess the test coverage.

Participants wished for a regression test suite with standard test cases and for regression testing guidelines at different stages of a project with respect to quality aspects. Some participants were satisfied with their impact analysis and with their test management systems. As a response to the test selection problem, exploratory testing was recommended and also to have a static test set used for each release. No specific test selection technique was referred to, such as the ones reviewed by Engström *et al.* [3].

The results from the questionnaire responses are in this respect not conclusive. The responses are divided evenly across the whole spectrum, with a slight shift towards satisfaction. However, in terms of processes for impact analysis and assessment of test coverage the challenges identified in the focus group where confirmed by a third of the respondents even though as many were satisfied. [Q47-51].

Test case design. Lack of time and resources for regression testing was a recurring complaint in the discussions. So also in the case for test case design. Among respondents to the survey were as many satisfied as dissatisfied in this matter [Q52]. One proposal mentioned in the focus group was to focus on test driven development and thus make developers take test responsibility, hence building test automation into the development process, which may be reused for regression testing purposes as well.

Automated and manual regression testing. Automating regression testing causes problems and manual testing is time and resource consuming. Both problems and proposals were discussed in the focus group. Within the focus group, participants were satisfied and dissatisfied with automation as well as with their manual testing. Most participants wanted a better balance between automated and manual testing and support in determining cost benefit of automating regression testing.

It is not only costs for implementing the automated tests that need to be considered, but also costs for maintaining the test suites and in many cases manual analysis of results. It was proposed to define interfaces for automation below the user interface level in order to avoid frequent changes of the test scripts, due to user interface changes. Use of manual testing was recommended for testing of user experience and for exploratory testing.

The problems of automation was confirmed by questionnaire responses. 60% of the respondents were dissatisfied with the balance between manual and automated regression testing [Q56], the assessment of cost/benefit, execution of automated regression tests as well as the environment for automated regression testing. In contrast, as many were satisfied with their manual testing, 60% [Q59].

Regression testing problem areas. Specific problem areas for regression testing, mentioned in the discussion forum were: regression tests in real target environment and in simulated target environment, regression testing of third party products and of GUI's. For each problem mentioned, were among the participants both those who had problems and those who were satisfied with their solutions. None of the problem areas was confirmed by a majority of negative answers in the questionnaire even though between 10-25% were dissatisfied in each case [Q60-64]. As testing of databases is subject to regression testing research, this area was added to the questionnaire, although not mentioned in the focus group.

Test results. Several of the participants in the focus group were unsatisfied with how test results were presented and analyzed. In many cases verdict reporting is inconsistent and often there is no time to do a thorough analysis. Some participants said that their reporting of results and analysis works well and gave examples of good factors, such as having an independent quality department and having software quality attributes connected to each test case, which is good not only for for reporting results but also for prioritization and selection of test cases.

The questionnaire responses were generally neutral regarding consistency of verdict reporting and processes and practices for analyzing results, but agreed that practices for presentation of results from automated tests were not good enough [Q68].

Test suite maintenance. The focus group named maintenance of test suites and test cases as a problem. Participants stated that much of the regression testing is redundant with respect to test coverage and that there is a lack of traceability from tests to requirements. Some of the participants were satisfied with their tools and processes for traceability and claimed that they are good at maintenance of test cases in case of changes in the product. A recommendation was to have independent review teams reviewing the test protocols.

Questionnaire responses confirmed the lack of good tools for documenting traceability between test cases and requirements but otherwise the variation in the responses to the questions regarding maintenance was great [Q69-71].

Testability. An issue brought up in the focus group were the amount of dependencies in the software and its relation to testability. Participants expressed a wish for a test friendly design where the structure enables a simple delimitation of relevant tests. There is a need for design guidelines considering testability, modularization of the software and clearer dependencies in order to make it easier to set test scopes.

Questionnaire responses indicate satisfaction with coordination/communication between designers and testers [Q72] and neutrality to modularization of the system [Q74]. Further they confirmed the need for minimization of dependencies in the system [Q73] as well as for testability issues in design guidelines [Q75].

Test planning. Finally some needs and recommendations regarding the test planning was given. Again a cost model was asked for: *It would be nice to have a cost model for environments and technical infrastructure covering; automated testing, test data, test rigs, unit tests, functional tests, performance tests, target/simulator and test coverage.*

Everyone in the focus group agreed that it is better to test continuously than in large batches. A rule of thumb is to plan for as much test time as development time even when the project is delayed. It is also good to have a process with a flexible scope for weekly regression tests, e.g. core automated scope, user scenarios, main regression scope, dynamic scope, dynamic exploratory scope etc. In order to broaden the coverage, it was proposed to vary the test focus between different test rounds.

4 Conclusions

Regression testing increases in software projects as software becomes more and more complex with increasing emphasis on systematic reuse and shorter development cycles. Many of the challenges, highlighted in the study, are *not* specific to regression testing but are general to all testing. However, they have a significant impact on how effective the regression testing becomes. Questions involving automated testing is of course particularly important for regression testing, as the same tests are repeated many times. Similarly, a test-friendly design is of great importance when one wants to do a selective retesting. Literature on regression testing tends to focus on the selection of test cases based on changes in the code, but for practitioners it does not seem to be the most important issue.

Regression testing definitions (RQ1) are very much the same across all surveyed companies and in line with formal definitions [1] although the regression testing practices differ. Regression testing is applied differently in different organizations, at different stages of a project, at different levels and with varying frequency. Regression testing is not an isolated one-off activity, but rather an activity of varying scope and preconditions, strongly dependent on the context in which it is applied. In most development organizations, regression testing is applied continuously and at several levels with varying goals. This further underlines the need for industrial evaluations of regression testing strategies, where context information is clearly reported, as was previously noted [3].

Regression testing challenges (RQ2) relate to test case selection, trade-offs between automated and manual testing and design for testability. Issues related to test automation are:

- Assessment of cost/benefit of test automation
- Environment for automated testing and the presentation of test results.

Design issues affect regression testing since there is a strong relation between the effort needed for regression testing and the software design. Design for testability, including modularization with well defined and observable interfaces, helps verifying modules and their impact on the system. This could be addressed by including testability in design guidelines. Except for the design issues, coordination and communication between designers and testers work well.

Good practices (RQ3) were also reported on:

- Run automated daily tests on module level.
- Focus automation below user interface.
- Visualize progress monitoring.

These practices are not specific to regression testing. The latter item is not specific testing at all, but is a management practice that becomes critical to regression testing as it constitutes a key part of the development project progress. This indicates that regression testing should not be addressed nor researched in isolation; rather it should be an important aspect of software testing practice and research to take into account.

Acknowledgment

The authors would like to thank Per Beremark for moderating the focus group meeting and to all participants in the focus group and questionnaire. The work is partly funded by The Swedish Governmental Agency for Innovation Systems (VINNOVA) in the UPPREPA project under grant 2005-02483, and partly by the Swedish Research Council under grant 622-2004-552 for a senior researcher position in software engineering.

References

1. IEEE: IEEE standard for software test documentation. IEEE Std(829-1983, Revision) (1998)
2. Chittimalli, P.K., Harrold, M.J.: Recomputing coverage information to assist regression testing. IEEE Transactions on Software Engineering 35(4), 452–469 (2009)
3. Engström, E., Runeson, P., Skoglund, M.: A systematic review on regression test selection techniques. Information and Software Technology 52(1), 14–30 (2010)
4. Engström, E., Runeson, P., Wikstrand, G.: An empirical evaluation of regression testing based on fix-cache recommendations. In: Proceedings of the 3rd International Conference on Software Testing Verification and Validation, pp. 75–78 (2010)
5. Skoglund, M., Runeson, P.: A case study of the class firewall regression test selection technique on a large scale distributed software system. In: International Symposium on Empirical Software Engineering., pp. 72–81 (2005)
6. White, L., Robinson, B.: Industrial real-time regression testing and analysis using firewalls. In: Proceedings 20th IEEE International Conference on Software Maintenance, pp. 18–27 (2004)
7. Rooksby, J., Rouncefield, M., Sommerville, I.: Testing in the wild: The social and organisational dimensions of real world practice. Computer Supported Cooperative Work (CSCW) 18(5), 559–580 (2009)
8. Flink, A.: The survey handbook, 2nd edn. SAGE Publications, Thousand Oaks (2003)
9. Onoma, A.K., Tsai, W.T., Poonawala, M.H., Suganuma, H.: Regression testing in an industrial environment: Progress is attained by looking backward. Association for Computing Machinery. Communications of the ACM 41(5), 81–86 (1998)

10. Causevic, A., Sundmark, D., Punnekkat, S.: An industrial survey on contemporary aspects of software testing. In: Proceedings of the 3rd International Conference on Software Testing Verification and Validation, pp. 393–401 (2010)
11. Grindal, M., Offutt, J., Mellin, J.: On the testing maturity of software producing organizations. In: Testing: Academia & Industry Conference-Practice And Research Techniques, TAIC/PART (2006)
12. Runeson, P.: A survey of unit testing practices. IEEE Software 23(4), 22 (2006)
13. Runeson, P., Andersson, C., Höst, M.: Test processes in software product evolution - a qualitative survey on the state of practice. Journal of Software Maintenance and Evolution: Research and Practice 15, 41–59 (2003)
14. Robson, C.: Real World Research, 2nd edn. Blackwell Publishing, Malden (2002)
15. Runeson, P., Beremark, P., Larsson, B., Lundh, E.: SPIN-syd - a non-profit exchange network. In: 1st International Workshop on Software Engineering Networking Experiences, Joensuu, Finland (2006)
16. Surveygizmo (December 2009) a web tool for questionnaires and polls, `http://www.surveygizmo.com`
17. Runeson, P., Höst, M.: Guidelines for conducting and reporting case study research in software engineering. Empirical Software Engineering 14(2), 131–164 (2009)
18. Zachman, J.A.: A framework for information systems architecture. IBM Systems Journal 26(3), 276–293 (1987)

Investigating the Temporal Behavior of Defect Detection in Software Inspection and Inspection-Based Testing

Dietmar Winkler, Stefan Biffl, and Kevin Faderl

Vienna University of Technology, Institute of Software Technology
Favoritenstrasse 9-11/188, A-1040 Vienna, Austria
{Dietmar.Winkler,Stefan.Biffl,Kevin.Faderl}@qse.ifs.tuwien.ac.at

Abstract. A major goal of analytical quality assurance (QA) activities, e.g., inspection and testing, is detecting defects in software artifacts to increase product quality and decrease rework effort and cost. Inspection aims at identifying defects early and traditional testing focuses on test case generation and execution late in the development process. Combining inspection and test-case generation to inspection-based testing (UBT-i) can help identifying defects early, increasing testability by systematically capturing requirements and quality attributes, and generating most valuable test cases based on inspection results. This paper reports on a controlled experiment to investigate the temporal behavior of UBR inspection and inspection-based testing regarding defect detection performance, i.e., effectiveness, efficiency, and false positives. Main findings of the study are that there are no significant advantages of UBR and UBT-i regarding defect detection performance and the temporal behavior of defect detection delivered contradictory results in two sessions of the study.

Keywords: Software Inspection, Inspection-based Testing, Temporal Behavior of Defect Detection, Controlled Experiment.

1 Introduction

Defects can have a high negative impact on the software quality of deliverables and can result in high rework effort and costs, even if defects are detected late in the development process [16]. Modern software engineering approaches include (a) software processes (e.g., V-Modell XT, Rational Unified Process, and agile development practices) to plan, monitor and control the sequences of steps within a software development project, (b) constructive approaches to efficiently construct artifacts (e.g., specification documents, test cases, and software components), and (c) analytical approaches to verify and validate deliverables with respect to given specification documents and customer requirements. In general, a common goal of analytical quality assurance approaches is to identify defects early.

Software inspection (SI) is a well-investigated and established approach for defect detection in all phases of software development [6], [13]. SI is applicable to all software engineering artifacts because no executable software code is required for inspection application. Reading techniques [12], e.g., checklists, perspectives, and use cases support reviewers and inspectors in systematically reading the artifact under inspection by providing the defect detection process actively [23]. Software testing requires

M. Ali Babar, M. Vierimaa, and M. Oivo (Eds.): PROFES 2010, LNCS 6156, pp. 17–31, 2010.
© Springer-Verlag Berlin Heidelberg 2010

textual requirements, specifications, models, and executable software code to construct and execute defined test cases. Thus, test case execution is located even late in the development process. Traditional testing approaches include test case definition and test execution [10]. The concept of test-driven (test-first) development (TDD) [4], an established approach in agile software development practice, leads to closing the temporal gap between test case generation and execution because test cases are generated prior or at least in parallel to code construction [4]. Nevertheless, we believe that software inspection, embedded within a testing approach, can support test-case generation for TDD by systematically identifying defects and generating test cases in parallel. Thus, bundling the benefits from SI and software testing [5] can lead to synergy effects regarding defect detection performance and test case generation.

Nevertheless, project and quality managers have to identify best-practice approaches for a most valuable application of selected verification and validation (V&V) approaches [7] because these activities require additional effort. Thus, an important question is whether or not, an inspection-based testing approach can provide additional benefits with respect to defect detection and test case generation. Another question includes the required effort to achieve best cost/benefit defect detection performance and the temporal behavior of defect detection. In this paper we apply two V&V approaches, best-practice software inspection with usage-based reading (UBR) and inspection-based testing (UBT-i), to investigate the temporal behavior of defect detection effectiveness, efficiency, and false positives in a controlled experiment. Temporal behavior refers to measuring defect detection performance in defined time intervals (30 minutes intervals for effectiveness and false positives and efficiency as defects found per hour) as a reasonable granularity of observing the temporal behavior.

The remainder of this paper is structured as follows: Section 2 describes related work on best-practice software inspection with UBR and UBT-i. Section 3 summarizes the research issues and hypothesis. We present the study design and arrangements in section 4, show the results of the study in section 6, and discuss the findings in section 6. Finally, section 7 concludes and identifies further work.

2 Related Work

Software inspection (SI) and software testing are well-investigated techniques in academia and industry settings. Several empirical studies have investigated defect detection techniques, inspections, and testing in isolation. Aurum *et al.* [2] summarize 25 years of empirical research on software inspections, including more than 30 individual studies on software inspection. Juristo *et al.* [9] summarize 25 years of empirical research on software testing based on more than 20 studies. This section summarizes related work regarding important aspects of software inspection with focus on usage-based reading (UBR) and inspection-based testing (UBT-i).

2.1 Inspection with UBR Reading Technique

Software inspection is a systematic and static verification and validation approach with respect to identifying defects and conducting quality assessment in software engineering projects. The individual application area of software inspections has enlarged its focus from only comprehension, initially proposed by Fagan [8] to comprehensive defect finding processes [12]. Reading techniques, e.g., checklist-based, perspective-based, and usage-based reading techniques guide inspectors through the reading process systematically [11]. Various studies were conducted to investigate the performance of individual reading technique approaches, e.g., in [2], [6], and [18], and identified UBR inspection as the most promising reading technique approach for business IT software projects [14], [23]. The basic idea of usage-based reading (UBR) is to focus on detecting most critical defects in software artifacts under inspection [6], [19] based on prioritized use cases and scenarios. In business IT software development use cases and scenarios support engineers to model system behavior from user perspective. Additionally, use cases prioritization enables focusing on most critical and important use cases from the perspective of involved stakeholders. Note that prioritized use cases help to focus on most valuable requirements [7]. Thus, UBR utilizes a set of use cases as a vehicle for focusing the inspection effort. Figure 1 shows the input and the result of UBR inspection.

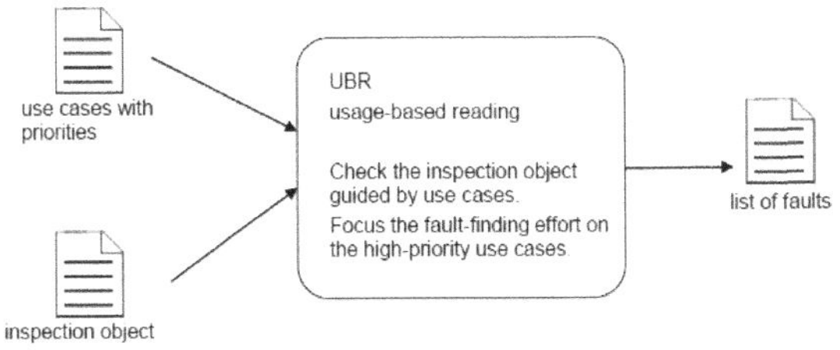

Fig. 1. Input and results of UBR

Prioritizing use cases is a central task in UBR inspection processes, as use case priorities are ranked by the perceived importance of customers (value-based) [7] or on risks (risk-based). Depending on the scope of prioritization (e.g., value and/or risk), use cases drive the inspection process. Note, that use cases can be utilized for various inspection variants (e.g., requirements, design, and code) in a specific project. The reviewers apply prioritized use cases and actively read the document under inspection by manually executing the use cases [14]. Note that guidelines support engineers in defect detection tasks.

2.2 Inspection-Based Testing

Software testing is an analytical and dynamic quality assurance activity requiring executable software code [10]. Common techniques of software testing focus on risks (risk-based testing), requirements (requirements-based testing) and components (unit tests). Usage-based testing (UBT) takes the use cases from user perspective applying black-box testing approaches. Note that black-box testing is typically based on customer requirements and specification documents. The focus is not to test how the software is implemented, but how it fulfills its intended purpose from the users' perspective [15]. The main goal of UBT seems to be similar to UBR with focus on prioritized use cases. Figure 2 shows the relationship of UBR inspection and usage-based

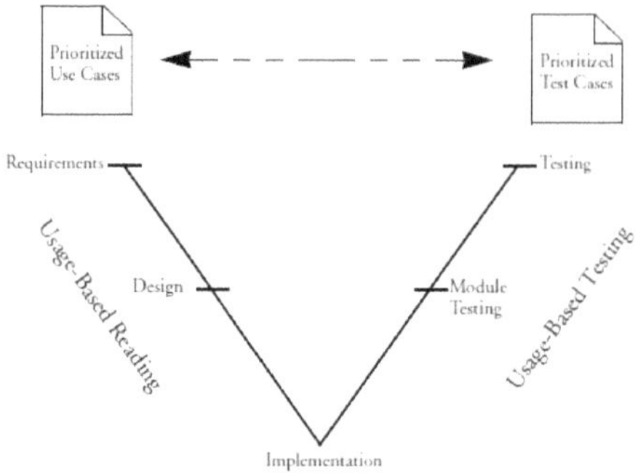

Fig. 2. UBR Inspection vs. Usage-based Testing

testing. Note that UBR inspection can be applied in the analytical phase of software development (e.g., defect detection of requirements specification documents) and UBT focuses on executable software code (defect detection of code related to prioritized use cases and test cases).

Several testing techniques have been empirically evaluated and compared to various inspection techniques [3], [17]. Andersson *et al.* [1] reported on an empirical study comparing usage-based testing and inspection approaches and introduced expert prioritized use cases and test cases to drive the testing process in code documents. Nevertheless, additional effort is necessary to identify and prioritize use cases and test cases prior to test execution. This paper applies a modified approach of UBT including a best-practice inspection approach to identify and prioritize use cases according to risk and business value [22]. Bundling benefits of UBT and UBR inspection leads to inspection-based testing (UBT-i) and includes two major benefits: (a) Defect detection approaches are applicable to design specification and code documents (UBR inspection contribution); (b) Test case generation based on use cases, architecture, design and identified defects as foundation for test execution in later phases of software development. Note that the test case generation is an added value of software inspection (which typically refers to a defect detection approach). Applying UBT-i can support defect detection and test case generation in parallel. Reports on a previous study [22] showed benefits of the UBT-i approach with respect to defect detection performance using an isolated inspection approach. Nevertheless, the temporal behavior of defect detection and test case generation remains open.

3 Research Issues and Hypotheses

Previous studies showed that UBR inspection and UBT-i perform similarly regarding defect detection performance, i.e., effectiveness and efficiency [22]. Note that the investigations of theses studies focus on the overall study duration. A consideration of performance measures within shorter time intervals seems to be worthwhile to investigate the temporal behavior of defect detection. We decided to select 30 minutes time intervals of observation because of a reasonable and manageable granularity of defect detection activities, i.e., best-practice UBR inspection and UBT-i. To investigate the temporal behavior of defect detection, we conducted a controlled experiment in academic environment to measure performance values (effectiveness and false positives) in 30 minutes time intervals and efficiency (defects per hour) intervals up to 300 minutes (5h) overall defect detection duration. To focus on the most risky defects, we applied three different severity classes (crucial, high important and less important defects) according to defect severity and the impact of the defect, if the defect will not be identified during inspection and testing. This paper focuses on the investigation of important (crucial and high important) defects. Main goals of this study were to investigate effectiveness, efficiency, and false positives of UBR inspection and UBT-i and with respect to analyzing the temporal behavior of defect detection performance in defined time intervals.

3.1 Variables

Following a standard practice of empirical software engineering [24], we define dependent and independent variables:

Dependent variables are performance measures (effectiveness, efficiency, and false positives) and time variables (timestamp of defect detection). Effectiveness is the number of found defects related to the number of seeded defects (i.e., crucial and high important defects); efficiency is the number of real defects found per time unit; false positives refer to the number of defects wrongly reported by participants. Temporal behavior refers to performance measures within defined time intervals.

The *independent variables* are defect location, defect classification, and the defect detection approach applied by the participants.

3.2 Hypothesis

The main goal of this paper is to report on the results of a controlled experiment to investigate the temporal behavior of performance measures regarding UBR inspection and UBT-i for design specifications. Note that suggestions regarding software reviews and inspections define the duration to some 120 minutes as optimum timeframe for inspection processes [6], [12]. Thus, our hypotheses focus on this time interval as foundation for investigating the temporal behavior of defect detection performance.

H1.0. UBR is significantly more effective than UBT-i during the first 120 minutes because participants, applying UBT-i have to (a) identify defects and (b) derive test cases. Thus, additional effort for test case generation will result in higher defect detection effectiveness for UBR. The alternative hypothesis (H1.1) is that UBR is not significantly more effective than UBT-i within the first 120 minutes.

H2.0. UBR is significantly more efficient than UBT-i regarding defect detection efficiency in the first 120 minutes because of additional effort regarding test-case generation (similar to H1.0). The alternative Hypothesis (H2.1) is that UBR is not significantly more efficient than UBT-i within the first 120 minutes.

H3.0: UBR inspectors report significantly more false positives than UBT-i applicants within the first 120 minutes. Assuming benefits from test case generation processes (requirements and quality attributes must be testable) false positives will be excluded from candidate defect lists by participants applying UBT-i approaches. The alternative Hypothesis (H3.1) is that UBR inspectors do not report significantly more false positives than UBT-I applicants.

4 Study Description

This section summarizes the study process, applied artifacts, study participants and identifies a set of threats to validity.

4.1 Study Process

The study includes three main phases in a sequential order, (a) study preparation phase, (b) study execution, and (c) evaluation phase:

The *study preparation phase* includes the preparation of the study material, i.e., requirements specifications, design documents, use cases, and source code fragments. Additionally, experts prepared questionnaires (experience and feedback questionnaires), guidelines and data capturing material.

The *study execution phase* consists of three major steps: (a) short tutorial to provide a brief overview on the study setting and a short sample application to explain the individual tasks, (b) individual defect detection and test case generation task in a first session for one part of the system *(taxi-part)* and (c) similar tasks in a second session for a more complex second part of the system *(central-part)*. The participants reported candidate defects (including the timestamp of defect detection) in a paper-based way and submitted the collected data in a separated defect submission session.

During the *study evaluation phase* the experiment team (guided by the authors) scanned the reported defects (noted defects) and assigned them to seeded defects (matched defects) for further analysis. Note that matched defects were assigned at the first time of reporting (including the time of detection). Multiple reported candidate defects were excluded from analysis and remain noted defects. We applied a set of tests regarding consistency and correctness of submitted data. Note that we provided feedback on the results of the study to the participants after the initial analysis of the data. For statistical evaluation we used descriptive statistics and conducted the Mann-Whitney Test at a significance level of 95% for hypothesis testing of two groups and the Kruskal-Wallis Test for testing more than two groups to identify significant differences.

4.2 Study Artifacts

The main artifacts of this study include a well-known application domain – a taxi management system – consisting of two parts, a taxi part representing the driver role in session 1 and a central part for dispatching and distributing calls in session 2. The material was based on two previous studies described in [20] and [21] and an improved study reported in [22]. Figure 3 shows the two basic components of the taxi management system. The systems design was described in a textual requirements document including 8 pages and 2 component diagrams, a design document (8 pages), and 24 prioritized use cases. Note that the requirements document and the use cases were considered to be correct. Additionally, we provided source code fragments

Fig. 3. Taxi Management System

(comparable to a snapshot from an agile development project) including some 1400 LOCs and a 9 pages method description (JavaDoc).

To measure defect detection performance the experiment team (supervised by the authors) introduced an overall number of 60 pre-defined defects (seeded defects) in two document locations (design documents and source code documents) including common defect types (e.g., missing and wrong information). 29 defects (48.3%) were seeded in the taxi part and 31 defects (51.7%) in the central part of the system. To enable value-based and risk-based consideration we assigned the seeded defects to three severity classes according to their importance. Class A defects (crucial defects) can have a strong impact on the fundamental functionality of the product. Class B (high important) defects are only rarely occurring but important defects or less important frequent defects of medium risk. Class C defects are rarely occurring and only have a minor impact on the functionality and quality of the software product.

Table 1. Allocation of seeded defects

System Part	Crucial Defects (class A)			High Important Defects (class B)			Less important (class C)		
	Taxi	Cent.	Total	Taxi	Cent.	Total	Taxi	Cent.	Total
Design Docs (DD)	7	3	10	6	6	12	2	3	5
Source Code (SC)	8	11	19	5	7	12	1	1	2
Total	15	14	29	11	13	24	3	4	7

Table 1 presents the nominal number of seeded defects according to defect severity classes and document location. Note that we focus on the important defects (i.e., crucial and high important defects) and design documents to investigate the temporal behavior of defect detection performance.

Additional material includes *guidelines* providing step-by-step instructions for the participants and questionnaires to capture individual prior knowledge of inspectors (*experience questionnaire*) and *feedback questionnaires* to capture information on method application after every session.

4.3 Subjects

The subjects in the study were 41 master students at TU Vienna with software engineering and quality assurance background. Additionally, most of the students work at least part time in a professional environment in industry. The study was fully integrated in the practical part of two advanced courses for software engineering and software quality assurance with focus on early software product improvement aspects and testing. The participants were assigned randomly to one of the two techniques, (UBR and UBT-i). We changed the technique assignment in the second session.

4.4 Threats to Validity

In order to increase internal and external validity we consider a set of threats to validity and implemented appropriate countermeasures.

To address *internal validity* we avoided *communication* of individuals during the study execution phases. In order to increase inspector performance *individual breaks* were allowed. Note that the break duration was reported to identify the real working effort. The *duration* of the study was limited to an overall duration of 300 minutes (5h). *Prior knowledge* of the participants was collected at the beginning of the study by applying an experience questionnaire. We used a *feedback questionnaire* to get knowledge of the individual course of action and to see if the participants followed the study process properly. We performed intensive reviews of the study package to verify the *correctness* of the document package. Note that a similar package was used in previous studies e.g., in [22].

To improve *external validity* we used a *well-known application* domain to avoid domain-specific interpretation problems and to focus on the improvement of method application regarding individual inspector skills. Additionally, the specification describes a real world application to enable comparability to industrial settings. The participants passed an intensive training session in previous lectures and a short tutorial prior to the study. We applied a class-room setting for study execution.

5 Experiment Results

This section summarizes the results of the empirical study with respect to performance measures and the temporal behavior of defect detection.

5.1 Effort

Inspection effort summarizes the overall working effort (mean and standard deviation) of two the experiment sessions (see Table 2). Note that we did not observe any significant difference regarding study effort (p-value 0,497(-)) between UBR and UBT-i. Comparable effort strengthens our expectations that UBT-i can deliver comparable results including the additional benefit of additionally generated test cases as a by-product of defect detection. We observed similar durations session 2.

Table 2. Effort for UBR and UBT-i in Session 1 and Session 2

Duration [min]	Session 1 (Taxi)		Session 2 (Central)	
	UBR	UBT-i	UBR	UBT-i
No of Subjects	20	21	21	20
Mean	272.5	268.8	281.3	276.2
Std.Dev.	38.01	29.13	35.32	30.11

5.2 Effectiveness

Effectiveness is the number of matched defects (real defects) related to the number of defects per defect severity class (we focus on crucial and high important defects in this evaluation, i.e., class A and class B). The first analysis showed comparable mean values defect detection effectiveness: 18.9 defects for UBR and 16.9 defects for UBT-i. Applying the Mann-Whitney-Test we did not observe any significant differences (p-value: 0.317(-)). These results confirm previous studies [22] that there is no significant difference regarding defect detection effectiveness for the overall experiment duration.

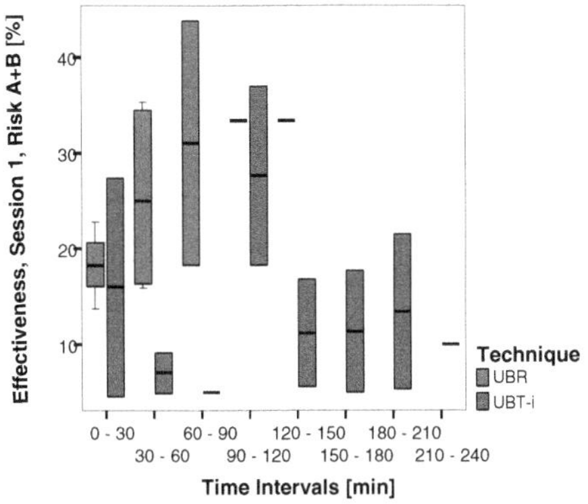

Fig. 4. Effectiveness of Session 1

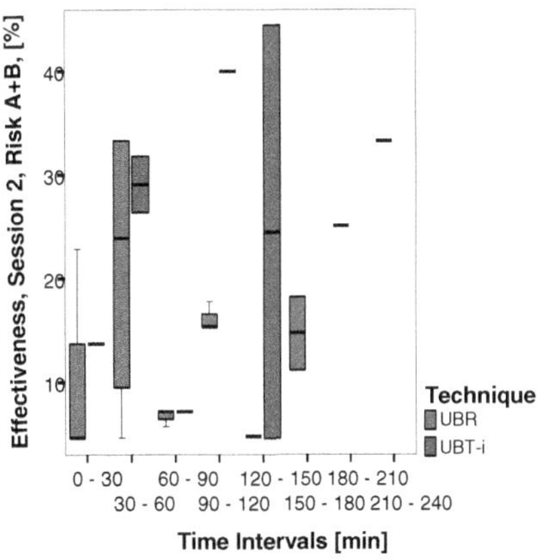

Fig. 5. Effectiveness of Session 2

A more detailed analysis of defect detection performance in defined 30 min time intervals enable the investigation of the temporal behavior of defect detection effectiveness. Note that already identified defects in the first time frame were excluded from the investigation of following time intervals (identified defects will decrease the number of remaining seeded defects). This step enables the comparison of different time intervals. Note that we present the findings up to 240 minutes because no additional defect was reported during the last hour of UBR and UBT-i application; the overall study duration was limited to 300 minutes (5h). Figure 4 presents the results of this evaluation for the first session (taxi part). Applying the Kruskal-Wallis test we observed significant differences between both groups in the first session regarding all time intervals > 30 minutes. No significant differences within the first 30 minutes of defect detection. Defect detection performance increases for UBR inspectors up to 150 minutes durations. Regarding UBT-i we observed comparable results during the first 30 minutes, lower effectiveness up to 150 minutes, and a higher effectiveness for all time intervals >150 minutes. Assuming an additional effort for test case generation, a lower effectiveness during the first 120 minutes is an explanation for these results.

Analyzing the results in the second session (see Figure 5) we observed completely different findings. We observed benefits for UBR at the beginning and at the end of the overall inspection process. Regarding UBT-i all defects were identified within the timeframe up to 150 minutes. This finding might indicate a modified defect detection approach in the second session, i.e., the UBT-i inspectors identified defects first and construct test cases afterwards. Ongoing effectiveness values for UBR inspectors might indicate an increased complexity of the second systems part (i.e., the central part of the system). Table 3 summarizes the results for both sessions.

Table 3. Effectiveness for Session 1 and 2, Risk A+B

Time Interval [min]	Session 1 (Taxi), Risk A+B				Session 2 (Central), Risk A+B			
	UBR		UBT-i		UBR		UBT-i	
	Mean	SD	Mean	SD	Mean	SD	Mean	SD
0 – 30	18.2	3.71	15.9	11.36	9.1	7.87	13.6	0
30 – 60	28.1	8.77	6.9	2.16	21.4	12.44	29.1	2.75
60 – 90	26.2	12.43	5.0	0	6.6	0.75	7.1	0
90 – 120	33.3	0	27.5	9.33	16.1	1.07	40.0	0
120 – 150	33.3	0	11.1	5.56	11.5	6.71	24.5	19.95
150 – 180	0	0	11.3	6.32	11.1	0	0	0
180 – 210	0	0	13.4	8.08	25.0	0	0	0
210 – 240	0	0	10.0	0	33.3	0	0	0

5.3 Efficiency

Efficiency refers to the number of real defects found per hour. Again, we focus on important defects, i.e., crucial and high important defects for evaluation purposes. Note that we apply a defined time interval in steps of 60 minutes as we measured efficiency in defects per hour. Figure 6, Figure 7, and Table 4 present the results of efficiency evaluation results for UBR and UBT-i participants in both sessions.

Our observation in session 1 showed that UBR inspectors are most efficient in the first time interval (0-60 min) and decreases in time interval 2 and 3. No additional defect was identified after 180 minutes of inspection. As assumed after investigating effectiveness for UBT-i, the efficiency value is highest in the second time interval (i.e., 60-120 min). Note that defects were identified up to 240 minutes.

We observed similar and surprising results in session 2, because UBT-i outperforms efficiency in the first 2 time intervals, i.e., 0-60 minutes and 60-120 minutes, respectively. Again we assume a separation of defect detection and test case generation. Regarding UBR inspectors we observed the highest efficiency in the time interval 180-240 minutes.

Table 4. Efficiency for Session 1 and 2, Risk A+B

Time Interval [min]	Session 1 (Taxi), Risk A+B				Session 2 (Central), Risk A+B			
	UBR		UBT-i		UBR		UBT-i	
	Mean	SD	Mean	SD	Mean	SD	Mean	SD
0 – 60	15.6	3.42	5.0	2.36	8.3	4.59	13.3	1.67
60 – 120	8.6	4.64	14.5	7.87	6.8	2.26	10.3	8.60
120 – 180	6.3	0	7.1	3.63	1.9	0.19	0	0
180 – 240	0.0	0	3.2	1.22	10.6	0	0	0

Further investigations, e.g., based on the feedback questionnaire to investigate the applied sequence of defect detection and test case generation, are necessary to identify reasons for these results. Applying the Kruskal-Wallis Test, we observed significant differences regarding all groups.

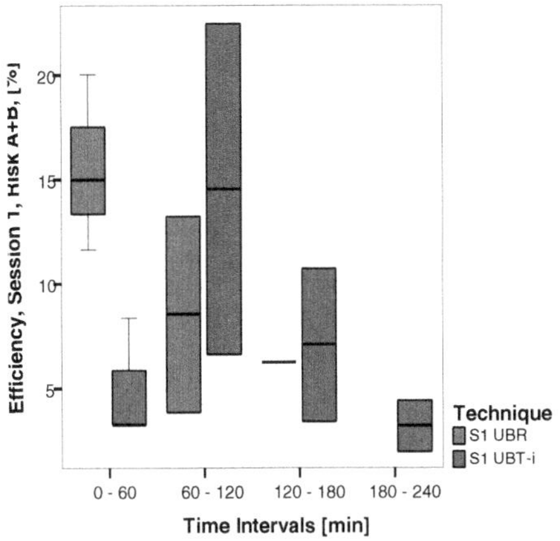

Fig. 6. Efficiency of Session 1

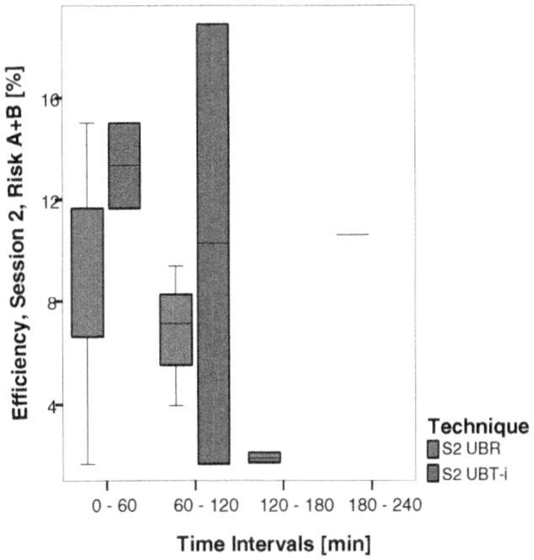

Fig. 7. Efficiency of Session 2

Because of these partly surprising findings, the time for the first reported defect can deliver an insight in the defect detection and test case generation process. Table 5 illustrates the time interval until the first matched (real) defect reported by the participants in every group.

Table 5. First Matched Defect Detected

	Session 1 (Taxi)		Session 2 (Central)	
	UBR	UBT-i	UBR	UBT-i
Mean	12.2	17.6	15.4	17.4
Std.Dev.	10.59	10.39	10.93	10.42

We observed that UBR reported the first matched defect significantly earlier than UBT-i participants both sessions; Mann-Whitney Test: p-value< 0.001(s)). Additionally, UBT-i inspectors reported the first defect between 17-18 minutes after starting their tasks. Note that UBR inspectors require some 3 additional minutes in the more complex second session, i.e., the central part.

5.4 False Positives

False positives (FP) are important issues regarding defect detection techniques, because they focus on the number of "wrong" candidate defects which are no real seeded defects. Note that we scanned all candidate defects for correctness to add them to reference defect list, if candidate defects are considered to be real defects. This task was conducted by the experiment team prior to the analysis. Assuming that candidate defects are the foundation for test case generation by UBT-i participants, we assumed

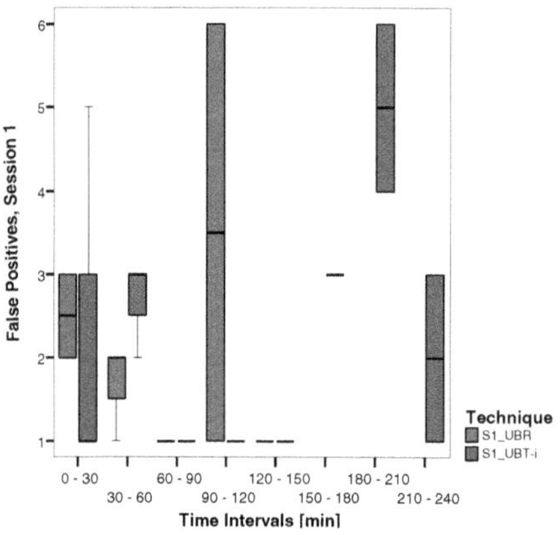

Fig. 8. False Positives of Session 1

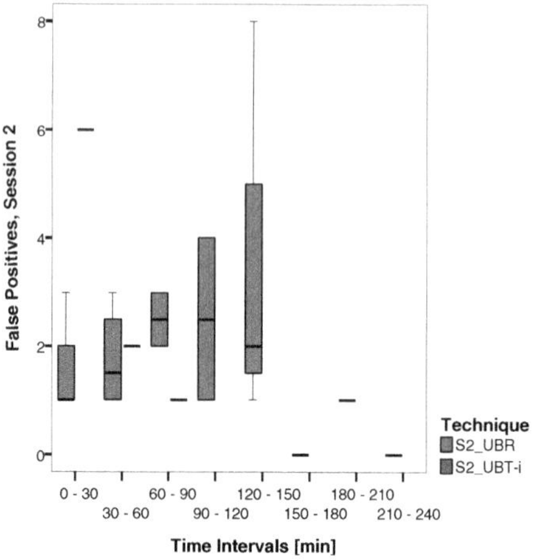

Fig. 9. False Positives of Session 2

that the number of false positives is lower for UBT-i participants. Figure 8 presents the results of the first session, Figure 9 illustrates the findings of the second session.

Regarding UBR in session 1 (see Figure 8), we observed a higher number of FP in the first time interval (0-30min) and in the time interval from 90-120 min. We observed similar trends for UBT-i participants, i.e., higher amount of FP at the beginning and at the end of the study. Concerning the second session (see Figure 9), we observed a high number of FP for UBT-i and a decreasing number of FP in the course of the study. In contrast, UBR starts with a low number of FB and an increasing number of FP up to 150 minutes. This finding (especially in the second session) is quite interesting as there seems to be strong advantages for UBT-i participants who also focus on test case generation, i.e., testability considerations. Table 6 depicts the mean value and the standard deviation of the False Positives (FP) of session 1 and session 2. We observed significant differences within these sessions after applying the Kruskal-Wallis Test.

Table 6. False Positives for Session 1 and 2, Risk A+B

Time Interval [min]	Session 1, Risk A+B				Session 2, Risk A+B			
	UBR		UBT-i		UBR		UBT-i	
	Mean	SD	Mean	SD	Mean	SD	Mean	SD
0 – 30	2.5	0.5	2.33	1.89	1.7	0.94	6.0	0.00
30 – 60	1.7	0.5	2.67	0.47	1.8	0.83	2.0	0.00
60 – 90	1.0	0.0	1.00	0.0	2.5	0.50	1.0	0.00
90 – 120	3.5	2.5	1.00	0.0	2.5	1.50	0.0	0.00
120 – 150	1.0	0.0	1.00	0.0	3.7	3.09	0.0	0.00
150 – 180	0.0	0.0	3.00	0.0	0.0	0.00	0.0	0.00
180 – 210	0.0	0.0	5.00	1.00	1.0	0.00	0.0	0.00
210 – 240	0.0	0.0	2.00	1.00	0.0	0.00	0.0	0.00

6 Discussion

Previous controlled experiments, reported in [22], showed that an inspection-based testing, i.e., UBT-i, performed similarly with respect to best-practice software inspection processes using UBR reading techniques. In this paper we reported on a replicated study to (a) confirm the findings in previous studies and extend the results with respect to the temporal behavior. We used effectiveness, efficiency, and false positives to measure defect detection performance for design documents in defined time intervals.

The study results showed a *comparable overall effort* for both techniques in both sessions without identifying significant differences regarding technique application effort. Thus, seems to be UBT-i a reasonable approach for defect detection (contribution of software inspection) and early test case generation.

H1. Effectiveness. Assuming an additional effort for test case generation (UBT-i), we expected a higher effectiveness for UBR inspectors, who focus on defect detection. In the first time interval of session 1 we did not observe any significant differences between both groups from 0-30 minutes. Additionally, we observed significant differences for all time intervals from 30 minutes to 150 minutes. These results confirm our expectations that UBT-i participants require additional time for test case generation. The analysis of the second session shows different findings. We observed that most of defects were identified by UBT-i inspectors in the timeframes up to 150 minutes. This finding might indicate a modified defect detection process in the second session, i.e., the UBT-i inspectors identified defects first and construct test cases afterwards. Ongoing effectiveness values for UBR inspectors might indicate an increased complexity of the second systems part (i.e. the central part). The hypothesis H1.0 can be confirmed for the first session but must be rejected for the second session.

H2: Efficiency. Consequently, we expected a higher efficiency, i.e., number of identified defects per hour for UBR inspectors. Similar to H1.0 the hypothesis can be confirmed for the first session, but cannot be confirmed for the second session. Especially, the results of the second hour differ significantly.

H3: False Positives. False positives refer to candidate defects reported by the participants which are no real defects. Assuming benefits from test case generation process (requirements and quality attributes must be testable) we expect significantly less false positives for participants applying UBT-i approaches. The results did not confirm our assumption, as the number of false positives increase at the end of tasks for UBR and UBT-i. Nevertheless, our assumptions (H3.0) were confirmed in the second session.

7 Conclusion and Further Work

Software inspection and testing are appropriate approaches for defect detection in various phases of software development. Software inspection focuses on early defect detection and software testing is applicable to executable code documents late in the development process. Bundling benefits from best-practice software inspection (UBR) and inspection-based test case generation can lead to synergy effects regarding defect detection performance and test-case generation based on inspection results. This integration approach trends towards the concept of test-driven development. Various studies report on defect detection performance of isolated techniques regarding software inspection variants and testing approaches. This paper focuses on the investigation of the temporal behavior of the software defect detection techniques UBR and UBT-i.

UBR performed very effective and efficient in a time interval up to 120 minutes. UBT-i in contrary requires more time for test case generation to achieve comparable defect detection results. The findings can provide an important indicator for planning analytical quality assurances in consideration of the scheduled inspection time for UBR as well as UBT-i. The outcome of this paper can help project and quality managers in more precisely define the inspection and testing duration efforts to support quality assurance activities and drive process and product improvement. Nevertheless, we observed differences in two sessions of the controlled experiment. The differences between the sessions were partially remarkable in the context of the investigated measures. Additional investigations are required to deepen the knowledge on the temporal behavior of defect detection performance. Another aspect for further investigation covers possible learning effects and/or modified defect detection processes, conducted by the UBT-i participants in the second session.

Further work also includes a more detailed investigation of the findings of this study and a replication of the controlled experiment to broaden the understanding of time effects in defect detection techniques.

References

1. Andersson, C., Thelin, T., Runeson, P., Dzamashvili, N.: An experimental evaluation of inspection and testing for detecting of design faults. In: ACM-IEEE International Symposium on Empirical Software Engineering (ISESE), pp. 174–184 (2003)
2. Aurum, A., Petersson, H., Wohlin, C.: State-of-the-Art: Software Inspections after 25 years. J. Software Testing Verification, and Reliability 12(3), 133–154 (2002)
3. Basili, V.R., Selby, R.W.: Comparing the Effectiveness of Software Testing Strategies. IEEE Transaction on Software Engineering 12(13) (1987)
4. Beck, K., Andres, C.: Extreme Programming Explained - Embrace Change. Addison-Wesley, Reading (2004)
5. Biffl, S., Winkler, D., Thelin, T., Höst, M., Russo, B., Succi, G.: Investigating the Effect of V&V and Modern Construction Techniques on Improving Software Quality. In: International Symposium on Empirical Software Engineering (ISESE), Poster Proceeding, Los Angeles, USA (2004)
6. Biffl, S.: Software Inspection Techniques to support Project and Quality Management. Shaker (2001)
7. Biffl, S., Aurum, A., Boehm, B., Erdogmus, H., Grünbacher, P. (eds.): Value-Based Software Engineering. Springer, Heidelberg (2005)
8. Fagan, M.E.: Design and Code Inspections to Reduce Errors in Program Development. IBM System Journal 15(3), 182–211 (1976)

9. Juristo, N., Moren, A.M., Vegas, S.: Reviewing 25 Years of Testing Technique Experiments. J. Empirical Software Engineering 9(1-2), 7–44 (2004)
10. Kaner, C., Bach, J., Pettichord, B.: Lessons Learned in Software Testing: A Context-driven Approach. Wiley, Chichester (2001)
11. Laitenberger, O., DeBaud, J.-M.: An Encompassing Life Cycle Centric Survey of Software Inspection. J. of Systems and Software 50(1), 5–31 (2000)
12. Laitenberger, O.: A Survey of Software Inspection Technologies, Handbook on Software Engineering and Knowledge Engineering. Technical Report, Fraunhofer IESE (2002)
13. Parnas, D.L., Lawford, M.: The role of Inspection in Software Quality Assurance. IEEE Transactions on Software Engineering 29(8) (2003)
14. Porter, A., Votta, L.: Comparing Detection Methods for Software Requirements Inspection: A Replication Using Professional Subjects. J. Empirical Software Engineering 3(4), 355–380 (1998)
15. Runeson, P., Regnell, B.: Derivation of an Integrated Operational Profile and Use Case Model. In: 9th International Symposium on Software Reliability Engineering, pp. 70–79 (1998)
16. Sommerville, I.: Software Engineering. Addison-Wesley, Reading (2007)
17. So, S.S.: An Empirical Evaluation of Six Methods to Detect Faults in Software. J. Software Testing, Verification, and Reliability 12(3), 155–172 (2002)
18. Thelin, T., Runeson, P., Wohlin, C.: An Experimental Comparison of Usage-Based and Checklist-Based Reading. In: International Workshop on Inspection in Software Engineering, WISE (2001)
19. Thelin, T.: Empirical Evaluations of Usage-Based Reading and Fault Content Estimation for Software Inspections. Lund University (2002)
20. Thelin, T., Andersson, C., Runeson, P., Dzamashvili-Fogelström, N.: A Replicated Experiment of Usage-Based and Checklist-Based Reading. In: Metrics (2004)
21. Thelin, T., Runeson, P., Regnell, B.: Usage-Based Reading – An Experiment to Guide Reviewers with Use Cases. J. Information and Software Technology 43(15) (2001)
22. Winkler, D., Biffl, S., Riedl, B.: Improvement of Design Specifications with Inspection and Testing. In: 31st Euromicro SEAA Conference, pp. 222–231. IEEE, Los Alamitos (2005)
23. Winkler, D., Biffl, S., Thurnher, B.: Investigating the Impact of Active Guidance on Design Inspection. In: Profes, pp. 458–473 (2005)
24. Wohlin, C., Runeson, P., Höst, M., von Mayrhauser, A., Regnell, B., Anders, W., Ohlsson, M.C.: Experimentation in Software Engineering: An Introduction. In: Kluver International Series in Software Engineering, Springer, Heidelberg (1999)

Analysis of Bug Fixing Processes Using Program Slicing Metrics

Raula Gaikovina Kula, Kyohei Fushida, Shinji Kawaguchi, and Hajimu Iida

Graduate School of Information Science, Nara Institute of Science and Technology
Takayamacho 8916-5, Ikoma, Nara 630-0101, Japan
{raula-k,kyohei-f,kawaguti}@is.naist.jp, iida@itc.naist.jp

Abstract. This paper is a report of a feasibility study into an alternative assessment of software processes at the micro-level. Using the novel approach of applying program slicing metrics to identify bug characteristics, the research studied relationships between bug characteristics and their bug fixing processes. The results suggested that specific characteristics such as cyclomatic complexity may relate to how long it takes to fix a bug. Results serve as a proof of concept and a starting point for this proposed assessment methodology. Future refinement of the metrics and much larger sample data is needed. This research is an initial step in the development of assessment tools to assist with Software Process Improvement.

Keywords: Program Slicing, Software Bug, Bug Fixing Process, Software Process Improvement.

1 Introduction

The quality and improvement of software processes are seen as vital to any software development project. Traditionally, software processes usually refer to the main phases in the software development life cycle. Improvement of these processes is a major activity for larger software organizations as benefits are seen in the cost and business value of improvement efforts, as well as the yearly improvement in productivity of development, early defect detection and maintenance, and faster time to market [1].

Capability Maturity Model Integration (CMMI) [2] is the most common form of rating software development organization's quality of performance. Other models such as International Standards (ISO 9000), [3] have been used for the quality of an organization's software development processes. There have been a number of studies on the issues relating to the implementation of these CMMI and ISO 9000 [4], [5], [6]. Much of the issues lie with the size of the organization as these models are expensive to assess and implement from small software organization [7]. These studies show that the processes assessments are sometimes tedious and usually not tailored for specific companies. Also additional studies show that higher management support, training, awareness, allocation of resources, staff involvement, experienced staff and defined software improvement process implementation methodology is critical for software process improvement [8].

M. Ali Babar, M. Vierimaa, and M. Oivo (Eds.): PROFES 2010, LNCS 6156, pp. 32–46, 2010.
© Springer-Verlag Berlin Heidelberg 2010

There has been several related work into trying to make the models easier and better to use. Yoo el al [9] suggests a model that combines CMMI and ISO methods. Armburst el al [10] takes a different approach by treating software as manufacturing product lines, therefore making the processes systematic and generic.

In contrast to such frameworks macro-level process assessments and improvement, an alternative measure of software processes can be done through the inspection of process execution histories. This analysis however is performed at the developer's level, and measures the fine grained processes called 'micro processes'. One such research has been done by Morisaki el al [11]. This research analyzes the quality of micro processes by studying the process execution histories such as change logs. Quality of the process is measured by the execution sequence, occurrences of missing or invalid sequences. This paper is based on this research and seeks improvement of micro-level processes will contribute to Software Process Improvement.

Our motivation is to develop a quantitative assessment model of software process at the micro level. It is aimed towards improving the efficiency of the software developer's workload at the maintenance phase of bug fixing. Current models of process assessment are focused on a higher software life cycle level and need complicated assessment such as CMMI and ISO 9000, which, as mentioned earlier are expensive as they require highly trained assessors. The author's goal is to work towards the development of models that assess the quality of micro processes.

More specifically, a proof of concept towards a prediction model based on estimating the bug processes execution time is the perceived contribution of this research. Being able to estimate the bug fixing process will improve the development process as more developers can manage resources and time based on how long it will take to fix a bug.

It is envisioned this study may aid developers in the micro process of bug fixing. The concept is that aiding the developer with tools to better manage bugs, leads to better quality in software processes at this level, influencing the overall improvement of the software development process.

The paper's objective is to provide a proof of concept that how a bug fixing process is executed may be related to a certain characteristic of a bug. For instance, perhaps bugs that have a lengthy fixing process have certain similar characteristics as compared to bugs that are easily fixed in just a couple of days. Bug characteristic is defined as the properties of the fragments of code prone to the bug fix. Based on this concept, the following hypotheses are presented for testing:

- Hypothesis 1: Bugs with similar bug characteristics share similar bug fixing process executions
- Hypothesis 2: Bugs that do not follow the usual micro process occur due to some bug characteristic.

In this paper, Section 2 presents the methodology, describing the terms and definitions used in the research as well as the proposed approach. Section 3 then explains the experiment using the approach and tools to carry out the experiments. The section also presents the findings of the experiments. Section 4 is the discussion and analysis of the results. Also the validation of the research is discussed as well as the application of the research is included. Finally, Section 5 outlines the conclusion and the future works.

2 Methodology

As mentioned in the research objectives, the research aims to find a relationship between a bug characteristic and the processes used to fix the bug. The approach taken was to first reconstruct a bug fixing process. Then using program slicing techniques identify bug prone fragments as well as define certain characteristics of a bug. Finally comparisons are performed to group and find relationship between bugs with similar bug fixing processes and similar bug characteristics.

2.1 Bug Fixing Process Definitions and Analysis

This research focuses on the day to day processes performed in the development of software. This paper assumes data repositories including following two locations in which bug information is stored daily.

1)Bug Tracking System
Typically a software development team uses a system to manage bugs in a medium to large scale project. The tracking system usually tracks progress of bug. This research utilizes the bug tracking systems to gather various properties of the bug.

2)Source Code Repository
The source code repository refers the system manages changes to source code in a software project. The two main system used is the Subversion (SVN) and Concurrent Versioning System (CVS). For this research, both SVN and CVS repositories were used to gather data on bug characteristics.

The generalized model of micro processes of bug tracking system used in the MPA model by Morisaki was used. The research showed that bug fixing comprises of these steps illustrated in Figure 1.

Step-1. *Bug Reported:* This is the start of the micro process. It signifies that there is a request to check and fix source code. Usually this event is signified when a new bug is created in the system.

Step-2. *Bug Assigned:* This is where the bug gets assigned to a developer. It is signified when the bug changes status indicating that the bug is being worked on. This event is signified by a change in status of the bug to 'assigned'.

Step-3. *Bug Fixed*: This stage is when code is being fixed. When code is being updated means that the bug fix is being applied to the source code, therefore captures the real time of when the bug is being fixed. This is signified by editing code in the source code repository and a reference to the bug is made in the change log or comments section of the changes.

Step-4. *Bug Closed*: This is the final stage of the bug fixing process. This is when the bug is acknowledged as fixed. This is signified when the bug status is changed to 'closed'.

These steps are generalized and is differs based on organization and project needs.

The quality of the micro process analysis is evaluated by how well the different phases are executed. Bugs were evaluated on whether they followed this model. Grouping of the bugs would be according to how well the model is followed. The groupings are identified as either correct sequences or incorrect sequences.

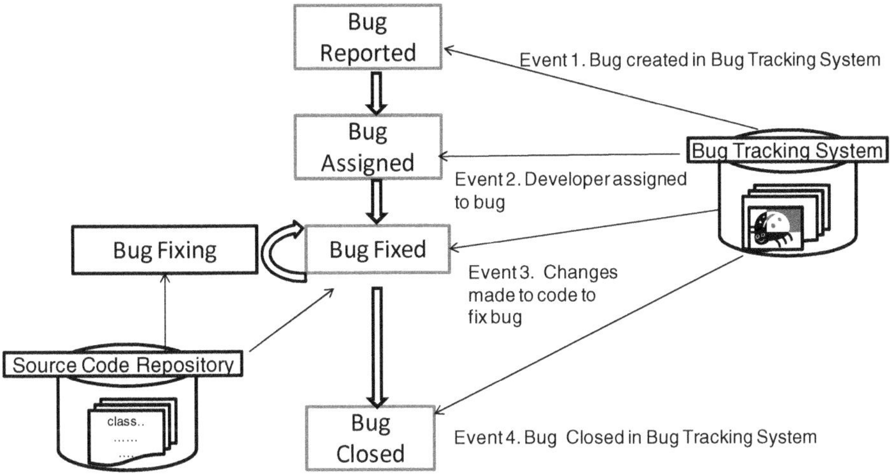

Fig. 1. Bug Fixing Process Model

2.2 Program Slicing Metrics for Bug Characteristics

To assess the bug characteristics, program slicing metrics is used in this approach to describe bug characteristic metrics. Program slicing is a concept first described by Weiser [12] as a method to study the behavior of source code through the flow dependency and control dependency relationship among statements. This work however has been used in the field of Software Evolution [13].

Previous work has been done on using program slicing metrics to classify bugs. Pan el. al. [14] showed proved that program slicing metrics work as well as conventional bug classification methodologies.

Since this is the initial research on applying program slicing metrics to micro process analysis, two of the most basic code metrics, Lines of Code (LoC) and Cyclomatic Complexity (CC) [15] were employed to express characteristics of the program slices.

2.3 Experiment Approach

The analysis of the bug fixing process includes three steps: 1) micro process extraction and analysis and 2) program slice extraction and analysis, and 3) comparison and analysis of data.

1) Micro process extraction and analysis:
This step involves data mining and extraction of bug related attributes from both the source code repository and the bug tracking system. Table 1 and 2 shows the data that is extracted from the bug tracking system and the data extracted from source code repository, respectively.

2) The program slices extraction and analysis:
This step involves analysis of the code using the program slicing metrics. The methodology used was to first identify the file edited during the bug fix, then extract the

Table 1. Data extracted from the bug tracking system

Attribute	Description
Bug ID	Used to identify the bug
Date Opened	When the bug was reported
Date Closed	When the bug was reported as fixed
Bug Priority	Understand bug's importance

Table 2. Data extracted from source code repository

Attribute	Description
Revision ID	Identification number used to track changes made to source code
Bug ID	References the changes made to a bug with bugID
Commit Date	Date when the bug fix was applied

associated files directly affected by bug fix using program slicing. Then the code metrics for the affected files were calculated. The following explains in detail how each metric was used to for bug classification.

- Bug LoC (Lines of Code): This metric is proposed to measure how much of the code is potentially affected by the bug. This is measured using the program slicing metric Lines of Code (LoC). The range of a bug is summarized in the equation below:

$$BugCC = \sum_{f \in affectedfiles} LoC(f) \tag{1}$$

where *affectedfiles* refers to the source code files that were affected when the bug was being fixed, and *LoC(f)* is lines of code of file *f*. The affected files include files that are dependent code related to the files edited during the bug fix.

- Bug CC (Cyclomatic Complexity): This metric is proposed to calculate the potential complexity of the code affected by the bug. This will be measured using the program slicing metric CC as explained in section 2.2. The severity of a bug is:

$$BugCC = \sum_{f \in affectedfiles} CC(f) \tag{2}$$

where *affectedfiles* refers to the source code files that were affected when the bug was being fixed, and *CC(f)* is cyclomatic complexity of file *f*. Since CC is calculated per function, Bug CC is sum of all the cc for each function in the affected files. The affected files include files that are dependent code related to the files edited during the bug fix.

3) Comparison and Analysis of data
Using the MPA data extracted and the program slicing metrics extracted from the software project, the bugs are grouped according to similar program slicing metrics characteristics.

3 Experiment

We conducted an initial experiment using Open Source Software (OSS) repositories. The main reason for choosing OSS was that it is easily accessible as well as does not require special permission or software licenses to analyze datasets.

3.1 Experiment Tools

We used following tools selected for both the program slicing and the tool used to extract the MPA data:

Program Slicing Tool
Based on previous surveys [16] on the available program slicing tools, three program slicing tools [17], [18], [19] were tested and the most appropriate tool selected. In the end CodeSurfer [19] was chosen because it met the needs of the research as well as being used in Pan's use of program slicing metrics for bug classification. The main limitation of CodeSurfer is that only projects in the C/C++ programming languages can be analyzed.

Bug Extraction Tool (Extract the MPA Data)
Using the micro process model we designed a bug extraction tool that would help search and extract the needed data related to this research. Published tools such as Kenyon [20] are available, however because data to be extracted are specific to this study, it was justified to develop the tool in-house.

Our extraction tool which was developed in java, acted as a web spider searching the online data repositories, and then parsing extracted data. In order to make the tool more flexible and not become a constraint on the research, the tool was developed to search both SVN and CVS repositories. The extracted data is mentioned in section 2.3. All bugs were verified to be bugs and not change requests.

3.2 Test Subjects

Due to the limitations of the CodeSurfer slicing tool only being able to analyze projects based on the C programming language, projects were selected based on program slicing capability (C++ projects were selected.) and on quality of bug extraction (if there was a reference between the bug tracking system and the source code repository). Using Sourceforge.net as a source of the OSS projects, the following three software projects met the selection criteria:

- *Scintilla*(Up to Ver. 2.01): Scintilla is an editing component for Win32 and GTK+. It comes bundled with SciTE, which is a Scintilla based text editor. It is used when editing and debugging source code.

- *WxWidgets*(Up to Rev. 62931)*:* WxWidgets is a C++ library that lets developers create applications for Windows, OS X, Linux and UNIX on 32-bit and 64-bit architectures, as well as several mobile phones platforms including Windows Mobile, iPhone SDK and embedded GTK+. Like Filezilla, WxWidgets used subversion and houses its bug tracking system outside Sourceforge.net.
- *Filezilla* (Up to Rev. 3295)*:* Filezilla is the open source File Transfer Protocol solution. The client component of the project was used for analysis. Filezilla used the subversion repository system and hosts its own bug tracking system.

The bugs used in the experiment were all that had complete data. This means all bugs in the projects that had its bug fixing process reconstructed and bug characteristics calculated were used. All bugs from project start date till the experiment date, December 2009 were analyzed. Figure 2 summarizes the collected data.

3.3 Findings

The general approach taken in analysis of the information was to do various comparisons of bug characteristics against their bug fixing process. Comparisons and groupings were: 1) Duration of bug fix and 2) Assessment of bug fixing process.

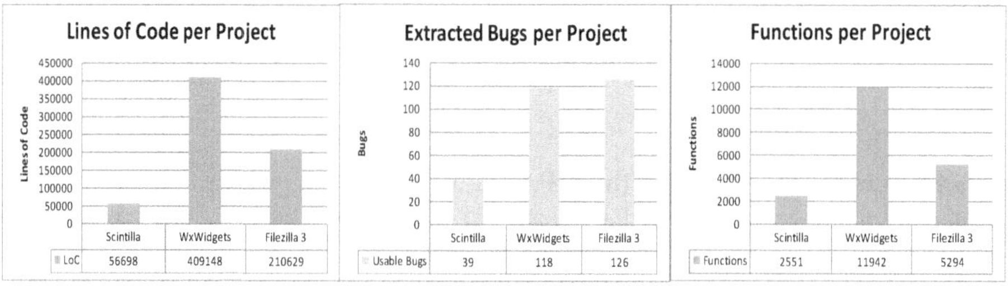

Fig. 2. General Comparisons between Projects

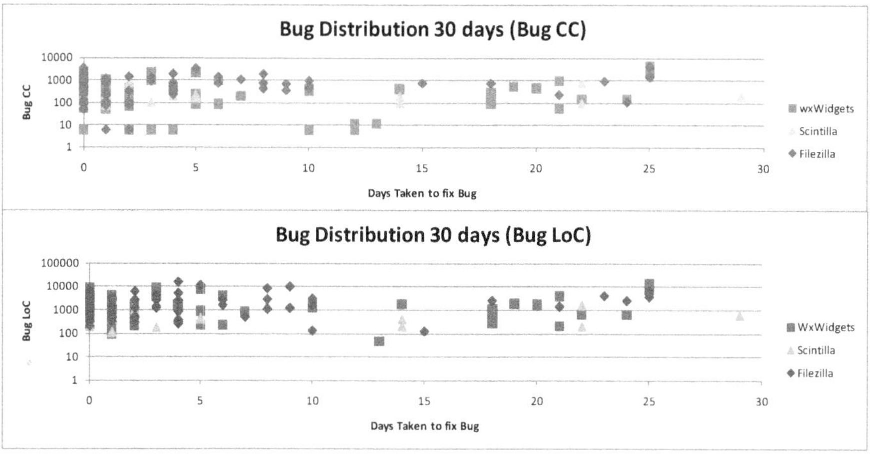

Fig. 3. Bug Distribution for the first 30 days

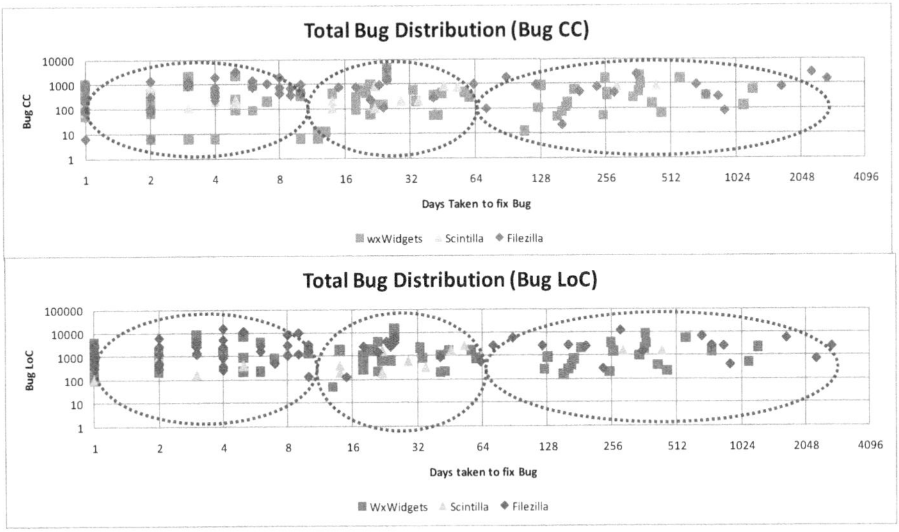

Fig. 4. Total Bug Distribution on log-log graph

With these two groupings, bug characteristics were applied to the groups to compare and attempt to find some similarities.

1) For the duration of the bug fix, the proposed analysis method used the number of days it took to fix a bug. This was calculated as:

$$\textit{Days taken to fix a bug} = \textit{Date of Bug Fix} - \textit{Date of Bug Detected} \tag{3}$$

where bug fix is the date when the code changes are committed to the code and bug detected being the date when the bug was first reported. Bug Fix was used instead of 'Bug Close' status as it is more accurate representation of when the bug was addressed.

As seen from Figure 3 the distribution of bugs seem to differ from 10 days onwards, thus identified as a cluster. Since the distribution covers a very large range of data, logarithmic graphs were used to plot the rest of the data. Using visual identification shown in Figure 4, it was seen that around bugs that are older than 64 days have a wider distribution compared to the bugs fixed in less than 64 days. With this observation, the second group of bugs was proposed from 11 to 64 days and the remaining third group from 64 days onwards.

2) Assessment of bug fixing process

The following groupings were applied based on the MPA model:

- *Standard Sequence:* Bugs that have all the processes sequenced in correct order.
- *Incorrect Sequence*: This group of bugs has incorrect sequences of the bug process compared the proposed model. The term 'incorrect' refers to abnormal sequence and behavior with the bug fixing process.

Significantly, 71%-83% of each project bugs were being *Fixed and Closed on the same day*. Therefore it was added as a separate group. It was noticed that Filezilla and WxWidgets were missing the 'assign' step for the MPA model.

Figure 5 illustrates the comparison of bug fixing process groups against the duration of bug fix groups. For Scintilla, the incorrect sequences occur in Bugs fixed in 0-10 days only. Also bugs that were fixed and closed the same day occur in all three groups. Finally bugs that took more than 64 days were all closed on the same day as being fixed. In the case of WxWidgets, there is an even distribution of the different types of bug fixing process executions, however, bugs fixed and closed on the same day always is greater than the other groups. Finally with Filezilla, Figure 5 indicates that the incorrect sequence, although very small, occurs in bugs that took up to 10 days to fix and more than 64 days to fix. As with WxWidgets, the bugs that were fixed and closed in the same day occur in all bug groups, however, most are found in bugs that took up to 10 days to fix. As seen below, results do not to show a clear trend.

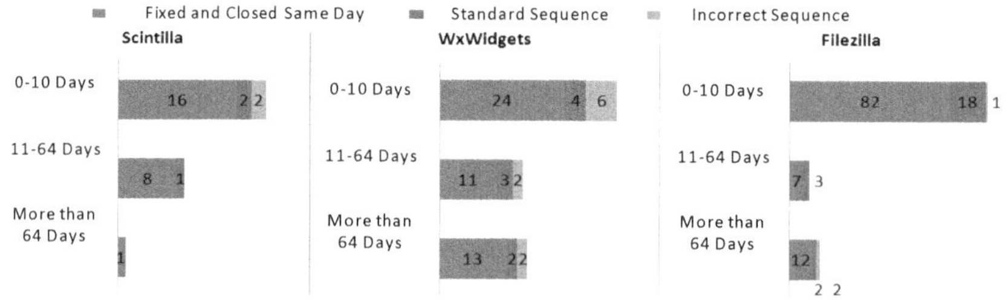

Fig. 5. Bug fixing process compared with bug classifications

Program Slicing Metrics
Using the assessment of bug fixing processes groupings, comparisons are made against the bug characteristics.

- Bug CC Analysis: The graphs in Figure 6 illustrate the distribution of cyclomatic complexity of the bugs. The results indicate that the 11 to 64 days group has the largest distribution compared to the other groups. Also 11 to 64 days has higher bug CC compared as well. This suggests that bugs that are fixed in 11 to 64 days have a larger range of bug CC and are higher in complexity as compared to the other groupings. It is also interesting to note that bugs that took than 64 days to fix have low complexity and a lower distribution.

- Bug LoC Analysis: The box plots illustrated in Figure 7 show the Bug LoC for bugs within the bug classifications. The graphs clearly show that bugs that took 11-64 days to fix have the highest lines of code in all projects. Apart from the highest lines of code we cannot make other similar characteristics. It seems that there is no clear trend from the three projects. Scintilla and WxWidgets seem to indicate that the 11 to 64 days has a largest distribution of Bug CC, however Filezilla suggest that maybe all groups have a similar distribution. These results indicate that further analysis with a larger test group need to be done.

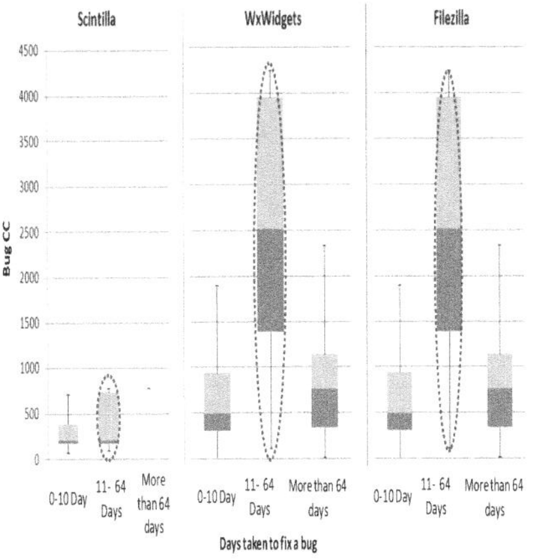

Fig. 6. Bug CC Distribution using Bug Classification across Projects

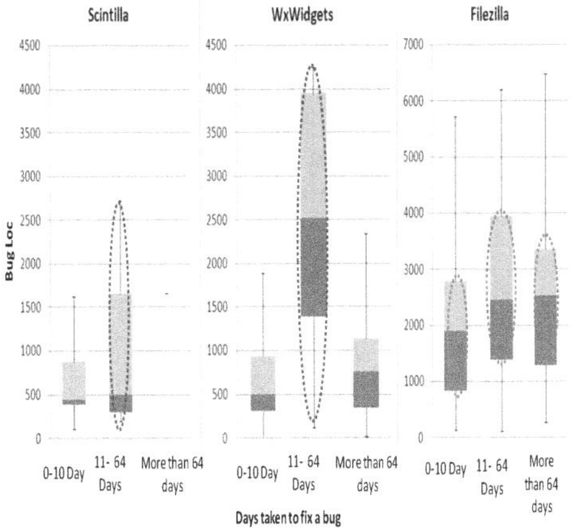

Fig. 7. Lines of Code Distribution using Bug Classification across Projects

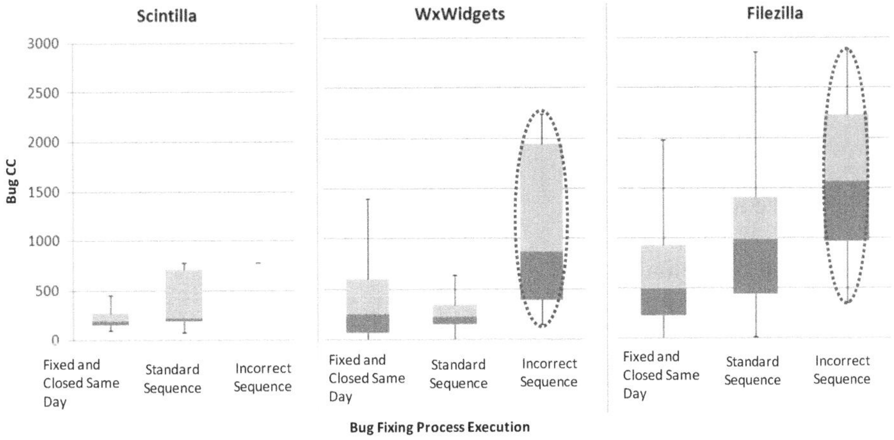

Fig. 8. Bug CC and Process Classifications

Total Data Analysis

Finally, we performed an analysis combining both the micro process execution and program slicing metrics. Results are as follows:

- Bug CC: The graphs in Figure 8 are the distribution of Bug CC metric of bugs grouped according to the bug fixing process per project. The graphs suggest that in each project, bugs with incorrect sequences have the highest distribution and maximum bug CC. The interpretation could be misleading as seen in the previous section, incorrect sequences account for only 2% to 15% of the sample size. However shows that further analysis is needed and the direction is promising.

- Bug LoC: Figure 9 show the results of when the groupings of bugs according to execution process were measured using the Bug LoC metric. Similar to the results seen in Bug CC, Bug LoC also displays incorrect sequences as having the widest range and highest lines of code as compared to the other groups. Similar to Bug CC analysis with program slicing, this information could be misleading as the sample sizes for the incorrect sequences are extremely low.

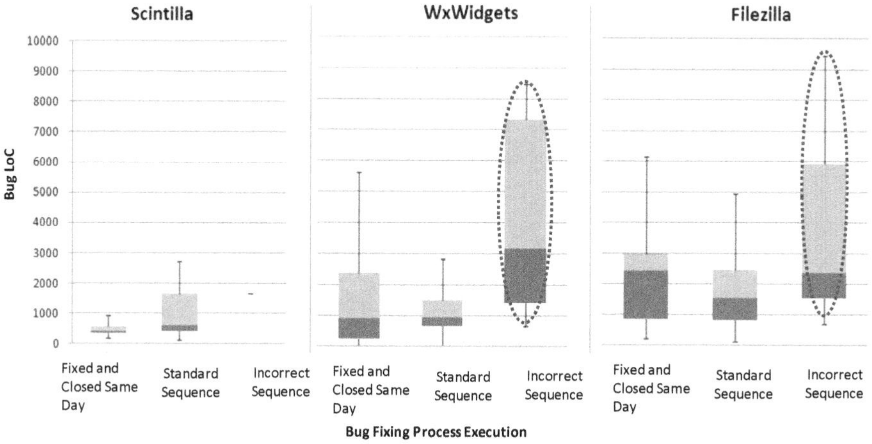

Fig. 9. Bug LoC and Process Classification

4 Discussion

4.1 Threats to Validity

This paper shows that the bug classification has some many challenges and validation issues with getting the correct datasets for experiments. Firstly the extraction methods are messy due to the many variations in the way the data repositories are managed, for example CVS and SVN. Additionally many of the software projects have subtle differences that make data extraction difficult. Other research have also encountered these perils, making OSS analysis data validation questionable [21]. Also the analysis only covered bugs that the bug fixing process could be re-constructed as well as have generated bug characteristics. This constraint also contributed to the small data we had to use for the analysis.

Another threat would be the accuracy of the metrics. Currently the slices are at file level, which could be arguably too broad a scope. However we do plan to do calculations of Bug CC and Bug LoC at function level to get more accurate results. It is stressed that what was more important was the results and feasibility of this new approach.

Though all the difficulties, the research did find feasible projects and was able to successful experiment and draw results. Since this is a proof on concept, emphasis was placed more on the results and methodology rather than the validation of the approach. The total final analysis in Figure 8 and 9 show very interesting results, however due to the small amount of data statistical analysis could not be performed. It is envisioned that with more accurate metrics, statistical analysis will be applied.

4.2 Findings in Analysis

The approach taken proves that bugs could be grouped based on program slicing based metrics. Using our proposed approach results firstly showed that using the program slicing metrics, the bugs were grouped according to how long it takes to fix the bug. With visual analysis of the distribution, it was found that the bug distribution changed after 10 days and 64 days. One theory based on project management, 10 days is 2 man weeks therefore developers may be pushed by deadlines to fix the bugs before 10 days.

To better understand the bug classification, the distributions of program slicing metrics were analyzed according to the bug groupings. Findings in Figure 6 and 7 suggest that bugs fixed within 10 days show lower complexity. Bugs between 11 and 64 days show a wider range of complexity and bugs that took more than 64 days had a much lower complexity. Since most bugs lie in the 0-10 day group, it can be concluded that bugs with lower complexity are fixed in less days. However another conclusion could be related to project management, 10 days is 2 weeks so maybe a project manager may require a set of bugs to be completed by that deadline. In relation of lines of code per bug, there seem some trends but nothing concrete enough to propose, therefore further analysis and review of the lines of code metric need to be performed.

The second part of the research aimed at analyzing the micro process execution, and grouped using the bug classifications. Results firstly show not all projects follow the proposed model for bug fixing. Both Filezilla and WxWidgets omitted the 'assign to developer' activity in the bug fixing process. Possible reasons would be the limitations of the bug tracking tool or the assignment process is not part of that projects bug fixing process related to two of the three projects. Also this shows the real time-frame in which the bug was fixed.

Another interesting finding was the appearance of bugs that were closed on the same day that it was fixed. In all test subjects, results indicated that the majority of bugs had bug closed the same day they were fixed. It was found that bugs closed in 0-10 days were most prone to errors in the bug fixing process. All projects indicated more bugs with incorrect sequences occur in bugs fixed in ten days. Bugs older than 10 days have a lesser chance of having incorrect sequences.

Finally, the main part of the analysis was done combining both the micro process execution and program slicing metrics. Bugs were grouped according to their bug fixing process execution against both Bug CC and Bug LoC. These results suggest that bugs with incorrect sequence in their bug fixing processes show a wide distribution with very high cyclomatic complexity and lines of code as compared to bugs that follow the general bug fixing model and bugs that are closed in the same day as being fixed. This data however may not be reliable as the sample set for incorrect sequence is too small to have any statistical significance.

4.3 Testing Hypothesis

Putting together the bug classifications and the analysis of the micro process as a proof of concept, there is enough evidence to suggest that there is indeed a relationship between bug characteristics and its processes executed. For example for bugs taking up to 10 days to fixing generally have low complexity and lines of code show a tendency to be closed in the same day and have a higher likelihood to have errors in its process execution.

In response to the hypotheses, the findings support Hypothesis 1 as our research shows groupings of similar bugs having similar bug characteristics. For example, bugs with incorrect micro process execution show much higher Bug CC metric than the correct standard and fixed and closed in same day bugs. Hypothesis 2 is also supported by the evidence that higher Bug CC is more prone to incorrect sequences. The experiments therefore suggest a relationship between bug characteristics and how they were fixed. However, further research it needed to have more confidence in these hypotheses.

5 Conclusion and Future Works

As mentioned throughout the paper, this work is seen as proof of concept with the final aim of developing a prediction model for bug fixing process based on the bug's characteristics. Future work will be to refine the tools and metrics used. For this research, only two program slicing metrics were introduced. As indicated by the results, extensive analysis is needed to make more concrete judgments.

Current results of the research act as a proof of concept for the use of program slicing in the inspection of the bug fixing processes in a software development project. It is envisioned that the research will help contribute to a better understanding and classification of bugs based on the nature of code. Currently the program slicing is performed according to file level code metrics. Future work will attempt to program slice at function level, giving precise metrics. A larger sample data that can give statistical analysis will be experimented to further validate the results.

If successful, the research can used to help create 'prediction models' for bugs. For example, based on a history of previous bugs and the trends of a specific project, a bug's fixing process could be estimated from its bug characteristics , thus assist developers handle the bug faster. This would then contribute to software improvement at this micro level.

The implementation could be a tool that is used during the bug detection and assignment stage of the bug fixing process. It would be able to analyze what part of the code are affected, and based on the classification, predict how long the bug would normally take to fix as well code based metrics such as the complexity of code.

In the bigger picture, this work contributes towards a predictive process model based on the program slicing metrics. As this is a novel approach, this study contributes as a starting point towards this goal.

Acknowledgements

This work is being conducted as a part of the StagE project, The Development of Next-Generation IT Infrastructure, supported by the Ministry of Education, Culture, Sports, Science and Technology.

References

1. Herbsleb, J., Carleton, A., Rozum, J., Siegel, J., Zubrow, D.: Benefits of CMM-Based Software Process Improvement: Initial Results, CMU/SEI-94-TR-13, Software Engineering Institute. Carnegie Mellon University, Pittsburgh, Pa (1994)
2. Margaret, K.K., Kent, J.A.: Interpreting the CMMI: A Process Improvement Approach, Auerbach Publications. CSUE Body of Knowledge area: Software Quality Management (2003)
3. Schmauch, C.H.: ISO 9000 for Software Developers, 2nd edn. ASQ Quality Press (1995)
4. Beecham, S., Hall, T., Rainer, A.: Software process problems in twelve software companies: an empirical analysis. Empirical Software Engineering 8, 7–42 (2003)
5. Baddoo, N., Hall, T.: De-Motivators of software process improvement: an analysis of practitioner's views. Journal of Systems and Software 66(1), 23–33 (2003)
6. Niazi, M., Babar, M.A.: De-motivators for software process improvement: an analysis of Vietnamese practitioners' views. In: Münch, J., Abrahamsson, P. (eds.) PROFES 2007. LNCS, vol. 4589, pp. 118–131. Springer, Heidelberg (2007)
7. Brodman, J.G., Johnson, D.L.: What small businesses and small organizations say about the CMMI. In: Proceedings of the 16th International Conference on Software Engineering. IEEE Computer Society, Los Alamitos (1994)
8. Rainer, A., Hall, T.: Key success factors for implementing software process improvement: a maturity-based analysis. Journal of Systems and Software 62(2), 71–84 (2002)
9. Yoo, C., Yoon, J., Lee, B., Lee, C., Lee, J., Hyun, S., Wu, C.: A unified model for the implementation of both ISO 9001:2000 and CMMI by ISO-certified organizations. The Journal of Systems and Software 79(7), 954–961 (2006)
10. Armbrust, O., Katahira, M., Miyamoto, Y., Münch, J., Nakao, H., Campo, A.O.: Scoping software process lines. Software Process Improvement and Practice 14(3), 181–197 (2009)
11. Morisaki, S., Iida, H.: Fine-Grained Software Process Analysis to Ongoing Distributed Software Development. In: 1st Workshop on Measurement-based Cockpits for Distributed Software and Systems Engineering Projects (SOFTPIT 2007), Munich, Germany, pp. 26–30 (August 2007)
12. Weiser, M.: Program slicing. In: Proceedings of the 5th international Conference on Software Engineering, San Diego, California, United States, March 09 - 12, pp. 439–449. IEEE Press, Piscataway (1981)
13. Hall, T., Wernick, P.: Program Slicing Metrics and Evolvability: an Initial Study. In: IEEE International Workshop Software Evolvability, pp. 35–40 (2005)
14. Pan, K., Kim, S., Whitehead Jr., E.J.: Bug Classification Using Program Slicing Metrics. In: IEEE International Workshop Source Code Analysis and Manipulation, pp. 31–42 (2006)
15. Watson, A., McCabe, T.: Structured testing: A testing methodology using the cyclomatic complexity metric. In: National Institute of Standards and Technology, Gaithersburg, MD, pp. 235–500 (NIST) Special Publication (1996)
16. Xu, B., Qian, J., Zhang, X., Wu, Z., Chen, L.: A brief survey of program slicing. SIGSOFT Softw. Eng. Notes 30(2), 1–36 (2005)
17. Ranganath, V.P., Hatcliff, J.: Slicing concurrent Java programs using Indus and Kaveri. International Journal on Software Tools for Technology Transfer (STTT) 9(5), 489–504 (2007)
18. Wang, T., Roychoudhury, A.: Dynamic slicing on Java bytecode traces. ACM Trans. Program. Lang. Syst. 30(2), 1–49 (2008)

19. Anderson, P., Zarins, M.: The CodeSurfer Software Understanding Platform. In: Proceedings of the 13th International Workshop on Program Comprehension, May 15-16, pp. 147–148 (2005)
20. Bevan, J., Whitehead, E.J., Kim, S., Godfrey, M.: Facilitating software evolution research with Kenyon. In: Proceedings of the 10th European Software Engineering Conference Held Jointly with 13th ACM SIGSOFT International Symposium on Foundations of Software Engineering, ESEC/FSE-13, Lisbon, Portugal, September 05-09, pp. 177–186. ACM, New York (2005)
21. Howison, J., Crowston, K.: The perils and pitfalls of mining SourceForge. Presented at Mining Software Repositories Workshop, International Conference on Software Engineering, Edinburgh, Scotland, May 25 (2004)

Systematic Piloting of Agile Methods in the Large: Two Cases in Embedded Systems Development

Jeanette Heidenberg[1,2], Mari Matinlassi[1], Minna Pikkarainen[3], Piia Hirkman[2], and Jari Partanen[1]

[1] EB, Elektrobit Corporation, Finland
{mari.matinlassi,jari.partanen}@elektrobit.com
[2] Åbo Akademi University/Turku Centre for Computer Science, Finland
{jeanette.heidenberg,piia.hirkman}@abo.fi
[3] VTT Technical Research Centre of Finland
minna.pikkarainen@vtt.fi

Abstract. Deploying agile methods in a large, diverse, geographically distributed setting is a challenging task. In this paper, we propose that systematic piloting is to be used in order to build experience and to overcome the most common challenges of agile deployment, such as resistance to change. We approach this by developing a method for piloting agile. This method is developed based on multiple-case study in a large embedded systems company. Based on two cases, we describe a method that transcends the encountered challenges and can help meld an agile method with a plan-driven organization.

Keywords: Software process improvement, agile deployment, pilot.

1 Introduction

Industry surveys indicate that the acceptance and knowledge of agile methods are still limited in industrial settings, especially in organizations that have used a traditional software development approach for years. Typically, the deployment of agile methods is resisted and wanted in these companies at the same time [1]; deployment is challenging [1] particularly for large and globally distributed software enterprises [2]. Some efforts have been made to tackle the deployment problem (see, e.g., [3] and [4]), but current research reports are scarce in providing clear methods and advice with regard to deploying agile methods and principles. Furthermore, the reports do not concentrate on what so often lies at the very beginning of software process improvement undertakings going agile: a pilot project. A pilot applies agile methods on a small scale in order to verify and adapt the methods before general deployment.

This paper presents a multiple-case study with research data from two pilot cases allowing cross-case analysis and, thus, more general research results compared to a single-case study [5]. The case study method [6] is a suitable research approach for studies in which the goal is to investigate contemporary phenomena in real-life contexts; in our case agile deployment in a large embedded systems company. This goal can be formulated as a research question: How to deploy agile methods in large, diverse organizations? At the beginning of the study we inferred that piloting is a means

M. Ali Babar, M. Vierimaa, and M. Oivo (Eds.): PROFES 2010, LNCS 6156, pp. 47–61, 2010.
© Springer-Verlag Berlin Heidelberg 2010

of deployment that can help in overcoming resistance to change, a proposition that was directly related to the challenges present at the case company (see Sections 2-3). This proposition gave further rise to a second research question: How to systematically implement agile pilots as part of the overall deployment process in a plan-driven environment? The defined research questions were addressed in the two cases in which an agile piloting method was developed. The research was based on rich data that was collected with workshops, semi-structured interviews and pilot follow-ups (as described in Section 5), reflected in the method that resulted from analytically generalizing the cases (Section 4).

2 Piloting in Context

According to the Oxford English dictionary [7], piloting refers (among other things) to "the testing of a scheme, project, etc., on a small scale before its wider introduction". The concept is used in very different contexts, such as research methods and software engineering. For example, it is used as a transition strategy in product family engineering [8] and as a deployment method for software process improvement (SPI) undertakings. This article approaches piloting mostly from the SPI point of view: here piloting means first applying a method in a small amount of real product projects or customer projects in order to identify risks and test the method, then adapting the methods based on learning and finally deploying the piloted method to other projects. The pilot project has to be a fairly good representative of a typical project in the organization. After a pilot, it is easier to decide whether to launch wide scale adoption of piloted practices to the whole organization – or not.

Piloting has been recommended for SPI-deployment in more traditional as well as in agile initiatives. Traditionally, piloting is regarded to be a part of SPI [9] or recommended by deployment methods such as QIP [10] and IDEAL [11] that are typically used in model- or standard-based improvement efforts (e.g., CMMI [12] and ISO 15504 [13]). With regard to agile methods, deployment has proven to include a number of difficulties both specific to an agile method [14],[15] and more general in nature [3],[16],[17],[18],[19]. Due to its testing nature, piloting can be recommended also for an agile context; piloting responds to some common needs in deploying agile methods (method tailoring - common especially in large projects [2],[20], evaluation of needs and identifying risks, and doing assessments [21],[22],[23]). As Reifer [24] mentions, pilots were used by early adopters of agile methods to see whether the methods work in the context in question and to make agile processes work with existing ones (or the other way around). Indeed, piloting has been increasingly reported by the software intensive organizations and research communities describing experiences of agile methods [25]. Piloting has also been included as a distinct step in a process for iterative improvement within agile software development projects suggested by Salo and Abrahamsson [26].

Moitra [27] suggests that while there are benefits in piloting, unsuccessful pilots may lead to resistance and skepticism for SPI; the need for piloting should depend on several factors, such as the level of support for SPI, how well the effects of SPI are understood, and the complexity of change [27]. That is, piloting is not a playground but an important phase where assistance is needed. Some recommendations do exist

(Kulpa and Johnson present five life-cycle phases similar to those of process improvement [9]; Moitra [28] lists nine analogous steps that relate to piloting in the implementation phase of an SPI-shaped change initiative) but these recommendations are generic and do not account for details in implementations in practice.

3 Background and Motivation

EB, Elektrobit Corporation, is a large, geographically distributed company specialized in demanding embedded software and hardware solutions for the wireless and automotive industries. The net sales for the year 2008 were MEUR 172.3 in total. As is the situation for many companies in the software industry, the case company has to meet an ever increasing demand for high-quality products while at the same time hitting tighter marketing windows. The right functionality has to be delivered at the right time, and the company has to be able to react to changing circumstances and requirements quickly. In order to meet these needs, the top management of the company decided to move in a more agile direction.

The products developed within the business areas of the case company are typically quite complex, including hardware/software codesign and real-time requirements. The company has very diverse project settings, ranging from small co-located projects to large, geographically distributed ones. The staff of the larger projects will typically consist of people with diverse competence areas. In this case, the project is often divided into dedicated specialist teams, responsible for, e.g., systemization, hardware development, software development, and testing. Furthermore, the operational mode of the projects will vary depending on their respective customer and partner interfaces.

Due to the large scale of the company and the many different types of projects run within the company, the need for a piloting method arose. The need to pilot was obvious, since general deployment of a new method is such a large company would be risky and difficult without testing it on a smaller scale first. Furthermore, the resistance to change among the stakeholders needed to be bridged. But due to the diversity of the project settings, just one pilot was not enough. A successful pilot would only be seen as a success story for that type of project. We needed to create enough success stories to prove the concept on a general level. For this we needed a method for setting up and running pilots.

In EB, piloting was not merely seen as testing something on a smaller scale; the piloting was also regarded as a means for introducing change into the organization. Organizational change in general and in the context of SPI share similar traits as also noted with early adopters of agile methods [24]. Studies of organizational change in SPI (for example, see [28],[29],[30]) prescribe elements of success related to an overall vision, clear goals, and both planning and managing change. Another issue concerns understanding: the environment and starting point as well as the method to be used should be fully understood. Further issues include creating and sustaining a (positive) need for change by management sponsorship, change agents, and allowing for those touched by the change to participate actively (involvement).

Due to this involvement ("organizations change one person at a time" [29]), the people perspective should be present from the start. (Naturally, this is nicely in harmony with the agile principles [31].) The people aspect is explicitly considered in a general model for individual and organizational change called ADKAR [32], the name of which stands for the five steps on the people side of change: building awareness, having a desire to support and to participate in change, creating and providing knowledge of how to change, fostering ability to implement new skills and behaviors, and reinforcement to sustain the change. Somewhat similar core ideas are reflected in phases for supporting organizational change in SPI [27] and for adopting new culture in software engineering organizations [33].

Based on the existing methods and recommendations above, and drawing from the guidelines for piloting mentioned in Section 2, we extracted the main level steps for the method, i.e., Marketing the pilot, Preparing the pilot and Executing the pilot (see Section 4). Empirical data and experiences collected from two real pilot cases (see Section 5) provided the more detailed definitions for each step.

4 A Method for Agile Piloting

Fig.1 shows the big picture of the piloting method developed for the case company. The method is composed of three main stages: marketing the pilot, preparing the pilot and executing the pilot. Marketing the pilot is about achieving company internal acceptance – both formal and informal acceptance – before starting the pilot. In the pilot preparation stage a decision to start the pilot is already there. However, some preparation and setting up needs to be done before pilot kick-off. After the kick-off the actual pilot execution stage starts. This is an iterative process of doing and learning. Each stage is composed of two steps, which are described in detail below.

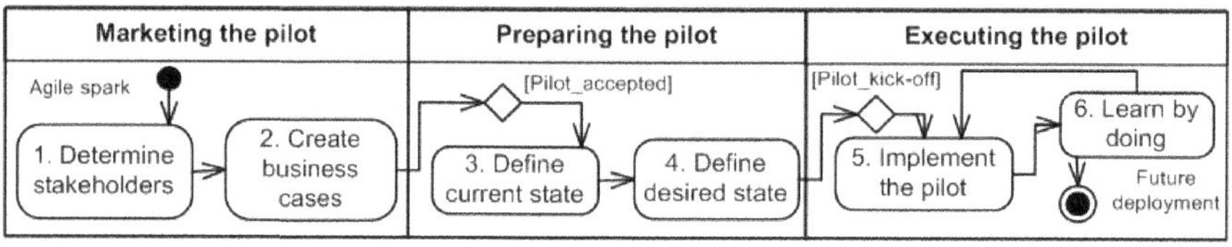

Fig. 1. Overview of the piloting method

4.1 Marketing the Pilot

Start with agile spark. Agile spark is the initiation point for agile piloting. If conventional engineering and communication problems within the projects drive the initiation of the agile drive, the agile spark is said to be bottom-up. On the other hand, the agile spark may be introduced top-down when, e.g., top management wants significant improvements in productivity of the organization.

Determine stakeholders. Committed stakeholders are interest groups that need to accept the pilot before it starts. Acceptance does not only mean formal acceptance, but also mental acceptance of the pilot and the ideas it represents. Mental acceptance is crucial for the success of the pilot. Related interest groups need to be aware of what is going on. However, we need neither their commitment nor permission to start the pilot. Both interest groups – committed and related – need to be recognized and their interests need to be determined.

Create business cases. A business case motivates a stakeholder to mentally accept the pilot. The interests of each stakeholder are different and business cases need to be created to address the needs of the stakeholders.

4.2 Preparing the Pilot

Once the pilot has been formally accepted pilot preparation can start.

Define current state. The importance of defining the current state cannot be emphasized enough. The following methods can be used for defining the current state: interviews (structured or open); workshops (with different interest groups, especially with committed stakeholders), and external help for analyzing the results.

Both the positive and negative issues in the current state are summarized and documented in order to monitor the progress of the pilot later.

Define desired state. Desired state definition is as important as defining the current state. Without the desired state definition, it is difficult to select or adapt agile methods for piloting. The best way to perform desired state definition is through workshops. The desired state definition may include both (1) minimum requirements/expectations on the pilot and (2) longer term deployment desires.

4.3 Executing the Pilot

The kick-off marks the official start of the implementation stage and serves as a means to build a sense of involvement.

Implement the pilot. The practical steps of how to implement the pilot depend heavily on the current and desired states and further, on the properties of the pilot project. That is, general steps for doing pilot implementation cannot be defined explicitly. However, our piloting method lists the most important points to be considered in pilot implementation.

Select the agile methods/practices to apply. Start with a method that fits the needs of the pilot. Ensure that the selected method is clearly understood before it is adapted or before more methods are included. Often it is necessary to apply the method for some time before it is clearly understood.

Adapt the selected method. Like software development methods in general, also agile methods usually need adaptation [2],[17],[34] and also here, the special requirements of the target environment need to be taken into account.

Adapt the company processes to integrate with the agile methods to be piloted. An agile method in a plan-driven context is a difficult combination. Therefore, at least the interfaces to the related company processes/practices need to be adapted to fit agile. Otherwise there is a risk that the new agile method will be adapted to a plan-driven approach – and not the other way around – which may fail the pilot in the end.

Prepare the infrastructure to meet the pilot needs. Infrastructure may mean anything from team rooms and software tools to pens and paper and digital cameras.

Organize training. It is important to ensure that the project staff and stakeholders have the correct skill set to use the selected methods efficiently. For this, different forms of training may be needed. One should consider both general purpose method training and training in the specific methods adapted for the pilot. General purpose training may include, e.g., courses for Scrum Masters or tutorials in test-driven development. Specific training may include presentations or workshops with the purpose of explaining the methods to be used in the pilot and how they are integrated with the surrounding processes.

Learn by doing. Even if the major part of the effort is done already before the actual pilot project is started, it is important that the pilot is not abandoned later. Experience gathered during the pilot should be used to adapt the way of working in the pilot as the understanding of the piloted methods improves. In our method, we provide the following advice in order to ensure that the pilot is learning by doing.

Organize pilot follow-up practices. A (more or less formal) steering group regularly follows up on the status and risks of the pilot. One important aspect of this is the collection of metrics in order to know whether the pilot is headed in the right direction. These metrics should measure the progress from the current state towards the desired state. The metrics collected can be both quantitative and qualitative. Examples of quantitative metrics are software quality and cycle time, while examples of qualitative metrics are work satisfaction and customer satisfaction. The steering group follows up on the progress of the pilot, identifying risks and organizing extra support and training if needed.

Adapt the methods if needed. The methods chosen at the beginning of the pilot may need further adaption to suit the specific setting of the pilot project. The metrics collected will tell the project whether it is headed in the right direction. But this information alone is not enough to know how to adapt the methods further. During the pilot, it is important to ensure that feedback is collected regularly from the pilot participants. They have the first-hand experience of using the piloted methods, and their growing understanding needs to be captured. One method for this is retrospectives, as defined in Scrum [35]. The feedback should be used to improve and further adapt the way of working during the pilot, keeping the desired state in mind.

5 Pilot Implementation in EB

In this paper, we present two pilots run at the company. Both pilots were started in 2008 and were set up according to the proposed methodology. However, due to the overall financial situation, both pilots were put on hold towards the end of the year. At the time of writing this paper, the first pilot is still on hold, while the second was continued in mid 2009.

The first pilot, which we will refer to as TeleAgile below, was a typical example of a telecommunications project at EB with respect to size and context. The planned size of the project was 60 people. Of these, 20 were included in the pilot team, in which the roles of project manager, system designer, software developer, software integrator, software tester, product owner and technical coordinator were all represented. The pilot team held full responsibility for their part of the system, and if they were to fail, the project would fail. Another 10 people were involved in other interest groups (program management, resource management, etc.). The project itself was a software centric project, part of a larger program. Within the program, the project had interfaces towards other software projects, hardware projects, FPGA (field programmable gate array) projects and mechanics projects. Of these, some were company internal projects and some were run by subcontractors. The project was geographically distributed over a total of five sites: three in Finland, one in China and one in India.

The second pilot (MultiTechScrum) was prepared at the same time as TeleAgile. MultiTechScrum is a smaller and local project with 15 people in development and 15 people in other interest groups (marketing, customer support, product planning etc.). MultiTechScrum seemed to be an easy case for piloting agile due to its size and local nature. However, it still presented some challenges. MultiTechScrum develops a multi-technological product involving engineers on several technology domains: (1) software, (2) hardware, (3) RF (radio frequency), (4) FPGA and (5) mechanics. Further, the pilot project product development applies a product family engineering approach where reuse is maximized, i.e., the major part of the development effort is spent on reusable assets and domain engineering.

In the next sections we go through the steps defined in the method presented in Section 4. For each of the steps we explain how that step was implemented in practice in our two cases.

5.1 Marketing the Pilot

Start with agile spark. In TeleAgile, the "agile spark" was initiated in several levels of the organization. Program and project management were the driving force, but with strong support from business unit management. On the team level, there was also a strong will to improve the work methods. The reasons for the willingness to change were mainly issues of communication as well as challenges in balancing changing requirements with a tight delivery schedule. Scrum [35] was not the explicit wish of the pilot – they were rather looking for a bespoke solution for their specific setting.

In MultiTechScrum, the "agile spark" was initiated in project management. The challenge was that the project team and other interest groups had become isolated in silos – even though they were co-located – and the interest groups suffered from mutual mistrust and communication problems. Project management wanted to overcome these problems and when they were introduced to Scrum, they wanted to try it out.

Determine stakeholders. The main stakeholders for both pilots were (1) program and project management, whose concerns are the scope, quality, budget and timeliness of the product; (2) business line management, who act as the customer interface and maintain the product roadmaps based on the customers' needs; (3) line management, who are responsible for the human resources aspect of the projects and manage the overall budget; (4) project staff, who needs to have the right information at the right time in order to design the required software, hardware, gate arrays, radio frequency circuits and mechanics. There also are related stakeholders such as customer support, marketing and production; however, the work of these interest groups is not directly affected by the agile pilot.

Create business cases. The business cases that were used to motivate the committed stakeholders to mentally accept the pilot were many. Here, we provide some examples. (1) Project and program management: "the projects will be smaller and therefore easier to manage" and "you will have better visibility into what the real status of the project is". (2) Product planning: "the projects will not be delayed" and "you will have new features to sell every 6 month". (3) Line management: "project costs will be reduced through improved communication" and "the well-being of the project staff and the quality of the product will increase". (4) Project staff: "you will be allowed to concentrate on the goals of the ongoing sprint and have more control over your own tasks".

5.2 Preparing the Pilot

Once we had common acceptance for the pilot projects as well as a formal decision to go ahead, we started preparing for the pilots themselves.

Define current state. In TeleAgile, the current state was established by workshops and semi-structured interviews. In order to ensure transparency into the pilot, a steering group was set up to which all levels of management were invited. At the very beginning of the pilot preparation step, this steering group gave its view on the current state. This was further refined by performing semi-structured individual interviews with the pilot team. For the interviews, external consultants were used. A total of nine interviews were held for the development team. Each interview took approximately 1-2 hours and they were all tape recorded and transcribed. The interview questions were based on the general question framework of the CMMI project and requirements management process areas as well as on agile practices. However, the framework was specifically tailored based on the needs of the pilot project.

Based on the outcome of the interviews, the current state was summarized and a proposal for the new way of working was defined. The results were discussed in the steering group as well as in a workshop with the interviewees, where they gave feedback to the current state collected as well as on the new working methods.

In MultiTechScrum, the current state was defined by first conducting one-on-one interviews with software design engineers. The interviews were semi-structured and included questions such as what is working well at the moment (regarding tools, processes, communication, co-operation) and what are the typical problems you face daily. The interviews were followed by workshops to define the current process and its strengths and challenges. The workshops were conducted in two phases and the attendants were project managers, line managers and an external agile consultant. In the first workshop, the participants collected challenges with the current way of working as well as good practices they would not change. They drew the current product development process and mapped the challenges and good practices to the current process. Between the two workshops, the external consultant created a proposal of how to adapt the Scrum method to meet the pilot project requirements.

Define desired state. In TeleAgile, the desired state was established in the same way as the current state. The steering group expressed their view of the desired state in the early phases of pilot preparation and this was refined through the interviews and workshops with the pilot team. The risks of the pilot were also defined by both the pilot team and the steering group, and included in the risk list that was monitored by the steering group.

In MultiTechScrum, the desired state was defined in the second workshop. The proposal for the new way of working was presented by the consultant and the attendants worked out the potential desired state they would like to see after successful deployment of the proposed process. Also potential risks related to the pilot were identified.

The desired states for the two pilots had many similarities. For example, the projects expected improvement in *visibility and predictability*. They expected, e.g., that the new product features would be more visible not only to the product managers but also to the development teams. From the viewpoint of the whole organization, the visibility for the near future (1-3 months) would be clearer and the transparency of the current development status would be better for the sales and marketing department. The design engineers would also see the big picture more easily and the project team would be able to control the focus of their own work and schedule the work tasks more effectively. Considering predictability, the desire would be to provide a more predictable product release schedule and more exact schedules (even if the content varies). From the viewpoint of project planning, the project cost and schedule predictability was expected to improve and the planning of tasks would be easier (when planning is done more often). The better predictability would provide more reliable deliveries – which is extremely important from the business point of view. As the goals of the project were qualitative in nature, we used qualitative methods for collecting the metrics. Interviews before and after the pilot serve to recognize whether the stakeholders had perceived an improvement in visibility and predictability. The project also collected standard metrics, such as defect rates and delivery times in order to mitigate risks.

5.3 Executing the Pilot

Implement the pilot. After defining the current state and the desired state, it was clear that major changes were needed in order to reach the desired state. We proceed by describing the steps taken in implementing the pilot according to the method described in Section 4.

Select the methods to apply. In both pilots, the agile method used as a starting point was Scrum. In TeleAgile the word "Scrum" was never used, even though the practices suggested as solutions for the challenges were taken from Scrum. In MultiTechScrum Scrum was selected by the team as the agile method thought to meet most of the needs of the pilot project. The main practices used in the pilots were: timeboxed deliveries, increased face-to-face communication through meetings (planning meeting, daily meeting, sprint demos), product and sprint backlogs, nightly build and early testing.

Adapt the selected method. It was not possible to use Scrum off the shelf in either of the pilots, so the method was tailored to meet the needs of the specific pilot. However, the main goal was to really change the way of working in both pilots. Therefore, Scrum was only slightly tailored without violating the agile principles. The refinements of Scrum are described below.

In TeleAgile, the purpose of the tailoring was to fit the methods to a large-scale, geographically distributed project. In MultiTechScrum, the purpose was to meet the specific needs introduced by product line engineering and a multi-technology environment. The tailoring was the most challenging part of the pilot implementation since there was little existing guidance in the literature.

In order to deliver in a timeboxed fashion, TeleAgile had to ensure that the contents of the timeboxes were synchronized throughout the entire program. MultiTechScrum had to ensure synchronization between the different technology teams. This requires short-term up-front planning, especially with regards to systemization. For this, we agreed to secure a system team that would also work in a timeboxed fashion, slightly ahead of the development teams. The system team would perform continuous requirement analysis, to ensure that the relevant system input is available at the start of every sprint. This approach was inspired by just-in-time approaches common in the agile world [36].

The meeting practices were the easiest to set up. In both pilots, the daily team meeting was extended to include members of other teams as well, in order to facilitate communication across team borders. The meeting structure was slightly more complex in the TeleAgile project, since the scale and distribution of the project implied a larger number of teams on different levels.

The product and sprint backlogs proved to not be sufficient for the needs of the pilots. TeleAgile needed an innovation backlog, where new features would be added before analysis and possible inclusion in the product backlog. MultiTechScrum needed a reuse backlog in order to manage product line requirements.

Adapt the company processes to integrate with the agile methods to be piloted. At the time of the pilot, the company desired to keep the plan-driven, traditional end product process and project milestone thinking through the pilot. Still, we were able to modify the end product process slightly in order to keep the pilot agile.

The main changes done were in the communication between the different stakeholders. For both pilots, we changed the meeting culture by replacing large, lengthy project meetings with shorter, timeboxed meetings that were clearly defined with respect to time, place, who should be present and what should be discussed.

Prepare the infrastructure to meet the pilot needs. The need arose for some infrastructural changes to support the pilots. Team rooms needed to be set up. We needed to organize support for light-weight documentation methods. This support would include devices such as digital cameras, white boards and flip charts. Since TeleAgile was a geographically distributed project, some computer based tools needed to be set up, such as a wiki-based support system for clarifying design decisions and a dedicated tool for error handling.

Organize training. Three types of training were used. We trained Certified Scrum Masters and Product Owners, using an international training provider. This proved to be a very powerful way to change the people's mindsets from plan-driven to agile thinking. Due to financial challenges, we also had to make use of more cost-effective training methods. In MultiTechScrum, we trained the engineers, product planning, management and related stakeholders in lectures given by in-house personnel supported by visiting agile gurus. Finally, we also had an existing in-house training set for software processes. We modified this to include the agile methods to be used and trained the project staff of the TeleAgile project using this training set. This was highly appreciated, though not as efficient in changing people's mindsets.

Learn by doing. During the writing of this paper, the TeleAgile pilot is no longer running, because the entire TeleAgile project was put on hold, its operational mode was changed and eventually it continued as an outsourced project. The MultiTech-Scrum pilot has been running for 6 months, i.e., is in the learn by doing stage. The TeleAgile pilot had a formal steering group with the responsibility to follow up on the progress and risks of the pilot. They were also responsible for collecting metrics in order to better understand the impacts of the changes. The MultiTechScrum pilot's steering group is less formal, but still performs the same tasks. The most important means of learning by doing, however, are the retrospectives. The pilot teams are asked to perform regular retrospectives where they evaluate their way of working and suggest improvements. These improvements can either be implemented immediately by the team itself or be escalated for the steering group to promote to other teams as well.

6 Discussion

The piloting mode used at EB derives from piloting and change management guidelines (see Section 3). The approach has some similarities to existing SPI deployment models such as QIP. However, in addition to the existing approaches, our method emphasizes the marketing and learning aspects. We now proceed to discuss the main challenges we encountered, how these are addressed in the literature and how we addressed them. We also discuss the implications of our work.

Resistance to change. The main challenge to overcome when introducing any changes is the inherent resistance to change. The main stakeholders that needed help with their resistance to change in our pilots were the engineers and the project managers. The engineers may feel threatened by the new way of working and the project managers may feel they lose power and status. Training has been recognized as an important success factor for agile practice adoption [1],[3]. We found our agile awareness trainings to be crucial for overcoming this resistance. In addition to training, Misra et al. [3] point out the importance of continuous learning. Agile methods support the ability to innovate and use the opportunity provided by change, that is, learning denoted as "generative" as opposed to "adaptive" [37]. The frequent retrospective approach was used for this purpose in our pilots.

We also suggest that one pays attention to the motivation level in the project at the time of the pilot. If there are motivational issues in the project that cannot be addressed by the pilot itself, it may be better to wait until the motivation levels are more normal. Marketing has been recommended for increasing motivation for SPI in an organization [38]. Although contrary evidence has recently been presented [39], the support of top management is an important incentive that encourages developers to use agile methods and engage in the knowledge transferring [1]. In our case, a good practice for EB was found to be collecting experiences of the agile pilot cases for information sharing purposes. However, the risk of an unsuccessful pilot that increases resistance should be taken into account as suggested by Moitra [27].

Preconceptions about agile. Even though agile methods are quite established in the industry today, some may still interpret agile as an approach that promotes "no design, no documentation". If this is the case, it may be beneficial to use a different vocabulary when discussing the pilot. We sometimes avoided using the words "Scrum" and "agile" and talked about terms like time-driven or timeboxed development instead.

Challenges in setting up a team room. Team environment is an important factor affecting the quality of agile development [38]. The open office space and the importance of the room environment have often been emphasized [40]. This is because agile teams should rely on continuous face to face interaction [41]. Any organization adopting agile needs to consider how the agile team could efficiently use both the advantages of the physical form and its translation to the digital medium [41]. Designing the team room proved to be a challenging task in our pilots. A team room requires more office space than a regular open office layout, so the same space will fit less people. Inform line management of the team room plans well ahead of time and be prepared that this may need negotiations. It is also important to take the current company culture and expectations on privacy into account when designing the team room, in order to reduce the resistance to this change.

Cultural differences. Cultural aspects is a significant factor affecting the agile adoption success: the project adopting agile should be able to be dynamic and make rapid decisions [3]. Cultural differences may occur in unexpected places, e.g., between two sites in the same country with different background in company culture, as was the case in our pilots. Situations in which the project members were accustomed to different types of traditional process-based development approaches and documentation structures were one such instance. It is important to be empathic and try to understand the needs and way of thinking of the stakeholders. We found that our decision to use external help for the interviews helped in understanding and bridging cultural differences. Our external consultants were perceived as more objective and brought in a fresh viewpoint.

Measuring pilot implications. Measuring the pilot implications quantitatively proved to be difficult. We investigated quantitative metrics, such as lead time, person-hours, productivity (e.g., lines of code), quality (e.g., defect rate), but none of these really objectively capture the improvements that we were aiming for. We believe that more qualitative metrics, like the ones proposed by the lean community [42] serve our purpose better. We especially want to capture the experience of the project staff. For this purpose, we suggest that interviews are used to determine the current state before and after the change has been implemented. Interviews also serve the additional purpose of creating commitment and a feeling of being heard.

Implications. As a result of applying the pilot method defined for the case company, a clear change in attitude was perceived. Before the pilots, the teams were not very keen on participating or eager to change. After the initiative and the pilots had been promoted, several teams were more than willing to participate. As the pilots progressed, there was overall a more positive attitude towards the agile methods used.

One could even say that resistance to change was overcome and thus one important goal with the pilots had been reached.

Another result of applying the pilot method is the experience gathered from tailoring both the agile methods used and the end product process in order to fit each other better. This enables an agile project to run in a non-agile context. The experience is accumulated as more pilots are implemented and will undoubtedly prove invaluable when deploying agile methods on a larger scale.

Although both of our cases used the same piloting approach, they had different culture, scope and context. However, neither of the cases did end up using a pure agile approach, but rather an adapted approach with traditional and agile elements as suggested by Boehm and Turner [43]. As the contents of different pilots may turn out to vary when running pilots in multiple environments within the same organization, one should consider what needs to be investigated with the pilots. If there is a need for truly investigating exactly the same thing in all of the pilots, the piloting steps should be consolidated to apply them all. On the other hand, if the need is to assess practices and determine risks, for example, the variations can prove to be useful.

The ultimate goal of the piloting effort is general deployment of agile methods in the company. As we can see such a clear change in the attitude towards agile methods already, we are fairly confident that systematic piloting is an efficient means of paving the way for general deployment in a large, diverse, geographically distributed organization.

7 Conclusion and Future Work

Introducing agile in a large, geographically distributed company is a challenging undertaking. Piloting is a well-known approach to SPI, both in agile and more traditional settings, and can be used to reduce risk and bridge resistance to change. However, in a diverse setting, such as the one in the case company, one pilot is often not enough to build global trust in the new method. Multiple pilots, preferably one in each type of project, may be needed.

In the case company, we realized that we needed support for the task of setting up pilots. As presented in this paper, a method for piloting agile in a large corporation was defined based on a multiple-case study. The method was proven successful in the goals of (1) overcoming resistance to change and (2) ensuring that a pilot project can run agile even if the rest of the organization is non-agile. However, it is too early to evaluate the long-term implications of the method for company-wide deployment.

Future work concerns mostly the current limitations of the study and includes further validation and refinement of the method as we further apply it in pilots in the case company. We are also interested in validating the applicability of the method in other companies struggling with the challenge of agile piloting in the large. Furthermore, the long-term impacts of piloting on the general deployment of agile methods still need to be evaluated.

Acknowledgements. Part of the work was done in connection to the ITEA2 project called Flexi funded by TEKES and coordinated by VTT.

References

1. Chan, F.K.Y., Thong, J.Y.L.: Acceptance of Agile Methodologies: A Critical Review and Conceptual Framework. Decis. Support Syst. 46(4), 803–814 (2009)
2. Lindvall, M., Muthig, D., Dagnino, A., et al.: Agile Software Development in Large Organizations. Computer 37(12), 26–34 (2004)
3. Misra, S.C., Kumar, V., Kumar, U.: Identifying some Important Success Factors in Adopting Agile Software Development Practices. J. Syst. Software 82(11), 1869–1890 (2009)
4. Pikkarainen, M., Salo, O., Still, J.: Deploying Agile Practices in Organizations: A Case Study. In: Richardson, I., Abrahamsson, P., Messnarz, R. (eds.) EuroSPI 2005. LNCS, vol. 3792, pp. 16–27. Springer, Heidelberg (2005)
5. Benbasat, I., Goldstein, D.K., Mead, M.: The Case Research Strategy in Studies of Information Systems. MIS Quarterly 11(3), 369–386 (1987)
6. Yin, R.K.: Case Study Research Design and Methods. Sage Publications, Thousand Oaks (2003)
7. Piloting, N.: OED online. Oxford University Press, Oxford (2009)
8. Pohl, K.: Software product line engineering. In: Foundations, principles, and techniques. Springer, Berlin (2005)
9. Kulpa, M.K.: Interpreting the CMMI: A process improvement approach. Auerbach, Boca Raton (2003)
10. Basili, V.R.: Software Development: A Paradigm for the Future. P. In: 13th Annual International Computer Software and Applications Conference (COMPSAC 1989), pp. 471–485. IEEE CS Press, Los Alamitos (1989)
11. McFeeley, R.: IDEAL: A User's Guide for Software Process Improvement CMU/SEI-96-HB-001 (1996)
12. CMMI: Capability Maturity Model® Integration for Development, Version 1.2. Technical Report CMU/SEI-2006-TR-008 (2006)
13. ISO: (SPICE) ISO TR 15504. Part 5. Information Technology. Software Process Assessment. Part 5: An Exemplar Process Assessment Model, JTC 1/SC 7. ISO TR 15504 (2006)
14. Derbier, G.: Agile Development in the Old Economy. In: Proceedings of the Agile Development Conference (ADC 2003), pp. 125–131. IEEE Computer Society, Washington (2003)
15. Rising, L., Janoff, N.S.: The Scrum Software Development Process for Small Teams. IEEE Software 17(4), 26–32 (2000)
16. Cohn, M., Ford, D.: Introducing an Agile Process to an Organization. Computer 36(6), 74–78 (2003)
17. Drobka, J.: Piloting XP on Four Mission-Critical Projects. IEEE Software 21(6), 70–75 (2004)
18. Grenning, J.: Launching Extreme Programming at a Process-Intensive Company. IEEE Software 18(6), 27–33 (2001)
19. Rasmusson, J.: Introducing XP into Greenfield Projects: Lessons Learned. IEEE Software 20(3), 21 (2003)
20. Fitzgerald, B., Hartnett, G., Conboy, K.: Customising Agile Methods to Software Practices at Intel Shannon. European Journal of Information Systems 15(2), 200–213 (2006)
21. McCaffery, F., Pikkarainen, M., Richardson, I.: Ahaa – Agile, Hybrid Assessment Method for Automotive, Safety Critical Smes. In: International Conference on Software Engineering (ICSE 2008), pp. 551–560. ACM, New York (2008)
22. Pikkarainen, M., Wang, X., Conboy, K.: Agile Practices in use from an Innovation Assimilation Perspective: A Multiple Case Study. In: International Conference of Information Systems (ICIS 2007), pp. 1–17 (2007)

23. Svensson, H., Host, M.: Introducing an Agile Process in a Software Maintenance and Evolution Organization. In: Proceedings of the Ninth European Conference on Software, Maintenance and Reengineering (CSMR), pp. 256–264. IEEE Computer Society, Washington (2005)
24. Reifer, D.J.: How Good are Agile Methods? IEEE Software 19(4), 16–18 (2002)
25. Dybå, T., Dingsøyr, T.: Empirical Studies of Agile Software Development: A Systematic Review. Inform. Software Tech. 50(9-10), 833–859 (2008)
26. Salo, O., Abrahamsson, P.: An Iterative Improvement Process for Agile Software Development. Software Process Improvement and Practice 12(1), 81–100 (2007)
27. Moitra, D.: Managing organizational change for software process improvement. In: Acuña, S.T., Juristo, N. (eds.) International Series in Software Engineering, vol. 10, pp. 163–185. Springer, New York (2005)
28. Moitra, D.: Managing Change for Software Process Improvement Initiatives: A Practical Experience-Based Approach. Software Process: Improvement and Practice 4(4), 199–207 (1998)
29. Mathiassen, L., Ngwenyama, O.K., Aaen, I.: Managing Change in Software Process Improvement. IEEE Software 22(6), 84–91 (2005)
30. Stelzer, D., Mellis, W.: Success Factors of Organizational Change in Software Process Improvement. Software Process: Improvement and Practice 4(4), 227–250 (1998)
31. Beck, K., Beedle, M., Van Bennekum, A., et al.: Manifesto for Agile Software Development (2001)
32. Hiatt, J.M.: ADKAR – a model for change in business, government and our community. Prosci Research, Loveland, CO (2006)
33. Böckle, G., Muñoz, J., Knauber, P., et al.: Adopting and Institutionalizing a Product Line Culture. In: Chastek, G.J. (ed.) SPLC 2002. LNCS, vol. 2379, p. 49. Springer, Heidelberg (2002)
34. Fitzgerald, B.: The use of Systems Development Methodologies in Practice: A Field Study. Inform. Syst. J. 7(3), 201–212 (1997)
35. Schwaber, K., Beedle, M.: Agile software development with scrum. Prentice-Hall, Upper Saddle River (2002)
36. Griswold, W.G.: Just-in-Time Architecture: Planning Software in an Uncertain World. In: SIGSOFT 1996 Workshops Isaw-2 and Viewpoints 1996, pp. 8–11. ACM Press, New York (1996)
37. Nerur, S., Balijepally, V.: Theoretical Reflections on Agile Development Methodologies. Comm. ACM 50(3), 79–83 (2007)
38. Baddoo, N., Hall, T.: Motivators of Software Process Improvement: An Analysis of Practitioners' Views. J. Syst. Software 62(2), 85–96 (2002)
39. Chow, T., Cao, D.: A Survey Study of Critical Success Factors in Agile Software Projects. J. Syst. Software 81(6), 961–971 (2008)
40. Beck, K., Andres, C.: Extreme programming explained: Embrace change. Addison-Wesley, Boston (2005)
41. Sharp, H., Robinson, H.: Collaboration and Co-Ordination in Mature eXtreme Programming Teams. Int. J. Hum-Comput. St. 66(7), 506–518 (2008)
42. Poppendieck, M., Poppendieck, T.: Implementing lean software development: From concept to cash. Addison-Wesley Professional, Upper Saddle River (2006)
43. Boehm, B., Turner, R.: Using Risk to Balance Agile and Plan-Driven Methods. Computer 36(6), 57–66 (2003)

Optimized Feature Distribution in Distributed Agile Environments

Ákos Szőke

Department of Measurement and Information Systems,
Budapest University of Technology and Economics, Budapest, Hungary
aszoke@mit.bme.hu
http://home.mit.bme.hu/~aszoke/

Abstract. In recent years, agile software development methods have gained increasing popularity. Distributed software development have been becoming a common business reality also. Software development organizations are striving to blend agile development methods like Scrum and distributed development to reap the benefits of both. However, agile and distributed development approaches differ significantly in their key tenets. While agile methods mainly rely on informal processes to facilitate coordination, distributed development typically relies on formal mechanisms. This paper aims at implementing modular design of software products to identify feature clusters that can be implemented colocated to minimize the communication needs between distributed teams. Presented method is evaluated with simulations that demonstrate how this method can produce 1) lower-risk feasible plans, 2) balanced workload on teams, and 3) provide higher quality feature distributions. Finally, the paper analyzes benefits and issues from the use of this method.

Keywords: distributed software development, agile release planning.

1 Introduction

Agile methods have gained acceptance in the mainstream software development community. A recent survey [1] showed that 84% of the respondents used agile development practices to some degree. The popularity of agile development ideas [2] can be explained by other surveys, which pointed out that agile teams are often more successful than traditional ones [3], [4]. Several studies demonstrated 60% increase in productivity, quality and improved stakeholder satisfaction [4], [5], 40% faster time-to-market and 60% and 40% reduction in pre-, and post-release defect rates [5] comparing to the industry average. The most popular agile methods are Scrum [6](50%), Extreme Programming (XP) [7](6%), and Scrum/XP Hybrid (24%) [1].

At the same time, distributed software development (DSD) is another trend, which have been becoming a common practice in today's industry [8]. The previously cited survey [1] pointed out that 58% of the respondents worked in distributed development teams – where the members of the teams are not physically

M. Ali Babar, M. Vierimaa, and M. Oivo (Eds.): PROFES 2010, LNCS 6156, pp. 62–76, 2010.
© Springer-Verlag Berlin Heidelberg 2010

co-located. Team member dispersion ranges from being over adjacent buildings to being over different continents. The key advantages that DSD aspires to achieve are 1) lower cost of labor, 2) increase or decrease work forces without employing or laying-off, and 3) obtain locally not available expertise [9].

Global software development (GSD) is the special case of DSD in which team distribution extends national boundaries [10]. GSD allows organizations to overcome geographical distances, to benefit from accessing a larger resource pool and to reduce development costs [8].

In distributed agile software development, additional challenges may be observed comparing to the co-located situations [10], [11], [12]. These challenges can be categorized into the following areas [12]:

- **Communication:** Agile development relies more on frequent informal interactions. However in DSD the teams cannot see or speak in person that result from geographical separation. Additional communication impedance raises from time zone differences that also hinders the communication between distributed teams. As a solution, DSD mandates that the development relies on formal documentation (such as specifications, designs) to mitigate impediments of communications between the teams.
- **Trust:** Agile development relies on shared view of goals that are difficult to observe in dispersed locations. To improve team cohesion in distributed software development, frequent personal communication is often required.
- **Control:** In agile development people-oriented control is applied, which based on informal commitments. The development is usually based on ongoing negotiation on the requirements between the developers and the customers. Due to the lack of communication, DSD often relies on process-oriented development and upfront commitments to meet the customer expectations on every location of the development.

In previous research [13] it was shown that, distributed projects take about two and one-half times longer to complete as similar projects where the project team is co-located. The delays can be explained by the communication and coordination issues rather than the size or complexity of the cross-site work [13]. As a consequence, distributed agile development requires significant effort from the team in order to be truly successful [14].

1.1 Related Work

In [15] a method is offered to calculate the degree of relatedness of the work items at different sites using code change history. The calculated relatedness is used to distribute work in a way that minimizes the need for coordination across sites. In [16] experiences of a rapid production process are described using software components suited for distributed development in a large, geographically distributed situation. In this approach, each component can be owned by a particular site to promote independent work and to minimize the need of coordination and communication.

Software outsourcing is an increasingly attractive business model for many large organizations. In [8] three outsourcing strategies are presented to maximize business value. In [17] good practices are presented that were observed in a very large (5.000 engineers) globally distributed development situation at Alcatel.

It compared to the extensive research on distributes software development in general, only few research dealt with DSD in the agile environment in specifically [11]. Lately Scrum [6], an agile management practice, has gained considerably popularity (see Sec.1). Experiences and practices of the adoption of Scrum by large companies such as Yahoo! or Microsoft is presented in [18], and in [19] respectively. In [14] experiences and proven practices to address challenges faced by geographically distributed agile teams are presented by the Microsoft's Patterns & Practices group. It pointed out that the decision makers must understand risk/reward tradeoff needs before deciding to distribute software development, because it decreases the project's likelihood of success, increases the delivery time and quality, and reduces the team's performance. Besides cross-locations, differences in culture and language also results in low progress in globally distributed environments. To cope with these issues, in the literature, some strategies are proposed including the use of straddlers (technical or managerial liaisons) [8], bridgehead teams [20], or rotation of management [17].

1.2 Problem Statement and Analysis

DSD has brought about its own unique set of challenges additional to the agile software development in itself. The majority of these challenges (see them in Sec. 1) can be rooted from the obstacles of communication – particularly informal communication i.e. when personal physical interactions occur [12], [13]. Team members at the different development sites often suffer from inhibited communication because they are geographically separated from each other. This plays the critical role in the success of a distributed agile team [15].

The obstacles of informal communication seem a contradiction to the ideas of agile methods [2],[21],[3],[13],[12] and seems to preclude the use of agile methodologies. Communication and coordination problems result in reduced productivity of the team (**P1**), increased production interval (**P2**), increased communication cost (**P3**), and difficult process control across distributed teams (**P4**).

If a team is distributed, one solution is to minimize the effects of the informal communication deficiency. It can be accomplished by *increasing the formality (ceremony) of the interactions*. In this case, with detailed documentation (i.e. specifications, design plans, project plans) and conventions (i.e. coding standards, templates) the lack of communication can be (theoretically) replaced. Although, this rule reacts and contradicts to the ideas of agility, but it is a well-tried approach to deal with geographical distances. Another solution can be realized by *decreasing the need of interactions* between the distributed teams. With this approach, the communication needs are minimized, which is also a good solution to the communication problem.

1.3 Objectives

Our proposed method intends, on the one hand, to minimize communication needs to minimize their negative effects of **P1-P4**, and on the other hand, to provide optimized distribution of software development work items across sites considering team capacity constraints. Our contribution is inspired by David Parna's work that recommends division of labor along with software modularity [22]. As a part of our proposed solution we defined: 1) a method to determine features (deliverable functional and non-functional requirements) that could be developed roughly independently (**S1**), 2) an optimization model to distribute features on different development sites (**S2**), and 3) a feature distribution method – which utilizes **S1** and **S2** – to support agile release planning in the distributed environment (**S3**).

Structure of the Paper. The rest of the paper arranged as follows: Sec. 2 presents background information; Sec. 3 outlines the proposed feature distribution method; Sec. 4 shows experiments with our prototypic tool; Sec. 5 discusses our solution and findings; and finally Sec. 6 concludes the paper.

2 Background

In this section, first, we introduce the agile development process, then different strategies of DSD, and finally the concept of architecture modularity – to provide the necessary background information for the proposed method.

2.1 Agile Software Development Process

From the project management point of view, agile software development process is made up of the following phases: 1) *conceptualization* to define a vision, high level ranked deliverables and project roadmap, 2) *release planning* to estimate deliverables and assign them into releases, 3) *iteration planning* to break down selected deliverables into technical tasks, 4) *iteration* to discuss the daily progress concerning writing tests, codes and fixing defects, 5) *iteration review* to demonstrate product increments to stakeholders and conduct iteration retrospective for the next iteration, and finally 6) *release* to package and deploy software to customers [23], [24], [25] (see Fig. 1).

Our proposed feature distribution method (**S3**) intends to complement the Release planning step up front in the distributed environment with the determination of roughly independently implementable features (**S1**) and their optimal distribution on different sites (**S2**).

2.2 Agile Distribution Strategies

Two important parameters are observed in practice relating to agile DSD [11], [9]: *team cross-functionality* (*cross-functional* or *not cross functional*) and *team distribution* (*co-located* or *across sites*). We define the cross-functional agile team

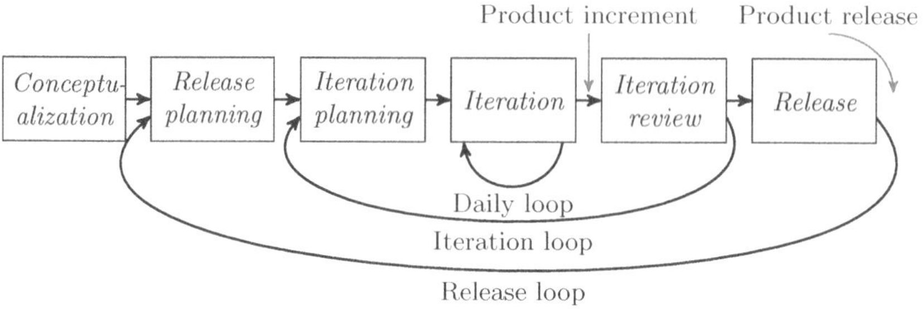

Fig. 1. Agile Development Cycles

as a group of people working toward the common goal on every site. Whereas, non-cross functional team is working toward a sub-goal on each site. We can derive the following three distribution strategies from these parameters:

- **Co-located:** the single agile team is co-located and cross-functional.
- **Isolated:** agile teams are isolated across sites and not cross-functional.
- **Distributed:** agile teams are isolated across sites and cross-functional.

In agile, face-to-face communication is far the most important since it requires the most intensive communication [6]. Both Isolated and Distributed strategies require communication across sites to remove dependencies between work units, but the communication intensities are very different. The latter strategy provides better load balance of resources since all team members form the common pool of resources. However, in Isolated case, each team removes most dependencies locally (within the given site), while in Distributed case dependencies must be resolved across sites. As a consequence Distributed case is more difficult to implement due to delays in all parties. Consequently, the former model is more often observed in practice [11], [9], and suggested by the Scrum Alliance [26].

Our proposed feature distribution method (**S3**) follows the Isolated strategy as its goal is to specify independently implementable features on different sites.

2.3 Modular Design

The concept of architecture and modularity are central in product development. Product architecture can be defined as the way in which functional elements of a product are arranged into modules in that way these units interacts with each other [22]. Modularity deals with the mapping from functional elements to modules, so it decomposes the system into units. Modular design emphasizes the minimization of interaction between modules, which enables modules to be developed independently. The independently developed modules are integrated using interfaces between the modules to form the whole product. It points out the two important activity of product development: decomposition and integration.

The two important characteristics of modularity are the *cohesiveness of modules* and the *coupling between modules*, which describe the interaction intensity between functional elements. Modules are identified in such a way that inter-module (between modules) interactions are relatively minimal (i.e. they are loosely coupled) while intra-module (within each module) interactions relatively high (i.e. they jointly serve a functionality, so they are cohesive) [27].

This underlines the importance of decomposition in distributed software development. Modularity enables development of different functional element groups (modules) at different sites independently, and integration ensures that the whole functionality can be delivered to the customer's site.

3 Feature Distribution Method for Agile DSD

In this section, we detail our previously outlined feature distribution method, namely Assembly Model Design, which aims to support agile release planning in the distributed environment (**S3**). As a part of this solution, we introduce the Feature Cluster Analysis step (Sec. 3.2) to determine features that could be developed roughly independently (**S1**), and the Feature Package Distribution step (Sec. 3.2) to provide optimized distribution of features across sites (**S2**).

3.1 Assembly Model Design Method

To determine a cohesive feature that can be developed in parallel in different sites a three-step method, namely Assembly Model Design method (AMD) (**S3**), is introduced. The next steps constitute the method 1) Usage analysis, 2) Feature analysis, and 3) Feature assembly analysis (including **S1-2**). The AMD method is visualized in Fig. 2, and detailed in the following.

Usage Analysis. Usage analysis defines stakeholders' needs in the form of scenario-based *Usage model* to describe possible ways to use a system to accomplish some desired functions or implicit purposes (see Fig. 2). Scenarios are operational examples of system usage, they can help to describe (*what*) and understand (*how*) emergent behavior of complex and dynamic systems [28]. Captured Usage model helps to determine client-valued functions, drive the whole development process and provide traceability of realization [29], [30]. During Usage analysis, the main goal is to devise what are the needs of the customer. Features, which identify customers' needs, can be collected with User stories and prioritized according to their importance [6]. Details on agile Usage analysis can be found in [24], [6].

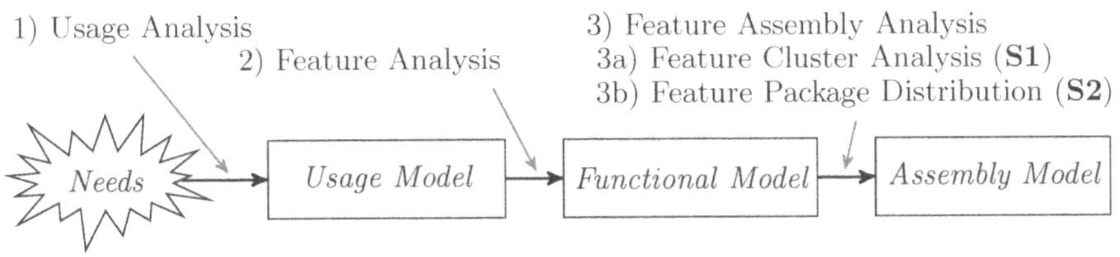

Fig. 2. Assembly Model Design Method for Determining Feature Packages

Feature Analysis. The Usage model can be used to identify features. Feature analysis converts the Usage model into a *Functional model* (see Fig. 2) by preparing a list of features (new and changed (non-)functional requirements) needed to meet the customer's primary needs. Functional requirements are abstractions of product function required to satisfy customer needs, provide information about what the product under investigation is supposed to do. They may be calculations, data manipulation and processing that define what a system is supposed to accomplish in terms of particular results of a system. Functional requirements are usually completed with non-functional requirements (a.k.a. quality requirements), which impose constraints on the design or implementation (such as performance, security, or reliability) [29]. From now on, functional and non-functional requirements are commonly called as features and denoted as FR. Realizing a feature usually requires cooperation of developers, which consists in accomplishing several technical tasks in some modules [31]. Details on Feature analysis can be found in [24], [6], [31].

3.2 Feature Assembly Analysis

The aim of Feature assembly analysis is to identify parts that can be treated logically independently. It deals with arranging features into feature packages in the manner by which the resulting *Assembly model* (see Fig. 2) can be used to structure the development teams needed. Features with high degree of cohesiveness should be grouped together into packages. Feature assembly analysis consists of two steps 3a) *Feature cluster analysis*, and 3b) *Feature package distribution*, which are detailed in the following.

Feature Cluster Analysis. Our aim is to minimize communication between teams. Therefore objects of feature implementations should be identified in order to help in separation of independent objects. Consequently, we introduce a binary relation between features (FRs) and system modules (SMs), called `ImplementedIn`, to express the fact that a given FR is implemented in some SMs (i.e. directed, one-to-many relation). We also developed a so-called Feature-Module Dependency matrix (FMD) to draw this relation, where on the vertical dimension FRs, and on the horizontal dimension SMs are listed. This approach is very similar to the widely known design structure (DSM) matrix [32], apart from the fact that DSMs have limited direct utility for inter-domain analysis (i.e. squared matrix form). For example, the Fig. 3 shows three different situations between FRs and SMs (in the cells '×' and '◯' notations denote relation and lack of relation between elements – respectively). It can be read across an element's row to see its targeted module.

The examples (Fig. 3) show the two possible connection types between FRs:

- **Coupled:** the FR_1 and FR_2 implementations relate to (`ImplementedIn`) both SM_1 and SM_2 (left) or the SM_1 only (middle).
- **Uncoupled:** the FR_1 and FR_2 implementations are unrelated, therefore FR_1 and FR_2 are uncoupled.

	SM_1	SM_2
FR_1	×	×
FR_2	×	×

	SM_1	SM_2
FR_1	×	○
FR_2	×	×

	SM_1	SM_2
FR_1	×	○
FR_2	○	×

Fig. 3. Coupled (left, middle) and Uncoupled (right) relations

As a consequence, we introduce a binary (`CoupledWith` – non-directed, many-to-many) relation between FRs to express that two given FRs are coupled – therefore, they should be implemented jointly. Uncoupled connection type means that the two FRs can be implemented independently.

The `ImplementedIn` relation sheds light on, at higher level, communication issues that the team must resolve emanating from the fact that they must be working on the same set of modules. Therefore, communication demand and coordination complexity can be reduced if the elements are clustered such a way that communications predominately occur within clustered FRs rather than between clustered FRs. In this regard, the elements of the FMD have to be transformed into coupled and uncoupled sub-matrices to express interdependent and independent FR sets. To identify independently implementable FR sets, we apply cluster analysis, which is a common technique for data analysis used in many fields, including machine learning, and data mining [33].

Cluster analysis is the assignment of a set of elements into subsets so that elements in the same cluster are similar, in some sense. In our case, similarity is expressed such a way that FRs are connected across SMs (i.e. they are in `ImplementedIn` relation), in other words, FRs are in `CoupledWith` relation. With this approach, arranging development work (FRs) according to the identified clusters, it can significantly decrease the communication needs and coordination complexity of the distributed team.

If we consider an initial FMD matrix as shown on the left in Fig. 4, the result of clustering is shown on the right – which is obtained by rearranging rows and columns based on `ImplementedIn` relations. In these figures, the targeted modules and FR implementation are represented on y-axis and x-axis respectively, and darken cells denote `ImplementedIn` relation between FRs and SMs. Comparing to the left figure, the right one sheds the light on the FR packages (the four blocks) that can be implemented independently.

Feature Package Distribution. After FR packages are identified, the next step is to distribute them on different teams. Now we discuss the application of binary integer programming (BIP) to realize optimal distribution [34].

To model this problem as an BIP, we use $n * m$ variables denoted by x_{ij}, where the variable x_{ij} ($1 \leq i \leq n$ and $1 \leq j \leq m$) indicates that the FR j is implemented by team i. For example, we would interpret an BIP solution with $x_{1j} = 1$ and $x_{2j} = 0$ as assigning FR j to team 1 and not assigning to team 2. Assignment does not include sequencing of work just allocating teams to FRs.

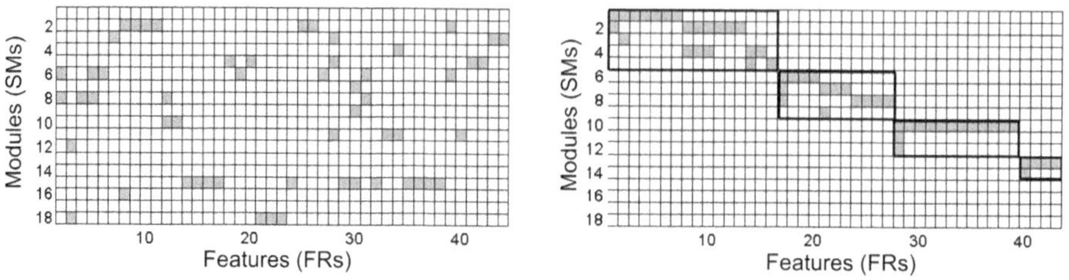

Fig. 4. Initial FMD matrix (left) and Transformed FMD matrix (right)

The amount of effort (e.g. Story point [24]) that FR j require and developed entirely by team i is represented w_{ij}. Sum of assigned work for team i can be calculated as $\sum_{j=1}^{n} w_{ij}x_{ij}$. Our objective is to maximize the work assignment to the distributed teams while all constraints are satisfied. Therefore, we can determine the objective as: Maximize $\sum_{i=1}^{m}\sum_{j=1}^{n} w_{ij}x_{ij}$.

Now, we have to consider what sort of linear constraints on the x_{ij} are necessary to ensure that they describe a valid solution. Firstly, FR j must be assigned to only one team $\sum_{j=1}^{n} x_{ij} = 1$, which produces n constraints. Secondly, for each team we must ensure that the aggregated effort of assigned work cannot be greater than the capacity of team i (c_i – i.e. available resources during a release). Finally, all FRs' assignments must be $x_{ij} \in 0,1$ (binary variables) to express the fact that an FR j is developed or not developed by a team i during the release, which results in $n * m$ constraints. As a summary, the FR package distribution binary integer optimization model (FRPD) is formulated as the following:

$$\text{Maximize} \sum_{i=1}^{m}\sum_{j}^{n} w_{ij}x_{ij} \tag{1a}$$

$$\sum_{i=1}^{m} x_{ij} = 1 \qquad : \text{for } j = 1..n \tag{1b}$$

$$\sum_{j=1}^{n} w_{ij}x_{ij} \leq c_i \qquad : \text{for } i = 1..m \tag{1c}$$

$$x_{ij} \in 0,1 \tag{1d}$$

where $i = 1..m$ and $j = 1..n$. If j is assigned to team i then $x_{ij} = 1$, otherwise $x_{ij} = 0$. The equations denote: 1a) maximization of deliverables, 1b) FR j must be assigned to only one team, 1c) assigned work cannot be greater then the team capacity of site i, and finally 1d) an FR is developed or not developed.

We will suppose, as is usual, that the efforts w_{ij} are positive integers. Without loss of generality, we will also assume that c_i is a positive integer, and $w_{ij} \leq c_i$ for $\forall i, j$. If the former assumption is violated, c_i is replaced by $\lfloor c_i \rfloor$. If an item violates the latter assumption, then the instance is treated as trivially infeasible.

3.3 Tool Support

To obtain a proof-of-concept of Feature assembly analysis method (see Sec. 3.2) we implemented a prototype in Matlab [35]. This prototype realizes the rank order clustering (ROC) [36] algorithm and formulates the FRPD optimization problem (see Sec. 3.2) which is solved by the Matlab's built-in BINTPROG function for binary integer programming problems. The previously presented partial example in Fig. 4 was produced with the prototype.

4 Experiments

To evaluate our proposed Feature assembly analysis method (see Sec. 3.2) simulations were carried out. Applying the historical release planning data, as an input for the method, made it possible to compare them [37]. The five past data sets were extracted from the backlog of IRIS application that is developed by Multilogic Ltd [38]. In this section, first we set research questions, then we present necessary background information, and finally we interpret our findings.

4.1 Research Questions

Our initial intends (see Sec. 1.2 **P1-3**) was to minimize the effects of the informal communication deficiency. To validate our method the next questions were addressed: *How does Feature assembly analysis-based feature distribution can be compared with the historical one in terms of **Q1**) resource workload, **Q2**) quality and **Q3**) feasibility.*

4.2 Context and Methodology

IRIS is a client risk management system (approx. 2 million SLOC) for credit institutions for analyzing the non-payment risk of clients. It has been a continual evolution since its first release in the middle of 90s. The system was written in Visual Basic and C# the applied methodology was a custom agile process.

The planning process was made up of the following steps. During *release planning*, the features were selected (expressed in User stories [24]) from the backlog – considering stakeholders' demands. Then every User story was estimated by two teams and assigned to these teams taking teams' resource capacities into account *intuitively*. The two teams worked in different locations in Budapest, so they could not see or speak often in person that resulted from geographical separation. Communication was mostly based on video conferences, phone calls and emails; since all developers were Hungarians, there was no language, cultural or time zone barriers.

4.3 Data Collection

Five data sets (five releases: R_{1-5}) were selected to make a comparison between the algorithmic and the intuitive method. All releases had the same iteration length (80 working hours i.e. 2 weeks), domain, customer, and development methodology, but they were characterized by different number of User stories (US – deliverable features), team capacities (TC – the amount of deliverable Story points [24] by the team in the release – see Sec. 3.2), effective developer

Table 1. Historical Requirements Dispersion

	US	TC_P (TC_{T1}, TC_{T2})	ED	RUS_P (RUS_{T1}, RUS_{T2})
R_1	34	115 (65,50)	6 (3.5,2.5)	117.0 (70.0,47.0)
R_2	25	115 (65,50)	6 (3.5,2.5)	85.5 (51.0,34.5)
R_3	27	115 (65,50)	6 (3.5,2.5)	137.5 (74.5,63.0)
R_4	44	115 (65,50)	6 (3.5,2.5)	116.5 (60.5,56.0)
R_5	26	115 (65,50)	6 (3.5,2.5)	120.0 (73.0,47.0)

Table 2. Feature Packages

	FR Packages
R_1	34.0; 55.0; 11.0; 15.0; 2.0
R_2	85.5
R_3	46.5; 5.0; 73.0; 13.0
R_4	52.5; 29.0; 25.0; 10.0
R_5	29.0; 2.0; 7.0; 64.0; 5.0; 13.0

workforce (ED – available developers), and delivered User stories at the end of the release (RUS – in Story point). Table 1 summarizes the *state variables* that were used to capture facts that were likely affecting the findings, where values between round brackets pointing out how these variables were divided between the sites of team 1 and team 2 – respectively. These variables were collected from the IRIS's backlog.

We constructed three *response variables* to test **Q1** – namely Δ^{P}, Δ^{T1}, Δ^{T2} to express the deviation of the planned team capacities from the planned deliverable features at project ($\Delta^{P} \triangleq TC_P - RUS_P$), at team 1 ($\Delta^{T1} \triangleq TC_{T1} - RUS_{T1}$) and team 2 level ($\Delta^{T2} \triangleq TC_{T2} - RUS_{T2}$). Explanations of **Q2**,and **Q3** were answered with the analysis of the solution's inherent properties.

4.4 Results and Analysis

To answer to the questions **Q1-3**, two kinds of simulations were performed on the input data (Table 1) to compare with the characteristics of our proposed approach. In Table 2, the result of our Feature Cluster Analysis step (Sec. 3.2) is presented using User stories as an input collected from the backlog. Using these FR packages as an input to our Feature Package Distribution step (Sec. 3.2), the simulations' output is summarized in Table 3. One of them was carried out such a way that teams capacities were the same as in the historical case ($\text{Sim}_{=\text{TC}}$), while the other one ($\text{Sim}_{\sim\text{TC}}$) was realized with alternation of TC_{T1} and TC_{T2} – with the utilization of what-if-analysis – to avoid resource over/under-loading.

In Table 3, values between round brackets show how the variables were divided between the two sites; and values between square brackets shows which feature packages were assigned in the given site (i.e. team 1/2). The $\Delta_{=TC}$ and $\Delta_{\sim TC}$

Table 3. Results of Feature Package Distribution

	Hist.	$\Delta_{\text{Hist.}}$	$\text{Sim}_{=\text{TC}}$	$\Delta^{\text{P(T1,T2)}}_{=\text{TC}}$	$\text{Sim}_{\sim\text{TC}}$	$\Delta^{\text{P(T1,T2)}}_{\sim\text{TC}}$
R_1	(70,47)	-2.0	([55.0,2.0],[34.0,15.0])	9.0(8.0,1.0)	([55.0,11.0],[34.0,15.0,2.0])	0(0,0)
R_2	(51,34.5)	29.5	(*Unsat*, *Unsat*)	-(-,-)	([85.5],0)	0(0,0)
R_3	(74.5,63)	-22.5	([46.5,5.0,13.0],0)	50.5(0,50.0)	([73.0],[46.5,5.0,13.0])	0(0,0)
R_4	(60.5,56)	-1.5	([52.5],[29.0,10.0])	23.5(12.5,11)	([29.0,25.0,10.0],[52.5])	0(0,0)
R_5	(73,47)	-5	([64],[29.0,2.0,5.0,13.0])	2.0(1.0,1.0)	([7.0,64.0],[29.0,2.0,5.0,13.0])	0(0,0)

columns show the differences between the allocated team capacities and the assigned deliverable features in case of $\mathrm{Sim}_{=\mathrm{TC}}$ and $\mathrm{Sim}_{\sim\mathrm{TC}}$ simulations.

Interestingly, in R_2, one can see a possible extreme situation where all features are grouped into one cluster so without changing the team capacity ($\mathrm{Sim}_{=\mathrm{TC}}$) the optimization problem is unsatisfiable (*Unsat*). Contrary, with some alternation of team capacities ($\mathrm{Sim}_{\sim\mathrm{TC}}$) the single cluster is assigned to one team.

Comparing the different cases, one can realize that 1) the historical one usually significantly under-load (R_2: $29.5/115 * 100\% = 25.7\%$) or overload ($R_3$: $-22.5/115 * 100\% = -19.6\%$) the available resources, 2) the $\mathrm{Sim}_{=\mathrm{TC}}$ case – due to the team capacity constraint – produced resource under-load (all $\Delta_{=\mathrm{TC}}$ values are positive), and finally 3) the $\mathrm{Sim}_{\sim\mathrm{TC}}$ case realized neither resources overload nor under-load (all $\Delta_{\sim\mathrm{TC}}$ values are zeros due to resource adjustment).

To compare the historical and the algorithmic cases statistical analysis was performed on the response variables. The result is presented in Table 4. From these, we conclude that – although the $\mathrm{Sim}_{=\mathrm{TC}}$ case did not exceed the resource limit, which means lower level scheduling risk – it includes too many contingencies at project (Std.dev. = 21.46) and team levels (Std.dev. = (3.85, 23.31)). Although, if we compare the historical and the $\mathrm{Sim}_{\sim\mathrm{TC}}$ cases, we can recognize that the optimized case 1) did not exceed the resource capacity due to resource adjustment ($\Delta_{\sim\mathrm{TC}}^{\mathrm{P(T1,T2)}} = 0$), which means lower-risk feasible plans (c.f. **Q3**); 2) produces balanced workload on teams (c.f. **Q1**); and 3) can easily resolve complex decision situations with the utilization of semi-automatic feature distribution generations, which support more informed and more established decisions. As a consequence, it ensures higher quality feature distribution plans compared to the historical case (c.f. **Q2**).

Table 4. Comparison of Team Assignments

	Δ^{P}			Δ^{T1}			Δ^{T2}		
	Hist.	$=\mathrm{TC}$	$\sim\mathrm{TC}$	Hist.	$-\mathrm{TC}$	$\sim\mathrm{TC}$	Hist.	$-\mathrm{TC}$	$\sim\mathrm{TC}$
Mean	12.10	21.25	0.00	8.20	5.50	0.00	8.10	15.75	0.00
Min	1.50	2.00	0.00	0.00	4.50	0.00	3.00	1.00	0.00
Max	29.50	50.50	0.00	9.50	14.00	0.00	15.50	50.00	0.00
Std.dev.	13.00	21.46	0.00	3.31	3.85	0.00	5.81	23.31	0.00

5 Discussion and Future Work

The obstacles of informal communication seem to preclude the use of agile methodologies in distributed environments [21], [3], [13], [12]. Communication and coordination problems result in 1) reduced productivity of the team, 2) increased production interval, 3) increased communication cost, and 4) difficult process control across distributed teams (c.f. Sec. 1.2 – **P1-4**). Although, there can be found some strategies and practices to deal with DSD in agile environment (Sec. 1.1), any planning method – specifically to release planning – for work distribution was not found.

To take advantages of both agile and DSD, we proposed a method, namely Assembly Model Design (AMD) method, to determine module-induced *assembly model* in software systems that can be developed independently in different development sites (Sec. 3.1). The main contribution of this method lays in the Feature assembly analysis phase which made up of two steps: *Feature cluster analysis* (**S1**), and *Feature package distribution* (**S2**).

In Feature cluster analysis (Sec. 3.2), we introduced a `ImplementedIn` relation between requirements (FRs) and system modules (SMs), and constructed the Feature-Module Dependency matrix (FMD) to draw this relation. This helped us to identify intensive communication needs between FRs in order to structure the development teams. Next, we applied cluster analysis and implemented the rank order clustering (ROC) [36] algorithm to form FR packages such a way that FRs are connected across SMs. With this approach, arranging development work (FRs) according to the identified clusters, it can significantly decrease the communication needs and coordination complexity of the distributed team. Although, there are many matrix clustering algorithms in the literature which use certain functions to sort the matrix – for example, the bond energy algorithm (BEA) and modified rank order clustering (MODROC) [39] – we selected the rank order clustering (ROC) [36] due to its relatively easy implementation and fast computation on not too large problems. After the FR packages identified, in Feature package distribution step (Sec. 3.2), we constructed an FRPD binary integer programming model to distribute FR packages among sites considering team capacities. This interpretation made it possible to adapt existing algorithms to realize optimal distribution easily.

This approach not only gives the communication needs increased visibility with the FMD matrix, but the algorithmic approach to clustering and optimized distribution steps help decision makers to accommodate quick what-if scenarios and re-planning on-the-fly during agile release planning. However, as our simulation carried out post mortem analysis, in-depth investigation (e.g. performing multiple case studies) of the method is recommended in industrial environments.

6 Conclusions

In recent years, software development organizations have been striving to blend agile software development methods and distributed development to reap the benefits of both. The obstacles of informal communication seem to preclude the use of agile methodologies in distributed environments. To address this situation, we have presented a method including a novel approach to feature clustering and optimized feature distribution for wide-ranging distributed agile release planning problems. To evaluate our method five simulations were carried out that demonstrated how the method could produce 1) lower-risk feasible plans, 2) balanced workload on teams, 3) higher quality feature distribution plans, and 4) provide more informed and established decisions. We believe the results are even more impressive in more complex (more of teams, features, etc.) situations.

We think that our proposed method is a plain combination of the present theories and methods thus it leads us to generalize our findings beyond the result of the simulations.

Acknowledgements. The development is supported in part by the GVOP grant (GVOP-3.3.3-05/1.-2005-05-0046/3.0).

References

1. VersionOne: 4rd annual survey: 2009, the state of agile development (2009), `http://www.versionone.com`
2. Manifesto for agile software development, `http://www.agilemanifesto.org`
3. Dybå, T., Dingsøyr, T.: Empirical studies of agile software development: A systematic review. Inf. & Softw. Techn. 50, 833–859 (2008)
4. Ambler, S.W.: Survey says: Agile works in practice. Dr. Dobb's Journal (2006), `http://www.ddj.com`
5. Layman, L., Williams, L., Cunningham, L.: Motivations and measurements in an agile case study. J. of Sys. Arch. 52, 654–667 (2006)
6. Schwaber, K., Beedle, M.: Agile Software Development with Scrum. Prentice Hall PTR, Englewood Cliffs (2001)
7. Beck, K., Andres, C.: Extreme Programming Explained: Embrace Change, 2nd edn. Addison-Wesley Professional, Reading (2004)
8. Heeks, R., Krishna, S., Nicholsen, B., Sahay, S.: Synching or sinking: global software outsourcing relationships. IEEE Software 18, 54–60 (2001)
9. Sutherland, J., Schwaber, K.: The scrum papers: Nuts, bolts, and origins of an agile process. PatientKeeper (2007)
10. Layman, L., et al.: Essential communication practices for extreme programming in a global software development team. Inf. & Softw. Techn. 48, 781–794 (2006)
11. Marchenko, A., Abrahamsson, P.: Scrum in a multiproject environment: An ethnographically-inspired case study on the adoption challenges. In: Proc. of the AGILE 2008, pp. 15–26. IEEE Press, Los Alamitos (2008)
12. Ramesh, B., Cao, L., Mohan, K., Xu, P.: Can distributed software development be agile? ACM Comm. 49, 41–46 (2006)
13. Herbsleb, J., Mockus, A.: An empirical study of speed and communication in globally distributed software development. IEEE Trans. on Soft. Eng. 29, 481–494 (2003)
14. Miller, A.: Distributed agile development at microsoft patterns & practices (2008), `http://www.microsoft.com`
15. Mockus, A., Weiss, D.M.: Globalization by chunking: A quantitative approach. IEEE Software 18, 30–37 (2001)
16. Repenning, A., Ioannidou, A., Payton, M., Ye, W., Roschelle, J.: Using components for rapid distributed software development. IEEE Software 18, 38–45 (2001)
17. Ebert, C., Neve, P.D.: Surviving global software development. IEEE Software 18, 62–69 (2001)
18. Cloke, G.: Get your agile freak on! agile adoption at yahoo! music. In: Proc. of the AGILE 2007, pp. 240–248. IEEE Press, Los Alamitos (2007)
19. Begel, A., Nagappan, N.: Usage and perceptions of agile software development in an industrial context: An exploratory study. In: Proc. of the Int. Symp. on Empirical Soft. Eng. and Measurement, pp. 255–264. IEEE Press, Los Alamitos (2007)

20. Krishna, S., Sahay, S., Walsham, G.: Managing cross-cultural issues in global software outsourcing. ACM Comm. 47, 62–66 (2004)
21. Abrahamsson, P., Salo, O., Ronkainen, J., Warsta, J.: Agile software development methods - review and analysis. Technical Report 478, VTT Publications (2002)
22. Parnas, D.L.: On the criteria to be used in decomposing systems into modules. ACM Commun. 15, 1053–1058 (1972)
23. Chow, T., Cao, D.B.: A survey study of critical success factors in agile software projects. J. of Sys. and Softw. 81, 961–971 (2008)
24. Cohn, M.: Agile Estimating and Planning. Prentice Hall PTR, Upper Saddle River (2005)
25. Szőke, A.: Agile release planning through optimization. In: Proc. of Int. Conf. on Evaluation of Novel Approaches to Software Engineering, INSTICC, pp. 149–160 (2009)
26. Scrum Alliance homepage, `http://www.scrumalliance.org`
27. Ulrich, K.T., Eppinger, S.D.: Product Design and Development, 3rd edn. McGraw-Hill, New York (2003)
28. Liu, L., Yu, E.: Designing information systems in social context: a goal and scenario modelling approach. Inf. Sys. 29, 187–203 (2004)
29. Aurum, A., Wohlin, C.: Engineering and Managing Software Requirements. Springer, New York (2005)
30. Szőke, A.: A Proposed Method for Release Planning from Use Case-based Requirements. In: Proc. of the Euromicro Conf. on Software Engineering and Advanced Applications, pp. 449–456. IEEE Press, Los Alamitos (2008)
31. Szőke, A.: Decision support for iteration scheduling in agile environments. In: Proc. of the Int. Conf. on Product Focused Software Process Improvement. LNBIP, vol. 32, pp. 156–170. Springer, Heidelberg (2009)
32. Eppinger, S., Salminen, V.: Patterns of product development interactions. In: Proc. of the Int. Conf. On Eng. Design, pp. 610–619. Pergamon Press, Oxford (2001)
33. Romesburg, C.: Cluster Analysis for Researchers. Lulu Press (2004)
34. Schrijver, A.: Theory of linear and integer programming. Wiley & Sons, USA (1986)
35. Mathworks homepage, `http://www.mathworks.com/`
36. King, J.R.: Machine-component grouping in production flow analysis: An approach using a ROC algorithm. Int. Journal of Prod. Research 18, 213–232 (1980)
37. Kellner, M., Madachy, R., Raffo, D.: Software process simulation modeling: Why? what? how? J. of Sys. & Softw. 46, 91–105 (1999)
38. Multilogic homepage, `http://www.multilogic.hu`
39. Chandrasekharan, M.P., Rajagopalan, R.: Modroc: An extension of rank order clustering for group technology. Int. J. of Prod. Research 24, 1224–1233 (1986)

Approaches to Agile Adoption in Large Settings: A Comparison of the Results from a Literature Analysis and an Industrial Inventory

Anna Rohunen[1], Pilar Rodriguez[1,2], Pasi Kuvaja[1], Lech Krzanik[1], and Jouni Markkula[1]

[1] University of Oulu, Department of Information Processing Sciences, P.O. Box 3000, 90014 University of Oulu, Finland
[2] Technical University of Madrid (UPM), E.U. Informatica, Ctra. Valencia Km. 7, E-28031 Madrid, Spain
{Anna.Rohunen,Pilar.Rodriguez,Pasi.Kuvaja,Lech.Krzanik, Jouni.Markkula}@oulu.fi

Abstract. – Nowadays the software industry is applying agile methods widely. However, there appears to be a lack of comprehensive guidelines and strategies addressing agile adoption. In addition, agile methods and practices often have to be tailored to be integrated into existing processes. In this study, agile adoption frameworks and strategies discussed in the literature, especially in the context of agile in the large, are analysed. The findings from the literature are validated by and compared to an industrial inventory. Based on the validation and the comparison, new approaches for agile adoption in large settings have been identified: incremental agile adoption approaches combining both bottom-up and top-down strategies; the important role of identified key practices that enable quick feedback and adaptation in the early adoption stages; and approaches derived from the multidimensional nature of agility. These approaches make possible to overcome the restrictions of conventional agile methods.

Keywords: Adoption of agile methods, strategies in agile adoption, agile adoption frameworks, agile in the large.

1 Introduction

Software industry today knows well agile values, principles and practices that are applied in agile methods and approaches. However, the problem appears when all the elements have to be combined and implemented in practice. The reason behind this appears to be a lack of complete strategies and associated guidelines addressing agile adoption, at least in the public domain. Since agile adoption process is dependent on organizational environment, agile methods and practices have to be often tailored to be integrated into existing processes.

In the field of agile software development, several literature reviews have been conducted [1], [2], [3], [4], [5]. However, none of the reviews have been focused merely on agile adoption. The study by Racheva, Daneva and Sikkel [1] discusses value creation concepts and is intended to discover ways in which agile projects and practices

M. Ali Babar, M. Vierimaa, and M. Oivo (Eds.): PROFES 2010, LNCS 6156, pp. 77–91, 2010.
© Springer-Verlag Berlin Heidelberg 2010

create business value. Dybå and Dingsøyr [2] have reviewed empirical studies and classified them into four categories, including a category "Introduction and adoption of agile development methods". Agile adoption was not the focus of their study, and only seven studies out of 36 were included in this category. The rest three studies mentioned above contain overviews of agile software development [3], [4], [5].

In order to amass current knowledge of diverse agile adoption topics and to identify essential future research issues for empirical studies, for agile in the large settings, a comprehensive study has been carried out in FLEXI project (see acknowledgements). The study consists of two main elements: an extensive literature analysis about agile adoption topics, and an industrial inventory on agile adoption experiences. The inventory was carried among the industrial companies of the project consortium in the large settings. Industrial companies in FLEXI project are all leading edge companies of their business areas and the first-ones to apply agile in large and very large projects in global setting. In this way, the study provides extensive knowledge on what the academic (research) is proposing and what the current status of agile adoption in industry is. The results have a special relevance if it is considered that, differently from other software engineering topics conceived in academia and then adapted and transferred to industry, agile mainly grows up in industry directly.

One of the main objectives of the literature analysis was to discover theoretical agile adoption frameworks and strategies in software industry, especially in the context of agile in the large. The findings of the literature analysis were evaluated, synthesized and presented by a systematic way [6]. In the literature analysis, the main findings show that there is still a need for investigating agile adoption frameworks and strategies, especially in the context of agile in the large. In the industrial inventory, the agile adoption experiences of the companies were analysed in order to validate the findings of the literature analysis and to discover new issues present in the industry but not reported in the literature. The results from both the literature analysis and the industrial inventory were compared and synthesized. The synthesis contained new approaches to agile adoption in the large settings. These approaches concern strategy types in agile adoption, stages of agile adoption, key practices and management of dependencies between different agile practices during their adoption.

This paper has been organized as follows. In Section 2 the research setting is described. Section 3 presents the outcomes of the literature analysis. Section 4 summarizes the results of the industrial inventory. In Section 5, the synthesis of the results from the literature analysis and industrial inventory is presented. Finally, in Section 6, the results of this study as well as its limitations are discussed.

2 Research Setting

The research setting of this study consists of three elements: the literature analysis, the industrial inventory, and agile in the large aspect. Challenges that are specific to agile adoption in large settings are identified through agile in the large aspect.

2.1 Performing Literature Analysis

The literature analysis study presented here is focused on diverse agile adoption problems. The research question addressed by this study is "What are currently the strategies to adopt agile methods that are used in the software market?". This study aims to amass current knowledge about agile adoption and to identify essential future research issues for empirical studies, especially on agile in the large settings.

To guarantee the topicality and validity of the results, the search was conducted on the studies published during years 2000-2009. The search was carried out using six electronic multidisciplinary databases and databases specialized in the field of computer sciences and business administration (ABI/Inform (ProQuest), Academic Search Premier (EBSCO), Emerald Journals (Emerald), Science Direct (Elsevier), ACM and IEEE Xplore – IEEE/IEE Electronic Library). Non research studies such as prefaces, article summaries, overhead presentations, interviews, short-papers, introductions to special issues, tutorials or mini-tracks were excluded from the analysis. In the search stage of the literature analysis, 120 research studies discussing adoption of agile software development methods were identified. The findings of the literature analysis were evaluated, synthesized and presented in a systematic way based on the guidelines for systematic literature reviews by Kitchenham [6]. Hence a data extraction form was designed to collect information from individual studies. Also selection criteria and quality assessment were designed to ensure proper quality of the studies that were finally included in the research material. The selection criteria concerned e.g. the focus of the study, publication date, and clarity and contents of the outcomes. The quality assessment included the following items: objective and context description, research design, data collection and analysis, justified findings and conclusions, applicability of the results, minimized threats, and use of references. The quality assessment forms were modified for different study types included in the analysis: quantitative empirical studies, qualitative empirical studies, non-empirical studies and experience reports. The analysis process was conducted by a team of three members.

Thus far 48 studies have been evaluated. From these 48 studies, 38 studies were accepted and included into the research material. The rest of the material was excluded from the research material due to not passing the minimum quality threshold (at least half of the maximum score in the quality assessment). In the study 13 journal articles and conference papers were found relevant as they focused on agile adoption strategies.

2.2 Industrial Inventory

Industrial inventory on agile experiences aimed to summarize adoption of agile methods, practices and tools among FLEXI project consortium. The project consortium included 8 large scale industry partners, 14 SMEs and 11 research or university partners in 8 European countries. In the consortium, there were partners from different industry sectors who are developing products for global markets. The consortium represented leadership in many industry sectors and excellent performance in both economical and technical sense. The main characteristics of the consortium partners and projects were the following: many locations, many stakeholders, distributed organizations and projects, global projects, large scale projects, and short time to market.

The research process was based on the guidelines of systematic literature reviews by Kitchenham [6] to appropriate extent. Again, a similar research question, tailored for the new context, was considered: "What are currently the strategies to adopt agile methods that are used in FLEXI project?". Documentation from both industrial and academic partners was reviewed, provided that the material discussed specifically industrial experiences. Research material included all type of material that could include knowledge about the adoption of any agile method: conference and journal publications from the project consortium, industrial trials providing an experimental basis for the theoretical considerations, PhD thesis, master thesis, deliverables, internal documents, etc. The search for the research material was conducted manually using project's internal publication database, and contacting partners. In the search process 31 studies were identified. Like in the literature analysis, a data extraction form was designed to collect information from individual studies. Also selection criteria and quality assessment were designed to ensure the quality of the studies. Again, the inventory process was conducted by a team of three members. All the material included in the industrial inventory was considered credible, relevant, and having rigor in the study design and data collection.

2.3 Agile in the Large

Agile in the large settings encompass distributed, large and global software development projects and organizations with many locations and stakeholders. Agile in the large organizations often have a long history in waterfall development with top-down deployment. In these settings selecting or tailoring agile practices and combining them with traditional practices may be required. In this study, aspects of agile in the large were identified and amassed in both the literature analysis and the industrial inventory. They were recorded in data extraction forms described above.

3 Literature Analysis Results

In this section, examples of different theoretical, structured agile adoption frameworks found in the literature analysis are presented. After that, the main findings in this area are summarized.

3.1 Agile Adoption Framework Analysis

Five frameworks that are general approaches to agile adoption are presented [7], [8], [9], [10], [11]. From the 13 journal articles and conference papers focused specifically on agile adoption strategies found in the literature analysis, only five can be considered as structured agile adoption frameworks since the rest of the studies provided recommendations and lessons learned following not clearly structured strategies. One of these frameworks describes a pilot project in a large environment [9]. Also a framework for mission and life-critical systems is presented [8]. Besides, a model for agile adoption in distributed environments is included in the analysis [11]. In most of these studies, the agile methods to be adopted were not specified, and the frameworks were independent of any specific agile methods. However, also XP, Scrum and hybrid methods were discussed in these studies.

Sidky et al. [7] present in their study a structured and repeatable approach to agile adoption. This agile adoption framework consists of two components: an agile measurement index and a four-stage process, that together guide and assist agile adoption efforts in organizations. The four-stage process helps to determine whether or not organizations are ready for agile adoption, and guided by their potential, what set of agile practices can and should be introduced. The four-stage process takes into account both project level and organizational level. The agile adoption framework by Sidky et al. is independent of any one particular agile method or style.

Mission and life-critical systems are typically large and complex, and have long development periods [8]. Another study by Sidky and Arthur [8] presents an agile adoption framework tailored for mission and life-critical systems. It presents a three-stage process that provides guidance to organizations on how to identify the agile practices they can benefit from without causing any negative impact to the mission and life-critical system being developed. Three fundamental actions are related to this challenge: identification of the ability of the organization to adopt agile practices, determination of the suitability of agile practices in the development of mission and life-critical systems, and determination of the suitability of agile practices for the organization developing mission and life-critical systems. Agile practices such as minimal documentation, evolutionary requirements and refactoring are found as unsuitable for mission and life-critical systems. It is also emphasized that some practices are dependent on the presence of other practices during their adoption, e.g. test driven development is dependent on the use of unit testing, continuous integration is dependent on automated unit tests, and having self organizing teams is dependent on having motivated and empowered individuals.

Qumer and Henderson-Sellers present in their study [9] an Agile Adoption and Improvement Model (AAIM) for adoption, assessment and improvement of an agile software development process. AAIM is based on both the results from existing research studies and the findings from the software industry, and tested on a pilot project in a large software development organization. AAIM consists of three agile blocks, six agile stages and an embedded agility measurement model. Each block and stage specifies the agile practices to be followed in order to achieve a particular AAIM level. For example, in AAIM level 1, three basic agile properties are introduced and established: speed, flexibility and responsiveness. These properties establish a foundation to achieve the rest of the agile levels, and they include e.g. test first approach. AAIM is a method-independent model and it aims to continuous improvement and incremental success.

Qumer and Henderson-Sellers also point out [10] that only few organizations are psychologically and technically able to adopt agile approach rapidly and effectively. They claim that a full transition to an agile process takes years. In [10], they propose Agile Software Solution Framework (ASSF). ASSF provides an overall context for the exploration of agile methods, knowledge and governance. ASSF contains Agile Toolkit, and together these two elements link business aspect to software development so that business value and the agile process are well aligned. ASSF assists managers in assessing the degree of agility they require and how to identify appropriate ways to introduce this agility to their organizations.

Finally, Sureshchandra and Shrinivasavadhani present in [11] a model to transfer from a traditional agile method to an agile method in a distributed environment. The aim of the model is to get information flow unobstructed, and flexibility and agility preserved. The model establishes a gradual transition with four stage process: evaluation, inception, transition and steady state. In the evaluation stage it is decided if the project can work in a distributed mode. Inception and transition are the intermediate stages where ownership, self-organization of the distributed teams and direct customer interaction of all teams takes place progressively. Finally, during steady state the distributed teams take complete ownership of their stories and become self-organized, and a direct communication between distributed satellite teams and the customer/business users is completely established.

3.2 Outcomes of the Literature Analysis

The first finding of the literature analysis based on the analysis of agile adoption frameworks was the identification of two agile adoption strategy types. These strategy types were wholesale strategies and incremental strategies. In wholesale strategies the entire agile process is adopted at once [12]. In incremental strategies new practices are gradually taken into use [7], [8], [9], [10], [11], [12], [13], [14], [15], [16], [18], [19]. Intention to continuous improvement was specifically emphasized in a few studies as regards incremental agile adoption [7], [9], [12]. Although adoption of any technology, product or method can take place wholesale or incrementally, it was discovered that the most of analyzed strategies bet on an incremental adoption in the case of agile methods. Except for one of the studies, the studies discussed only incremental agile adoption strategies. Incremental adoption strategies were used in both general agile adoption approaches and approaches for large settings. Hodgetts describes two case studies about wholesale adoption [12]. Both of these cases had not been successful because of a lack of consensus of the team, and a lack of substantial preparation for agile adoption. Hodgetts also considers wholesale agile adoption process as a risky approach, compared to incremental approaches.

The second finding of the literature analysis was three characteristic features of agile adoption frameworks that are: agile adoption frameworks are usually composed of stages, an agility measurement model that guides and assists the agile adoption is generally used, and there is intention to manage the dependencies between different agile practices during their adoption. This study focuses only on agile adoption stages and managing dependencies between practices because of the fundamental role of these matters. When it comes to agile adoption stages, it was observed that in the research material commonly considered stages were evaluation stage and introduction stage [7], [8], [9], [10], [11]. In evaluation stage the ability of the organization to adopt agile methods is assessed, and the suitable agile practices to be implemented are selected. Evaluation stage is followed by incremental introduction of agile practices. In most of the studies, specific agile practices were not indicated but each concrete agile team, in evaluation stages, has to tailor the method and discover the suitable agile practices. Dependencies between agile practices were discussed in [8], [10], [17].

The findings of the literature analysis were summarized into three categories as follows:

- Strategy types in adoption of agile methods
- Stages of agile adoption
- Managing dependencies between different agile practices during their adoption

This classification is used further in this study when presenting both the main findings from the industrial inventory and the synthesis of the literature analysis and industrial inventory. In conclusion, it was found that with very few exceptions, agile adoption studies consider very high-level strategies and certainly lack the technical substance. Also, the analysed frameworks were found as initial contributions, and studies that clearly indicate how to exactly answer the complex question of how to adopt agile practices were not found.

4 Industrial Inventory Results

Like in the literature analysis, the agile methods to be adopted were not specified in the majority of the industrial inventory research material, but in many cases Scrum, XP and lean development were discussed. The findings of the industrial inventory are presented as generalized results, independent of any specific agile methods.

4.1 Strategy Types in Adoption of Agile Methods

In the research material gained in the industrial inventory, only incremental agile adoption strategies were discussed. In some cases of the industrial inventory also continuity of the adoption process was emphasized, so on the basis of these cases incremental agile adoption process could also be defined "taking gradually and continuously new practices into use" [20], [21]. It was observed that incremental strategies suit well to the context of agile in the large [20], [21], [22], [23]. In big organizations *"Start next Monday"* -thinking is important in order to get the adoption started and the learning process going on [24].

Besides, in the industrial inventory also bottom-up and top-down strategies were discussed as well the importance of using both of them in parallel during the adoption, especially in the context of agile in the large. Potential application areas for bottom-up strategies could be team level choosing and adoption of agile practices, self-organization and empowerment. Top-down strategies cover defining and/or operating lean development, business objectives, transformation process and transformation backlog, organizational values, and changing the management culture and behavior. This has been done by the management level of the organization. [24], [25]

In the industrial inventory material also key practices that should be implemented in the beginning of the agile adoption were observed [20], [21]. How to manage dependencies between agile practices and how to define the key practices are discussed more detailed in section "4.3 Managing dependencies between different agile practices during their adoption".

In addition, tailoring agile practices and combining them with existing processes and past experiences was mentioned as an important aspect in several studies in the industrial inventory [22], [23], [25], [26], [27], [28], [29], [30], [31], [32], [33].

As a whole, agile adoption can be seen as an iterative process with short feedback cycles and continuous learning and development. In the industrial inventory observing the response to changes and adjusting the adoption process accordingly were discovered as prerequisites of a successful change process. This is crucial especially in the context of agile in the large where incremental agile adoption strategies suit well. [20], [21]

4.2 Stages of Agile Adoption

Evaluation stage was missing or not reported almost in all industrial inventory cases. However, in one case [31] three stages for agile adoption had been defined. This case took into account also multidimensional nature of agility meaning: selecting agility goals, selecting means of agility, and making sure that enabling conditions had been fulfilled in order to implement the goals. In this model the kind of agility the company needs (project and software development/product/enterprise agility) was defined by agility goals. When it comes to the means of agility, agile software methods can be seen only as one subset of such means. Enabling conditions can be e.g. human factors. Based on this description of the multidimensionality of agility, it can be concluded that multidimensional nature of agility could be studied in the context of agile in the large in order to manage the restrictions of conventional agile methods.

In some industrial inventory studies also retrospectives can be seen as a kind of initial evaluating activity used in the beginning of an incremental adoption process for inspection and adaption purposes [20], [21].

4.3 Managing Dependencies between Different Agile Practices during Their Adoption

Based on the industrial inventory, two key practices were identified as starting points of the adoption process. These are short iterations to enable quick feedback, and retrospectives for inspection and adaptation purposes. Incremental agile adoption strategies and observing the response in the change process suit well to agile in the large, as the key practices enable quick feedback and adaptation. The key practices are seen as enablers for a successful agile adoption in this context. [20], [21]

Possible synergies between practices being adopted were also discussed in the industrial inventory. For example, Pikkarainen et al. [32] suggest that in order to improve communication or coordination in teams or organizations, it might be best at first to adopt only a set of agile practices that are evaluated as most beneficial to team coordination and from a communication perspective. After that the adoption process could continue to incorporate other practices if they have some other added value for the teams or companies.

5 Synthesis of the Results

In this section, comparison tables and a synthesis for the main findings in the agile adoption literature analysis and the industrial inventory are presented. The synthesis contains also a summary of agile in the large aspects that were identified during both the literature analysis and the industrial inventory.

5.1 Strategy Types in Adoption of Agile Methodologies

On the one hand, there are incremental and wholesale strategies and, on the other hand, strategy types "bottom-up" and "top-down" were identified. In both the literature analysis and the industrial inventory, it was discovered that agile adoption strategies are often incremental. In the industrial inventory the importance of using bottom-up and top-down adoption strategies in parallel was discovered. Both of these strategies are needed at the same time when adopting agile in big organizations. In the industrial inventory also observing the response to changes and adjusting the adoption process accordingly was discovered as a prerequisite for a successful change process. Further, tailoring agile practices and combining them with existing processes and past experiences still seem to be important topics in large environments.

The results concerning agile adoption strategy types have been summarized in Table 1.

Table 1. Comparison of the agile adoption strategy types

	Literature analysis	Industrial inventory	Agile in the large
Incremental strategies	Incremental process adoption, taking gradually new practices into use [7], [8], [9], [10], [11], [12], [13], [14], [15], [16].	Incremental strategies were promoted among the case companies: Agile adoption can be seen as an iterative process with short feedback cycles and continuous learning and development [20], [21], [22], [23], [24].	Incremental strategies suit well to the context of agile in the large. "Start next Monday" -thinking is important to get started with something and get the learning process going on in big organizations.
Wholesale strategies	1 wholesale process adoption case study including 2 cases [12]. Unsuccessful results.		
Bottom-up strategies		Agile practices are chosen and adopted by teams, self-organization and empowerment [24], [25].	Both bottom-up and top-down approaches have their roles in agile adoption. Especially, in the context of agile in the large, they exist in parallel.
Top-down strategies		Lean development, business objectives, transformation process and backlog, organizational values, the management culture and behavior change are defined and/or operated by the management level [24], [25].	

5.2 Stages of Agile Adoption

According to the information from both the agile adoption literature analysis and the industrial inventory, two rough stages of agile adoption were defined: 1) Preliminary activities assessing the ability of the organization to adopt agile methods, defining agility goals, considering the means of agility, selecting the suitable agile practices to be implemented, and fulfilling enabling factors and conditions, and 2) Implementation activities including actual agile practices introduction and implementation.

The results concerning agile adoption stages types have been summarized in Table 2.

Table 2. Comparison of the agile adoption stages

	Literature analysis	Industrial inventory	Agile in the large
Preliminary activities	Evaluation stage [7], [8], [9], [10], [11]. Assessment of the ability of the organization to adopt agile methods and selection of the suitable agile practices to be implemented.	Multidimensional nature of agility in large-scale settings can be taken into account via the following steps: 1) Defining agility goals 2) Considering the means of agility 3) Enabling factors and conditions must be fulfilled In some industrial studies also retrospectives used in the beginning of an incremental adoption process for inspection and adaption purposes can be seen as a kind of evaluating activity. [20], [21], [31]	Considering multidimensional nature of agility in large-scale environment should be included in the preliminary activities.
Implementation activities	Agile practices introduction stage (often incremental) [7], [8], [9], [10], [11].		

5.3 Managing Dependencies between Different Agile Practices during Their Adoption

In an incremental agile adoption process possible dependencies and synergies between practices affect the order in which the practices will be adopted. In the industrial inventory the role of certain key practices that enable quick feedback and adaptation (e.g. short iterations and retrospectives) was highlighted.

The results concerning intention to manage dependencies between agile practices during agile adoption have been summarized in Table 3.

Table 3. Comparison of the intention to manage dependencies between agile practices during their adoption

	Literature analysis	Industrial inventory	Agile in the large
Key practices	Some agile practices are dependent on the presence of other practices during their adoption [8], [10], [17].	Key practices acting as starting points of the adoption process to provide quick feedback and enable adaptation (e.g. short iterations and retrospectives) [20], [21].	Using key practices that enable quick feedback and adaptation could be seen as an enabler for a successful agile adoption
Synergy effects	Synergies between practices [8], [10], [17].	Synergies between practices, e.g. when sprint planning, open office space and daily meeting are used together, informal communication works as a factor which decreases the need for documentation [32].	

6 Conclusions and Limitations of the Study

The aim of this study was to analyze current understanding about agile adoption, and to identify fruitful starting points for future empirical studies especially for agile in the large settings. Due to a lack of complete strategies and associated guidelines addressing agile adoption, this study started with a literature analysis on existing agile adoption frameworks and strategies. The findings from the literature were complemented and validated with the results of an industrial inventory on agile adoption experiences. Finally, new approaches to agile adoption were discovered via synthesis of the results of the literature analysis and the industrial inventory. Throughout the study, a special emphasis was put on the aspects of agile in the large.

As a general answer to the research question addressing the study: "What are currently the strategies to adopt agile methods that are used in the software market?" it was concluded that we could find no study which clearly and deeply indicates how to adopt agile methods. It was found that with very few exceptions, most of the analysed studies view the adoption process from somewhat high-level perspective. Although some studies provide initial contributions such as frameworks shedding light on the area of agile adoption, a key implication for the research is that there is still need for investigating agile adoption frameworks and strategies, especially in the context of agile in the large.

The main findings of this study were classified into three categories as follows: 1) strategy types in adoption of agile methods, 2) stages of agile adoption, and 3) managing dependencies between different agile practices during their adoption.

1) In both the literature analysis and the industrial inventory, it was discovered that agile adoption strategies are often incremental. In the industrial inventory research material, also continuity was seen as an important feature of the incremental adoption process. In other words, the importance of taking continually new agile practices into use was emphasized. Incremental strategy to adopt agile methods step by step seems to be suitable especially in the context of agile in the large. Further, when it comes to the aspect of agile in the large, the industrial inventory also convinced of the importance of using bottom-up and top-down adoption strategies in parallel when adopting agile in big organizations. Compared to the literature analysis, this is a new aspect. In the future studies it could be combined to incremental approaches that also suit well in the context of agile in the large. In the industrial inventory, also observing the response to changes was discovered as a prerequisite of a successful change process. Accordingly, adoption process should be adjusted based on the response. As a whole, when used all together, these strategies can be seen as a starting point to make agile adoption an agile process itself.
2) According to the literature, incremental agile adoption strategies include an evaluation stage assessing the ability of the organization to adopt agile methods and selecting the suitable agile practices to be implemented. This stage is followed by an incremental introduction of agile practices. In the industrial inventory instead, any classification of stages usually did not exist. Hence one fruitful area for future research could be discovering evaluation stage in the context of agile in the large. This could also be combined to the considerations of multidimensional nature of agility that discusses e.g. product and enterprise agility. Discussion of multidimensional nature of agility should be included in the preliminary activities in the context of agile in the large in order to manage the restrictions of conventional agile methods.
3) In an incremental adoption process it also has to be taken into account that there can be dependencies and synergies between practices. This affects the order in which the practices will be adopted. In the industrial inventory the role of certain key practices that enable quick feedback and adaptation (e.g. short iterations and retrospectives) was highlighted. These practices should be implemented already in the beginning of the agile adoption process. How to define, select, adopt and use the key practices in a proper way, especially in the context of agile in the large, could be investigated more detailed. In addition, in this context tailoring agile practices and combining them with existing processes and past experiences still seem to be important topics that are waiting for organization level solutions.

On the other hand, both the literature analysis and industrial inventory convinced us that agile methods are not applicable just for small scale projects. Agile methods can be effectively deployed in large settings if agile in the large aspect is properly taken into account. However, the applicability of agile methods in different domains should be managed carefully. For example, when developing safety critical systems risks related to the adoption and use of agile practices have to be discussed systematically before formulating the adoption strategy. Certain agile practices are clearly not suitable for safety critical systems (minimal documentation, evolutionary requirements or refactoring).

Although the industrial inventory was conducted among a diverse set of companies with large settings, its external validity has to be discussed when interpreting the findings of the study. A few companies were actively reporting their experiences, whereas material from the rest of the consortium was scarcer. Those companies that extensively provided this study with the industrial inventory material are big companies with large settings, and they represent expert knowledge in their industries. However, the findings could be still validated and specified using a bigger sample of companies. Also the literature analysis should be more precise. Despite this, we have been able to discover agile in the large strategies and find evidence of its applications in large environments.

In this study, several future research issues for empirical studies were found: combining different agile adoption strategies, discovering evaluation stage in large environments, and the use of key practices when adopting agile. Agility measurement model (discussed in section 3.2) can also be added to the discussion on agile adoption as the work on this issue progresses. In the future, we will enhance our analysis of industrial experiences. For example surveys can be conducted to obtain more extensive and detailed information from the industry. Aggregate level results of this type could also be used for a basis of comparison and benchmarking among practitioners.

Acknowledgments. This study has been carried out in ITEA2 project E06022 FLEXI, "Flexible global product development and integration: From idea to product in 6 months."

References

1. Racheva, Z., Daneva, M., Sikkel, K.: Value Creation by Agile Projects: Methodology or Mystery? In: Bomarius, F., Oivo, M., Jaring, P., Abrahamsson, P. (eds.) Product-Focused Software Process Improvement. LNCS, vol. 32, pp. 141–155. Springer, Heidelberg (2009)
2. Dybå, T., Dingsøyr, T.: Empirical Studies of Agile Software Development: A Systematic Review. Information and Software Technology 50, 833–859 (2008)
3. Erickson, J., Lyytinen, K., Siau, K.: Agile modeling, agile software development, and extreme programming: the state of research. Journal of Database Management 16, 88–100 (2005)
4. Cohen, D., Lindvall, M., Costa, P.: An introduction to agile methods. Advances in Computers 62, 2–67 (2004)
5. Abrahamsson, P., Salo, O., Ronkainen, J., Warsta, J.: Agile Software Development Methods: Review and Analysis. VTT Technical Report (2002)
6. Kitchenham, B.A.: Guidelines for Performing Systematic Literature Reviews in Software Engineering Version 2.3. Technical Report, Keele University and University of Durham (2007)
7. Sidky, A., Arthur, J.: A Disciplined Approach to Adopting Agile Practices: The Agile Adoption Framework. Innovations in Systems and Software Engineering 3, 203–216 (2007)
8. Sidky, A., Arthur, J., Bohner, S.: Determining the Applicability of Agile Practices to Mission and Life-critical Systems. In: Proceedings of the 31st Annual IEEE Software Engineering Workshop, pp. 3–12. IEEE Computer Society, Washington (2007)

9. Qumer, A., Henderson-Sellers, B., McBride, T.: Agile Adoption and Improvement Model. In: Rodenes, M. (ed.) Proceedings of European and Mediterranean Conference on Information Systems 2007, EMCIS (2007)
10. Qumer, A., Henderson-Sellers, B.: A Framework to Support the Evaluation, Adoption and Improvement of Agile Methods in Practice. Journal of Systems and Software 81, 1899–1919 (2008)
11. Sureshchandra, K., Shrinivasavadhani, J.: Adopting Agile in Distributed Development. In: Proceedings of the 2008 IEEE International Conference on Global Software Engineering, pp. 217–221. IEEE Computer Society, Washington (2008)
12. Hodgetts, P.: Refactoring the Development Process: Experiences with the Incremental Adoption of Agile Practices. In: Proceedings of the Agile Development Conference, pp. 106–113. IEEE Computer Society, Washington (2004)
13. Mahanti, A.: Challenges in Enterprise Adoption of Agile Methods – A Survey. Journal of Computing and Information technology 14, 197–206 (2006)
14. Bahli, B.: The Role of Knowledge Creation in Adopting Extreme Programming Model: an Empirical Study. In: Proceedings of ITI 3rd International Conference on Information & Communication Technology, pp. 75–87 (2005)
15. McDowell, S., Dourambeis, N.: British Telecom Experience Report: Agile Intervention – BT's Joining the Dots Events for Organizational Change. In: Concas, G., Damiani, E., Scotto, M., Succi, G. (eds.) XP 2007. LNCS, vol. 4536, pp. 17–23. Springer, Heidelberg (2007)
16. Rayhan, S.H., Haque, N.: Incremental Adoption of Scrum for Successful Delivery of an IT Project in a Remote Setup. In: Proceedings of the Agile 2008, pp. 351–355. IEEE Computer Society, Washington (2008)
17. Griffiths, M.: Crossing the Agile Chasm: DSDM as an Enterprise Friendly Wrapper for Agile Development. Quadrus Development Inc. (2003)
18. Striebeck, M.: Ssh! We Are Adding a process.... In: Proceedings of the Conference on AGILE 2006, pp. 185–193. IEEE Computer Society, Washington (2006)
19. Long, K., Starr, D.: Agile Supports Improved Culture and Quality for Healthwise. In: Proceedings of the AGILE 2008, pp. 160–165. IEEE Computer Society, Washington (2008)
20. Vilkki, K.: Juggling with the Paradoxes of Agile Transformation. In: Agile Processes in Software Engineering and Extreme Programming (2008) (Keynote Speech)
21. Project internal unreported, unpublished material
22. Project internal unreported, unpublished material (2008)
23. Project internal unreported, unpublished material (2007)
24. Vilkki, K.: Juggling with the Paradoxes of Agile Transformation or How to survive in a large scale agile transformation. FLEXI Newsletter 2(2008), 3–5 (2008)
25. Aalto, J.-M.: Large-scale Agile Development of Nokia S60 Software. OO Days, Tampere (2008)
26. Lindvall, M., et al.: Agile Software Development in Large Organizations. Computer 37, 26–34 (2004)
27. Karlström, D., Runeson, P.: Combining Agile Methods with Stage-Gate Project Management. IEEE Software 22, 43–49 (2005)
28. Dybå, T., Dingsøyr, T.: Empirical Studies of Agile Software Development: A Systematic Review. Information and Software Technology 50, 833–859 (2008)
29. Salo, O.: Enabling Software Process Improvement in Agile Software Development Teams and Organisations. VTT Technical Report (2006)

30. Srinivasan, J., Dobrin, R., Lundqvist, K.: 'State of the Art' in Using Agile Methods for Embedded Systems Development. In: Proceedings of the 2009 33rd Annual IEEE International Computer Software and Applications Conference, pp. 522–527. IEEE Computer Society, Washington (2009)
31. Kettunen, P., Laanti, M.: Combining Agile Software Projects and Large-scale Organizational Agility. Software Process Improvement and Practice 13, 183–193 (2008)
32. Pikkarainen, M., Haikara, J., Salo, O., Abrahamsson, P., Still, J.: The impact of agile practices on communication in software development. Empirical Software Engineering 13, 303–337 (2008)
33. Järvilehto, M.: AGILE NOKIA – Large, fast and commited. FLEXI Newsletter 1(2008), 3 (2008)

Applying DPPI: A Defect Causal Analysis Approach Using Bayesian Networks

Marcos Kalinowski[1], Emilia Mendes[2], David N. Card[3], and Guilherme H. Travassos[1]

[1] COPPE/UFRJ – Federal University of Rio de Janeiro,
68511 Rio de Janeiro, Brazil
[2] Computer Science Department – The University of Auckland,
92019 Auckland, New Zealand
[3] Det Norske Veritas, 32937 Florida, USA
mkali@cos.ufrj.br, emilia@cs.auckland.ac.nz, card@computer.org,
ght@cos.ufrj.br

Abstract. Defect causal analysis (DCA) provides a means for product-focused software process improvement. A DCA approach, called DPPI (Defect Prevention-based Process Improvement), was assembled based on DCA guidance obtained from systematic reviews and on feedback gathered from experts in the field. According to the systematic reviews, and to our knowledge, DPPI represents the only approach that integrates cause-effect learning mechanisms (by using Bayesian networks) into DCA meetings. In this paper we extend the knowledge regarding the feasibility of using DPPI by the software industry, by describing the experience of applying it end-to-end to a real Web-based software project and providing additional industrial usage considerations. Building and using Bayesian networks in the context of DCA showed promising preliminary results and revealed interesting possibilities.

Keywords: Bayesian Networks, Defect Causal Analysis, Defect Prevention, Defect Prevention-based Process Improvement, DPPI, Product Focused Software Process Improvement.

1 Introduction

Causal analysis and resolution encompasses the identification of causes of defects and other problems, and ways to prevent them from occurring in the future. It is part of many software process improvement models and approaches, such as CMMI [1], ISO/IEC 12207 [2], and Six Sigma [3]. Defect causal analysis (DCA) [4] represents the application of causal analysis and resolution to a specific type of problem: defects introduced in software artifacts throughout a software lifecycle.

Thus, DCA can be seen as a process to discover and analyze causes associated with the occurrence of specific defect types, allowing the identification of improvement opportunities for the organization's process assets and the implementation of actions to prevent the recurrence of those defect types in future projects. Effective DCA has helped to reduce defect rates by over 50%, in organizations such as IBM [5], Computer Science Corporation [6], HP [7], and InfoSys [8]. Once used, DCA reduces the

M. Ali Babar, M. Vierimaa, and M. Oivo (Eds.): PROFES 2010, LNCS 6156, pp. 92–106, 2010.
© Springer-Verlag Berlin Heidelberg 2010

rework effort [8] and increases the probability of achieving other process-based quality and performance goals [1].

However, despite its benefits and broad industry adoption, there are still numerous unanswered questions concerning DCA implementation in software organizations and a small number of related publications [9]. Therefore, in order to provide guidance on how to efficiently implement DCA in software organizations, a systematic review was conducted in 2006 and replicated in 2007 [10]. The results of both systematic review trials, besides allowing producing DCA guidance, revealed opportunities for further investigation [11]. For instance, "the DCA state of the art did not seem to include any approach integrating learning mechanisms regarding cause-effect relations into DCA meetings". This means that, in all of the approaches found, the knowledge about cause-effect relationships gathered during each DCA session was only used to initiate actions to improve the development process, and afterwards discarded.

To our knowledge, the first effort to bridge this gap is reported in the initial concept of a DCA approach described in [12]. In this initial concept the integration of knowledge gathered in successive causal analysis events as means to assemble a deeper understanding of the defects` cause-effect relations is suggested by using Bayesian networks. Such integration aims to facilitate the creation and maintenance of common causal models to be used to support the identification of causes of defects, allowing efficient process improvement in each DCA event. For instance, such causal models can help to answer the following questions during DCA meetings: "Given the past projects within my organizational context, which causes led to which types of defects?", or "Given the past projects within my organizational context, with which probability did a certain cause lead to a specific defect type?". Further this initial concept was evolved and tailored into the DPPI (defect prevention based process improvement) approach, based on an additional systematic review trial (conducted in 2009) and feedback gathered from experts in the field. DPPI, besides using and feeding Bayesian networks to support DCA, addresses all the specific practices of the CMMI CAR (Causal Analysis and Resolution) process area.

In this paper we extend the knowledge regarding the feasibility of using DPPI by the software industry, by (i) describing the experience of applying DPPI to a large scale Web-based software project detailing how its activities and tasks could be performed in the context of a real software project, and (ii) providing industrial considerations for DPPI with additional insights from a practitioner's point of view into its underlying usage assumptions, the need for tools, and other usage possibilities.

The remainder of this paper is organized as follows. In Section 2 a theoretical background on DCA is described. In Section 3, an overview of DPPI and its activities is provided. Section 4 describes the experience of applying DPPI to a Web-based software project. Section 5 contains the industrial considerations. Finally, conclusions and comments on future work are given in Section 6.

2 Defect Causal Analysis

To have a clear understanding of what defect causal analysis represents in the scope of this paper it is important to first understand what the term defect means. The IEEE standard terminology for software engineering [13] states that when a defect is found through peer reviews it is related to a fault in the artifact being reviewed. When a defect is found through testing activities, on the other hand, it is related to a failure in the software product being tested. In this paper the term defect is used to represent faults revealed by software inspections.

Card [9] summarizes the DCA process in six steps: (i) to select a sample of the defects; (ii) to classify selected defects; (iii) to identify systematic errors; (iv) to determine the main cause; (v) to develop action proposals; and (vi) to document meeting results. In this context, a systematic error is an error that results in the same or similar defects being repeated in different occasions. Finding systematic errors indicates the existence of significant improvement opportunities for the project or organizational process assets. Besides listing these six steps, the importance of managing the implementation of the action proposals until their conclusion and communicating the implemented changes to the development team is highlighted [9].

A representation of the traditional software defect prevention process [14], consistent with the DCA process described above, is shown in Fig. 1. DCA can be considered part of defect prevention, which also addresses implementing improvement actions to prevent the causes (action team activity) and communicating changes to the development team (stage kickoff activity). The depicted experience base indicates defect prevention as a means for communicating lessons learned among projects.

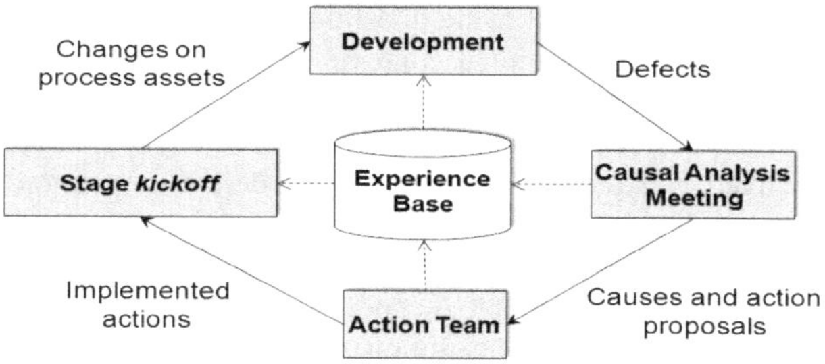

Fig. 1. Defect Prevention Process [14]

In order to provide an unbiased and fair review regarding DCA's the state of the art, a systematic review was planned and executed in three different years (2006, 2007, and 2009). We chose to use a systematic review (SR) for the initial research step, as it tends to be unbiased and more reliable than an ad-hoc review [15]. More details on the SR can be found in [10], where the review protocol and the 2006 and 2007 trials are described in detail. At all, considering the three trials, the SR analyzed 198 research papers, and 55 were filtered using the protocol's inclusion criteria (44 in 2006 + 6 in 2007 + 5 in 2009). The protocol was applied against the following digital libraries: ACM Digital Library, EI Compendex, IEEE, Inspec, and Web of Science.

Based on the first two SR trial results, some guidance on how to efficiently implement DCA in software organizations could be elaborated [11]. Afterwards, the guidance was updated, based on the 2009 trial. This updated guidance helps to answer the following questions commonly faced by practitioners when implementing DCA in software organizations: "Is my organization ready for DCA?", "What approach should be followed?", "Which techniques should be used?", "What metrics should be collected?", "How should DCA be integrated with Statistical Process Control?", "How should defects be categorized?", "How should causes be categorized?", and "What are the expected costs and results of implementing DCA?". More details on this guidance can be found in [11].

Using the initial guidance, a proposal towards a defect prevention based software process improvement approach could be outlined [12], addressing an identified opportunity for further investigation by suggesting the use of Bayesian networks to integrate cause-effect learning mechanisms into DCA meetings. Afterwards this approach was evolved and tailored into DPPI based on the updated guidance, feedback gathered from experts in the field, and the experience of instantiating some of its concepts based on real project data. DPPI, besides using and feeding Bayesian networks to support DCA, addresses all the specific practices of the CMMI CAR process area. The next section provides a brief DPPI overview.

3 DPPI Overview

DPPI represents a practical approach for defect prevention that follows the framework of the traditional defect prevention process, described by Jones [14]. Thus, although slightly rearranged, the DCA meeting, action team, and stage kickoff activities, shown in Fig. 1, are also considered.

When comparing DPPI to the traditional defect prevention process, the main innovation is the integration of knowledge gathered in successive causal analysis events in order to provide a deeper understanding of the organization's defect cause-effect relations; this addresses an opportunity for further investigation identified in our SRs and highlighted in [11]. To our knowledge this opportunity was first addressed in the initial concept that led to DPPI, described in [12], and so far no other approach considers this integration. Such integration allows establishing and maintaining common causal models to support the identification of causes for efficient process improvement in each causal analysis event. Those causal models could support diagnostic reasoning, helping to understand, for instance, given similar projects of the organization, which causes usually lead to which defect types.

Additionally, DPPI follows the guidance for implementing DCA efficiently in software organizations [11] in order to tailor the defect prevention activities into more specific tasks, providing further details on the techniques to be used to accomplish these tasks efficiently. Moreover, it integrates defect prevention into the measurement and control strategy of the development activity for which defect prevention is being applied, allowing one to observe whether the implemented improvements to the development activity brought real benefits. The tailored approach addresses all CMMI CAR specific practices. Thus, following the DPPI approach results in CMMI compatibility regarding the analysis of causes of software defects.

Given that DPPI aims at continuous improvement by enhancing the development activity's sub-process performance and capability, as suggested by the guidance, it was designed to take place right after the inspection of the artifacts of each main software lifecycle development activity.

DPPI includes four activities: (i) Development Activity Result Analysis; (ii) DCA Preparation; (iii) DCA Meeting; and (iv) Development Activity Improvement.

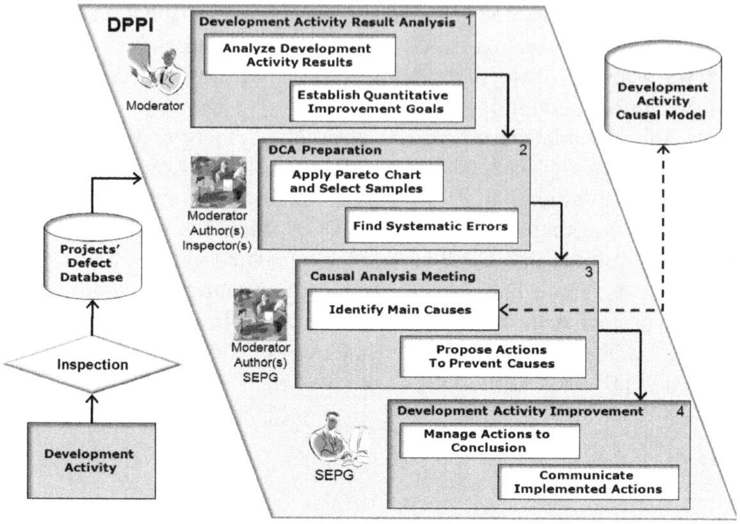

Fig. 2. DPPI Approach Overview

The main tasks for each of these activities, as well as the roles involved in their execution, are depicted in Fig. 2. Note that the software development activity itself and its inspection are out of DPPI's scope.

This figure also highlights the proposal to maintain information regarding the organization's defect cause-effect relations (causal model) for each development activity. DPPI considers those causal models to be dynamically established and maintained by feeding and using Bayesian networks. Pearl [16] suggests that probabilistic causal models can be built using Bayesian networks, if concrete examples of cause-effect relations can be gathered in order to feed the network. In the case of DPPI the examples to feed the Bayesian network can be taken from each DCA meeting results. A brief description of the four DPPI activities and their tasks is provided in the following subsections.

3.1 Development Activity Result Analysis

This activity, which is not mandatory (unless CMMI compatibility is desired), aims at the quantitative measurement and control of the development activity, but is suggested by the guidance as essential to understand the DCA's efficiency, as highlighted in [17]. It comprises two tasks to be performed by the DPPI moderator (could be the same moderator of the inspection in which the defects where revealed). Further details on these tasks follow.

Analyze Development Activity Results. In this task the development activity's defect related results should be analyzed, comparing it against the same development activity historical defect related results. For DPPI this analysis focuses on changes in defect rates, and changes in the activities' input and output quality. Thus, as suggested by the guidance, the following metrics should be analyzed against historical data by using a statistical process control chart: (i) number of defects per unit of size, (ii) number of defects found per inspection hour, (iii) Phase Input Quality (PIQ, which indicates the percentage of defects found in the analyzed development activity that were actually introduced in prior activities), and (iv) Phase Output Quality (POQ, which indicates the percentage of defects of the analyzed development activity that leaked into other development activities). The PIQ and POQ metrics allow to comprehend an activity's input and output quality, and are described in further details in [18], however, sometimes data to calculate them might not be available.

Moreover, as suggested by [19] and indicated by the guidance, the type of the statistical process control chart for the first two of those metrics should be a U-chart, given that defects follow a Poisson distribution. For the PIQ and POQ metrics (which represent a relative percentage) a standard individuals (xMR) chart can be plotted. Those charts can easily indicate if the defect metrics of the development activity sub-process are under control by applying some basic statistical tests (more details on those tests can be obtained in [20]).

Establish Quantitative Improvement Goals. This task concerns establishing improvement goals for the development activity sub-process. A typical example of quantitative improvement goal is: "reducing the defect rate by X percent". If the sub-process related to the development activity is out of control the focus of the causal analysis meeting becomes revealing assignable causes and the improvement goal should be related to stabilizing the sub-process. If it is under control the focus is on finding the common causes and the improvement goal should be improving the process performance and capability.

3.2 DCA Preparation

This activity comprises the preparation for defect causal analysis by selecting the samples of defects to be analyzed and identifying the systematic errors that have been committed leading to several of those defects.

Apply Pareto Chart and Select Samples. This task refers to finding the clusters (samples) of defects where systematic errors are more likely present. Since systematic errors lead to defects of the same type, as indicated by the guidance [11], the Pareto chart can be used to find those clusters, by using the defect categories as the discriminating parameter.

Find Systematic Errors. This task comprises analyzing the defect sample (reading the description of the sampled defects) in order to find its systematic errors. Examples of systematic errors can be found in [21]. Only the defects related to those systematic errors should be considered in the DCA meeting. At this point the moderator could receive support from representatives of the document authors and the inspectors involved in finding the defects.

3.3 DCA Meeting

In this activity the moderator should be supported by representatives of the authors (which know the project context) and the software process engineering group (SEPG). A description of the two tasks involved in this activity follows.

Identify Main Causes. This task comprises analyzing the descriptions of the defects related to the systematic errors in order to find the main causes for each systematic error. It receives great support from having a causal model represented as a Bayesian network and can be stated as the core of our approach. Given the causal model elaborated based on prior DCA meetings for the same development activity, the probabilities for causes to lead to the defect type related to the systematic error being analyzed can be calculated by using the Bayesian network inference. Afterwards those probabilities can be used to support the DCA meeting team in identifying the main causes. Therefore it can be represented as a probabilistic cause-effect diagram [12] for the type of defect related to the systematic error being analyzed.

This diagram was designed based on the cause-effect diagram [24], suggested by the guidance for identifying causes. The probabilistic cause-effect diagram extends the cause-effect diagram by (i) showing the probabilities for each possible cause to lead to the analyzed defect type and (ii) representing the causes using grey tones, where the darker tones are used for the causes with higher probability. This representation can be easily interpreted and highlights the causes with greater probabilities of causing the analyzed defect type. A concrete example of how such diagram can be built based on the Bayesian network is shown in Section 4.

At the end of the meeting the Bayesian network should be fed with the resulting causes for the defect type, so that the probabilities of the causes can be updated for the next DCA event.

Propose Actions to Prevent Causes. In this task, actions should be brainstormed to improve the process assets in order to prevent the identified causes. The overall meeting results (current defect rates, improvement goals, main defect categories, systematic errors, causes, and action proposals) should be documented.

3.4 Development Activity Improvement

Finally, in this activity, the action proposals should be implemented by a dedicated team and managed until their conclusion. After implementation, the changes to the process should be communicated to the development team.

Given this brief overview of DPPI, the next section describes the proof of concept experience of applying DPPI to a real large scale Web-based software project.

4 DPPI Proof of Concept

As a proof of concept, DPPI was applied retroactively to perform defect causal analysis on the functional specification activity of a real Web-based software project. The scope of this project, called SIGIC, was to develop a new information system to manage the activities of the COPPETEC Foundation. Thus the project involved several departments from the Foundation, such as: human resources, financial, protocol, among others. The system to be implemented was modularized and developed in an iterative and incremental lifecycle. Based on this lifecycle, a development process was defined, in which software inspections were performed on each of the modules' functional specifications, using the ISPIS framework [22].

In total, more than 10 iterations were performed and more than 200 use cases were specified, implemented and delivered to the client over a three years development period. By the end of the project, all inspection data was available, including details on over 1000 defects found and removed from the functional specifications before the actual implementation. In this context, DPPI was applied retroactively to the functional specification activity of the fourth developed module regarding protocol of bound solicitations, called MPTV. The details of how each DPPI activity (except the improvement activity, which could not be performed since the application was retroactive) could be performed are described hereafter.

4.1 Applying Development Activity Result Analysis

To understand the current scenario and changes in defect rates comparing the SIGIC MPTV module to the prior ones (MSL, MGU, and MPT), as suggested by DPPI, a U-chart was plotted for defects per inspection hour and defects per unit of size (use case point). This chart is shown in Fig. 3.

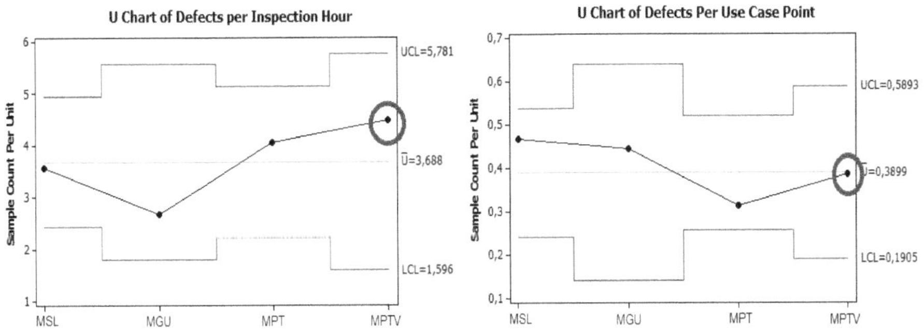

Fig. 3. U-charts for defects per inspection hour and defects per use case point

Note that the number of defects revealed per inspection hour in the MPTV module was higher than the average, whereas the number of defects per use case point was average. The U-chart shows a scenario of stability (none of its control limits were exceeded). Since the functional specification is the first development activity, its PIQ is 0, and unfortunately its POQ could not be calculated since defect data from other activities was not available.

Given this scenario, the improvement goal was reducing defect rate per use case point from 0.39 to 0.31, which was the best defect rate obtained so far.

4.2 Applying DCA Preparation

This activity comprises applying a Pareto chart to select samples and finding systematic errors in those samples. The Pareto chart built to analyze the defects of the MPTV module is shown in Fig. 4. It considers the defect categories described in [23] and shows that most of the defects are of type incorrect fact, and that the sum of incorrect facts and omissions represents about 60% of all defects found. Incorrect facts were chosen as the sample to identify systematic errors.

The following two systematic errors could be identified by reading incorrect fact defects: writing invalid business rules; and linking use case descriptions incorrectly.

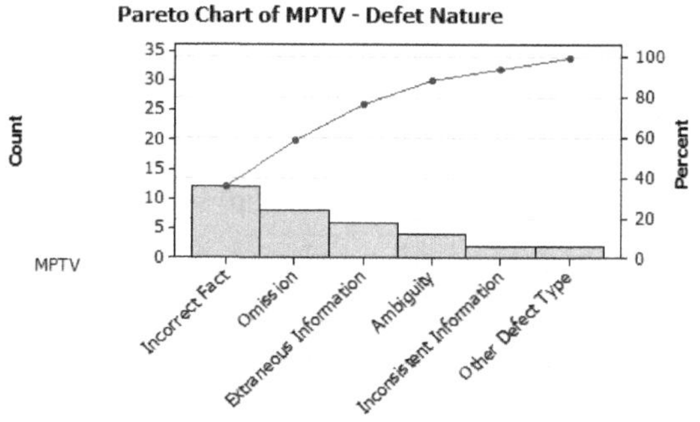

Fig. 4. MPTV defect category Pareto chart

4.3 Applying DCA Meeting

Before describing how the DPPI DCA meeting activity was accomplished, some details are provided on how the defect causal model could be built retroactively.

Building the Bayesian Network. Since no prior DCA events had been performed in the SIGIC project, the Bayesian causal model had to be built retroactively based on the existing defect data in order to be used for the MPTV DCA event. First a meeting with the SIGIC project team was conducted to brainstorm possible causes for functional specification defects based on the cause categories (method, people, tools, input and organization) suggested in the guidance. The brainstorm result is shown in Fig. 5.

Afterwards, descriptions of the 163 functional specification defects revealed prior to the MPTV module were analyzed with the support of the document authors, SEPG members and inspectors responsible in finding those defects in order to associate each defect to one of the brainstormed causes. During this attempt other causes could have been added, but in the case of the SIGIC project this was not needed.

As a result, each defect had information on the module, the size of the module, the total inspection effort, the defect category, defect severity, cause, and cause category. Those were also the nodes of the Bayesian network. The causal relations of our interest could be easily modeled by having the cause and the cause category nodes both affecting the defect category node. The values and the ranges for those nodes were obtained by using the defect data as learning cases.

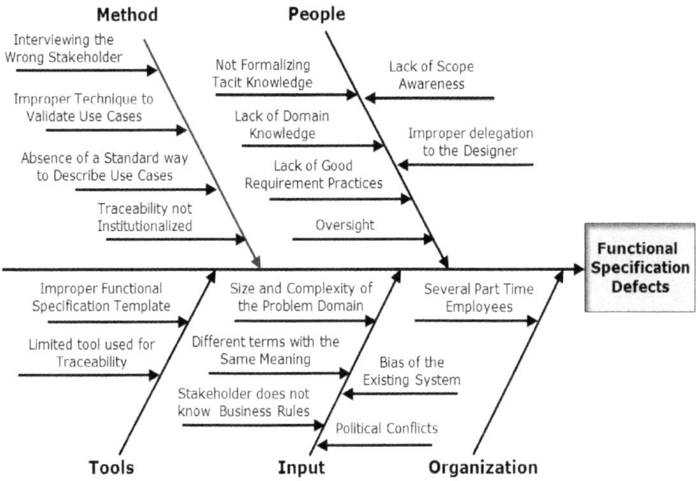

Fig. 5. Defect causes brainstorm result

Note that, in this case, the Bayesian network was built retroactively, since no prior DCA sessions were conducted in the project. Otherwise the learning cases could have been the other DCA session results and thus the Bayesian network could have been built dynamically, without the need to classify all defect data. In this case, the Bayesian network should be fed also with the results of DCA sessions of other similar projects in the organization, so that more Bayesian learning cases are available. More details on the needed similarity between projects will be provided in Section 5.

Conducting the DCA Meeting. At the start of the DCA meeting activity a probabilistic cause-effect diagram should be available for the defect category being analyzed. This diagram can be built by simply reading the Bayesian inference for that defect category. The Bayesian inference shows the probabilities with which each cause led to this defect category in past modules (or similar projects) of the same organizational context.

The Bayesian diagnostic inference and the corresponding probabilistic cause-effect diagram for incorrect facts in functional specifications of the SIGIC project are shown in Fig. 6. This figure shows that in this project typically the causes for incorrect facts were "Lack of Domain Knowledge" (25%), "Size and Complexity of the Problem Domain" (18,7%), "Oversight" (15,6%), and "Limited tool used for Traceability" (12.5%). We believe that such probabilistic cause-effect diagram could help to effectively use the defect related cause-effect knowledge stored in the causal model.

In fact, during the SIGIC MPTV DCA meeting the identified causes for the systematic error of writing invalid business rules were "Lack of Domain Knowledge" and "Size and Complexity of the Problem Domain". For the systematic error of linking use case descriptions incorrectly it was "Oversight". Those causes correspond to the three causes of the probabilistic cause-effect diagram with highest probabilities and were identified by reading the defect descriptions and involving the author, inspectors, and SEPG members. Thus, the probabilistic cause-effect diagram might be helpful, although further investigation into this issue is required.

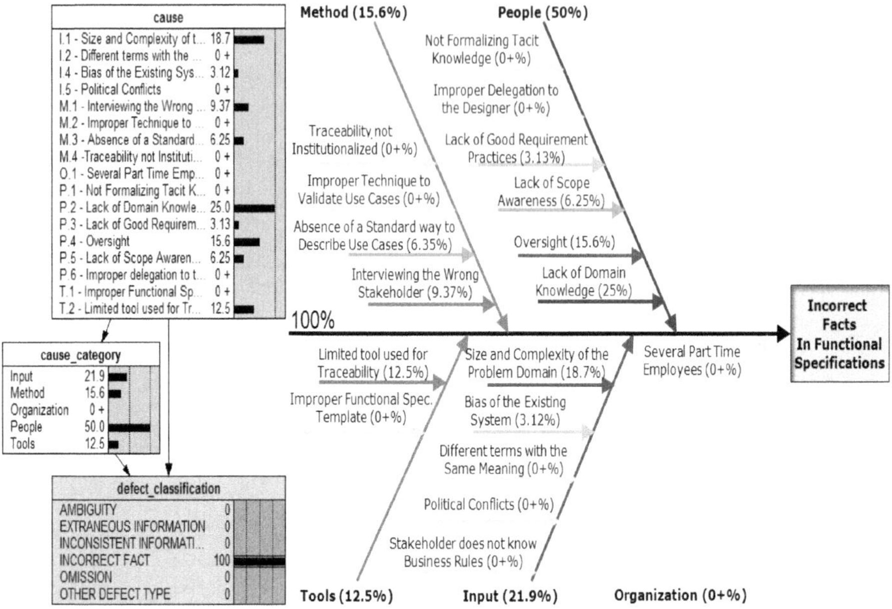

Fig. 6. Bayesian network inference for incorrect facts in functional specifications and the corresponding DPPI probabilistic cause-effect diagram

The proposed actions addressing the causes "Lack of Domain Knowledge" and "Size and Complexity of the Problem Domain" were: (i) studying the domain and the pre-existing system; and (ii) modifying the functional specification template, creating a separate session for the business rules, listing them all together and separate from the use case description. For the cause "Oversight" the action was publishing relevant examples of incorrect fact oversight related defects and presenting them to the functional specification team.

However, as mentioned before, the development activity improvement was not performed, since the proof of concept was performed retroactively and the next module was already specified. Therefore, quantitative results of applying DPPI (which would be shown in the U-charts of the upcoming module after implementing proposed improvement actions) could not be obtained.

In the next section we present some industrial considerations for DPPI with additional insights into what it would take to make the approach a regular industry practice. Therefore, its underlying usage assumptions, the need for tools, and other usage possibilities are discussed from a practitioner's point of view.

5 Industrial Considerations

As mentioned before, feedback on DPPI was gathered from three software engineering experts, with large academic and professional experiences (having participated in several software process consulting projects and holding PhDs in software engineering), by presenting them the approach. During this feedback session one of the main discussions was concerning DPPI's underlying usage assumptions, which are presented hereafter.

5.1 Underlying Usage Assumptions

The underlying assumptions for using DPPI include the existence of a defined process for the project, as suggested by [9], and the execution of software inspections during which information regarding the detected defects is stored. The information regarding defects should include the activity in which the defect was introduced, the activity in which the defect was found and the defect type. More details on defect categorization can be found in the guidance described in [11].

Moreover, DPPI has to be used to improve the same activity for different modules of the same or similar projects. In case of using it between different projects, they should share the same defect categorization scheme, follow similar processes, be related to domains of similar complexity, use teams of similar experience, and use the same type of technology. Basically, in this case, the assumptions are the same as for grouping different projects for statistical process control, described in [20]. Otherwise the U-charts and even the causal model would not be meaningful. Regarding the U-charts, in particular, in order for them to be useful to control the sub-process of the development activity being analyzed, inspections need to be performed following a defined and stable inspection process (so that defect data can be related to the performance of the development activity sub-process).

Regarding the causal model, causes identified in prior DCA events for the same development activity concerning similar projects/modules need to registered with their category (considerations on this categorization can be found in [11]) and the related defect type, so that the Bayesian network for the development activity can be built dynamically using that data as learning cases. Otherwise the causal model would have to be built retroactively (as done in Section 4 of this paper), which requires much more effort, resulting in a difficulty to scale in order to consider defect cause-effect knowledge reflecting several projects of the organization during the DCA sessions. Other considerations regarding effort, more specifically related to tool support follow in the next subsection.

5.2 Considerations on Tool Support

Some tool support can be used in order to facilitate the application of DPPI. For instance, plotting the U-charts and the Pareto diagram manually would require much effort. Several statistical tools can be used for this purpose, during the experience described in this paper, the U-charts and the Pareto diagram were plotted using the MiniTab software.

Another aspect for which tool support is required is building the Bayesian network from the learning cases and performing the Bayesian inference. Again several tools can be used for this purpose; during the experience described in this paper the Bayesian network was built using Netica software, which was also used for the Bayesian inference.

Besides these tools, the application described in this paper used ISPIS [22], which facilitated conducting a well defined and stable inspection process and registering defect data. However, inspections are out of the DPPI scope and could have been performed manually as well.

5.3 Other Usage Possibilities

Practitioners might want to use DPPI to support CMMI implementation. Table 1 contains a mapping of the specific practices of the CMMI CAR process area to the DPPI activities.

Table 1. Mapping of CMMI CAR process area specific practices to DPPI activities

CMMI CAR Specific Goal/Practice	Related DPPI Activities
SG 1 Determine Causes of Defects	DCA Preparation and DCA Meeting
SP 1.1 Select Defect Data for Analysis	DCA Preparation
SP 1.2 Analyze Causes	DCA Meeting
SG 2 Address Causes of Defects	Development Activity Result Analysis and Development Activity Improvement
SP 2.1 Implement the Action Proposals	Development Activity Improvement
SP 2.2 Evaluate the Effect of Changes	Development Activity Result Analysis
SP 2.3 Record Data	Throughout DPPI, by using its templates

Another usage possibility is for defect prediction. Since the causal model with defect related knowledge obtained by applying DPPI is stored as a Bayesian Network it can be used for two reasons, diagnosis and prediction [16]. In this paper we only explored the diagnosis perspective. However, the Bayesian network can be traversed in the opposite direction, in order to support the definition of risk mitigation strategies by performing "what-if" scenario simulation on the causes. For instance, "What happens to the defect profile if the wrong stakeholder was interviewed?".

6 Conclusions

The DPPI approach was assembled based on DCA guidance obtained from SRs and on feedback gathered from experts in the field. DPPI provides a framework for conducting, measuring and controlling DCA in order to use it efficiently for process improvement. It represents the only approach that integrates cause-effect learning mechanisms into DCA meetings. Those learning mechanisms consider a concrete characteristic of the product, the defects introduced in its artifacts, to enable the construction of a causal model for the organization, represented through a Bayesian network. In order to allow using such Bayesian network to support DCA meetings a graphical representation, called probabilistic cause-effect diagram, was designed.

In this paper we extended the knowledge regarding the feasibility of using DPPI by the software industry, by: (i) describing the experience of applying DPPI to a large scale Web-based software project detailing how its activities and tasks could be performed in that context, and (ii) providing industrial considerations for DPPI with additional insights from a practitioner's point of view into its underlying usage assumptions, the need for tools, and other usage possibilities.

In general, the experience of applying DPPI end-to-end to a real software project provides preliminary feasibility indication of using it as a means for product-focused process improvement. In particular, its main innovation, the causal model represented through a Bayesian network which represents knowledge regarding a concrete characteristic of the product (its defects), could be built successfully. Moreover, in the context of the project in which the network was applied, the Bayesian diagnostic inference, represented in the probabilistic cause-effect diagram, predicted the main causes efficiently. However, the benefits of using the network to support DCA meetings have not been evaluated objectively so far.

Regarding the industrial considerations, the application of DPPI allowed providing additional insights into its underlying usage assumptions and the needs for tool support. Additionally, the possibility of using DPPI as a step by step for analyzing software defect causes in compliance with the CMMI CAR process area was discussed. Moreover, the possibility of using the resulting Bayesian network for defect prediction in order to support the definition of risk mitigation strategies by performing "what-if" scenario simulation was mentioned.

In our point of view, building and using Bayesian networks in the context of DCA showed promising preliminary results and interesting possibilities. Hence, we invite academy and industry for further investigation on this topic.

Acknowledgments. We would like to thank the SIGIC project team, without their support the experience described in this paper would not have been possible. Thanks also to the experts which provided us feedback on DPPI.

References

1. SEI: CMMI for Development (CMMI-DEV), Version 1.2. CMU/SEI-2006-TR008. Software Engineering Institute, Carnegie Mellon University, Pittsburgh, PA (2006)
2. ISO/IEC: ISO/IEC 12207:2008 Systems and software engineering – Software life cycle processes (2008)
3. Eckes, G.: The Six Sigma Revolution: How General Electric and Others Turned Process Into Profits. John Wiley and Sons, Chichester (2000)
4. Card, D.: Defect Causal Analysis Drives Down Error Rates. IEEE Software 10(4), 98–99 (July 1993)
5. Mays, R.G., Jones, C.L., Holloway, G.J., Studinski, D.P.: Experiences with Defect Prevention. IBM Systems Journal 29(1), 4–32 (1990)
6. Dangerfield, O., Ambardekar, P., Paluzzi, P., Card, D., Giblin, D.: Defect Causal Analysis: A Report from the Field. In: Proceedings of International Conference of Software Quality, American Society for Quality Control (1992)
7. Grady, R.B.: Software Failure Analysis for High-Return Process Improvement Decisions. Hewlett-Packard Journal 47(4), 15–24 (1996)
8. Jalote, P., Agrawal, N.: Using Defect Analysis Feedback for Improving Quality and Productivity in Iterative Software Development. In: 3rd ICICT, Cairo, pp. 701–713 (2005)
9. Card, D.: Defect Analysis: Basic Techniques for Management and Learning. Advances in Computers ch. 7, 65, 259–295 (2005)
10. Kalinowski, M., Travassos, G.H.: A Systematic Review Regarding Software Defect Causal Analysis. Technical report (in portuguese), 158 p, COPPE/UFRJ (2008)

11. Kalinowski, M., Travassos, G.H., Card, D.N.: Guidance for Efficiently Implementing Defect Causal Analysis. In: VII Br. Sym. Soft. Qual (SBQS), Florianópolis, Brazil (2008)
12. Kalinowski, M., Travassos, G.H., Card, D.N.: Towards a Defect Prevention Based Process Improvement Approach. In: 34th Euromicro SEAA, Parma, Italy, pp. 199–206 (2008)
13. IEEE: IEEE Standard Glossary of Software Engineering Terminology. Standard 610. IEEE Press, Los Alamitos (1990)
14. Jones, C.L.: A process-integrated approach to defect prevention. IBM Systems Journal 24(2), 150–167 (1985)
15. Brereton, P., Kitchenham, B.A., Budgen, D., Turner, M., Khalil, M.: Lessons from applying the systematic literature review process within the software engineering domain. Journal of Systems and Software 80(4), 571–583 (2007)
16. Pearl, J.: Causality Reasoning, Models and Inference. Cambridge University Press, Cambridge (2000)
17. Jantti, M., Toroi, T., Eerola, A.: Difficulties in establishing a defect management process: A case study. In: Münch, J., Vierimaa, M. (eds.) PROFES 2006. LNCS, vol. 4034, pp. 142–150. Springer, Heidelberg (2006)
18. Damm, L., Lundberg, L.: Company-wide Implementation of Metrics for Early Software Fault Detection. In: International Conference on Soft. Eng. (ICSE 2007), Minneapolis (2007)
19. Hong, G., Xie, M., Shanmugan, P.: A Statistical Method for Controlling Software Defect Detection Process. Computers and Industrial Engineering 37(1-2), 137–140 (1999)
20. Florac, A.W., Carleton, A.D.: Measuring the Software Process: Statistical Process Control for Software Process Improvement. Pearson Education, London (1999)
21. Leszak, M., Perry, D.E., Stoll, D.: Classification and evaluation of defects in a project retrospective. Journal of Systems and Software 61(3), 173–187 (2002)
22. Kalinowski, M., Travassos, G.H.: A Computational Framework for Supporting Software Inspections. In: Int. Conf. on Automated Soft. Eng. (ASE 2004), Linz, Austria, pp. 46–55 (2004)
23. Shull, F.: Developing Techniques for Using Software Documents: A Series of Empirical Studies. Ph.D. thesis, University of Maryland, College Park (1998)
24. Ishikawa, K.: Guide to Quality Control. Asian Productivity Organization, Tokyo (1976)

Evaluating Three Approaches to Extracting Fault Data from Software Change Repositories

Tracy Hall[1], David Bowes[2], Gernot Liebchen[1], and Paul Wernick[2]

[1] Brunel University, Department of Information Systems & Computing, Uxbridge, Middlesex, UK
{tracy.hall,gernot.liebchen}@brunel.ac.uk
[2] University of Hertfordshire, School of Computer Science, Hatfield, Hertfordshire, UK
{d.h.bowes,p.d.wernick}@herts.ac.uk

Abstract. Software products can only be improved if we have a good understanding of the faults they typically contain. Code faults are a significant source of software product problems which we currently do not understand sufficiently. Open source change repositories are potentially a rich and valuable source of fault data for both researchers and practitioners. Such fault data can be used to better understand current product problems so that we can predict and address future product problems. However extracting fault data from change repositories is difficult. In this paper we compare the performance of three approaches to extracting fault data from the change repository of the Barcode Open Source System. Our main findings are that we have most confidence in our manual evaluation of diffs to identify fault fixing changes. We had less confidence in the ability of the two automatic approaches to separate fault fixing from non-fault fixing changes. We conclude that it is very difficult to reliably extract fault fixing data from change repositories, especially using automatic tools and that we need to be cautious when reporting or using such data.

Key words: Software, fault, data, prediction.

1 Introduction

Identifying and fixing faults in software is a major software development cost. Preventing and removing faults is reported to cost the US between $50 and $78 billion per year [1,2]. Code faults remain a significant source of problems in software with a great deal of resources dedicated to software testing and debugging [3]. Identifying where faults are before testing could lead to higher quality software and better use of resources [4,5,6].

It is important that we understand more about the nature and cause of faults in code so that we can target our search for faults more effectively both before and during testing. Research indicates that about 60-80% of software faults are found in about 20% of the code modules (eg. [7]), with around half of code modules usually fault free [8]. Clearly there are potential resource savings if fault handling efforts are focussed on the code that actually contains faults.

M. Ali Babar, M. Vierimaa, and M. Oivo (Eds.): PROFES 2010, LNCS 6156, pp. 107–115, 2010.
© Springer-Verlag Berlin Heidelberg 2010

Many previous researchers have explored how faults in code can be targeted and identified, with a variety of code fault prediction models reported in the literature. Building reliable fault prediction models depends on the availability and dependability of historical fault data. Most models are built on the assumption that the causes of faults in the past are similar to the causes of faults in the future. This means that models built on historical fault data should enable unfound future faults to be located.

However identifying historical fault data is not straightforward in either commercial or open source projects. The first difficulty is that it is impossible to identify all faults. Residual faults always remain in the system. Consequently previous work predominately uses fault fixing data as a proxy for faults and clearly this represents only a sub-set of faults in the system. This is a problem we do not address in this study. The second difficulty is that recording and documenting fault data is an overhead that many developers avoid. Consequently fault data is rarely maintained and very few projects use bug reporting tools like Bugzilla. Where fault data is maintained it has been reported to not be terribly reliable. As a result most researchers extract fault data from change data (eg from CVS records). Although change data accurately represents changes implemented to the system, these changes include not only fault fixes but all enhancements, improvements and refactorings made to the system. Consequently it is important to identify only those changes that represent fault fixes.

The aim of the paper is to identify the most reliable approach to identifying fault fixing changes from a change repository. We compare the effectiveness of three approaches to identifying fault fixing data using the change repository of the Barcode open source system. In the first approach we manually analyse change diffs (textual changes in code between revisions) and classify each as either a fault fixing diff or not. The other two approaches we investigate automatically analyse CVS records. The first searches the change repository for fault related key words, and the second searches for small sized changes.

In the next section we outline related previous work extracting fault data from change repositories. In Section Three we explain our methodology and describe the open source system used in this study. Section Four presents the results of collecting fault fixing data using each of the three approaches compared in this study. In Section Five we conclude and summarise our findings.

2 Background

The most common automatic method for extracting fault fixing change data from project repositories is based on searching for fault related key words in comment fields. This approach has been extensively evaluated by Zimmermann et al (eg [9,10,11]). Their work is mainly in the context of open source projects and is based on the use of CVS records and Bugzilla records. Although they report promising results they also acknowledge that natural language ambiguities reduce the success rate of the approach.

Weyuker and Ostrand [12] compare the performance of two approaches to using keywords to identify fault fixes within an industrial context. First, a system's change comments are searched through automatically for keywords indicating if a change was the result of a fault fix or if it was the result of a change of functionality. Second a change is categorised as a fault fix if an additional fault identifying field was set by developers during testing or once deployed. Their study showed that the technique using the additional field performed better than the keyword approach. Again, natural language ambiguities limited the performance of the keyword search technique.

A less common approach to identifying fault fixing changes has been proposed by Ostrand et al [13]. Following a suggestion made by developers they introduced the idea that fault fixing changes are only likely to affect one or two files. They tested this approach on a sample of 50 change submissions by reading manually through change messages [13]. Their results are promising and Ostrand et al report that they perform better than the key word search. However they applied and tested this approach only within a graphical systems development environment.

Unfortunately implementing Ostrand et al's [13] number of files involved in a change approach is hard if CVS is the only tool used to manage changes. This is because CVS does not clearly identify the set of individual changes making up one change. Other change control systems such as Subversion automatically maintain records of change sets, whereas with CVS these change sets must be reconstructed. Consequently methods for recognising the constituent changes in change sets have been developed. Zimmermann et al [14] identify a change set by either adopting a fixed window or a sliding window approach. Both techniques rely on the assumption that file submissions in a change set are carried out by the same author and within a certain time frame. The fixed window approach uses a 200 second time frame in which related submissions must occur to be part of a given change set. The sliding window approach moves the frame along after each file to see if the next file should be included. This results in a variable time frame in which submissions in a change set can be made.

3 Methodology

3.1 The Barcode Open Source System

In this study we use the change repository for the Barcode open source system (http://ar.linux.it/software/#barcode). We chose this system because initially we wanted to replicate Meyers and Binkley's program slicing metrics work [15], as our overall aim was to investigate the relationship between program slicing data and fault data. To do this we needed to extract fault data from the Barcode system and compare it to our program slicing metrics data.

Barcode is a small open source system (approx 9 KLOC) written in the C language. The program slicing tool that we use (CodeSurfer) only analyses C and C++ code, so language is a key consideration for us. Barcode is a tool for the conversion of text strings to printed bars. The Barcode project started in 1999 and a change history is available as CVS data. Although several developers participate in the project, all entries into the CVS system are carried out by one person. The Barcode project does not employ an automated fault reporting system, such as Bugzilla, but a file containing additional information about CVS submits, including pointers to issues in source code (the changelog), is maintained.

3.2 Procedures for Implementing the Three Approaches

Manual classification of change diffs. We use a manual analysis of Barcode's diffs to classify changes made to the system as either fault fixing or non fault fixing changes. Our aim is to use this classification as a baseline with which to compare the two automatic approaches. Our assumption is that manual classification of changes for a small project like Barcode is likely to be more accurate than automatic methods. However this manual classification approach is highly resource intensive and is only practical for small studies.

For manual classification we first extracted 199 module level diffs from the CVS repository for Barcode. Each diff contains the code and comments logged with the checked-in change. This data was then given to 3 researchers to independently classify each of these diffs as either: a fault fix; not a fault fix; don't know.

After this independent classification of the diffs, an inter-rater reliability analysis and a Cohen's Kappa score was calculated to measure classification agreement between the three researchers (described in Section 3.3). Disagreements in the classification of diffs were then discussed by all three researchers, the basis of these disagreements were resolved and the diffs classified for a second time.

Key word searching. We identified fault fixing changes from Barcode's change repository using a key word search based on previous studies (eg [14]) We searched the change comments logged in CVS for keywords: "bug", "fix(ed)" and "update(d)". The resulting classification of fault fixing and non fault fixing changes was compared to the manual classification of diffs using an inter rater reliability measure (described in Section 3.3).

Identifying changes involving only 1 or 2 files. We applied Ostrand et al's [13] approach to identifying fault fixing changes as those involving only one or two files. To identify how many files are involved in a given change all changes in a change set must be first identified. Identifying change sets is not straightforward for Barcode which maintains its change records only under CVS control.

In addition to implementing a fixed window approach to identifying change sets we also introduce an enhanced sliding window approach. Our sliding window approach estimates the bandwidth of an upload (bytes per second) to determine the size of the sliding window rather than use the conventional constant sized sliding window. This then allows us to calculate a more accurate variable timeframe for a particular author downloading a particular change set.

The resulting classification of fault fixing and non fault fixing changes is compared to the manual classification of diffs using an inter rater reliability measure (described in Section 3.3).

3.3 Inter Rater Reliability Measurement

We compare the performance of all 3 fault fix finding approaches using inter rater reliability scores using the Cohen's Kappa statistic. We report both the κ value of this statistic together with its categorical scale, as proposed by Landis and Koch:

< 0 No agreement
0.00 — 0.20 Slight agreement
0.21 — 0.40 Fair agreement
0.41 — 0.60 Moderate agreement
0.61 — 0.80 Substantial agreement
0.81 — 1.00 Almost perfect agreement

3.4 Limitations of the Study

The limitations of this study are mainly related to the quality of data on which it is based. As in many change repositories CVS comment fields are not always completed and when they are not always accurately or comprehensively. However this is no different to any metrics data, as in the real world most metrics data is noisy and has missing values and our methods must be able to cope with this. In addition because each of the methods that we are evaluating tries to indirectly identify fault fixing changes, the classification will never be 100% accurate. For example there will be misclassifications in our manual diff method; ambiguity and idiosyncrasy in natural language will mean we miss keywords in our key work search; check-in variations will also mean that we will misclassify some changes involving one or two files as a fault fix when they were not. Furthermore Ostrand et al's approach may not work as well with program that do not have a graphical user interface.

4 Results

4.1 Manual Classification of Change Diffs

Table 1 shows how each researcher manually classified each of the 199 Barcode diffs.

Table 1. Overall diff classifications

		Classifications		
		F	DK	NF
Researchers	R1	58	0	141
	R2	70	43	85
	R3	54	51	94

F=Fault fix; DK=Don't know; NF=not fault fix

Table 1 shows the different classification levels of each researcher and Table 2 shows the spread of those disagreements across the categories.

Table 2. Comparison of diff classifications between researchers

Researcher 1 \ Researcher 2	F	DK	NF
F	37	13	8
DK	0	0	0
NF	33	31	77

Researcher 3 \ Researcher 2	F	DK	NF
F	31	15	8
DK	7	5	39
NF	32	24	38

Researcher 1 \ Researcher 3	F	DK	NF
F	29	8	21
DK	0	0	0
NF	25	43	73

F=Fault fix; DK=Don't know; NF=not fault fix

114/199 agreements Kappa .28 (fair) 74/199 agreements Kappa .027 (slight) 102/199 agreements kappa .17 (slight)

Table 2 shows substantial classification disagreement between the 3 researchers. This is likely to be the result of several factors. The first factor is the decision that Researcher 1 made to allow no Don't Know classifications and instead to assign diffs to the most likely class. The second factor is varying programming experience. Although all 3 researchers are familiar with C programming, two of them have extended experience of C programming due to working on projects in industry and academia. The other researcher's knowledge was based on being taught C during his first degree. The third factor may also be related to the difficulty of interpreting the intentions of a programmer based only on diffs.

As a result of this high level of disagreement all three researchers got together and discussed the classification of each of the 199 diffs. They decided not to allow any Don't Knows as the other two approaches did not include such classifications. During this process 68 of the 199 diffs were excluded from future analysis as, on closer inspection they were based on inappropriate data (for example changes only to header files). This means that the other 2 approaches were applied to a 'cleaned' data set of 131 diffs. The following diff classification consensus was achieved: 47 fault fixing changes; 84 non fault fixing changes.

4.2 Keyword Search

We searched comments in the CVS logged changes as described in Section 3. As a result the 131 changes were classified as: 27 fault fixing changes and 104 non fault fixing changes. Table 3 compares the classification of this approach to the manual classification of diffs.

Table 3 shows that there is significant disagreement between the two approaches in the classification of fault fixing and non fault fixing changes. In particular the keywords classify far fewer changes as fault fixes than the manual diff classifications (27 as opposed to 47). This may be the result of missing comment data on which to search, as well as unexpected comments used to describe a fault fixing change. Our key words do not include for example 'patched' or 'mended' (though clearly our key word list could be extended).

Table 3. Key word compared to diff classification

Change log analysis	Diff results: F	NF	Total
F	21	6	27
NF	26	78	104
Total	47	84	131

F=Fault fix; NF=not fault fix
99/131 agreements kappa 0.4 (fair)

4.3 Size of Change Search

We applied both the fixed and sliding window timeframe approaches to identify those changes that involved only one or two files. Such changes are classified as fault fixing changes. Using the fixed window approach changes were classified as: 44 fault fixes; 87 non fault fixes. Using the sliding window approach changes were classified as: 50 fault fixes; 81 non fault fixes. Table 4 compares the classification of both of these timeframe approaches to our manual diff classifications.

Table 4. Size of change compared to diff classification

Fixed window	Diff results: F	NF	Total
F	25	19	44
NF	22	65	87
Total	47	84	131

F=Fault fix; NF=not fault fix
90/131 agreements kappa 0.3 (fair)

Sliding window	Diff results: F	NF	Total
F	29	21	50
NF	18	63	81
Total	47	84	131

F=Fault fix; NF=not fault fix
92/131 agreements kappa .3 (fair)

Table 4 shows that the approach used to calculate the timeframe in which downloaded files are assumed to be related make little difference to the classification of changes. The sliding window timeframe classifies 6 more changes as fault fixing than the fixed window timeframe. Table 4 also shows that both approaches have significant disagreement with the manual diff classification of fault fixing and non fault fixing changes.

5 Conclusions

Our results suggest that extracting fault fixing data from CVS change repositories can be unreliable. There are many factors that contribute to this. A significant factor is the completeness and quality of the data stored. Missing and unclear checked-in CVS comments make it difficult for the key word search technique to be accurate. This, together with the readability of code, also makes it difficult to manually identify fault fixing diffs. As a result it is difficult to have confidence in the precision of techniques for separating fault fixing changes from other changes. Added to which fault fixing changes represent only a sub-set of faults in the system as they are only faults that have been found, latent faults certainly remain in the system. Although our study is based on an open source system these problems are just as likely in the commercial domain where data is reported to be incomplete and have quality issues.

Our results could have important implications for researchers and practitioners. It is difficult for practitioners to have confidence in some fault prediction models as the historical fault data on which they are based could lack quality. This is likely to reduce the accuracy of predicting real faults or fault proneness. It is also difficult for researchers to build reliable fault prediction models without access to high quality data. Such data is not widely available, especially in projects which do not use fault management tools such as Bugzilla. Some projects do appear to adopt a more systematic approach to managing faults and it is these projects that are likely to generate more reliable data for analysis.

Our overall conclusions are that the quality of data used to build fault prediction models is critical to the reliability of those models and is an aspect of those models that needs to be addressed by researchers. And finally, the collection of reliable data on faults by projects is critical to improving our understanding of product quality.

Acknowledgements. This work was funded by the UK's Engineering and Physical Sciences Research Council under grant number: EP/E063039/1, Investigating code fault proneness using program slicing. We would also like to thank Sarah Beecham, Sue Black and Steve Counsell for their support during the work reported here.

References

1. Levinson, M.: Let's stop wasting $78 billion a year. CIO Magazine (2001)
2. Runeson, P., Andrews, A.: Detection or Isolation of Defects? An Experimental Comparison of Unit Testing and Code Inspection. In: ISSRE 2003, pp. 3–13 (2003)
3. Di Fatta, G., Leue, S., Stegantova, E.: Dis-criminative Pattern Mining in Software Fault Detection. In: SOQUA Workshop (2006)
4. Turhan, B., Kocak, G., Bener, A.: Data mining source code for locating software bugs: A case study in telecommunication industry. Expert Syst. Appl. 36, 6 (2009)
5. Bezerra, M.E.R., Oliveira, A.L.I., Adeodato, P.J.L., Meira, S.R.L.: Enhancing RBF-DDA Algorithm's Robustness: Neural Networks Applied to Prediction of Fault-Prone Software Modules. In: Artificial Intelligence in Theory and Practice II (2007)
6. Oral, A.D., Bener, A.: Defect prediction for embedded software. In: Proceedings of the 22nd International Symposium on Computer and Information Sciences, pp. 1–6 (2007)
7. Pai, G.J., Dugan, J.B.: Empirical Analysis of Software Fault Content and Fault Proneness Using Bayesian Methods. IEEE Trans. Software Eng. 33(10), 675–686 (2007)
8. Tomaszewski, P., Håkansson, J., Grahn, H., Lundberg, L.: Statistical models vs. expert estimation for fault prediction in modified code – An industrial case study. Journal of Systems and Software 80(8), 1227–1238 (2007)

9. Zimmermann, T., Premraj, R., Zeller, A.: Predicting defects for eclipse. In: Proceedings of the Third International Workshop on Predictor Models in Software Engineering (2007)
10. Sliwerski, J., Zimmermann, T., Zeller, A.: When do changes induce fixes? In: Proceedings of the Second International Workshop on Mining Software Repositories, pp. 24–28 (2005)
11. Schröter, A., Zimmermann, T., Premraj, R., Zeller, A.: Where do bugs come from? SIGSOFT Softw. Eng. Notes 31(6), 1–2 (2006)
12. Weyuker, E.J., Ostrand, T.J.: Comparing methods to identify defect reports in a change management database. In: DEFECTS 2008: Proceedings of the 2008 workshop on Defects in large software systems, pp. 27–31 (2008)
13. Ostrand, T.J., Weyuker, E.J., Bell, R.M.: Predicting the location and number of faults in large software systems. IEEE Trans. Software Eng. 31(4), 340–355 (2005)
14. Zimmermann, T., Weissgerber, P.: Preprocessing cvs data for fine-grained analysis. In: Proceedings of the First International Workshop on Mining Software Repositories, pp. 2–6 (2004)
15. Meyers, T.M., Binkley, D.: An empirical study of slice-based cohesion and coupling metrics. ACM Trans. Softw. Eng. Methodol. 17(1), 1–27 (2007)

Regularities in Learning Defect Predictors

Burak Turhan[1], Ayse Bener[2], and Tim Menzies[3]

[1] Department of Information Processing Science, University of Oulu, Oulu 90014, Finland
burak.turhan@oulu.fi
[2] Department of Computer Engineering, Boğaziçi University, Istanbul 34342, Turkey
bener@boun.edu.tr
[3] Lane Dept. of CS&EE, West Virginia University, Morgantown, WV, USA
tim@menzies.us

Abstract. Collecting large consistent data sets of real world software projects from a single source is problematic. In this study, we show that bug reports need not necessarily come from the local projects in order to learn defect prediction models. We demonstrate that using imported data from different sites can make it suitable for predicting defects at the local site. In addition to our previous work in commercial software, we now explore open source domain with two versions of an open source anti-virus software (Clam AV) and a subset of bugs in two versions of GNU gcc compiler, to mark the regularities in learning predictors for a different domain. Our conclusion is that there are surprisingly uniform assets of software that can be discovered with simple and repeated patterns in local or imported data using just a handful of examples.

Keywords: Defect prediction, Code metrics, Software quality, Cross-company.

1 Introduction

It is surprisingly difficult to find relevant data within a single organization to fully specify the internal parameters inside a complete software process model. For example, after 26 years of trying, Barry Boehm's team of researchers from the University of Southern California collected less than 200 sample projects for their COCOMO effort estimation database [1].

There are many reasons for this, not the least being the business sensitivity associated with the data. Software projects are notoriously difficult to control: recall the 1995 report of the Standish group that described a $250 billion dollar American software industry where 31% of projects were canceled and 53% of projects incurred costs exceeding 189% of the original estimate [2]. Understandably, corporations are reluctant to expose their poor performance to public scrutiny.

Despite this data shortage, remarkably effective predictors for software products have been generated. In previous work we have built:

- *Software effort estimators* using only very high-level knowledge of the code being developed [3] (typically, just some software process details). Yet these estimators offer predictions that are remarkably close to actual development times [4].

M. Ali Babar, M. Vierimaa, and M. Oivo (Eds.): PROFES 2010, LNCS 6156, pp. 116–130, 2010.
© Springer-Verlag Berlin Heidelberg 2010

- *Software defect predictors* using only static code features. Fenton (amongst others) argues persauively that such features are very poor charactizations of the inner complexities of software modules [5]. Yet these seeingly naive defect predictors out-perform current industrial best-practices [6], [7].

The success of such simple models seems highly unlikely. Organizations can work in different domains, have different process, and define/measure defects and other aspects of their product and process in different ways. Worse, all to often, organizations do not precisely define their processes, products, measurements, etc. Nevertheless, it is true that very simple models suffice for generating approximately correct predictions for (say) software development time [4], the location of software defects [6].

One candidate explanation for the strange predictability in software development is that: *Despite all the seemingly random factors influencing software construction, the net result follows very tight statistical patterns.* Other researchers have argued for similar results [8], [9], [10], [11], [12] but here we offer new evidence. The performance of a data miner improves as the size of the training set grows. At some point, the performance *plateaus* and further training data does not improve that performance. Previously, we showed in commercial domain (NASA aerospace software and white-goods controller software) that for defect prediction, plateaus occur remarkably early (after just 30 examples) [7]. Furthermore, we showed that with certain limitations, defect predictors can be learned across projects, i.e. training on project A and testing on project B.

In this paper, we investigate the same effects in open source domain with two different products. Observing an effect in different entities of commercial domain (NASA, white-goods) might be a coincidence. However, observing the same effect in a relatively unrelated domain, we will no longer be able to dismiss the effect as quirks in one domain. Therefore, the goal of this paper is to further investigate the issue of regularities in learning defect predictors by replicating our previous experiments (i.e. [6], [13], [7]) on an additional domain (open-source) in order to strengthen the evidence base for the following assertions:

- The regularities we observe in software are very regular indeed;
- We can depend on those regularities to generate effective defect predictors using *minimal information from projects*[1].

The rest of this paper is structured as follows. We give examples of statistical patterns from general software research and briefly discuss the role of defect predictors in Section 2. Then we focus on defect predictors in detail and introduce observed regularities in defect prediction research (for commercial domain) in Section 3. Section 4 extends the analyses of these regularities to open source domain. Discussions of our observations are given in Section 5 and we conclude our research in Section 6. Please note that the results of Section 3 have appeared previously [6], [13], [7]. The rest of this paper is new work.

[1] This second point is a strong endorsement for our approach since, as discussed above, it can be very difficult to access details and extensive project data from real world software development.

2 Background

2.1 Examples of Regularities in General SE Research

Previous research reports much evidence that software products confirm tightly to simple and regular statistical models, For example, Veldhuizen shows that library reuse characteristics in three unix based systems (i.e. Linux, SunOS and MacOS X), can be explained by Zipf's Law, that is most frequently used library routines [14] are inversely proportional to their frequency ranks. As shown in Figure 1, the distribution is highly regular.

Figure 2 shows a summary of our prior work on effort estimation [4] using the COCOMO features. These features lack detailed knowledge of the system under development. Rather, they are just two dozen ultra-high-level descriptors of (e.g.) develeper

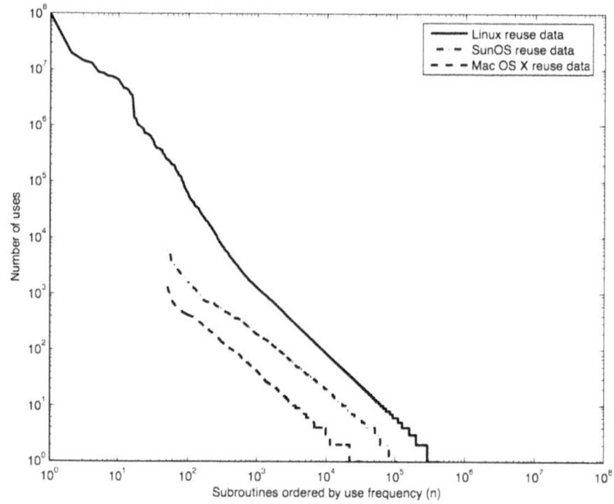

Fig. 1. Distribution of reuse frequencies in three unix based systems [14]

	$100 * (pred - actual)/actual$		
	50% percentile	65% percentile	75% percentile
mode=embedded	-9	26	60
project=X	-6	16	46
all	-4	12	31
year=1975	-3	19	39
mode=semi-detached	-3	10	22
ground.systems	-3	11	29
center=5	-3	20	50
mission.planning	-1	25	50
project=gro	-1	9	19
center=2	0	11	21
year=1980	4	29	58
avionics.monitoring	6	32	56
median	-3	19	39

Fig. 2. 158 effort estimation methods applied to 12 subsets of the COCO81 data

experience, platform violatily, software process maturity, etc. In Figure 2, different effort estimation methods are applied to the COC81 data[2] used by Boehm to develop the original COCOMO effort estimation model [15]. Twenty times, ten test instances were selected at random and effort models were built from the remaining models using 158 different estimation methods[3]. The resulting predictions were compared to the actual estimation times using relative error. COC81's data can be divided into the 12 (overlapping) subsets shown left-hand-side of Figure 2. The right-hand-columns of Figure 2 show MRE at the median, 65%, and 75% percentiles. The median predictions are within within 3% of the actual. Such a close result would be impossible if software did not conform to very tight statistical regularities.

Figure 3 shows Koru and Liu's analysis of two large-scale open source projects (K-office and Mozilla). As shown in those figures, these different systems confirm to nearly an identical Pareto distribution of change-prone classes: 80% of changes occur in 20% of classes [12]. The same 80:20 changes:fault distribution has been observed by Ostrand, Weyuker and Bell in very large scale telecommunication projects from AT&T [8], [9], [10], [11]. Furthermore, the defect trends in Eclipse also follows similar patterns, where they are explained better by a Weibull distribution [17] .

2.2 On Learning Defect Predictors

Figures 1, 2, 3 and 4 show that statistical regularities simplifies predictions of certain kinds of properties. Previously [6], we have exploited those regularities with data miners that learn defect predictors from static code attribtues. Those predictors were learned either from projects previously developed in the same environment or from a continually expanding base of current project's artifacts.

To do so, tables of examples are formed where one column has a boolean value for "defects detected" and the other columns describe software features such as lines of code; number of unique symbols [18]; or max. number of possible execution pathways [19]. Each row in the table holds data from one "module", the smallest unit of functionality. Depending on the language, these may be called "functions", "methods", or "procedures". The data mining task is to find combinations of features that predict for the value in the defects column.

The value of static code features as defect predictors has been widely debated. Some researchers vehemently oppose them [20], [21], while many more endorse their use [22], [23], [6], [24], [25], [26], [27], [28]. Standard verification and validation (V&V) textbooks [29] advise using static code complexity attributes to decide which modules are worthy of manual inspections. The authors are aware of several large government software contractors that won't review software modules *unless* tools like the McCabe static source code analyzer predicts that they exhibit high code complexity measures.

Nevertheless, static code attributes can never be a full characterization of a program module. Fenton offers an insightful example where *the same* functionality is achieved using *different* programming language constructs resulting in *different* static measurements for that module [5]. Fenton uses this example to argue the uselessness of static code attributes for fault prediction.

---

[2] Available from `http://promisedata.org`

[3] For a description of those methods, see [16].

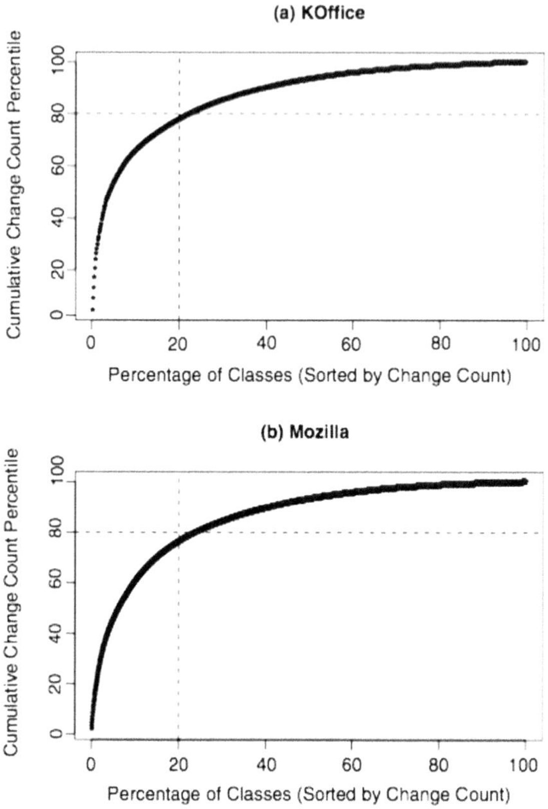

Fig. 3. Distribution of change prone class percentages in two open source projects [12]

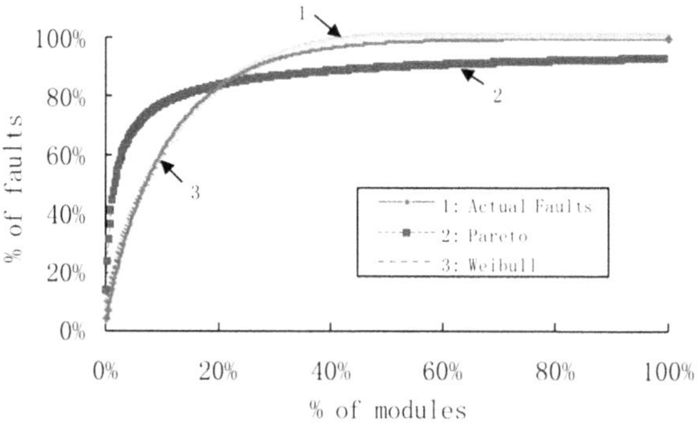

Fig. 4. Distribution of faulty modules in Eclipse [17]

Using NASA data, our fault prediction models find defect predictors [6] with a probability of detection (pd) and probability of false alarm (pf) of $mean(pd, pf) = (71\%, 25\%)$. These values should be compared to baselines in data mining and industrial practice. Raffo (personnel communication) found that industrial reviews find $pd = TR(35, 50, 65)\%$[4] of a systems errors' (for full Fagan inspections [30]) to $pd = TR(13, 21, 30)\%$ for less-structured inspections. Similar values were reported at a IEEE Metrics 2002 panel. That panel declined to endorse claims by Fagan [31] and Schull [32] regarding the efficacy of their inspection or directed inspection methods. Rather, it concluded that manual software reviews can find $\approx$60% of defects [33];

That is, contrary to the pessimism of Fenton, our $(pd, pf) = (71, 25)\%$ results are better than currently used industrial methods such as the $pd{\approx}60\%$ reported at the 2002 IEEE Metrics panel or the $median(pd) = 21..50$ reported by Raffo. Better yet, automated defect predictors can be generated with a fraction of the effort of alternative methods, even for very large systems [24]. Other methods such as formal methods or manual code reviews may be more labor-intensive. Depending on the review method, 8 to 20 lines of code (LOC) per minute can be inspected. This effort repeats for all members of the review team (typically, four or six [34]).

3 Regularities in Defect Predictors in Commercial Domain

In prior work [13], [7], we have used the NASA and SOFTLAB data of Figure 5 to explore learning defect predictors using data miners. To learn defect predictors we use a Naive Bayes data miner since prior work [6] could not find a better data miner for learning defect predictors. In all our experiments, the data was pre-processed as follows:

- Since the number of features in each data table is not consistent, we restricted our data to only the features shared by all data sets.
- Previously [6], we have observed that all the numeric distributions in the Figure 5 data are exponential in nature. It is therefore useful to apply a "log-filter" to all numerics N with $log(N)$. This spreads out exponential curves more evenly across the space from the minimum to maximum values (to avoid numerical errors with $ln(0)$, all numbers under 0.000001 are replaced with $ln(0.000001)$).

Inspired by the recent systematic review of within vs cross company effort estimation studies by Kitchenham et al. [35], we have done extensive experiments on Promise data tables to analyze predictor behavior using a) local data (within the same company) b) imported data (cross company). For each NASA and SOFTLAB table of Figure 5, we built test sets from 10% of the rows, selected at random. Then we learned defect predictors from:

- the other 90% rows of the corresponding table (i.e. local data).
- 90% rows of the other tables combined (i.e. imported data).

We repeated this procedure 100 times, each time randomizing the order of the rows in each table, in order to control *order effects* (where the learned theory is unduly affected

[4] $TR(a, b, c)$ is a triangular distribution with min/mode/max of a, b, c.

source	data	(# modules) examples	features	%defective
NASA	pc1	1,109	22	6.94
NASA	kc1	845	22	15.45
NASA	kc2	522	22	20.49
NASA	cm1	498	22	9.83
NASA	kc3	458	22	9.38
NASA	mw1	403	22	7.69
NASA	mc2	61	22	32.29
SOFTLAB	ar3	63	29	12.70
SOFTLAB	ar4	107	29	18.69
SOFTLAB	ar5	36	29	22.22
OPEN SOURCE	cav90	1184	26	0.40
OPEN SOURCE	cav91	1169	26	0.20
OPEN SOURCE	gcc	116	26	100.0

Fig. 5. Datasets used in this study

by the order of the examples). We measured the performance of predictor using pd, pf and $balance$. If $\{A, B, C, D\}$ are the true negatives, false negatives, false positives, and true positives (respectively) found by a defect predictor, then:

$$pd = recall = D/(B + D) \quad (1)$$

$$pf = C/(A + C) \quad (2)$$

$$bal = balance = 1 - \frac{\sqrt{(0 - pf)^2 + (1 - pd)^2}}{\sqrt{2}} \quad (3)$$

All these values range zero to one. Better and *larger* balances fall *closer* to the desired zone of no false alarms ($pf = 0$) and 100% detection ($pd = 1$). We then used the Mann-Whitney U test [36] in order to test for statistical difference.

Our results are visualized in Figure 6 as *quartile chaorts*. Quartile charts are generated from sorted sets of results, divided into four subsets of (approx) same cardinality. For example these numbers have four quartiles:

$$\{\overbrace{4, 7, 15}^{q1}, 20, 31, \overbrace{40}^{median}, 52, 64, \overbrace{70, 81, 90}^{q4}\}$$

These quartiles can be drawn as follows: the upper and lower quartiles are marked with black lines; the median is marked with a black dot; and vertical bars are added to mark the 50% percentile value. For example, the above numbers can be drawn as:

0% — ● | —— 100%

In a finding consistent with our general thesis (that software artifacts conform to very regular statistical patterns), Figure 6 shows the same stable and useful regularity occuring in both seven NASA data sets and three SOFTLAB data sets [7].:

- Using imported data dramatically increased the probability of detecting defective modules (for NASA: 74% to 94% median pd; for SOFTLAB: 88% to 95% median pd);

Nasa on local Nasa data.

	treatment	min	Q1	median	Q3	max
pd	Local	0	60	75	82	100
pf	Local	0	24	29	35	73

Nasa on imported Nasa data.

	treatment	min	Q1	median	Q3	max
pd	Imp.	81	84	94	98	99
pf	Imp.	26	60	68	90	94

Softlab on local Softlab data.

	treatment	min	Q1	median	Q3	max
pd	Local	35	40	88	100	100
pf	Local	3	5	29	40	42

Softlab on imported Nasa data.

	treatment	min	Q1	median	Q3	max
pd	Imp.	88	88	95	100	100
pf	Imp.	52	59	65	68	68

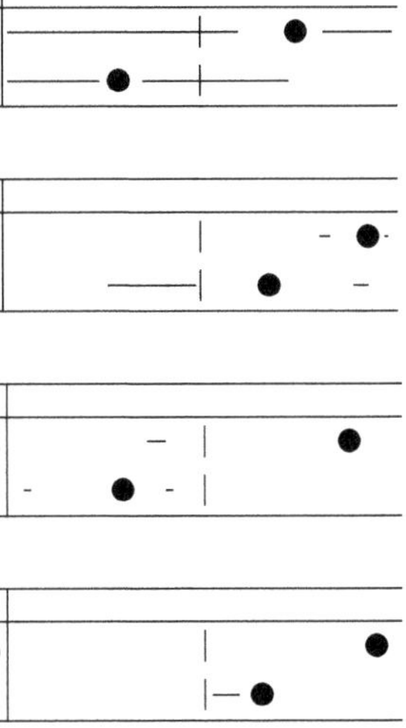

Fig. 6. Quartile charts for NASA and SOFTLAB data [7]. Numeric results on left; quartile charts on right. "Q1" and "Q3" denote the 25% and 75% percentile points respectively.

- But imported data also dramatically increased the false alarm rate (for NASA: 29% to 68% median pf; for SOFTLAB: 29% to 65% pd) . Our suspicion is that the reason for the high false alarm rates was the irrelevancies introduced by imported data.

We have then designed a set of experiments for NASA data tables to see the effects of sampling strategies on the performance and to determine the lower-limit on the number of samples for learning defect predictors, i.e. the point where a plateau is observed in the performance measure. In those experiments we applied over/under and micro-sampling (see [13]) to the data tables and observed that:

- the performance of predictors does not improve with over sampling.
- under-sampling improves the performance of certain predictors, i.e. decision trees, but not of Naive Bayes [13].
- with micro-sampling, the performance of predictors stabilize after a mere number of defective and defect-free examples, i.e. 50 to 100 samples.

The last observation suggests that the number of cases that must be reviewed in order to arrive at the performance ceiling of a defect predictor is very small: as low as 50 randomly selected modules (25 defective and 25 non-defective). In Figure 7 for Nasa tables, we visualize number of training examples (increments of 25) vs. balance performance of Naive Bayes predictor. It is clear that the performance does not improve with more training examples, indeed it may deteriorate with more examples.

We now report the results of the same experiment for SOFTLAB data. Note that SOFTLAB tables *ar3*, *ar4* and *ar5* have {36,63,107} modules respectively, with a total

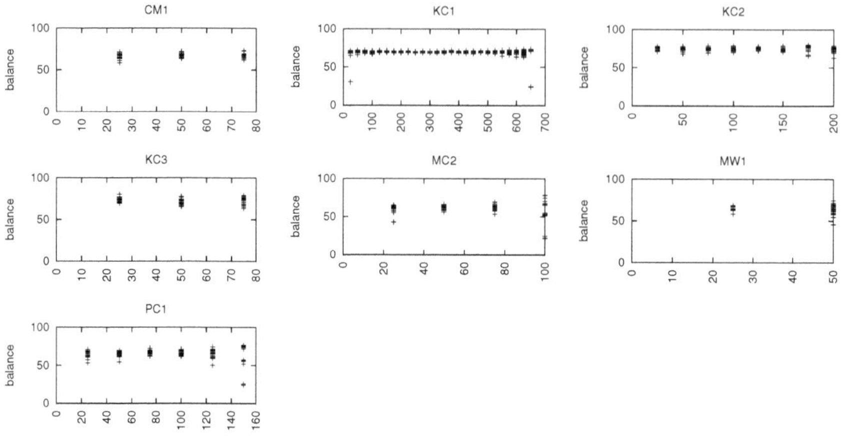

Fig. 7. Micro-sampling results for NASA data [7]

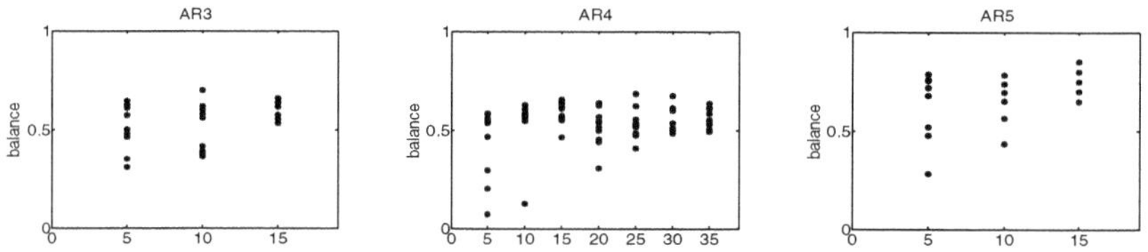

Fig. 8. Micro-sampling results for SOFTLAB data

of 206 modules of which only 36 are defective. Thus, local results in Figure 6 are achieved using a minimum of $(36 + 63) * 0.90 = 90$ and a maximum of $(107 + 63) * 0.90 = 153$ examples. Nevertheless we repeat the micro-sampling experiment for SOFTLAB data tables, with increments of 5 due to relatively lower number of defects. In Figure 8, we plot the results for SOFTLAB data tables. We observe the same pattern as in Figure 6: performance tends to stabilize after a small number of training examples.

Results for NASA and SOFTLAB data tables suggest that practical defect predictors can be learned using only a handful of examples. In order to allow for generalization, it is appropriate to question the external validity of the above two results: The data used for those results come from very different sources:

- The SOFTLAB data were collected from a Turkish white-goods manufacturer (see the the datasets ($\{$ar3, ar4, ar5$\}$) from Figure 5) building controller software for a washing machine, a dishwasher and a refrigerator.
- On the other hand, NASA software are ground and flight control projects for aerospace applications, each developed by different teams at different locations .

The development practices from these two organizations are very different:

- The SOFTLAB software were built in a profit- and revenue-driven commercial organization, whereas NASA is a cost-driven government entity.
- The SOFTLAB software were are developed by very small teams (2-3 people) working in the same physical location while the NASA software was built by much larger team spread around the United States.
- The SOFTLAB development was carried out in an ad-hoc, informal way rather than formal, process oriented approach used at NASA.

The fact that the same defect detection patterns hold for such radically different kinds of organization is a strong argument for the external validity of our results. However, an even stronger argument would be that the patterns we first saw at NASA/ SOFTLAB are also found in software developed at other sites. The rest of this paper collects evidence for that stronger argument.

4 Validity in Open Source Domain

This section checks for the above patterns in two open source projects:

- two versions of an anti-virus project: Clam AV v0.90 and v0.91;
- a subset of defective modules of the GNU gcc compiler.

In Figure 5, these are denoted as cav90, cav91 and gcc, respectively. Note that these are very different projects, build by different developers with very different purposes. Also note that the development processes for the open source projects are very different to the NASA and SOFTLAB projects studied above. Whereas NASA and SOFTLAB were developed by centrally-controlled top-down management teams, cav90, cav91 and gcc were build in a highly distributed manner. Further, unlike our other software, gcc has been under extensive usage and maintenance for over a decade.

Local/ imported data experiments are once more applied on cav90, cav91 and gcc data tables and the results are visualized in Figure 9. We again used Nasa tables as imported data, since they provide a large basis with 5000+ samples. Note that partial gcc data includes only a sample of defects, thus we are not able to make a 'local data' analysis for gcc. Rather, we report the detection rates of predictors built on imported data from Nasa and cav91. These predictors can correctly detect up to median 60% of the subset of bugs that we were able to manually match to functional modules.

Recall that cav91 has a defect rate of 0.20%. The probability of detection rates for cav91 are median 67% and 77% for local and imported data respectively, which is another evidence on the usefulness of statistical predictors.

At the first glance, the patterns in Figure 9 seem a bit different than those in Figure 6. There are still increases in probability of detection and false alarms rates, though not dramatically. However, this is not a counter example of our claim. We explain this behavior with the following assertions:

For our experiments:

- in commercial software analysis, local data corresponds to single projects developed by a relatively small team of people in the same company and with certain business knowledge.

cav90 on local cav90 data.

	treatment	min	Q1	median	Q3	max
pd	Local	0	40	40	60	100
pf	Local	22	32	35	37	44

cav90 on imported Nasa data.

	treatment	min	Q1	median	Q3	max
pd	Imp.	49	49	51	51	53
pf	Imp.	35	36	37	37	38

cav91 on local cav91 data.

	treatment	min	Q1	median	Q3	max
pd	Local	0	67	67	100	100
pf	Local	17	25	28	30	39

cav91 on imported Nasa data.

	treatment	min	Q1	median	Q3	max
pd	Imp.	77	77	77	77	77
pf	Imp.	36	38	38	39	40

gcc defects on imported cav91 data.

	treatment	min	Q1	median	Q3	max
pd	Imp.	53	53	53	53	53

gcc defects on imported Nasa data.

	treatment	min	Q1	median	Q3	max
pd	Imp.	60	60	60	60	60

Fig. 9. Quartile charts for OPENSOURCE data

- in commercial software analysis, imported data corresponds to a variety of projects developed by various people in different companies and spans a larger business knowledge.
- in open source software analysis, local data corresponds to single projects developed by a larger team of people at different geographical locations with various backgrounds.

We argue that, the above assertions differentiate the meaning of local data for open source projects from commercial projects. The nature of open source development allows the definition of local data to be closer to commercial imported data, since both are developed by people at different sites with different background. That's the reason why adding commercial imported data does not add as much detection capability as it does for commercial local data. Furthermore, the false alarms are not that high since there are less irrelevancies in local open source data than commercial imported data, which is the cause of high false alarms. That's because open source local data consist of a single project and commercial imported data consist of several projects, which introduce irrelevancies.

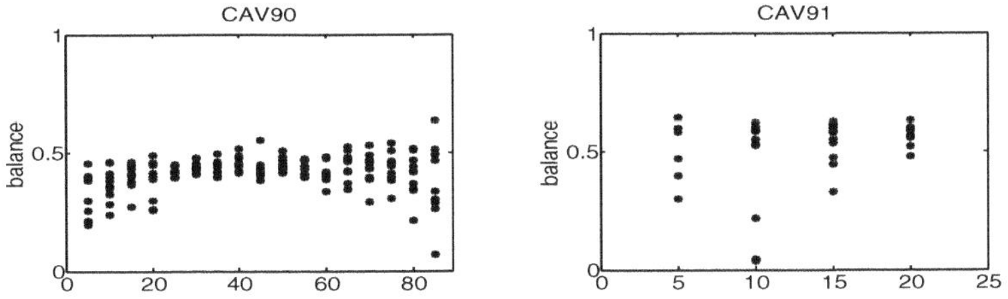

Fig. 10. Micro-sampling results for OPEN-SOURCE data

We also repeat the 10*10 way cross-validation micro-sampling experiment for cav90 and cav91 data tables, this time with increments of 5 due to limited defect data (Figure 7 used increments of 25). In Figure 10 we see a similar pattern:

- Balance values tend to converge using only 20-30 samples of defective and non-defective modules.
- Using less examples produce unstable results, since there are not enough samples to learn a theory.
- For cav90, using more than 60 training examples affects the stability of the results.

The importance of Figure 10 results is that our results in two commercial domains, considering the minimum number of examples to train a predictor, are once more validated in a third, open-source domain.

5 Summary of Results and Limitations

We can summarize our results on commercial and open-source data as follows:

- Using imported data increases the detection capability of predictors.
- Predictors can be learned using only a handful of data samples. In both commercial and open-source domain the performance of predictors converge after a small number of training examples.
- These results are generalizable through different cultural and organizational entities, since same patterns are observed in NASA, SOFTLAB and OPEN-SOURCE data tables.

Yet, these results have associated limitations. For instance imported data increase false alarm rates as well. We tried to avoid this by applying a relevancy filtering. This effect is less visible in open source domain for the reasons discussed above. We also observed that using larger training instances may cause variations in predictor performances. This should be controlled through incremental experiments on the training set size. Finally, though the data analyzed in this paper spans a large space of software products and provide strong evidence in favor of regularity, it is not possible to claim a formal generalization of our results due to their empirical nature. Nevertheless, please note that these result are observed: in a variety of projects (i.e. 7 NASA, 3 SOFTLAB, 2 OPEN-SOURCE) from different domains (i.e. commercial and open-source) spanning a wide range time interval (i.e. from 1980's to 2007). Therefore, we assert that:

There exists repeated patterns in software that can be discovered and explained by simple models with minimal information no matter what the underlying seemingly random and complex processes or phenomena are.

This assertion should be processed carefully. We do not mean that *everything* about software can be controlled through patterns. Rather, we argue that these patterns exist and are easy to discover. It is practical and cost effective to use them as guidelines in order to understand the behavior of software and to take corrective actions. In this context we will propose two directions for further research in our conclusions.

6 Conclusions

Building defect predictor models is easy, fast and effective in guiding manual test effort to correct locations. What is more important is that these automated analysis methods are applicable in different domains. We have previously shown their validity in two commercial domains and in this paper we observe similar patterns in two projects of the open source domain. We have also shown that although these models are sensitive to the information level in the training data (i.e. local/ imported), they are not affected by the organizational differences that generate them.

Based on our results, we argue that no matter how complicated the underlying processes may seem, software has a statistically predictable nature. Going one step further, we claim that the patterns in software are not limited to individual projects or domains, rather they are generalizable through different projects and domains. Therefore, we suggest two directions for further research:

- One direction should explore software analysis using rigorous formalisms that offer ironclad gaureentees of the corrections of a code (e.g. interactive theorem proving, model checking, or the correctness preserving transoftations discussed by Doug Smith[5]). This approach is required for the analysis of mission-critical software that must always function correctly.
- Another direction should explore automatic methods with a stronger focus on maximizing the effectiveness of the analysis while minimizing the associated cost.

There has been some exploration of the second approach using lightweight formal methods (e.g. [37]) or formal methods that emphasis the usability and ease of use of the tool (e.g. [38], [39]). However, our results also show that there exists an under-explored space of extrememly cost-effective automated analysis methods.

Acknowledgements

This research is partially supported: by Tubitak under grant number EEEAG 108E014 at Bogazici University, by Tekes under Cloud Software Program at University of Oulu, and

[5] Keynote address, ASE'07.

at West Virginia University under grants with NASA's Software Assurance Research Program. Reference herein to any specific commercial product, process, or service by trademark, manufacturer, or otherwise, does not constitute or imply its endorsement by the United States Government.

References

1. Menzies, T., Elrawas, O., Barry, B., Madachy, R., Hihn, J., Baker, D., Lum, K.: Accurate estimates without calibration. In: International Conference on Software Process (2008)
2. The Standish Group Report: Chaos (1995)
3. Menzies, T., Port, D., Chen, Z., Hihn, J., Stukes, S.: Specialization and extrapolation of induced domain models: Case studies in software effort estimation. In: IEEE ASE 2005 (2005)
4. Menzies, T., Chen, Z., Hihn, J., Lum, K.: Selecting best practices for effort estimation. IEEE Transactions on Software Engineering (2006)
5. Fenton, N.E., Pfleeger, S.: Software Metrics: A Rigorous & Practical Approach. International Thompson Press (1997)
6. Menzies, T., Greenwald, J., Frank, A.: Data mining static code attributes to learn defect predictors. IEEE Transactions on Software Engineering (2007)
7. Turhan, B., Menzies, T., Bener, A.B., Di Stefano, J.: On the relative value of cross-company and within-company data for defect prediction. Empirical Softw. Engg. 14(5), 540–578 (2009)
8. Bell, R., Ostrand, T., Weyuker, E.: Looking for bugs in all the right places. In: ISSTA 2006: Proceedings of the 2006 international symposium on Software testing and analysis (2006)
9. Ostrand, T., Weyuker, E., Bell, R.: Where the bugs are. ACM SIGSOFT Software Engineering Notes 29(4) (2004)
10. Ostrand, T., Weyuker, E.: The distribution of faults in a large industrial software system. In: ISSTA 2002: Proceedings of the 2002 ACM SIGSOFT international symposium on Software testing and analysis (2002)
11. Ostrand, T., Weyuker, E., Bell, R.: Automating algorithms for the identification of fault-prone files. In: ISSTA 2007: Proceedings of the 2007 international symposium on Software testing and analysis (2007)
12. Koru, A.G., Liu, H.: Identifying and characterizing change-prone classes in two large-scale open-source products. JSS (2007)
13. Menzies, T., Turhan, B., Bener, A., Gay, G., Cukic, B., Jiang, Y.: Implications of ceiling effects in defect predictors. In: Proceedings of PROMISE 2008 Workshop, ICSE (2008)
14. Veldhuizen, T.L.: Software libraries and their reuse: Entropy, kolmogorov complexity, and zipf's law. arXiv cs.SE (2005)
15. Boehm, B.: Software Engineering Economics. Prentice-Hall, Englewood Cliffs (1981)
16. Jalali, O.: Evaluation bias in effort estimation. Master's thesis, Lane Department of Computer Science and Electrical Engineering, West Virginia University (2007)
17. Zhang, H.: On the distribution of software faults. IEEE Transactions on Software Engineering 34(2), 301–302 (2008)
18. Halstead, M.: Elements of Software Science. Elsevier, Amsterdam (1977)
19. McCabe, T.: A complexity measure. IEEE Transactions on Software Engineering 2(4), 308–320 (1976)
20. Fenton, N., Ohlsson, N.: Quantitative analysis of faults and failures in a complex software system. IEEE Transactions on Software Engineering, 797–814 (2000)

21. Shepperd, M., Ince, D.: A critique of three metrics. The Journal of Systems and Software 26(3), 197–210 (1994)
22. Khoshgoftaar, T.M., Seliya, N.: Fault prediction modeling for software quality estimation: Comparing commonly used techniques. Empirical Software Engineering 8(3), 255–283 (2003)
23. Tang, W., Khoshgoftaar, T.M.: Noise identification with the k-means algorithm. In: ICTAI, pp. 373–378 (2004)
24. Nagappan, N., Ball, T.: Static analysis tools as early indicators of pre-release defect density. In: ICSE 2005, St. Louis (2005)
25. Nikora, A., Munson, J.: Developing fault predictors for evolving software systems. In: Ninth International Software Metrics Symposium, METRICS 2003 (2003)
26. Porter, A., Selby, R.: Empirically guided software development using metric-based classification trees. IEEE Software, 46–54 (1990)
27. Srinivasan, K., Fisher, D.: Machine learning approaches to estimating software development effort. IEEE Trans. Soft. Eng., 126–137 (1995)
28. Tian, J., Zelkowitz, M.: Complexity measure evaluation and selection. IEEE Transaction on Software Engineering 21(8), 641–649 (1995)
29. Rakitin, S.: Software Verification and Validation for Practitioners and Managers, 2nd edn. Artech House (2001)
30. Fagan, M.: Design and code inspections to reduce errors in program development. IBM Systems Journal 15(3) (1976)
31. Fagan, M.: Advances in software inspections. IEEE Trans. on Software Engineering, 744–751 (1986)
32. Shull, F., Rus, I., Basili, V.: How perspective-based reading can improve requirements inspections. IEEE Computer 33(7), 73–79 (2000)
33. Shull, F., Basili, V., Boehm, B., Brown, A., Costa, P., Lindvall, M., Port, D., Rus, I., Tesoriero, R., Zelkowitz, M.: What we have learned about fighting defects. In: Proceedings of 8th International Software Metrics Symposium, Ottawa, Canada, pp. 249–258 (2002)
34. Menzies, T., Raffo, D., Setamanit, S., Hu, Y., Tootoonian, S.: Model-based tests of truisms. In: Proceedings of IEEE ASE 2002 (2002)
35. Kitchenham, B.A., Mendes, E., Travassos, G.H.: Cross- vs. within-company cost estimation studies: A systematic review. IEEE Transactions on Software Engineering, 316–329 (2007)
36. Mann, H.B., Whitney, D.R.: On a test of whether one of two random variables is stochastically larger than the other. Ann. Math. Statist. 18(1), 50–60 (1947)
37. Easterbrook, S., Lutz, R.R., Covington, R., Kelly, J., Ampo, Y., Hamilton, D.: Experiences using lightweight formal methods for requirements modeling. IEEE Transactions on Software Engineering, 4–14 (1998)
38. Heimdahl, M., Leveson, N.: Completeness and consistency analysis of state-based requirements. IEEE Transactions on Software Engineering (1996)
39. Heitmeyer, C., Jeffords, R., Labaw, B.: Automated consistency checking of requirements specifications. ACM Transactions on Software Engineering and Methodology 5(3), 231–261 (1996)

Business Value Is Not Only Dollars – Results from Case Study Research on Agile Software Projects

Zornitza Racheva[1], Maya Daneva[1], Klaas Sikkel[1], and Luigi Buglione[2]

[1] University of Twente, Computer Science Department, PO Box 217, 7500 AE, Enschede, The Netherlands
[2] Engineering.it, Via Ricardo Morandi, Rome – 06 4453278, Italy
{z.racheva,m.daneva,k.sikkel}@utwente.nl
Luigi.Buglione@eng.it

Abstract. Business value is a key concept in agile software development. This paper presents results of a case study on how business value and its creation is perceived in the context of agile projects. Our overall conclusion is that the project participants almost never use an explicit and structured approach to guide the value creation throughout the project. Still, the application of agile methods in the studied cases leads to satisfied clients. An interesting result of the study represents the fact that the agile process of many projects differs significantly from what is described in the agile practitioners' books as best practices. The key implication for research and practice is that we have an incentive to pursue the study of value creation in agile projects and to complement it by providing guidelines for better client's involvement, as well as by developing structured methods that will enhance the value-creation in a project.

Keywords: Business value, agile software development, value-based approach, multiple case study.

1 Introduction

Demonstrating the linkages between investments in IT solutions and business benefits is becoming mandatory for an increasingly large number of organizations. This is particularly necessary in the context of agile software development, as new agile methodologies are being adopted and need to prove their merits. A key characteristic of any agile approach is its explicit focus on business value [1]. Essentially, in an agile software project, the development process is a value creation process. Indeed, the agile community established a common understanding [2] that (i) the main purpose of an agile project is to deliver maximum business value for the client and that (ii) agile approaches deliver business value fast and early in the project.

This paper builds on our previous work [17] that investigated the understanding of business value in agile projects from publications in the agile software engineering (SE) and requirements engineering literature. This systematic review [17] of literature showed that, with very few exceptions, most published studies take the concept of business value for granted and do not state what it means in general as well as in the specific study context. We could find no study which clearly indicates how exactly

M. Ali Babar, M. Vierimaa, and M. Oivo (Eds.): PROFES 2010, LNCS 6156, pp. 131–145, 2010.
© Springer-Verlag Berlin Heidelberg 2010

individual agile practices or groups of those create value and keep accumulating it over time. This finding motivated us to pursue further studies of value creation in agile projects by deploying empirical research methods, for example case study research [22]. In this paper, we present the results of a case study that investigated (i) the ways in which agile practitioners perceive the notion of business value, and (ii) those agile development practices that create value, in the practitioners' opinion.

We have set out to answer the following research questions (RQs):

RQ1: What concepts of business value do practitioners in the context of agile projects perceive?

RQ2: In which way do agile projects create business value (process of value creation)? In which way do specific or individual practices influence the creation of business value?

RQ3: Do practitioners perform value-driven decisions during agile development?

RQ4: How do developers combine value creation for their own organization with value creation for the client's organization?

To answer our research questions, we have performed a multiple case study [22] in eight software developing organizations. In the next section, we provide background on our motivation for this study and related work. Section 3 describes the details of our case study process and Section 4 presents the results. Section 5 assesses our answers to the research questions and discusses implications for researchers and practitioners. Section 6 analyses the possible validity threats, and Section 7 concludes the paper.

2 Background

2.1 Motivation

The literature of agile SE [12] has emphasized the value creation attributable to the nature of agile projects. Agile software practices are credited with saving failing projects and increasing the success chance of many others. In the understanding of the agile SE community, the value delivered to the client lies not only in what the final software product represents, but also in the development process as such, which significantly contributes to the amount of value delivered. For example, a recent study at Intel Shannon [12] reports on the application of agile practices which lead to reductions in code defect density by a factor of 7. Moreover, Favaro [11] points out that agile approaches generate two kinds of economic benefits: operational and strategic. This means that the value creation process is not limited to the development of a product. The operational benefits of agile practices include lower costs for the clients, better quality product, shorter time-to-market. The strategic benefits include flexibility to respond to changes and ability to take advantage of new information, which ensure longer-term additional benefits for the client. Our research attempts to capture the state of the practice in this respect, as practitioners in agile software organizations witness it. As already stated in the Introduction, our current case study research is strongly motivated by the fact that we could not find any published study which indicated how exactly the value creation happens in real-life projects. (We refer interested readers to [17] for more details on our earlier work which resulted in this finding.) We also felt motivated by a recent call by Petersen and Wohlin [16] who suggest that more qualitative studies are needed to make agile studies comparable and also to uncover issues that have not been explicitly identified in the agile literature. Moreover, Barney at al. [4], [5] point out that: "there is little research into the criteria used in the decision-making process around requirement selection for value creation".

2.2 Related Work

At the time of writing this paper, the topic of value creation receives increasing attention in the research community [3]. In SE, the sub-field of Value-based Software Engineering (VBSE) which focuses on the value analysis and value creation process in a software projects, has been gaining in importance [6]. Drawing on the value-based SE theories, Aurum and Wohlin [3] advocate a value-based approach in requirements engineering. In essence, this is about aligning clients' requirements, business requirements and technological opportunities when making requirements prioritization decisions. For example, recent studies by Barney et al. [4], [5] investigated the release-planning process to create software product value through requirements selection. These authors identified the factors that determine the decisions about inclusion of certain requirements for implementation. Next, Rönkkö et al. [18] present three aspects of software – as a technology, as a design, and as an artifact. They use these aspects to divide the value concept into three components that are relevant for software developing companies and their clients: intrinsic value, externalities and option value. The authors propose a value-decomposition matrix as a vehicle to reason about the various aspects of value. We make the note however, that they take a broader look at the development of software products, without discussing a specific development method. As these authors stress, the vagueness of the concept of value seems to be a central problem in the VBSE.

Furthermore, publications in agile SE converge on that agile methods get "more done with less" [10], [15], [20]. More specifically, in our earlier systematic review [17], we found that agile literature sources agree that business value is considered the key requirements prioritization criterion in most agile projects. For example, the study of Cao et al. [8] reached the conclusion that *"...agile RE practitioners uniformly reported that their prioritization is based predominantly on one factor – business value as the customer defines it."*

We make the note that unlike our study, the literature sources that form the related work in this section have not discussed the question of value definition and value creation *trough the agile process*. In fact, the focus of the studies of Barney et al [4], [5], is not the agile process itself, as most of the projects included in the studies followed incremental development. The authors do not discuss the process on itself and how the process affects the value creation. Although iterative development is in the focus of the study, the development approach does not play a role beyond the fact that the product is developed in multiple releases.

3 The Research Method

We conducted a multiple-case study [22] to explicate the decision-making process during an agile project in the context of changing requirements. The case study consisted of semi-structured open-end in depth interviews with practitioners that work in organizations that develop software by using agile approaches. The case study is a first step in discovering the way in which the agile requirements mid-course decision process contributes to the client's value creation.

The companies, included in the study, characterized themselves as following agile methodologies. Some of them did strictly follow Scrum principles such as daily stand–up meetings and release retrospective. More detailed discussion about the study participants can be found in section 'limitations'.

3.1 The Case Study Process and Participants

We executed a rigorous case study by performing the following steps: (1) Compose a questionnaire; (2) Validate the questionnaire through an experienced researcher; (3) Implement changes in the questionnaire based on the feedback; (4) Do a pilot interview to check the applicability of the questionnaire to real-life context. (5) Carry out open-end in-depth interviews with practitioners; (6) Sample (follow-up with those participants that possess deeper knowledge or a more specific perspective).

Each in-depth interview included a section with questions related to the business value perception and value creation. Those questions were:

- What does business value of a requirement mean for you?
- At your meetings with your clients/product owners, do they explicitly discuss the business value of the requirements, so that all meeting attendees understand why some requirements are of higher priority than others?
- Is 'value' connected to the business goals which the clients want to achieve by deploying the software system? If so, in which way does 'value' connect to clients' business goals?
- When judging the value of the requirements, do clients also consider any other factors (e.g. cost, size, risk)?
- Has the desired value been quantified? If yes, how?
- In which way, in your experience, does the agile process add value to the client? Can you give a specific example from your practice?
- For yourself, as part of the developing side – do you consider the value for your own organization, or is it more important what the client wants?
- Do you share knowledge about business value creation within the organization?

We make the note that no substantial changes in our interview protocol took place after the pilot interview, so that the pilot interview could be considered part of the case study. The study included 11 practitioners who were working for eight different companies/public organizations:

- 1 middle size company in the Netherlands (3 cases, 3 participants)
- 2 small companies in the Netherlands (3 cases, 3 participants)
- 1 small company in Bulgaria (1 participant)
- 1 middle size company in Bulgaria (1 participant)
- 1 university in Germany (1 student project)

- 1 country-specific business unit of a large international company, Italy (1 participant)
- 1 department in a large governmental organization, Turkey, (1 participant).

The participants described a total of 11 projects. The application domains for which software solutions were developed represent a rich mix of fields and include banking, ERP for small businesses, health care management, automotive, content management system, online municipality services system. In each organization we interviewed one or more representatives that were directly involved in the decision-making and the development process. Many of the participants performed multiple roles in the team and thus had a wide overview of the end-to-end process.

3.2 The Data Collection

We collected data from our case study participants by carrying out in-depth interviews. According to research methodologists [9], [22], in-depth interviews are intensive conversations with a small number of respondents to explore their perspectives on a particular project, practice or idea. We used this data collection technique because it is deemed useful when a researcher needs detailed and context-specific information so that he/she explores an issue in depth.

The interviews took place between July 15 and Nov 10, 2009. Nine interviews were done in face-to-face meetings. Two interviews took place over the phone. Each interview lasted between 60 and 90 minutes. Each interviewee was provided beforehand with information on the research purpose, the research process and the rights and responsibilities of the participating case study companies. At the meeting, the researcher and the interviewee walked through the questionnaire which served to guide the interviews.

We make the note that in each interview, the interviewer (that is the first author of this paper) used her judgment and tact to decide how closely to stick to the interview guide and how much to follow up the practitioners' answers and the new directions they might open up. Throughout the data collection, the interviewer attempted to verify her interpretation of participant's answers. She also summarized the key data immediately following the interview. The data was then transcribed and analyzed, which is described in the next section.

3.3 The Data Processing

The data analysis in this study was guided by the grounded theory method according to Charmaz [9] that is a qualitative method applied broadly in social sciences. This approach is explorative and well suited for situations where the researcher does not have pre-conceived ideas, and instead is driven by the desire to capture all facets of the collected data. On the next step the data can be used to build a theory. The data analysis followed the following steps (1) Coding, which was focused on attaching a 'code' to a portion of the text; (2) Clustering all portions of text with the same code; (3) Creating lists with codes and clustering them into families; (4) Identifying patterns, i.e. multiple occurrences of the same mechanisms or concepts. These steps were executed by the first two authors of the paper who worked independently at two different locations. Each researcher read through the practitioners' responses and searched for themes and patterns that appear to be common among the practitioners. The third author of this paper acted as a checker in the process of identifying patterns (step 4 of the list above). We got a variety of themes which we grouped in two ways that we found meaningful: by perspective (clients' versus developers' perspectives) and by company size (small, medium, large). For example, our analysis found that small agile software development companies who have small organizations as their clients set up their prioritization process differently compared to larger companies.

4 Results

This section presents the results in an order corresponding to our research questions formulated in Section 2.

1. What concepts of business value do practitioners in the context of agile projects perceive? Table 1 summarizes what the participants in the study perceive as a business value.

Table 1. Understandings of business value from the interviews

The business value…
"…is in the context of the main functionality: does the feature support our main scenario?"
"…what the organization will gain when we implement the requirement".
"…usually it is what they like to see, what is used most (from workflow perspective)."
"…what will it means if we implement this requirement – will the client become more efficient, more competitive, will it gain something"
"…is defined based on: how much the client uses certain feature; whether it works good, and to help them do their work (in this case – the work flow)

Table 1 indicates that in our observations, many of the business value definitions are context-dependent, that is, a definition could be traced back to a specific context characteristic of a project. For example, one of the participants, who worked on a project in the context of a software suppliers' network, defined the term business value as: *"Business value is to allow the client develop the functionality for which he/she is dependent on us"*. This perception clearly demonstrated the linkage between the perceived business value by this interviewee and the role he plays with respect to his clients in the suppliers' network. Another interviewee shared that *"perceptions of business value vary from project to project, even if you have the same client on site in both projects"*. Examples as these brought us to think that we can not expect one universal definition of BV. Moreover, practitioners also indicated that the definition of the same client would probably change from project to project, depending on (i) the different project-specific settings, (ii) the specific needs of the client (for example, the need to have highly reusable or highly scalable software), and (iii) the market position of the client's organization. To us, this all indicated that multiple layers of business value are clearly observable in agile project organizations and that it might make good sense to look into these layers in order to understand the underlying mechanisms responsible for the variation of perceived business value across agile projects within an organization. We consider it intuitive to think that agile projects may well vary in terms of how much of an agile approach they adopt in the project delivery cycle, and this, in turn, leads to variations in the perceived business value of both the system being delivered (that is, the product) and of the way it is delivered (the process). This reasoning motivates us to carry out a follow-up case study in which we plan to collect more observations on how business value is created and to understand the relationship which could possibly exist between the extent to which a project is agile and the perceived business value.

2. In which way do agile projects create business value or influence the creation of business value? All study participants agree on that agile development better suits the project objective to satisfy customer needs and, hence, it leads to increased customer satisfaction, regardless of other project context characteristics as level of customer involvement, organizational culture, type of product, level of risk and requirements volatility. More in detail, the answers by practitioners and the agile practices they addressed are presented in Table 2.

As suggested in Table 2, our observations from the interviews bring us to the conclusion that business value is created by a combination of agile practices and mechanisms at play in a project-specific context. For example, in short projects with limited resources and a short list with requirements, the client profits from the agile process through (1) the efficiency of the process, (2) the 'savings' made by the light-weight method, and (3) the ability to figure out early what they'll get and whether it is what they need. This profit-making mechanism is deemed by our participants important to obtain the best possible system for the money spent.

Another example is in a context of volatile or unclearly defined requirements. In this case, the value is ensured by the change management mechanisms and by incorporating learning loops in the process [19]. An interesting finding in our study was that the views by all participants agreed on that the agile paradigm has an effect on the social aspects of project delivery, such as work moral and atmosphere, as well as on the relationship between client and developing organizations.

3. Do practitioners perform value-driven decisions during agile development? While the concept of business value was deemed important to all participants, when it comes down to making requirements prioritization decisions at inter-iteration time, we found a surprising result: nine out of eleven participants stressed the importance of, what they called, a '**negative** value'. This is a prioritization criterion that the practitioners used in requirements prioritization and it means *'how big the damage for the client/product will be if a requirement is not implemented'*.

The practitioners explained that in their requirements prioritization experiences the important point of reasoning was not the estimation of the value being present in a certain feature, but instead – the question of how much this feature would detract from the product's value, if the developers do not implement it. The 'negative' value thus is equivalent to loss of value or damage to the business. In the experience of one practitioner, this reasoning reflects a professional pragmatic behavior especially in projects that have very limited resources and clients preoccupied with whether or not they derive maximum benefit from the project. Unlikely to contexts in which scarcity of project resources is an important concern, in projects which enjoy 'more generous' budgets, practitioners agreed on that their decisions were driven mainly by value consideration, namely supporting the main functionality of the software system being delivered and keeping in mind the 'negative value'. We note that making decisions by considering 'negative value' sounds intuitive, as the scarcer the resources, the more

Table 2. Agile practices and business value creation

Answers to the question of how agile software processes create business value	**Practices addressed:**	**Results in:**
"…The clients are included in the development process which enhances the understanding between the parties."	Client's involvement	Satisfied client, better relationship
"The process was adding value. The project included many relatively small requirements; there was a high through flow in the PB (product backlog) that you can not handle in a waterfall way."	Handling changing requirements	Creating a product that the client desires and that answers to changes
"The clients prefer to get something more often instead of one big thing once per year that might not be what they want."	Frequent releases	Satisfied client
"…by the efficiency of the process, the 'savings' made by the light-weight method, and by figuring early what they'll get and whether it's what they need. Gives the client peace of mind! Gives them the idea about what they'll get, at the same time they don't pay up front and don't have to sign a peace of paper; also they know that they can add something if they forget."	Close cooperation with the client Requirements' changes are allowed	Satisfied clients; Harmonious trustful relationship; peace of mind; less probability for requirements creep
"if it was not agile, we could have made a completely different system from what they want. Especially in this case where the requirements were not SMART. We discovered very early what they really want. Otherwise you need much more specific requirements. Also, for the developers – they have more voice, there is more interaction, they are happy. We have almost no cases of people that leave the company."	Small releases and frequent demos	The developers are happy! And work better; creating the right product, happy client, no waste of time and resources
"You can show very early what they can get; and you can manage expectations – what to expect and when."	Early release	Happy client, realistic expectations
"I don't believe in requirement documents; I think they are exactly as good as a card, and all the rest effort (specification, etc.) is a waste. Another good think is that you don't sign something up front. It is good for both sides, and for us to make expectation management; Agile makes products faster to market; you have de facto demo every 2 weeks, which is extremely helpful, as nobody can do everything right from the first time. It allows the client to collect feedback, observations and experience from the beta-versions, and so the first version in production is much better."	Slim RE process, less documentation, frequent releases, incorporate learning	Good use of resources, no waste, lower risk (do not sign something fixed up front), faster to market, creating the right product, higher quality
"You can make changes during the project; nobody knows in advance what they really want. This process helps them to see what happens, at an early stage."	Change management, early releases, incorporate learning and experience	Better product and right product via learning
"…to reduce the time for development…The project team is more cohesive, the experience is shared, also to the whole company."	Information sharing techniques	Faster time to market, better team work, information sharing
"The special benefit of agile is that the client can better influence/re-define what he gets for his money."	Client participation	Happy clients, more 'value for money'

conscious the project teams are on how to spend them. However, we also make the note that, to the best of our knowledge, the agile literature sources do not mention the concept of 'negative value'. Reflecting on the discrepancy between the business value concepts discussed in agile literature and our experience that the concept of 'negative value' surfaced during the interviews with the majority of the participants, regardless of their locations, company sizes, and cultures, we think that it is an under-researched topic which warrants further research. First, the concept of 'negative value' suggests that we may need to redefine the concept of business value in agile all together. Second, this concept clarifies the type of value that feeds into the decision-making processes in agile projects. Understanding the mechanisms that condition the use of 'negative value' in agile can bring us to restate the decision-making conceptual frameworks which we, the researchers, have been using to explain agile phenomena until now. We consider this a research problem for our immediate future. More specifically, we plan to get back to the case study sites and do follow-up in-depth interviews to explicate the meaning of 'negative value' and its use in agile decision-making.

4. How do developers combine value creation for their own organization with value creation for the client's organization? The practitioners shared the views that in the software project organizations, the developers regularly perform their own estimations and revise their understandings of how the business value from the client's standpoint relates to the bottom line of the developers' companies. They explained that this developers' value-conscious estimation happens, because of the pressure on the developers to maximize the value creation for the client, only while ensuring a descent level of profit for their own companies. This means that not all wants of the clients get implemented at inter-iteration time, and certainly, not all requirements that the client specified at project inception time are implemented. Overall, the practitioners agreed that the developers are active participants in the requirements decision-making processes. Their participation is deemed even stronger in cases of small projects, where the client is a small organization or company that does not possess knowledge in the IT domain and cannot afford paying extra for IT consulting services. Such a client may even find it very expensive to allocate a resource to the role of 'on-site client'. Often, it is economically unfeasible for the client organization to pool away a full-time employee from their every-day business and task him/her to serve 'on-site' in an agile project. In such a context, it happens that the client delegates the decisions influencing the value creation, to the developing team. Our case study participants indicated with certainty that a high level of trust is a prerequisite for such cooperation. Some participants described situations where they even had to 'save the clients from themselves', meaning to prevent unwise decisions or suboptimal choices that will be harmful in long term. The practitioners motivated this course of action with their experience from previous projects at the client's site as well as their profound knowledge of the client's business domain. The developers also justified this behavior by their desire to create maximal value for the client and, thus, to contribute to a successful project. In the experience of our interviewees *"this leads to high client satisfaction and good relationship with the client, which will, eventually, lead to future mutual projects"*. This observation represents an interesting point for further discussions and research, as it does not converge with the common understanding in the agile literature that the customer is responsible for making the (prioritization) decisions. We think, therefore, that knowing more about the variation in project contexts is key to understand how relevant project context characteristics possibly affect the choice of decision-making approach in a project.

That the developers strongly participate in the prioritization and decision-making gives us the hint that agile and traditional requirements engineering processes may not be that different, compared to what originally was thought, regarding who prioritizes the requirements. Our study suggests that in agile (as well in traditional) contexts, we can find examples of clients who essentially rely on developers to prioritize their project requirements; we, therefore, think that the difference between agile and traditional processes is not with respect to who prioritizes the requirements, but: (1) with respect to what competencies and (tacit) knowledge those, who prioritize, have of their client's business, (2) with respect to whether the client is able to participate in the process. Our interviewees suggested that the developers, who 'saved the clients from themselves' are experienced professionals (e.g. in the words of one interviewee, with 10 to 15 years of experience in IT systems delivery in a specific business sector) and this might indicate that for agile prioritization to be led by developers, it should include highly-competent and experience people. At the time of writing this paper, we consider this a hypothesis for future research and we feel motivated to carry out further case studies in company sites to confirm or disconfirm it.

Last, the observation that clients feel their knowledge of requirements priorities limited when it comes to inter-iteration decision-making opens up a question to those researchers that develop and evaluate requirements prioritization methods. The existing prioritization techniques rest on the assumption that clients are aware of the mechanics behind the application of requirements prioritization techniques and, as a minimum, they are conscious about their role of providers of the input that feeds into these techniques. It appears that our case study findings question the extent to which this assumption is realistic. Indeed, requirements prioritization methods take for granted that there are objective values to provide inputs into the methods. Now, looking at our case study findings, the suspicion grows that these objective values may not always exist and are difficult to make. Our findings are indicative for a limitation being present in the current requirements prioritization methods, and therefore, we think that future research is warranted to understand those cases in which the assumption is not realistic.

5 Discussion on the Results

We were surprised that our study yielded a few findings regarding essential aspects of business value creation in agile projects, which were misaligned with what agile literature says on these aspects. Reflecting on these findings, we formulated a number of interesting research questions for the future. Below, we present the research questions according to those findings which indicated a gap between agile project realities and the agile literature:

(1) Business value is more than just numbers. It comes out of a human judgment that is based on competencies and deep knowledge of the client's domain. An interesting question then is how a judgment about business value is formed and what tacit knowledge should be made explicit, so that knowledge about business value gets shared among developers and clients.

(2) Perceived business value varies from project to project, as projects vary in terms of amount of agile practices they use. Does any relationship exist between the extent to which a project is agile (i.e. the amount and the combination of agile practices) and the perceived business value? If so, what kind of relationship is it?

(3) The value-creation process plays an important role for the developers' organization. The agile practitioners' literature [2] seems to share the opinion that the only value-creating considerations that drive the development decisions are those of creating value for the *client*. During this study we made the consistent observation that, more often then not, the value creation for the developers has been considered as well. Clearly, developers and clients have some goals that ensure mutual benefits to incur e.g. "we want to make the client happy, so that he/she comes back", while other goals on the developers' side may not be related to one particular project or one particular client, and instead are related to issues like reuse, other concurrently running projects and distribution of resources for maximizing value for the organization. We need to consider more carefully in which ways development teams balance the client's business value with their own organizational bottom-line. We think this is an important topic for future research on its own right. We think, if we collect and analyze examples of good and not-so-good ways to balance client's and developers' value-creation perspectives, then we will be able to deduce patterns, principles, do's and don'ts, and other general understandings that help practicing requirements engineers build up a body of knowledge that can assist them in value-creation.

(4) As already noted in the previous section, the developers rely on their own estimations and understandings, even on common sense, in order to maximize the value creation for the client. The situations in which the developers had to 'save the clients from themselves' opens up perspectives for future research. For example, it would be interesting to see what level of trust is necessary in those situations when clients 'delegate' the value creation process to the developing team who delivers the system.

(5) The evidence from the study shows that, in contrast to the documented agile best practices in the literature [10], in most of the cases the developers are those who made inter-iteration decision making. Our interviewees agreed that more often than not the involvement of the clients consisted mainly of approving the plan/giving comments. Only in few cases practitioners were able to provide evidence that the client is really capable/interested/aware of the agile way of defining priorities, and thus able to navigate the functionality by the mid-course decision-making process. In Section 4 we already expressed the suspicion that this may question the fundamental assumption behind the contemporary agile requirements prioritization methods, namely that some objective values exist to feed as inputs into the methods. We think, this alone is worthwhile researching so that we understand the extent to which this assumption is realistic. In our case study, the interviewees went further to explain why developers are that strongly participating in the decision-making. In their view, the developers' company is the one to make sure that the project delivery process runs in a way that is profitable for the company. If developers accommodate all wishes which clients might come up with at inter-iteration time, the company may find it not sustainable in the long run. As said in the previous paragraph, while an agile software company lets its clients

prioritize the requirements, this decision-making process can take place only when the client's sense of flexibility is balanced against the company's sense of profitability. However, it remains to uncover the mechanisms that are at play in contexts where this balance is feasible.

(6) Throughout the interviews, it became explicit that there is a link between the project's settings and the way the decisions are made, i.e. how the value creation process is organized. In all projects where the client's company was a small company, the decision making was deliberately delegated to the developer. It could be a product owner, a project manager or another representative of the developing team that was responsible for the communication with the client.

6 Limitations

We explicitly addressed the possible threats to external and internal validity of the observations and conclusions in a case study as per the recommendations of qualitative case study research methodologists [21],[22]. First, the external validity addresses the generalizability of our observations and conclusions beyond the studied sample of companies, projects and participants. The following aspects of the study can be considered as possible threats to the validity: (i) the number of companies and projects that have been studied; and (ii) the choice of study participants. The scale of the study does not allow us to make statistically relevant observations. However, as discussed earlier, this was not the purpose of our study. For a qualitative study, the question is rather [21],[22]: to what extent the companies included in the study can be considered as representative for a broader range of companies? We deliberately included in the study representatives of companies of different sizes and business sectors. Some of the findings apply generally across the cases, despite the heterogeneity of the set of case studies. This gives confidence that the conclusions hold for other companies in similar context as well. It is for this reason we have searched for aspects that the cases have in common rather than aspects in which they might differ. Our findings correspond to the intuitive thought that agile companies in similar contexts would share similar approaches to business value in their projects, but, more importantly, it was also confirmed by participants in a panel discussion where first results of the study have been presented. Of course, the stress here is on the word 'context'. We believe that the most important aspects of the context, in this case, are: location of the company, company size and project size. As participants in the study indicated, the geographic zone, where a company is located implies the presence of a country-(or zone-) specific culture, which defines to a large extent the relationships between the clients' and developers' organizations. In addition, there are specific legal aspects in each country in respect to the contractual terms an agile project organization would adopt. Furthermore, the geographical location of the company is linked to the way in which the agile methodology is applied and the extent to which the agile way of thinking and working as a philosophy penetrates in a specific part of the world. This means to us that it is realistic to expect that the results of our study are generalizable to companies in a similar context, especially in companies of similar size, located in Central and South-European countries. We make the note that we are aware of the different level of penetration of the agile paradigm in the different geographic zones. E.g. in North

America, the increased awareness and usage of agile approaches have lead to the formation of professional communities and networks as well as to specialized professional certifications (e.g. scrum master). It will be very interesting to observe, compare and contrast the agile development and project management practices at companies working in different cultural settings. Furthermore, it would be interesting to compare their processes of value creation and their understanding of value with the observations in this paper.

It should be noted that our cases are limited to small and medium-sized companies. Due to their different nature, the findings cannot be generalized to large companies, which have a different, and often distributed, software delivery process. For example, in [13], the authors describe a large-scale Scrum-of-scrums approach that ensures multi-team coordination in large organizations (e.g. Nokia) and relies on a set of mechanisms unique to agile contexts in large companies. In this case, study, we did include one large organization, however, the project which we included in the case study was small. This meant, it had a smaller project organization, consisting of a few representatives of the country-specific business unit of the company (to which our interviewee belonged) and a representative of the client.

Second, with respect to internal validity, our key concern refers to the choice of the companies. As we are analyzing agile processes, we want to be sure that this is in fact what we are investigating. The important question to discuss is how did we (the researchers) know that the processes we studied were indeed agile ones. To minimize the effect of this threat on the results of the case study, we took some extra actions: We confirmed with all participants that they (or their team) apply an agile methodology. The participants stated that their organizations were known as agile method adopters and that they were committed to use agile in the projects that we collected information about. Next, during the interviews, we consciously looked for confirmation of whether the interviewees indeed referred to examples of their experiences in agile projects (and not in projects that used other approaches). Certainly, this is a philosophical question as well – where is the line between other iterative and incremental approaches and which characteristics of the project should be observable in order to claim a team or a project to be agile. This question is out of the scope of this paper, though. To the best of our knowledge, the projects included in our study are truly agile projects in the sense of the Agile manifesto [2]. Furthermore, our interviewees agreed on that the agile process helped them create rapport with their clients easier than it could have been possible in a project that uses a traditional delivery approach. The interviewees also agreed that the agile process makes it *"much easier than ever before"* to consistently maintain communication with the client organization. They felt that this all was instrumental to *"making the clients happy"*. Clearly, one could raise the concern that these observations are biased, as they are provided by agile practitioners. More than 70% of the interviewees were seasoned practitioners with more than 15 years of software project experience and that they accumulated a large part of this experience while working for organizations with traditional software development approaches. So, they had enough practice to compare the both worlds. However, we admit that there is a possible threat to validity as we interviewed only those people that are currently engaged in agile development. Theoretically, there could have been people that came back to traditional approach. However, this was not a feasible option within the resources we had.

7 Conclusions

This paper presents the results of empirical investigation on the understanding of agile software practitioners on the concept of business value and its creation during the development process. All participants in our explorative study expressed the opinion that agile projects make clients satisfied by the outcome of a project. This was a point of convergence across case study sites regardless of the significant variety in project characteristics (type of software project, organization size, culture) at these sites.

The study revealed an important gap between the realities of the practitioners in the studied projects and the agile literature. In our view, acknowledging the presence of this gap is a valuable input to agile project managers and practitioners when they make decisions on how to implement the agile practices concerning the interactions with their clients. Agile managers may choose to avoid certain practices if they deem this brings them closer to their project realities in which business value is to be created. Reflecting on the gap also brought us to research questions for the future.

We believe that value creation in agile projects is a lively, difficult and richly articulated research field and, therefore we think that our explorative case study can be just one step on the way to develop a deeper understanding of the agile phenomena related to essential aspects of business value. We consider it a work-in-progress that the community may want to adapt and expand.

Acknowledgments. This research is funded by the Netherland's Research Foundation (NWO) under the QUADREAD project. We thank all practitioners that took part in the case study and the three referees for their constructive comments.

References

1. Abrahamsson, P., Salo, O., Ronkainen, J., Warsta, J.: Agile Software Development Methods: Review and Analysis, VTT Technical Report (2002)
2. Agile Alliance, Manifesto for Agile Software Development, February 13 (2001), `http://www.agilemanifesto.org/`
3. Aurum, A., Wohlin, C.: A Value-Based Approach in Requirements Engineering: Explaining Some of the Fundamental Concepts. In: Sawyer, P., Paech, B., Heymans, P. (eds.) REFSQ 2007. LNCS, vol. 4542, pp. 109–115. Springer, Heidelberg (2007)
4. Barney, S., Aurum, A., Wohlin, C.: A Product Management Challenge: Creating Software Product Value through Requirements Selection. Journal of Software Architecture 54, 576–593 (2008)
5. Barney, S., Wohlin, C., Aurum, A.: Balancing software product investments. In: Proc. of the Symposium on Empiricl Software Engineering (ESEM), pp. 257–268 (2009)
6. Biffl, S., Aurum, A., Boehm, B., Erdogmus, H., Grünbacher, P. (eds.): Value-based Software Engineering. Springer, Heidelberg (2006)
7. Boehm, B.: Software Engineering Economics. Prentice-Hall Inc., Englewood Cliffs (1981)
8. Cao, L., Ramesh, B.: Agile Requirements Engineering Practices: An Empirical Study. IEEE Software 25(01), 60–67 (2008)
9. Charmaz, K.: Constructing Grounded Theory: a Practical Guide through Qualitative Research. Sage, Thousand Oaks (2007)
10. Cohn, M.: Agile Planning and Estimating. Prentice Hall Inc., Englewood Cliffs (2005)

11. Favaro, J.M.: That Elusive Business Value: Some Lessons from the Top. In: Baumeister, H., Marchesi, M., Holcombe, M. (eds.) XP 2005. LNCS, vol. 3556, p. 199. Springer, Heidelberg (2005)
12. Fitzgerald, B., Hartnett, G., Conboy, K.: Customising Agile methods to Software Practices at the Intel Shannon. European J. of Info. Syst. 15(2), 200–213 (2009)
13. Larman, C., Vodde, B.: Practices for Scaling Lean and Agile Development: Large, Multisite and Offshore Projects with Large-Scale Scrum. Addison-Wesley, Reading (2008)
14. Little, T.: Schedule estimation and uncertainty surrounding the cone of uncertainty. IEEE Software 23(3), 48–54 (2006)
15. Little, T.: Value Creation and Capture: a Model of the Software Development Process. IEEE Software, 48–54 (2004)
16. Peterson, K., Wohlin, C.: A Comparison of issues and Advantages in Agile and Incremental Development between State of the Art and an Industrial Case. Journal of Systems and Software 82, 1479–1490 (2009)
17. Racheva, Z., Daneva, M., Sikkel, K.: Value Creation by Agile Projects: Methodology or Mystery? In: 10th International Conference on Product-Focused Software Process Improvement, pp. 141–155. Springer, Heidelberg (2009)
18. Rönkkö, M., Frühwirth, C., Biffl, S.: Integrating Value and Utility Concepts into a Value Decomposition Model for Value-Based Software Engineering. In: 10th International Conference on Product-Focused Software Process Improvement, pp. 362–374. Springer, Heidelberg (2009)
19. Schwaber, K.: Agile Project Management with SCRUM. Microsoft Press, Redmond, Washington (2004)
20. Sutherland, J., Altman, I.: Take No Prisoners: How a Venture Capital Group Does Scrum. In: Proceedings of AGILE 2009, Chicago, MI (USA), August 24-28, pp. 350–355. Springer, Heidelberg (2009)
21. Wieringa, R.: Design Science and Software Engineering, In: ICSOFT (2009)
22. Yin, R.K.: Case Study Research: Design and Methods. Sage, Thousand Oaks (2004)

Critical Success Factors for Offshore Software Development Outsourcing Vendors: An Empirical Study

Siffat Ullah Khan[1], Mahmood Niazi[1], and Rashid Ahmad[2]

[1] School of Computing and Mathematics, Keele University, Keele, ST5 5BG, UK
s.khan@epsam.keele.ac.uk, mkniazi@cs.keele.ac.uk
[2] College of EME, National University of Science & Technology, Rawalpindi, Pakistan
rashid@ceme.edu.pk

Abstract

CONTEXT – Offshore software development outsourcing is a contractual business of high quality software production with significant cost-saving.

OBJECTIVE – The objective of this research paper is to analyse the factors that influence software outsourcing clients in the selection of offshore software outsourcing vendors.

METHOD – We have performed questionnaire surveys with 53 experts. We asked the participants to rank each success factor on a five-point scale to determine the perceived importance of each success factor. Our survey included success factors identified in the previous findings of systematic literature review study.

RESULTS – Our study reveal both cost-saving and appropriate infrastructure as the most influential factors in the selection of outsourcing vendors. Our results also indicate that appropriate infrastructure, cost-saving and efficient project management are common success factors across different groups of practitioners.

CONCLUSIONS – Cost-saving and appropriate infrastructure should be considered as the prime factors in the selection process of software development outsourcing vendors.

1 Introduction

Software development outsourcing is a contractual business between client and vendor organisations in which a client(s) contracts out all or part of its software development activities to a vendor(s), who provides agreed services for remuneration [1]. Offshore software outsourcing is dramatically changing the business economics in the overall outsourcing industry due to the availability of skilled human resource and provision of high quality software at low cost [2].

This research focuses on the need to gain an in-depth understanding of the range of criteria used by the software development outsourcing clients for the selection of software development outsourcing vendors. Understanding the selection criteria will help software development outsourcing vendors in addressing those criteria in order to be fully ready for software development outsourcing initiatives. This may also help to ensure the successful outcome of offshore outsourcing projects and long lasting relationships between clients and vendors.

M. Ali Babar, M. Vierimaa, and M. Oivo (Eds.): PROFES 2010, LNCS 6156, pp. 146–160, 2010.
© Springer-Verlag Berlin Heidelberg 2010

There are many reasons for software development outsourcing [3]. Client organisations benefit from offshore outsourcing because vendors in developing countries (offshore vendors) usually cost one-third less than onshore vendors and even less when compared with in-house operations [4]. Moreover, offshore vendors improve their skills and service quality with the experience of offshore outsourcing projects, learning new ways to satisfy the clients' needs. However, in addition to the outsourcing benefits there are many risks in an outsourcing process [5], [6].

Many challenges have been reported in the offshore software outsourcing process. One of the key challenges is handling complex communication and coordination problems due to language and cultural barriers as well as lack of face-to-face communication [7]. Other challenges include lack of client involvement, hidden costs, the development of software development outsourcing practices and creating and maintaining trust among the outsourcing companies [8], [9], [7]. However, despite the importance of offshore software development outsourcing, little empirical research has been carried out on offshore software development outsourcing practices in general and the identification of factors that have a significant impact on client organisations in particular. To do this we intend to address the following research questions:

RQ1. What factors do offshore software outsourcing vendors need to address in order to have a positive impact on software outsourcing clients?

RQ2. Do the identified factors vary across the different level of experts?

This paper is organised as follows. Section 2 describes the background. Section 3 describes the research methodology. In Section 4 findings are presented and analysed with some discussion. In Section 5 summary is provided. Section 6 describes the limitations. Section 7 provides the conclusion and future work.

2 Background

Offshore software development outsourcing is a contractual business of high quality software production at offshore destinations with significant cost-saving. This is because organisations (clients) in the developed countries outsource their software development activities to other organisations at low wages countries (offshore vendors) who provide agreed services with significant cost-saving. Software development outsourcing has been growing steadily and an 18-fold increase in the outsourcing of IT-enabled business processes is projected [10]. A survey report reveals that the interest in outsourcing has been increased by many companies (client organisations) in the developed countries [2]. Similarly the new report by Gartner predicts that the current economic downturn will accelerate offshore software outsourcing activities [2]. "Global economic uncertainty remains, but the outsourcing market could be the first to benefit as companies in Europe and the US seek to reduce costs" [2]. Many firms in the US have outsourced their software development projects to offshore countries for gaining better quality IT services at comparatively cheaper rate and in a shorter time period [11]. India was the first outsourcing destination and is still leading the outsourcing industry [2]. Many Indian vendor organisations are creating global reach (overseas offices) in Northern Ireland in order to offer services to those European clients who desire onshore or nearshore presence [2]. However, new outsourcing destinations are emerging which may offer a better deal to clients [2]. India, Philippines,

China, Ireland and Brazil are ranked as the top 5 mature outsourcing destinations where as the report predicts Canada, Russia, Mexico, Vietnam and Poland as the next 5 emerging offshore destinations [12].

Forrester Research 2002 predicted that 3.3 million US professional jobs and $136 billion in wage will be outsourced offshore by 2015 [13]. According to Forrester Research 2007, 65% of American and European firms (with 1,000 or more employees) currently benefit from offshore vendors for their software development; another 13% firms intend to outsource next year. Whereas two years earlier only 45% of these firms were the users of offshore outsourcing for the software applications development [13].

However significant outsourcing failure rates have also been reported [14]. Nam et al. [15] in their investigation of 93 client companies found that 36 did not intend to continue their relationships with vendors. King [16] reports that JP Morgan decided to perform many software activities that it previously outsourced, and did not renew its $5 billion contract with IBM. At the root of many failures is the increased complexity that outsourcing brings to development projects. This complexity results in: high coordination costs [17], information security problems [18], lack of direct communication [19], perceived loss of expertise in the outsourced activity [20], cultural misunderstandings [21] and infrastructure problems [22].

There are several tasks relating to software development, such as programming, software architecture design and software testing, which are outsourced. There are many reasons for software development outsourcing [3]. Small and medium sized companies with limited resources and technical expertise are best served by outside contractors. Large companies may use an outsourcing strategy in order to experiment with new information technologies without making an upfront investment. Large companies may also use software development outsourcing due to limited availability of software development expertise at the host companies and to reduce processing costs [23]. However the scope of software development outsourcing is expanding from focusing only on reducing cost to improving organisations' overall business performance. This change has led to a realisation that the organisations readiness plays a vital role in the success or failure of software outsourcing initiatives [24], [25].

Understanding factors relating to criteria used by the software development outsourcing clients for the selection of software development outsourcing vendors can help ensure the successful outcome of projects and long lasting relationships between clients and vendors in different geographical locations [8], [9], [26], [1].

3 Research Methodology

3.1 Measure Development

Considering the objectives of our research and available resources, we decided to use a survey research method to understand software development outsourcing practitioners' perception of the factors that influence software outsourcing clients in the selection of offshore software outsourcing vendors. A survey research method is considered suitable for gathering self-reported quantitative and qualitative data from a large number of respondents [27]. A survey research can use one or a combination of several data gathering techniques such as interviews, self-administered questionnaires and others [28]. We decided to use a questionnaire as a data collection instrument due to several factors such as collecting data from diverse range of respondents and available resources.

A questionnaire was developed at Keele University based on existing literature [29], [30]. We used a closed format questionnaire as an instrument to collect self-reported data. The questionnaire was based on the success factors reported by Khan et al. [31], [32]. In order to gain the tacit knowledge on success factors some open ended questions were also included in the questionnaire to find any other factors apart from the identified factors. The questionnaire was also designed to elicit the importance that each respondent placed on each factor identified. In order to describe the importance of success factors, the respondents were asked to note each factor's relative value (i.e., strongly agree, Agree, Strongly disagree, Disagree, or Not sure).

The piloting of the questionnaire was conducted through four software engineering researchers at Keele and necessary changes were made to the questionnaire. Our questionnaire is divided into 4 sections: sections one is about demographics data, in section two success factors to software development outsourcing are provided, in section 3 practices for each success factor are described and in section 4 instructions about the questionnaire submission are provided.

3.2 Data Sources

Since the goal of this research was to gain an understanding of software development outsourcing practitioners' perceptions of factors that influence software outsourcing clients in the selection of offshore software outsourcing vendors, we needed to collect data from diverse range of outsourcing practitioners involved in outsourcing activities across the world. The traditional way of approaching the target population was not appropriate as we did not have the contact details of these experts and we also could not find any database which has such information. Based on the discussions with different colleagues at Keele and also speaking to few outsourcing experts we have decided to use some new ways in order to locate and approach the target population. In this connection, we joined various relevant outsourcing online groups to find outsourcing experts for participation in the research survey. All these online groups are hosted by LinkedIn website. A request was posted to these groups to invite experts for participation. Our invitation letter included a brief description of the research project and the nature of the commitment required. This request can be viewed at http://groups.google.com/group/icgse/browse_thread/thread/d234dbae0fab31cb. We believe that this request was received by 13268 members of the outsourcing groups specified in Table 1. Amongst these a total of 106 experts showed their willingness through email for participation in the research survey. Finally, 43 responses were received, giving the response rate of 41%.

Apart from this online collection, a request was made at the poster session of ICGSE09, Limerick, Ireland where 15 experts showed their willingness for participation. Finally 10 experts returned completed questionnaires. Thus raising the total no of experts participated in the survey to 53 and the overall response rate is almost 44%. These participants are from a total of 20 different countries with a majority from US, UK and Canada.

Table 1. Summary of online outsourcing experts groups

Group Name	Group members (At Request posting Time)	Request posted Date
ICGSE (Google groups)	28	April, 2009
Poster session, ICGSE09 (Limerick, Ireland)	Almost 100	15 Jul 2009
Global Sourcing Professionals (LinkedIn group)	1601	April, 2009
ICT Outsourcing Professionals (LinkedIn group)	426	April, 2009
IT/Software Development Outsourcing and Offshoring (LinkedIn group)	4015	April, 2009
Offshoring & Outsourcing Forum (LinkedIn group)	1452	April, 2009
Outsourcing 2 India (LinkedIn group)	297	April, 2009
Outsourcing & Offshoring (LinkedIn group)	2470	April, 2009
Outsourcing to Ukraine (LinkedIn group)	595	May, 2009
Outsourcing@UK (LinkedIn group)	2127	Jul, 2009
Outsourcing in the Central and Eastern Europe (LinkedIn group)	257	Jul, 2009

3.3 Data Analysis Method

First way of organising qualitative or quantitative data is to group scores or values into frequencies [33], because frequency analysis is helpful for the treatment of descriptive information. The number of occurrences and percentages of each data variable can then be reported using these frequency tables. Frequencies are helpful for comparing and contrasting within groups of variables or across groups of variables and can be used for both nominal/ordinal as well as numeric data. For most of the data analysis, we used frequency analysis. In order to analyse each identified success factors, the occurrence of each factor in each questionnaire was counted. By comparing the occurrences of one success factor against the occurrences of other success factors, the relative importance of each success factor has been identified.

4 Analysis and Results

4.1 Success Factors Identified through Empirical Study

In order to answer RQ1, Table 2 shows the list of success factors identified through empirical study. The results suggest that out of 22 success factors, 18 factors have greater than 50% of occurrences where as the remaining 4 success factors have greater than 30% occurrences in the positive list. 'Skilled human resource' is the most common success factor in our positive list, i.e. 94%. Research suggests that half of the companies that have tried outsourcing have failed to realise the anticipated results [25]. One of the reasons for software development outsourcing failures is the difficulties in creating good relationships among the outsourcing companies [1], [34]. We argue that 'skilled human resource' can play a vital role in establishing a good relationship between client and vendor organisations as this will help vendor organisations to provide adequate services to client organisations. Different studies have also described the importance of 'skilled human resource' factor:

- High-quality skilled staff are the backbone of the IT industry and vendors should employ high skilled workers with professional degrees in Computer Science, Engineering, Management and similar fields [35].
- Often a client organisation is eager to know the technical capability of vendor organisation [8].

Our results also indicate that 'cost-saving' (92%) is the 2nd most significant factor for the selection of vendor organisations. This suggests that low cost software production or to charge a fair price has a positive impact on the outsourcing clients in the selection process of outsourcing vendors. Due to this factor the western countries are outsourcing projects to developing countries to take advantage from the reduced labour costs. In order to be competitive, vendors organisations should provide better and cheaper services to the clients [36].

We also found 'timely delivery of the product' and 'vendor's responsiveness' as the 3rd most significant factors in our positive list (i.e. 87%). Other frequently cited positive factors are: Organisation's track record of successful projects – 85%, Quality of Products and Services – 83%, Appropriate Infrastructure- 79%, Efficient Outsourcing Relationships Management – 75% and SPI Certification (CMMI, ISO, etc) – 75%. These results validate the findings of our systematic literature review [31].

The results suggest that out of 22 success factors, 5 factors have greater than 30% of occurrences in the negative list of Table 2. These factors are 'industry-university linkage' (45%), 'company size (large and medium) (43%), 'overseas offices' (43%), 'knowledge exchange' (36%) and risk sharing (32%). As these factors in the negative list are not considered in the selection of outsourcing vendors we suggest that outsourcing vendors should not worry to implement these factors.

In the neutral list (not sure) of Table 2, 19 success factors have been cited where as the remaining 3 success factors have zero occurrences in the neutral list. These 3 factors are 'skilled human resource', 'quality of product and service' and 'timely delivery of the product'. This suggests that all practitioners in the sample were completely sure about the role of these factors in vendor selection process.

4.2 Success Factors in the Opinions of Junior, Intermediate and Senior Level Experts

In total 53 outsourcing experts have participated in this research. We have categorised these experts into three categories based on their experiences. These three categories are junior level experts having experience range of 1-5 years, intermediate level experts having experience range of 6-10 years and senior level experts having 11 years and above experience as shown in Appendix. Due to non-existence of a proven theory about categorisation of outsourcing experts, this categorisation was done based on the discussion with different outsourcing experts and researchers at Keele. However, other researchers can define their own criteria in order to decide different levels of outsourcing experts.

Our results indicate that out of 22 success factors, 21 success factors have been reported as "strongly agree" in the sample of junior level experts. The remaining one factor company size (large and medium) has zero frequency. Amongst these 21 success factors, 4 factors have been cited in >=50% of the sample of "strongly agree" of junior experts. These 4 factors are 'appropriate infrastructure' – 67%, 'cost-saving' – 61%, 'quality of products and services' – 50%, 'efficient project management' – 50%.

Table 2. Summary of success factors from experts' perspective SA=Strongly Agree, A=Agree, SD=Strongly Disagree, D= Disagree, NS=Not sure

Success Factors	Experts' perception (n=53)							
	Positive			Negative			Neutral	
	SA	A	% of Positive	SD	D	% of Negative	NS	%
Cost-saving	32	17	92	0	3	6	1	2
Skilled Human Resource	19	31	94	0	3	6	0	0
Appropriate Infrastructure	32	10	79	0	7	13	4	8
Quality of Products and Services	23	21	83	1	8	17	0	0
Efficient Outsourcing Relationships Management	22	18	75	2	4	11	7	13
Organisation's track record of successful projects	20	25	85	0	6	11	2	4
Efficient Project Management	18	12	57	0	8	15	5	9
Efficient Contract Management	20	15	66	0	10	19	8	15
SPI Certification (CMMI, ISO, etc.)	17	23	75	1	9	19	3	6
Knowledge of the Client's Language and Culture	17	19	68	2	10	23	5	9
Timely Delivery of the Product	15	31	87	4	3	13	0	0
Knowledge Exchange	7	21	53	4	15	36	6	11
Data Protection Laws	11	25	68	4	7	21	6	11
Financial Stability	9	28	70	2	8	19	6	11
Company Size (Large and Medium)	1	25	49	4	19	43	4	8
Risk Sharing	4	22	49	1	16	32	10	19
Pilot Project Performance	10	27	70	3	9	23	4	8
Vendor's Responsiveness	14	32	87	2	2	8	3	6
Political Stability	6	29	66	4	7	21	7	13
Overseas Offices	7	16	43	3	20	43	7	13
Soft Deliverable	10	26	68	1	10	21	6	11
Industry-University Linkage	7	14	40	7	17	45	8	15

It is worth noting that 'appropriate infrastructure' has the highest percentage (67%) for junior level experts. By 'appropriate infrastructure' we mean:

- IT infrastructure/Network infrastructure/ Telecommunication infrastructure.
- Physical infrastructure (related both with the country and the company) which includes Telecom, power/electric supply, roads, transportation, physical buildings, office layouts, Internet access and sewer and water system etc.
- Sufficient resources including hardware and software to maintain large development projects.

Our findings indicate that developing an appropriate infrastructure by vendor organisations has a positive impact on client organisations. Hence, in order to succeed in outsourcing projects vendor organisations should check the IT resources, including the number of servers, the intranet structure and the performance of the systems resources prior to undertake outsourcing activity [37].

Cost-saving got the 2nd rank and is strongly agreed by 61% of the junior experts. Quality of products and services' and 'efficient project management' receive the 3rd rank and strongly agreed by 50% of junior experts.

We found 7 success factors as the least significant (strongly disagree) in the views of junior level experts. The factors 'company size (large and medium)' and 'industry-university linkage' have the highest percentage (17%) of occurrence in the strongly disagree list. Similarly 'overseas offices' has 11% of occurrence whereas 'efficient outsourcing relationships management', 'knowledge exchange', 'political stability' and 'soft deliverable' have 6% occurrences in the strongly disagree list.

For intermediate level experts we found all 22 success factors in the 'strongly agree' list as shown in Appendix. Five success factors have been strongly agreed by >=50% of intermediate level experts. The success factor 'cost-saving' has the highest percentage (68%) of occurrence among intermediate level experts. Vendor organisations should concentrate on providing cheaper software production as per clients' requirements. 'Appropriate infrastructure', 'efficient outsourcing relationships management', 'efficient project management' and 'organisation's track record of successful projects' are the 2nd most significant success factors having 53% of occurrences by the intermediate level experts.

We found 12 success factors as the least significant (strongly disagree) in the views of intermediate level experts. The factors 'timely delivery of the product', 'knowledge exchange' and 'industry-university linkage' have the highest percentage (11%) of occurrence in the strongly disagree list. Other factors have 5% of occurrence in the strongly disagree list.

For senior experts a list of 21 success factors was found in the 'strongly agree' list. Four success factors have been strongly agreed by >=50% of the senior experts. The factor 'appropriate infrastructure' has the highest percentage (63%) of occurrence. Similarly 'efficient project management' and 'knowledge of the client's language and culture' are the 2nd most significant factor having 56% occurrence. 'Cost-saving' has 50% occurrence and is the 3rd most significant factor in the view of senior level experts.

We found 12 success factors as the least significant (strongly disagree) in the views of senior level experts. The factor 'data protection laws' has the highest percentage (19%) of occurrence in the strongly disagree list. Similarly 'timely delivery of the product', 'pilot project performance', 'political stability', and 'industry-university linkage' got the 2nd rank having 13% occurrence in the strongly disagree list. The remaining seven factors have 6% of occurrence.

Due to the ordinal nature of data, we have used linear-by-linear Chi-square test to find the significant difference amongst junior, intermediate and senior level experts for the success factors. The linear by linear association test is preferred when testing the significant difference between ordinal variables because it is more powerful than Pearson Chi-square test [38]. However, no significant difference was found across the variables. This shows that all outsourcing experts are well aware what is required in selecting the appropriate outsourcing vendors.

5 Summary and Discussions

The success factors which can influence clients in the selection of offshore software outsourcing vendors have been identified through the empirical study. Our research goal is to provide software outsourcing practitioners with a body of knowledge that can help them to design and implement successful outsourcing initiatives. Success factors represent some of the key areas where management should focus their attention in order to better design software outsourcing initiatives. In order to decide the importance of a success factor, we have used the following criterion:

- If a success factor is strongly agreed by >=50% of the practitioners then we treat that success factor as a critical success factor.

We have used the similar criterion in our previous research [39], [40], [31], [41]. However, software outsourcing practitioners can define their own criteria in order to decide the criticality of listed outsourcing success factors.

In order to address RQ1, using the above criterion we have identified the 2 critical success factors that have a positive impact on outsourcing clients during the selection of outsourcing vendors. These critical success factors are: cost-saving (60%) and appropriate infrastructure (60%). However, other factors which have frequency percentage >=30 (strongly agree) may need to be addressed by the vendors in order to win outsourcing projects. These factors are: quality of products and services (43%), efficient outsourcing relationships management (42%), organisation's track record of successful projects (38%), efficient contract management (38%), skilled human resource (36%), efficient project management (34%), , SPI certification(CMMI, ISO etc) (32%) and knowledge of the client's language and culture (32%). These findings complement and validate the findings of our systematic literature review [31].

For RQ2, using the criterion for critical success factors, we have identified:

- Three success factors common across three types of experts (i.e. junior, intermediate and senior): Appropriate infrastructure, cost-saving and efficient project management.
- Quality of products and services is critical in the opinion of junior level experts.
- Efficient outsourcing relationships management and organisation's track record of successful projects are critical in the opinion of intermediate level experts.
- Knowledge of the client's language and culture is critical in the opinion of senior level experts.

Comparisons of the factors identified in three levels of experts confirm more similarities than differences between the factors as no significant difference was identified. Table 3 shows that 21 factors are strongly agreed by junior experts, 22 factors by intermediate and 21 factors by senior experts. The summary of our findings for RQ2 is given in Table 3.

Table 3. Distribution of success factors across various experts

Experts' experience level	Total number of success factors cited as strongly agree	No. of critical success factors (cited in >=50% of the "strongly agree" list)
Junior (n=18)	21	The following 4 CSFs have been identified. • Appropriate infrastructure (67%) • Cost-saving (61%) • Quality of products and services (50%) • Efficient project management (50%)
Intermediate(n=19)	22	The following 5 CSFs have been identified. • Cost-saving (68%) • Appropriate infrastructure (53%) • Efficient outsourcing relationships management (53%) • Efficient project management (53%) • Organisation's track record of successful projects (53%)
Senior (n=16)	21	The following 4 CSFs have been identified. • Appropriate infrastructure (63%) • Efficient project management (56%) • Knowledge of the client's language and culture (56%) • Cost-saving (50%)

6 Limitations

Construct validity is concerned with whether or not the measurement scales represent the attributes being measured. The attributes used in this research were taken from a substantial body of previous research reported in [40], [42], [43] and conducting a systematic literature review [31]. The responses from the participants show that all the attributes considered were relevant to their work. Internal validity provides support for an overall assessment of the results. The results of the pilot studies provide an acceptable level of internal validity as the variables included in our study were taken from extensive literature review and piloting of questions. External validity is concerned with the generalisation of the results to environments other than the one in which the initial study was conducted [44]. External validity is addressed as these results represent opinions of 53 practitioners from 20 different countries; although we cannot say that all respondents from these 20 countries would agree with them, we believe that they provide a representative sample.

We have used questionnaires and one disadvantage of the questionnaire survey method is that respondents are provided with a list of possible factors and asked to identify the factors that have positive impact on clients during the selection of outsourcing vendors. This tends to pre-empt the factors investigated and to limit them to those reported by the existing studies - respondents may only focus on the factors provided in the list. We tried to address this issue by encouraging the respondents to also mention if they could think of success factor other than those already mentioned on the questionnaire. However, like the researchers of many studies based on experience data (e.g. [39,45,46]), we also have full confidence in our findings because we have collected data from practitioners working in quite diverse roles and directly involved in outsourcing activities within their organisations. In addition, practitioners' experiences were explored independently and without any suggestions from the researchers.

7 Conclusion and Future Work

We investigated through the empirical study factors that are generally considered critical by clients in the selection of offshore software outsourcing vendors. We suggest that focusing on these factors can help software development outsourcing vendors in improving their readiness for software outsourcing activities.

Our findings indicate that 'cost-saving' and 'appropriate infrastructure' are critical for software development outsourcing vendors as most of the practitioners in the sample strongly agreed with these factors. In addition to these factors, other factors are also important for outsourcing vendors such as 'efficient project management', 'quality of products and services', 'efficient outsourcing relationships management', 'organisation's track record of successful projects' and 'knowledge of the client's language and culture'.

We encourage independent studies on this topic. This will increase confidence in our findings and also track changes in attitudes to offshore software outsourcing over time. We believe that a good understanding of these factors is vital in developing the vendor organisations' readiness for offshore software development outsourcing activities. From the findings of this study, we have identified the following goals that we plan to follow in future:

- To determine the reasons of why some factors are not significant in the views of outsourcing experts.
- Perform more analysis of the identified critical success factors based on different variables like company's size, company's scope, job, county etc.
- Analyse the critical barriers in the selection process of offshore outsourcing vendors.
- Conduct empirical studies to determine how to implement those factors which have been frequently cited in our study.

Our ultimate aim is to develop a Software Outsourcing Vendors' Readiness Model (SOVRM). This paper contributes to only one component of the SOVRM, i.e. the identification of the success factors. The eventual outcome of the research is the development of SOVRM to assist offshore software outsourcing vendors in assessing their readiness for software development outsourcing activities. The SOVRM proposed will bring together and advance the work that has been undertaken on frameworks and models for offshore software outsourcing. Our contribution to improving software development outsourcing processes will provide other researchers with a firm basis on which to develop different outsourcing processes that are based on an understanding of how and where they fit into the software development outsourcing activities. New outsourcing practices could then be developed targeting software development outsourcing projects.

Acknowledgements

We are thankful to University of Malakand, Pakistan and Higher Education Commission, Pakistan for sponsoring the PhD research studies under FDP scholarship. We are also thankful to all participants of the research survey, organizers of the poster session at ICGSE09, the reviewers of the questionnaire design and participants of the questionnaire piloting, especially Professor Pearl Brereton, Clive Jefferies, Ahmad Ryad Soobhany, John Butcher and James Rooney for providing assistance in the empirical study.

References

1. Ali-Babar, M., Verner, J., Nguyen, P.: Establishing and maintaining trust in software outsourcing relationships: An empirical investigation. The Journal of Systems and Software 80(2007), 1438–1449 (2007)
2. Op2i.com: Outsourcing Survey Report, 2008 (2008), http://www.op2i.com
3. Bush, A.A., Tiwana, A., Tsuji, H.: An Empirical Investigation of the Drivers of Software Outsourcing Decisions in Japanese Organizations. Information and Software Technology Journal (2007) (in press for publication)
4. McLaughlin, L.: An eye on India: Outsourcing debate continues. IEEE Software 20(3), 114–117 (2003)
5. Holmstrom, H., Conchúir, E.Ó., Ågerfalk, P., Fitzgerald, B.: Global Software Development Challenges: A Case Study on Temporal, Geographical and Socio-cultural Distance. In: International Conference on Global Software Engineering, pp. 3–11 (2006)
6. Damian, D., Izquierdo, L., Singer, J., Kwan, I.: Awareness in the Wild: Why Communication Breakdowns Occur. In: International Conference on Global Software Engineering, pp. 81–90 (2007)
7. Islam, S., Joarder, M.M.A., Houmb, S.H.: Goal and Risk Factors in Offshore Outsourced Software Development From Vendor's Viewpoint. In: IEEE International Conference on Global Software Engineering, ICGSE 2009, Limerick, Ireland, pp. 347–352 (2009)
8. Nguyen, P., Ali-baber, M., Verner, J.: Trust in software outsourcing relationships: an analysis of Vietnamese practitioners' views. In: EASE, pp. 10–19 (2006)
9. Oza, N.V., Hall, T., Rainer, A., Grey, S.G.: Trust in software outsourcing relationships: An empirical investigation of Indian software companies. Information & Software Technology 48(5), 345–354 (2006)

10. United-Nations: World Investment Report. The shift towards services, New York and Geneva (2004)
11. Palvia, S.C.J.: Global Outsourcing of IT and IT Enabled Services: Impact on US and Global Economy. Journal of Information Technology Case and Applications 5(3), 1–8 (2003)
12. Global Services (2009), `http://microsites.globalservicesmedia.com/research`
13. McCarthy, J.: 3.3 Million U.S. Services Jobs to Go Offshore, Forrester Research (2002)
14. Foote, D.: Recipe for offshore outsourcing failure: Ignore organization, people issues. ABA Banking Journal 96(9), 56–59 (2004)
15. Nam, K., Chaudhury, A., Rao, H.R., Rajagopalan, S.: A Two-Level Investigation of Information Systems Outsourcing. Communications of ACM 39(7), 36–44 (1996)
16. King, W.: Outsourcing becomes more complex. IT Strategy and Innovation - ISM Journal, 89–90 (2005)
17. Aubert, B., Dussault, S., Patry, M., Rivard, S.: Managing the risks of IT outsourcing (1998)
18. Blackley, J., Leach, J.: Security considerations in outsourcing IT services. Information Security Technical Report 1(3), 11–17 (1996)
19. Pyysiainen, J.: Building trust in global inter-organizational software development projects: problems and practices. In: International Conference on Software Engineering: Global Software Development Workshop (2001)
20. Gonzalez, R., Gasco, J., Llopis, J.: Information systems outsourcing risks: a study of large firms. Industrial management and data systems 105(1), 45–62 (2005)
21. Kobitzsch, W., Rombach, D., Feldmann, R.L.: Outsourcing in India. IEEE Software, 78–86 (March-April 2001)
22. Barthelemy, J.: The hidden cost of IT outsourcing. Sloan Management Review 42(3), 60–69 (2001)
23. Beaumont, N., Khan, Z.: A taxonomy of refereed outsourcing literature. Business and Economics. Monash University, Australia, working paper 22/05 (2005)
24. Oza, N.V.: An empirical evaluation of client - vendor relationships in Indian software outsourcing companies, PhD thesis, University of Hertfordshire, UK (2006)
25. Bradstreet, D.: Dun & Bradstreet's Barometer of Global Outsourcing (September 2000), `http://findarticles.com/p/articles/mi_m0EIN/is_2000_Feb_24/ai_59591405`
26. Holmstrom, H., Conchuir, E., Agerfalk, P., Fitzgerald, B.: The Irish Bridge: A case study of the dual role in offshore sourcing relationships. In: 27th International Conference on Information Systems, Milwaukee (2006)
27. Kitchenham, B., Pfleeger, S.L.: Principles of Survey Research, Parts 1 to 6. Software Engineering Notes (2001-2002)
28. Lethbridge, T.C.: Studying Software Engineers: Data Collection Techniques for Software Field Studies. Empirical Software Engineering 10, 311–341 (2005)
29. Lee, J.-N.: The impact of knowledge sharing, organizational capability and partnership quality on IS outsourcing success. Information & Management 38, 323–335 (2001)
30. Niazi, M., Wilson, D., Zowghi, D.: A Maturity Model for the Implementation of Software Process Improvement: An empirical study. Journal of Systems and Software 74(2), 155–172 (2005)
31. Khan, S.U., Niazi, M., Rashid, A.: Critical Success Factors for Offshore Software Development Outsourcing Vendors: A Systematic Literature Review. In: Fourth IEEE International Conference on Global Software Engineering, ICGSE 2009, Lero, Limerick, Ireland, pp. 207–216 (2009)

32. Khan, S.U., Niazi, M., Rashid, A.: Factors influencing clients in the selection of offshore software outsourcing vendors: an exploratory study using a systematic literature review. Journal of Systems and Software (submitted to 2010)
33. Black, T.: Doing qualitative research in the social sciences: An integrated approach to research design, measurement and statistics. Sage, London (1999)
34. Heeks, R., Krishna, S., Nicholson, B., Sahay, S.: Synching or Sinking: Global Software Outsourcing Relationships. IEEE Software, 54–60 (March/ April 2001)
35. Nauman, A.B., Aziz, R., Ishaq, A.F.M., Mohsin, M.: An analysis of capabilities of Pakistan as an offshore IT services outsourcing destination. In: Proceedings of IEEE 8th International INMIC, Multitopic Conference, December 2004, pp. 403–408 (2004)
36. Bhalla, A., Sodhi, M.S., Son, B.-G.: Is more IT offshoring better? An exploratory study of western companies offshoring to South East Asia. Journal of Operations Management 26, 322–335 (2008)
37. Hongxun, J., Honglu, D., Xiang, Y., Jun, S.: Research on IT outsourcing based on IT systems management. In: ACM International Conference Proceeding Series, vol. 156, pp. 533–537 (2006)
38. Martin, B.: An Introduction to Medical Statistics, 3rd edn. Oxford medical publications (2000)
39. Niazi, M., Wilson, D., Zowghi, D.: Critical Success Factors for Software Process Improvement: An Empirical Study. Software Process Improvement and Practice Journal 11(2), 193–211 (2006)
40. Niazi, M., Ali-babar, M.: De-motivators for software process improvement: An empirical investigation. Software Process Improvement and Practice Journal (Perspectives on Global Software Development: special issue on PROFES 2007) 13(3), 249–264 (2008)
41. Khan, S.U., Niazi, M., Rashid, A.: Critical Barriers for Offshore Software Development Outsourcing Vendors: A Systematic Literature Review. In: 16th IEEE Asia-Pacific Software Engineering Conference, APSEC 2009, Penang, Malaysia (2009)
42. Niazi, M., Ali-Babar, M.: Identifying High Perceived Value Practices of CMMI Level 2: An Empirical Study, in press for publications. Information and Software Technology (2009)
43. Kitchenham, B., Charters, C.: Guidelines for performing Systematic Literature Reviews in Software Engineering, Keele University and Durham University Joint Report, EBSE 2007-001 (2007)
44. Regnell, B., Runeson, P., Thelin, T.: Are the Perspectives Really Different-Further Experimentation on Scenario-Based Reading of Requirements. Empirical Software Engineering 5(4), 331–356 (2000)
45. Baddoo, N., Hall, T.: Motivators of software process improvement: An analysis of practitioner's views. Journal of Systems and Software (62), 85–96 (2002)
46. Beecham, S., Hall, T., Rainer, A.: Software Process Problems in Twelve Software Companies: An Empirical Analysis. Empirical software engineering 8, 7–42 (2003)

Appendix: Distribution of success factors based on Experts' experience

SA=Strongly Agree, A=Agree, SD=Strongly Disagree, D= Disagree, NS=Not sure

Success Factors	Junior (1-5) years experience (n=18)					Intermediate (6-10) years experience (n=19)					Senior (11+) years experience (n=16)					Chi-square Test (Linear-by-Linear) α = .05, df=1	
	SA	A	D	SD	NS	SA	A	D	SD	NS	SA	A	D	SD	NS	X^2	P
Cost-saving	11	7	0	0	0	13	4	1	0	1	8	6	2	0	0	.792	.373
Skilled Human Resource	6	10	2	0	0	9	10	0	0	0	4	11	1	0	0	.014	.906
Appropriate Infrastructure	12	3	1	0	2	10	4	4	0	1	10	3	2	0	1	.005	.943
Quality of Products and Services	9	8	1	0	0	9	7	3	0	0	5	6	4	1	0	3.489	.062
Efficient Outsourcing Relationships Management	7	5	1	1	4	10	6	1	0	2	5	7	2	1	1	.525	.469
Organisation's track record of successful projects	7	7	3	0	1	10	8	0	0	1	3	10	3	0	0	.017	.895
Efficient Project Management	9	2	5	0	2	10	6	2	0	1	9	4	1	0	2	.334	.563
Efficient Contract Management	7	4	2	0	5	7	7	3	0	2	6	4	5	0	1	.870	.351
SPI Certification (CMMI, ISO, etc.)	7	6	2	0	3	6	10	2	1	0	4	7	5	0	0	.225	.635
Knowledge of the Client's Language and Culture	3	7	6	0	2	5	9	2	1	2	9	3	2	1	1	2.206	.137
Timely Delivery of the Product	6	10	2	0	0	7	10	0	2	0	2	11	1	2	0	2.134	.144
Knowledge Exchange	2	10	4	1	1	3	5	5	2	4	2	6	6	1	1	.235	.628
Data Protection Laws	6	6	1	0	5	3	12	3	1	0	2	7	3	3	1	.013	.908
Financial Stability	3	10	3	0	2	4	9	2	1	3	2	9	3	1	1	.014	.907
Company Size (Large and Medium)	0	8	5	3	2	1	10	7	0	1	0	7	7	1	1	.436	.509
Risk Sharing	2	7	5	0	4	1	7	6	1	4	1	8	5	0	2	.221	.639
Pilot Project Performance	2	9	5	0	2	6	9	2	1	1	2	9	2	2	1	.046	.830
Vendor's Responsiveness	6	10	0	0	2	6	12	0	1	0	2	10	2	1	1	.763	.382
Political Stability	2	10	3	1	2	3	8	4	1	3	1	11	0	2	2	.026	.871
Overseas Offices	3	5	6	2	2	3	5	7	1	3	1	6	7	0	2	.006	.941
Soft Deliverable	3	9	4	1	1	3	11	2	0	3	4	6	4	0	2	.012	.911
Industry-University Linkage	2	4	7	3	2	3	4	5	2	5	2	6	5	2	1	.512	.474

Impact of Corporate and Organic Growth on Software Development

Natalja Nikitina and Mira Kajko-Mattsson

School of Information and Communication Technology,
Royal Institute of Technology, Stockholm, Sweden
{nikitina,mkm2}@kth.se

Abstract. Many small software companies grow in an organic and corporate manner. When growing, they have to make many organizational changes, mature their processes and adapt them to the rapidly growing customer base and product demands. This may be a challenging task bearing in mind the fact that software organizations lack guidelines for how to grow and mature their software processes in the context of business growth. In this paper, we map out one software company's corporate and organic growth in the course of its historical events and identify its impact on the company's software production processes and capabilities. We also list benefits, challenges, problems and lessons learned as experienced by the company studied. The paper rounds up with the suggestion for incorporating business growth elements into software process improvement models.

Keywords: business growth, process change, process improvement.

1 Introduction

Many of today's software start-up companies grow and expand at fast rate. They do it either in an *organic* and/or *corporate* manner where *organic* means growth in form of increased output and/or sales and *corporate* means growth by being merged with, acquired, or taken-over by some other company [3].

Companies encounter many challenges with respect to sustaining and furthering their business growth rate [15]. They have to think in the long term about business and its environment and quickly adapt to the changing or emerging markets. They have to manage their increasing customer portfolio, and grow their products in quick and strategic manner [15].

Organic business growth implies radical changes to the ways in which companies develop and maintain their software products. Many times start-up companies do not have any software processes in place. Or, if they have any, then the processes may not always be mature and scalable enough to meet the business growth.

Corporate business growth, on the other hand, often forces the acquired companies to adapt to their acquirers' process portfolios. This may be a big challenge bearing in mind the fact that many of these organizations may not be mature or willing enough to change their process cultures overnight [6], [17].

M. Ali Babar, M. Vierimaa, and M. Oivo (Eds.): PROFES 2010, LNCS 6156, pp. 161–175, 2010.
© Springer-Verlag Berlin Heidelberg 2010

Even if the majority of the software organizations encounter strong organic and corporate growth, little has been done about finding out their effects on software development processes [3], [14], [15]. Hence, today, we do not have much insight into how much software development processes are impacted by business growth. Neither do we have any guidelines aiding organizations in maturing their processes while growing their businesses. Current process maturity models and frameworks, such as ISO 15504, CMM and CMMI, are not directly helpful [1], [4], [5], [10]. They are focused on what to change to mature the process and not how to adapt it to business growth.

In this paper, we report on the effects of a corporate and organic business growth on the software development process over the course of its eleven-year history. Our goal is to study the impact of organic and corporate growth on software development and identify issues that might contribute to process improvement models. The organizational body under study is a product development group that has started as a small and independent start-up company. It has undergone two acquisitions and ended up as part of a multinational software corporation.

Due to the sensitivity of the results presented herein, we do not disclose the names of the companies involved. Hence, we are referring to the acquired company as *Virtual Software Group (VSG),* its product development group as *Virtual Computing Product* group (*VCP* group) and to its acquirers as *Software Infrastructure Group (SIG)* and *Enterprise Software Provider (ESP).*

The remainder of this paper is organized as follows. In Section 2, we report on our research method. In Section 3, we provide historical perspective of the changes within the company. In Section 4, we describe the impact of corporate and organic growth on software development. Finally, in Section 5, we present the conclusions of this study and list the lessons learned as experienced by the acquired company.

2 Research Method

In this section, we report on our research method. First, Section 2.1 describes research method steps and then Section 2.2 presents the questionnaire used in this study.

2.1 Method Steps

Our case study consisted of three following steps: (1) *Choice of the company*, (2) *Semi-structured Interviews*, and (3) *Data Analysis*. Below, we briefly describe them.

We started our research by choosing a company. We first identified a company which encountered business growth. We then contacted its employees and tried to confirm whether the company fit the aim of our research and was willing to participate in it. This was done by a few unstructured interviews and the reviews of the online information about the company, its business and business growth history.

As a second step, we chose five company employees. The choice was based on their employment length, knowledge of the organization and the experiences of the changes within the past eleven years. We interviewed two team leaders (software developers), a release manager, a system architect and a product manager. All of them have been working in the company for at least five and at most ten years. Hence, they were appropriate candidates for our study. When interviewing them, we used a semi-structured and open-ended questionnaire presented in Figure 1 and described in Section 2.2. The interviews were aimed to follow the history of software process evolution and identify challenges brought into it by the business growth.

I – Information about the company

I.1: What is the name of the company?
I.2: What is your position within the company?
I.3: What is the size of the company (in terms of people)?
  a. Whole company
  b. Development department
I.4: What does the company work with?
I.5: Which software development method does the company use?

II - Business growth

II.1: Has the company had any business growth?
II.2: Does the company encounter the continuous growth or is it coming in intervals?
  In case of the continuous growth:
  a. Since when has the company had a business growth?
  In case of growth in intervals:
  a. How many business growths has the company had?
  b. How frequently does the company encounter business growth?
  c. What is a business growth in the context of your company?
  d. For how long do the intervals of business growth last? (i) The last one, (ii) The former ones

III – People relation

III.1: Did the amount of employees change as a result of business growth(s)? If yes, how?
  a. Have the roles of the employees changed as a result of business growth(s)? If yes, how and why?
  b. Were new employees hired as a result of business growth(s)? If yes, how many and to which positions?
  c. Were the company employees fired as a result of business growth(s)? If yes, how many and why?
III.2: How has the hiring of new employees affected the software development process?
  a. What training techniques were introduced for newly employed?

IV – Influence of business growth on the software development process

IV.1: If the business growth was coming in intervals (Q. 2.2): For each business growth under discussion:
  a. What was the software development process like before the business growth? Did you use any software development method? Which one? Did you use it fully?
  b. What was the software development process like after the business growth? Did you use any software development method? Which one? Did you use it fully?
IV.2: Was the software development process affected by the business growth?
  a. If yes, how was the process changed and adapted to the growing team? What was done? Please list the changes to the process. For each change/adaptation:
    i. Please name the change:
    ii. Please describe the change: Was this change for better or for worse? Please comment on it.
    iii. How did this change impact the development process?
    iv. Was the change intentional or accidental? Was a change reactive or proactive?
    v. Why did each change occur? What caused the change?
    vi. Who initiated the change? Who supported the initiation?
    vii. What other challenges were met in order to implement the change?
  b. If not, how come that it was not changed?
IV.3: What challenges has the business growth created? Please list the challenges.
IV.4: Please list the problems you have met due to the business growth. For each problem:
  a. What was the problem?
  b. How did you address each problem?

V – The cause of business growth

V.1: What was/were the reason(s) of business growth(s)?
V.2: Was the development process scalable before business growth? Is it scalable now?
V.3: Were the development teams prepared for business growth when it happened? If yes, how?
V.4: Does the company have any business growth plan? If yes, please briefly describe what such a plan covers?
V.5: Do you think business growth will happen again/ continue in this company?
V.6: How is the company prepared for future business growth?
V.7: Does the company plan for business growth? In what way?

VI – Lessons learned from business growth

VI.1: What lessons did you learn from business growth?
VI.2: What is your suggestion to avoid negative impact of future business growth?
VI.3: What can be done to adapt the process for smooth future business growth?
VI.4: How can we keep or even improve the maturity of the process during the business growth? Is it possible?

Fig. 1. Interview Questionnaire

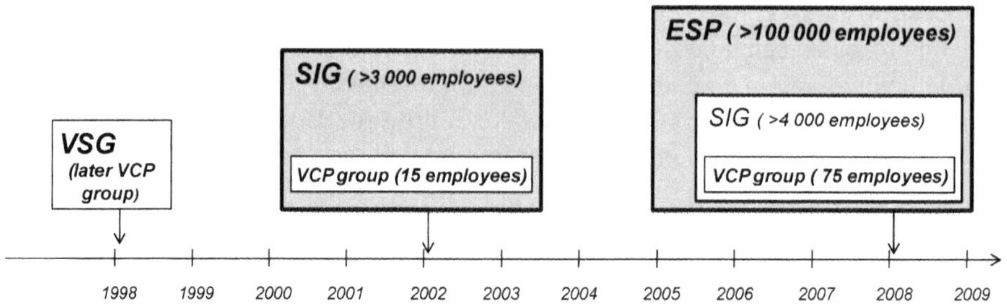

Fig. 2. Historical perspective of corporate growth of *VCP* group

Finally, we transcribed the interviews, analyzed the data using a hermeneutics approach and later confirmed the results of our analysis with the interviewees. In this step, we also identified and analyzed the changes made, benefits gained, problems encountered, challenges met and lessons learned from the business growth.

2.2 Interview Questionnaire

We designed our questionnaire with the purpose of inquiring about the business growth and its influence on the software development process. As can be seen in Figure 1, the questionnaire consists of six sections where each section is dedicated to a specific subject of interest. These are:

I. *Information about the company:* finding out information about the company, its size and development method.
II. *Business growth:* aiming at identifying the scope of business growth and its impact on the company.
III. *People relation:* inquiring about how the business growth has affected the employees of the company.
IV. *Influence of business growth on the software development process:* gathering information about changes done to the process due to the business growth. It also inquires about challenges and problems brought by the business growth.
V. *The cause of business growth:* asking about the reasons for the business growth and the company's state of readiness and preparation to meet future business growth.
VI. *Lessons learned from the business growth:* eliciting the lessons the interviewees have learned and their suggestions for process adaptation for achieving smooth business growth in the future.

3 Corporate and Organic Business Growth

The *Virtual Computing Product group* (*VCP* group) has undergone three major periods. As illustrated in Figure 2, we call them *VSG Period*, *SIG Period* and *ESP Period*. In the *VSG Period* occurring in the years 1998-2002, the *VCP* group was the only development team of a small company called *Virtual Software Group (VSG)*. By then, it developed a *Virtual Platform Product (VPP)*. In the *SIG Period* taking place in the years 2002-2008, *VSG* was acquired by *Software Infrastructure Group (SIG)*, an application infrastructure software company. Hence, *VSG*'s development team, the *VCP* group, became one of *SIG*'s development teams and continued to develop the *VPP* products. Finally, in the *ESP Period*, starting in 2008, *SIG* was acquired by *Enterprise Software Provider (ESP)*, a world leading multinational software corporation. As a result, the *VCP* group became a development group within *ESP* where it is still working on the same product line.

The acquisitions by *SIG* and *ESP* have led to substantial corporate growth of the *VCP* group. Besides this, the *VCP* group has undergone a continuous organic growth. This has strongly impacted its organization and processes. Below, we report on these two growths and their impact. The description is based on Figures 2 and 3.

3.1 Historical Perspective of the VSG Period

In the *VSG Period*, *VSG* was a small start up company. It developed initial versions of the *VPP* product for a few customers and users. At that time, the company had only a few developers, who created a small development team called *VCP* group. The team had no role specializations and no process in place. The developers were responsible for all kinds of business and engineering tasks ranging from management, development, to maintenance and support. All their processes were run in an ad hoc manner.

3.2 Historical Perspective of the SIG Period

In the *SIG Period*, *VSG* was acquired by *SIG*. Hence, the *VCP* group became a development group within *SIG* and continued working on the same product. As a result of corporate growth, right after the *SIG* acquisition, the *VPP* product's user base expanded and continued growing thereafter in an organic pace. The *VCP* group also expanded its product portfolio from one to four products altogether. For the first two years, it was managed by managers in the US to be then overtaken by local managers in Sweden in 2004.

Fig. 3. Historical changes of corporate and organic growth of *VCP* group

In 2002, the *VCP* group had no processes in place whereas *SIG* had many structured and rigid processes in place. Despite this, *SIG* did not force the *VCP* group to change their process cultures. All process introductions were optional. With time, however, due to the fact that *VCP's* customer base grew and consequently the number of developers, the *VCP* group felt forced to introduce some processes. To address the most urgent process problems, they started with the most critical processes such as support, product and release management. Below, we briefly elaborate on this.

Due to fast organic growth, in terms of rapidly growing customer base and increased number of customer demands, the company created a separate support team in the year of 2002. By 2003-2004, they created a two-tier support where a customer support team was placed on the front-end support level and developers on the back-end support level [7]. A few years after, several new customer support teams were created in other countries. Due to the fact that customer support teams are service oriented and are not primary involved in development, those teams are not included in the *VCP* group today.

By 2003, the *VCP* group in Stockholm had grown to 35 people. It was no longer possible for one person to know and manage the whole system. For this reason, the developers became organized into different vertical teams where one team specialized in one or a few product areas.

In the same year, corporate changes were done and the *VCP* group introduced product and release management processes and the role of a product manager. A few years after, these were enriched by introduction of risk management. The group also introduced a requirement management process and an engineering specification. Based on the requirement document, the engineering specification became the main product documentation to be created by developers.

By 2003-2004, the growing *VCP* group tried to introduce Waterfall process to define and structure development method. Development teams however were not satisfied with it. Hence, some tried to introduce Scrum in 2007. As a result, today, the development teams use an unspecified pseudo-agile process evolved from an intersection between Waterfall-like method and some Scrum practices such as Scrum meetings and iterations.

In 2003, the *VCP* group employed a writer whose role was to create and update support and technical documentation for all the *VPP* products. A few years later, a second writer joined the group, both situated in the US. During the last few years, three additional writers were employed in India.

As part of the corporate growth in 2005-2006, the *VCP* group took over *SIG*'s QA and testing process model which they then customized to their own needs. Initially, the QA and testing process model were centralized within the whole organization. They were not smoothly integrated with the *VCP* group' processes. To remedy this, the QA team got integrated with the development teams of *VCP* group.

By 2007, the *VCP* group had reached 75 employees including developers, QA engineers, architects and development managers, all situated in Sweden, 20 additional employees in the US, including QA engineers, managers and writers, and three writers in India. Two QA teams, one in Sweden and one in the US, grew in size and became too large to be managed easily. Since the most important competitive advantage of *VPP* was performance and the QA teams dedicated majority of their time to it, *SIG* split the QA unit into one QA and one performance testing team in Sweden, and two performance testing teams in the US.

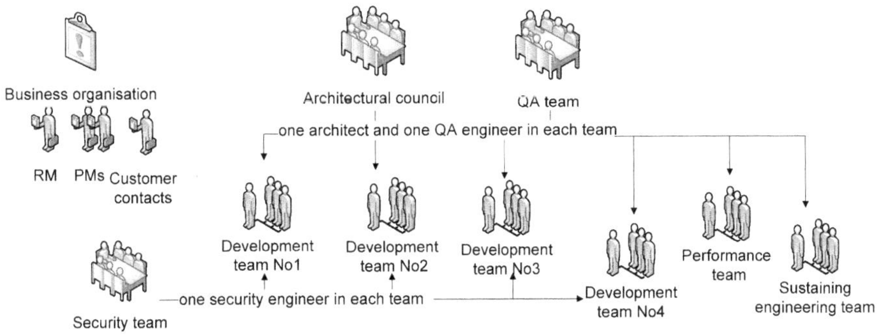

Fig. 4. Organizational structure of *VCP* group in Sweden

By that time, the product had also grown in size and complexity, and it was difficult to get an understanding of its overall system architecture. This led to a creation of an architectural council, which was responsible for creating an overall system architecture and for bringing consistency into the system structure by providing common standards and guidelines. It consisted of senior developers, who originally were part of *VSG* and who had deep knowledge of the product.

3.3 Historical Perspective of ESP Period

In 2008, *ESP* bought *SIG*. This, in turn, implied substantial changes to the *VCP* group. From the beginning, *ESP* decided that large part of its products should use *VPP* (the *VCP* group's product) as a base. Therefore, the amount of customers increased ten times comparing to the amount in 2005. The *VCP* group was not prepared for managing such a large customer base so abruptly.

Since *ESP* is a big company and has many processes in place, they enforced all their newly acquired organizations to follow their processes. All the processes were mandatory. Those who could not introduce them at once had to provide a roadmap on how and when they were going to implement them. The processes that were affected or introduced by this enforcement within the *VCP* group were support process, release management, problem management, risk management and security management.

After being bought by *ESP*, the *VCP* group continued organic growth; however the amount of developers in the group has not changed. Because of the recession and economical crisis, the company only hired the replacements of few *VCP* group members, who quit just after the acquisition. Therefore, the *VCP* group still consists of 75 engineers in Stockholm with a somewhat changed role portfolio including three product managers, a release manager, developers, architects, QA, performance, sustaining and security engineers (see Fig. 4). The group represents a standard research and development department and it is situated in Stockholm. Another 23 engineers involved in developing the products' line are situated in the US and India. Those are performance testing teams and a documentation team.

3.4 Changes

The above presented course of events shows that the *VCP* group has experienced many changes due to the organic and corporate growth. These changes affect organizational concepts such as roles, market, organization and processes in the following ways:

- *Roles*: The role portfolio of the *VCP* group has been substantially changed for the last eleven years. In 1998-1999, during the *VSG Period*, the *VCP* group did not have any clearly defined roles apart from developers and managers. Since 2002, the *VCP* group has been continuously introducing new roles covering various management and development responsibilities.
- *Market changes*: The corporate growth has helped the *VCP* group to find and assure the niche of its product on the market. Today, the *VPP* products are widely used worldwide.
- *Organization*: The acquisitions and organic growth have stimulated substantial changes to the *VCP* group's organizational infrastructure. The group has evolved from one team to nine teams. As shown in Fig. 4, these are four development teams, and one QA, one performance, one architecture, one security and one sustaining engineering team.
- *Processes*: Until 2002, the *VCP* group did not have any process in place. Substantial expansion and acquisitions of the *VCP* group by *SIG* and *ESP* stimulated it to introduce nine processes supporting their development and operation. These are customer support, QA, testing, problem management, requirement management, release management, sustaining engineering, risk management and security management processes.

4 The Impact of Corporate and Organic Growth

The business growth has brought many changes to the process resulting in many benefits, problems and challenges. Organic growth stimulated the *VCP* group to add changes to their organizational structure and to mature their development processes. The corporate growth, on the other hand, enforced some process steps and provided support for the *VCP* group for scaling up their processes. Due to the interdependencies and relation between organic and corporate growths, it is difficult to separate impacts of each growth. Later on, however, we will make an attempt to address benefits, problems and challenges of the two growth types. Before proceeding with their presentation, we would like to clarify our understanding of the terms problems and challenges.

In this paper, we define a problem as an issue or difficulty that needs to be resolved and a challenge as a difficulty of acting upon and dealing with some problem. The problems and challenges described in this paper are interrelated. Some problems are input to some challenges and vice versa. Hence, it is difficult to draw any clear lines of relationship. However, we try to identify the most obvious ones when it is relevant.

4.1 Benefits of Corporate and Organic Growth

Corporate and organic growth at the *VCP* group has lead to five benefits. These concern better utilization of development skills and resources, better control of corrective maintenance and risks, and improved product quality and its quality management. Below, we report on them.

Benefit 1: *Better utilization of development skills and resources:* In the *VSG Period*, the *VCP* group consisted of a few developers. The roles of these developers corresponded to some form of a "*skilled generalist*", a role developing a system from top to bottom. This approach was effective as long as the system, the development team and the customer base were small and easy to manage. With time, however, the developers experienced that they were too much burdened with increasing customer demands and many strongly diversified and time consuming engineering tasks. For this reason, the *VCP* group gradually introduced different roles, thus freeing developers from a broad range of strongly diversified responsibilities and allowing them to become more focused on the clearly specialized ones. In their opinion, specialization of roles has led to more effective utilization of human resources.

Benefit 2: *Better control of the corrective maintenance process:* During the *VSG Period*, software problems were reported and solved in an ad hoc manner. They were not recorded in a structured way, their severity and priority were not analyzed and some critical problems could be left unattended. This has lead to many difficulties. For this reason, *SIG* and *ESP* continuously improved the corrective maintenance process by mainly introducing a two-tier support infrastructure. This has relieved developers from support tasks and from solving minor problems. Instead, they could spend all their time on system development, enhancements and resolution of critical problems. In addition, the *VCP* group introduced problem management process, testing and QA process, and supporting tools. All this has led to better control over the corrective maintenance process and more predictable release plans.

Benefit 3: *Improved quality of the product:* During the *VSG period*, the *VCP* group had a simple testing process, performed by the developers. The company focused on feature development rather than on product stability and system quality. Therefore, the first versions of the product were unstable and customers reported many problems on them. Later on, *SIG* introduced QA and testing infrastructure and new testing roles to the *VCP* group. This has resulted in more quality checks, tests and code reviews. As a result, the *VPP* products today are stable enough to be used as a base for large part of *ESP* products.

Benefit 4: *Better control over the risks:* At the beginning of the *SIG Period*, the *VCP* group did not have risk management process in place. With time, however, due to high product complexity and its wide customer and usage profiles, the *VCP* group realized that they needed to have the process to track and mitigate the risks. They felt that it was important because a delay of major releases could cause bigger problems for the *VPP* products and other products that depended on it. As a result, today, project risks are not only identified at the beginning of each release, but also continuously analyzed, tracked and monitored throughout the whole release cycle.

Benefit 5: *Automated testing and QA environment:* During the *VSG Period* and at the beginning of the *SIG Period*, testing process suffered due to lack of automated testing environment. To support developers, the QA group was created and testing and QA infrastructure were introduced and automated. This saved substantial testing effort and made the code base more robust against faults introduced by new code.

4.2 Problems of Corporate and Organic Growth

Business growth has also brought some problems to the development. These concern lack of a unified development process, loss of productive time, extensions of processes with unnecessary steps and various communication problems. Below, we report on them.

Problem 1: *Lack of a unified development process in the VCP group:* The *VCP* group has not defined and does not follow any unified development process. This, however, was not considered to be a problem when having very few software development teams. Growing in the amount of developers and teams, the *VCP* group has still not achieved any consensus on what process to use and in what context. As a base, the group uses an unspecified pseudo-agile process based on Waterfall-like method and some Scrum practices. The method is supplemented with Scrum and XP techniques in different manner by different teams. As a result, different development teams use different techniques and methods. Also, the involvement of product owners varies among the teams. Some teams have short iterations, frequent demonstrations and meetings with the product owner, whereas other teams work on one specification for half a year and only demonstrate the end product. This contributes to inefficient communication between the teams, and adds to some of the problems described below.

Problem 2: *Loss of productive time due to corporately mandated environmental changes:* Due to the corporate growth and acquirer's company policies, the *VCP* group was forced to change its technical and tool environment concerning customer relationship management tool and hypervisors. All these changes required substantial adaptation effort thus leading to strongly decreased productivity. For instance, it took nearly a year for the group to change to a new hypervisor.

Problem 3: *Misunderstandings and insufficient communication between developers and QA engineers:* When initially created, due to the corporate change, QA was a central organ within the organization. The developers' responsibilities were to develop system code and QA engineers' responsibilities, on the other hand, were to assure that the system code was of high quality. In order to maintain system quality, QA engineers added many checks and processes, which developers had to follow. The centralization of QA and traditional software development resulted in a communication and collaboration problem. Both groups had difficulties in working towards common goals.

The communication problem was solved by adapting an agile technique and by decentralizing QA (one QA engineer became part of a development team, see Fig. 4). Today, QA engineers are integrated with development teams in an agile manner. They perform QA and testing activities already during the implementation process and they guide development decisions to assure that the final product is testable. Thanks to this change, many of the testing problems are solved earlier in the process.

Problem 4: *Unnecessary or redundant process steps:* Development processes at *VCP* group have continuously evolved and matured. At the same time, more and more unnecessary or redundant process steps were added to the development process. This was because the new processes and standards have been continuously enforced; however, they have been seldom reviewed or analyzed. During the last few years, this problem was partially addressed and some process steps were removed from the development process. Still, however, many unnecessary and redundant steps remain.

4.3 Challenges of Corporate and Organic Growth

Corporate and organic growth has brought many challenges to the development process. These concern tackling growing product complexity and quality, managing maintenance, communication, scalability, and delivery, management of inertia to process changes and upkeep of developer creativity. Below, we report on them.

Challenge 1: *Challenge to manage growing complexity:* During the last ten years, due to the substantially increased customer demands, the product has grown in size and complexity. The number of developers and development teams has grown and the tacit knowledge of the product has become distributed among many developers. All this has led to difficulties to manage and maintain consistency and the growing system complexity. In order to address this difficulty, an architectural council has been created whose role is to bring structure and consistency into the architecture and code.

Challenge 2: *Evolution and maintenance challenge:* Today, developers have to be very careful when making new changes to the system. Because it is already used by many customers and products, the developers have to make sure that the changes do not introduce new problems. Such problems may have substantial ripple effect on the products reliant on the *VPP* products. For this reason, developers put extra effort into studying all complex dependencies both within the product and its environment.

Challenge 3: *Challenge to improve system quality:* The complex system is hard to test. Its testing is challenged mostly by the fact that the product is used both as an independent product and as a base for a large number of other products. Furthermore, customers often use the product in the ways that have not been initially intended for and specified. This has led to an increase of many different problems generating many different testing scenarios and tests. Since the QA resources have not increased, it has become very challenging to maintain satisfactory product quality.

Challenge 4: *Communication challenge:* The bigger the system, the more developers are developing it and the more communication is required [2], [13], [18], [19]. Since the *VCP* group does not have any unified development process (Problem 1) or any inter-team communication pattern, the communication has become a challenging task. Especially challenging is the communication between employees in Sweden and the US, due to the physical distance and time difference.

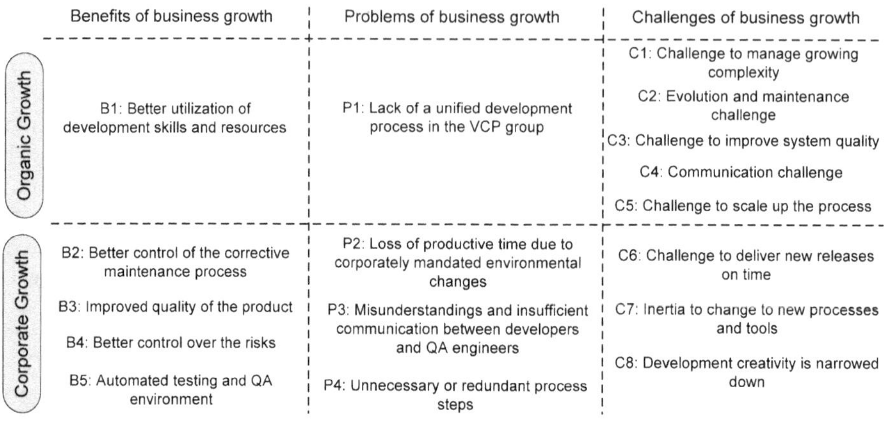

Fig. 5. Impact of corporate and organic growths on the *VCP* group's development processes

Challenge 5: *Challenge to scale up the process:* The process was not scalable during the *VSG Period*. There was no sufficient organizational structure or distribution of responsibilities, which contributed to the communication challenge (Challenge 4). The introduction of processes in the *SIG Period* somewhat improved the scalability problem. The scalability, however, was hampered by solutions such as, for instance, centralized QA and testing at those times. Even, if they have become decentralized, the process at the *VCP* group is still not fully scalable, due to the reasons such as lack of a uniform development process in the group.

Challenge 6: *Challenge to deliver new releases on time:* After *ESP* acquisition, other *ESP* products have become dependent on *VPP*. As a result, *ESP* imposed corporate release schedules. The release scope and time cannot be changed once it is communicated to other development units. This makes the developers of *VCP* group feel challenged to deliver all the desired features within the specified deadline.

Challenge 7: *Inertia to change to new processes and tools:* During the corporate growth, many changes were forced on the *VCP* group. Even if everyone agreed on process or tool related problems, not everyone agreed on their proposed solutions. The *VCP* group was not involved in deciding whether and which processes or tools to implement. Instead, the tools and processes were imposed on them. This has led to a strong resistance to most of the process changes and tools.

Challenge 8: *Development creativity is narrowed down:* By adding more and more corporately mandated processes to the software development, the *VCP* group started to narrow down and loose its development creativity. The processes were added as a solution to every process problem. However, they did not always improve the process but often made it more rigid thus making the development teams less flexible and creative. Because of the limited opportunity to utilize their creativity and other reasons, several employees quit the *VCP* group right after it got acquired by *ESP*.

5 Conclusions and Lessons Learned

In this paper, we have presented a historical perspective of organic and corporate business growth and identified its impact on the software organization and its development process. As summarized in Figure 5, both organic and corporate growths have made the company experience benefits, problems and challenges, which have led to the following lessons learned:

- *Lesson 1*: *Create a support team early in the process if you wish to improve your productivity*. Otherwise developers will be overloaded with support related tasks instead of developing new features.
- *Lesson 2*: *Implement a communication pattern on an intra and inter organizational level*. Otherwise, you will arrive at spending time on ineffective communication instead of business value creation. The importance of communication pattern in a growing business has been reported in [15]. Its significance has also been recognized in distributed development environments in [2], [12], [13], [18] and [19].
- *Lesson 3*: *Focus on quality from the very beginning*. It is only in this way you will be able to grow your customer base and product portfolio in a controlled manner. This lesson has been learned in all types of development contexts [9]. It is however very important for the organizations which grow fast. Not having a stable customer base and product portfolio and trying to put a foot in the very competitive market, the start-up companies may quickly be out of business due to product quality problems.
- *Lesson 4*: *Implement a uniform development process within a development group or unit*, however allow some team-adapted process variants and flexibility. This lesson has been learned in all types of distributed and non-distributed development contexts. From the perspective of growing organizations, it is important to have a control over the whole process without compromising on the developers' needs and well-being and without restraining their creativity. In this way, one may avoid personnel turnover, which may otherwise have a strong impact on companies' future business success.
- *Lesson 5*: *Reflect on and improve the processes on a continuous basis*. Only then, you will be able to adapt to the changing business environment and be capable of evaluating the existing and new process steps. This lesson has also been learned in [2], [6] and [17]. It has proven to minimize the pain of process change and to raise awareness of and spread the best practices along the organization.
- *Lesson 6*: *Plan for process changes and introduce them one by one*. Otherwise, you will not meet satisfactory process acceptance and your productivity rate may suffer. This lesson learned has also been reported in [6] and [16] where the benefit of introducing new processes in a careful stepwise manner was recognized.
- *Lesson 7*: *Educate on newly introduced processes or process steps*. This will help developers understand the reasons behind process changes and be more capable of providing feedback to process improvement. All this will further contribute to the prevention of process inertia.
- *Lesson 8*: *Involve developers in process changes*. It is only in this way they will get convinced to adapt to the new processes.

Lessons 7 and *8* have been recognized in many different contexts throughout recent decades both in agile and non-agile contexts [8], [11]. They are also important in the business growth context, where business growth is strongly dependent on how process improvement steps are accepted by the roles involved in them [15].

The *VCP* group has an intention to continue to grow their business and improve their processes. They would strongly benefit from guidelines on how to change software processes and organization when growing their business. Those guidelines should clarify the following:

- How to coordinate organizational changes with process changes in the context of organic and corporate growth?
- How to evolve inter and intra organizational communication while growing in an organic and corporate manner?
- How to introduce/enforce new or acquirer's processes with minimum resistance and disruption, in the context of corporate growth?
- How to adapt and tailor processes enforced by the acquirer to the needs of the team or organization in the context of corporate growth?
- How to keep processes slim but effective enough during organic and corporate business growth? How to evaluate and reflect on them in a continuous manner?
- How to communicate to and involve developers in newly introduced process changes?
- In what way should start-up companies grow in quality of their products while growing their businesses?
- How to smoothly implement a unified development process and still allow some team-adapted process variants and flexibility both in the context of organic and business growth?

The above-listed guidelines constitute a number of research questions that might be useful for the software community to explore. Putting the research questions into guidelines however, is not enough. In our opinion, organic and corporate business growth should be put as constituents in today's process improvement models. It is only in this way we may make sure that business growth will be considered in all types of process improvement contexts.

Acknowledgement

We would like to thank Mr. Marcus Lagergren, Mrs. Tuva Palm and Mr. Mathias Axelsson for their contribution into this paper, as well as Mr. Bengt Rutisson and Mr. Staffan Larsen for sharing their knowledge and experience.

References

1. CMMI Product Team: Capability Maturity Model Integration: CMMISM for Systems Engineering, Software Engineering, Integrated Product and Process Development, and Supplier Sourcing. Technical report, Software Engineering Institute (2002)

2. Drummond, B., Francis, J.: Yahoo! Distributed Agile: Notes from the World Over. In: Agile 2008 Conference, pp. 315–321. IEEE, Los Alamitos (2008)
3. Dalton, D., Dalton, C.: Corporate growth: Our advice for directors to buy "organic". J. Business Strategy 27(2), 5–7 (2006)
4. Glazer, H., Dalton, J., Anderson, D., Konrad, M., Shrum, S.: CMMI or Agile: Why Not Embrace Both. Technical note, Software Engineering Institute (2008)
5. International Organization for Standardization and International Electrotechnical Commission: ISO/IEC 15504: Information Technology-Software Process Assessment: Part 1- Part 9. Technical Report, ISO (1998)
6. Jochems, R., Rodgers, S.: The rollercoaster of required agile transition. In: 2007 Agile Conference, pp. 229–233. IEEE, Los Alamitos (2007)
7. Kajko-Mattsson, M.: Maturity Status within Front-End Support Organisations. In: 29th International Conference on Software Engineering, pp. 652–663. IEEE, Los Alamitos (2007)
8. Kajko-Mattsson, M., Nikitina, N.: From Knowing Nothing to Knowing a Little: Experiences Gained from Process Improvement in a Start-Up Company. In: 2008 International Conference on Computer Science and Software Engineering, pp. 617–621. IEEE, Los Alamitos (2008)
9. Khan, S.-A., Kajko-Mattsson, M., Tyrberg, T.: Comparing EM3: Predelivery Maintenance Model with its Industrial Correspondence. In: International Conference on Principles of Information Technology and Applications, pp. 573–582. IEEE, Los Alamitos (2009)
10. Masters, S., Bothwell, C.: CMM Appraisal Framework. Technical report, Software Engineering Institute (1995)
11. Nikitina, N., Kajko-Mattsson, M.: Historical perspective of two process transitions. In: The Fourth International Conference on Software Engineering Advances, pp. 289–298. IEEE, Los Alamitos (2009)
12. Paasivaara, M., Durasiewicz, S., Lassenius, C.: Distributed agile development: Using Scrum in a large project. In: The Third IEEE International Conference on Global Software Engineering, pp. 87–95. IEEE, Los Alamitos (2008)
13. Paasivaara, M., Durasiewicz, S., Lassenius, C.: Using Scrum in the Distributed Agile Development: A multiply case study. In: The Fourth IEEE International Conference on Global Software Engineering, pp. 195–204. IEEE, Los Alamitos (2009)
14. Page, A.S., Jones, R.C.: Business Growth Part 1: Fast Growth. J. Management Decision 28(1), 40–47 (1990)
15. Page, A.S., Jones, R.C.: Business Growth Part 2: Growth Management. J. Management Decision 28(3), 55–63 (1990)
16. Pinheiro, C., Maurer, F., Sillito, J.: Improving quality, one process change at a time. In: International Conference on Software Engineering, pp. 81–90. IEEE, Los Alamitos (2009)
17. Roche, G., Vaquesz-McCall, B.: The amazing team race – a team based on the agile adoption. In: 2009 Agile Conference, pp. 141–146. IEEE, Los Alamitos (2009)
18. Sutherland, J., Schoonheim, G., Kumar, N., Pandey, V., Vishal, S.: Fully distributed Scrum: Linear Scalability of Production between San Francisco and India. In: 2009 Agile Conference, pp. 339–344. IEEE, Los Alamitos (2008)
19. Turk, D., France, R., Rumpe, B.: Limitations of Agile Software Process. In: The Third International Conference on eXtreme Programming and Agile Processes in Software Engineering, pp. 43–46. IEEE, Los Alamitos (2002)

Prioritizing Countermeasures through the Countermeasure Method for Software Security (CM-Sec)

Dejan Baca[1,2] and Kai Petersen[1,2]

[1] Blekinge Institute of Technology Box 520,
SE-37225 Ronneby, Sweden
[2] Ericsson AB,
Sweden

Abstract. Software security is an important quality aspect of a software system. Therefore, it is important to integrate software security touch points throughout the development life-cycle. So far, the focus of touch points in the early phases has been on the identification of threats and attacks. In this paper we propose a novel method focusing on the end product by prioritizing countermeasures. The method provides an extension to attack trees and a process for identification and prioritization of countermeasures. The approach has been applied on an open-source application and showed that countermeasures could be identified. Furthermore, an analysis of the effectiveness and cost-efficiency of the countermeasures could be provided.

1 Introduction

Software security has recently become an important business case for companies to protect information availability [1]. Therefore, it is important to make security an integral part throughout the software development process which has been done through security touch-points introduced by Gary McGraw [2].During the development of software, bugs and vulnerabilities are unintentionally introduced into the end product. The cost of removing these vulnerabilities increases the further the product has reached in its development cycle. It is therefore preferable to detect them as early as possible in the development process. Vulnerabilities are introduced into two different phases of development, namely architecture/design and implementation. Implementation vulnerabilities such as buffer overflows are added to the source while the developer writes it. For these types of vulnerabilities, static code analysis tools can be used for early detection [3,4]. Design vulnerabilities on the other hand can be introduced into the product before there is any source code to examine. Early vulnerability prevention therefore has to focus in the architect of the product instead of the implementation, and hence security touch points have to be introduced early.

Different approaches have been introduced to detect threats/attacks on the system, namely risk analysis, and attack trees. Many if these methods are not

M. Ali Babar, M. Vierimaa, and M. Oivo (Eds.): PROFES 2010, LNCS 6156, pp. 176–190, 2010.
© Springer-Verlag Berlin Heidelberg 2010

specific for software development and some require UML diagrams or other information of the end product that might not be available (see e.g. [5]). This if often done with risk analysis and other threat modeling techniques. Attack tree are specifically proposed in the software development context and only require an understanding of the intended end product. Hence, they can be used as a security touch point early, even before implementation has been started. However, there are a few challenges related to the use of attack trees:

- From our experience of working with software security in industry we know that it can be difficult for non-security professionals to create an attack tree.
- The focus of attack trees and risk analysis is on identifying and prioritizing attacks, but not on the protection on the end-product (cf. [6,7,8]).
- The way of prioritizing the attacks is done by assigning estimated risks, which are dependent on many factors not known to the software developer (cf. [6]).

In response to these challenges we present a novel method to prioritize countermeasures to prevent security vulnerabilities, and by that focus the prioritization on the protection of the end-product. The Countermeasure Method for Software Security (CM-Sec) is an extension to attack trees. The method has the following features:

- It aids non security developers in identifying and prioritizing attacks and countermeasures by providing a process that guides them to the solution step by step. The introduction of why the system could be attacked and who could attack the system is used as a trigger to identify attacks and countermeasures.
- Instead of evaluating the risk of an attack for each individual attack ACM-Sec focuses on the prioritization of attacks through cumulative voting, i.e. a fixed number of points is distributed, attacks having a higher threat level receiving more points.

The method has been applied on an open-source system by the authors to demonstrate its applicability. The first author has good knowledge of the system as he is participating in the open source project developing it. The application showed that a broad range of countermeasures could be identified and linked to attacks, and that the distance of the criticality of the countermeasures can be consistently determined.

The remainder of the paper is structured as follows: Section 2 presents the background and related work. Thereafter, Section 3 presents the CM-Sec method. The application of the method on an open source system is illustrated in Section 4. Section 5 discusses the application of the method and Section 6 concludes the paper.

2 Background and Related Work

The related work focuses on approaches to identify and prioritize attacks on software systems early in development, i.e. before coding starts. The motivation for doing so is that the earlier problems in software development are discovered, the easier and less costly they are to fix [9].

A traditional way of identifying threats to a system would be a quantitative risk analysis like that described in Peltier [10]. The first step in the risk analysis would be to enumerate all assets and include their values for the system and then determine the threats that might exist for these values. The second step is to estimate the probability that a threat will occur and the damage it could cause. By combining these two values you get a priorities list of the top risks for the system. Determining what an asset is for a software product can be problematic, also immediately identifying threats to that assets often requires security expertise.

Attack trees were introduced by Bruce Schneier [11] and are structured by stating (1) the goal of the attack (e.g. obtaining a key); (2) what type of attack to be used (e.g. obtaining a private key from a user); and (3) how to implement the attack (e.g. break into the users machine and read the key from the disc) [12]. The implementations of the attack can be connected to conditions, e.g. one could choose either one of two or more implementation (OR) or several implementations are to be done together [12]. Attack trees have been applied on examples of software systems (cf. [13]). After identifying the attacks should be evaluated based on their risk, i.e. the likelihood of their occurrence multiplied with the damage done [6,7,8]. However, Buldas et al. [6] point out that the damage could be determined, but the risk of the occurrence is hard to estimate. Therefore, they propose to model the probability of the attack as a game for the attacker taking the following parameters into account: gains for the attacker, costs of the attack for the attacker, success probability, probability of getting caught, and penalty of getting caught. A potential drawback of the proposal by Buldas et al. is that the software developers need to have a good understanding of the motivations of the attacker. Furthermore, attackers are different based on each individual's attitude towards risk (see [14] for the distinction between risk averse vs. risk loving).

A process for managing risk is the Riskit method [15], which is used to continuously prioritize and control risks. The method prioritizes risk based on probability and utility loss. In the prioritization of risks and actions the process depends on the estimation of the probability for ranking purpose.

The related work shows that the solutions for addressing security issues prior to implementation have been focusing on the identication and prioritization of attacks and threats, and use this as input for the prioritization of actions (see e.g. [15]). However, few methods focus on the prioritization of actions. However, from a software development perspective it is of interest to know which actions should be taken to avoid the occurrence of attacks. In addition, all approaches focused on prioritizing risks based on the estimations of probability and damage. As pointed out by Buldas the estimation of probability and damage are hard, and as two parameters have to be estimated the likelyhood of unaccurate estimations is high. Hence, our method proposes to prioritize the countermeasures/actions using hierarchical cumulative voting.

3 Countermeasure Method for Software Security (CM-Sec)

The method consists of two parts, the first part is an extension of attack trees. The second is a process for conducting the analysis to arrive at the prioritized list of countermeasures. For the second part a tool has been implemented which supports practitioners in conducting the prioritization.

3.1 Countermeasure Graphs: An Extension to Attack Trees

Three extensions are made to attack trees, which only focus on attacks and describe conditions under which the attacks can occur. The extensions are made explicit in the meta model shown in Figure 1. The model consists of goals (why to attack), actors (who attacks), attacks (how to attack), and countermeasures (how to avoid attack), each described as a comment in the Figure.

The first extension is the relationship between goals, actors, and attacks. In attack trees there exists a 1..∗ relationship between the classes as they are trees, i.e. one goal is related to several attacks while one attack is only related to one goal. However, in practice an attack could be executed by several actors, or an actor could pursue more than one goal. Hence, these relationships were extended to ∗..∗.

The second extension is the inclusion of priorities assigned to goals, actors, attacks, and countermeasures. The priorities are an integer number assigned by the person conducting the prioritization. The prioritization method is further explained when presenting the process of creating the countermeasure graph (see Section 3.2).

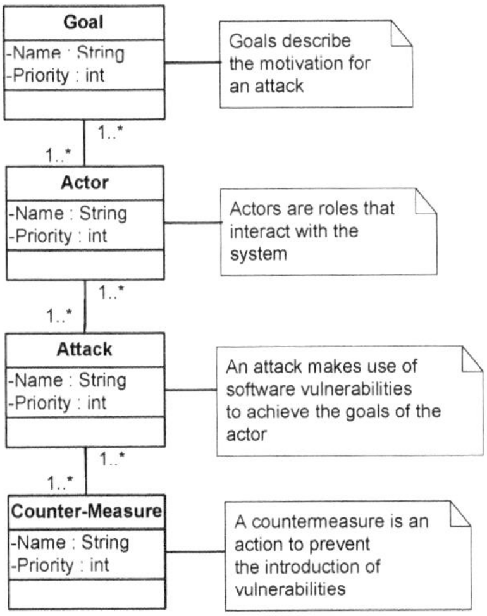

Fig. 1. Metamodel of the Extension to Attack Trees

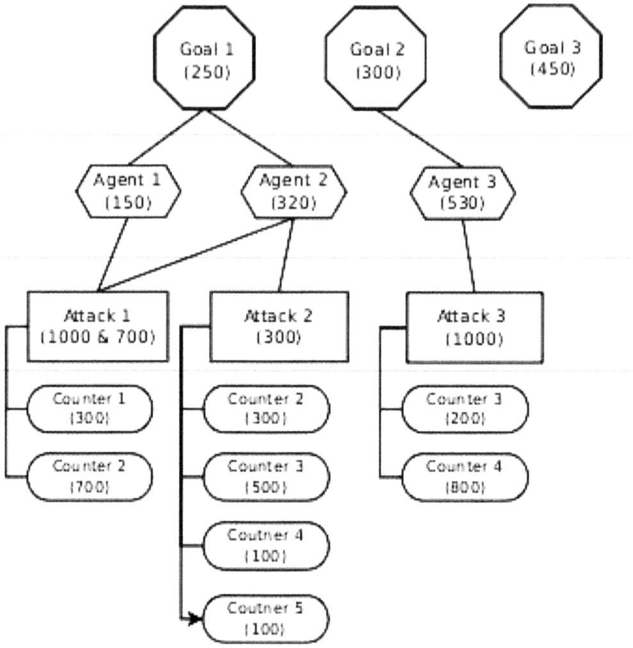

Fig. 2. Example of a Countermeasure Graph

The third extension is the inclusion of countermeasures which are actions by the developers to avoid vulnerabilities to be introduced into the software product in the first place. Hence, from an implementation perspective it is important to prioritize the countermeasures which is done by considering the priority of attacks, as well effort to realize the countermeasure. With the inclusion of countermeasures the protection of the end-product is supported.

An example of the countermeasure graph is shown in Figure 2. The nodes of the graph show the goals, actors, attacks, and countermeasures. The edges connect:

- Goals to agents if the agent pursues the goal.
- Agents to attacks if the agent is likely to be able to execute the attack.
- Attacks to countermeasures if the countermeasure is able to prevent the attack.

Furthermore, the priorities are assigned to each of the nodes. As can be seen agent two is higher prioritized than agent one, meaning that the agent is more likely to execute the attack and hence is a higher threat to the system. The agent has two attacks where attack one is prioritized higher as it does more damage to the system. The figure also shows the prioritization of the countermeasures, countermeasure two being the most efficient in preventing the attack. It is important to observe that the prioritization does not only allow to prioritize the order of attacks and countermeasures, but also shows the distance between them.

3.2 Process

Identify Goals, Actors, Attacks and Countermeasures. The purpose of the countermeasure graph is to determine what security countermeasures would be useful to include in the product and at the same time identify what countermeasures already exist. At the same time we determine what the greatest threat to the product is and how well we prevent them. To achieve this we need to discover what attacks can be made and how they are stopped, with traditional threat analysis or attack trees this process is direct and tries to immediately identify attacks. We instead divide the work in four distinct steps and then use hierarchical cumulative voting [16] to calculate the impact of every step.

Goals: The first step is to understand why anyone would attack the product and what their gain would be. This is often the same as the intended usage of the product and is used as a guideline to see the big picture.

Agents: Thereafter the *Agents* are identified. *Agents* are users, roles and software that interact with the products. Preferably the entire range of possible users should be presented in this step, form end users to administrators and outside software that interact with the product.

Attacks: Combining the *Agents* with a *Goal* we then look for *Attacks.* This step of the threat analysis is made easier because we have a more clear idea who and why the attack would accrue. We do not focus on if the attack would work, only if it is a possible route for the *Agent* to take to achieve his desired *Goal.*

Countermeasures: The final step is identifying what *Countermeasures* could be used to prevent an attack. A countermeasures can prevent one or more attacks.

Having identified the goals, agents, attacks, and countermeasures we are interested in which countermeasures are most effective.

Prioritization of Countermeasures. The attack graph consists of sets of goals, agents, attacks, and countermeasures. In the following we present the prioritization questions asked to the developers, and also provide further explanation of the voting on each hierarchy.

- Goals: To what degree would the achievement of the goal damage the system from either a cost or stability perspective? These are at first general goals that the different *Agents* might be interested in achieving. While the first iteration of the attack tree has general goals further iteration will focus the goals on specific requirement and features and are abuse cases based on them. The *Goals* are also connected to what *Agents* would be interested in them. Voting on the *Goals* is focused on the damage that specific goal would sustain on the product. Depending on the goal the damage could be economical or system stability.

- Agent: How large is the threat of the agent for the system? With the *Agents* we determine how threatening the different roles are to the product. Votes are based on how "scared" the product should be from that *Agent*. As an example a server product would consider end user more threatening then system administrators while privacy software might be the opposite.
- Attack: How likely is the success of the attack for the agent it belongs to? The attack voting is per *Agent* and determines how likely it is for that *Agent* to successed with the attack.
- Countermeasures: How efficient is the countermeasure in preventing an attack? When voting on *Countermeasurs* the focus is on their ability to prevent the attack compared to each other. In some cases two *Countermeasurs* might be equally effective, but one of them might aid in preventing other attacks as well. The attack graphs would then put higher priority on that *Countermeasur*.

Each of the sets is prioritized according to the rules of hierarchical cumulative voting (HCV) [16]. Cumulative voting in itself has the benefit of (1) that it is simple to do, and (2) the distance of importance between two items is visible. The voting is done by providing a number of points (e.g. 100 dollars) and then distributing them between a set of items. In HCV the prioritization is done on each level of the hierarchy (in this case goals, agents, attacks, and countermeasures).

Figure 3 shows the principle of HCV. The prioritization is done on all level, in this case on level 0 (L0) no prioritization is necessary as there is only one node on that level. On level H1 three nodes compete against each other for the points, i.e. nodes two, three, and four. On the lowest level H2 nodes within a group (H2.1, H2.2, and H2.3) compete. When the votes are completed the value of a node is calculated by multiplying the path of its parent nodes. For example, to know the value of node 11 we calculate the product of points assigned to node 11, 4, and 1. As there are different number of nodes within the groups the votes have to be adjusted by the number by the number of nodes in each group (cf. [16]).

In the case of our analysis an n to n relationship exist between nodes on different levels of the hierarchy. If an attack is related to several agents then this should raise the prioritized value of the attack. As an example we calculate the value of countermeasure two in Figure 2, which prevents two attacks that can be

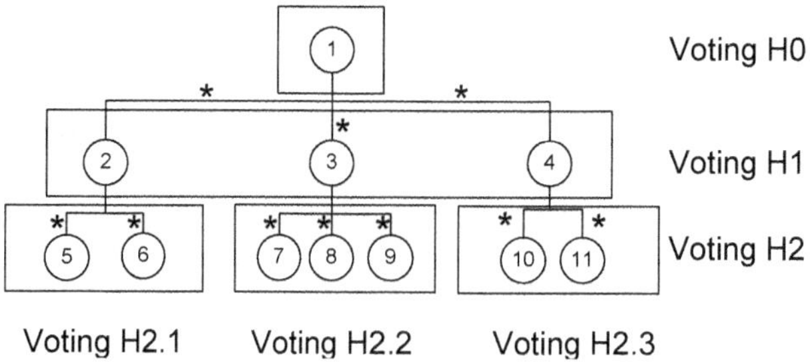

Fig. 3. Cumulative Hierarchical Voting

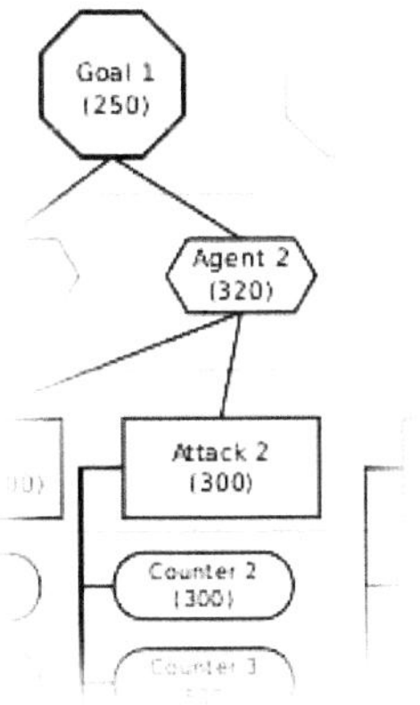

Fig. 4. Countermeasure 2 values from Attack 2

exploited by two different agents. First, we calculate the value for counter two ($C2_2$) related to attack 2 as shown in figure 4 (remaining zeros removed):

$$C2_2 = 250 * 320 * 300 * 300 = 7200 \tag{1}$$

Thereafter, counter two is calculated for attack 1 ($C2_1$). Because Attack 1 only has two countermeasuers its values need to be normalized to the countermeasuers from Attack 2 that has the highest number of coutnermeauers. As such, Countermeasure 2 with a value of 700 is normalized worth 280 points. Observe also that for Attack 1 two agents can perform the same attack, as seen in Figure 5. However, they do not provide the same risk, neither do they have the same likelihood of succeeding with the attack. They are therefore prioritised individually and then added to the equation individually. By doing so countermeasures that prevent several attacks especially attacks that are possible from multiple Agents are rated higher, and hence the threat level increases:

$$C2_1 = (250*150*1000*280(norm)) + (250*320*700*280(norm)) = 26100 \tag{2}$$

Overall, the value of the attack is the sum of $C2_1 + C2_2 = 33380$. The two are added because the countermeasure prevents two attacks and hence is more effective. Knowing the prioritization of the countermeasures with regard to effectiveness allows to combine them with costs in a matrix. The cost can either determined by HCV just as the prioritizations of if it possible use real man-hour estimations. The matrix, as seen in figure 8, shows different areas for the interaction of effectiveness and cost that can be used as a support in deciding which ountermeasures to focus on. The bottom-right area contains countermeasures that are effective and have low costs. Hence, these should be implemented first. The top-left area contains countermeasures that are ineffective and at the same time costly, hence they should be avoided. In the middle of the two areas

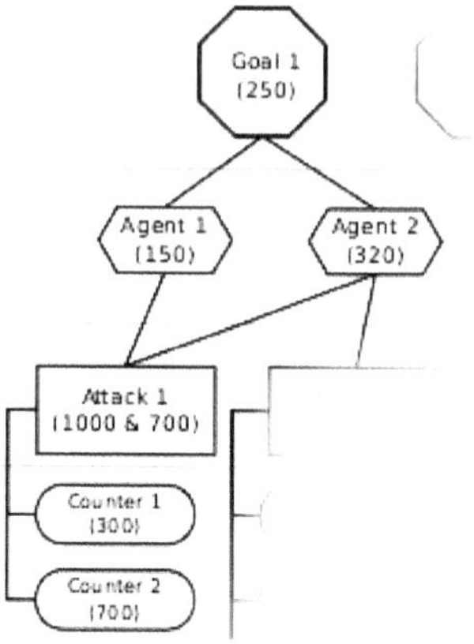

Fig. 5. Countermeasure 2 values from Attack 1, including two Agents

the borderline-cases are shown, which could be implemented if there are enough resources available.

4 Application

To demonstrate the method we applied it on an open source system, called Code 43.

4.1 System Description and Development Environment

We examined an open source product, which is an online first person shooter game. An overview of the architecture of the system is provided in Figure 6. In the center of the system is the master server providing server lists to clients, storing clients authentication information (e.g. authorization data), and client statistical data showing the performance of the players. Connected to the master server are the servers hosting the games. The clients are the ones logging into the servers that they receive through the server list provided by the master server. Because servers are setup by users they can not be trusted and information from them can be corrupt. Only the master server is in the trusted zone, all other actors in the system are outside this zone (servers are untrusted and clients are considered unsecured).

The game is a complex product consisting of 400,000 lines of code not including blanks or comments. This project has matured from other products, i.e. it is reusing source code. In total there has been 26 major active developers.

4.2 Result of Applying ACM-Sec

In this example we have identified four Agents that interact with the system. They have five distinct goals that can be archived via six attacks. From these six

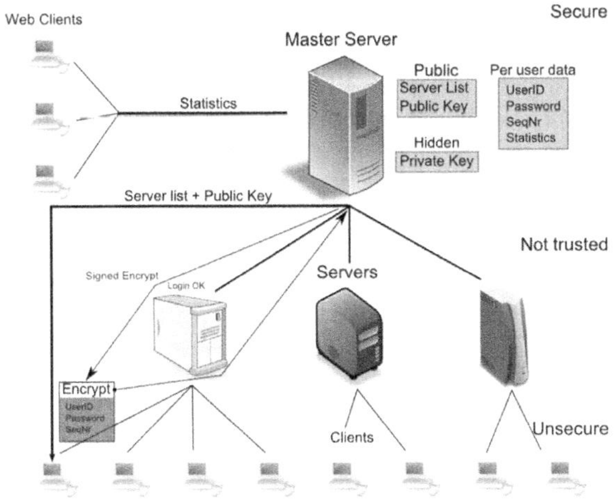

Fig. 6. Application Network Overview

attacks we devised eleven countermeasures that would in different effectiveness prevent one or several attacks. An overview of the countermeasure graph is shown in Figure 7. Inside the nodes the value assigned during the prioritization is shown. All values have been normalized according to the approach illustrated in Section 3.2. If there is more than one number in a node then this is for the different ages (see, for example, nodes *ask for password* and *fake statistics*).

In the following we provide the details for the goals, agents, attacks and countermeasures. This includes a detailed description of each of them.

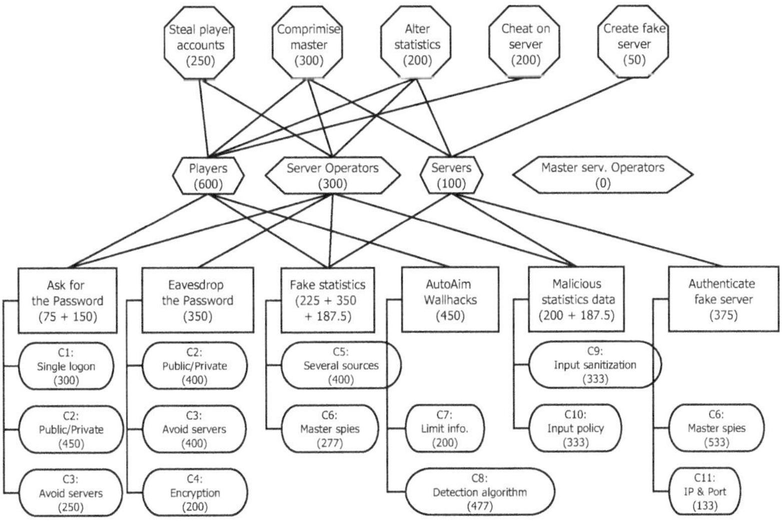

Fig. 7. Countermeasure Graph for Open Source Game

Table 1 provides an overview of the goals attackers might have. The majority of the goals are focused on cheating, like alter statistics and cheat on server. The motivation is either to steal an edge (steal an account), to gain an edge (client-site cheating), or to edit and modify ones edge (alter statistics). Thus, its primarily about the gaming experience.

Table 1. Goals and Their Damage

Goal	Description
G1: Steal user accounts	All clients have a private account that stores their statistics and aliases. Other users and server operative could steal their clients' identities.
G2: Compromise master	The master server is the only trusted source in the network architect. It is therefore a lucrative target for malicious users.
G3: Alter statistics	Clients compete with each other. All users are therefore interested in faking their success and cheat at their rankings.
G4: Cheat on server	Clients compete with each other. Client might try to alter the game rules to their benefit to gain an edge against other clients.
G5: Create fake server	Clients receive server lists from the trusted master. Servers that want more clients might create fake servers that all point to the same servers. Therefore showing up several times in the server list and creating a larger exposure to clients. This is unfair to other servers.

As can be seen in Figure 7 the players are the agent with the highest threat, the reason being that the goals are all related to the gaming experience. Server operators also can have an interest as sometimes they are players themselves or can be influenced by gamers (e.g. due to ties to other gamers).

Table 2. Agents and Their Threat

Agents	Description
A1: Players	These are clients and the end users of the system. They are also the least trusted source and present the greatest threat.
A2: Server Operators	Any client can create and add servers to the system. As such the servers can not be trusted and server operative can have the same motives as players.
A3: Servers	Being open source software the server can be altered to behave differently than the master server expects. It is therefore also a threat to the system.
A4: Master Server Operators	The operator of the master server has total command over the system. While he/she is an agent he/she does not provide any threats as the master server operator already can do whatever he/she wants.

An overview of the attacks is provided in Table 3. The attacks focus on either stealing other users accounts or cheating to improve ones own statistics. In both cases the threat does not only come from client but also from servers that are run by other clients. The administrators of these servers might have the same interest in other clients' account and statistics, just as other clients might.

The countermeasures which are the main outcome of this analysis are shown in Table 4. As can be seen in Figure 7 one countermeasure is able to prevent several attacks, which raises its value in the prioritization (see, for example, C2).

Table 3. Attacks

Attack	Description
At1: Ask for the password	Social engineering attack where either other clients, server operators or servers send fake login request to other users in an attempt to get the clients password.
At2: Eavesdrop the password	Servers can intercept the clients' login information as it passes thought the server to the master server. Servers also need to know that the client as passed the login procedure.
At3: Fake statistics	Clients and server can send any statistics to the master server and thus increasing their own ranking.
At4: AutoAim / Wallhacks	There exists several client side cheats where players use unauthorized software to gain an edge against their competitors.
At5: Malicious statistical data	A large source of user input to the master servers comes from statistical data. As such it is a big threat and way in for attackers. The attacks can vary from buffer overflows to injection attacks on the master servers database or webpage that presents the statistical data.
At6: Authenticate fake server	Any server can authenticate to the master server. They therefore can create multiple entries of their server in the master server list.

Table 4. Countermeasures

Agents	Description
C1: Single logon	Have a single point of login for the user during game start. With a specific login window that can not be replicated or requested by servers or other users.
C2: Public/ private	User public/ private keys signings for client identification.
C3: Avoid servers	Use direct client and master server communication for client authentication. However, servers still need verification from master that the client has authenticated.
C4: Encrypt	Encrypt the password with a master server public key before sending it. Would require a sequence number or timestamp to prevent replay attacks.
C5: Several sources	Verify statistical data by comparing it from several sources. From both client in the game and the server hosting the game.
C6: Master spies	User random samples and make the master join servers to verify that the servers are not duplicates and that the statistical information is correct.
C7: Limit info.	Limit the information sent to the client so automated processes can not aid the player unfairly. For example do not send other players location unless they are within the clients' field of view.
C8: Detection algorithm	Nonhuman actions can be detected by the server by analyzing the clients behavior and comparing it with normal dataset.
C9: Input sanitization	Cleaning all input strings and removing any harmful characters.
C10: Input policy	Having a strict input protocol that drops any incorrect input before it is processed for storage.
C11: IP and Port	Verify unique servers by examining both IP address and the destination Port. The same server can however run several games on different ports.

After having prioritized the effectiveness of the countermeasures using our prioritization approach introduced in Section 3.2 the countermeasures are combined with cost. Cost is the estimated effort required to implement them. The result is shown in Figure 8.

From this the following interpretations can be made: Countermeasures C2, C5, and C6 should be implemented as they are in the zone of countermeasures that are effective and have low cost. As can be seen in Figure 7 C2 affects the

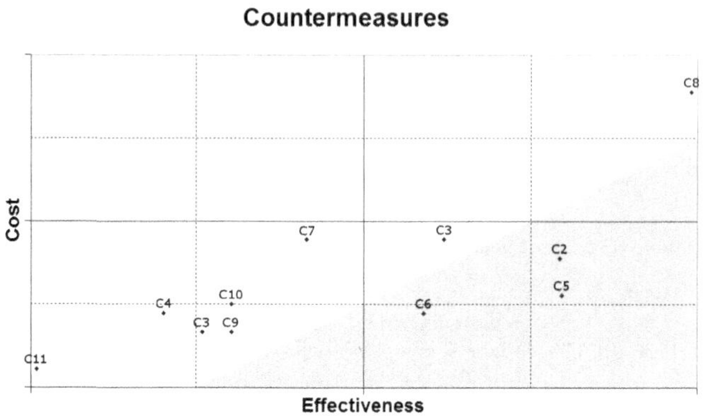

Fig. 8. Combination of Effectiveness with Cost

same attack as C3 and C4. Hence, the implementation of C2 would reduce the effectiveness of these two countermeasures. Countermeasure C8 is very costly to implemented, but is highly effective. As often project resources are limited this countermeasure should be taken into consideration for future releases, i.e. it should be handled as a requirement instead of a quick fix. Countermeasure C11 should not be implemented as it has very low effectiveness, i.e. its implementation does not make a difference. The Figure also shows that C9 and C10 are equally effective, but have different costs. Hence, the analysis also allows prioritization on cost whenever countermeasures are close to each other with regard to effectiveness. In this example we did not find any countermeasures with high cost and low effectiveness. However, in a different context such countermeasures might very well be identified.

5 Discussion

5.1 Practical Implications

Focus on End-product: We would like to stress that it is important to prioritize countermeasures as those are directly related to the end-product. That means they result in actions that could be taken early in the development process to avoid the introduction of vulnerabilities in the first place. Furthermore, it is important to mention that our method can be applied throughout the whole development life-cycle, independently of whether a new product is implemented, or an existing product is analyzed. When an existing product is analyzed it is important to take into account the countermeasures already implemented, this needs to be taken into account when doing the re-prioritization.

Problems of objectivity: Risk analysis and attack trees assume that developers have a good understanding of how an attacker would think as probabilities have to be estimated for many different factors (cf. [6]). Furthermore, it is hard for developers without security experience to identify attacks without guidance. Hence, the proposed methods addressed this problem in two different ways: First, the attack trees were extended by agents as this allows the developers to put themselves in the shoes of the attacker, knowing who the attacker might be. Secondly, a process is proposed that the developers can follow. Furthermore, the process focuses on comparing different attacks and countermeasures with each other. Having the comparison makes it easier to value the attacks and countermeasures.

Implementation of Triangulation: When conducting the prioritization we recommend that it should be done by several developers. The averages and variances of the points assigned provide an understanding of to what degree the developers agree on voting. If there is a large discrepancy the data will show the need for discussions and further investigations.

Tool support: To support the developers in the prioritization process we are developing a tool. The main feature of the tool is to (1) work in groups during the identification of the goals, agents, attacks, and countermeasures (shared canvas), (2) support in the prioritization. The support should be handled thorough sliders which allow easy re-priortization and show the impact of the change of one prioritization in real-time. This makes the method particularly suited for agile development as changes in the system can be very easily prioritized for each iteration.

5.2 Research Implications

The presented method focuses on countermeasures instead of only attacks and is novel with this regard. Hence, research needs to focus on testing the approach in an industrial application. We plan to conduct case studies in industry to evaluate the method with empirical data.

6 Conclusion

This paper presented a novel method to identify and prioritize countermeasures to increase the security of software systems. The method provides an extension to attack trees, as well as a process for the identification and prioritization of the countermeasures. We applied the method on an open source system, the application showing that several countermeasures could be identified. Furthermore, an analysis of the quantitative results is presented, showing that the proposed method has a potential in guiding managers in choosing the most effective and cost-efficient countermeasures. In future work empirical evaluations of the proposed method in industry are needed.

References

1. Frühwirth, C.: On business-driven it security management and mismatches between security requirements in firms, industry standards and research work. In: Proceedings of the 10th International Conference on Product-Focused Software Process Improvement (PROFES 2009), pp. 375–385 (2009)

2. McGraw, G.: Software security: building security in. Addison-Wesley, Upper Saddle River (2006)
3. Baca, D., Carlsson, B., Lundberg, L.: Evaluating the cost reduction of static code analysis for software security. In: Proceedings of the International Workshop on Programming Languages and Analysis for Security (PLAS 2008), pp. 79–88 (2008)
4. Baca, D., Petersen, K., Carlsson, B., Lundberg, L.: Static code analysis to detect software security vulnerabilities - does experience matter? In: Proceedings of the The 4th International Conference on Availability, Reliability and Security (ARES 2009), pp. 804–810 (2009)
5. Howard, M., LeBlanc, D.: Writing Secure Code. Microsoft Press, Redmond, Washington (2003)
6. Buldas, A., Laud, P., Priisalu, J., Saarepera, M., Willemson, J.: Rational choice of security measures via multi-parameter attack trees. In: López, J. (ed.) CRITIS 2006. LNCS, vol. 4347, pp. 235–248. Springer, Heidelberg (2006)
7. Moore, A.P., Ellison, R.J., Linger, R.C.: Attack modeling for information security and survivability. Technical Report Technical Report CMU/SEI-2001-TN-001, Software Engineering Institute (2001)
8. Mauw, S., Oostdijk, M.: Foundations of attack trees. In: Won, D.H., Kim, S. (eds.) ICISC 2005. LNCS, vol. 3935, pp. 186–198. Springer, Heidelberg (2006)
9. Damm, L.O., Lundberg, L., Wohlin, C.: Faults-slip-through - a concept for measuring the efficiency of the test process. Software Process: Improvement and Practice 11(1), 47–59 (2006)
10. Peltier, T.R.: Information security risk analysis. Auerbach, Boca Raton (2001)
11. Schneier, B.: Attack trees. Dr. Dobb's Journal 24(12), 21–29 (1999)
12. Viega, J., McGraw, G.: Building secure software: how to avoid security problems the right way. Addison-Wesley, Reading (2002)
13. Saini, V., Duan, Q., Paruchuri, V.: Threat modeling using attack trees. J. Comput. Small Coll. 23(4), 124–131 (2008)
14. Hederstierna, A.: Decisions Under Uncertainty - The Usefulness of an Indifference Method for Analysis of Dominance. EFI The Economic Research Institute, Stockholm School of Economics (1981)
15. Kontio, J.: Risk management in software development: A technology overview and the riskit method. In: Proceedings of the IEEE International Conference on Software Engineering (ICSE 1999), pp. 679–680 (1999)
16. Berander, P., Svahnberg, M.: Evaluating two ways of calculating priorities in requirements hierarchies - an experiment on hierarchical cumulative voting. Journal of Systems and Software 82(5), 836–850 (2009)

Feedback in Context: Supporting the Evolution of IT-Ecosystems

Kurt Schneider, Sebastian Meyer, Maximilian Peters, Felix Schliephacke, Jonas Mörschbach, and Lukas Aguirre

Software Engineering Group, Leibniz Universität Hannover
Welfengarten 1, 30167 Hannover, Germany
{Kurt.Schneider,Sebastian.Meyer}@inf.uni-hannover.de
{maximilian.peters,felix.schliephacke,
jonas.moerschbach}@stud.uni-hannover.de,
lukasaguirre@gmail.com

Abstract. IT ecosystems consist of dynamically interacting subsystems, components, and services containing software. Companies provide parts of IT ecosystems, e.g. for airports, train stations, and shopping malls. Due to the complex interaction of subsystems, overall behaviour cannot be completely anticipated or engineered. IT ecosystems constantly evolve by adapting to new user requirements and to changes in their environment. On-going improvement requires feedback from users. However, feedback is not easy to get. This paper presents an approach facilitating feedback in context. It is gathered by mobile devices like Smartphones. Effective support for evolution needs to cover (1) identifying the component or subsystem a user wants to address, (2) the ability to send feedback at very low effort and cost, and (3) support for interpreting incoming feedback. We present an architecture, a framework, and an application example to put stakeholder feedback into context. Contextualized feedback supports providers in driving the IT ecosystem evolution.

Keywords: IT ecosystem, feedback, context, architecture, improvement cycle.

1 Introduction: Evolution in IT Ecosystems

Today, many technical systems and devices interact with each other. In public places like airports, train stations, or universities, citizens become stakeholders of tightly interwoven systems. Their mobile phones can be used to make reservations, pay tickets, and receive confirmations from banks, ticket counters, and train information systems. Software controls subsystems and services, all of which are developed independently. They often depend on each other to provide higher level services. Subsystems interact with other subsystems, and with users. We call a system an "IT ecosystem", if those parts act and react autonomously or semi-autonomously [1]. This term is used as a metaphor. Bosch presents a taxonomy of ecosystems [2]. He starts from biological ecosystems and distinguishes human, social, and economic ecosystems. In particular, he is interested in software ecosystems: "A software ecosystem consists of the set of software solutions that enable, support and automate the activities and transactions by the actors

M. Ali Babar, M. Vierimaa, and M. Oivo (Eds.): PROFES 2010, LNCS 6156, pp. 191–205, 2010.
© Springer-Verlag Berlin Heidelberg 2010

in the associated social or business ecosystem and the organizations that provide these solutions." Our notion of *IT ecosystems* emphasizes emergent behaviour similar to an ecosystem in nature, where different species and animals interact autonomously.

Stakeholders perceive resulting system behaviour as a complex "smart environment". IT ecosystems are not designed as a whole; they rather evolve. Components and requirements change often, and new parts are added. Lentz and Bleizeffer state: "Modern IT ecosystems have evolved organically into complex systems of hardware, software, middleware components, applications, organizations, practices, application lifecycles, and job specializations." [3]. Changes in requirements are not easily recognized in IT ecosystems. Nevertheless, getting feedback on acceptance of their products or services is vital for providers to tune and improve their software. Traditional requirements engineering is not appropriate for software in an IT ecosystem for several reasons, as a comparison shows:

- ***In traditional, individual software projects***, requirements engineering has been a distinguishable project activity. Requirements could be elicited, analyzed, and validated before implementation started. Iterations and prototypes may be advisable, but requirements are still elicited before they are implemented. Usually, there is a defined user community. Interviews and workshops are the recommended approach for eliciting and validating requirements. There is a good chance to reproduce observations and problems. When a small system does not behave as expected or desired, users have a good chance to recognize the deviation. They will be able to identify the responsible software system and to contact the developers.
- ***In "IT ecosystems",*** new requirements and suggestions need to be identified while the system is already running. They result from on-going changes in environment, interaction, and user expectations. Stakeholder will recognize unforeseen or undesired system behaviour, but will often not be able to identify the responsible subsystem. Even if they could, it would take time to find provider contact information. In most cases, stakeholders may be angry or annoyed, but not provide feedback. From the provider perspective, opportunities for improvement are missed.

  Eliciting requirements proactively (instead of a reaction to a problem) is also difficult: Requirements of different user groups may diverge and will depend on context. Representative samples of users need to cover all groups and many contexts or conditions. It is expensive and ineffective to conduct interviews or workshops with such a large sample of users: Instead, companies use questionnaires, marketing studies and other tools to reach many (potential) customers [4], which is again a suboptimal solution:

  - Stakeholders are interrupted in their original tasks.
  - They will often not remember or report a problem - unless they encounter it just before they were asked.
  - Emergent effects may occur in an IT ecosystem with all its interacting subsystems. Some phenomena might not be reproducible in a laboratory setting or user test if the context and conditions differ.

- ***Our approach to "IT ecosystems":*** Focused feedback channels are made available to stakeholders *when and where* they encounter a situation or problem they consider worth reporting. Feedback can be given via Smartphone. By integrating this feedback into an improvement cycle, stakeholders engage in a community effort for improving their own environment – and for their own benefit.

The tools that are required to support this approach need to facilitate and guide the identification of appropriate addressee subsystems in the IT ecosystem. Whatever is "close" might be the responsible part. Therefore, we suggest using heuristics on geographical and logical proximity to identify addressees for feedback: Context can be captured implicitly and at minimal effort by locating users automatically. In addition, tailor-made mechanisms for pre-sorting feedback are proposed to facilitate analysis of feedback and fast improvement reaction.

Accordingly, this paper makes a three-fold contribution:

1. We present a technical concept that enables feedback in context. It contains an architecture and a framework to be used in different applications.
2. We argue how providers of subsystems can benefit from feedback in context. Empirical evaluation of this aspect (acceptance, benefit) is not covered in this paper.
3. We show the technical feasibility of our concept by implementing it using technology that is currently available and in wide use.

Section 2 presents the main assumptions and concepts that underlie our approach. Related work is described in Section 3. In Section 4, we explain the architecture of our distributed support framework. An implementation of our concepts is presented in Section 5. We illustrate our approach and framework by applying it to an example (Section 6). With these mechanisms at hand, user evaluation and optimization of heuristics can now be the next step. We discuss the current status and conclude.

2 Assumptions, Opportunities, and Concepts

A number of trends in modern technology and society have created a new situation. So far, the only way for unsatisfied customers of software and systems to complain was by calling or writing to providers. However, spending extra time and effort for identifying and contacting the responsible provider prevented most people from giving feedback. Why would someone spend time and money to report requirements? And why would providers care to collect complaints after they already sold a product?

Assumption: *Competitiveness in IT ecosystems depends on available feedback*
Providers of systems, software, or services compete with others in an IT ecosystem. For example, traffic providers like Deutsche Bahn (German railways) or airports will depend on embedded software that interacts with mobile phones, proprietary business systems, and the internet. Dissatisfied users may turn away from services and look for a similar service from a competitor. In order to keep customers, and to keep customers satisfied, providers will need to improve their processes and their software-based products while they are running. The ability to recognize problems and implement

suggestions for improvement quickly will be a key to success in IT ecosystems [4]. Stakeholders (i.e., subscribed and potential customers) could be encouraged to indicate their feedback and desires. Thus, an important new communication channel could be opened. Providers could play an active role in shaping their portion of the evolving IT ecosystem.

Opportunity: *Stakeholders are familiar with new and ubiquitous technology*
Our work tries to support the upcoming generation of stakeholders who are familiar with video-equipped mobile phones and multimedia handhelds. Two new developments encouraged us to explore ad-hoc video and light-weight feedback in context (as explained in more detail in [5]):

(1) The advent of inexpensive ubiquitous recording and sending devices. For example, digital cameras, Smartphones and flatrates are in wide use today.
(2) A generation of stakeholders who have grown up using Smartphones and PDAs voluntarily in their private life. Today's high school and university students represent that generation. They are current and future customers.

Many people recognize faults and weaknesses in public systems (e.g., airport displays, navigation or information services). We assume that many citizens will be *able* to use their familiar mobile devices for giving feedback. We further assume that many technology-affine citizens are *willing* to provide feedback if that causes no or marginal cost and effort. According to Davenport [6], incentives do not need to be financial. Stakeholders may be happy to provide short feedback to enhance the systems they use themselves. When stakeholders wait for a service or a system reaction (e.g. at an ATM), this is an opportunity to get feedback. There is a two-fold benefit: waiting time appears shorter, and stakeholders can express frustration.

Concept: *Context from object perspective*
Context is an important issue for feedback. Many context-aware systems consider the *context of users* and adapt system behaviour to the context observed. In Fig. 1, they would consider objects A and B to be in the context of stakeholder S (dashed line). Our perspective in this paper is slightly different: The geographical and logical position of a user in an IT ecosystem is identified along several dimensions (GPS, WLAN, Bluetooth etc.). When a user indicates the intention to give feedback, the multi-dimensional position of his or her Smartphone is used to identify those components of the IT ecosystem that are most likely to be the intended addressee of that feedback. Administrators can define under which circumstances a stakeholder is considered "close". There can be individual definitions for each object. Instead of asking: "What objects are in the context of S?" (dashed line in Fig. 1), we ask: "What objects would consider S to be close enough for giving useful feedback to them?"

In Fig. 1, S is in the context of B. Object A has defined a narrow context and would not consider S close enough. If S triggers feedback, the Smartphone of S displays only B as a potential addressee, since only B considers S close enough. Please note that Fig. 1 maps the multiple context dimensions to a geographical model of "closeness" for visual presentation.

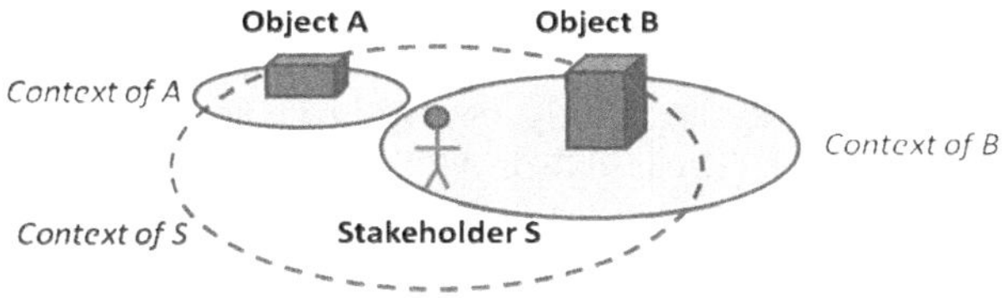

Fig. 1. Context depends on perspective: S is close enough to B, but not to A

Concept: *Context as a key to low-threshold feedback*
The main contribution of this paper is the use of multi-dimensional context of feedback for lowering effort and threshold to participate. As outlined in the introduction, we assume that proximity or closeness indicate appropriate addressees. Context is established by *physical* proximity to a real-world object (display, ticket machine, tree, car), by *logical* proximity to a Web site (as identified by the URL currently connected), or by being *in the range* of a bluetooth or Wi-Fi sender. We assume that "participating objects and systems" will be registered as potential feedback receivers. When a stakeholder wants to submit feedback, "close" objects are identified, and the stakeholder selects the best addressee for his or her feedback.

In [7] and [5], we suggest using ad-hoc video-clips for eliciting feedback and supporting requirements validation. In this paper, we will not discuss videos as a feedback medium, but focus on the framework and infrastructure for feedback.

3 Related Work

Non-traditional requirements engineering. In most traditional development environments, requirements are elicited early from stakeholders. Validating those requirements is an important prerequisite for good quality. Interviews and workshops are often used for bridging the gap between customers and software developers. Ethnographic approaches were recommended for observing and analyzing complex situation that are difficult to explore by asking stakeholders [8]. When a system is developed for an entire market rather than an individual customer, product management and market-driven requirements engineering [4] are more relevant than individual up-front interrogation. In that case, phases of building and phases of analysis and validation must take turns. Karlsson et al. [4] point to the drastically growing importance of feedback when an operational version of a system is supposed to be improved.

Fickas and Feather [9] state that requirements change over time. Requirements monitoring helps to automatically detect mismatches between the system functions and desired goals. Goals that have not been made explicit cannot be observed automatically. Our approach utilizes the users of the system directly to detect mismatches. User feedback can uncover mismatches between the system and their own personal goals - which may contribute to making tacit goals explicit.

Video clips are a straight-forward extension to the concepts presented in this paper. As discussed in [5], some researchers have investigated high-effort approaches in using videos [10]. For getting contextualized feedback from everyday situations, we advocate ad-hoc videos recorded on mobile devices by normal citizens. A video shows a concrete situation in context, which is an advantage over textual feedback. Audio explanations can provide the intention of recording this situation. In text, however, context must be described explicitly, or it will be ignored.

Zachos and Maiden [11], [12] used their ART SCENE system on mobile devices to guide stakeholders through scenarios. By following those scenarios in concrete and contextualized situations, misunderstandings and invalid assumptions can be detected. Again, this approach is directed towards requirements engineers and stakeholders who are willing to spend a considerable amount of time on requirements validation. Our approach is complementary in nature. It enables ordinary citizens to send a short, but contextualized feedback within a minute. If many people participate, even small pieces may help to get a picture.

Sitou and Spanfelner [13] propose a set of possible models to capture the usage context and users expectations. They argue for the **multi-dimensionality** of the context in order to be helpful for requirements engineering. Sitou and Spanfelner observe users while they interact with the system in order to elicit new or changed requirements. We do not observe users, but enable them to provide feedback in context.

Dey et.al. suggest a software infrastructure for **smart environments** [14]. They gather context data from sensors and use it as a substitute for user input to trigger defined processes. Again, we do not substitute users and their activity but enable them to give feedback actively. Context is used to identify possible addressees. Sutcliffe, Fickas and Sohlberg propose a method for requirements engineering that takes into account the context of a person as parameter for requirements [15]. Rather than eliciting requirements from feedback directly, we encourage and gather light-weight feedback. It indicates where more in-depth requirements engineering is needed.

The concept of **derivating implicit feedback** is a common task in information retrieval to obtain better results by adapting to the user's needs. Fox et al. described how implicit ratings like the number of returned result sets or the duration of a session can be used to get an indication of user satisfaction [16]. Another class of sources for implicit feedback is analyzing clicktrough data from web logs as described by Dupret and Liao [17]. These approaches rely on observing the user during the interaction with a system. Contrary to this, our approach is dedicated to an environment where observing the user is not an option, although recognizing the surroundings of the user is possible.

4 Architecture and Process of Feedback in IT Ecosystems

An IT ecosystem consists of several subsystems, components, and services. Not all parts of such a system will participate in soliciting feedback. For example, only the passenger-related parts of an airport may be in focus, while baggage handling, human resources, or runway services may not be taking feedback. Therefore, elements must register in order to qualify for feedback. We call registered elements "SmartObjects".

There will be many registered elements. Their representatives, SmartObjects, are managed by a central feedback management unit. Although that unit can be distributed for increased efficiency or robustness, we consider it *one central unit* from a logical perspective. It contains software to represent and manage all SmartObjects. Management includes features for defining new SmartObjects and for specifying the circumstances under which a given stakeholder will be considered "in the current context" of that SmartObject.

We postulate stakeholders to use a mobile device with several sensors for different dimensions of context, such as Bluetooth, Wi-Fi, GPS, or the URL of a website. When stakeholders want to provide feedback, they connect to the central unit. Context information provided by the mobile device is evaluated in the central unit. According to a matchmaking algorithm (as exemplified in Section 5), a list of SmartObjects is presented. They are potential addressees since the stakeholder is in their context. The final selection of the addressee SmartObject is made by the stakeholder. Depending on the definition of that SmartObject, a few questions may be displayed on the mobile device. Answers are sent back to the SmartObject as part of the feedback interaction.

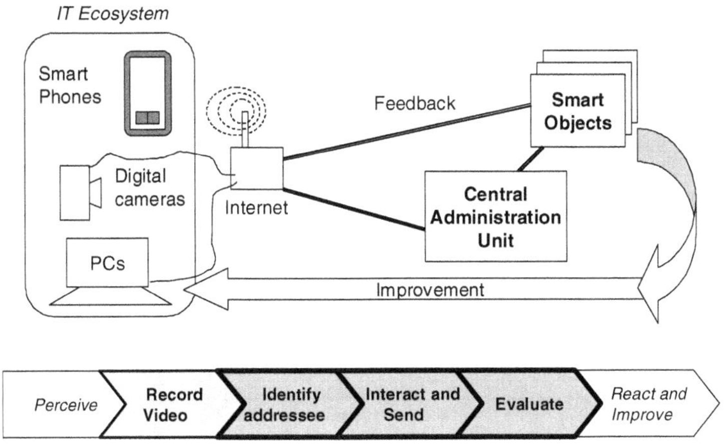

Fig. 2. Architecture of a framework and process for feedback in context

See Fig. 2 for an overview of the distributed architecture and the improvement process for feedback in context. Dark process steps are at the core of this paper, while video recording is mentioned only briefly. White process steps are required to close the improvement cycle, but they are beyond the scope of this paper: A stakeholder must perceive a trigger for giving feedback; and a service or software provider company must react to feedback. We do not discuss these steps here.

The architecture as sketched in Fig. 2 is characterized by several aspects:

- Feedback in context is achieved by a distributed framework of interacting parts: (1) The Central Administration Unit, (2) SmartObjects, and (3) software embedded in participating mobile device or digital cameras. This architecture reflects the distribution and flexibility of the IT ecosystem.
- Each of the three parts can be integrated with provider or mobile device systems. All parts together make up the *feedback in context* framework.
- There is a difference between a real-world object (subsystem, software, service) and the SmartObject representing it in the framework: Note that even software-free objects like restaurants or escalators can be represented by SmartObjects.

For example, a stakeholder can be specified to be in the context of a house whenever their GPS coordinates are within 100 m of each other.

- Feedback for all SmartObjects is first received by the central unit. Once the addressee SmartObject is identified, the feedback call is handled by the SmartObject software. It also collects data for evaluation.

Fig. 3 shows an overview sequence chart of the feedback interaction. While Fig. 2 is a static view of the architecture, Fig. 3 highlights dynamic aspects.

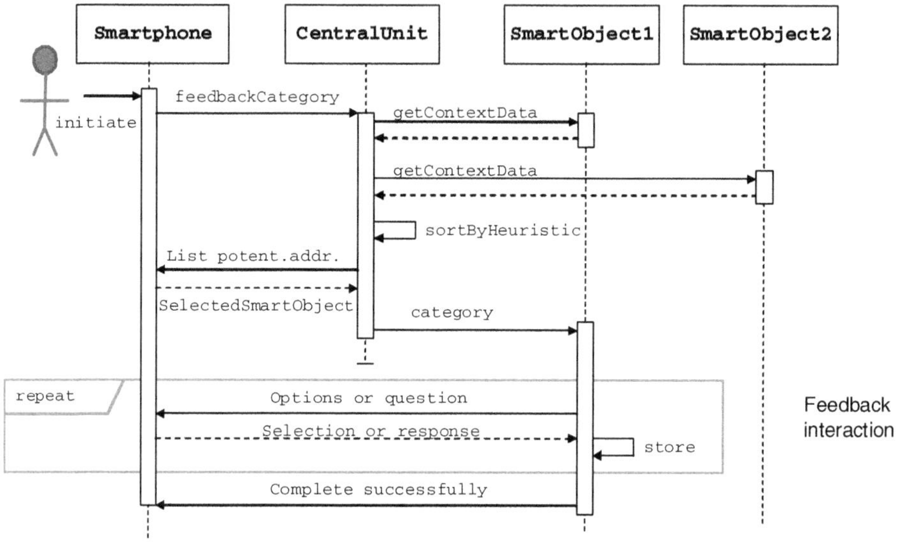

Fig. 3. Sequence chart of general interaction during feedback in context

Submitting feedback in context can vary in detail, but it always takes the steps sketched in Fig. 3:

1. Something triggers a stakeholder to send feedback, e.g. a problem concerning the behavior of a ticket machine or a software service.
2. The mobile device has software which connects it to the Central Unit.
3. According to the multi-dimensional context specifications, several SmartObjects may qualify as addressees ("within range of our service Wi-Fi" or "in 20m range of GPS…"). Their context definition is evaluated heuristically by the Central Unit.
4. The Central Unit determines a list of SmartObject "in context" and submits it to the user's Smartphone. This is the list of potential addressees.
5. The Smartphone displays the list, and the stakeholder selects the objects he or she wants to provide feedback to, e.g. SmartObject1 in Fig. 3.
6. The selected SmartObject may establish a short feedback interaction by presenting options for selection, or by asking simple questions.

5 Implementation of the ConTexter Framework

ConTexter is an implementation of the architecture and technical concepts described above. The ConTexter framework was implemented in four parts which can run on independent computer systems. They can be mapped to the architecture.

1. The GUI is used by the administrator to create, define, and edit SmartObjects. It is a Java Swing Application and works as a client that connects to the Central ConTexter Unit as well as to the SmartObjectAdministration (part of the Central Unit) via Java Remote Method Invocation (RMI).
2. The mobile part is used by the Smartphone user to submit feedback by mobile phone. We used a G1 Smartphone running the Android operating system.
3. The Central Unit identifies relevant SmartObjects by the context data provided by the G1. It returns information on how to connect to different SmartObjects.
4. The SmartObjectAdministration in the Central Unit provides an interface between the G1 Smartphone and selected SmartObjects.

Mobile ConTexter components use standard Android APIs. The accuracy of different modules of the G1 was a problem in general. In particular, the calculated GPS positions differ and depend on the current environment. To handle this problem, the administrator can define and adjust the range of tolerance with each SmartObject that has a GPS context. The actual context (via GPS, URL, WLAN, Bluetooth) is identified by a separate program thread to let the stakeholder use the GUI meanwhile.

URL context is retrieved by searching the browser's cache for the last visited website. URL context is only classified as relevant if the visit of this website was within the last three minutes.

The **SmartObjectAdministration** is necessary because the Android API does not provide any remote method invocation (RMI) functionality. We had to run the communication based on standard sockets communicating with our own protocol. In real applications, it is infeasible to assign each SmartObject a separate port. To avoid the need for one port per SmartObject the SmartObjectAdministration uses only one port and listens for incoming requests from the G1. It forwards its socket to the currently chosen SmartObject. Along the same lines, the SmartObjectAdministration is implemented as one process only, which dynamically instantiates SmartObjects on demand - instead of running one process per SmartObject permanently. This also opens the opportunity to run several SmartObjectAdministrations in parallel on different machines. This may be useful in a commercial setting where more than one software provider uses ConTexter feedback independently.

Heuristic for sorting potential addressee SmartObjects. When a call reaches the server, it calculates a preference value for each potential addressee (SmartObject). To determine the relevance of a SmartObject as potential addressee, a "context relevance index" is calculated. More relevant objects are displayed higher on the mobile phone SmartObject list. For each SmartObject: The administrator can adjust priorities of different context type via adjustment factors. A SmartObject's relevance is not only determined by its context alone, but also by the number of calls in which it was finally selected to be the intended addressee by the stakeholder. This heuristic is based on the assumption that an existing problem will trigger several feedbacks. Counting calls and finally selected SmartObjects is an element of learning and adaptation.

Many other heuristics can be formalized and compared: Time and environment conditions, even weather and history could be included. We decided to start simple and investigate refinements later, during usage evaluation.

In our implementation, we decided to implement the management of actual context data in a central database located in the Central Unit: The request for context data is implemented by database queries in the Central Unit instead of involving SmartObjects. Fig. 3 is a good representation of the logical interaction, while our implementation uses one of many performance optimizations one could imagine.

6 Example Case Study: UniImprove

Our concept of multi-dimensional context of feedback and the framework architecture are independent of any particular implementation. In the previous section, core aspects of our implementation in the ConTexter framework were presented. In this section, we illustrate the concepts introduced above.

In this example, Leibniz Universität Hannover is considered an IT ecosystem. Our scenario pretends the university board decided to start the UniImprove initiative. It uses ConTexter to guide improvement of university services, software, and other objects under university control. Enrolled students are invited to register (as stakeholders) at the Central ConTexter Unit. Registration is carried out over the internet. Fig. 4 illustrates some contexts and SmartObjects on a Google Earth map: The main gate in front of our university building (a) is specified by its GPS coordinates and by a Bluetooth sender (b). When students follow path (c), they reach the information display in the entrance hall, which is a registered SmartObject. Its context is defined by a Wi-Fi network (d). There is also the University Restaurant (e: GPS context and URL for menu) and the pathway to the next building (f: GPS). The pathway is included and represented by a SmartObject since there were many complaints about dirt and poor lighting in the past. Finally, there is a Bluetooth antenna of our department (g).

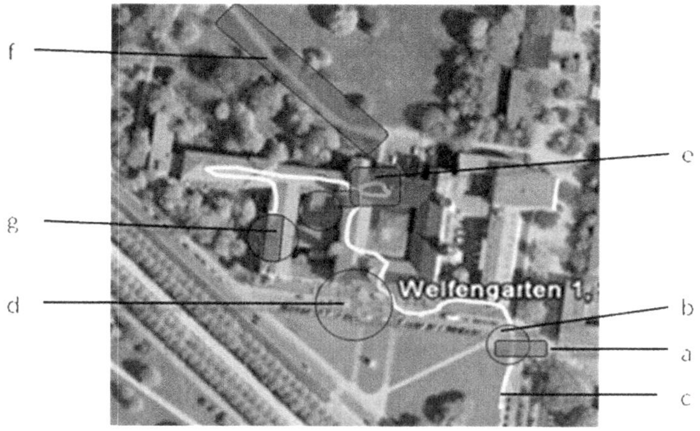

Fig. 4. Example of registered objects and context areas along a path at Universität Hannover

Fig. 4 is for illustration only. Real ranges and areas may differ, and there are far more registered objects in a real IT ecosystem. When a new *object* is registered at the Central ConTexter Unit, multi-dimensional context conditions are specified. A registered real object (e.g. tree, pathway, display, software, service) can be relevant when the stakeholder is "close" in any of the available dimensions. Fig. 5 shows a situation in which the online syllabus (list of offered classes) is being registered as "Syllabus" SmartObject. For demonstration purposes, URL, GPS, and Wi-Fi dimensions have already been specified. A specific Bluetooth connection is just being added. Whenever a stakeholder is in range of any of those context dimensions, the Syllabus will be considered a potential addressee of feedback.

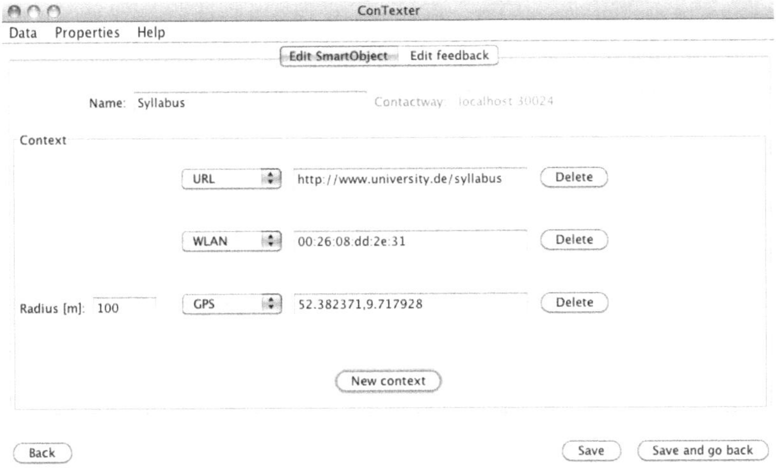

Fig. 5. Central ConTexter Unit during specification of multi-dimensional context

As soon as some SmartObjects have been registered, UniImprove can be used. When ConTexter is activated on a Smartphone, it asks for the category of feedback: complaint, compliment, or neutral remark. In Fig. 6 (left) a complaint is about to be made. In the next step (centre) all SmartObjects in the current context are displayed. In this example, the stakeholder selects Syllabus as the addressee. Since the SmartObject list was sorted by a heuristic, stakeholders make the final selection. Depending on the SmartObject definition, a few feedback options may be offered (right).

Fig. 6. Choosing category of feedback, final addressee, and submitting feedback

Stakeholders can check boxes and type free text if they wish. In an extended version of ConTexter, even previously recorded video clips can be attached to the feedback message. This short example covers most concepts introduced above. However, it illustrates only one possible implementation. We implemented other variants of the fine-grained interaction and heuristics. For example, the initial choice of a feedback category can be dropped. There is room for more optimizing heuristics. The goal is to present a reasonable list of possible addressees that most likely contains the object intended by the stakeholder.

7 Semi-automatic Feedback Evaluation

Soliciting feedback is an important yet difficult task. Submitted feedback must be used to the benefit of providers and stakeholders in order to justify the effort invested. In the introduction (Section 1), semi-automatic evaluation of submitted feedback was identified as one of the core opportunities. If many stakeholders participate, a large number of feedbacks will be received. By that time, a strategy for evaluation must be implemented and ready.

We present an example solution that supports simple pre-evaluation in many cases. As Fig. 7 shows in the realm of the UniImprove example, feedback options are defined in the Central ConTexter Unit when a SmartObject is registered and defined. So far, two compliments, a neutral type of feedback, and two types of complaints have been introduced. A third type of complaint ("confusing presentation") is just about being added. In all cases, stakeholders may include free text with their selections. During operation of the ConTexter framework, administrators and providers can use a similar interface to review the current status of feedbacks received. At this point, pre-defined options help classifying and visualizing the distribution of feedbacks.

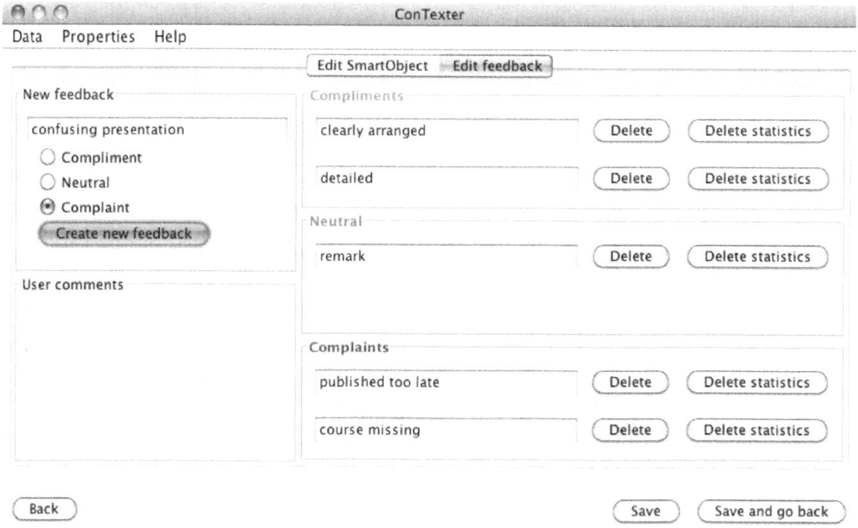

Fig. 7. Feedback options are defined during SmartObject registration

In Fig. 8, there is an overview of feedback types on the left, and a detailed view on all pre-defined options on the right. Free text annotations are shown in the lower left corner. In a more detailed view, original feedbacks (selected options with free text) can be seen for fine-grained analysis. In Fig. 8, two complaints refer to the title of a missing course.

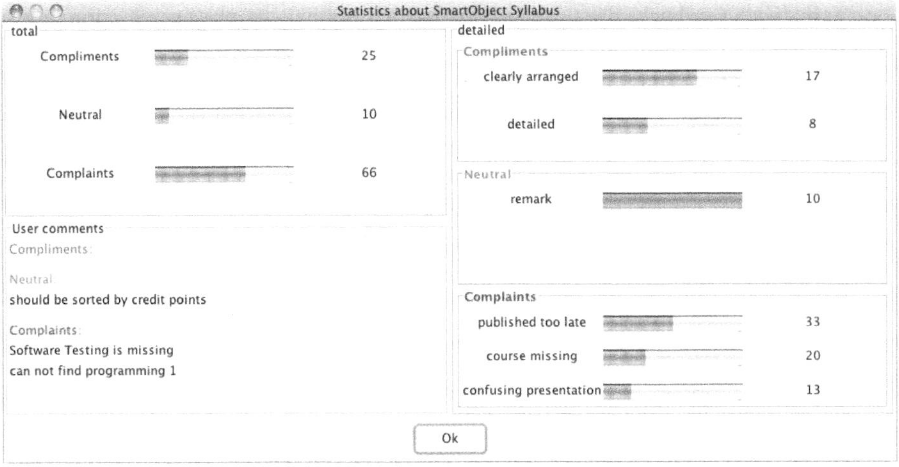

Fig. 8. Automatic classification of incoming feedback based on selected options

Obviously, the simple counters and visualizations can be refined and combined by marketing or requirements experts in a provider organization. Providers who registered more than one SmartObject can compare and use their respective feedback for advanced analysis. ConTexter is an implementation of a *framework* for contextualized feedback. Thus, providers can integrate the SmartObject statistics API into their internal evaluation systems by using the ConTexter framework. As presented in this paper, all aspects are integrated and facilitate installation and operation of that framework in a new application domain or software environment. After several feedbacks have been received, the above statistics screen Fig. 8 is created from specified feedback options and received feedbacks.

The components of the ConTexter framework offer the infrastructure for seamless interaction around feedback. When a new application is set up, administrators (i.e., providers) must register and specify SmartObjects with feedback types etc. Immediately afterwards, feedback can be sent and received. Writing or compiling code is not required.

8 Summary and Conclusions

Technical systems and software-controlled subsystems continue to interact more and more. Once this interaction exceeds central control, IT ecosystems start to emerge and evolve. The interaction of their subsystems is difficult to understand and may be impossible to anticipate.

Commercial software and service providers need to update and improve their subsystems if they want to stay competitive. Feedback from users and stakeholders is an essential input to continuous improvement. Stakeholders perceive an IT ecosystem as a smart environment and may not be able to distinguish all its parts. For the first time, the new generation of customers and stakeholders have the technical prerequisites and personal ability to recognize sub-optimal system behaviour – and to report it through contextualized feedback. This is a new opportunity, and we present an approach of seizing that opportunity.

Our approach consists of a technical framework, infrastructure, and concepts for applying them in an improvement processes. We first describe the architecture and framework in general. Then, we present the ConTexter implementation of that framework. ConTexter framework and UniImprove application example demonstrate that our concepts can be implemented with current technology. They establish a feedback and learning cycle for continuous improvement of IT ecosystem. We will continue exploring applications and extensions, such as the potential of ad-hoc video clips attached to contextualized feedback.

There are numerous open research questions in this field. Many interesting questions were actually stimulated by the work presented in this paper: How many stakeholders will provide feedback? Is it sufficient to lower effort, or do providers need to grant incentives for good feedback? What is the optimal proximity heuristic for SmartObjects? How should related SmartObjects be organized? Empowering semi-automatic interpretation is another research area that we have only touched upon in Section 7. We expect answers to vary significantly over different application areas and implementation alternatives. For example, acceptance might depend on perceived reaction and improvement time as much as on feedback mechanisms. The impact of our approach will be influenced by the personality of users such as their affinitiy to technology. Even the brand of supported Smartphones could have an influence. We are currently developing an iPhone interface to be used in addition to Android Smartphones to study that effect.

By applying our approach, subsystems of IT ecosystems can be explored and continuously evaluated by affected stakeholders. For example, an airport or an entire city could open that new feedback channel. Frameworks like ConTexter can support the evolution of IT ecosystems. Both service providers and their users can benefit from seamless feedback in context.

Acknowledgments. This work was inspired by our work in the NTH School for IT Ecosystems. NTH (Niedersächsische Technische Hochschule) is supported by Leibniz Universität Hannover, TU Braunschweig, and TU Clausthal.

References

1. Singer, L., Brill, O., Meyer, S., Schneider, K.: Leveraging Rule Deviations in IT Ecosystems for Implicit Requirements Elicitation. In: Second International Workshop on Managing Requirements Knowledge (MaRK 2009) at RE 2009 (September 2009)

2. Bosch, J.: Software Product Lines to Software Ecosystems. In: 13th International Software Product Line Conference (SPLC 2009), San Francisco, CA, August 24-28 (2009)
3. Lentz, J.L., Bleizeffer, T.M.: IT Ecosystems: Evolved Complexity and Unintelligent Design. In: CHIMIT 2007, Cambridge, MA, USA, March 30-31 (2007)
4. Karlsson, L., Dahlstedt, Å.G., Natt och Dag, J., Regnell, B., Persson, A.: Challenges in Market-Driven Requirements Engineerng - an Industrial Interview Study. In: Proceedings of Eighth International Workshop on Requirements Engineering: Foundation for Software Quality, Essen, Germany (2002)
5. Schneider, K.: Anforderungsklärung mit Videoclips. In: Proceedings of Software Engineering 2010, Paderborn, Germany (2010)
6. Davenport, T.G.P.: Knowledge Management Case Book - Best Practises. Publicis MCD, John Wiley & Sons (2000)
7. Brill, O., Schneider, K., Knauss, E.: Videos vs. Use Cases: Can Videos Capture More Requirements Under Time Pressure? In: Proceedings of REFSQ 2010, Essen, Germany (2010)
8. Hughes, J., O'Brien, J., Rodden, T., Rouncefield, M., Sommerville, I.: Presenting ethnography in the requirements process. In: Second IEEE International Symposium on Requirements Engineering, March 27-29, IEEE Computer Society, York (1995)
9. Fickas, S., Feather, M.S.: Requirements monitoring in dynamic environments. In: Proc. Second IEEE International Symposium on Requirements Engineering, March 27-29, pp. 140–147 (1995)
10. Creighton, O., Ott, M., Brügge, B.: Software Cinema: Video-based Requirements Engineering. In: 14th IEEE Internat. Requirements Engineering Conference (2006)
11. Zachos, K., Maiden, N.: ART-SCENE: Enhancing Scenario Walkthroughs With Multi-Media Scenarios. In: Proceedings of Requirements Engineering Conference (2004)
12. Zachos, K., Maiden, N., Tosar, A.: Rich-Media Scenarios for Discovering Requirements. IEEE Software 22, 89–97 (2005)
13. Sitou, W., Spanfelner, B.: Towards Requirements Engineering for Context Adaptive Systems. In: COMPSAC 2007: Proceedings of the 31st Annual International Computer Software and Applications Conference, Washington, DC, USA, pp. 593–600. IEEE Computer Society, Los Alamitos (2007)
14. Dey, A., Abowd, G., Salber, D.: A Context-based Infrastructure for Smart Environments. In: Proceedings of the 1st International Workshop on Managing Interactions in Smart Environments (MANSE 1999), pp. 114–128 (1999)
15. Sutcliffe, A., Fickas, S., Sohlberg, M.M.: PC-RE: a method for personal and contextual requirements engineering with some experience. Requirements Engineering 11(3), 157–173 (2006)
16. Fox, S., Karnawat, K., Mydland, M., Dumais, S., White, T.: Evaluating implicit measures to improve web search. ACM Trans. Inf. Syst. 23(2), 147–168 (2005)
17. Dupret, G., Liao, C.: A model to estimate intrinsic document relevance from the clickthrough logs of a web search engine. In: WSDM 2010: Proceedings of the third ACM international conference on Web search and data mining, pp. 181–190. ACM, New York (2010)

Comparing Agile Processes for Agent Oriented Software Engineering

Alma M. Gómez-Rodríguez and Juan C. González-Moreno

D. de Informática (University of Vigo)
Ed. Politécnico, Campus As Lagoas,
Ourense E-32004, Spain,
{alma,jcmoreno}@uvigo.es
http://gwai.ei.uvigo.es/

Abstract. Multi-agent Systems are at the moment an important new paradigm in software development. Several methodologies have been proposed for developing systems within this approach. Besides new agile process have been proposed to be used combined with the meta-models of such methodologies. This paper studies how the use of one of those Agent Oriented methodologies following an agile process such as Scrum produces improvements in the time consumed in the development that could shorten the learning time. This may have as outcome the possibility of using smaller groups in development.

1 Introduction

Agents represent a powerful abstraction tool in software development. The inherent characteristics of agents: autonomy, reactivity, proactivity, etc. provide a very good approach in the solution of distributed complex problems [1]. Therefore, Agent-Oriented Computing has become in the last decade a new Software Engineering paradigm [2]. The interest in software development with agents is focused in multi-agent systems (MAS) [3], [4], [5] that is, a set of autonomous agents which work cooperatively using high level communication languages and protocols.

There are many applications implemented using agents, nevertheless agent tools, methodologies and process have not yet a sufficient level of maturity for being used under warranty in commercial software development [2]. Two issues are essential if the agents are to be used in software industry: the availability of tools or frameworks which simplify multi-agent systems implementation and the use of suitable methodologies and development processes which guide the engineer during the system construction. At the moment much work is being carried out in all these fields. Many agent oriented methodologies have been proposed and applied to MAS development with good results [6], [7], [8], [9], [10], [11], [12], [13]. Some of these methodologies introduce a tool supporting the development, such as IDK [14], Metameth [15], etc.

This work focusses on the importance of processes in software development. So, we consider a software development process as a simple dependency graph

M. Ali Babar, M. Vierimaa, and M. Oivo (Eds.): PROFES 2010, LNCS 6156, pp. 206–219, 2010.
© Springer-Verlag Berlin Heidelberg 2010

with three basic components: the process participants (*roles or workers*), the consumed and generated products (*work products*) and the *activities* and *tasks* achieved during the process, which constitute particular instances (*work definitions*) of the works that must be done. Methodology, in contrast, defines the models to construct and the concepts and notation used in these models.

Among all the methodologies for Agent Oriented development, we have chosen INGENIAS for the case study proposed. INGENIAS methodology covers analysis and design of MAS, and it is intended for general use, with no restrictions on application domain [16], [6], [17]. It has two supporting tools: the INGENIAS Development Kit (IDK) and the INGENIAS Agent Framework (IAF) [17], [18]. The intended process of INGENIAS is Unified Development Process (UDP), but some previous works [19], [20] have shown that methodology and process can be considered independently. A previous work [19] has adapted INGENIAS to follow agile processes, in particular Scrum. The adaptation has been done by identifying common tasks in the different development processes and reordering them to construct a new process.

New processes for INGENIAS have been defined theoretically in previous works [19], [20]. So it is an important issue to When defining a process, it is very important to prove the applicability in practice of these definitions. We consider that a first step when approaching this verification is to apply the process to a particular development and consider its suitability. Following this idea, this paper focuses on the results obtained in the application of two different development processes to a MAS. The aim of this paper is to compare this two processes mainly in productivity. In this way, we try in this way to confirm the suitability of both of them.

The structure of the remaining of the paper follows. Section 2 introduces the methodology used in the development: INGENIAS while 3 details the process defined for the development: Scrum for INGENIAS. Section 4 explains the experiment done and show the results. Finally, Section 5 addresses the conclusions and future work.

2 INGENIAS Methodology

The original purpose of INGENIAS was the definition of a specific methodology for the development of Multi-agent Systems (MAS), by integrating results from research in the area of agent technology and from traditional Software Engineering Methodologies. Initially, the definition of the INGENIAS Methodology was based on the well-established Rational Unified Process (RUP) in order to define its lifecycle, and on the definition of a set of meta-models that describe the elements needed to specify and develop a MAS. These meta-models describe the system from five viewpoints: *agent*, *interactions*, *organization*, *environment* and *goals/tasks*.

The integration of the INGENIAS MAS specification language with software engineering practices is achieved by defining a set of activities that guide the analysis and design phases, with the statement of the results that have to be produced by each activity. As in the rest of modern methodologies, the key point in INGENIAS is its meta-model language. As stated before, INGENIAS introduces five kinds of meta-models in order to define a MAS. The entities of the meta-models could appear in different diagrams, but are unique regarding the global system specification.

- **Organization meta-model.** It defines the global organization of the system, where organization is the equivalent to MAS architecture. An organization has a structure and a functionality. The structure is similar to the one stated in AALAADIN framework [21], and is defined attending to how agents should be grouped. Functionality is determined by defining the goals of the organization and the workflows it should execute.
- **Environment meta-model.** The environment model is composed of environment diagrams. The environment is what surrounds the MAS and what originates mainly agent perception and action. As a developer, one of the first tasks is to identify system resources, applications, and agents. System resources are represented using TAEMS [22] notation. Applications are wrappers of whatever is not an agent or a resource, and could be understood in INGENIAS as equivalent to objects in Object Orientation. Using these elements, a developer should be able to define how the MAS interact with the systems surrounding.
- **Tasks/Goals meta-model.** It describes how the mental state of agents change over the time, what is the result of executing a task over the agent the mental state, how to achieve goals, and what happens when a goal cannot be achieved.
- **Agent meta-model.** It defines the primitives to describe a single agent. It can be used to define the capabilities of an agent or its mental state. The mental state is an aggregate of mental entities that satisfy certain conditions. The initial or intermediate mental state is expressed in terms of mental entities such as those of AOP [23] and BDI [24].
- **Interaction meta-model.** These kind of diagrams show how two or more agents interact. The interaction behavior is described using different languages, such as UML collaboration diagrams, GRASIA interaction diagrams, or AUML protocol diagrams. An interaction has a purpose that has to be shared or partially pursued by interaction participants. Usually, this purpose is related with some organizational goal.

Recently in [25] the FAML meta-model has been proposed. Potentially, FAML is a an interesting candidate for future standardization of engineering agent modeling languages. FAML is composed by two layers: *design-time* and *runtime*, and each layer has two scopes: *an agent-external* and *an agent-internal*. In [25], INGENIAS meta-model (see Fig. 1) was considered by authors as one of the five more extant current agent-oriented approaches.

Originally the development process proposed for INGENIAS was an adaptation of the Rational Unified Process according to the modification showed in Table 1. Afterwards, in [26], [27] an agile version of INGENIAS based on

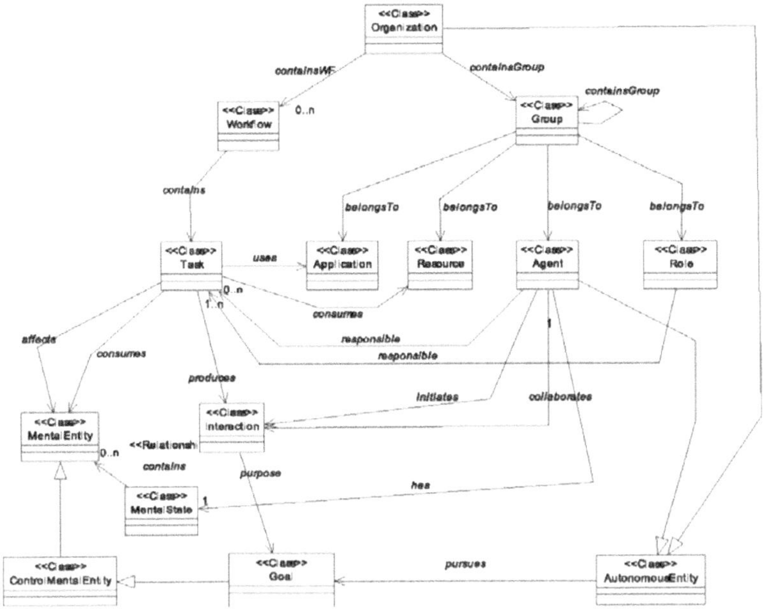

Fig. 1. INGENIAS Metamodel

OpenUp was presented. From the evidence that an agile process could be used with the INGENIAS metamodel language, a framework for deploying MAS over the JADE platform [28] appears in a natural way, this was the IAF [18], [29]. Besides, based on the use of this framework a modification of the Scrum process for INGENIAS was proposed in [19].

Section 3 introduces a more detailed explanation of how to use Scrum Process for INGENIAS.

3 The Scrum Process for INGENIAS

A Scrum is a mechanism in the sport of rugby for getting an out-of-play ball back into play. The term was adopted in 1987 to describe hyper-productive development. Ken Schwaber formalized the process in the first published paper on Scrum at OOPSLA 1995 [30]. As pointed in [31], Scrum is an empirical Agile project management framework which is used to iteratively deliver to the customer software increments of high value. Scrum relies on self organizing, empowered teams to deliver the product increments. It also relies on a customer, the Product Owner, to provide the development team with a list of desired features using business value as the mechanism for prioritization. Scrum is a model for management of the process of software development. It is not a methodology, because it does not propose models or concepts to address, but a framework

Table 1. Results to be obtained in each phase of the INGENIAS Process

	PHASES		
	INCEPTION	ELABORATION	CONSTRUCTION
ANALYSIS	To generate use cases and identify actions of these use cases with the corresponding Interaction Model To outline the system architecture with an Organization Model To generate Environment Models which reflects Requirement elicitation	To refine use cases To generate Agent Models that detail the elements of the system architecture To continue with the Organization Models, identifying workflows and tasks To obtain Task and Goal Models to highlight control constraints (main goals, goal decomposition) To refine the Environment Model including new elements	To study the remaining use cases
DESIGN	To generate a prototype using RAD tools such as ZEUS or Agent-Tool	To focus the Organization Model on workflow To refine Tasks and Goal Models reflecting the dependencies and needs identified in workflows and the relationships with system's goals To show how tasks are executed using Interaction Models To generate Agent Models which show required mental state patterns	To generate new Agent models or refining existing ones To study social relationships in order to refine the organization

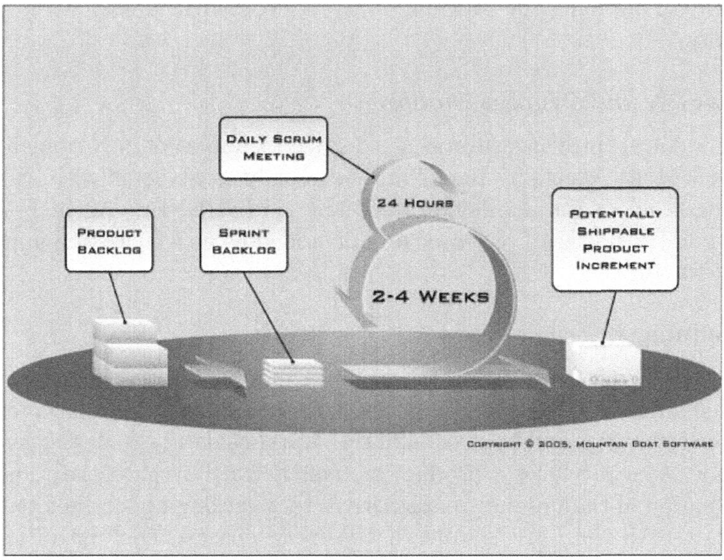

Fig. 2. Scrum lifecycle

where different methodologies can fit. The Scrum process is particularly suitable for Knowledge Engineering Developments based on the use of Multi-Agent Systems, because of the agile development and the user implication.

An initial view of Scrum process, as proposed by its authors in [31], can be seen in Fig. 2.

Previous works [27] have determined that when trying to map a well established methodology/process into a new process, it is necessary to define the steps to be done. In [27] several steps that must be followed in the definition of a new development process models for AOSE are defined, adopting SPEM [32] as model specification. These steps are:

1. *Identify the process model with an existent process model* if possible, if not define from zero the new one taking as basis the next steps.
2. *Define the lifecycle view.* Identify the phases, iterations and sequence of application. This step is essentially a temporal step in which other resources different from time are not considered.
3. *Define the disciplines.* Disciplines in SPEM determine process packages which take part in the process activities, related with a common *subject.* That is, disciplines represent a specialization of selected sub-activities, where these new sub-activities can not appear in other packages or disciplines. In this step, resources are the subject of the activities defined.
4. *Define the guidance and suggestion view.* The *Guidances* provide information about certain model elements. Each *Guidance* is associated to a *Guidance Kind.* This step is focused in exemplifying and documenting the activities previously defined.

The results of applying the previous steps to INGENIAS are shown in the next subsections.

3.1 Identify the Process Model

The methodology provides several pre-defined examples of development. These means that Multi-Agents Systems could be quickly constructed with INGENIAS by reusing previous developments. Recently, the INGENIAS Agent Framework (IAF) for JADE has been proposed and documented as a successful approach in this context [18].

3.2 Defining Lifecycle View

In Scrum, each release is produced within a number of iterations from 2 to 4 weeks called Sprints (see Fig. 2). Sprint goal is defined by the product owner, taking both priorities and team capabilities into consideration. At the end of each Sprint, the team produces a product increment which is potentially releasable. The evaluation of the product release drives to a backlog update before the next sprint starts. All the work is done in two basic phases: the *Preparation Phase* (before the first sprint) and the *Sprint Phases* (successive sprints leading to the release).

Although, Scrum does not describe engineering activities required for product development, INGENIAS-Scrum process must do it in order to adjust to IAF recommendations. IAF allows combining the classic approach of coding applications with modern techniques of automatic code generation.

IAF requires the use of the INGENIAS Development Kit (IDK), that contains a graphical editor for working with the specification model. Accordingly to IDK, the Scrum definition for the *Preparation Phase* comprises the tasks: *Initiate Product Backlog*, *Plan Release* and *Preparation Tasks*. The *INGENIAS Product Backlog* contains the product requirements established using the IDK. This process can be done by adapting a known model from a previous project (i.e. IDK-IAF distribution comes with a complete cinema project which can be used for other distributed e-commerce developments) or defining a completely new product backlog with the editor. After this initial model is completed, in the *Preparation Tasks*, the *Scrum Master* and the *Product Owner* establish the *Plan Release* in which the needed *Sprints* are defined.

From the Scrum perspective and taking into account that IAF bases on the automatic generation of code approach, the project team must be completely involved in getting the release within the planned sprints. So, the INGENIAS specification must be established with the IDK as the core of the development. From this core, the different scripts and sources will be automatically produced. Nevertheless, at the first stage, the generated code for the tasks may be incomplete and the programmer should add, if necessary, code in the tasks.

3.3 Define the Disciplines View

As previously pointed, in the INGENIAS-Scrum approach the disciplines are the tasks required in each sprint, so the intended meaning of each task, according to IAF, must be explained. But first, the roles and products involved in the development must be introduced [27]. The roles, in this case, are:*Product Owner*, this role must be play by an active *customer* as in eXtreme Programming (XP); *Scrum Master*, the *coach* and main of the development team; *Scrum Team*, this is a *collective role* that must be played by any of the team members; *Stakeholder*, anyone that does not directly participate on the project but can influence the product being developed, that is, an *interested party*.

The products or artifacts involved in a Scrum development process are: *Product backlog*, *Sprint backlog* and *Product increment*. The *product backlog* contains the product requirements and has the purpose of listing all the functionalities to implement from a customer perspective. The *sprint backlog* is the list of things to do from the development team point of view. It could be understood as a fine-grained planning on detailed tasks. At last, the *product increment* is a partial product obtained at the end of each sprint, which can be deployed in the production environment or simply made available to users. From the INGENIAS-Scrum perspective those artifacts are referred to the INGENIAS model and JADE code produced in each release. An INGENIAS model documented with the IDK can accomplish a low o high level of detail. Also, in the description of each model the *Scrum Master* can fix the work to be done in the next release, where release can be identified with the *package* entity of the INGENIAS model.

3.4 Define Guidances View

Developing a system with code generation facilities requires some guidance. In IAF documentation [18] several guidelines for development are proposed. In multi-agent systems, we recommend specially the use of two kinds of guidance: *Technique* and *Guideline*. The *technique* provides an algorithm to create a work product. The *guideline* is a set of rules and recommendations about a work product organization.

4 Case Study and Results

This section addresses the comparison of INGENIAS following the Scrum Process using the IAF on the IDK and the RUP for INGENIAS using the full version of the IDK tool. This comparison is based on the development of the same MAS by different groups of students and in measuring during the development some variables that can determine the productivity and performance of the processes selected. As authors teach Software Engineering Courses at Computer Science Faculty on the Vigo University, it was decided to use the students for this study. The students were divided into groups of 4-6 people and were asked to develop a complete agent oriented system. The groups were homogeneous in the number of members, but defer among them in the knowledge of development processes, in particular RUP. Three of the groups have a good knowledge of RUP, another three have a superficial knowledge and the rest do not know anything of RUP. None of the groups have notions about what was Scrum process of development.

Moreover, people that conforms the teams do not know the INGENIAS methodology, neither its meta-modeling language. So the challenge for the teams was twofold: to learn INGENIAS methodology and meta-model and to understand Scrum process.

With this set of students, we plan an experiment, which tries to constitute a first approach in the study of the influence of the development process selected over productivity. Data of the experiment were collected along the Software Engineering Course, while the students develop the system that was mandatory. The requirements of the system to obtain are explained next.

4.1 Case Study Description

As stated before, all the groups were asked to develop the same agent-oriented system. In particular, every team must develop a web site for managing software development projects based on the Scrum Development Process. This selection was made to increase the level of knowledge about Scrum in the groups in the first steps and phases of the development. The portal must allow:

1. *The Creation, Modification, Project Monitoring and Closure* of a Software Project that is being constructed using Scrum Process.
2. *The Establishment of the teams and the assignation of the roles* that each member team will assume along the project. The system must also allow changes in team composition or roles assignation. These changes may be done dynamically during development.
3. *The Management of each Project Sprint.*
4. *The Creation, Identification, Modification and Monitoring* of every meeting held during the Sprints.
5. *The Storage, Retrieval and Collaborative modification* of any work product obtained along the development.

The different teams were asked to provide some intermediate deliverables along the development, in order to have some control on their evolution with independency of the process selected. The first deliverable demanded was a simulation of the proposed solution to the portal modeled using Alice [33]. This first deliverable had a double utility. In the one hand, it served as a control point in the degree of knowledge of Scrum achieved by the teams. On the other, it was used as the way of establishing the system functional requirements for each group. Obviously, if the prototype was wrong, the students had to modify it until considered correct.

Besides, three more deliverables were established one of them each two months. Excluding the first one described that must be finished one month after the beginning.

These deliverables were used to measure the degree of functionality accomplished, according to the functionality proposed by each team in the prototype provided.

4.2 Experiment and Results

Several variables were taken into account in the study, as we considered that they may influence the final productivity of the teams developing the system.

Each team is identified by a number (it appears in first column of Table 2). This is just a way of having the possibility of referring to a particular team, if needed.

The experience column expresses the background of each team regarding the knowledge of RUP or any other development process. We consider that previous knowledge of processes can influence in learning new ones. Nevertheless, as said before, none of the groups have previous knowledge of Scrum.

The process column shows what kind of process was used by the team during the development. The process that they have to follow was assigned randomly by the teachers and independently from previous background of the teams.

The prototype column indicate the kind of solution chosen by each team. Three are the possibilities in this column:

- *Server-oriented solution.* A server-oriented solution is a classic client-server solution in which features are provided by a single central server to different kind of users. Each user has its own privileges to operate in the web site.
- *Service-oriented solution.* A service-oriented solution describes the site as a set of distributed services that may be requested concurrently by the user. It is also possible in this kind of solution that certain services are automatically offered to selected users that satisfy some condition.
- *User-oriented solution.* An user-oriented solution prioritizes a centralized and sequential management of the development process. In this kind of solution users interact with the system and decide when and which data should be entered.

From a theoretical perspective, the more suitable solution from MAS point of view is the second one, because a distributed net could be easier established over an agent platform. Each service could be offered by a particular agent or by a group of agents. Each agent could have their own goals, that have to be satisfied by a set of tasks and that require some interaction with other agents. So that, this drives to a collaboration or coordination on the tasks to satisfy agent's goals. The rest of solutions present some drawbacks in the deployment, because the methodology is not so suitable for them. Nevertheless, all solutions are still feasible to be adopted in a MAS approach, although some of them will imply an extra cost of time.

The four latest columns measure the rate of functionality achieved for each of the deliverables provided. As stated before, this rate is calculated referring to those proposed by each team in their prototype and are ordered by their final achievement.

Table 2 presents the results obtained from the case study.

Table 2. Teams' performing results

Team	Experience	Process	Prototype	1st Del.	2nd Del.	3rd Del.	Final
6	High	Scrum	Service Oriented	15%	30%	55%	85%
2	High	Scrum	Server Oriented	15%	25%	50%	80%
1	High	RUP	Service Oriented	20%	35%	50%	75%
5	Medium	Scrum	User Oriented	15%	25%	45%	75%
8	Low	Scrum	Service Oriented	15%	22%	45%	75%
3	Medium	RUP	Server Oriented	15%	30%	40%	70%
7	Low	Scrum	Server Oriented	15%	30%	50%	70%
4	Medium	RUP	Server Oriented	15%	25%	45%	65%
9	Low	RUP	User Oriented	10%	20%	40%	60%

4.3 Discussion

An initial analysis of the results tries to address productivity of the teams. We consider that teams are more productive when they achieve a higher rate of functionality for the same increment. This consideration could make sense as far as all the teams have the same time available for delivering the increment. The results show that the productivity on the teams using Scrum as process was higher in average, even when taking into consideration the kind of solution adopted. The study shows also that the learning time is shorter for members of the development group that follow an Scrum processes, because the increments in the rate of functionality are higher. This could allow the use of smaller groups of development, due to the higher productivity.

A second issue to consider in results shows that the ratio of evolution in the productivity is higher in the last deliverables for Scrum teams. This suggests, in our opinion, that Scrum process is a better solution to manage the lifecycle for INGENIAS methodology than the RUP originally proposed.

Other factor that can influence the results, is the previous knowledge or background of the teams. We do not have a quantitative measure of the background, instead we consider a rough measure of it, idenfying three possible values: High, Medium or Low. Nevertheless, in order to improve the study in the future a quantitative measure will be incorporated. Moreover, although experience must have an impact on productivity, we thought that the process has a more important influence. This is justified by the fact that less experienced groups have a better productivity using Scrum than more experienced groups using RUP.

The kind of solution chosen (column Prototype of Table 2) can also influence productivity of teams. Nevertheless we consider that it is not so important, because teams using *ServerOriented* Prototype have good productivity results.

As said in previous subsection, the selection of what process must follow each group was assigned randomly by the teachers of Software Engineering. Productivity may be affected if the choice were free. Other studies in the future may address the changes in productivity when groups can choose the process to follow. At present, this objective was not in the scope of the experiment.

The results obtained have exceeded expectations. For instance, a medium experienced and a novice team got the same productivity results using Scrum than one of the expert teams using the RUP. Moreover, the worst results were obtained by a novice team and a medium experience team using the RUP approach. These results could be interpreted as an evidence that the RUP approach needs much more time to be learned and used with solvency.

However, some results not expected were found. First, one of the worst results was gotten using RUP with a server oriented solution. Secondly, a good rate of productivity was obtained by team with an user oriented solution using the Scrum development Process.

Results obtained by team number five seem to be a surprise because the kind of solution chosen is not the most suitable for the problem. This can be explained by the fact that the team has dynamically chosen to apply a shorter cycle of deliverables and to associate an agent to each kind of user. This has increased the interaction between agents, and in fact, the architecture proposed by the group represents each of the Scrum roles by an agent. This change has increased the productivity of the final two deliverables.

5 Conclusions and Future Work

In previous sections the MAS methodology INGENIAS was presented jointly with two different approaches for their process development. In order to compare productivity and suitability of both a case study has been also presented. The case study was solved by nine teams that have no knowledge about the Scrum process, that was *the object of the study.* Teams have a different preparation on Process Development: *three are experts, three are novices, and the rest have an average training.* This selection was chosen in order to get a complete information about the real productivity of the Scrum approach when compared with the OpenUp approach.

Summarizing results, the conclusion is that the ratio of evolution in the productivity is higher in the last deliverables for all the Scrum teams. At first glance, at attending these results, Scrum process seems a better solution to manage the lifecycle of the INGENIAS approach that the OpenUp one. Of course these results constitute an initial approach in the comparison of the processes (OpenUp and SCRUM) for INGENIAS methodology.

This first approach suggest that SCRUM is better suited but more studies have to be done. In particular, we consider that more data are needed, so that we will go on with the experiment next years. Other studies will be also valuable, such as fixing as object of the study the OpenUp approach to compare the results, or doing the comparative with teams with the same level of capacitation on the two development processes. Other possibility, considered as a future work, is to have a new structure for teams (for instance, 4 or 6 people working by pairs as suggested by XP). Besides, it is worth considering in the future other variables that may influence the results such as the kind of system to construct, the size of groups, etc.

In any case the results obtained are very promising in order to experiment with new agile process for AOSE development with INGENIAS.

Acknowledgement. This work has been supported by the project *Novos entornos colaborativos para o ensino* supported by Xunta de Galicia with grant 08SIN009305PR.

References

1. Jennings, N.R., Wooldridge, M.: Agent-Oriented Software Engineering. In: Bradshaw, J. (ed.) Handbook of Agent Technology. AAAI/MIT Press (to appear, 2001)
2. Wooldridge, M., Ciancarini, P.: Agent-Oriented Software Engineering: The State of the Art. In: Ciancarini, P., Wooldridge, M.J. (eds.) AOSE 2000. LNCS, vol. 1957, pp. 1–28. Springer, Heidelberg (2001)
3. DeLoach, S., Wood, M., Sparkman, C.: Multiagent Systems Engineering. International Journal of Software Engineering and Knowledge Engineering 11(3), 231–258 (2001)
4. Henderson-Sellers, B., Giorgini, P.: Agent-Oriented Methodologies. Idea Group Inc., USA (2005)
5. Ricordel, P.M.: Programmation Orientée Multi-Agents: Développement et Déploiement de Systemes Multi-Agents Voyelles. PhD thesis, Institut National Polytechnique De Grenoble (2001)
6. Pavón, J., Gómez-Sanz, J.: Agent Oriented Software Engineering with INGENIAS. In: Mařík, V., Müller, J.P., Pěchouček, M. (eds.) CEEMAS 2003. LNCS (LNAI), vol. 2691, pp. 394–403. Springer, Heidelberg (2003)
7. O'Malley, S.A., DeLoach, S.A.: Determining when to use an agent-oriented software engineering pradigm. In: Wooldridge, M.J., Weiß, G., Ciancarini, P. (eds.) AOSE 2001. LNCS, vol. 2222, p. 188. Springer, Heidelberg (2002)
8. Cuesta, P., Gómez, A., González, J., Rodríguez, F.J.: The MESMA methodology for agent-oriented software engineering. In: Proceedings of First International Workshop on Practical Applications of Agents and Multiagent Systems (IWPAAMS 2002), pp. 87–98 (2002)
9. Bernon, C., Cossentino, M., Pavón, J.: Agent-oriented software engineering. Knowl. Eng. Rev. 20(2), 99–116 (2005)
10. Mas, A.: Agentes Software y Sistemas Multi-Agentes. Pearson Prentice Hall, London (2004)
11. Padgham, L., Winikoff, M.: Prometheus: A Methodology for Developing Intelligent Agents. In: Proceedings of the Third International Workshop on Agent Oriented Software Engineering, at AAMAS (2002)
12. Chella, A., Cossentino, M., Sabatucci, L., Seidita, V.: Agile PASSI: An Agile Process for Designing Agents. International Journal of Computer Systems Science & Engineering. Special issue on Software Engineering for Multi-Agent Systems (May 2006)
13. Cossentino, M., Sabatucci, L.: Agent System Implementation. In: Agent-Based Manufacturing and Control Systems: New Agile Manufacturing Solutions for Achieving Peak Performance. CRC Press, Boca Raton (2004)
14. INGENIAS Development Kit, `http://ingenias.sourceforge.net/`
15. Cossentino, M., Sabatucci, L., Seidita, V., Gaglio, S.: An Agent Oriented Tool for New Design Processes. In: Proceedings of the Fourth European Workshop on Multi-Agent Systems (2006)

16. Pavón, J., Gómez-Sanz, J.: Agent Oriented Software Engineering with INGENIAS. In: Mařík, V., Müller, J.P., Pěchouček, M. (eds.) CEEMAS 2003. LNCS (LNAI), vol. 2691, pp. 394–403. Springer, Heidelberg (2003)
17. Pavón, J., Gómez-Sanz, J.J., Fuentes-Fernández, R.: IX. In: The INGENIAS Methodology and Tools, pp. 236–276. Idea Group Publishing, USA (2005)
18. Gómez-Sanz, J.: Ingenias Agent Framework. Development Guide V. 1.0. Technical report, Universidad Complutense de Madrid (2008)
19. García-Magariño, I., Gómez-Rodríguez, A., Gómez-Sanz, J., González-Moreno, J.C.: INGENIAS-SCRUM Development Process for Multi-Agent Development. In: International Symposium on Distributed Computing and Artificial Intelligence (DCAI 2008), Advances in Software Computing (2008)
20. Fuentes-Fernández, R., García-Magariño, I., Gómez-Rodríguez, A.M., González-Moreno, J.C.: A technique fordefining agent-oriented engineering processes with tool support. Engineering Applications of Artificial Intelligence 23(3), 432–444 (2010)
21. Ferber, J.: Multi-Agent Systems. Addison-Wesley, Reading (1999)
22. Wagner, T., Horling, B.: The struggle for reuse and domain independence: Research with taems, dtc and jaf. In: Proceedings of the 2nd Workshop on Infrastrucutre for Agents, MAS and Scalable MAS (2001)
23. Shoham, Y.: Agent-oriented programming. Artificial Intelligence 60, 51–92 (1993)
24. Kinny, D., Georgeff, M.: Modelling and design of multi-agent systems. In: Jennings, N.R., Wooldridge, M.J., Müller, J.P. (eds.) ECAI-WS 1996. LNCS (LNAI), vol. 1193, pp. 1–20. Springer, Heidelberg (1997)
25. Beydoun, G., Low, G.C., Henderson-Sellers, B., Mouratidis, H., Gómez-Sanz, J.J., Pavón, J., Gonzalez-Perez, C.: Faml: A generic metamodel for mas development. IEEE Trans. Software Eng. 35(6), 841–863 (2009)
26. García-Magariño, I., Gómez-Rodríguez, A., González, J.C.: Modeling INGENIAS development process using EMF. In: 6th International Workshop on Practical Applications on Agents and Multi-agent Systems, IWPAAMS 2007, Salamanca Spain, November 12-13, pp. 369–378 (2007) (in Spanish)
27. García-Magariño, I., Gómez-Rodríguez, A., González-Moreno, J.C.: Definition of process models for agent-based development. In: Luck, M., Gomez-Sanz, J.J. (eds.) AOSE 2009. LNCS, vol. 5386, pp. 60–73. Springer, Heidelberg (2009)
28. Bellifemine, F., Bergenti, F., Caire, G., Poggi, A.: JADE - A Java Agent Development Framework. Multiagent Systems, Artificial Societies, and Simulated Organizations 15(2), 125–147 (2005)
29. García-Magariño, I., Gómez-Sanz, J.J., Fuentes-Fernández, R.: Model transformations for improving multi-agent systems development in ingenias. In: The 10th International Workshop on Agent-Oriented Software Engineering, AOSE 2009, Budapest, Hungary (with the annex), May 11 (2009)
30. Sutherland, J.: Business object design and implementation workshop. In: OOPSLA 1995: Addendum to the proceedings of the 10th annual conference on Object-oriented programming systems, languages, and applications, pp. 170–175. ACM, New York (1995)
31. Schwaber, K., Beedle, M.: Agile Software Development with Scrum. Prentice Hall PTR, Upper Saddle River (2001)
32. OMG.: Software Process Engineering Metamodel Specification. Version 2.0, formal/2008-04-01 (2008), `http://www.omg.org/`
33. Dann, W.P., Cooper, S., Pausch, R.: Learning To Program with Alice, 2/E. Prentice Hall, Englewood Cliffs (2009)

Standardizing the *Software Tag* in Japan for Transparency of Development

Masateru Tsunoda[1], Tomoko Matsumura[1], Hajimu Iida[1], Kozo Kubo[2], Shinji Kusumoto[3], Katsuro Inoue[3], and Ken-ichi Matsumoto[1]

[1] Graduate School of Information Science, Nara Institute of Science and Technology, 8916-5 Takayama, Ikoma, Nara, Japan
{masate t@is,tomoko-m@is,iida@itc,matumoto@is}naist.jp
[2] Research Center for Advanced Science and Technology, Nara Institute of Science and Technology, 8916-5 Takayama, Ikoma, Nara, Japan
kubo@rsc.naist.jp
[3] Graduate School of Information Science, Osaka University, 1-5 Yamada-Oka, Suita-shi, Osaka, 565-0871 Japan
{kusumoto,inoue}@ist.osaka-u.ac.jp

Abstract. In this paper, we describe the *Software Tag* which makes software development visible to software purchasers (users). A software tag is a partial set of empirical data about a software development project shared between the purchaser and developer. The purchaser uses the software tag to evaluate the software project, allowing them to recognize the quality level of the processes and products involved. With Japanese government support, we have successfully standardized the software tag named *Software Tag Standard* 1.0, and have developed various associated tools for tag data collection and visualization. For its initial evaluation, the software tag has been applied to several projects. This paper also presents various activities aimed at promoting the use of the software tag in Japan and the world.

Keywords: Information sharing, empirical data, project management, offshore development.

1 Introduction

Software systems are becoming huge and complex, with our everyday life heavily dependent on such software systems. One of the major concerns of software purchasers (users) in Japan is the quality of the software systems. Japanese society generally demands high-quality software systems with low fault rates and high operability levels.

On the other hand, many software purchasers in Japan are not knowledgeable about the nature of software. It is reported that only 40% of Japanese major companies employ a full-time Chief Information Officer (CIO) and that only 20% of all CIOs are confident of their knowledge about information technologies [10].

Without a sufficient understanding of software quality and software projects, many companies try to purchase software systems from software developers (vendors). This produces a very risky situation. For example, purchasers cannot specify

M. Ali Babar, M. Vierimaa, and M. Oivo (Eds.): PROFES 2010, LNCS 6156, pp. 220–233, 2010.
© Springer-Verlag Berlin Heidelberg 2010

system requirements very well, and they do not oversee the project properly. Such situations often lead to project failures. It is reported that only 31.1% of software projects are recognized as 'successful projects' in Japan [11]. To confront these issues, there is strong demand to provide transparency of software projects to the software purchaser and improve communications between purchaser and developer.

The *Software Tag* is a new scheme to provide information feedback about the project from the developer to the purchaser. It establishes transparency of the software development project by allowing purchasers to view and analyze the elements of the tag. It also provides support for quantitative and qualitative communications between stakeholders. The Software Traceability and Accountability for Global Software Engineering (*StagE*) project [1] is a government-supported project that pursues standardization and promotion of the software tag scheme. In this project, we have defined the detailed structure of the software tag and developed various support tools. The software tag has been applied to real projects of major Japanese organizations. Along with technical development, we have also started various promotion activities, such as formal standardization of the software tag in both domestic and international standards, and exploration of new trade laws for software using the software tag scheme.

An early concept of how software tags could be used for software maintenance was shown in [5]. In this paper, we mainly explain use of the software tag for software development, together with activities and outcomes from the StagE project. In section 2, we describe an overview of the software tag scheme, and in section 3 explain the details of the software tag structure. In section 4, we describe activities of the project. In section 5 we provide some discussion, while in section 6 we outline conclusions and future research topics.

2 Overview of the Software Tag Scheme

A software tag is a packaged data set about a software project. It is currently composed of 41 characteristic elements of project data and progress data, as defined in section 3.1. Fig. 1 shows an overview of the software tag scheme.

1. A software purchaser orders development of a software system. The purchaser includes both the final products and the software tag in their requirements.
2. During software development, various kinds of empirical data are created and generated. For example, requirements documents, software design documents, source code, test cases, issue tracking logs, manual documents, review logs, and quality analysis records may be produced. These are collected and archived. Note that we collect not only the final data at the end, but also interim snapshot data during development.
3. The collected data is analyzed for process improvement of the development organization, as is the usual process improvement scheme for software development organizations.
4. The collected data is used to construct the software tag. Parts of the empirical data are selected and abstracted into the software tag format.
5. The software tag is delivered to the software purchaser periodically during the development and/or finally at the end of the development together with the final

software product. The software purchaser evaluates the software development by viewing and analyzing the tag, and accepts the delivered software product.

If a controversy such as a question about the quality of the product occurs between the software purchaser and the developer, the delivered software tag and (if necessary) the empirical data are analyzed, providing a basis for exploring a resolution to the controversy.

The software tag is a key to improving *transparency* of software projects. By examining the software tag, the software purchaser can identify and understand the development process, which has been mostly hidden from the purchaser. The purchaser can evaluate the quality of the processes and products of the project.

For the software developer, the software tag is useful to prove that they have conducted the proper activities in the software project. Also, it can be used to trace the quality of the activities of sub-contractors and sub-sub-contractors... (such contracting chains are very popular in Japan).

This scheme can be very useful for offshore and global development, because transparency and traceability of software development can be established with a fairly low overhead for the developers.

Standardizing the software tag will help to establish a minimum baseline for project quality, and to improve negotiations over software development contracts. Evaluation of software products and projects based on the objective empirical data contained in the software tag will lead to more healthy use of software in society.

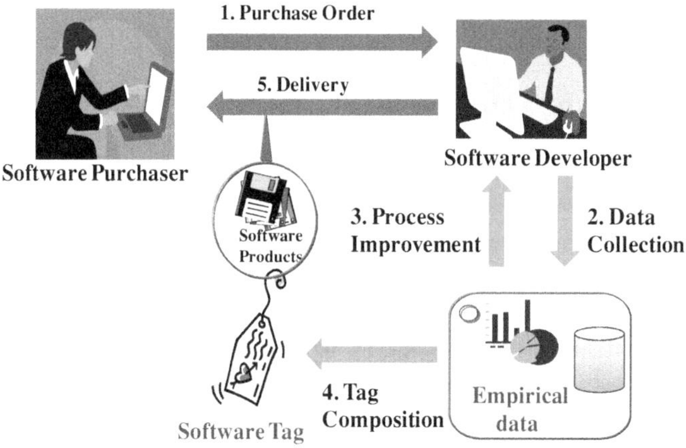

Fig. 1. Overview of Software Tag Scheme

3 Development of Software Tag Technologies

3.1 Software Tag Standard 1.0

We have defined the elements of the software tag as shown in Table 1, named *Software Tag Standard 1.0*. It is composed of 41 tag elements, which are categorized into *project information* and *progress information*. The project information depicts the overall sketch of the project with various basic pieces of information. The progress information provides qualitative and quantitative indices of project achievement with various measures of the development phases. The tag standard provides more precise explanations and example metrics for each tag element which are not presented here.

We divided project information into five categories described below, and settled tag elements for each category (see Table 1).

- basic information of the software project (*Basic Information*)
- information of the system developed by the project (*System Information*)
- information of development framework applied to the project (*Development Information*)
- information of relationships between target project and other projects (*Project Organization*)
- other information (*Others*)

To settle progress information, we referred to ISO/IEC 12207 Software Life Cycle Processes and activities [7], and included process, quality and effort information described below into it.

- information of requirements, design, programming and test for the software (*Requirements*, *Design*, *Programming*, and *Test*)
- information of quality assurance activities on the project (*Quality*)
- information of development effort on the project (*Development Cost*)
- information of project plan and management on the project (*Schedule and Management*)
- other information for the products attached to the software (*Other Products*)

It is not mandatory to use all 41 elements in the software tag in all cases. The purchaser and the developer can negotiate and select elements to use. Also, they can discuss and determine the details of the metrics. For example, #19, Scale of Programming, might be agreed to be measured by lines of code without comments. Based on the software tag standard, the purchaser and the developer should decide followings before using the software tag.

- tag elements to be used
- metrics used for tag elements
- measurement targets of metrics (e.g. whole system, sub systems, or files)
- frequency of measurement
- timing of offering the software tag to the purchaser (e.g. every week, every month, or the end of respective process)

In this standard, we have included various kinds of information that are considered important to the purchasers. The overall structure should be simple for the purchaser to understand, so we have tried to keep it as simple as possible. Also, we have tried to keep in mind the balance of the tag elements. This standard does not include tag elements that are computable from other tag elements. There are a number of standards and reports such as SWEBOK, CMMI, ISO/IEC 15939, and reports by the Software Engineering Center in Japan (SEC) which can help interpret the tag elements.

Table 1. Software Tag Standard 1.0

Classification	Category	No.	Tag Element	Explanation
Project Information	Basic Information	1	**Project Name**	Unique name of project
		2	**Organization**	Information of development organization
		3	**Project Information**	Information needed to identify the project characteristics
		4	**Customer Information**	Information identifying the purchaser or owner
	System Information	5	**System Configuration**	Information identifying system configuration to label the type of system
		6	**System Scale**	Development system scale
	Development Information	7	**Development Approach**	Development process type or techniques
		8	**Organizational Structure**	Structure of development organization
		9	**Project Duration**	Information of development length
	Project Organization	10	**Super-Project Information**	Name of super project which creates this project
		11	**Sub-Project Information**	Name of sub projects which is created by this project
	Other	12	**Special Notes**	Other necessary or useful data for interpreting or analyzing tag data
Progress Information	Requirements	13	**User Hearing Information**	Information of user-requirements hearing
		14	**Scale**	Amount of requirements
		15	**Revisions**	Amount of changed requirement
	Design	16	**Scale**	Amount of design products
		17	**Revisions**	Amount of changed design
		18	**Design Coverage by Requirements**	Implementation ratio of design for requirements
	Programming	19	**Scale**	Amount of programming products
		20	**Revisions**	Amount of changed programs
		21	**Complexity**	Complexity of programs
	Test	22	**Scale**	Amount of testing
		23	**Revisions**	Amount of changed test
		24	**Density**	Ratio of test to system size
		25	**Progress Status**	Test progress to plan
	Quality	26	**Review Status**	Quantity information of review
		27	**Review Density**	Ratio of review to system size

Table 1 (*Continued*)

Classification	Category	No.	Tag Element	Explanation
Progress Information	Quality	28	**Review Effectiveness**	Ration of found defects to amount of review
		29	**Defect Count**	Number of defects found by test
		30	**Fixed Defect Count**	Number of fixed defects
		31	**Defect Density**	Ratio of defects to system size
		32	**Defect Detection Rate**	Ratio of detected defects to consumed test
		33	**Static Check Results**	Report of static checker
	Development Cost	34	**Overall Cost**	Development and maintenance cost
		35	**Productivity**	Ratio of amount of products to overall cost
	Schedule and Management	36	**Process Management**	Information on management of development process
		37	**Purchaser-Developer Meeting Status**	Amount of user-vendor communication
		38	**Total Risk Item Count**	Number of risk items in the development
		39	**Risk Item Existence Period**	Time length between a risk item creation and deletion
	Other Products	40	**Scale**	Amount of product metrics not listed above
		41	**Revisions**	Amount of change in products not listed above

The definition process was based on discussions with industry and academic collaborators such as:

Purchasers: Tokyo Stock Exchange, Japan Aerospace Exploration Agency, DENSO.
Developers: Fujitsu Lab, Hitachi, NEC, SHARP, SRA Key-Tech Lab, Toshiba, NTT Data.
Others: Information Technology Promotion Agency, Ministry of Economy, Trade and Industry, Japan (IPA), Nara Institute of Science and Technology, Osaka University.

Thorough the discussion, we recognized that appropriate metrics (tag elements) set and calculation methods of them are different for organizations or projects. Therefore, we made tag elements selective, and on the tag standard, calculation methods of corresponding metrics of tag elements were not included but examples of the metrics are included.

To store, exchange and reuse the software tag, a standard data format is needed. So we settled the draft of the *standard software tag format* which is based on XML format, and are making the tool which converts existing tools' data into standard software tag format data. Software tag support tools explained in the next section treats software tag format data.

3.2 Support Tools

We are developing various support tools to promote the software tags scheme. In this paper, we introduce three essential tool prototypes that have been created for planning, collection, and visualization of the software tag.

Software Tag Planning Tool (*TagPlanner*)
TagPlanner supports planning software tag data collection. With TagPlanner, users such as project managers can fix tag data definition and its structure easily before starting a software project. Each tag element is connected to a project's task, and users can browse structure of the tasks and details of tag elements by TagPlanner. With TagPlanner, users can see how to collect tag elements. TagPlanner has a typical example of project's tasks and tag metrics, and which can be edited by uses.

Fig. 2 is a screenshot of TagPlanner. Details of functions of each pane are described below.

Process pane: Using some process model, this pane exhibits standard process of an organization. In the figure, the process is shown by WBS (work breakdown structure).
Task pane: This pane presents tasks selected at the process pane and metrics related to the tasks. When a metric is clicked, measurement method and other information are shown in the detail information pane.
Detail information pane: This pane shows how to measure and analysis a metric, person in charge of measurement, and other information. Information on the pane is updated by operating on the task pane or the tag element pane. Frequency of measurement and metrics included in the software tag is settled on the pane.
Tag element pane: Tag elements are listed on the pane. Metrics used to compute tag elements are also listed.

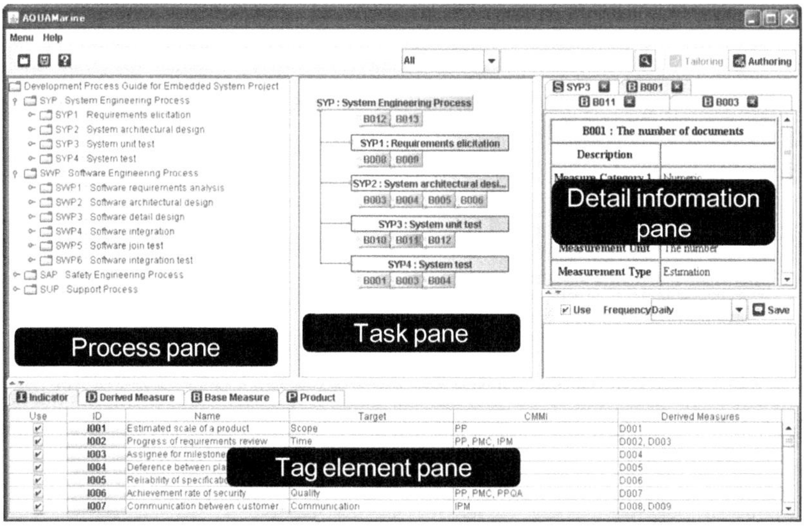

Fig. 2. TagPlanner Screenshot

The software tag data plan made by TagPlanner is saved as the standard software tag format explained in section 3.1. Software tag plan made by TagPlanner is useful when the purchaser and the developer agree to which tag elements are used. TagPlanner is also useful as the guideline of tag data collection and tag elements selection by referring the typical example of project's tasks and metrics for tag elements.

Software Tag Data Collection Tool (*CollectTag*)

CollectTag supports collection of empirical data from software projects and creation of a software tag. CollectTag uses a wizard as a user interface, allowing the user (developer) to easily input the necessary data for the software tag. For each project, the purchasers and developers determine the metrics for the tag elements. To provide generality, we implemented CollectTag as a translator that converts a set of empirical data provided by the developer into the standard software tag format. That is, the developer periodically inputs values for each tag element, and then CollectTag outputs a software tag.

First, a user selects a tag element, and settles a metric for the element. For example, when [Programming]-[Scale] (#19) is selected, the user can select [Lines of code] or [Function point] (Fig. 3).

Next, the user selects data input method (Fig. 4). To reduce the effort of data input, CollectTag provides automatic data collection mechanisms for 11 of the tag elements in the progress information, if the target project uses common software development tools for configuration management and bug tracking. For example, LOC (#19: Scale) and CK (#21: Complexity) metrics [3] can be automatically collected and calculated from configuration management tools such as CVS or Subversion. When data is input manually, empirical data should be related to the data.

Finally, CollectTag generates the software tag elements in standard software tag format. This makes it easy to provide the output to other visualization and analysis tools for further processing.

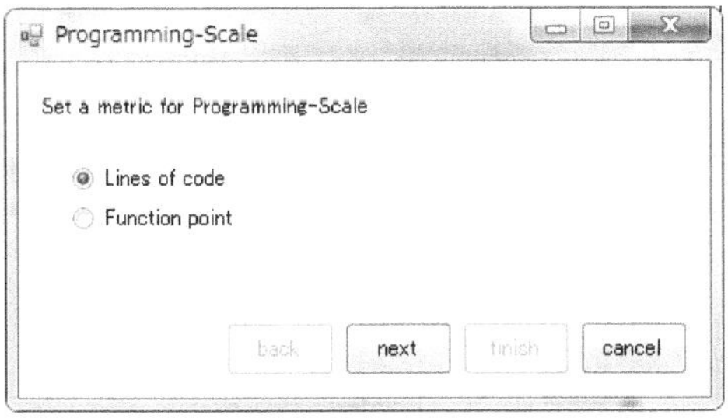

Fig. 3. Selecting a Metric (CollectTag)

Software Tag Visualization Tool (*TagReplayer*)

TagReplayer provides fundamental features for integrated visualization of various historical data included in standard software tag format data. TagReplayer employs the metaphor of video player manipulation for its user interface so that users can replay the progress of the project just like watching video on TV. Users can also instantly recall the details of any points along the timeline based on the software tag. TagReplayer aligns progress information from the software tag as a series of events.

Fig. 4. Selecting an Input Method (CollectTag)

Fig. 5 is a screenshot of TagReplayer. Details of TagReplayer are explained below.

Time bar: The time bar indicates a point of time which TagReplayer replays a project. By moving slider, replay goes to a certain point of time. Replay interval can be changed, and stopping, fast forward or fast rewind of replay are also available.
Event list view: On the event list view, tag data is listed by time series. A user knows events happened on a certain day from the view.

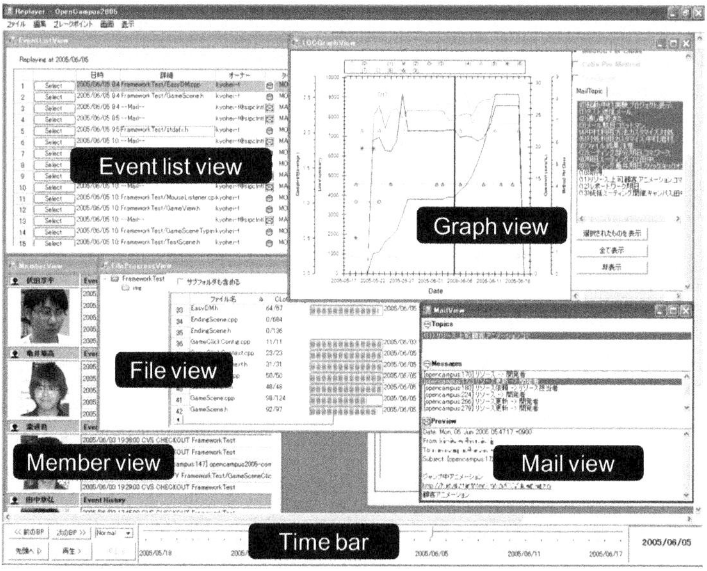

Fig. 5. TagReplayer Screenshot

Graph view: The graph view shows transition of lines of code (LOC) during a project using line graph. Moreover, topics made from natural text mining and clustering of mail archive are overlaid on the chart, and it helps understanding what was happened on the project.
Member view: The member view displays assigned tasks and completed task history of each project member. A user also sees workload of each member from the view.
File view: The file view indicates completion rate of each file at time point of replaying. The completion rate is computed using cumulative changed LOC at the end of the project. Using the view, a user recognizes dilatory files.
Mail view: The mail view shows detail of topics shown in the graph view. The view includes topics list, mail subject list, and a mail body.

Also, TagReplayer has the breakpoint function which stops replay if a certain condition is true, and the function which shows source code at time point of replaying.

To confirm effectiveness of TagReplayer, software development process in which some students engaged was replayed to subjects who did not engaged in the project, using TagReplayer. As a result, subjects recognized stagnant period and the reason of stagnant. This experience shows that TagReplayer is very useful for postmortem project reviews.

3.3 Applications of the Software Tag

We present here three example cases of application of the software tags scheme to real software projects.

- A course registration system for a university with 26K LOC in Java was developed for five months by a medium-sized software company in Japan. 32 elements of tag data were collected, and we analyzed data to know the project status. Comparing test density (#24) and defect density (#31) with the publicly available benchmark values from the Software Engineering Center in Japan (SEC), they are lower than the benchmark value. It means that using the software tag, the purchasers and developers see the probability of insufficient testing density. Also, we analyzed transition of total amount of source code (#19; programming scale), modified amount of source code (#20; programming revisions), and static check results (#33). They varied at a certain day during test phase, and from a commit comment on a SCM, refactoring was done on the day. So, such tag elements are useful to know characteristic event in the project.
- A medium-sized stock exchange system for a stock market was enhanced by a Japanese major software development company for more than two years. Projects data is offered from the company to us, and we made the software tags from it. We speculated project status based on the analysis of them, and interviewed the company to confirm actual status of the projects. According to the results, we concluded that comparing tag elements related to the requirements phase such as requirements revisions (#15), number of defects about design (#29; defect count), and number of review (#26; review status) between functions, the purchaser and developer were able to identify problems with the requirements completeness caused by frequent changes.

– A Japanese software development company ordered several small-sized projects such as development of a project management support system from various offshore companies in China and Korea. Three finished projects data is offered from the company to us. We analyzed it and interviewed the company to confirmed actual status of the projects. As a result, we concluded that although remotely located from each other, the purchasers and developers could understand the progress of the specifications comparing tag elements such as the number of review (#26; review status), the number of user hearing (#13; user hearing information), and number of defects about design (#29; defect count) between functions.

4 Activities for Promotion and Diffusion

The StagE project is also actively promoting and diffusing the software tags scheme in industry as follows.

International/Domestic Standardization
Interviews with several Japanese software purchasers and developers, along with offshore software developers for Japanese companies in some countries, convinced us that most software purchasers and developers would strongly demand that the software tag and tools should be international and/or domestic technical standards in software engineering. To support this, we are now serving ISO as a committee member of the working group on process assessment, ISO/ITC JTC1/SC7/WG10. We are also working with some software tool developers to construct a de facto standard software project management system that includes the tag support tools mentioned in Sec. 3.2.

International Collaboration
Offshore software development is one of the most useful application areas of the software tag scheme. To encourage and accelerate international collaboration to have various kinds of case studies and experiments of the software tag in offshore software development, we established Asia-Pacific Software Engineering Research Network (APSERN) in 2008 with software engineering researchers in NICTA (National ICT Australia), ISCAS (The Institute of Software, Chinese Academy of Sciences), and so on.

Professional Discussion of Legal Issues
In the case of a legal dispute between software purchasers and developers, the software tag can clarify their liabilities and has the potential to help resolve such legal issues in software development. The StagE project has a committee examining the legal issues of software development. Members of this committee include lawyers, patent attorneys, and software engineers. The committee has interviewed many software developers in Japan and China to compile data about troubles between software purchasers and developers. It also distributed questionnaires to more than a hundred software developers in Japan to analyze the trends of such troubles. The software tag provides an opportunity for collaboration between software engineering and software trade law.

5 Discussion

Discussions about the software tag scheme are described below.

- There are metrics repositories aimed at improving and benchmarking development organizations [6], along with some software measurement paradigms [2], [4], [8], [9]. Also, there are projects which involve some companies and are now coping with establishment of software quality [12] [13]. However, the software tag provides a unique approach to involve software purchasers in the quality improvement framework by providing development transparency. As far as we know, there is no similar approach presented in the technical literature.
- We believe that the benefits of the software tag scheme for software purchasers will be substantial because the development processes and the developed products become more visible and understandable. However, purchasers will need to collaborate more closely with developers, providing effort and enthusiasm to create successful projects.
- We have presented the first standard of the software tag with 41 elements. In some sense, these are very basic data for indicating development quality, and they may be insufficient to perform detailed analysis. However, as a standard used for various software development projects, the set should be minimal and low cost. As presented in Sec. 3.1 and 3.2, our tag standard 1.0 is a lightweight set with low collection and assembly cost. It is important to continue practical applications of the software tag, and to get feedback for further improvement of the standard.
- Some developers disclose information whose role is similar to the software tag with the progress report meeting. The progress report meeting and software tag bring similar effects. Metrics used in the activity may be similar to tag elements, so tag elements are considered to be not uncommon. Still the software tag is effective to propagate such a good practice involved the purchaser.
- The role of the software tag is similar to the medical checkup and financial statements. On the medical checkup, many bodily data are collected and evaluated, and the results are shown to the person to see his/her health condition. Financial statements which are used for settlement of accounts indicate amount and flow of capital by various money amounts. They are disclosed investors and business partners to exhibit soundness of the company. In the similar way, the software tag discloses various project and product metrics to the purchaser to signify soundness of process and products.
- Although there may be the risk of tampering software tag data, it is difficult to tamper several tag elements with keeping consistency through some versions of software tags. On the other hand, it is not difficult to rebuild the software tag from stored source data. Hence, tampering software tag data would not get along. It may be a good way that a third party stores source data of the software tag, and verify correctness of the software tag when conflict occurs. Also, the third party may analyze data to guarantee independence of the evaluation and reliability of the results.
- Software tag standard 1.0 does not include concrete metrics. However, it would be not easy to settle metrics for many tag elements from scratch. A catalog of typical metrics set for software tag elements should be made to support planning software tag in the future. The catalog will be organized by the purpose, and explain how to

collect and analyze tag elements. The catalog will be browsed on TagPlanner (see Sec. 3.2). With analyze methods and benchmarks on the catalogue, purchasers csn confirm validity of evaluation of software tags to some extent.

6 Conclusions

We have introduced our activities for standardization of the software tag in Japan. The software tag contains software development data, and it brings purchasers transparency of software development. We identified 41 items for seeing software process and products, and defined them as the standard tag element set. To support software tag scheme, we made tools for planning, collecting, and analyzing tag data. From three example cases of application of the software tags scheme, it is expected that the software tag scheme is useful to find problems of requirement analysis or to grasp progress of offshore software development.

Through these activities, the concept of the software tag is becoming well understood in Japan. From discussion with purchasers and developers, we think that their interest toward development data sharing gets higher than before, and they seem to be realizing how to use the software tag in detail. It appears that for purchasers and developers who have software development management skill, the software tag scheme has small disadvantage but has possibility of big advantage.

Our future work will focus on making international/domestic standards of the software tag. With such standardization, the software tag is expected to be used in various software industries, where we think it will strongly promote participation and understanding of software development by purchasers. Also, to reduce adaptation cost of the software tag, we will delivery software tag support tools and the software tag guidebook which explains how to use the software tag. That would accelerate incorporating the software tag scheme in the industrial practices. Moreover, we will make a template of the contract document, considering software tag and legal issues of software development.

Acknowledgments

This work is being conducted as a part of the StagE project, The Development of Next-Generation IT Infrastructure, supported by the Ministry of Education, Culture, Sports, Science and Technology. We are grateful to the members of the StagE project, especially to Michael Barker, Akito Monden, Makoto Matsushita, and Shuji Morisaki.

References

1. Barker, M., Matsumoto, M., Inoue, K.: Putting a TAG on Software: Purchaser-Centered Software Engineering. In: Ramachandran, M., Carvalho, R.A. (eds.) Handbook of Research on Software Engineering and Productivity Technologies: Implications of Globalization, pp. 38–48. Information Science Reference, Hershey (2009)
2. Basili, V.R., Rombach, H.D.: The TAME Project: Towards Improvement-Oriented Software Environments. IEEE Trans. Software Eng. 14(6), 758–773 (1988)

3. Chidamber, S.R., Kemerer, C.F.: A Metrics Suite for Object Oriented Design. IEEE Trans. Software Eng. 20(6), 476–493 (1994)
4. Chirinos, L., Losavio, F., Bøegh, J.: Characterizing a data model for software measurement. Journal of Systems and Software 74(2), 207–226 (2005)
5. Inoue, K.: Software Tag for Traceability and Transparency of Maintenance. In: Proceedings of 24th IEEE International Conference on Software Maintenance, ICSM 2008, pp. 476–477 (2008)
6. International Software Benchmarking Standards Group (ISBSG): ISBSG Estimating: Benchmarking and research suite (2004)
7. ISO/IEC 12207: Systems and software engineering - Software life cycle processes. International Organization for Standardization (2008)
8. ISO/IEC 15939: Software engineering - Software measurement process framework. International Organization for Standardization (2002)
9. Kitchenham, B.A., Hughes, R.T., Linkman, S.G.: Modeling Software Measurement Data. IEEE Trans. Software Eng. 27(9), 788–804 (2001)
10. Nikkei Business Publications, Inc.: Survey Report on IT Investment and CTO in Japan. Nikkei Information Strategy (March 2008) (in Japanese)
11. Nikkei Business Publications, Inc.: Second Survey of Japanese Software Projects. Nikkei Computer, December 1, pp. 36–53 (2008) (in Japanese)
12. The Consortium for IT Software Quality: CISQ – The Global Standard for IT Software Quality, `http://www.it-cisq.org/`
13. The Quamoco Consortium: Quamoco – The Benchmark for Software Quality, `https://quamoco.in.tum.de/wordpress/?lang=en`

Discovering Software Process and Product Quality Criteria in Software as a Service

Maiara Heil Cancian[1], Jean Carlo Rossa Hauck[2], Christiane Gresse von Wangenheim[3], and Ricardo José Rabelo[1]

[1] Department of Automation and Systems - Federal University of Santa Catarina - Brazil
[2] Graduate Program in Knowledge Engineering and Management, Federal University of Santa Catarina - Brazil
[3] Graduate Program in Computer Science (PPGCC), Federal University of Santa Catarina - Brazil
maiara@das.ufsc.br, {jeanhauck,gresse}@gmail.com, rabelo@das.ufsc.br

Abstract. SaaS (Software as a Service) has become one of the fastest-growing innovative fields of the IT sector. Yet, as any other software intensive organizations, SaaS providers also need to deliver the service quality they offer. And, although, today exist a multitude of software quality models, so far, a specific adaptation does not exist to the SaaS context. Therefore, we present the results of our research on discovering software process and product quality criteria in the SaaS scenario. We adopted a research methodology, including, domain analysis, stakeholders interviews and literature review to elicit quality criteria and a survey to validate and prioritize the identified criteria. Such a set of identified quality criteria may help service clients to select providers as well as serve as a basis for a mapping relevant software process areas and best practices in order to adapt existing capability/maturity models and standards to this specific domain.

Keywords: Software process quality, software product quality, SaaS - Software as a Service.

1 Introduction

The Service Oriented Architecture (SOA) paradigm has introduced a new outlook on system design and integration, where all system features are treated as independent and self-contained software services. There are many technologies to implement SOA solutions and web services are currently the most used [1], [2]. Following this trend, business models that employ this paradigm have been widely adopted, like in the case of Software as a Service (SaaS). SaaS is an availability model for software services offered to clients through the Internet that are accessed on demand and paid per use [3]. Among the advantages we can highlight that software solutions can be more rapidly composed, avoiding high investments on infrastructure and IT administration. So, the provider (organization that delivers a service) offers the service through the Internet and creates a Service License Agreements (SLA) [4]. In this model, clients seek

M. Ali Babar, M. Vierimaa, and M. Oivo (Eds.): PROFES 2010, LNCS 6156, pp. 234–247, 2010.
© Springer-Verlag Berlin Heidelberg 2010

and select services that, when invoked, will be used by their local applications, no matter, if it is isolated or integrated into a Business Process Management (BPM) environment. As such, clients need to assure that the quality of the evocable services is reliable [5]. On the other hand, in order to be competitive within the market and to provide quality services that meet the SLA established with the clients, SaaS providers must deliver the service quality they offer. And, as any other kind of software intensive organization today, organizations that provide SaaS solutions also need to improve the maturity of their software process as a whole.

Yet, the remaining question is: what are exactly software process and product quality criteria to be considered in the SaaS scenario. In general, quality is defined as the satisfaction of a product or a service to specific customer needs [6]; perception and satisfaction of the market needs, use adequacy and/or process results homogeneity [7]; and/or alignment to the product requirements [8]. Considering software development, in general, there is a large number of models and standards related to software quality, such as, ISO 9126 [9], as well as software process maturity/capability models and standards, including, CMMI [10] or ISO/IEC 15504 [11] and ISO/IEC 12207 [12]. Yet, considering that those models and standards are intended to provide a generic support for a large range of software organizations, they typically need to be customized to a specific domain or sector to adequately support the specific needs of this environment [13]. In fact, we can observe a current trend to the customization of process capability/maturity models and standards for various domains, such as, OOSPICE [14] for component-based development, S4S [15] for space applications and CMCM [16] for the medical device industry. And, although, there are a great variety of such customizations is being performed, so far, there is not one directed specifically on the SaaS scenario. The existing models focus on traditional acquisition business models. Recently new models have attempted to cope with SOA requirements or services, but not with SaaS in particular. Quality and trustworthiness in loosely coupled computational systems – which is the case of SaaS – have received great attention in the last recent years [17]. Actually, there is neither a largely adopted definition for it nor for the best way to manage it [18].

In this regard, we can observe that also the SaaS scenario, which combines clients' needs and providers' support, a number of specific requirements meed to be considered in order to assure the necessary global reliability and trustworthiness. But, so far, there does not yet is a customized model indicating important software process and product quality criteria for SaaS [19]. The existence of such a customized process reference model indicating a set of best practices specifically relevant within the SaaS scenario could optimize software process improvement investments and improve the quality of the provided services.

In this context, we describe in this paper a first step regarding the customization of existing quality and process capability/maturity models by systematically discovering relevant software product and process quality criteria in the SaaS scenario. In the second section of this paper, we describe related work, followed by section 3, where our research methodology is presented. Results of this work are stepwise described in section 4 to 7 and the conclusions are presented in section 8.

2 Related Work

Today there is a large variety of software quality and process maturity/capability models [13], [20]. Among then, there is the standard ISO/IEC 25000 (SQuaRE - Software Product Quality Requirements and Evaluation) [21], which establishes a view of software product quality criteria by the definition of quality requirements and evaluation. On the other hand, there is a multitude of process capability/maturity models, including, the CMMI framework, ISO/IEC 15504, ISO/IEC 12207, which define a set of best practices for software process improvement and assessment. And, although those models provide a generic set of best practices applicable on a large scope of software processes, they are not specifically adapted to the SaaS scenario.

Recently, reference models focused on services have received increased attention, such as, the constellation CMMI for Services (CMMI-SVC) [22] or ITIL [23]. Yet, these models refer to services in a broader sense than considered in the SaaS scenario. For example, the CMMI for services constellation covers the activities required to establish, deliver, and manage services, which are defined as intangible, non-storable products. And early users of CMMI-SVC have used the model for services as varied as training, logistics, lawn care, etc. In contrast, within the SaaS context, the concept of a service is defined as a component of SOA. Therefore, those models also are not specifically adapted to the SaaS business model.

On the other hand, we can observe a general trend to develop domain-specific reference models, adapting and customizing those generic reference models. Based on the results of a systematic literature review [24], we can observe that there exist more than 50 domain-specific reference models today, covering a large range of domains, such as, automotive software [25], space software [26], component based software development [14], among others. Yet, so far there is not a specific reference model for the SaaS scenario.

3 Research Methodology

In this context, our long term research goal is the development of a customized software process capability/maturity model for the SaaS scenario. In this context, we observe that currently there is not a systematic methodology on how to perform such an adaptation for a specific domain [24] and most of the current customizations have been done in an ad hoc manner. Exceptions are the works done by [27], [28], which describe the adaptation process in detail.

Thus, based on the approach presented by [27], we firstly identify software process and product quality criteria, which will then in a future research step be used as a basis to identify relevant process areas and best practices required to satisfy those quality criteria.

In this paper, we describe the first step of our research, the identification of software process and product quality criteria.

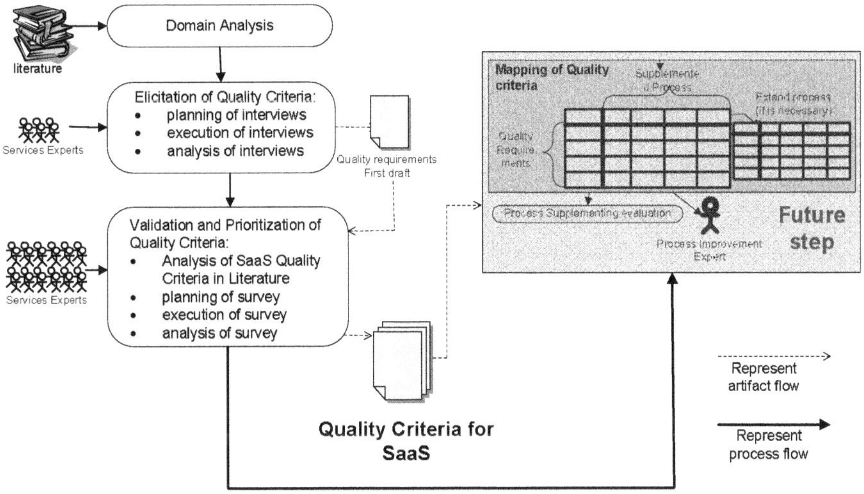

Fig. 1. Research Methodology

In order to identify the software process and product quality criteria we performed the following steps (Figure 1):

Domain Analysis: in order to characterize the specific context of the SaaS scenario and to identify relevant characteristics as well as to identify relevant stakeholders. This step has been done based on literature review. Within this step, we also identified a set of quality criteria for the SaaS scenario described in literature.

Elicitation of Quality Criteria: in order to elicit relevant software process and product quality criteria for services and processes to be considered or demanded from SaaS service providers. Therefore, we conducted interviews with a small group of experienced professionals involved in the use, development and provision of software services. The interviews were planned, executed and analyzed resulting in a list of relevant quality criteria. As result, a set of quality criteria was identified.

Validation and Prioritization of Quality Criteria: in order to review the quality criteria obtained in the previous step and to prioritize them by their importance in the SaaS scenario. Therefore, we mapped and completed the quality criteria obtained in the previous step to quality criteria identified in literature. In a second step, we performed a survey by consulting a greater number of stakeholder representatives and experts, who reviewed (and, if necessary, included new criteria) as well as prioritized the criteria according to their relevance within the SaaS business model.

Based on the results obtained in these steps, we are planning as a future research step the mapping of the identified quality criteria to relevant software process areas and practices by adapting software process capability/maturity models (CMMI and

ISO/IEC 15504) following the methodology presented in [27] in order to specify relevant process profiles within the SaaS scenario.

4 Domain Analysis

SaaS is a software solution offered as a service, which is developed using SOA [29]. The solution is accessed through the internet, saving the implementation and maintenance of a TI infra-structure by the client as the complete structure demanded to develop, process and maintain remains stored at the provider [30]. The client keeps the rights on their data and the software usage. At no point, s/he needs to authorize or buy the software as if it was a product [31]. Those aspects are well known in the Cloud Computing world [32].

Using SaaS, the client assembles their software service portfolio in accordance with their necessity. It can be easily altered, featuring new service or excluding some service hired previously. This is possible, because the release is detached and on-line.

This scenario comes with many benefits. From the client's perspective, they pay only for real usage. Additionally, there is the possibility to use the service for some time, and in case s/he finds the service unsatisfactory, terminate the contract, considering the fact that, in the SaaS scenario, the clients do not own a software license. On the provider's perspective, they can assist the needs of the client more precisely. Figure 2 shows a hypothetical example of a client provider relation in the SaaS model. In this example, the provider provides five services and the client assembles her portfolio with three services.

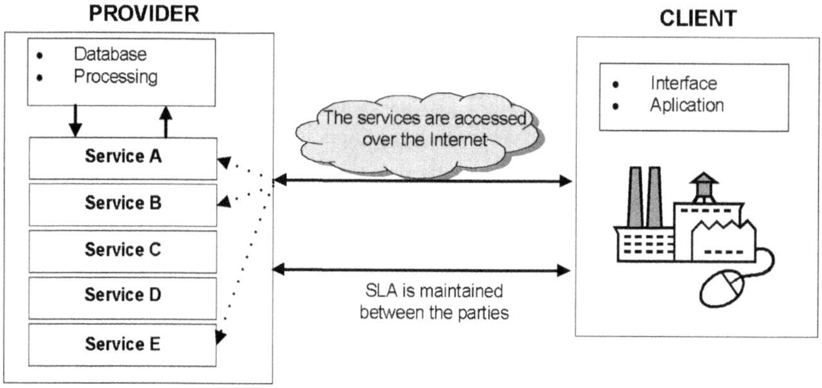

Fig. 2. Overview on the SaaS scenario

What rules a bureaucratic negotiation (referring to usage, execution and service access) between the client and the provider is an Service Level Agreement (SLA) [33].

5 Elicitation of Quality Criteria

Based on the domain analysis, we conducted a series of interviews in order to elicit relevant software process and product quality criteria in the SaaS scenario. As a result of the domain analysis, we identified various relevant stakeholders (Figure 3).

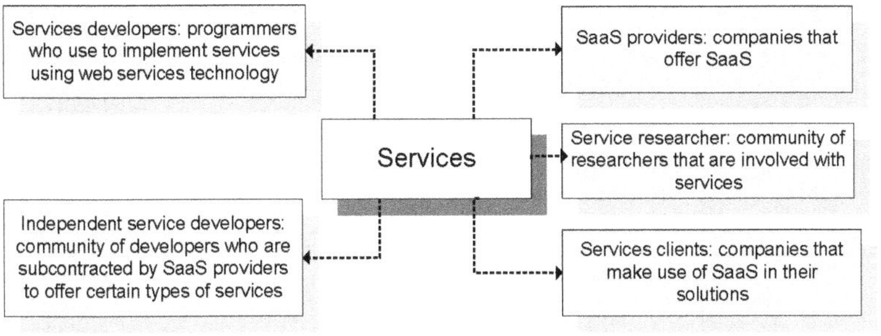

Fig. 3. Stakeholder categories in the SaaS scenario

Based on the domain analysis, structured interviews were planned, including mainly open-ended questions. The goal of these interviews was to identify software product and process quality criteria in the SaaS scenario. To achieve this goal, the following questions were posed:

- General information about the interviewee (experience, work place, etc.);
- Differences between the traditional scenario and SaaS, problems the interviewees observed and their expectations;
- Quality needs when selecting/ providing services in the SaaS scenario.

In total, we performed 6 individual interviews during August/September 2008 with representatives of each of the stakeholder categories. The interviewee's categories are:

- Interviewee 1: service researcher;
- Interviewee 2: independent service developer;
- Interviewee 3: service client;
- Interviewee 4: service developer;
- Interviewee 5 and 6: SaaS provider.

In average, the interviews lasted about 90 minutes.

As a result of the interviews, we analyzed and synthesized the collected information by attributing a formal description to each of the elicited criteria and by unifying items with the same meaning into a unified list of relevant software process and product quality criteria (Table 1).

Table 1. Quality criteria elicited through the interviews

Criteria	Description	Source
Acquisition	Refers to the acquisition process from the point of view of the customer.	Interviewee 1 Interviewee 5
Availability	Refers to the availability of the service for immediate use.	Interviewee 2 Interviewee 4
Change control	Refers to the change control process in order to minimize the impact of changes.	Interviewee 4 Interviewee 5
Help desk	Refers to the support process focusing on the way customers will be assisted when using the service.	Interviewee 2 Interviewee 3 Interviewee 4
Infrastructure capability	Refers to the extent to which the available infrastructure is adequate and sufficient.	Interviewee 4
Interoperability	Refers to the capability of communicating as transparently as possible to other systems.	Interviewee 1
Maintenance	Refers to the maintenance process in order to perform changes in software according to requests.	Interviewee 1 Interviewee 2 Interviewee 4 Interviewee 5
Prevision of continuity of service	Refers to extent to which an organization is able to provide the continuation of technical resources and IT systems / services	Interviewee 4 Interviewee 6
Process improvement	Refers to the process improvement process focusing on the improvement of software process capability.	Interviewee 1 Interviewee 3
Quality control	Refers to the quality control process in order to ensure that the process of the provided service meets the requirements.	Interviewee 4
Requirements development and management	Refers to the requirements development and management process to ensure that the service meets specifications.	Interviewee 1 Interviewee 3 Interviewee 4 Interviewee 5
Security	Refers to the protection of a dataset, in the sense of preserving their value for a person or organization. They are attributes of confidentiality, integrity and availability, security of computational systems, electronic information and data.	Interviewee 1 Interviewee 2 Interviewee 4 Interviewee 5 Interviewee 6
Technically competent employees	Refers to the extent to which employees have sufficient and adequate technical competencies.	Interviewee 1 Interviewee 2 Interviewee 5
Technically competent in business	Refers to the extent to which employees have sufficient and adequate business competencies.	Interviewee 1 Interviewee 3 Interviewee 5
Testing	Refers to the test process in order to verify and validate that the service corresponds to the defined requirements.	Interviewee 1 Interviewee 6
Utilization of standards	Refers to the extent to which services can be accessed and visualized by any person or technology, independently of hardware/software platforms.	Interviewee 4 Interviewee 6
Version control	Refers to the version control process to establish and keep the integrity of versions.	Interviewee 2

This set of quality criteria represents just the first step for the elicitation of SaaS quality criteria, and is being validated and prioritized in the next step.

6 Validation and Prioritization of Quality Criteria

The objective of this step was to validate and prioritize the quality criteria obtained in the previous step. Therefore, we first compared and completed the obtained quality criteria based on quality criteria identified in literature.

Due to the fact, that, currently there do not yet exist quality models specifically for the SaaS scenario, we amplified the scope of related literature, analyzing quality criteria related to the context of web services, which are strongly related to the SaaS scenario. In this regard, a main contribution is the work by Sabata [34] and Mani et al [35]. As a result, the following quality criteria (Table 2) have been identified based on a literature analysis and considered adequate also within the SaaS scenario.

Table 2. Quality criteria based on literature analysis

CRITERIA	DESCRIPTION	SOURCE
Accessibility	Refers to the extent in which a service really provides a service, because a service can be available, but not accessible.	[35], [36], [37]
Integrity	Refers to the behavior of a service executing a transaction. After finishing a transaction, the state of information must be free of inconsistencies.	[36], [38], [39]
Performance	Refers to the throughput (number of requisitions per time unit) and latency (time between sending the requisition and receiving the answer).	[35], [39], [40]
Reliability	Refers to the availability and reliability of IT resources.	[35], [38], [41]
Robustness	Refers to the extent to which a service keeps working even in the presence of inconsistent or incomplete data.	[36], [37]
Scalability	Refers to the capability of processing more requisitions in a time interval without compromising the service.	[36], [41]

Based on this completed set of quality criteria, we performed a survey in order to validate and prioritize the criteria. In order to do so, we prepared a questionnaire listing and describing the elicited quality criteria and requesting the respondents to prioritize each one on a 4-point ordinal scale ranging from essential to unnecessary. Respondents also could include new criteria or make comments. In addition, we also collected demographic information on the background of the respondents. The survey has been made available online using the tool LimeSurvey (http://www.limesurvey.org).

With the objective to involve a larger sample in the survey, we selected stakeholder representatives from various countries by inviting:

- Research groups and individuals, who have been working on software services and are known by the authors through international research projects, mailing lists and special interested groups;
- Authors of related scientific papers of conferences and journals concerning software services;
- A search for relevant professionals based on their resumes posted in the Internet.

We run the survey in 2008 inviting a group of 280 professionals. The survey was available for 60 days and in total we received 84 responses, representing a response rate of 30%. For the analysis of the collected information, we excluded 2 completed questionnaires, as they had been completed by people without sufficient experience regarding the SaaS scenario. The obtained information has been analyzed considering the following objectives:

1. Completeness: in general the respondents confirmed the identified quality criteria. Only two new criteria were indicated (Governance and Reputation) and incorporated into the set of qualities criteria (yet, as these criteria were included only during the survey they were not considered for the prioritization).

	ESSENTIAL	VERY IMPORTANT	IMPORTANT	UNNECESSARY	ESSENTIAL	VERY IMPORTANT	IMPORTANT	UNNECESSARY	TOTAL
Weights:	4	3	2	1	weight x responses number				
	Responses number								
Integrity	57	21	5	0	228	63	10	0	**301**
Reliability	48	30	4	1	192	90	8	1	**291**
Security	45	31	7	0	180	93	14	0	**287**
Accessibility	49	21	13	0	196	63	26	0	**285**
Requirements development and management	41	29	13	0	164	87	26	0	**277**
Infrastructure capability	28	48	6	1	112	144	12	1	**269**
Quality control	32	37	14	0	128	111	28	0	**267**
Acquisition	28	40	15	0	112	120	30	0	**262**
Testing	26	44	12	1	104	132	24	1	**261**
Performance	22	47	13	1	88	141	26	1	**256**
Utilization of standards	29	34	18	2	116	102	36	2	**256**
Change control	26	39	16	2	104	117	32	2	**255**
Interoperability	23	42	17	1	92	126	34	1	**253**
Robustness	24	39	19	1	96	117	38	1	**252**
Availability	28	34	16	5	112	102	32	5	**251**
Maintenance	24	37	20	2	96	111	40	2	**249**
Version control	18	46	18	1	72	138	36	1	**247**
Technically competent in business	19	42	21	1	76	126	42	1	**245**
Technically competent employees	24	31	27	1	96	93	54	1	**244**
Prevision of continuity of service	24	34	21	4	96	102	42	4	**244**
Scalability	17	41	24	1	68	123	48	1	**240**
Help desk	17	40	25	1	68	120	50	1	**239**
Process quality certification	5	30	39	9	20	90	78	9	**197**
Governance	complementation								
Reputation	complementation								

Fig. 4. Priorization results

2. Prioritization: in order to visualize an order of importance based on the classification of each of the criteria by the respondents, we calculated the rating by attributing weights to the classification (4-essential to 1- unnecessary) and then added up the weighted responses of all respondents per criteria. Figure 4 illustrates the results of the prioritization by indicating in the column Total the total weighted sum of each of the criteria.

In general, we can observe that basically all criteria identified in the previous steps were considered relevant within the SaaS context. An exception is the criteria "process quality certification" of the provider, which has been excluded from the set of relevant criteria due to its low prioritization, indicating the unimportance of the item. The requirements which are marked as "Complementation" were suggested by the survey participants and were considered relevant for this scenario.

7 Results: Quality Criteria for SaaS

Summarizing the results from our research, we obtained a set of relevant quality criteria in the SaaS scenario. The resulting criteria have been classified in:

- Product-related quality criteria: criteria related to the provided product and/or service.
- Process-related quality criteria: criteria related to the software process adopted for the development, operation and maintenance of the provided software product/service.
- Organization-related quality criteria: criteria related to the organization providing software products/services within the SaaS business model.

Table 3, 4 and 5 list the identified quality criteria.

Table 3. Product related quality criteria

Criteria	Description
Accessibility	Refers to the extent in which a service really provides a service, as a service can be available, but not accessible.
Reliability	Refers to the extent of the availability and reliability of IT services or resources
Performance	Refers to the throughput (number of requisitions per time unit) and latency (time between sending the requisition and receiving the answer).
Availability	Refers to the availability of the service for immediate use.
Scalability	Refers to the capability of processing more requisitions in a time interval without compromising the service.
Security	Refers to the protection of a dataset, in the sense of preserving their value for a person or organization as an attribute of confidentiality, integrity and availability, security of computational systems, electronic information and data.
Integrity	Refers to the behavior of a service executing a transaction. After finishing a transaction, the state of information must be free of inconsistencies
Interoperability	Refers to the capability of communicating as transparently as possible to other systems.
Robustness	Refers to the extent to which a service keeps working even in the presence of inconsistent or incomplete data.

Table 4. Process related quality criteria

Criteria	Description
Acquisition	Refers to the acquisition process from the point of view of the customer.
Change control	Refers to the change control process in order to minimize the impact of changes.
Quality control	Refers to the quality control process in order to ensure that the process of the provided service meets the specified requirements.
Version control	Refers to the version control process to establish and keep the integrity of versions.
Requirements dev. and management	Refers to the requirements development and management process to ensure that the service meets specifications.
Maintenance	Refers to the maintenance process in order to perform changes in software according to requests.
Process Improve-ment	Refers to the process improvement process focusing on the improvement of software process capability.
Help desk	Refers to the support process focusing on the way customers will be assisted when using the service.
Testing	Refers to the test process in order to verify and validate that the service corresponds to the defined requirements.

Table 5. Organization related quality criteria

Criteria	Description
Infrastructure capability	Refers to the extent to which the available infrastructure is adequate and sufficient.
Technically competent employees	Refers to the extent to which employees have sufficient and adequate technical competencies.
Prevision of continuity of service	Refers to extent to which an organization is able to provide the continuation of technical resources and IT systems / services
Technically competent in business	Refers to the extent to which employees have sufficient and adequate business competencies.
Utilization of standards	Refers to the extent to which services can be accessed and visualized by any person or technology, independently of hardware/software platforms.
Governance	Refers to factors that show how a company is directed, administered or controlled.
Reputation	Refers to the conceptualization of the provider in the community/market (image).

7.1 Discussion

With this research, we made a first step into the direction of identifying a set of software process and product quality criteria relevant within the SaaS business model. Yet, it is important to consider some limitations of the validity of the results of the research. A question in this context is the representativeness of the obtained results. Within the first step, the elicitation of the quality criteria, we performed only a small number of interviews (6) with representatives of different viewpoints on the SaaS scenario. As a result, this may limit the generaly of the results. Yet, in order to increase the validity, we performed in a second step a validation and prioritization of the obtained results in form of a survey involving a total of 84 participants. Regarding the survey, on the other hand, the response rate of about 30% of the 280 invited participants may be a limitation. Although, this represents an acceptable response rate, the derived results may not comprehensively represent the knowledge of experts in this domain and therefore may restrict the external validity of the results.

Another question, may be the level of expertise of the participants, as the SaaS scenario is still very recent and the participants experiences may vary largely, affecting the validity of their responses. This is further complicated by the fact, that as SaaS is an emergent area, there is not a solid theoretical foundation yet. This may also have affected the construct validity of the results due to a lack of well-understood terminology in this domain and thus causing misunderstandings by the participants. As much as possible, descriptions and explanations were provided to sustain the questions.

8 Conclusions

In this paper, we identify a set of software process and product quality criteria relevant within the SaaS business model. Within this context, this may contribute to increase its acceptance in a larger scale by helping service clients to evaluate and select service providers. Such a set of quality criteria may be a useful instrument to help services companies to create new sustainable models as well as help to a larger adoption of SaaS models. Especially, when considering the current paradigm shift from local computing systems to several pervasive-based systems running under SaaS model, the demand on service quality tends to become even greater.

In addition, such a set of software process and product quality criteria also creates a basis for the customization of a software process capability/maturity model pointing out relevant best practices specifically within the SaaS domain, guiding software process assessment and improvement. Therefore, one of our next steps is to map the identified quality criteria to software process areas and best practices adapting and evolving existing software process capability/maturity models and standards (such as, ISO/IEC 15504-5/ISO/IEC 12207 and CMMI).

Acknowledgements

This work was supported by the CNPq (Conselho Nacional de Desenvolvimento Científico e Tecnológico) and CAPES (Coordenação de Aperfeiçoamento de Pessoal de Nível Superior), both entities of the Brazilian government focused on scientific and technological development.

References

1. Singh, M.P., Huhns, M.N.: Service-Oriented Computing Semantics, Processes, Agents. John Wiley & Sons, Ltd., Chichester (2004)
2. Tsai, W.T.: Service-oriented system engineering: a new paradigm. In: IEEE International Workshop on Service-Oriented System Engineering, SOSE 2005, Beijing, China, pp. 3–6 (2005)

3. Eliadis, H., Rand, A.: Setting Expectations In Saas: The Importance of the Service Level Agreement to Saas Providers and Consumers. In: SIIA Software as a Service Working Group Software & Information Industry Association (2007)
4. Arenas, A., Wilson, M.: Contracts as Trust Substitutes in Collaborative Business. Computer 41(7), 80–83 (2008)
5. Kourtesis, D., et al.: Discovery and Selection of Certified Web Services Through Registry-Based Testing and Verification. In: Pervasive Collaborative Networks, pp. 473–482 (2008)
6. Juran, J.M.: Juran Planejamento para a qualidade, Pioneira, São Paulo, p. 394 (1990)
7. Ishikawa, K.: TQC, Total Quality Control: Estratégia e Administração da qualidade. IMC Internacional sistemas educativos São Paulo (1986)
8. Crosby, P.B.: Qualidade falada a sério. Mc Graw - Hill do Brasil São Paulo (1990)
9. ISO/IEC, International Organization for Standardization (ISO) / International Electrotechnical Commission (IEC). Standart 9126: Software engineering - Product quality (2004)
10. Team, C.P.: CMMI for Development (CMMI-DEV), in Technical Report CMU/SEI-2006-TR-008, V. 1.2, Editor Carnegie Mellon University / Software Engineering Institute: Pittsburgh (2006)
11. ISO/IEC, International Organization for Standardization and International Electrotechnical Commission, ISO/IEC 15504-5: Information Technology - Process Assessment, in Part 5: An exemplar Process Assessment Model, Genebra (2006)
12. ISO/IEC, International Organization for Standardization and International Electrotechnical Commission, ISO/IEC 12207: Standart for Information Technology. IEEE, New York (1998)
13. Paulk, M.C.: Surviving the Quagmire of Process Models, Integrated Models, and Standards. In: Annual Quality Congress Proceedings, Toronto, Ontario, Canada, pp. 429–438. Carnegie Mellon University, Pittsburgh (2004)
14. Henderson-Sellers, B.B., Rout, J., Patrick, T.: Creating the OOSPICE model architecture, A case of reuse. In: SPICE 2002: the thired international confernce on software process improvement and capability determination (2002)
15. Automation, S.E.a. OOSPICE (2008), `http://www.oospice.com/` (10/06/2008)
16. Caffery, F.M., Coleman, G.: Developing a configuration management capability model for the medical device industry. International Journal of Information Systems and Change Management 2(2), 139–154 (2007)
17. Terzis, S.: Trust Management. Guest Editor's Intoduction - The many faces of trust (2009), `http://www.computer.org/portal/web/computingnow/archive/april2009`
18. Bhargava, B., et al.: The pudding of trust intelligent systems. IEEE Intelligent Systems, 74–88 (2004)
19. Wangenheim, C.G.v., et al.: Systematic Literature Review of Software Process Capability/Maturity Models. In: SPICE 2010 Conference, Pisa/Italy (2010)
20. Sarah, A.S.: Evolution of the Framework's Quagmire. Computer Management, 96–98 (2001)
21. ISO/IEC, International Organization for Standardization and International Electrotechnical Commission, ISO/IEC 25000: Software Engineering - Software Product Quality Requirements and Evaluation (SQuaRE) (2004)
22. Team, C.P.: CMMI for Services (CMMI-SVC) in Technical Report CMU/SEI- PA 15213-3890. Carnegie Mellon University / Software Engineering Institute, Pittsburgh (2008)
23. Taylor, S.: ITIL Service Management Practices - V3 Qualification scheme. Editor, p. 31 (2007), `http://www.itil-officialsite.com/Qualifications/Examiners/SharonTaylor.asp`

24. Wangenheim, C.G.v.: How domain-specific process reference models and standarts are developed. In: Working Paper, LAPIX/INE/CTC/UFSC, Editor Florianópolis, Brazil (2010)
25. SIG, A.: Automotive SPICE - Process Assessment Model. In: The procurement Forum (2007)
26. Cass, A., et al.: SPICE for SPACE trials, risk analysis, and process improvement. In: Software Process: Improvement and Practice (2004)
27. Richardson, I.: SPI Models: What Characteristics are Required for Small Software Development Companies. Software Quality Journal, 101–114 (2002)
28. Beecham, S., Hall, T., Rainer, A.: Defining a Requirements Process Improvement Model. Software Quality Journal 13(3), 247–279 (2005)
29. Ma, D.: The Business Model of Software-As-A-Service. In: IEEE International Conference on Services Computing, SCC 2007, Salt Lake City, Utah, USA, pp. 701–702 (2007)
30. Lin, G., Dasmalchi, G., Zhu, J.: Cloud Computing and IT as a Service: Opportunities and Challenges. In: IEEE International Conference on Web Services, ICWS 2008, Beijing, China, p. 5 (2008)
31. Kaufman, L.M.: Data Security in the World of Cloud Computing. IEEE Security & Privacy 7(4), 61–64 (2009)
32. Menasce, D.A.: QoS issues in Web services. IEEE Internet Computing 6, 72–75 (2002)
33. Cancian, M.H., Rabelo, R.J., Wangenheim, C.G.v.: Uma proposta para elaboração de Contrato de Nível de Serviço para Software-as-a-Service (SaaS). In: Proceedings of the 8th International Information and Telecommunication Technologies Symposium, I2TS 2009 (2009)
34. Sabata, B., et al.: Taxonomy for QoS Specifications. In: Proceedings of the Third International Workshop on Object-Oriented Real-Time Dependable Systems, Washington. EUA (1997)
35. Mani, A., Nagarajan, A.: Understanding Quality of Service for Web Services (2002), `http://www.ibm.com/developerworks/library/wsquality.html` (10/07/2008)
36. Hosamani, M., Narayanappa, H., Rajan, H.: How to Trust a Web Service Monitor Deployed in an Untrusted Environment? In: Third International Conference on Next Generation Web Services Practices, NWeSP 2007, pp. 79–84 (2007)
37. Hongqi, L., Zhuang, W.: Research on Distributed Architecture Based on SOA. In: International Conference on Communication Software and Networks, ICCSN 2009, pp. 670–674 (2009)
38. Azuma, M.: Applying ISO/IEC 9126-1 Quality Model to Quality Requirements Engineering on Critical Software. In: Security Standards (2004)
39. Juric, M.B., et al.: Web Services and Java Middleware Functional and Performance Analysis for SOA. In: Digital EcoSystems and Technologies Conference, DEST 2007, Inaugural IEEE-IES, pp. 217–222 (2007)
40. Momm, C., Gebhart, M., Abeck, S.: A Model-Driven Approach for Monitoring Business Performance in Web Service Compositions. In: Fourth International Conference on Internet and Web Applications and Services, ICIW 2009, pp. 343–350 (2009)
41. Lee, K., et al.: QoS for Web Services: Requirements and Possible Approaches. W3C Working Group Note 25 (November 2003)

A Maturity Model for IT Dependability in Emergency Management

Kim Weyns, Martin Höst, and Yeni Li Helgesson

Department of Computer Science, Lund University
P.O. Box 118, SE-211 00 Lund, Sweden
{kim.weyns,martin.host,yeni.li_helgesson}@cs.lth.se

Abstract. In many organisations a gap exists between IT management and emergency managemement. This paper illustrates how process improvement based on a maturity model can be used to help organisations to evaluate and improve the way they include IT dependability information in their emergency management. This paper presents the IDEM3 (IT Dependability in Emergency Management Maturity Model) process improvement framework which focuses especially on the cooperation between IT personnel, emergency managers, and users, to proactively prevent IT dependability problems when the IT systems are most critical in emergency situations. This paper describes the details of the framework, how the framework was developed and its relation to other maturity models in related fields.

Keywords: Dependability, Emergency Management, Maturity Model, IT Management.

1 Introduction

In recent years governmental actors have come to depend more on IT systems for all their everyday tasks. For communication, they depend on landline telephone networks, mobile phone networks, web servers, email servers, etc. Other important systems are used for patient administration in health care and social care, school administration or city planning.

Just as for their everyday tasks, governmental actors now depend on all kinds of IT systems for their responsibilities in crisis situations [1]. These systems include not only specially built systems for emergency situations but also the everyday systems described above. The latter category of systems is of special interest, because under normal conditions an occasional unavailability of these IT systems is fully acceptable, but in emergency situations, when time is a critical factor, any unexpected unavailability can have disastrous consequences [2], [3].

Therefore it is important that these IT systems are an integral part of all major risk and vulnerability analyses conducted. This way information about the dependability of the different IT systems can be combined with information about how critical the systems are in different situations [4]. IT dependability management for organisations with a critical role in emergency situations is a

M. Ali Babar, M. Vierimaa, and M. Oivo (Eds.): PROFES 2010, LNCS 6156, pp. 248–262, 2010.
© Springer-Verlag Berlin Heidelberg 2010

complex process of managing software in terms of IT systems. The occurrence of a number of critical IT incidents in the recent past shows that there is room for improvement. Earlier research [5] has shown that there is a particular need for improvements with respect to the communication between emergency managers and IT-management. This is a complex problem for which no quick solutions exist that fit all organisations. Instead, organisational improvements in this area must be based on the organisation's current situation and its goals for the future, that is through a process improvement approach.

This paper presents a maturity model for the coordination of emergency management and IT dependability management. The main focus of the framework is on the cooperation between emergency managers and IT personnel. The purpose of this maturity model is to help organisations to identify, evaluate and improve their IT dependability processes.

2 Background

The maturity model presented in this paper is based on the result of a series of case studies on how governmental organisations deal with IT dependability issues in emergency management [3], [5]. The main conclusion from these studies was that many organisations today experience problems and frustrations concerning IT dependability in emergency management. The main cause of many of these problems could be traced back to communication and cooperation problems between the personnel in different roles involved. Further these studies also pointed out a lack of useful tools that support IT dependability improvements across a whole organisation. This maturity model is meant to offer a process improvement model that is simple and general enough to be applicable to many organisations and at the same time effective enough to make a substantial difference in an organisation's IT dependability practices.

3 Related Work

In the field of IT management a number of international standards and best practice frameworks have been published, among those ITIL [6], COBIT [7] and ISO/IEC 27002 [8]. These frameworks are more suited to be used by large corporations with very large IT resources and are less suited for smaller organisations and often do not take into account the special requirements for organisations with an operative role in crisis relief. Of these frameworks, COBIT is structured as a maturity model. Frühwirth [9] has discussed the mismatch of software dependability management and industry standards today.

The maturity model presented in this paper is based on a number of maturity models from related fields. The first successful maturity models were developed by the Carnegie Mellon Software Engineering Institute [10]. Since the development of the Capability Maturity Model, maturity models have been applied in many other fields. The problems between emergency management and IT management are related to some of the problems in software requirements management and therefore the process improvement methods that have been successfully applied in software engineering can also benefit IT management.

In 2008, SEI published a preliminary version of the CERT Resiliency Engineering Framework [11] for the use in the field of business continuity management with a special focus on IT systems. In the field of IT management, Luftman [12] presents a simplified maturity model with a strong focus on the business value of IT systems. In the field of safety management, maturity models have also been proposed as a way of assessing an organisation's safety culture [2], or product design safety [13]. Section 8 focuses especially on how each of these maturity models relate to the maturity model presented in this paper. The maturity model presented in this paper does not try to replace any of these maturity models or to cover any of these related fields completely. From each related field, this maturity model contains only those attributes that are specifically important for the dependability of IT systems in emergency management.

Recently, Santos et al. [1] have published a maturity model for the use of information technologies in emergency response organisations. Their model does not cover the dependability of the IT systems in emergency situations, but instead focuses on information management practices. The IDEM3 maturity model described in this paper is most suited for an organisation where the IT services are provided by an IT department that is part of the organisation. For evaluating the resiliency of IT services provided by external suppliers, Bhamidipaty et al. have developed the Resiliency Maturity Index [14], a framework for characterizing and evaluating the resiliency of an IT services organization. However this model does not evaluate the relationship between the resiliency of the service supplier and the dependability requirements of the organisation.

4 Methodology

To support organisations that want to evaluate and improve their IT dependability practice, this paper presents the IDEM3 (IT Dependability in Emergency Management Maturity Model) process improvement framework.

The research that resulted in the IDEM3 maturity model was conducted in a number of steps: the identification of the attributes, followed by mapping the different levels of each of the attributes to the five levels of the maturity model, then an off-line validation and currently the maturity model is being evaluated in a practical setting. This process is presented in Figure 1.

First, the case studies [5] that describe the need for this kind of maturity model also resulted in a list of factors that are important for the coordination of IT dependability management and emergency management. These key factors formed the first basis for the attributes of the maturity model.

Secondly, the factors were mapped to the general architecture of a maturity model with five levels as found in other maturity models such as CMMI [15]. For the model to be applicable by small organisations, it was necessary to simplify the structure by replacing the concept of 'key process areas' by the more modest 'attributes' found in the model.

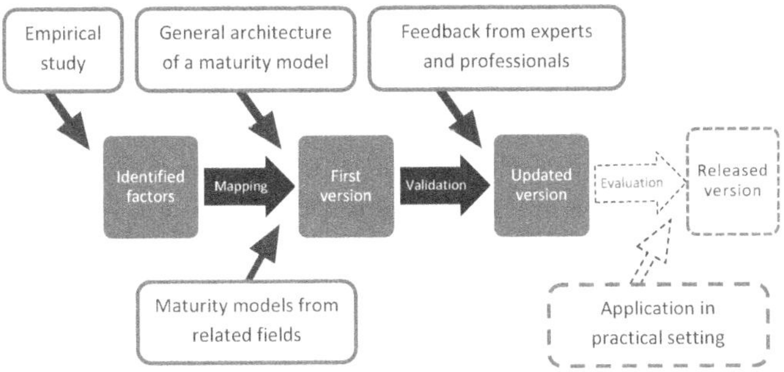

Fig. 1. Development process of the maturity model. Dotted lines indicate ongoing activities.

In this mapping the attributes were also compared and complemented with similar attributes found in maturity models from related fields, as described in more detail in Section 8. Before the model was applied in a practical setting, the model was validated with the help of experts and practitioners in the field. Finally, the model is currently being evaluated through the application of the model in a series of large case studies. The validation and the first results from the evaluation are further discussed in Section 9.

5 Process Improvement with IDEM3

This section shortly explains how IDEM3 can be used as part of an organised process improvement effort. First, the model can be used to assess the current maturity of the organisation in dealing with IT dependability in emergency management. For this assessment the current practices in the organisation should be matched with the attributes described in Section 6. The recommended way to do this is to select some of the most critical systems, preferably systems that are quite different in nature and together are representative for the critical IT systems in the organisation. For each of these systems, personnel with different roles should be interviewed individually based on a detailed questionnaire, where they are each asked to describe how they are currently experiencing each of the attributes of the maturity model. The involvement of personnel from different parts of the organisation is an essential part of this maturity model to make sure that IT dependability is not only evaluated from a technical point of view. The interviews should at least include users of each of the systems, system managers, safety managers in the domain where the systems are used and of course IT personnel.

The responses from all these interviews should be analysed in detail by the process manager overseeing the assessment with special attention for differences between the answers of different respondents and between the different systems. The analysis of the interviews should then be the basis for a focus group meeting where the organisation can be assessed on the maturity scale for each of the different attributes presented in the maturity grid shown in Table 1. The 22 attributes are ordered in such a way that attributes are most strongly correlated to those attributes just above and below. Therefore the maturity of an organisation in these 22 attributes can be presented in a spider web diagram, offering a clear representation of the organisation's strengths and weaknesses.

Finally, after this assessment, the organisation can decide whether the measured level of maturity is sufficient for the organisation. Not all organisations need to aim for the highest maturity level, mostly depending on how critical the role of the organisation is. The process improvement needed to reach a higher level of maturity is a long term project and should be organised as such. This means that a realistic time plan with explicit long and short term goals should be agreed upon. For the long term planning, it is important to realise that after each step from one maturity level to the next, some time is needed to make sure all procedures are well incorporated in the organisation and to make sure improvements are not too easily lost again. An improvement of more than one maturity level per year is probably unrealistic. Organisations should not try to skip certain levels or to implement a new level too quickly after the previous one since each level builds on the achievements of the previous level being well understood. For the short term planning, the organisation can focus most of all on those attribute for which they received the lowest maturity score. The organisation as a whole should focus on achieving a stable IT dependability management at this new maturity level. The actual improvements can be implemented with the help of those project management mechanisms that are most suited for the organisation in question. While implementing these planned improvements, it is important that regular critical self-assessments are held to evaluate the organisation's progress and to make sure the selected improvements are correctly implemented and are not easily lost again. A single assessment based on the IDEM3 maturity model can also be done separately from any planned process improvement based on the 5 maturity levels. An organisation can conduct a one-time assessment of its IT dependability based on this maturity model to identify its current strengths and weaknesses in this field. The results of this assessment will then form an excellent basis for a discussion on how to involve all stakeholders to improve the organisation's IT dependability in emergency management. Unlike with some other maturity models, IDEM3 assessment is not meant to be used as a basis for certification or for direct, objective comparison between different organisations.

6 Maturity Levels

Just like most other maturity models discussed in Section 3, the IDEM3 model has five maturity levels. The levels have similar names as in these other maturity models, and the basic idea behind each of the levels are also comparable. The Initial level is the most basic level, representing an organisation where some critical IT systems have not been analysed from a dependability point of view and nobody takes responsibility for initiating a more strategic discussion about

IT dependability. The second, Managed, level is characterised by an organisation where the dependability of all critical IT systems is managed on a system-by-system basis leaving the organisation very dependent on the competence of the system managers for every system.

The third level is referred to as the Established level. This means that the organisation has established a centrally coordinated approach for dealing with IT dependability. This will usually be established by appointing one central IT dependability manager who distributes standard procedures for dependability analysis to all system managers. A standardised approach is a prerequisite for being able to implement future improvements across the whole organisation. A level 3 organisation also has clearly defined roles and responsibilities concerning IT dependability. The fourth level, called Quantitatively Managed, is similar to level 3, but also requires that the centrally coordinated approach is supported by extensive quantitative data collection. Regular measurements and testing with special usage scenarios in mind can make IT dependability statistically predictable and allow for strategic improvements in IT dependability. The Continually Improving level, which is the fifth and final level of the maturity model, is reached by an organisation that can use the feedback obtained from the practices from level 4 to continually improve not only their IT systems, but also their own IT management procedures. IT systems will then be naturally included in risk and vulnerability analyses and their dependability will be regularly re-evaluated.

To define the levels in more detail the levels can be compared on 22 attributes. Of course all these attributes are in some way related and none of them can be changed completely independent of the others. Nevertheless they each add their own focus to the maturity model and stress a special aspect of an organisation's maturity.

The 22 attributes can be divided in 4 categories: Outcomes, IT management, Cooperation and Organisational Issues. A detailed summary of these attributes can be found in Table 1 and the attributes in each category are also described in the following subsections. The attributes are ordered in such a way that those attributes that are most strongly related are placed next to each other.

6.1 Outcomes

The first category of attributes is different from the three other categories in that it contains those attributes that can not directly be influenced by an organisation, but only indirectly. These attributes should mainly be considered as the consequence of an organisation's maturity, while the other categories are the causes of the maturity level. At the same time the outcome attributes are also the most important because the main goal of this maturity model is improving the outcomes of the IT dependability. This category also contains those attributes that are the most visible to stakeholders outside of the organisation.

Table 1. Overview of the 22 attributes of the maturity model across the 5 maturity levels

			Level 1: Initial	Level 2: Managed	Level 3: Established	Level 4: Quantitatively Managed	Level 5: Continually improving
Outcomes	1	Action	Reactive	Responsive	Preventive	Predictive	Pro-active
	2	Problems that can be identified	Failures	Technical system faults	Insufficient reliability, too high dependence and interdependencies	Faults in risk analysis	Faults in risk analysis procedures
	3	Basis for improvements	Fixing failures	Personal judgement	Standards	Quantitative risk analysis	Safety culture
	4	Improvements	Few, changes can be both positive and negative	For some systems, not sustained	For all systems, sustained	Regular, organised	Continuous
	5	Successes	Not repeatable	Repeatable	Sustainable	Measurable	Source for organisational learning
	6	Success factor	Luck, Competence of key personnel	Personal competence of system managers	Central coordination	Cooperation, Measurements	Continuous improvement effort by everyone
	7	Role of IT in emergency situations	Cause of problems	Varying between systems	Under control, backup solutions available	Predictable behaviour	Valuable asset
	8	Dependability problems	Accepted, create chaos	Solved on individual basis	Possible problems identified and prevented	Possible problems predicted and prevented in a prioritised way	Continuously prevented
	9	IT dependability	Low	Mixed	Stable	Controlled	Continually improving
IT management	10	Results of IT incident management	None	Improvement for one system	Improvement for all systems	Improvements in procedures	Improvement in organisational culture
	11	IT incident management	Ad-hoc	System-based	Formal incident management procedure	Basis for learning	Basis for deeper learning
	12	IT dependabiltiy management	Sporadic, Technical focus	Single initiatives, Techincal focus	Basic level, linked to requirements	Detailed level	Continuously improved
	13	Dependability Requirements	Unknown	For some systems	Documented	Measurable	continuously updated
Cooperation	14	Service Levels	None	For some systems	Basic service level for entire organisation and for all systems	SLAs with measurable service levels for all systems	Continuously evaluated SLAs
	15	IT dependability analysis and emergency planning	separate activities, not combined	Activities with a shared goal, contact for some systems	Input for each other	Measurable values exchanged, direct connection	Naturally combined activities
	16	Presence of IT dependability in emergency plans	not included	Included for some systems	Risk and vulnerability analysis for all IT systems included in plans	Measurable values included, regularly tested	Naturally included, continuously improved
	17	Relationship IT personnel - emergency managers	Conflict	Personal relations	Cooperation between departments	Cooperating, with shared risk and reward	Partnership
Organisational Issues	18	Involvement	Nobody	Individual system managers and some stakeholders	All internal stakeholders	All internal stakeholders, some external stakeholders	All stakeholders, internal and external
	19	Responsibility	'Someone else'	Individual System managers	(delegated by) IT safety manager	Shared by System, Process, IT, and Safety managers	Everyone
	20	Management Mechanism	Sanctions	Warnings	Instructions	Guidelines	Education
	21	Organisational learning	None	Reactive ("Don't do that again")	Following rules ("Do like this"), Open loop	Following policy ("Think like this"), Single loop learning ("Improve what you do")	Double loop learning ("Improve the way you think")
	22	Resource allocation	Reactive, Ad hoc	To individual projects	Divided equally over the whole organisation	Divided in prioritised way	Optimized for best results

The outcomes category contains 9 attributes: Actions taken, Problems that can be identified, Basis for improvements, Nature of improvements, Successes, Success factor, Role of IT in emergency situations, Attitude towards dependability problems and IT dependability.

These 9 attributes together describe the dependability experienced by an organisation at each maturity level, and how the organisation deals with these results.

A level 1 organisation will typically experience many problems with IT dependability and will focus most of its effort on trying to fix the problems as they appear. Because of the lack of an organized approach, some problems will not get solved and implemented changes can cause problems for other parts of the organisation. This will lead to a lot of frustrations, and although many of the minor problems will not come as a surprise, a serious failure in a critical system during an emergency situation can still do a lot of damage.

An organisation at level 2 will employ a system-by-system approach towards IT dependability allowing it to respond effectively to most of the problems and even to prevent some problems that only affect one system. Lessons learned from problems they experience will often lead to improvements in the affected system only as there is no centralised approach to IT dependability. This method of working leads to a higher dependability than in level 1, but places a large amount of responsibility on each system manager and much will depend on his skill and experience in dealing with the risks of IT dependability problems.

An organisation at level 3, on the other hand, uses a basic centralised approach towards IT dependability. The same basic techniques for risk and vulnerability analysis are applied to all systems and many dependability problems can systematically be prevented. Because of the coordination between different systems, also problems with interdependencies can be detected and dealt with. The main success factor from level 3 on will be the quality of the centrally coordinated dependability measures being used across the whole organisation. This will also make it easier for the organisation to efficiently share important resources such as backup facilities and emergency power supplies between all critical systems.

A level 4 organisation will supplement the basic centralised approach from level 3 with a large-scale systematic data collection and analysis concerning IT dependability. This will make IT dependability more predictable. The data collection will make it possible to measure improvements and their effects and to prioritise the usage of IT dependability resources. A level 4 organisation will also have an improved cooperation between all involved stakeholders which is an important factor for the IT dependability.

Finally a level 5 organisation will continuously work on evaluating and improving its IT dependability. The safety culture in an organisation at level 5 will even make it possible to regularly identify possibilities for improvement in their risk analysis procedures. At level 5, IT dependability is generally working very well and the level of success that can be achieved depends mostly on whether a continuous improvement effort can be sustained throughout the organisation. This makes that IT systems will not only be a source of risks or problems in emergency situations but also a valuable asset that can be depended upon.

6.2 IT Management

The second category of attributes collects those attributes that are directly related to IT management. Unlike some other maturity models, this maturity model does not seek to cover the complete field of IT management, but focuses exclusively on those aspects that are most important for IT dependability in emergency management. This category contains the following 4 attributes: Results of IT incident management, IT incident management, IT dependability management and Dependability requirements. A level 1 organisation lacks organised IT incident management, and the dependability requirements of most systems will typically never have been analysed. At level 2 incident management is handled for each system separately and for many systems there will be no explicit link to risk analysis or emergency management. A level 3 organisation is expected to have a centralised IT incident management system allowing information sharing between different parts of the organisation. Further centralised guidelines for IT dependability management will require the main dependability requirements for each system to be explicitly documented and available to all stakeholders. From level 4, IT incidents can be analysed in detail and can lead not only to direct improvement in all systems but also to improvements of the procedures used for IT dependability and even lead to improvement in the safety culture of the organisation at level 5. At the two highest levels of maturity dependability requirements for all systems should contain detailed measurable values and these requirements should be updated in the case of changes in the systems' functionality or usage.

6.3 Cooperation

A third set of attributes concerns the cooperation between the different parties involved in IT dependability. This is in the first place IT personnel, system managers, the system's users and also the personnel responsible for conducting risk and vulnerability analyses, for example emergency managers. The 4 attributes in the category are: Service level agreements, IT dependability analysis and emergency planning, Presence of IT dependability in emergency plans and Relationship IT personnel - emergency managers. A level 1 organisation will typically lack service level agreements or any other documents clearly linking IT dependability and emergency management. The frustrations and conflicts between different parts of the organisation will hinder a necessary cooperation on these important issues. In a level 2 organisation some of these issues will be taken care of for some systems, while there will be many problems with other systems, mostly depending on whether there are good contacts between the system manager of each system and the IT department. A level 3 organisation is expected to have basic, standardised service level agreements in place for all systems. Further, dependability estimates for all systems will be used as input for emergency management and the requirements discovered while making emergency plans will be used as input in the prioritising the IT dependability activities. From level 4 an organisation's SLA's should contain clear, quantitative dependability goals and measurements. The link between dependability requirements and risk and vulnerability analyses for all systems should be explicitly documented. By clearly defining the responsibilities of all parties in detail, all successes will be shared success and when problems should arise the blame cannot just be shifted around as is often the case on the lower levels of maturity. Finally, in a level 5 organisations there is a real partnership between the different departments cooperating on IT dependability and continuously striving to improve their cooperation.

6.4 Organisational Issues

A last category of attributes collects those issues that concern the whole organisation and how it is managed. There are 5 attributes in this category: Involvement, Responsibility, Management Mechanisms, Organisational learning and Resource allocation.

In a level 1 organisation, in the worst case, nobody is actively involved with IT dependabilities and most stakeholders will feel the responsibility lies with someone else. After an incident, often the blame is shifted around and no learning takes place. In a level 2 organisation, the responsibility for IT dependability lies explicitly with the individual system managers who deal with the issue as they see fit. Therefore learning about IT dependability will mostly happen on an individual basis and improvements will depend on whether the system manager can find the resources to invest in IT dependability for each system. In a level 3 organisation, all the responsibility lies in the first place with central IT safety manager who is responsible for the coordination of IT dependability procedures. The IT safety manager distributes detailed dependability instructions and directions that are meant to be followed strictly by all stakeholders. This coordination allows the organisation to learn as a whole from past failures and successes. In a level 4 organisation, the detailed service level agreements for each system will make it possible for the responsibility to be shared by all actors in the IT dependability process. Through the detailed feedback from the collected data in a organisation at level 4, the organisation can achieve organisational learning by adapting its centralised procedures and guidelines based on measured outcomes. System managers are expected to be experienced enough to be able to apply the centralised guidelines and tools to manage IT dependability without detailed instructions. In level 5 organisations, not only the dependability guidelines are regularly updated, but also the way the organisation learns is continuously re-evaluated. This is called double-loop learning. In a well functioning level 5 organisation everyone will be aware of their own part of the responsibility for IT dependability and resources for improvements in IT dependability can be distributed in a prioritised way.

7 Transition from One Level to the Next

To further clarify the different levels of the maturity model, this section explains the main elements of the transition process from one level to the next. Although not every organisation will be at level 1 initially, and not every organisation will aim for level 5, the levels are meant to be taken successively without skipping over any level. A transition from level 2 to level 4 can only be achieved by first implementing level 3.

7.1 From Level 1 to Level 2

There are no requirements for the first level of maturity, and at this level it is common that there are some critical IT systems for which there is no control over the dependability. For an organisation to rise to level 2 the responsibilities for each system need to be well defined. Usually this will mean that the coordination for all dependability issues is done by the system manager for each system who organises the work with dependability in the way that suits each particular situation best. The main advantage with this approach is the clear definition of responsibilities which makes that the main problems can be discovered and solved. The main disadvantage is that it is nearly impossible for the organisation to evaluate the quality of the dependability analyses done by the system managers since they each use their own methods.

7.2 From Level 2 to Level 3

To go from level 2 to 3, an organisation needs to standardize the way all system managers deal with IT dependability. First an organisational standard needs to be defined and then all system managers need to be instructed in this standard. The standard can be compiled based on national or international standards or on some of the procedures that were already previously used for some IT systems with good results.

7.3 From Level 3 to Level 4

While level 3 is mostly concerned with qualitative data about the dependability of IT systems, level 4 also requires the use of substantial amounts of quantitative dependability goals and measurements. A level 3 organisation might for example classify the availability requirements of a system according to a simple scale, Low-Medium-High, but a level 4 organisation is expected to use more detailed, numeric values. Setting up a central system to collect all service level agreements and to facilitate the analysis of all this data is a requirement for the transition from level 3 to 4.

7.4 From Level 4 to Level 5

Level 5 is characterised by a continuous effort to improve the processes in the organisation. This is only possible if the processes are well understood throughout the whole organisation and even across the borders of the organisations to include suppliers and network operators. To go from level 4 to 5 all procedures from level 4 need to become completely institutionalised throughout the organisation and all stakeholders need to be working together in a natural way. This way the data collected can form the basis for deeper, double-loop learning for the organisation. This means the lessons learned are not only used to improve the organisation's dependability practices but also to optimise the improvement process itself.

7.5 Commitment Required

It should be clear that there is a large difference between the commitment and resources required of an organisation to reach each level of dependability. Level 1 represents the lowest commitment to IT dependability. Becoming a level 2 organisation only requires a serious commitment from the individual system managers who needs to drive IT dependability forward and need to collect input from all other personnel involved. Reaching level 3 maturity requires a regular commitment from all personnel involved with IT dependability to maintain a basic level of IT dependability across the whole organisation. Level 4 is very similar, but requires a larger effort for data collection and analysis. Reaching and sustaining level 5 maturity definitely requires the largest overall commitment to IT dependability, although in practice all efforts for IT dependability should feel more as a natural part of the daily workings of the organisation than as a special effort for IT dependability.

8 Relation to Other Maturity Models

As mentioned before, the maturity model presented in this paper is based on a number of maturity models from related fields. Table 2 illustrates how the attributes in the IDEM3 model correspond to similar concepts in these maturity models. For most attributes, similar maturity levels as in IDEM3 can also be found in one or more of these maturity models. The compatibility of the IDEM3 model with each of these models not only makes it easier to combine the usage of this model with the other models, it also increases the validity of each of the attributes and therefore of the whole model. IDEM3 does not in any way try to be an alternative for any of the models presented below, but has a different, very specific focus that is not explicitly present in any of the other models.

Of course, not all attributes can be matched with corresponding areas in all other maturity models. This can be for a number of different reasons. First of all, each of the maturity models referred to here has its own scope, which only partly overlaps with the scope of this maturity model. Therefore there are, for example, no attributes concerning IT management in maturity models from the area of design safety. When an attribute is clearly outside the scope of a certain maturity model, this is marked in Table 2 as n.a., not applicable. Secondly, there are some attributes that are not explicitly mentioned in certain maturity models, for example, organisational learning in all but one of the models. Such attributes are nevertheless generally compatible with these models, they were just not selected as process areas or explicitly used in the description of the different maturity levels. This is marked in Table 2 with a minus sign (-).

Table 2. Traceability of the attributes of the maturity model to other maturity models [12], [7], [11], [13], [2]

			Luftman	COBIT	CERT REF	DCMM	Safety Culture	Comments
Outcomes	1	Action	n.a.	n.a.	concepts used, but not as exact	=Approach	-	idea taken from DCMM
	2	Problems that can be identified	n.a.	n.a.	-	-	-	Own input
	3	Basis for improvements	n.a.	n.a.	n.a.	~ Practice used in decision making	= part of Safety Culture	Adapted from DCMM, original from UKOOA
	4	Improvements	n.a.	n.a.	-	-	-	from CMMI
	5	Successes	-	-	discussed in organisational characteristics, but different levels	in level descrtiption	-	from CMMI
	6	Success factor	-	-	similar idea in level description	-	-	adapted from CERT
	7	Role of IT in emergency situations	~ business perception of IT value	-	n.a.	n.a.	n.a.	adapted from Luftman
	8	Dependability problems	n.a.	-	discussed in organisational characteristics, but different levels	-	= part of Safety Culture	idea taken from SCMM
	9	IT dependability	n.a.	n.a.	in organisational characteristics	n.a.	n.a.	adapted from CERT res
IT management	10	Results of IT incident management	-	-	-	n.a.	n.a.	Own input
	11	IT incident management	-	DS8	Incident Management and Control, no levels	n.a.	n.a.	Own input
	12	IT dependabiltiy management	n.a.	DS4, DS5	in organisational characteristics	n.a.	n.a.	adapted from CERT res
	13	Dependability Requirements	n.a.	-	in organisational characteristics + Resiliency Requirements	Key process area	n.a.	adapted from CERT res
Cooperation	14	Service Levels	= part of Competency/value measurements	DS1	-	n.a.	n.a.	idea taken from Luftman
	15	IT dependability analysis and emergency planning	= part of Competency/value measurements	part of PO9	in organisational characteristics	n.a.	n.a.	idea taken from Luftman
	16	Presence of IT dependability in emergency plans	= part of Competency/value measurements	part of PO9	in organisational characteristics	n.a.	n.a.	idea taken from Luftman
	17	Relationship IT personnel - emergency managers	= Partnership	P04.15, no levels	n.a.	n.a.	n.a.	idea taken from Luftman
Organisational Issues	18	Involvement	~ part of Scope	consistent with PO4	attribute discussed in organisational characteristics, but different levels	-	similar idea present	adapted from Luftman
	19	Responsibility	n.a.	consistent with PO4	attribute discussed in organisational characteristics, but different levels	-	= part of Safety Culture	adapted from SCMM
	20	Management Mechanism	-	-	-	Even more levels present	-	Selection of DCMM, original source not found
	21	Organisational learning	-	-	-	Key process area	-	idea taken from DCMM
	22	Resource allocation	-	PO05	in organisational characteristics + Financial Resource Management	n.a.	n.a.	adapted from COBIT

9 Evaluation of the Maturity Model

IDEM3 is the result of a long development process during which many of the details of the model have regularly been updated. The model has been evaluated and validated in a number of ways. First of all, the case studies [5] provide an empirical grounding [16] and the relationships with in well-established maturity models are a strong external theoretical grounding [16] of the maturity model.

For a further external validation, IDEM3 has, at a number of different occasions, been presented in detail to researchers and practitioners with long experience in the field, such as representatives of the Swedish Civil Contingencies Agency. At each of these presentations the model has received a positive reception, and many practitioners, both from the field of IT dependability and emergency management have expressed an interest in putting the ideas of this model into practice. Their comments and recommendations, both on the form and the details of this model, have all been taken into account in the version presented in this paper.

Further, the model is currently being used to assess certain aspects of IT dependability at two Swedish hospitals and to formulate improvement suggestions. First results of this assessment and the improvements suggested by the model were very positively evaluated by the participating organisations. These four rounds of evaluations give us confidence that the model in its current form can be an effective tool in improving an organisation's IT dependability in emergency management. The final validation of this model, in the form of a large-scale implementation of this model at a number of organisations, is currently taking place. The practical evaluation of a complete maturity model is in no way an easy task, and proving that the model leads to an efficient improvement in an organisation's IT dependability requires a huge research effort.

10 Conclusions

This paper has shown that process improvement based on a maturity model can help organisations close the critical gap between IT dependability management and emergency management. The IDEM3 maturity model contains 22 attributes in four categories: Outcomes, IT Management, Cooperation and Organisational Issues. The model is based upon a number of established maturity models from related fields and upon a number of problems identified in an earlier case study.

The maturity model is not a quick fix that will solve all of an organisation's IT dependability problems. The main value of the maturity model is that it offers a way for an organisation to quickly capture its strengths and weaknesses in how it combines IT management and emergency management. IDEM3 can help an organisation to involve all stakeholders in this process improvement effort and to visualise it progress. The model has been evaluated and improved based on feedback from experts and professionals in the field, and is currently being evaluated by case studies in the field of application.

References

1. Santos, R.S., Borges, M.R.S., Gomes, J.O., Canós, J.H.: Maturity levels of information technologies in emergency response organizations. In: Briggs, R.O., Antunes, P., de Vreede, G.-J., Read, A.S. (eds.) CRIWG 2008. LNCS, vol. 5411, pp. 135–150. Springer, Heidelberg (2008)
2. Fleming, M.: Safety culture maturity model. Offshore Technology Report, 2000/049, HSE Books, Norwich, UK (2001)
3. Zimmerman, R., Restrepo, C.: Information technology (IT) and critical infrastructure interdependencies for emergency response. In: Proceedings of the 3rd International Information Systems for Crisis Response and Management (ISCRAM) Conference (2006)
4. SEMA: Basic Level for IT Security. SEMA recommends 2003:2. Swedish Emergency Management Agency (2003)
5. Weyns, K., Höst, M.: Dependability of IT systems in municipal emergency management. In: Proceedings of the 2009 Information Systems for Crisis Response and Management (ISCRAM) Conference (2009)
6. Office of Government Commerce: Information Technology Infrastructure Library, Version 3 (2007)
7. ISACA: Control objectives for information and related technologies (COBIT) (3rd edn.) (2000)
8. International Organization for Standardization: ISO-IEC 27002: Information technology - Security techniques - Code of practice for information security management (2005)
9. Frühwirth, C.: On business-driven IT security management and mismatches between security requirements in firms, industry standards and research work. In: Bomarius, F., Oivo, M., Jaring, P., Abrahamsson, P. (eds.) PROFES. Lecture Notes in Business Information Processing, vol. 32, pp. 375–385. Springer, Heidelberg (2009)
10. Konrad, M., Chrissis, M.B., Ferguson, J., Garcia, S., Hefley, B., Kitson, D., Paulk, M.: Capability maturity modeling at the SEI. Software Process: Improvement and Practice 2, 21–34 (1996)
11. Caralli, R.A.: Introducing the CERT resiliency engineering framework improving the security and sustainability processes. Carnegie Mellon University, Software Engineering Institute, Pittsburgh, PA (2007)
12. Luftman, J.: Managing the Information Technology Resource: Leadership in the Information Age. Prentice-Hall, Englewood Cliffs (2003)
13. Strutt, J., Sharp, J., Terry, E., Miles, R.: Capability maturity models for offshore organisational management. Environment International 32, 1094–1105 (2006)
14. Bhamidipaty, A., Lotlikar, R., Banavar, G.: RMI: a framework for modeling and evaluating the resiliency maturity of IT service organizations. In: IEEE International Conference on Services Computing (SCC 2007), pp. 300–307 (2007)
15. SEI: Capability Maturity Model Integration, Version 1.2. Volume CMU/SEI-2006-TR-008(2008). Carnegie Mellon Software Engineering Institute (2008)
16. Ågerfalk, P.J.: Grounding through operationalization - constructing tangible theory in IS research. In: Proceedings European Conference on Information Systems (ECIS 2004) (2004)

Dependency Analysis between CMMI Process Areas

Paula Monteiro[1], Ricardo J. Machado[1], Rick Kazman[2], and Cristina Henriques[3]

[1] Universidade do Minho
{pmonteiro,rmac}@dsi.uminho.pt
[2] Software Engineering Institute
kazman@sei.cmu.edu
[3] I2S, Informática Sistemas e Serviços, SA
cristina.henriques@i2s.pt

Abstract. SPI and in particular CMMI is being widely use by several organizations to improve their product quality. However, the SMEs are reluctant in adopting it and in particular maturity level 2 of CMMI, because they think that achieving this level is too expensive and do not see a clear benefit on it. Our solution to captivate the interest of SMEs in CMMI is the anticipation of some process areas of maturity level 3 considered as a benefit by the organization and implement those process areas at the same time of maturity level 2 of CMMI. In this paper, we identify the dependencies among all the process areas of CMMI and between all the process areas of each maturity level. Our study was conducted to identify the impact on the dependencies of maturity level 2 when we introduce some process areas of maturity level 3 in the implementation effort.

Keywords: dependency analysis, CMMI, process areas, maturity levels.

1 Introduction

CMMI-DEV (Capability Maturity Model Integration for Development) [1], [2] is a well-known Software Process Improvement (SPI) model developed by the Software Engineering Institute (SEI). It is concerned in helping organizations to improve their processes. This SPI model has been implemented by several organizations [3], [4] that report a great improvement in reducing costs, improving the productivity, and the performance. According to [5] the most frequent reasons given by organizations for adopting a CMM[1]-based SPI model, like CMMI, were the improvement of their software quality, development time, development costs and productivity. However, customer satisfaction and staff motivation were referred in some SMEs [5].

Coleman and Connor performed a study [6] of how SPI models are applied in the software industry and they concluded that the software managers reject the implementation of SPI models because of the implementation costs. In what concerns why

---

[1] The Capability Maturity Model (CMM), originally developed as a tool for objectively assessing the ability of government contractors' processes to perform a contracted software project, has been superseded by CMMI, though the CMM continues to be a general theoretical process capability model used in the public domain.

M. Ali Babar, M. Vierimaa, and M. Oivo (Eds.): PROFES 2010, LNCS 6156, pp. 263–275, 2010.
© Springer-Verlag Berlin Heidelberg 2010

organizations do not adopt the maturity level 2 of CMMI, according to [7] the most frequent reasons given were: small organization, too costly, no time, using other SPI and no clear benefit in this CMMI level. Wilkie *et al.* [8] have concluded that small organizations are mainly focused on the product quality assurance instead of the process quality assurance and medium organizations consider process quality important but not so important as CMMI suggests. Organizations do not consider the maturity level 2 a high-value improvement since the process areas of this maturity level are mainly concerned on the process quality and the organizations are concerned with the product quality. To make CMMI widely used in small organizations, Wilkie *et al.* [8] suggest that CMMI should be recasted to cover the needs of this type of organizations. Other studies [9], [10], [11], [12] have become aware that to persuade SMEs in the adoption of an SPI model it is important to show to the organizations the benefits of its adoption, lower their costs and make the benefits perceptible in a short time. The SEI has had several research projects dedicated to this issue; SEI called them "Improving Processes in Small Settings". The original URL is no longer available, but the results of those projects could be found in [13]. However, no solution for the dependency analysis and cross-ML|CL improvement roadmaps in SMEs have been tackled.

Taking into account that the problem of software is a management problem and not a technical one [14], we can state that organizations do not see that when they implement maturity level 2 they are solving the historical problems of software projects like: understand and break the project scope, frequent requirements changes, deadline and cost issues. All these issues are addressed in this CMMI maturity level.

Our solution to make CMMI widely used in SMEs does not consist in recasting the CMMI, but to propose to the organizations the implementation of the process areas of the maturity level 2 and, at same time, to implement some process areas of the maturity level 3. These process areas could be chosen by the organization according to their needs of improvement or chosen according the higher benefit to the organization.

To analyze the impact of this approach, we decided to study the dependencies between the process areas, to better understand which other process areas than those chosen for implementation must be at least taken into account because of the dependencies between them.

SPI models and, in particular, CMM model have a long history of evolution [15]. The CMM model was initially published in 1987 and has evolved into the currently CMMI-DEV v1.2. We should not consider that the CMMI-DEV v1.2 is a silver bullet; CMMI will keep its evolution. This means that need to conducted studies about this framework. Namely, the study of dependencies between the process areas remains relevant to build assessment schemes tailored to the organizations' needs.

There are some studies focusing on the analysis of the dependencies between the process areas and the specific practices of maturity level 2 [16], [17] in order to discover an implementation sequence of the process areas. They do not conceive a global view of the dependencies, unlike the ISO 9001:2000 [18] (or the newer 9001:2008 [19]) already do. One of the mandatory requirements from ISO 9001 is the clause 4.1b): "the organization shall [...] determine the sequence and interaction of these processes".

This paper is organized as follows. Section 2 presents a brief description of CMMI, section 3 describes the dependencies between the maturity levels 2 and 3 of CMMI, section 4 describes the dependencies between the maturity levels 2 and the validation and verification process areas, and, finally, in section 5, some conclusion are presented.

2 CMMI for Development Model

CMMI-DEV is composed by a set of 22 process areas divided by categories and by maturity levels. In Table 1, we present the list of the 22 process areas grouped by maturity levels. To help the discussion, we add {PAn} to the CMMI acronym defined in [1], [2]. *PA* stands for *process area*, and *n* corresponds to the number of the process area.

Table 1. Table of all CMMI process areas

	Category	PA	Acronym	
	Engineering	Requirements Management	{PA 1}	REQM
	Project Management	Project Monitoring and Control	{PA 2}	PMC
	Project Management	Project Planning	{PA 3}	PP
MATURITY LEVEL 2	Project Management	Supplier Agreement Management	{PA 4}	SAM
	Support	Measurement and Analysis	{PA 5}	MA
	Support	Configuration Management	{PA 6}	CM
	Support	Process and Product Quality Assurance	{PA 7}	PPQA
	Engineering	Product Integration	{PA 8}	PI
	Engineering	Requirements Development	{PA 9}	RD
	Engineering	Technical Solution	{PA 10}	TS
	Engineering	Validation	{PA 11}	VAL
	Engineering	Verification	{PA 12}	VER
MATURITY LEVEL 3	Process Management	Organizational Process Definition	{PA 13}	OPD
	Process Management	Organizational Process Focus	{PA 14}	OPF
	Process Management	Organizational Training	{PA 15}	OT
	Project Management	Integrated Project Management	{PA 16}	IPM
	Project Management	Risk Management	{PA 17}	RSKM
	Support	Decision Analysis and Resolution	{PA 18}	DAR
MATURITY LEVEL 4	Process Management	Organizational Process Performance	{PA 19}	OPP
	Project Management	Quantitative Project Management	{PA 20}	QPM
MATURITY LEVEL 5	Process Management	Organizational Innovation and Deployment	{PA 21}	OID
	Support	Causal Analysis and Resolution	{PA 22}	CAR

All the CMMI process areas have established specific goals (SG). These specific goals are unique characteristics that must be performed in order to satisfy each process area. In Table 2, we have an example of the specific goals of two process areas: the validation (VAL) and the verification (VER) process areas. We do not present all the specific goals, since they are listed in the official CMMI documentation. In our study, we are not considering the integrated product and process development (IPPD) "addition". Table 2 shows that each specific goal can be divided into specific practices (SP). The specific practices describe all the activities that must be performed to accomplish the specific goals.

Beside the specific goals and specific practices, CMMI model defines a set of generic goals (GG) and generic practices (GP). The generic goals, as the name says, are generic to all process areas. They are characteristics that must be performed to institutionalize the processes of each process area. The generic practices describe all the activities that must be performed to accomplish the generic goals. Table 3 lists all the generic goals and generic practices of CMMI.

Table 2. CMMI specific goals example

	PA	Specific Goals
ML3	{PA 11} VAL	**SG 1 Prepare for Validation** SP 1.1 Select Products for Validation SP 1.2 Establish the Validation Environment SP 1.3 Establish Validation Procedures and Criteria **SG 2 Validate Product or Product Components** SP 2.1 Perform Validation SP 2.2 Analyze Validation Results
	{PA 12} VER	**SG 1 Prepare for Verification** SP 1.1 Select Work Products for Verification SP 1.2 Establish the Verification Environment SP 1.3 Establish Verification Procedures and Criteria **SG 2 Perform Peer Reviews** SP 2.1 Prepare for Peer Reviews SP 2.2 Conduct Peer Reviews SP 2.3 Analyze Peer Review Data **SG 3 Verify Selected Work Products** SP 3.1 Perform Verification SP 3.2 Analyze Verification Results

Table 3. CMMI generic goals for the continuous and staged representations

Generic Goal	Continuous	Staged
GG 1 Achieve Specific Goals GP 1.1 Perform Specific Practices	CL1	
GG 2 Institutionalize a Managed Process GP 2.1 Establish an Organizational Policy GP 2.2 Plan the Process GP 2.3 Provide Resources GP 2.4 Assign Responsibility GP 2.5 Train People GP 2.6 Manage Configurations GP 2.7 Identify and Involve Relevant Stakeholders GP 2.8 Monitor and Control the Process GP 2.9 Objectively Evaluate Adherence GP 2.10 Review Status with Higher Level Management	CL2	ML2
GG 3 Institutionalize a Defined Process GP 3.1 Establish a Defined Process GP 3.2 Collect Improvement Information	CL3	ML3, ML4, ML5
GG 4 Institutionalize a Quantitatively Managed Process GP 4.1 Establish Quantitative Objectives for the Process GP 4.2 Stabilize Subprocess Performance	CL4	
GG 5 Institutionalize an Optimizing Process GP 5.1 Ensure Continuous Process Improvement GP 5.2 Correct Root Causes of Problems	CL4	

2.1 Staged vs. Continuous Representations

CMMI has two representations that can be followed by an organization to become a CMMI assessed company. These representations are: the staged and the continuous representation. In the continuous representation, the organization can choose the order of the improvements to meet the organization objectives by choosing one or more process areas. This kind of representation uses the term Capability Level (CL) to characterize the improvement. Capability levels are a means for incrementally improving the processes corresponding to a given process areas. In the staged representation, the organization uses a set of pre-defined process areas, imposed by the CMMI model. In this case, the term used to characterize the improvement is Maturity Level (ML).

Levels are used in CMMI to describe an evolutionary path recommended for an organization that wants to improve the processes it uses to develop and maintain its products and services. To achieve a capability level the organization must satisfy all the specific goals and generic goals for the process areas selected to be improved.

To achieve a maturity level the organization must satisfy all the specific and generic goals for the pre-defined set of process areas imposed by the maturity level under implementation. It is important to notice that in the continuous representation GG1 to GG5 are applied, but in the staged representation only the GG2 and GG3 are applied.

To illustrate the concepts of continuous and staged representation we will explain how to achieve CL1 to CL3 for the {PA11} and how to achieve ML2 and ML3. To support our approach, these capability and maturity levels are analyzed in this manuscript to establish cross-ML|CL improvement roadmaps, as stated by the formula (6).

2.2 Introduction to Notation

Achieving CL1.{PA11} implies to execute all the specific goals for {PA11} and the GG1.

$$\begin{aligned} CL1.\{PA11\} = GG1.\{PA11\} = \textstyle\sum_{i=1}^{2} SGi.\{PA11\} = SG1.\{PA11\} \wedge \\ SG2.\{PA11\} = \textstyle\sum_{i=1}^{3} SP1.i.\{PA11\} \wedge \textstyle\sum_{i=1}^{2} SP2.i.\{PA11\}\,. \end{aligned} \tag{1}$$

The previous equation expresses this effort. Executing all the specific goals for {PA11} is the same of executing the entire specific practices for {PA11}.

To achieve CL2 to {PA11} we have to perform all the specific goals for {PA11} and the GG2. In the next equation we see that to achieve CL2.{PA11} we have to achieve CL1.{PA11} and, at the same time, to execute all the specific goals for GG2.

$$\begin{aligned} CL2.\{PA11\} = CL1.\{PA11\} \wedge GG2.\{PA11\} = \\ CL1.\{PA11\} \wedge \textstyle\sum_{i=1}^{10} GP2.i.\{PA11\}\,. \end{aligned} \tag{2}$$

The equation

$$\begin{aligned} CL3.\{PA11\} = CL2.\{PA11\} \wedge GG3.\ \{PA11\} = \\ CL1.\{PA11\} \wedge \textstyle\sum_{i=1}^{10} GP2.i.\{PA11\} \wedge \textstyle\sum_{i=1}^{2} GP3.i.\{PA11\} \end{aligned} \tag{3}$$

represents the effort to achieve CL3 for {PA11}. This effort includes all the work to achieve CL2 for {PA11} and, at the same time, the effort to accomplish the GG3.

In what concerns to the maturity levels, we represent the improvement from ML1 to ML2 by ML1→ML2. This improvement corresponds to the execution of the activities illustrated by the following equation:

$$\begin{aligned} ML1 \rightarrow ML2 = \textstyle\sum_{i=1}^{7}(SGj.\{PAi\} \wedge GG2.\{PAi\}) = \\ (\textstyle\sum_{j=1}^{1} SGj.\{PA1\} \wedge \textstyle\sum_{k=1}^{10} GP2.k.\{PA1\}) \wedge (\textstyle\sum_{j=1}^{2} SGj.\{PA2\} \wedge \textstyle\sum_{k=1}^{10} GP2.k.\{PA2\}) \wedge \\ (\textstyle\sum_{j=1}^{3} SGj.\{PA3\} \wedge \textstyle\sum_{k=1}^{10} GP2.k.\{PA3\}) \wedge (\textstyle\sum_{j=1}^{2} SGj.\{PA4\} \wedge \textstyle\sum_{k=1}^{10} GP2.k.\{PA4\}) \wedge \\ (\textstyle\sum_{j=1}^{2} SGj.\{PA5\} \wedge \textstyle\sum_{k=1}^{10} GP2.k.\{PA5\}) \wedge (\textstyle\sum_{j=1}^{3} SGj.\{PA6\} \wedge \textstyle\sum_{k=1}^{10} GP2.k.\{PA6\}) \wedge \\ (\textstyle\sum_{j=1}^{2} SGj.\{PA7\} \wedge \textstyle\sum_{k=1}^{10} GP2.k.\{PA7\})\,. \end{aligned} \tag{4}$$

This equation says that attaining ML2 implies to perform all the specific goals from {PA1} to {PA7} and, at the same time, to perform the GG2 once again from {PA1} to {PA7}.

To achieve the ML3 we have to perform the following:

$$\text{ML2}\rightarrow\text{ML3} = \text{ML1}\rightarrow\text{ML2} \wedge \textstyle\sum_{i=1}^{18} \text{GG3.\{PAi\}} \wedge \sum_{i=8}^{18} \text{SGj.\{PAi\}} \wedge \sum_{i=8}^{18} \text{GG2.\{PAi\}} \tag{5}$$

which means that we have to achieve ML2 and perform, at the same time, the specific goals from {PA8} to {PA18}, the GG3 from {PA1} to {PA18} and the GG2 from {PA8} to {PA18}.

3 Discovering the Process Areas Dependencies

By looking into the official CMMI documentation [1], [2] we cannot have a global view of the dependencies between the all the process areas. By reading the "related process areas" section of each process area, we can only understand what are the dependencies of each process area independently.

To obtain the complete list and a graph representation of all the dependencies between all the process areas we started to analyze the "related process areas" section for all the process areas. Then, we decided to create a matrix (that contains the information of all the dependencies) and a set of graphs (that graphically represents the information stored in the matrix). The matrix rows represent the source process areas and the columns represent the destination process areas, in the dependency analysis perspective.

3.1 Elementary Dependency Analysis

Next, we describe our efforts to characterize the elementary dependency analysis of a particular process area; we also call this analysis the *PAn-centric dependency analysis* (*n* is the number of the process area; see Table 1). PPQA process area is next illustrated as an example.

In the "related process areas" section of the PPQA, we can read "*refer to the **Project Planning process area** for more information about identifying processes and associated work products that will be objectively evaluated*" and "*refer to the **Verification process area** for more information about satisfying specified requirements*". This means that the PPQA is related to the PP and VER process areas. This information is represented in the matrix by marking with an X the cell that corresponds to the PPQA row and to the PP column and also the cell that corresponds to the PPQA row and to the VER column (see Table 4). The matrix is capable of representing the dependency information about all the process areas. We also represent this information in graphs, for better understanding. The graph for this elementary dependency analysis example is presented in Fig. 1.

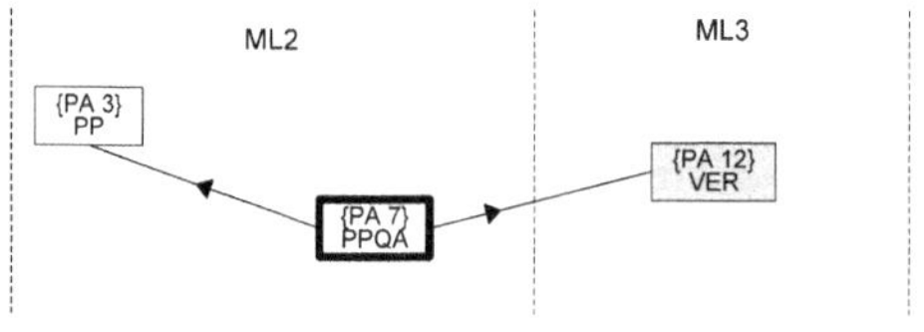

Fig. 1. Elementary Dependency Analysis Graph

Table 4. PPQA matrix line

	PA depended / PA depends	ML 2							ML 3											ML 4		ML 5	
		{PA 1} REQM	{PA 2} PMC	{PA 3} PP	{PA 4} SAM	{PA 5} MA	{PA 6} CM	{PA 7} PPQA	{PA 8} PI	{PA 9} RD	{PA 10} TS	{PA 11} VAL	{PA 12} VER	{PA 13} OPD	{PA 14} OPF	{PA 15} OT	{PA 16} IPM	{PA 17} RSKM	{PA 18} DAR	{PA 19} OPP	{PA 20} QPM	{PA 21} OID	{PA 22} CAR
ML 2	{PA 7} PPQA			X									X										

3.2 Dependencies of CMMI Process Areas

To create the complete matrix and graphs of the CMMI process areas we executed the elementary dependency analysis for all the process areas. The resulting matrix is presented in Table 5. To easily understand the impact of the dependencies between all the process areas, we organized the matrix by maturity level.

It is also possible to obtain a graph representation of the global matrix of Table 5. To ease the visualization of the dependencies of each CMMI maturity level, we decided to create 4 graphs, one for each maturity level. The explanation about how to create those graphs appears in the next section.

Each of those 4 graphs is denominated as *ML-n Centric Dependency Analysis Graph* (where n is the maturity level under study). In Fig. 2 and 3, we can see the ML-2 and the ML-3 centric dependency analysis graphs. The main idea behind the creation of these ML-n centric graphs is to allow us to see only the dependencies that

Table 5. Dependencies between all the CMMI process areas

	PA depended / PA depends	ML 2							ML 3											ML 4		ML 5		
		{PA 1} REQM	{PA 2} PMC	{PA 3} PP	{PA 4} SAM	{PA 5} MA	{PA 6} CM	{PA 7} PPQA	{PA 8} PI	{PA 9} RD	{PA 10} TS	{PA 11} VAL	{PA 12} VER	{PA 13} OPD	{PA 14} OPF	{PA 15} OT	{PA 16} IPM	{PA 17} RSKM	{PA 18} DAR	{PA 19} OPP	{PA 20} QPM	{PA 21} OID	{PA 22} CAR	Number of Dependencies
ML 2	{PA 1} REQM		X	X			X			X	X							X						6
	{PA 2} PMC			X		X																		2
	{PA 3} PP	X								X	X							X						4
	{PA 4} SAM	X	X							X	X													4
	{PA 5} MA	X	X	X			X			X				X							X			7
	{PA 6} CM		X	X	X																			3
	{PA 7} PPQA			X									X											2
ML 3	{PA 8} PI				X		X			X	X	X	X					X	X					8
	{PA 9} RD	X					X		X		X	X	X					X						7
	{PA 10} TS	X								X			X						X			X		5
	{PA 11} VAL									X	X		X											3
	{PA 12} VER	X								X		X												3
	{PA 13} OPD														X									1
	{PA 14} OPF													X										1
	{PA 15} OT			X										X					X					3
	{PA 16} IPM		X	X		X							X	X										5
	{PA 17} RSKM		X	X															X					3
	{PA 18} DAR			X													X	X						3
ML 4	{PA 19} OPP					X															X			2
	{PA 20} QPM		X			X								X			X			X		X	X	7
ML 5	{PA 21} OID					X								X	X	X	X		X	X				7
	{PA 22} CAR					X															X	X		3
	Number of Dependencies	6	7	9	2	6	4	0	1	8	6	3	6	6	2	1	3	5	5	2	3	3	1	

are concerned to the maturity level under study, by eliminating from the graph a huge number of dependencies that we do not want to take into account when we are studying a particular maturity level. However, we have also constructed the global graph with all the CMMI dependencies (also called *CMMI Dependency Analysis Graph*) to show the global view of the dependencies between the CMMI process areas and to verify what are the bi-directional dependencies between the process areas of different maturity levels (Fig. 4).

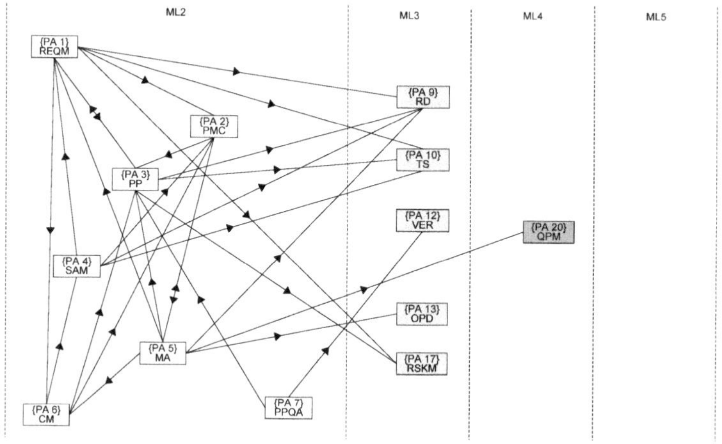

Fig. 2. ML-2 centric dependency analysis graph

3.3 ML-2 Centric Dependency Analysis

To study, discover and analyze the dependencies of the process areas of maturity level 2, we have to perform the ML-2 centric dependency analysis. Since we already have the matrix with all the dependencies between CMMI process areas (Table 5), we can use this information to analyze the dependencies of maturity level 2. We start by creating the ML-2 centric dependency analysis graph. To create this graph we select the rows from the matrix that corresponds to the maturity level 2 (the first 7 rows).

To better explain the creation of this graph, we will comment {PA3} Project Planning as an example. To represent in the graph the dependencies that {PA3} possesses from the others CMMI process areas, we parse the matrix row that corresponds to {PA3} as shown in Table 6. We can see that {PA3} has 4 dependencies from other process areas: {PA1} REQM, {PA9} RD, {PA10} TS and {PA17} RSKM.

In Table 6 we replaced the X from the original matrix with the symbol ►, in order to express that this connection starts in {PA3} and ends in {PA1}, for instance. We have also made some changes in the column {PA3}. In this column, we replaced the X by the symbol ◄, in order to express that this connection ends in {PA3} and starts in {PA2}, for instance. To construct the graph we only need to parse the rows.

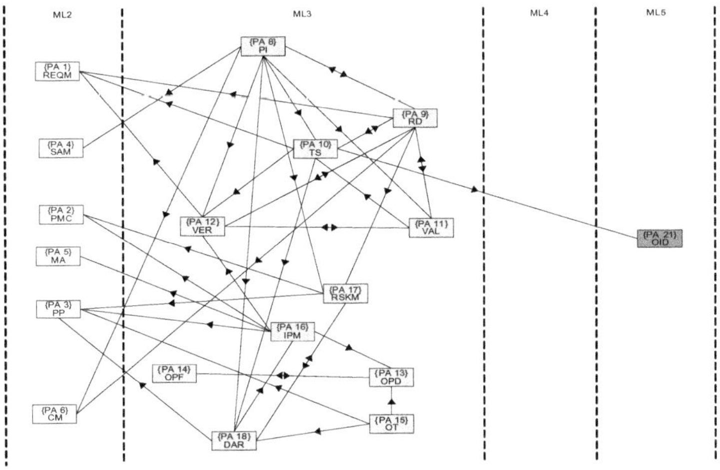

Fig. 3. Dependencies of process areas of the CMMI maturity level 3

Table 6. ML-2 centric dependency analysis for {PA3}PP

		ML 2							ML 3											ML 4		ML 5	
	depended PA / PA depends	{PA 1} REQM	{PA 2} PMC	{PA 3} PP	{PA 4} SAM	{PA 5} MA	{PA 6} CM	{PA 7} PPQA	{PA 8} PI	{PA 9} RD	{PA 10} TS	{PA 11} VAL	{PA 12} VER	{PA 13} OPD	{PA 14} OPF	{PA 15} OT	{PA 16} IPM	{PA 17} RSKM	{PA 18} DAR	{PA 19} OPP	{PA 20} QPM	{PA 21} OID	{PA 22} CAR
ML 2	{PA 1} REQM			◄																			
	{PA 2} PMC			◄																			
	{PA 3} PP	►								►	►							►					
	{PA 4} SAM																						
	{PA 5} MA			◄																			
	{PA 6} CM			◄																			
	{PA 7} PPQA			◄																			

In Fig. 2 we can observe the existence of a bi-directional dependency between {PA3} and {PA1}. To express this bi-directional dependency, in Table 7 we replaced the X by the symbol ◄►. Since the process areas are ordered in the same way both in rows and in columns, to easily identify the bi-directional dependencies we just need to check if the row n and column n are marked with an X.

Table 7. {PA3}PP bi-directional dependencies of ML-2 Centric Dependency Analysis

		ML 2							ML 3											ML 4		ML 5	
	depended PA / PA depends	{PA 1} REQM	{PA 2} PMC	{PA 3} PP	{PA 4} SAM	{PA 5} MA	{PA 6} CM	{PA 7} PPQA	{PA 8} PI	{PA 9} RD	{PA 10} TS	{PA 11} VAL	{PA 12} VER	{PA 13} OPD	{PA 14} OPF	{PA 15} OT	{PA 16} IPM	{PA 17} RSKM	{PA 18} DAR	{PA 19} OPP	{PA 20} QPM	{PA 21} OID	{PA 22} CAR
ML 2	{PA 1} REQM		X	◄►			X			X	X							X					
	{PA 2} PMC																						
	{PA 3} PP	◄►																					
	{PA 4} SAM	X																					
	{PA 5} MA	X																					
	{PA 6} CM																						
	{PA 7} PPQA																						

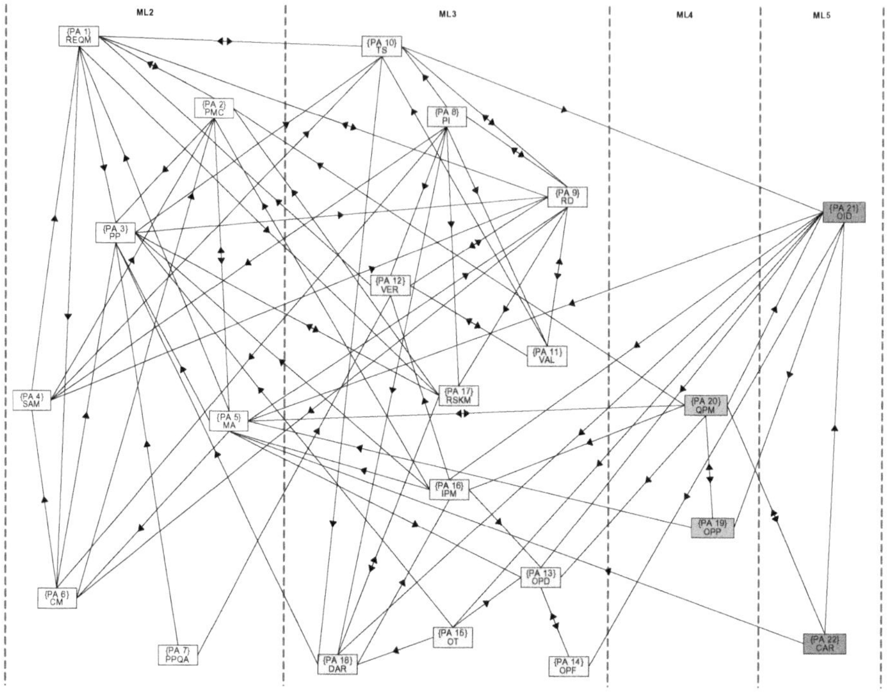

Fig. 4. Global dependencies between CMMI process areas

4 ML-2 Centric Dependency Analysis with Elementary Dependency Analysis for Validation and Verification Process Areas

As a motivation to convince SMEs that CMMI maturity level 2 brings real benefits, we decided study what are the theoretical dependencies we should expect when performing ML1→ML2 and, at the same time, prepare for one CL3 assessment for some process areas, namely CL3.{PA11} and CL3.{PA12}. The choice of {PA11} and {PA12} is based on the particular needs of I2S (the company where we will perform the complete dependency analysis with real data). The type of assessment we are considering is a combination of staged and continuous representations. The combination of maturity level 2 assessment and CL3.{PA11} and CL3.{PA12} is given by the following expression:

$$\mathrm{ML1} \rightarrow \mathrm{ML2} \parallel (\mathrm{CL3.\{PA11\}} \wedge \mathrm{CL3.\{PA12\}}) \;.. \qquad (6)$$

To analyze the dependencies we must expect from this case, we need to study the *{PA11} centric dependency analysis* and the *{PA12} centric dependency analysis*. To generate the {PA11} centric dependency analysis graph (Fig. 5a) we need to parse the row of {PA11} in the matrix of Table 5. Analogous exercise must be performed to generate the {PA12} centric dependency graph (Fig. 5b).

The global view of the dependencies when performing ML1→ML2 with the simultaneous assessment of CL3 for both {PA11} and {PA12} is depicted Fig.6. The information that represents the ML-2 centric dependency analysis graph is depicted in black. The information relative to the {PA11} centric dependency analysis graph and to the {PA12} centric dependency analysis graph is represented in red.

The graph represented in Fig.6 permits to conclude that the effort to perform ML1→ML2 and to achieve, simultaneously, CL3 for {PA11} and {PA12} should not be an obstacle to assume the maturity level 2 as the main organizational goal, in this considered case. All the existing dependencies are relative to process areas already imposed by the maturity level 2. The only extra effort that must be considered consists in implementing {PA11} and {PA12}.

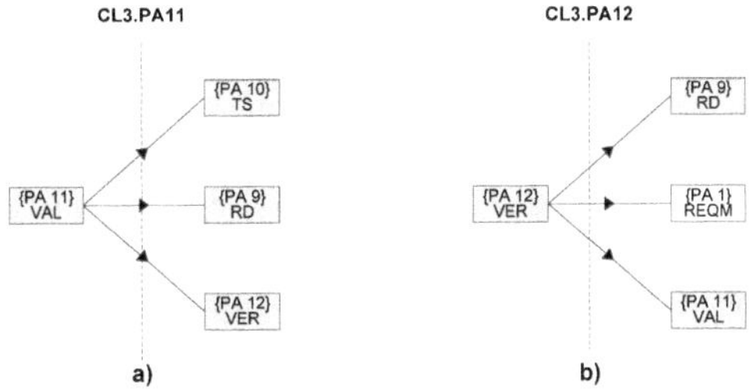

Fig. 5. a) Elementary Dependency Analysis for {PA11} and b) Elementary Dependency Analysis for {PA12}

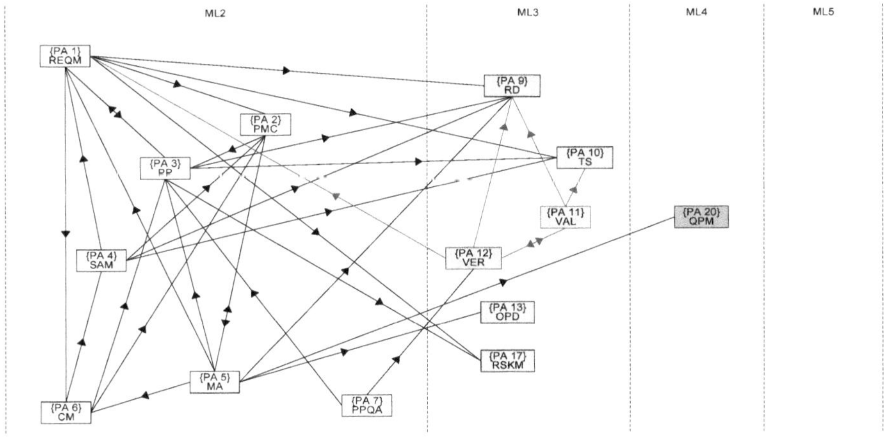

Fig. 6. Dependencies between CMMI ML2 and V&V ({PA11} and {PA12}) Process Areas

5 Conclusions

CMMI official documentation does not explicitly describe the existing dependencies among the process areas. To find out the global theoretical dependencies, we need to complement the reading of the documentation with special care and analysis capabilities, but, even after that, it is hard to obtain the global view of the dependencies. Our final goal is not to reach the global theoretical dependencies, but rather to use this view as a characterization of the framework limitations to be next confronted with the dependencies we can observe in the implementation of real SPI projects (by adopting SCAMPI appraisals whether for ML or CL assessments). This means that this paper will be considered as a baseline for future comparisons with empirical results.

In this paper we describe a set of techniques to identify the dependencies between all the process areas and to create a global view of those dependencies by means of some matrix and a set of graphs. We have also developed a notation that translates the meaning of achieving a particular capability and maturity level. This notation allows to understand which specific practices and specific goals have to be implemented to achieve a given capability and maturity level.

Our motivation to explicit the global dependencies between CMMI process areas arose when we tried to understand the impact of implementing the maturity level 2 simultaneously with some process areas from maturity level 3 as a way to make CMMI more widely used in Portuguese SMEs. As an example, we analyzed the dependencies between the process areas of maturity level 2 and two particular process areas of maturity level 3.

As future work, we will also complement our current dependency analysis study with the interactions between the process areas of each category in order to analyze if those interactions are already identified as a dependency between the process areas. For this study we will use the information described with the bird's-eye view presented in [1]. Another source of information that will be used to complement this dependency study is the SG descriptions of each PA. For instance, PP should be dependent also from OPD (SP1.4 for the Measurement Repository), having cross links in PP SP1.4 sub-practice 1.

This complementary study may lead us to a new set of dependencies that, again, are not well described in the CMMI official documentation.

References

1. CMMI Product Team: Capability Maturity Model Integration, version 1.2, CMMI for Development, CMU/SEI-2006-TR-008, ESC-TR-2006-008 (2006), http://www.sei.cmu.edu/publications/documents/06.reports/06tr008.html
2. Chrissis, M.B., Konrad, M., Shrum, S.: CMMI(R): Guidelines for Process Integration and Product Improvement. The SEI Series in Software Engineering, 2nd edn. Addison-Wesley Professional, Reading (2006)
3. Gibson, D.L., Goldenson, D.R., Kost, K.: Performance Results of CMMI®-Based Process Improvement. Software Engineering Institute, CMU (2006), http://www.sei.cmu.edu/library/abstracts/reports/06tr004.cfm
4. Goldenson, D.R., Gibson, D.L.: Demonstrating the Impact and Benefits of CMMI®: An Update and Preliminary Results. Software Engineering Institute, CMU (2003), http://www.sei.cmu.edu/library/abstracts/reports/03sr009.cfm
5. Staples, M., Niazi, M.: Systematic review of organizational motivations for adopting CMM-based SPI. Information and Software Technology 50, 605–620 (2008)

6. Coleman, G., O'Connor, R.: Investigating software process in practice: A grounded theory perspective. Journal of Systems and Software 81, 772–784 (2008)
7. Staples, M., Niazi, M., Jeffery, R., Abrahams, A., Byatt, P., Murphy, R.: An exploratory study of why organizations do not adopt CMMI. Journal of Systems and Software 80, 883–895 (2007)
8. Wilkie, F.G., McFall, D., McCaffery, F.: An evaluation of CMMI process areas for small-To medium-sized software development organisations. Software Process Improvement and Practice 10, 189–201 (2005)
9. Cater-Steel, A., Toleman, M., Rout, T.: Process improvement for small firms: An evaluation of the RAPID assessment-based method. Information and Software Technology 48, 323–334 (2006)
10. Wangenheim, C.G.v., Varkoi, T., Salviano, C.F.: Standard based software process assessments in small companies. Software Process: Improvement and Practice 11, 329–335 (2006)
11. Quality Management for Small Enterprises Project, `http://www8.cs.umu.se/~jubo/Projects/QMSE/`
12. Software Process Improvement in Regions of Europe Project, `http://www.cse.dcu.ie/spire/spire.html`
13. Improving Processes in Small Settings, `http://www.sei.cmu.edu/iprc/ipss.html`
14. Humphrey, W.S.: Introduction to the team software process. Addison-Wesley, Reading (2000), ISBN 0-201-47719-X
15. Paulk, M.C.: A History of the Capability Maturity Model for Software. ASQ Software Quality Professional 12, 5–19 (2009)
16. Villalón, J.A.C.-M., Agustín, G.C., Mejía, J., Gilabert, T.S.F., Sánchez, A.: CMMI-ACQ: A Formal Implementation Sequences of the Processes Areas at Maturity Level 2. In: Robotics and Automotive Mechanics Conference on Electronics, pp. 212–217 (2008)
17. Chen, X., Staples, M., Bannerman, P.L.: Analysis of Dependencies between Specific Practices in CMMI Maturity Level 2. In: O'Connor, R., Baddoo, N., Smolander, K., Messnarz, R. (eds.) EuroSPI, vol. 16, pp. 94–105. Springer, Heidelberg (2008)
18. International Organization for Standardization: ISO 9001:2000 - Quality management systems - Requirements. Geneva (2000)
19. International Organization for Standardization: ISO 9001:2008 - Quality management systems - Requirements. Geneva (2008)

Productivity Reanalysis for Unbalanced Datasets with Mixed-Effects Models

Sousuke Amasaki

Department of Systems Engineering
Okayama Prefectural University
111 Kuboki, Soja, Okayama, 719–1197, Japan
amasaki@cse.oka-pu.ac.jp

Abstract. Data analysis is a major and important activity in software engineering research. For example, productivity analysis and evaluation of new technologies almost always conduct statistical analysis on collected data. Software data are usually unbalanced because they are collected from actual projects, not from formal experiments, and therefore their population is biased. Fixed-effects models have often been used for data analysis though they are for balanced datasets. This misuse causes analysis to be insufficient and conclusion to be wrong. The past study[1] proposed an iterative procedure to treat unbalanced datasets for productivity analysis. However, this procedure was sometimes failed to identify partially-confounded factors and its estimated effects were not easy to interpret. This study examined mixed-effects models for productivity analysis. Mixed-effects models can work the same for unbalanced datasets as for balanced datasets. Furthermore its application is straightforward and estimated effects are easy to interpret. Experiments with four datasets showed advantages of the mixed-effects models clearly.

Keywords: productivity analysis, mixed-effects models, unbalanced datasets, estimation, data analysis.

1 Introduction

Software engineering research often collected software data for statistical analysis. Software data recorded characteristics of software development process, software product, or sometimes people in a project or an formal experiment. It has been used for productivity analysis, performance evaluation of new technology, demographic survey, etc.

Software data is often nested, heterogeneous, and unbalanced. When an organization collects software data from projects in several departments, this software data forms hierarchical structure. A project is nested in a department. If it is collected from multiple organizations in multiple countries, an organization is also nested in a country. These characteristics were recorded in software data because they can explain heterogeneity among, for instance, organizations. Software data is also heterogeneous even in the case that it is not nested. Each software project

M. Ali Babar, M. Vierimaa, and M. Oivo (Eds.): PROFES 2010, LNCS 6156, pp. 276–290, 2010.
© Springer-Verlag Berlin Heidelberg 2010

consists of different team members, project management practices, application domains, and so on. These characteristics are also recorded in software data.

Characteristics are not populated equally in software data. Projects with severe execution time constraint are less found in software data, for instance. Because software data is usually collected from actual projects, not from experiments. Furthermore, size of software data is relatively small. For these reasons, a certain combination of characteristics are lacked in a software data while other combinations are common. The word *unbalanced* means this characteristic of software data.

Software data consists of numeric and nominal values. Statistical analysis treats numeric values with continuous variables and nominal values with discrete variables. Analysis of variance (ANOVA) and analysis of covariance (ANCOVA) are common methods for analyzing software data including discrete variables as predictors. They are used for identifying variables effective on a response variable. They can also quantify effects of factor levels of discrete variables. With these estimated effects, an explanation model can be built.

Kitchenham pointed out, however, that ANOVA involved two problems in the case that software data is unbalanced: concealed impacts and spurious impacts[1]. Concealed impacts prevent a significant predictor from being identified. Spurious impacts make an insignificant predictor to be significant by mistake. These impacts lead wrong conclusion. For managing concealed and spurious impacts, she proposed an analysis procedure iteratively applying ANOVA to residuals obtained from the previous ANOVA application. She demonstrated usefulness of the proposed procedure for productivity analysis. However, this procedure was sometimes failed to identify an important factor and its estimated effects were not easy to interpret.

In this paper, we showed usefulness of mixed-effects models for analyzing unbalanced datasets. Mixed-effects models can produce correct results in case of unbalanced datasets. They can also consider group-level predictors which are valuable when analyzing dataset from multiple groups. This study compared mixed-effects models with the procedure proposed by Kitchenham. Experiments with several datasets showed advantages of the mixed-effects models clearly.

The rest of this paper organized as follows. First, related work and mixed-effects models are introduced in Sect. 2 and 3. Then, we asked three research questions and described experiment procedure in Sect. 4. Section 5 showed how mixed-effects models worked. We finally concluded this paper in Sect. 6.

2 Related Work

In the past research, fixed-effects models have been widely used for analyzing software data even if they were unbalanced. Commonly used fixed-effects models in software engineering research are: (generalized) linear regression models, non-linear regression models, analysis of variance(ANOVA), and analysis of covariance(ANCOVA).

Linear and non-linear regression models have often been used for cost estimation models and variable selection procedures. In addition, fault-prone module prediction models often used logistic regression models which are classified into generalized linear regression models.

For productivity analysis and evaluation of technologies, ANOVA and ANCOVA have been widely used. The difference between them is whether continuous and discrete variables are mixed into a model.

We could find only one work by Kitchenham[1] managing unbalanced datasets. She proposed a procedure based on residual analysis for productivity analysis. To select important discrete factors, this procedure first applies one-way ANOVA on a response variable and obtains the most significant factor. Then, it repeats one-way ANOVA on residuals from the previous ANOVA. Continuous variables are also selected with the similar way.

Some studies applied mixed-effects models for software data analysis[2,3,4,5]. Mixed-effects models were used for treating repeated measures in most of them. As mentioned in [1], repeated measures are cause of spurious impacts. These studies grouped instances corresponding to the same subject into a factor level of a group indicator. On the other hand, mixed-effects models were rarely used for identifying and quantifying important ones from many discrete factors. Furthermore, group-level predictors, which can treat group-level variables as predictors, have been less mentioned in software data analysis. Thus, this study demonstrated usefulness of mixed-effects models with software datasets.

3 Mixed-Effects Models

3.1 Overview

Mixed-effects models(MEM) are mixture of fixed-effects models (FEM) and random-effects models. FEM has often been used in software engineering research. The following formula corresponds to a simple linear FEM with one continuous predictor X:

$$y_i = \alpha + \beta x_i + \epsilon_i, \text{ and}$$
$$\epsilon_i \sim N(0, \sigma^2). \tag{1}$$

Here, suffix i specifies an instance of dataset. α and β are a intercept and a slope, respectively. ϵ_i is an error term following normal distribution with mean 0 and variance σ^2. In this case, coefficients α and β are constant(fixed) for all instances.

In random-effects models, in contrast to FEM, coefficients α and β vary among groups specified by j. The following formula is a simple linear random-effects model with one continuous predictor X:

$$y_i = \alpha_{j[i]} + \beta_{j[i]} x_i + \epsilon_i, \tag{2}$$
$$\alpha_{j[i]} = a_0 + b_0 u_{j[i]} + \eta_{1j[i]}, \tag{3}$$
$$\beta_{j[i]} = a_1 + b_1 u_{j[i]} + \eta_{2j[i]}, \tag{4}$$

$$\eta_{1j} \sim N(0, \sigma_\alpha^2), \tag{5}$$
$$\eta_{2j} \sim N(0, \sigma_\beta^2), \text{and} \tag{6}$$
$$\epsilon_i \sim N(0, \sigma^2). \tag{7}$$

$j[i]$ indicates a group in which an instance i participates. $\alpha_{j[i]}$ and $\beta_{j[i]}$ are indexed by group j. Hence each group has specific intercept and slope. In software engineering research, a group may correspond to an organization, a software development team, etc. A group indicator is represented using a discrete variable. $\alpha_{j[i]}$ and $\beta_{j[i]}$ can be explained by a group-level predictor u_j as shown by (3) and (4). Here, η_{1j} and η_{2j} are group-level errors.

MEM include FEM and random-effects models as follows:

$$y_i = \alpha_{j[i]} + \beta x_i + \epsilon_i. \tag{8}$$

This model means that mean of Y is different for each of groups but an effect of unit of X on Y is constant for all groups. Because only an intercept varies, this model is called *random intercept model.*

3.2 ANOVA and ANCOVA Using MEM

Analysis of variance (ANOVA) and analysis of covariance (ANCOVA) are common methods for identifying significant predictors and quantifying factor levels of each of these predictors in software data. In the past study, FEM-based ANOVA and ANCOVA were used.

In case of FEM-based ANOVA and ANCOVA, a discrete predictor of J levels are coded into $J-1$ binary predictors b_{1j} as follows:

$$y_i = \alpha + \alpha_{11}b_{11} + \alpha_{12}b_{12} + \ldots + \alpha_{1(J-1)}b_{1(J-1)} + \beta x_i + \epsilon_i. \tag{9}$$

This coding rule sets a certain level as a baseline and its effect is absorbed in a intercept α. Other levels are represented using binary predictors. For example, if an instance has a level 1 for that discrete predictor, $b_{11} = 1$; otherwise $b_{11} = 0$. Therefore, effects of other levels are estimated at α_{1j}. These effects are relative to their baseline.

In the case that software data includes many discrete factors, that coding rule is inappropriate. It is recommended that *degrees-of-freedom* of error term should be more than 4 and preferably more than 10[1]. The degrees-of-freedom is defined as: (the number of instances - 1) - (the number of parameters to be estimated.) The degrees-of-freedom deceases by 1 in the case that a continuous predictor is included in a model. By contrast, it decreases by $J-1$ in the case that a discrete predictor of J levels is included. That is, the degrees-of-freedom decreases more rapidly if many discrete predictors of more than 2 levels are included.

In case of mixed-effects models, the degrees-of-freedom does not decrease so rapidly at the time that a discrete factor is added. Mixed-effects models use (8) for ANOVA and ANCOVA. This random intercept model considers a discrete predictor of J levels as a group indicator.

Equation (3) explains effects of factor levels of this discrete predictor. a_0 is considered as a baseline. $b_0 u_{j[i]} + \eta_{1j[i]}$ corresponds to an effect of factor level $j[i]$. In case of no group-level predictor, the following equation is obtained from (3) and (8):

$$y_i = \alpha + \eta_{1j[i]} + \beta x_i + \epsilon_i. \tag{10}$$

Here, α is used instead of a_0. This is the same formula as (9) except for representation of effects of factor levels. $\eta_{1j[i]}$ is a sample from normal distribution of mean 0 and variance σ_α^2, does not a coefficient to be estimated. Hence, degrees-of-freedom decreases by 1 for one discrete predictor regardless of the number of its factor levels. Furthermore, ANOVA and ANCOVA using MEM work the same for unbalanced as for balanced datasets[6].

Importance of a group indicator is evaluated by its standard deviation. In case of (10), σ_α in (5) is evaluated. Roughly speaking, a group indicator is considered as insignificant if $\sigma_\alpha \ll \sigma$ or can be considered as 0. $\sigma_\alpha \ll \sigma$ means that uncertainty within a group is far larger than that between groups and therefore it is a trivial predictor.

For precise evaluation, the likelihood-ratio test is used. the likelihood-ratio test compares the one model including a predictor with the another model excluding it. If null hypothesis cannot be rejected, this predictor is removed because of favor of parsimony.

4 Experiment

4.1 Research Questions

This study examined three research questions:

RQ1: MEM can estimate effects of factor levels correctly from unbalanced datasets?

RQ2: MEM can produce a model better than the iterative procedure based on residual analysis proposed in [1] (IPR)?

RQ:3 MEM can improve a productivity model using group-level predictors?

RQ1 is related to accuracy of estimated effects. IPR was examined with artificial unbalanced datasets in [1]. As a result, it could identify significant factors the same from unbalanced datasets as from a balanced dataset. However, estimates of factor levels were not completely accurate.

RQ2 is related to quality of a productivity model obtained from IPR. IPR can identify significant factors but we think it has three problems.

First, IPR involves a risk that a partially-confounded factor might be removed unnecessarily. Confounded factors are factors which have the same effect on a response variable. Thus, it is sufficient to include one of them in a model. *Partially*-confounded factors are confounded factors each of which has some of its own effect. Thus, it is desired to include all of them in a model.

Second problem is that estimates of factor levels are not easy to interpret because it uses residual analysis. Each factor is identified by applying one-way

Table 1. Balanced dataset (DS1)[1]

		F1		
F2	F3	L1	L2	L3
	L1	5	8	13
L1	L2	5	8	13
	L3	5	8	13
	L1	7	10	15
L2	L2	7	10	15
	L3	7	10	15
	L1	11	14	19
L3	L2	11	14	19
	L3	11	14	19

ANOVA on residuals obtained from previous ANOVA results, except at most significant factor. Because effects of factor levels are estimated from residuals, each factors is not included in a productivity model as is. It prevents a model from a straightforward interpretation. This problem maybe critical for understandability which is an important factor for practical use.

Third, IPR is slightly complicated than ANOVA. Simple procedure is preferable for efficient analysis.

If MEM can identify and include partially-confounded factors with simple procedure, a better productivity model can be obtained.

Finally, RQ3 is related to MEM itself. As mentioned in Sect. 3, MEM can include group-level predictors and grouping factors simultaneously. This feature may be useful, for example, to explain the difference of productivity among teams by team factors such as average experience years.

4.2 Dataset

This study compared MEM-based ANOVA and ANCOVA with IPR proposed in [1]. Thus, we used the same four datasets used in [1]. Three of the four datasets were made artificially in order to show concealed and spurious impacts. They were named DS1, DS2, and DS3. Table 1, 2, and 3 show DS1, DS2, and DS3, respectively.

These three datasets have three factors F1, F2, and F3, each of which has three levels L1, L2, and L3. Numeric values are of a response variable. F1 and F2 are significant factors. F3 is an insignificant factor.

DS1 is a perfectly balanced dataset. For each combination of factor levels, exactly one instance is collected. Hence, its size is $3^3 = 27$. DS2 is a subset of DS1 which missed instances for twelve combinations of factor levels. The size of DS2 is 15. This dataset shows concealing impacts if FEM-based ANOVA is used. DS3 is also a subset of DS1 which missed instances for twelve combinations of

Table 2. Unbalanced dataset concealing effect of F2 (DS2)[1]

		F1		
F2	F3	L1	L2	L3
	L1		8	13
L1	L2		8	13
	L3	5		13
	L1	7	10	
L2	L2	7	10	15
	L3		10	15
	L1	11		
L3	L2	11		
	L3			

Table 3. Unbalanced dataset giving spurious for F3 (DS3)[1]

		F1		
F2	F3	L1	L2	L3
	L1	5, 5		
L1	L2	5	8	
	L3		8	13
	L1	7, 7		
L2	L2	7	10	
	L3		10	15
	L1	11		
L3	L2	11	14	
	L3		14	19

factor levels and duplicated instances for two combinations. The size of DS3 is 17. This dataset shows spurious impacts if FEM-based ANOVA is used.

One of the four datasets is the COCOMO dataset published in [7]. This dataset consists of 21 factors of different scale types and its size is relatively small ($n = 63$). In this dataset, productivity was defined as follows:

$$\text{productivity} = \frac{\text{Adjusted KDSI(Kilo of Delivered Source Instructions)}}{\text{Man-Months}} \tag{11}$$

Details of adjustment were shown in [7]. Table 4 shows factors and its types. It is hard to use FEM-based ANOVA as is because the number of discrete factors are large and they all have more than 2 levels.

The COCOMO dataset recorded numerical adjustments for each factor instead of factor levels. We replaced numerical adjustments by their corresponding

Table 4. Factors in COCOMO dataset

Name	Type (Discrete/Continuous)	Description
Type	D (6 lv.)	Type of project
RELY	D (6 lv.)	Required software reliability
DATA	D (5 lv.)	Data base size
CPLX	D (7 lv.)	Product complexity
TIME	D (5 lv.)	Execution time constraint
STOR	D (5 lv.)	Main storage constraint
VIRT	D (4 lv.)	Virtual machine volatility
TURN	D (5 lv.)	Computer turnaround time
Platform	D (4 lv.)	Type of platform
ACAP	D (7 lv.)	Analyst capability
AEXP	D (5 lv.)	Applications experience
PCAP	D (7 lv.)	Programmer capability
VEXP	D (4 lv.)	Virtual machine experience
LEXP	D (4 lv.)	Programming language experience
MODP	D (6 lv.)	Modern programming practices
TOOL	D (6 lv.)	Use of software tools
SCED	D (5 lv.)	Required development schedule
RVOL	D (6 lv.)	Requirement Volatility
Mode	D (3 lv.)	Software development mode
Year	C	Year completed
ln(Duration)	C	Logarithm of duration

factor levels as same as [1]. For example, 1.0 of *PCAP* is to "Nominal". In [1], TIME was converted from 11 to 5 levels because it had many factor levels. This study also followed this prepossessing procedure.

4.3 Experiment Procedure

We applied MEM-based ANOVA and ANCOVA for the four datasets. All discrete factors were assumed to be group indicators. MEM-based ANOVA and ANCOVA first try to include all indicators and all predictors in a model because the degrees-of-freedom remains more than 10 for all datasets. Then, one of them having no significant effects on productivity is removed from a model. The likelihood-ratio test was used for this decision with a significance level $\alpha = 0.01$. This backward elimination procedure is repeated until all insignificant factors are removed.

To answer RQ1, we compared estimated effects from DS2 and DS3 by MEM-based ANOVA with those from DS1 by FEM-based ANOVA. DS1 is perfectly balanced datasets and we can assume estimates from DS1 to be true values.

To answer RQ2, a productivity model obtained from the COCOMO dataset by MEM-based ANCOVA is compared with that by IPR. Here, understandability and applicability in practice are evaluated.

Table 5. Standard deviations of MEM-based ANOVA on DS2 and DS3

Factors	DS2	DS3
F1	1.92	1.87
F2	1.91	1.67
F3	0.00	0.00
Residual	0.00	0.00

Table 6. Estimated effects(coefficients) of factor levels tfrom DS1, DS2, and DS3

Factor/	DS1	DS2		DS3	
Level	FEM	FEM	MEM	FEM	MEM
F1L1	−3.66	−2.2	−3.66	−2.69	−3.66
F1L2	0.66	−1.2	0.66	−0.71	0.66
F1L3	4.33	3.4	4.33	5.71	4.33
F2L1	−2.66	−0.4	−2.66	−2.61	−2.66
F2L2	−0.66	0.2	−0.66	−0.61	−0.66
F2L3	3.33	0.6	3.33	3.23	3.33
F3L1	0	−0.6	0	−2.94	0
F3L2	0	0.3	0	−0.77	0
F3L3	0	0.3	0	3.23	0

To answer RQ3, we included a group-level predictor in a model obtained from the COCOMO dataset. Although the COCOMO dataset does not include group-level predictors, we tried to include typical group predictors gained from this dataset. This trial is to examine whether model extension by group-level predictor is valuable for improvement of a model.

5 Results

5.1 Comparison of Estimates between FEM-Based and MEM-Based ANOVA

Table 5 shows standard deviations of factors estimated from DS2 and DS3 by MEM-based ANOVA. A factor with standard deviation near to 0 is insignificant and a factor with large standard deviation is significant. MEM-based ANOVA clearly identified significant factors F1 and F2 and an insignificant factor F3. Thus, concealed and spurious impacts did not matter in case of straightforward application of MEM-based ANOVA.

Table 6 shows estimated effects of factor levels. Results of ANOVA using fixed-effects models were borrowed from [1]. ANOVA using fixed-effects models could not estimate effects correctly for some factor levels because of concealed and spurious impacts. By contrast, MEM-based ANOVA could estimate all effects exactly from DS2 and DS3 as same as fixed-effects ANOVA only did from DS1.

From these results, we concluded that MEM can tell importance of factors, and can estimate effects of factor levels correctly from unbalanced datasets.

5.2 Comparison of MEM-Based ANCOVA and IPR

Table 7 shows estimated effects of remained factors by backward elimination with MEM-based ANCOVA. Estimated effects of TIME, STOR, and SCED were consistent with order of factor levels. Estimated effects of PCAP and RVOL were not decreased or increased consistently with corresponding factor levels though the trend of each factor from positive to negative was roughly consistent. IPR also estimated inconsistent effects for PCAP and RVOL.

In case of PCAP and RVOL the difference among estimated effects was smaller than their standard errors. Thus, this inconsistency did not matter statistically. In the case that an consistent productivity model is required, IPR concatenated some factor levels such that linear relationship is satisfied among estimated effects.

Table 8 shows results of MEM-based ANCOVA with concatenation approach. Each factor was still significant after concatenation. In addition to PCAP and RVOL, SCED also had fewer factor levels by concatenating Lax and Nominal. As a result, each factor had consistent effects of its factor levels.

The study [1] used $MMRE$ and $PRED(20)$ as goodness of fit statistics. Table 9 shows these statistics for MEM-based ANCOVA and IPR. MEM-based ANCOVA clearly improved both statistics. Therefore, we concluded that MEM-based ANCOVA could make a better productivity model regarding goodness of fit.

MEM-based ANCOVA made a productivity model as follows:

$$\begin{aligned}\ln(\text{productivity}) = {} & \eta_{TIME} + \eta_{PCAP} + \eta_{RVOL} \\ & + \eta_{STOR} + \eta_{SCED} + \alpha + \beta \ln(\text{Duration}). \end{aligned} \tag{12}$$

Here, η_X corresponds to an effect of a factor level of X. All group-level intercepts were united in α as shown by (10).

IPR made the following productivity model:

$$\begin{aligned}\ln(\text{productivity}) = {} & \alpha_{TIME} + \alpha_{PCAP/TIME} + \alpha_{RVOL/TIMEandPCAP} \\ & + \alpha + \beta \ln(\text{Duration}). \end{aligned} \tag{13}$$

Here, for example, $\alpha PCAP/TIME$ indicates an effect of a factor level of PCAP which was estimated after that for TIME.

Equation (12) included all factors in (13). It also included STOR and SCED. SCED, STOR, and TIME were considered as confounded factors in [1]. It is sufficient to include one of them in a model if they were confounded factors because this means that they had the same effect on a response variable.

These contrast results, however, implicated that those factors were partially-confounded. Partially-confounded factors are confounded factors each of which

Table 7. Estimated effects of remained factors by MEM-based ANCOVA

Factor	Levels	Effects(coefficients)
TIME	Nominal	0.424
	High	0.176
	Very High	0.088
	Extra High	-0.115
	Super High	-0.573
PCAP	Super High	0.399
	Very High	0.140
	High	0.051
	Nominal	0.095
	Low	0.033
	Very Low	-0.438
	Super Low	-0.280
RVOL	Low	0.431
	Nominal	0.231
	High	0.439
	Very High	-0.257
	Extra High	-0.607
	Super High	-0.237
STOR	Nominal	0.423
	High	0.079
	Very High	0.026
	Extra High	-0.146
	Super High	-0.383
SCED	Lax	0.284
	Nominal	0.251
	Compressed	0.034
	Very Compressed	-0.569
ln(Duration)		-0.022
(Intercept)		5.130

has some of its own contribution to a response variable. Kitchenham said that IPR involves a risk that a partially-confounded factor might be removed unnecessarily. SCED and STOR were still significant factors and improved goodness of fit statistics even if TIME was included. We therefore concluded that they were partially confounded factors.

The difference between MEM-based ANCOVA and IPR was also found in interpretation of factor level effects. In case of IPR, we say that logarithm of productivity increases 0.681 when PCAP is Super High and after allowing for the effect of TIME. In case of MEM-based ANCOVA, we say that logarithm of productivity increases 0.333 when PCAP is Super High regardless of levels of other factors. Because IPR estimated factor level effects from residuals, interpretation of these effects was not straightforward and not intuitive.

Table 8. Estimated effects of remained factors by MEM-based ANCOVA(with concatenation approach)

Factor	Levels	Effects(coefficients)
TIME	Nominal	0.476
	High	0.209
	Very High	0.098
	Extra High	-0.137
	Super High	-0.647
PCAP	Super High	0.333
	Very High and High	0.104
	Nominal	0.00
	Low and Very Low and Super Low	-0.441
RVOL	Low and Nominal and High	0.465
	Very High	-0.061
	Extra High and Super High	-0.404
STOR	Nominal	0.413
	High	0.074
	Very High	-0.026
	Extra High	-0.122
	Super High	-0.340
SCED	Lax and Nominal	0.309
	Compressed	0.163
	Very Compressed	-0.472
ln(Duration)		-0.019
(Intercept)		4.864

From these results, we concluded that MEM-based ANCOVA can produce a model better than IPR. It is easy to apply, easy to interpret, and can include partially-confounded factors.

5.3 Examination of Usefulness of Group-Level Predictors

In the past research using FEM-based ANOVA, discrete factors of ordinal scale have often converted to continuous factors. Here, factor levels are converted to numeric values in consistent with their order.

This conversion is useful in two situations. First, a dataset includes many discrete factors and they make a model complicated, though it did not matter

Table 9. Goodness of fit statistics

Statistic	IPR	MEM-based ANCOVA (concat.)
$MMRE$	0.36	0.20(0.21)
$PRED(20)$	0.49	0.60(0.57)

Table 10. Effects of factor levels(with linear group-level predictor)

Factor	Levels	Effects(coefficients)
TIME	Nominal	0.000
	High	-0.240
	Very High	-0.479
	Extra High	-0.719
	Super High	-0.958
PCAP	Super High	0.508
	Very High	0.290
	High	0.162
	Nominal	0.044
	Low	-0.157
	Very Low	-0.354
	Super Low	-0.494
RVOL	Low	0.224
	Nominal	0.000
	High	-0.224
	Very High	-0.448
	Extra High	-0.673
	Super High	-0.897
STOR	Nominal	0.039
	High	-0.281
	Very High	-0.396
	Extra High	-0.484
	Super High	-0.841
SCED	Lax	0.171
	Nominal	0.084
	Compressed	-0.114
	Very Compressed	-0.708
ln(Duration)		-0.018
(Intercept)		6.221

in case of IPR and MEM-based ANOVA. Second, effects of factor levels are assumed to have linear relationship.

This conversion may be harmful in the case that effects of factor levels do not have linear relationship. Linear assumption produces an inappropriate model. In this case, it is preferable to use a discrete factor as is.

MEM can manage both possibilities using group-level predictors[6]. In the case that a group-level predictor is included, Equation (10) is as follows:

$$y_i = a_0 + b_0 u_{j[i]} + \eta_{1j[i]} + \beta x_i + \epsilon_i. \tag{14}$$

$u_{j[i]}$ is a group-level predictor and b_0 is a coefficient of u_j. Here, $b_0 u_{j[i]} + \eta_{1j[i]}$ corresponds to an effect of factor level $j[i]$. To assume linear relationship among these effects, a continuous factor converted from a discrete factor is used to u_j.

Table 11. The difference of power between MEM-based ANCOVA and IPR and its influence on productivity

Models	$\min(\text{Duration})^p$	$\max(\text{Duration})^p$
MEM-based ANCOVA(−0.018)	0.95	0.92
IPR(−0.177)	0.88	0.46

For example, PCAP has seven factor levels and therefore u_j may take -3, -2, -1, 0, 1, 2, or 3 in accordance with its factor levels.

If estimated effects would have complete linear relationship, standard deviation of η_{1j}, σ_α, decreases to be 0. If not, u_j is to be a insignificant factor. When estimated effects would not have linear relationship but they would keep order of factor levels, η_{1j} and u_j will contribute to effects.

Table 10 shows results of MEM-based ANCOVA with linear group-level predictors. Here, Nominal Level for each factor was converted to 0. In comparison with Table 7, each factor had consistently ordered effects while the difference between adjacent effects of each factor was not always equal. This modeling keeps goodness of fit statistics $MMRE = 0.21$ and $PRED(20) = 0.57$. For $PRED(10)$, simple, concatenated, and linear MEM-based ANCOVA showed $0.35, 0.30$, and 0.41, respectively. Thus, linear group-level predictors worked well.

This model also improved its understandability. Because Nominal Level of all factors were near 0, it was easy to understand how logarithm of productivity changes from Nominal level to other levels. Furthermore, we can easily obtain a standard productivity model which assumes all factors are Nominal by adding effects at Nominal Level and intercept. Here, standard productivity models from MEM-based ANCOVA and IPR are as follows:

$$(\text{productivity from MEM-based ANCOVA}) = 594.1 \cdot (\text{Duration})^{-0.018} \quad (15)$$

$$(\text{productivity from IPR}) = 625.2 \cdot (\text{Duration})^{-0.177} \quad (16)$$

Baselines of these models were different by approximately 5% ($625.2/594.1 \simeq 1.05$) and it did not matter here. The difference of their powers was critical. Table 11 shows how the difference of powers influences on interpretations of these productivity models. Here, a range of Duration in the COCOMO dataset is from 2.0 to 72.0.

In case of MEM-based ANCOVA, productivity is assumed to be almost constant between the shortest-term project and the longest-term project if they are average projects regarding PCAP, RVOL, SCED, STOR, and TIME. By contrast, a productivity model by IPR assumes that productivity of the longest-term project is as half as that of the shortest-term project. This study preferred MEM-based ANCOVA model to IPR model because of better goodness of fit.

From these results, we concluded that MEM can improve a productivity model using group-level predictors.

6 Conclusion and Future Works

This study examined how mixed-effects models worked well for analyzing unbalanced datasets. MEM-based ANOVA and ANCOVA could estimate all effects correctly from unbalanced datasets and they are easy to interpret. They also could identify partially-confounded factors and could include them into a productivity model simultaneously. As a result, $MMRE$ and $PRED(20)$ were improved to 0.21 and 0.57. Furthermore, it was confirmed that group-level predictors were useful for improving understandability of a model.

Group-level predictors can be used for other purpose such as multilevel analysis. By using multilevel analysis, the difference among software development organizations, teams, or countries may be explained by group-level characteristics while considering individual-level characteristics. Examining mixed-effects models for multilevel analysis is future work.

In terms of productivity analysis, other software data must be analyzed with mixed-effects models. For example, public datasets on PROMISE repository[8] such as cocomonasa datasets were easily obtained. We can expect new findings from comparisons among results of these analyses.

References

1. Kitchenham, B.: A procedure for analyzing unbalanced datasets. IEEE Trans. on Software Engineering 24(4), 278–301 (1998)
2. Kemerer, C.F., Paulk, M.C.: The impact of design and code reviews on software quality: An empirical study based on psp data. IEEE Trans. on Software Engineering 35(4), 534–550 (2009)
3. Bazeghi, C., Mesa-Martinez, F.J., Renau, J.: μComplexity: Estimating processor design effort. In: Proc. of 38th Annual IEEE/ACM International Symposium on Microarchitecture, pp. 209–218 (2005)
4. Reinhartz-Berger, I., Dori, D.: OPM vs. UML – experimenting with comprehension and construction of web application models. Empirical Software Engineering 10, 57–79 (2005)
5. Lawrie, D., Feild, H., Binkley, D.: Quantifying identifier quality: an analysis of trends. Empirical Software Engineering 12, 359–388 (2007)
6. Gelman, A., Hill, J.: Data Analysis Using Regression and Multilevel/Hierarchical Models. Cambridge University Press, Cambridge (2007)
7. Boehm, B.W.: Software Engineering Economics. Prentice-Hall, Englewood Cliffs (1981)
8. Shirabad, J.S., Menzies, T.J.: The PROMISE repository of software engineering databases. In: School of Information Technology and Engineering. University of Ottawa, Canada (2005)

SAS: A Tool for the GQM$^+$Strategies Grid Derivation Process

Vladimir Mandić and Markku Oivo

Department of Information Processing Science, University of Oulu, Finland
{vladimir.mandic,markku.oivo}@oulu.fi

Abstract. GQM$^+$Strategies is an approach designed to help the software industry develop measurement programs that are aligned with business goals. The resulting structure, which aligns metrics (GQM goals) and business goals, is called a grid. Usefulness (quality) of the grids depends on how well the environment is characterized by the grid elements. Our research objective was to construct a tool which would support and improve the context/assumption definition and strategy selection activities of the grid derivation process. The constructive research work took place between two pilot applications of the GQM$^+$Strategies approach. The first one identified key requirements, while the second one was used to test the tool. For the validation we used a questionnaire to assess practitioners' feedback regarding usefulness of the tool. We augmented the GQM$^+$Strategies toolbox with the SAS tool. The principles used to design the tool complement the grid derivation process and practices. Two industrial pilot applications of GQM$^+$Strategies demonstrated the usefulness of the SAS tool.

Keywords: GQM$^+$Strategies, GQM, SAS, Strategies Abstraction Sheet.

1 Introduction

Software engineering (SE) researchers are confronted with the influence of the context (environment) on empirical findings. The same influence is observable in the software industry. A good solution for one company may not be so good for or can even be disastrous for some other companies. Software metrics programs are especially vulnerable to the influence of context [1]. Kautz [2] pointed out that decoding context is a key to successful measurement programs; it is not a matter of following general principles and guidelines, but of adjusting each to suit a specific company [2], [3]. Umarji and Seaman [3] proposed contextual interviews to support metrics programs.

In the early 1990s, the GQM (Goal Question Metric) [4] approach was accompanied by the Quality Improvement Paradigm (QIP) [5]. QIP is a set of heuristics that applies iterative procedures to software quality improvement through systematic use of feedback information that is collected using goal-oriented measurements. The QIP cycle includes the activity of characterizing the current project and its environment (context). This provides a mechanism to deal with context when conducting GQM–based measurement programs. In recent years, Basili et al. developed the GQM$^+$Strategies[1]

[1] *GQM$^+$Strategies®* is a registered mark of the Fraunhofer Institute for Experimental Software Engineering, Germany and the Fraunhofer USA Center for Experimental Software Engineering, Maryland.

M. Ali Babar, M. Vierimaa, and M. Oivo (Eds.): PROFES 2010, LNCS 6156, pp. 291–305, 2010.
© Springer-Verlag Berlin Heidelberg 2010

approach [6] with the explicit purpose of bridging the gap between business goals and measurement programs at the operational level. The resulting structure, which aligns metrics (GQM goals) and business goals is called a *grid*. The second novelty of the new approach was that it was the first time a measurement approach was explicitly taking business environment into account. Environment related information is documented as a grid element, and is retrieved when interpreting metrics data.

Research work with GQM$^+$Strategies is in the early phase; there are no published practical experiences yet with the use of this method. The first version of the method was published in 2007 as a white paper [6]. A series of publications was published to illustrate the method's usefulness on hypothetical examples [7], [8].

As a part of our previous research, two pilot applications of the GQM$^+$Strategies method were carried out with Finnish ICT companies. These pilots provided us with valuable feedback about how to improve the derivation of the GQM$^+$Strategies grid. After the first pilot, we recognized the necessity of having appropriate tools that would accompany the GQM$^+$Strategies method. Under "tools" we consider not only software applications, but also some additional procedures and methods. For example, the toolbox should contain tools for structuring discussions, for visualization of the GQM$^+$Strategies grid, for analyzing relevant context, and so on.

In virtue of those needs we specified the objective of our constructive research as the development of a tool with the purpose of improving grid derivation activities, such as context/assumption definition and strategy selection. Based on feedback from the first pilot, we selected two of the most important requirements that such a tool should meet: ability to document relevant contextual information, and ability to guide/structure group-discussion sessions.

We designed a strategies abstraction sheet (SAS) tool for the second pilot. The pilot was used as early empirical validation of the tool. For the validation we used a questionnaire to assess participants' feedback regarding the usefulness of the tool.

The rest of the paper is structured as follows. Section 2 gives a short overview of the GQM abstraction sheet, and explains GQM$^+$Strategies' concepts and grid derivation process. The motivation for our constructive research is elaborated in Section 3 with discussion of the importance of context for the grid derivation. The strategies abstraction sheet tool is explained in Section 4. Early validation results are presented and discussed in Section 5. Section 6 concludes the paper and states our final remarks.

2 Background and Related Work

The foundation of the GQM paradigm was laid out at the Software Engineering Laboratory (SEL) in the beginning of the 1980s. Even though the method was originally developed for research purposes, in a relatively short period it was recognized by the software industry as a viable solution for establishing measurement programs. The method quickly evolved beyond its initial purpose. Almost 30 years after inception of GQM, the method's evolution culminated with recent development of GQM$^+$ Strategies.

2.1 GQM Paradigm and Abstraction Sheet

The main concepts of the GQM paradigm [4] are: goals, questions, and metrics. Goal documents the objectives of measurements. Basili *et al.* [4] specified five dimensions of a GQM goal as: object of study, purpose, quality focus, viewpoint, and context. Further on, a set of questions operationally defines a GQM goal. Answers to the set of questions should clearly indicate whether the goal is achieved or not. Finally, a set of measures is associated with every question so as to answer it in a quantitative way.

The GQM paradigm advocates top-down metrics derivation, with the purpose of ensuring a meaningful definition of metrics. The interpretation process goes bottom-up. One of the benefits of the goal-driven measurement approach is the definition of what data is really needed with the possibility to reuse metrics and questions for different GQM goals.

The GQM approach package includes a *GQM abstraction sheet* [9], a tool for derivation of questions and metrics from GQM goals. The tool is used during interviewing sessions or group discussions. One of the main advantages of the abstraction sheet tool is its ability to expose implicit models and to formulate them into questions and metrics [10]. The structure of a GQM abstraction sheet is depicted by four quadrants and a header. The header represents the GQM goal with five dimensions: object, purpose, quality focus, viewpoint, and environment, while the quadrants [9] represent: (I) variation factors, (II) quality focus, (III) baseline hypothesis, and (IV) impact of variation factors.

Interviewees are asked to propose relevant attributes to describe the goal's quality focus (second quadrant). Further on, the interviewees are expected to hypothesize values of the quality focus attributes (third quadrant). After that, a discussion of variation factors and their impact on the baseline hypothesis takes place (first and fourth quadrants). If needed changes in quality focus and the baseline hypothesis can be made, the entire process is iterative.

Because the interpretation process is seen as structured discussions and dialogs between the GQM measurement team and others (developers, managers, testers, analysts, etc.), it is important to expose implicit models at the beginning when specifying the data to be collected.

2.2 GQM$^+$Strategies

GQM$^+$Strategies [6], [8] is an extension of the GQM approach [4]. The GQM approach provides a method for an organization or project to define goals, refine those goals down to specifications of data to be collected, and then to analyze and interpret the resulting data with respect to the original goals. However, it does not provide a mechanism for linking high-level business goals to lower-level goals or supporting and integrating *different* goals at different levels of the organization, such mechanisms are provided by GQM$^+$Strategies.

GQM$^+$Strategies introduced several new concepts: goals, strategies, context/assumptions, and interpretation model. Discernment is made between *goal* and *GQM goal*. The goal is a business goal, and it can be very abstract and difficult to operationalize, while GQM goals are also referred to as measurable goals. Business goals are further refined

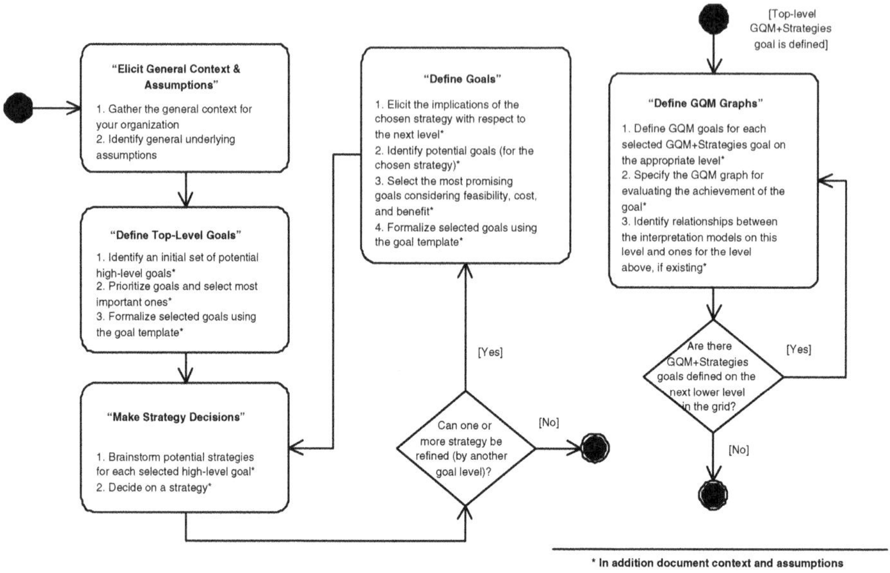

Fig. 1. GQM$^+$Strategies grid derivation process. Source: [7].

by *strategies*. The end result of applying strategies is more concrete goals. Using this mechanism, abstract business goals are brought to the level where operationalization is possible. Business goals are formalized by using the *business goal template* (Table 1). The template documents the basic activity that should be performed in order to accomplish the goal, the main (quality) focus of the goal, the object under consideration, the quantification of the goal specified by a magnitude, the timeframe in which the magnitude has to be achieved, the scope, and basic constraints that may limit accomplishing the goal. Furthermore, potential relationships with other goals are listed.

The *Goal+Strategies element* represents a single goal and derived strategies, including all context information and assumptions that explain the linkage between the goal and the corresponding strategies. The *GQM graph* is a single GQM goal that measures

Table 1. GQM$^+$Strategies goal formalization template with "Splash" product example [7]

Goal template	Example
Activity	Increase
Focus	Customer satisfaction
Object	"Splash" product
Magnitude	10% reduction in number of customer complains
Timeframe	12 weeks after release, beginning in one year
Scope (Context)	Web products development division, Splash product manager
Constraints	Splash price and functionality ability to sustain CMMI levels
Relations	Can conflict with development cost goals, schedule goals, etc.

the element. The *GQM$^+$Strategies grid* is an integrated collection of all GQM$^+$Strategies elements, GQM graphs, and all links.

GQM$^+$Strategies also introduces the concept of levels. Top-level business goals exist on strategic levels. Furthermore, the goal derivation process addresses lower levels (e.g., the operational level). The concept of levels is convenient for grouping and organizing GQM$^+$Strategies elements.

The entire process of deriving business goals and measurable goals is consolidated through the *interpretation model*. During the interpretation process, measured GQM goals and the status of the context/assumption variables influence assessment of business goal realization.

The GQM$^+$Strategies grid deviation process [7] is flexible and allows different approaches, starting from top-level business goals down to addressing lower-level goals or vice versa. During the derivation process, two parallel threads are running (Figure 1): (1) one is related to defining business goals, context/assumption elements, and strategies for addressing goals, and (2) the other is related to defining measurable goals and actually deriving the GQM graph.

In the following we give an overview of the grid derivation process [7].

Elicit General Context and Assumptions. The organizational (business) environment is modeled by specifying context factors and assumptions.For example, corporate vision and mission statement represent general context elements for top-level business goals.

Define Top-Level Goals. First, an initial set of high-level goals is identified. Second, the goals have to be prioritized and analyzed for potential conflicts. Third, the selected goals are formalized using the GQM$^+$Strategies goal template (Table 1).

Make Strategy Decisions. First, a list of potential strategies for achieving the business goals is identified. Second, the most promising strategy has to be selected, considering the cost and benefit analysis.

Define Goals. If it is possible to refine strategy by another goal level, first the implications of the chosen upper-level strategies with respect to lower level goals have to be determined. Second, potential lower-level goals are identified based on the analysis. Third, the most promising goal with respect to feasibility, cost, and benefit is selected. Fourth, the most promising goals are selected and formalized using the GQM$^+$Strategies goal template.

Creating the measurement branch of the grid for each goal and strategy level is not an isolated task; that is, the metrics derived across different levels of the GQM$^+$Strategies model will usually overlap. Moreover, an interpretation model for a higher-level goal may only be defined completely if the lower-level pieces have already been modeled.

Define GQM Graphs. The GQM Graph derivation process is well documented in the literature[2].

[2] For example, see: van Solingen, R., Berghout, E.: *The Goal/Question/Metric Method*. The McGraw-Hill Company, Maidenhead; England (1999).

3 Importance of Context

In everyday life, the term *context* is often used, and its meaning is understandable. According to *Webster Dictionary*[3]: **context** [noun] /Date: circa 1568/ *(1): the parts of a discourse that surround a word or passage and can throw light on its meaning (2): the interrelated conditions in which something exists or occurs: environment, setting.*

A more computer-science related formulation of the context is *circumstances or situations in which a computing task takes place* [11]. All these definitions refer to context as surroundings or environment. GQM$^+$Strategies specifies the concepts of context and assumptions which differ slightly, but at same time are related to the general understanding of context as environment. Context/assumption elements are used to document (model) environment. Facts about the environment are modeled with context variables, while uncertainties are modeled as assumptions (predictions) [6].

We differentiate external from internal environment. The most natural way to define external environment is as circumstances beyond corporate (organizational) boundaries (e.g., the market, technology, etc.), while internal environment is a characterization of the organization itself. This differentiation of environments is important, because often internal environment is neglected and more attention is given to external environment.

Context (environment) has much deeper implications on a grid derivation process than just documenting context/assumption elements. Any decision, especially a strategic one, depends on numerous contextual conditions, and on an infinite number of combinations of those conditions. Therefore, decisions are based on a simplified view of the context. Such simplification is possible because only the finite subset of context variables is *relevant* for a given situation and related decisions [12].

The decision about which business goals are selected/defined depends on the context. The decision about which strategies will be defined/used to achieve those business goals also depends on the context. Actually, the entire GQM$^+$Strategies grid is shaped by contextual information.

High-quality GQM$^+$Strategies grids have an ability to guide an organization in achieving their business goals and strategies. That ability depends on the methods capability to "capture" relevant context (internal and external environment). GQM$^+$Strategies adaptation can be successful only if it produces high-quality grids.

In the following section we will introduce the strategies abstraction sheet (SAS). Our intention is to emphasize the importance of context when defining or selecting strategies, and therefore we call it a *strategies* abstraction sheet.

4 Strategies Abstraction Sheet (SAS)

Our work extends the state of the art and practices by augmenting the GQM+Strategies toolbox with the SAS tool. The tool is designed for use with the GQM$^+$Strategies approach, with the purpose of exposing relevant contextual information. The relevant contextual information is of high significance for the context/assumption definition and strategy selection activities of the grid derivation process. The principles used to design the tool, such as *variation factors analysis* and *context dynamics analysis*, complement

[3] Merriam-Webster Online Dictionary: `http://www.merriam-webster.com`

the grid derivation process and practices. To the best of our knowledge, this is the first such tool.

4.1 SAS Research Requirements

SAS is designed as an effective tool[4] for the grid derivation process. We define effectiveness as the capability of the grid derivation process to maximize the impact of context on the resulting GQM+Strategies grid by documenting the relevant subset of contextual variables and assumptions. This we will consider as our main research requirement (R1).

Requirement R1: *Construct a tool which is able to elicit implicit knowledge about contextual variables and assumptions for GQM+Strategies business goals.*

Usually business related decisions are made in closed groups of people. Therefore, we recognize the need for the tool to be able to manage group sessions by guiding (focusing) and structuring discussions. This is the second research requirement (R2).

Requirement R2: *Construct a tool which is able to facilitate sessions of experts' group-discussion during the GQM+Strategies grid derivation process.*

An **implicit requirement** for a tool that aims to guide experts' group-discussion sessions is to address threats to the session results. The threats are *conformity*, *bias*, and *personality*. *Conformity* manifests the tendency of individuals to self-correct theirs opinion according to the group's opinion. Also, some individuals can be *biased* if their opinion is under the influence of seniors or executives. Naturally, different people have different *personalities*, some of them "speak loudly" and try to impose their opinion, while others are more closed and quiet.

Alike the GQM abstraction sheet, the *structure of SAS* is organized around four quadrants. Navigation through an abstraction sheet adds new principles to existing ones, and we refer to them as the *logic of SAS*.

In parallel with the description of the logic of SAS, a hypothetical example will follow. The purpose of the example is to illustrate steps and not to present a real-world case example. Even with a real-world example, it is impossible for an outside reader to determine the relevance of contextual elements. The example illustrates the hypothetical use of the SAS tool for the business goal given in Table 1 (the "Splash" product example), and it is not related to the pilot project used for validating the tool.

In the following sections we will present the structure, and explain the logic of SAS.

4.2 The Structure of SAS

The structure of SAS resembles GQM abstraction sheets, with four quadrants and a header, but with the addition of a footer (Figure 2). Some principles from the abstraction sheet were kept here, such as one sheet representing one business goal. The abstraction sheet is used for exposing implicit models; now in our case, those models are contextual variables and assumptions.

[4] At this point our definition of the tool is as a concept and a set of procedures for how to use it, not a software application.

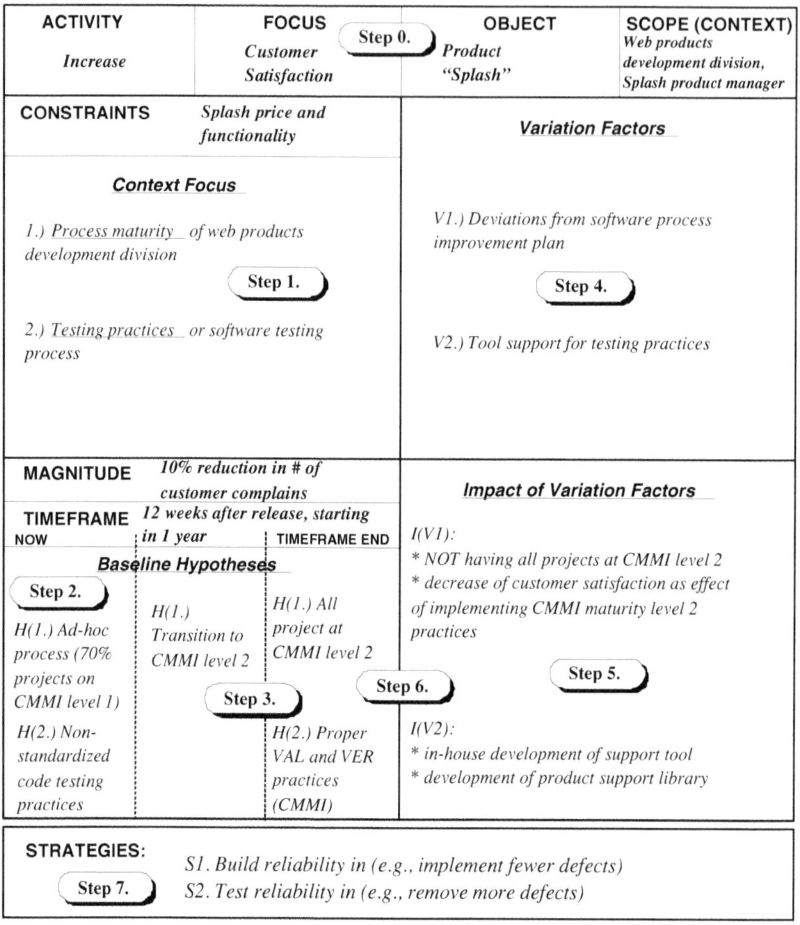

Fig. 2. Strategies Abstraction Sheet (SAS). Illustrated on "Splash"example.

The four quadrants of the strategies abstraction sheet are: (I) variation factors, (II) context focus, (III) baseline hypothesis, and (IV) impact of variation factors.

GQM$^+$Strategies business goals are more complex than GQM goals. They are defined by eight elements (goal formalization template Table 1); herein the SAS structure is more complex. The header of a SAS presents four elements (dimensions) of a business goal: *activity*, *focus*, *object*, and *scope*.

Constraints are presented as designated context focus elements in the second quadrant. They indeed represent the special context elements. They are special because we take them for granted, usually because we do not have mechanisms to affect them or to change them. It is possible that some context focus elements became constraints after analyzing variation factors.

The *magnitude* and *timeframe* of a business goal are depicted in the form of the third quadrant's header. The magnitude quantitatively characterizes the degree of change. The nature of the change is specified by activity and focus goal elements. Timeframe can be specified in a qualitative and/or quantitative manner, but in such a way that allows calculation of absolute time (calendar time).

The entire baseline hypothesis quadrant (third quadrant) is divided into three columns which represent a simplified time-line. The first column represents the current moment (NOW column, Figure 2), while the third column (TIMEFRAME END column) is reserved for the future moment when the achievement of the business goal is expected.

The first and fourth quadrants are used for analysis of variation factors. After documenting relevant contextual information for why a business goal is or is not realistic, strategy proposals are written down in the footer section.

4.3 The Logic of SAS

The business goals and strategies definition/selection is usually done by a group of people. Therefore, the SAS tool will rarely be used in one-on-one interviewing sessions. After having defined a business goal according to the GQM+Strategies goal formalization template (Table 1), the initial step is to collect context focus proposals. This is achieved by *SAS scoring*.

Step 0 and Step 1: SAS Scoring and definition of context focus elements. A convenient way to nominate relevant context focus elements is to use a simple scoring mechanism —*SAS scoring*. Before the scoring, the business goal is depicted in the abstraction sheet as described in Section 4.2 (Step 0). Scores are obtained by probing the question: ***Is the goal realistic (feasible)?***

The four-point scoring scale is defined as follows: (1) The goal is extremely unrealistic, (2) The goal's feasibility is questionable (uncertain), (3) The goal is feasible with acceptable level of uncertainties, and (4) The goal is realistic.

The purpose of scoring is to initiate discussion about relevant context focus elements. Accordingly, the scoring scale is designed in such way as to force opinion from participants, negative opinion (presented with lower points, 1 and 2), or positive opinion (3 and 4); there is no mid-point for neutral answer. Scoring is very useful in guiding group sessions; the extreme negative or positive opinions should be discussed first.

The initial definition of context focus elements (Step 1 in Figure 2) is done after analyzing (discussing) why participants believe that goal is or is not feasible.

EXAMPLE. For the business goal given in Table 1, the participants responded with negative opinions regarding goal feasibility. Their concerns were that a software development process has chaotic behavior and that testing practices were not uniform across the entire development process. As a result of discussion, an agreement was reached for two context focus elements (Figure 2): *1.) Process maturity of the web products development division,* and *2.) Testing practices or a software testing process.*

Step 2: Hypotheses setting. After defining relevant context focus elements, the next step is to determine the current status of context elements. It is possible to set hypotheses in quantitative or in qualitative (descriptive) form. Quantification, if possible, is welcomed because it can significantly increase understanding of context among participants.

The current status of context elements is documented in the first column of the *baseline hypotheses* quadrant (Step 2 in Figure 2).

EXAMPLE. For the context focus elements defined in the previous step (Figure 2) the baseline hypotheses were defined as: *H(1.) Ad-hoc process with 70% (majority) projects on CMMI level 1*, and *H(2.) Non-standardized code testing practices.*

Regarding testing it was noted that testing efforts are more focused on code (unit testing) than on other forms of testing.

Step 3: Analyzing the dynamics of context focus. Changes in environment are perceived through the time component. The ability to define/make good strategy is dependent on the ability to predict future changes or events in the environment (e.g., market changes or a shift to the new paradigm or technology, etc.). Therefore, in this step participants are asked to describe/predict how the baseline hypotheses will look in the future when it is expected to reach a business goal (when the timeframe expires).

EXAMPLE. The timeframe for analyzing context dynamics was about 1.5 years, according to the business goal timeframe: 12 weeks after release, starting after one year. The important question was how the context elements would look in 1.5 years' time. The predicted future status of the context focus elements were: *H(1.) All projects at least at CMMI level 2*, and *H(2.) Proper VAL and VER practices (CMMI terminology) implemented.*

For the first context focus *H(1.)*, it was known that it will be affected by software process improvement plans and the transition to CMMI level 2, while for the testing practices *H(2.)*, there was an evident need to implement validation and verification practices in order to increase satisfaction of customer needs and requests. However, those practices are CMMI level 3 practices, and participants were not specific as to when or how the implementation could occur (mid-column was left blank in Figure 2).

Step 4: Defining variation factors. Variation factors analysis (Steps 4 and 5) is one of the major benefits of using the SAS tool for grid derivation. Any strategic decision is a consequence of environment (context); therefore it is important to document relevant context information. However, we do not have the technology nor the capability to document all of the numerous contextual facts and variables, but just a limited subset. The objective is to ensure the presence of the most relevant contextual facts and variables inside that limited subset. One important mechanism to achieve that is variation factors analysis.

In Step 4 all related events that have or could have influence on context focus elements are discussed and the most significant ones are documented as variation factors.

EXAMPLE. The possible variation factors were specified as (Figure 2): *V1.) Deviations from the software process improvement plan*, and *V2.) Tool support for testing practices.*

For the majority participants, the software process improvement plan was considered ambitious. With a history of constant priority changes by managers, it is expected that some process improvement initiatives will be postponed. Secondly, the level of adopting new testing practices depends on adequate tool support. Particularly, it was pointed out that some changes in product architecture and design could enable efficient defects detection and reporting even before a customer reports them as issues.

Step 5: Specifying impact of variation factors. In this step, the possible implications of the variation factors are specified and documented.

EXAMPLE. For the identified variation factors (Figure 2), the impacts of variation factors were perceived as: *I(V1.) Not having all projects at CMMI level 2, and decrease of customer satisfaction as effect of implementing CMMI maturity level 2 practices,* and *I(V2.) The need for in-house development of a support tool, and development of a product support library.*

Step 6: Analysis of variation factors impact and documenting context/assumption elements. After having done the variation factors analysis (previous two steps), we analyzed the impact of variation factors on the baseline hypotheses. We see this step as the point when it is possible to determine if relevant information regarding environment (context) will be considered as a context or an assumption element of the GQM+Strategies grid. Also, it is possible that the impact of variation factors is so large that it reveals serious problems with the goal's dimensions, such as magnitude and timeframe. In that case, it is necessary to iterate the goal definition step and to change it.

Analysis of the impact of variation factors is crucial for shared understanding of context (environment) among participants, and only after a common understanding is reached it is possible to document the most relevant context and assumption elements.

EXAMPLE. For the example in Figure 2, the following context elements were documented:

[C1] Web products' development process is immature, with the majority of projects at CMMI level 1
[C2] Testing procedures are not standardized and are focused on code (unit) testing
[C3] A CMMI-based software process improvement initiative is ongoing

Assumptions:

[A1] In time for the first release after one year, all projects will be at least at CMMI ML2
[A2] Stabilizing the development process on ML2 will **not have** impact on customer satisfaction
[A3] Implementing VAL and VER practices will contribute to increasing customer satisfaction
[A4] In-house development of needed testing tool support and product support libraries is possible within given timeframe (1.5 years)

For example, without analysis of variation factors' impact, the assumption **[A1]** would be documented as a context element. Participants were so certain of the hypothesis

H(1.): "all projects at CMMI level 2" in Step 3 that they would took it as a context element instead of an assumption.

To establish proper VAL and VER practices, an additional effort has to be invested in establishing those practices and developing some custom-made in-house solutions. The question of whether all that could be done in one and half years was answered by assumption [A4], that such development is possible. The possible scenario might be that, on the lower level (operational level), developers who were supposed to do the actual work of development while at same time defining their goal, set an assumption which would negate (contradict) assumption [A4]. Even if they have sufficient evidence, they could set a context element which would negate assumption [A4]. Such a situation has to be addressed during feedback sessions when the entire grid is presented and discussed.

Step 7: Elicitation of strategy proposals. The result of the previous steps should be a common understanding of the business goal's context among participants and documented relevant context and assumption elements. The final step, Step 7, has an objective to elicit a set of strategy proposals. Those strategies are considered in the *"Make Strategy Decisions"* activity of the grid derivation process (Figure 1).

EXAMPLE. Strategy proposals for the example case (Figure 2) were: *S1. Build reliability in (e.g., implement fewer defects),* and *S2. Test reliability in (e.g., remove more defects)*

In general, the strategy proposals are in the direction of avoiding (minimizing) obstacles (problems) or in the direction of utilizing advantages, identified during context analysis, or a combination of both.

The SAS tool provides useful mechanisms to address conformity, bias, and personality threats. Those mechanisms are *SAS scoring* and *variation factors analysis*. Before the scoring, there are no discussions which could affect individual opinions; the act of scoring should be done simultaneously by all participants (we used printed cards with numbers; scoring was done by raising cards). The act of scoring provides the starting position, which is not affected by the threats. After collecting the initial context focus proposals, variation factors analysis is aimed at providing equal opportunity for all participants to justify their evaluation (score) through an analytical process. The most serious threat is personality; the moderator of the session should take care of different existing personalities. The bias, especially between senior executives and lower levels, can be significant. A good strategy to deal with it is to separate groups and to facilitate multi-sessions during the grid derivation process.

5 Early Validation

In our previous research we did two pilot applications of the GQM$^+$Strategies method with two Finnish companies. The first pilot was done within an ICT company which has been present in the market for more than 15 years. In that period it has grown from a small company to a multinational organization, having operations in nine countries worldwide. The main focus of the company is development of the tools for testing specific systems. The second pilot was carried out within a division of a large international

ICT company with 24 branches on three continents (North America, Europe, and Asia) and over 4.000 employees. The primary products of the company are the embedded systems used in telecommunications. The software development unit where the pilot was carried out is located in Finland, has about 20 software engineers, and the entire site employs over 100 people.

During our first pilot, we recognized the requirements for a tool. Therefore, in the preparation phase for our second pilot, we designed the first version of the tool. The second pilot project consisted of two group sessions. At the end of the second pilot, during the feedback session, we used a questionnaire to assess practitioners' opinions regarding the usefulness of the GQM+Strategies approach and the SAS tool.

5.1 Design of Questionnaire

The questionnaire contained multiple-choice questions regarding the GQM+Strategies method and the SAS tool. We decided to validate the tool requirements (R1 and R2, Section 4) with one question each. Here we will focus only on the SAS relevant questions.

Question A addresses requirement R1, *How well did the resulting grid represent and document your context (external and internal environment)?* The answers were given on a scale from 1—context is poorly represented and documented—to 5—all contextual elements are well represented and documented, or 0—do not know.

Question B addresses requirement R2, *How much did the SAS tool help in focusing and structuring brainstorming discussions?* The answers were given on a scale from 1—did not help at all—to 5—it helped significantly, or 0—do not know.

5.2 Results and Discussion

Results of the questionnaire are given in Table 2. Overall, 12 people participated in the study. Three (25%) were representatives of top-management, four (33%) were from mid-level management, and five (42%) were developers representing the operational level.

The practitioners agreed that the resulting GQM+Strategies grid documented their context adequately (*Mode=3,4*). While in the second question we identified one outlier, after further data examination we concluded that this one participant was not present in the sessions when the tool was presented and used. Therefore, we excluded that data point and recalculated the descriptive statistics (Question B*). According to the results, there was a consensus among practitioners that the SAS tool helped in structuring discussions during the GQM+Strategies grid derivation process ($Q_1 = Median = 3$ and $Q_3 = 4$).

Table 2. Descriptive statistics for the questionnaire results for the questions A and B. Outliers were identified as observation X for which: $X < Q_1 - 1.5 \cdot IQR$ or $X > Q_3 + 1.5 \cdot IQR$ is true.

	Requirement	N	Min.	Mode	Max.	Range	Q_1	Median	Q_3	IQR	Outliers
Question A	R1	12	2	3,4	4	2	3	3	4	1	0
Question B	R2	12	0	3	4	4	2.5	3	4	1.5	1
Question B*	R2	11	2	3	4	2	3	3	4	1	0

We refer to this study as an early validation because it is the very first application of GQM$^+$Strategies that used the SAS tool. In the case where participants have had no prior experience with or knowledge about GQM and the GQM abstraction sheet, we see these results as very encouraging.

To these results we will add our observations made during the pilot projects. Comparing the first pilot, where we had no tool for guiding group discussions, with the second, where we used the SAS tool, the result was documented, relevant contextual information with much less effort. Top-management representatives, who had no prior experience with the GQM abstraction sheet, at first tried to compare SAS with the SWOT (Strength, Weaknesses, Opportunities, Threats) tool. Therefore, a comparison of SAS and SWOT tools should be included when presenting SAS to such an audience.

5.3 Validation Validity

The major threat to internal validity was the small subject-group, which was at the same time one of the project constraints. For this type of project, it is very difficult to obtain a larger group of participants with adequate representatives from all hierarchical levels. One possibility to address small subject-groups is to ask more questions. We decided to limit the length of the questionnaire as the only way to get commitment from the top-level executives. Therefore, we find it important to replicate this study and to increase the tool's experience base. Further replications will also contribute to addressing external validity. The subjective opinion of the participants is in favor of the SAS tool helping them in their case, but still it is not a guarantee that it will be equally successful in other cases.

In similar empirical studies, introducing a couple of new things at the same time would be considered a threat to validity. In our case, introducing the concepts of the GQM$^+$Strategies method and the SAS tool had a positive-loop effect. The tool helped in understanding the method's concepts from a different angle, while the method helped in explaining the structure of SAS. The only disadvantage is that the method evaluation questions had priority over the tool evaluation questions when the limited space of the questionnaire has been distributed.

6 Conclusions

Without a proper understanding of context information it is virtually impossible to define and especially interpret software metrics. Context information needs to be defined in the early phases of measurement planning. GQM$^+$Strategies enhances the GQM approach with explicit linking of metrics and measurement goals to strategy and business goals. The definition of business context is required in GQM$^+$Strategies planning and interpretation activities. The main contribution of this paper is the introduction and early validation of the SAS (Strategies Abstraction Sheet) tool which helps in the GQM$^+$Strategies grid derivation process. The logic of the tool is described and the description is supported with a practical example.

The SAS tool supports and improves the context definition and strategy selection activities of the grid derivation process. The tool is based on a concept and set of procedures for how to use it. The SAS tool is not a traditional software application. The requirements for the tool have been elicited during an industrial pilot application of GQM+Strategies. The design principles include variation factors analysis and context dynamics analysis, complemented by the grid derivation process and practices. The validation of the tool has been carried out during the second pilot application of GQM+Strategies. The two pilot applications demonstrate the usefulness of the tool. The use of the tool helped structure discussions during the GQM+Strategies grid derivation process. The resulting GQM+Strategies grid documented their context adequately with much less effort by the tool users.

We recognize that the final validation of the tool requires further empirical research. Replication of this kind of study is challenging, but this early validation is already very encouraging.

References

1. Woodall, W.: Controversies and contradictions in statistical process control. Journal of Quality Technology 32(4), 341–350 (2000)
2. Kautz, K.: Making sense of measurement for small organizations. IEEE Software 2(16), 14–20 (1999)
3. Umarji, M., Seaman, C.: Why do programmers avoid metrics? In: 2nd ACM-IEEE international symposium on Empirical software engineering and measurement (ESEM 2008), Kaiserslautern, Germany, pp. 129–138 (2008)
4. Basili, V., Caldiera, G., Rombach, D.: Goal question metric paradigm. In: Marciniak, J. (ed.) Encyclopedia of Software Engineering, vol. 1, pp. 528–532. John Wiley & Sons, Inc., New York (1994)
5. Basili, V.: The experience factory and its relationship to other improvement paradigms. In: Sommerville, I., Paul, M. (eds.) ESEC 1993. LNCS, vol. 717, pp. 68–83. Springer, Heidelberg (1993)
6. Basili, V., Heidrich, J., Lindvall, M., Münch, J., Regardie, M., Rombach, D., et al.: Bridging the gap between business strategy and software development. In: Twenty Eighth International Conference on Information Systems, Montreal, Canada, pp. 1–16 (2007)
7. Basili, V., Heidrich, J., Lindvall, M., Münch, J., Seaman, C., Regardie, M., et al.: Determining the impact of business strategies using principles from goal-oriented measurement. In: Internationale Tagung Wirtschaftsinformatik, Wien, Austria, vol. 9, pp. 1–10 (2009)
8. Basili, V., Lindvall, M., Regardie, M., Seaman, C., Heidrich, J., Münch, J., et al.: Linking software development and business strategy through measurement. IEEE Computer 43(4), 57–65 (2010)
9. van Latum, F., Oivo, M., Hoisl, B., Ruhe, G.: No improvement without feedback: Experiences from goal-oriented measurement at schlumberger. In: Montangero, C. (ed.) EWSPT 1996. LNCS, vol. 1149, pp. 167–182. Springer, Heidelberg (1996)
10. Briand, L., Differding, C., Rombach, D.: Practical guidelines for measurement-based process improvement. Technical report, TR-ISERN-96-05, University of Kaiserslautern, Germany (1996)
11. Henricksen, K., Indulska, J., Rakotonirainy, A.: Modeling context information in pervasive computing systems. In: Mattern, F., Naghshineh, M. (eds.) PERVASIVE 2002. LNCS, vol. 2414, pp. 79–117. Springer, Heidelberg (2002)
12. DeRose, K.: Contextualism and knowledge attributions. Philosophy and Phenomenological Research 52(4), 913–929 (1992)

Understanding the Influential Factors to Development Effort in Chinese Software Industry

Mei He[1], He Zhang[2], Ye Yang[1], Qing Wang[1] and Mingshu Li[1]

[1] Laboratory for Internet Software Technologies
Institute of Software, Chinese Academy of Sciences
hemei@itechs.iscas.ac.cn
[2] National ICT Australia
University of New South Wales, Australia
he.zhang@nicta.com.au

Abstract. A good understanding of the influential factors to software development effort and further precise effort estimate are undoubtedly crucial to any cost-effective and controllable software development projects. In most effort estimation researches, a large dataset is always a necessary basis of estimation modeling, model calibration and method validation. Among them, different attributes and characteristics of project data will to a large extent affect the applicable scope of particular research result. This research aims to identify the factors that significantly influence development effort, and to investigate how the influence works in Chinese software industry. In this study, six factors and their relationships to development effort are analyzed, prioritized and discussed based upon the dataset recording 999 projects from 140 software organizations in China. In terms of our analysis and findings, some suggestions for effort estimation and control are extracted to assist software practitioners in coping with various types of software projects.

1 Introduction

Software development is considered to be a human-intensive process, and its main cost is largely determined by the effort taken in it. Thereby, a good understanding of the influential factors to software development effort and further precise effort estimate are undoubtedly crucial to any cost-effective and controllable software development projects. Moreover, as software process improvement has been widely accepted and adopted in software industry, the organizations need more reliable and effective methods in predicting and quantitatively controlling project cost in order to improve their process management.

In the research of software development effort estimation, various techniques, like expert judgment, algorithm-based models, analogy and machine learning, have been proposed and applied. However, it is difficult to get consensus on which model or method is better than the others [1], [2]. Furthermore, no matter what technique is used to estimate software development effort, it is always one of the key concerns of software practitioners: "*What factors do influence software development effort and how they influence?*" [1], [3].

M. Ali Babar, M. Vierimaa, and M. Oivo (Eds.): PROFES 2010, LNCS 6156, pp. 306–320, 2010.
© Springer-Verlag Berlin Heidelberg 2010

In most effort estimation researches, a large dataset is always a necessary basis of estimation modeling, model calibration and method validation. Among them, different attributes and characteristics of project data will to a large extent affect the applicable scope of particular research result. For example, the accuracy of some model might be relatively high, but the difficulty in obtaining model inputs would be the holdback to its wide application.

This paper aims to revisit the influence of the typical factors to software development effort, but in the context of Chinese software industry. The large-scale dataset used in this research stores the project data of 999 projects from 140 software organizations throughout China. It can be used to investigate the status quo of software development in China and to explore what factors affect development effort in these projects. Especially in this study, we attempt to identify the factors that significantly influence software development effort, and to investigate how they influence. Some suggestions for effort/cost estimation and control can be extracted to assist software practitioners in coping with different types of software project.

This paper is structured as follows. Section 2 briefly introduces the dataset used in this study, enumerates the typical influential factors to effort and the associated research questions. Next, modeling and analysis procedure and results are described in Section 3. Section 4 discusses the significance of the results for answering the research questions with comments. Our conclusions are drawn in Section 5.

2 Research Questions and Related Work

This section introduces the dataset used in this study, discusses the possible influential factors with the related work, and proposes the corresponding research questions.

2.1 CSBSG Dataset

The dataset used in this paper is from China Software Benchmarking Standard Group (CSBSG). The CSBSG was established in 2006, and it aims to encourage and establish domestic benchmarking standards for system and software process improvement in Chinese software industry. The database was founded and is being maintained by a number of Chinese organizations within China Software Process Improvement Network (CSPIN). The dataset used in our study is the latest version of CSBSG database, recording 999 software project data from 140 organizations located in 15 regions/provinces across China.

Although each project has many metrics recorded, this study only introduces those typical factors that possibly influence development effort and were relatively well recorded in the dataset. In fact, many of those factors have been discussed by other researchers, but there exist significantly different conclusions for each of them. For example, no agreement has been reached yet on whether new development costs more effort than enhancement. In this study, such influences with contradictious discussion are examined based on the analysis of our dataset.

2.2 Project Size

Obviously, Project Size (PS) is an essential parameter for effort estimation that the majority of mainstream and classical effort estimation models all have used it as a key estimator. Particularly during the development of algorithm-based effort estimation models, a number of researchers have chosen the very similar formula in general like Effort=A+B*(Size)^C, which explicates the close relationship between *size* and *effort*. For example, COCOMO, a well-known and widely adopted series of models for cost estimation, has continued to use the same form (as shown in Equation 1) for years.

$$PM = A \times \left(\sum Size\right)^{\sum B} \times \prod (EM) \quad (1)$$

Hereby, in terms of our dataset, the first research question emerges as:

RQ1: **How does project size influence software development effort?**

2.3 Team Size

Team Size (TS), in previous researches, has been identified as a variable influencing software productivity or effort [4], [5], [3], [6], and most of them agreed that increasing team size will reduce productivity or increase effort. In [3], [6], both the *average team size* and *peak team size* had been observed and recorded. In this paper, TS is referred to the maximum number of members involved in the entire project life-cycle, as it is easier to measure than *average team size* over the project.

RQ2: Will a larger team size cause extra expense in effort?

2.4 Duration

Duration (DUR) is measured with calendar days in this study, i.e. the number of days from the project commencement date to the end date (holidays inclusive). Some previous researches discussed the relation between productivity and duration. In [4], the authors found a seeming good regression model while adding duration, lines of code and team size together as independent variables, but they thought that is roughly the definition of lines-of-code (LOC) productivity and thus added nothing to their knowledge. In terms of our project data, the recorded DUR is much longer than the expected schedule by experience; whereas, some projects even spent less than 3 man-hours a day. One possible explanation is that project members took part in multiple projects concurrently, and it could be another case that the schedule pressure was not much. Then another practical question comes out:

RQ3: Will deadline extension cause additional waste of development effort?

2.5 Development Type

Development Type (DT) indicates whether a software project is new development, redevelopment, or enhancement. Some researchers considered new development costs more effort than enhancement [3], and explained that while new development starts everything from scratch, software enhancement simply adds, changes, or deletes software functionality of legacy systems to adapt to changes in business requirements

[7]. On the other hand, some found no significant difference between them [8]. Some new development projects in ISBSG database also show higher productivity [9]. There is no consensus so far, and here we intend to revisit the influence in our dataset.

RQ4: Does new development really cost more effort than enhancement?

2.6 Business Area

Business Area (BA) denotes the types of business within the organization or industry that the project/product will support. CSBSG dataset covers 13 business areas, i.e. Telecom, Transport, Finance, Retail & Inventory, Media, Energy, Generic, Health Care, Public Administration, Manufacturing, Construction, Education and Society Service. Nevertheless, the last three areas are not included in the later analysis due to the relatively small number of projects recoded in the dataset (less than 10).

BA has been identified as one of the most significant factors influencing productivity for times [4], [10], [8], [9]. However, the most productive area is not consistent among the results by different researchers. For example, banking and assurance, which are classified as "finance" in CSBSG, are the most productive areas reported in [10] but the least in [9]. In practice, many factors, such as personnel application experience, software complexity, requirement volatility etc., would affect the software development for different areas [10], [9]. The state of software development for different business areas in China needs to be further studied.

RQ5: Which business area is relatively more cost-effective?

2.7 Programming Language

The primary Programming Languages (PLs) in software project considered into this research are the ones with more than 10 observations in the dataset: ASP, C, C#, C++, COBOL, Java and VB.

Some previous researches removed the language effect either by merely considering programs written in the same language or by converting all data into one language using conversion factors. Nonetheless, a number of researchers have found that productivity varies with the level of the language [4]. As the language level increases, fewer lines of code are needed to deliver the same functionality. In [3], languages were classified by '*generation*', and the analysis was seldom on the basis of specific language. In terms of CSBSG dataset, most frequently applied languages are the third generation languages (3GLs), and accordingly the analysis of language influence on productivity is based on the specific languages in this study.

RQ6: Does programming language really matter in predicting effort?

3 Analysis Procedure and Result

3.1 Data Validation and Preliminary Analysis

Project Size is recorded as "Size Total" in CSBSG dataset. For all the 999 projects, 998 ones have their size measured by LOC, and only one exception of Project 867[1] is

[1] Each project was assigned an exclusive ID number from 1 to 999.

recorded in Function Points (FPs). Another 3 projects from the same organization (as Project 867) use the same primary language - Java, and have their sizes recorded in both FP and LOC. All ratios of LOCs per FP are 53, which is consistent with the transformation ratio reported in SPR documentation [11]. In that case, transforming the size of Project 867 into LOC metrics can be reasonable.

The maximum Team Size were not given in these four projects, 3 values are filled up by comparing the phased team size records and selecting the maximum value, while the remainder has no phased team size recorded and is therefore excluded.

In effort modeling, Actual Total Work Effort in man-hours is used as the dependent variable, and the factors are intended to add as independent variables in the model. The modeling procedure and final result may reveal the possible relationships between factors and effort based upon CSBSG dataset.

3.2 Model Development

First, Table 1 lists the modeling variables, scales and descriptions for reference.

Table 1. Summary of the variables considered in the modeling procedure

Variable	Scale	Descriptions
ln_effort	Ratio	Log-transformed Summary Work Effort
ln_size	Ratio	Log-transformed Total lines of code
ln_teamsize	Ratio	Log-transformed Maximum size of the development team
ln_dur	Ratio	Log-transformed Total working days from Start to End Date
DevType	Nominal	Development Type
BusiArea	Nominal	Business area within the organization/industry that the project/application will be supporting
Language	Nominal	Primary programming language

Prior to model development, Effort, Project Size, Team Size and Duration are all taken natural log transformation to redress the skewness for these variables. Fig. 1 is the histograms of log transformed Effort, Project Size, Team Size and Duration, which show normal distribution well.

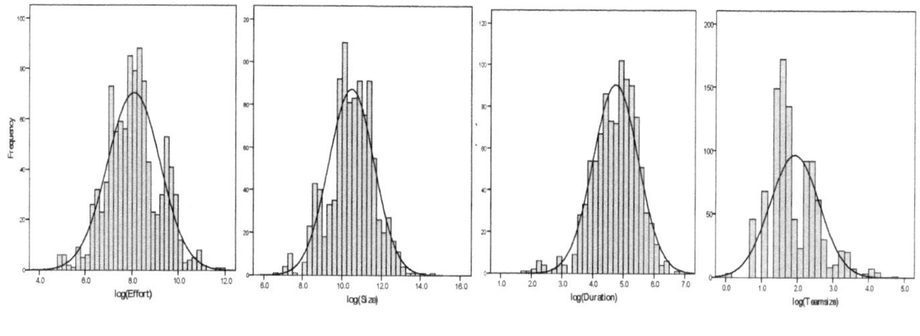

Fig. 1. Distribution of log-transformed numerical variables

After that, the potential relationships between Effort and the factors (Project Size, Team Size and Duration) after log transformation are explored. The three graphs below (see Fig. 2) indicate that linear model can be used to approximate their relationships with effort. A multiple linear regression can be applied to develop our model. The linear model is supposed to be in form of:

$$Y = \beta_0 + \beta_1 X_1 + \beta_2 X_2 + ... + \beta_k X_k + \mu \tag{2}$$

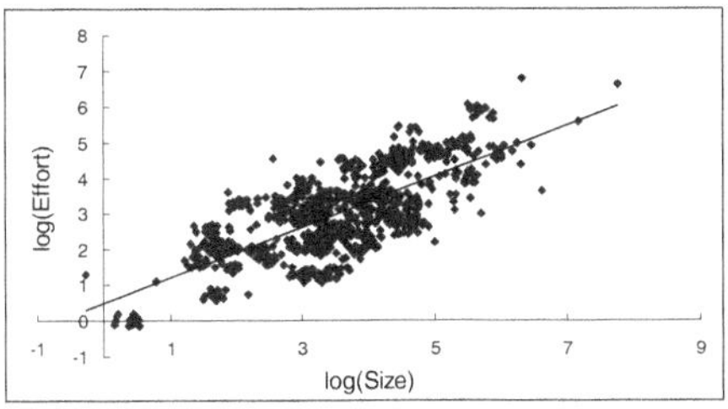

(a). log(Effort) against log(Size)

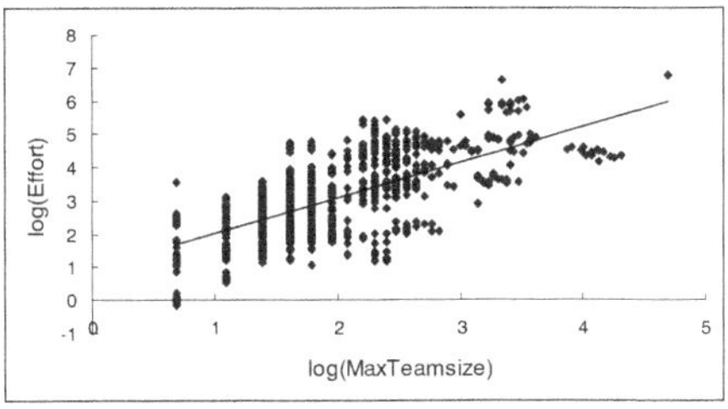

(b). log(Effort) against log(TeamSize)

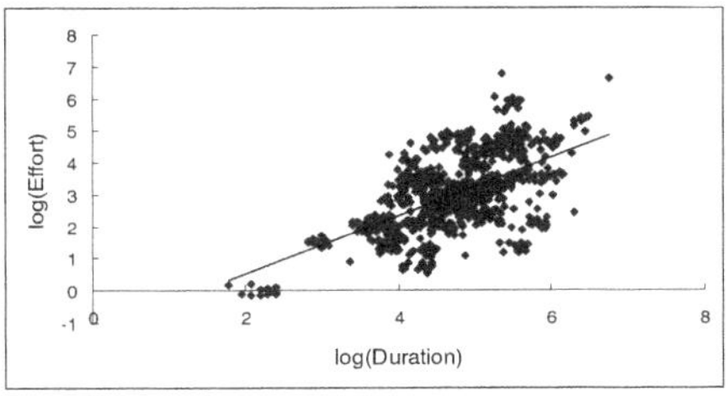

(c). log(Effort) against log(Duration)

Fig. 2. Scatter plots of effort against factors

Furthermore, the correlation analysis is employed to check whether the problem of multi-colliearity (strong correlations between independent variables) exists in the data. As recommended by Maxwell [12], Spearman's correlation analysis is done to check the numerical variables' independence; ANOVA (analysis of variance) is run to check the independence between the categorical variables and chi-square test for the relationship between the categorical and numerical variables. The result confirms that multi-colliearity within this data is not a problem.

In the modeling procedure, three numerical variables, Project Size, Team Size and Duration, passed the check and can be added into one model; but there exist some correlations between any two of the categorical variables, i.e. DevType, BusiArea and Language.

In addition, to explore the problem of missing values, the metrics with missing data are Duration (22), Development Type (13), and Team Size (1). According to the rule of thumb, a minimum sample size of 50+8k for multiple regression analysis is suggested [13]. The valid sample size here is acceptable.

Once the above issues are solved, the regression model can be developed by following the two steps recommended in [12]. At the same time, we also use the statistical tool (Stata [19]) to assist our analysis.

- **Step 1:** Stepwise regression analysis with numerical variables

Performing stepwise regression procedure helps to determine the relative importance of each numerical independent variable's relationship to the dependent variable. It only takes the variables available for nearly every project into consideration. In our dataset, missing value for the numerical variables, i.e. ln(size) (abbreviated as *lsize*), ln(duration) (as *ldur*), ln(TeamSize) (as *lteam*) in statistical analysis is very little as discussed above, and no problem to apply this procedure.

.sw regress In_effort In_size In_dur In_teamsize, pr(.05)
Begin with full model
P<0.0500 for all trems in model

Srouce	SS	df	MS
Model	900.266105	3	300.088702
Residual	371.92449	988	.376444787
Total	1272.19355	991	1.28374728

Number of obs = 992	F(3, 988) = 797.17	Prob > F = 0.0000
R-squared = 0.7076	Adj R-suqared = 0.7068	Root MSE = .61355

In effort	Coef.	Std. Err.	t	p > | t |	[95% conf.	Interval]
In_size	.2986532	.0238871	12.50	0.000	.2517778	.3455286
In_dur	.535817	.0323085	16.58	0.000	.4724159	.5992181
In_teamsize	.6862529	.0338465	20.28	0.000	.6198336	.7526723
cons	1.08979	.1897075	5.74	0.000	.7175139	1.462066

Fig. 3. Results for forward stepwise regression

The result of running a forward stepwise regression procedure is shown in Fig. 3 (a screen shot from Stata's running result). Given the criteria that if Prob>F is a number less than or equal to 0.05, the model can be accepted. In this case, the value of Prod>F is small enough, which means this model is significant. Thereafter, the result of running a backward stepwise regression procedure is also validated as a significant linear model.

- **Step 2:** Building the multi-variable model with "stepwise ANOVA" [12]

From this step, the best *one-variable* model, best *two-variable* model, best *three-variable* model and so on, are obtained one by one.

At first, to determine which variable (*lsize*, *ldur*, *lteam*, or *devtype*) explains the most variation in *leffort*, regression procedures are run for numerical variables, and ANOVA procedures for the categorical variables. As shown in Table 2, *lsize* explains the most variation in *leffort*. The result confirms the findings from many previous studies which make project size as the most important key variable for cost or effort estimation [14], [2], [1].

Then, *lsize* is added to the model in order to find the best two-variable model. As shown in Table 2, *Devtype* is then added to form the best two-variable model. Such procedure is repeated until there is no possible further improvement in the obtained model. All the outputs are recorded in Table 2.

Table 2. Statistical Output Summary Sheet

Variables	Num Obs	Effect	Adj R^2
1-variable models			
*ln_size	999	+	0.5180
ln_duration	993	+	0.3847
ln_teamsize	998	+	0.4454
DevType			0.0419
Language			0.0867
BusiArea			0.2415
2-variable models with lsize			
ln_duration	993	+	0.5860
ln_teamsize	998	+	0.6256
*DevType			0.6267
Language			0.5779
BusiArea			0.6041
3-variable models with lsize, DevType			
*ln_duration			0.6820
ln_teamsize			0.6772
Language			0.6725
BusiArea			0.6720
4-variable models with lsize, DevType, ldur			
*ln_teamsize			0.7465
Language			0.7330
BusiArea			0.7429
5-variable models with lsize, DevType, ldur, lteam			
Language			0.7778
*BusiArea			0.7854
6-variable models with lsize, DevType, ldur, lteam, BusiArea			
Language			0.8088

Finally, the best model is a six-variable model: *leffort* as a function of all the variables listed in Table 3. To be noticed that the default Development Type is enhancement, default Programming Language is 'Other', and the default development Business Area is manufacturing.

According to coefficients in Table 3, the model equation is extracted as:

$$\begin{aligned}&\ln(effort) = 0.38\times\ln(size) + 0.5\times\ln(teamsize)\\&+0.55\times\ln(duration) + \alpha_i \times I(DevType_i)\\&+\beta_j \times I(BusiArea_j) + \chi_k \times I(Language_k) + 0.31\end{aligned} \tag{3}$$

where the function $\boldsymbol{I}$ is the indicator function with binary values of 1 or 0 ('1' means the project belongs to such type or uses such language, otherwise '0'); and the coefficients α_i, β_j and χ_k are corresponding to the values in Table 3. The default coefficients for the default types (that is enhancement, 'Other' language, and manufacturing business area) are all zero.

The explanatory power of the fitted model is high at R^2 = 80.9%, which indicates that 80.9% of the variance in the dependent variable can be explained by this model.

As shown in Fig. 4, the predicted values and observed values conform well to each other.

However, we have to emphasize again, the motive of this paper is not to obtain another prediction model, but to revisit and validate the influencing relationship between development effort and these factors in the context of Chinese software industry. In that case, further investigation on the prediction accuracy and comparison with other effort estimation models are not taken into account in this paper.

Table 3. List of fitted coefficient in the final 6-variable model

Regression terms	Coef.	Std. Err.	*p*-value
ln_size	0.38	0.03	0.000
ln_teamsize	0.50	0.04	0.000
ln_dur	0.55	0.03	0.000
Re-Dev	-0.16	0.10	0.092
New Dev	-0.46	0.05	0.000
Telecom	0.32	0.09	0.000
Transport	-0.13	0.16	0.428
Finance	0.48	0.09	0.000
Retail	0.81	0.09	0.000
Media	0.87	0.18	0.000
Energy	0.120	0.09	0.183
Other	0.28	0.10	0.006
Generic	0.17	0.09	0.059
Health care	0.38	0.13	0.004
Public Admin.	0.123	0.08	0.113
Asp	-0.29	0.17	0.086
C	0.23	0.12	0.058
C#	-0.06	0.11	0.554
C++	0.34	0.11	0.002
Cobol	-0.24	0.15	0.115
Java	0.30	0.11	0.004
VB	0.65	0.14	0.000
_cons	0.31	0.26	0.228

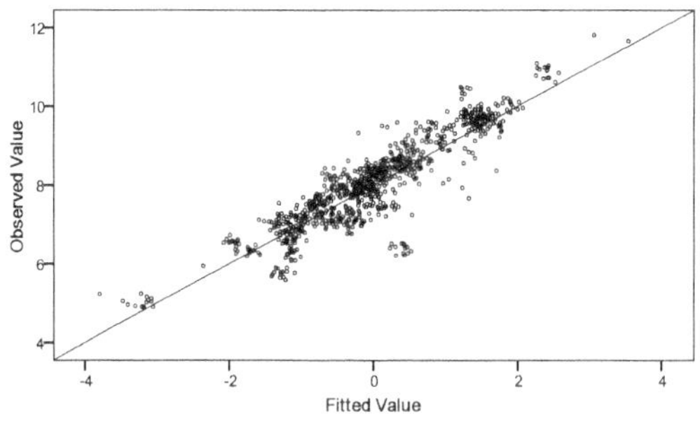

Fig. 4. Scatter plot of observed values versus fitted values

3.3 Model Validation

The model's underlying assumptions need to be checked before the final model obtained through the above steps.

- Assumption 1: In a well-fitted model, there should be no pattern to the errors (residuals) plotted against the fitted values.
- Assumption 2: The errors in the model should be randomly and normally distributed with mean zero.

In our model, "Fitted Value" here refers to the *leffort* predicted, and Fig. 5, where the residual versus fitted value graph is shown, indicates no obvious pattern. In addition, Fig. 6 shows the distribution of residuals which is normality with mean zero. Therefore, the assumption of normality of the residuals can be checked and confirmed.

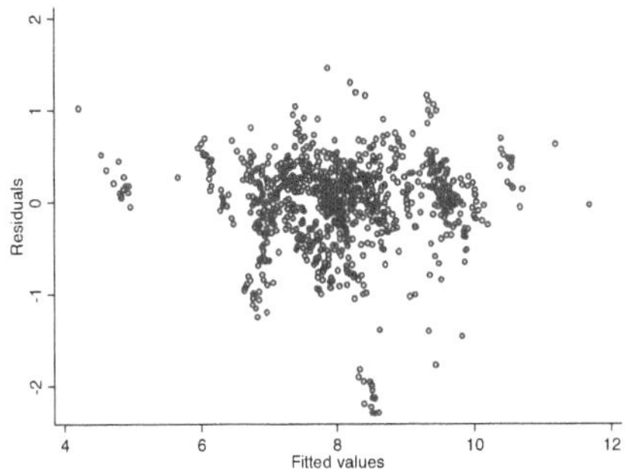

Fig. 5. Diagnostic plot of the residuals versus the fitted values

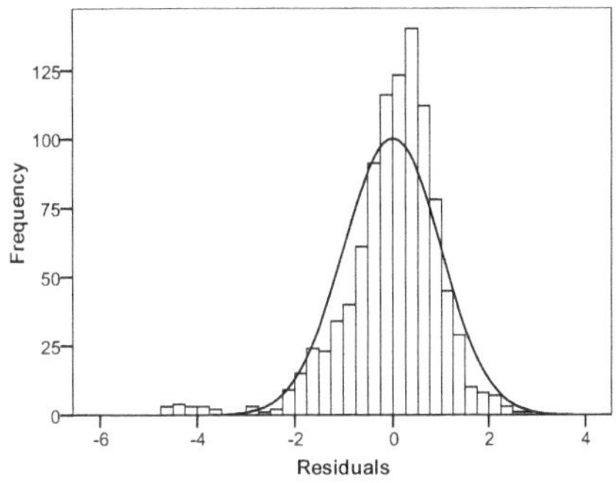

Fig. 6. Histogram of the residuals to check its normal assumption

4 Discussions

As shown in Table 3, on the basis of p-value < 5%, the final sets of factors that are significant to software development effort can be identified: Project Size, Duration, (maximum) Team Size, Development Type, (primary) Programming Language and Business Area.

Project Size (RQ1): The regression coefficient of effort on Project Size after log transformation is 0.38. It illustrates that Project Size is positively related to effort. While productivity is defined as size over effort, it also shows that productivity will increase with increasing Project Size. The result confirms the finding in [15], which compared the median productivity of different project size groups. Interestingly, the phenomenon of Economies of Scale for our dataset is consistent to some others' research [3], [6], but opposite to [14]. For the phenomenon of Economies of Scale, Agrawal et al. [6] explained that is due to the high maturity (CMM 5 level) for organizations in their study. However, this might be not the case in terms of our data due to the lack of supporting information. Another possible explanation is that small-sized projects came from low productivity organizations and the large ones from high productivity ones, but these all need to be further investigated with more evidence in the future data collection and analysis. In addition, while adding size alone, the explanatory power of the fitted model is high at R2 = 51.8%, which indicates that project size is indeed an intrinsic driver of software development effort. This result is also in agreement with many classic effort estimation researches which identify software Project Size as a fundamental factor in dealing with software development effort or cost [14], [2], [16].

Team Size (RQ2): The regression coefficient of effort on Team Size after log transformation is 0.50, which indicates more effort need to be spent for larger team size while other attributes' values do not change. This result is consistent with the finding in [15]. It is quite frequent that some managers are used to adding new personnel for a challenging project. However, adding personnel is not always a wise decision since organizations have to pay more attention and effort to maintain their process control, personnel coordination and resource harmony for an increased team size.

Duration (RQ3): The regression coefficient of effort on project Duration after log transformation is 0.55, the positive value implies that increasing project duration is very likely to lead to a decrease in productivity. In other words, to implement the same size of software, increasing project calendar time will increase total effort. Sometimes, due to the pressure from concurrently developed multiple projects, development teams have to decrease their effort on every single project and postpone their schedule. The result here reminds managers to balance the additional effort caused by schedule slack.

Development Type (RQ4): By modeling analysis, Development Type is confirmed to be another significant factor to influence effort. Table 3 shows that the regression coefficients of re-development and new development are -0.16 and -0.46 respectively, and these values are relative to the coefficient 0 of enhancement as the default development type. This means that given the other attributes with the unchanged values, the enhancement projects may consume the most effort, while re-development may need less effort than enhancement, and new development may consume even less than re-development. In other words, new development projects in the CSBSG dataset show the highest productivity than the other two types, which also confirms the finding in [15]. In contrast with the findings in some other research [3], [7], the possible reasons for the low productivity in enhancement are explored. If the manager often changes the development team or key personnel, it might add the effort in assimilation process. At the same time, in new development, rush to get high productivity with the lack of disciplined documentation may also cause many problems for future maintenance or enhancement work. All of these give project managers a noticeable reminder.

Business Area (RQ5): The diversity of Business Area within the organization or industry that the project/product will support is also confirmed to significantly influence software development effort. With reference to the default manufacturing area (Coef. 0), all the business areas can be ranged in descending order of the number of effort needed: Media (Coef. 0.87), Retail & Inventory (Coef. 0.81), Finance (Coef. 0.48), Health Care (Coef. 0.38), Telecom (Coef. 0.32), Generic (Coef. 0.17), Public

Admin (Coef. 0.123), Energy (Coef. 0.120), Manufacturing (Coef. 0) and Transport (Coef. -0.13). By fixing the other attributes' values, projects in such business areas like Media, Finance and Retail & Inventory may cost more effort, while other areas like Public Admin, Energy and Manufacturing may cost less, in other words, they are more productive. Compared to productivity ascending order shown in [15], the consistency is that software development in Energy, Manufacturing and Public Admin was more productive, and the Finance and Retail & Inventory areas were less productive. There is an inconsistency for Telecom area, based on the modeling analysis, Telecom was not as inefficient as described in [15].

With interests in this inconsistency, 171 projects from Telecom area are further examined. From the aspect of Development Type, only 28% projects are new development; from the Project Size, 87% of them are smaller than 64KLOC, and 57% are even smaller than 16KLOC. In addition, as shown in Fig. 7, C++ and Java are two languages dominated the Telecom projects, while they show relative low productivity as discussed later, that could be a possible reason for the low productivity in this Telecom subset from CSBSG.

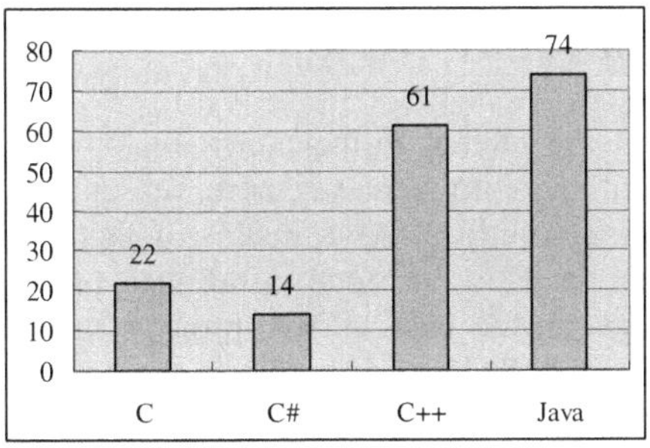

Fig. 7. Language application state for Telecom projects

Because of the diversity of Business Area, software development is affected by multiple aspects. As to Finance area, there exists some other research reporting its low productivity [17]. Since financial software requires real-time, excessive data exchange, vast data processing, high level security and other complex technologies, the productivity is easier to decrease than other business sectors. Meanwhile, due to considerations on confidential information, some banks or investment companies insist implementing internal software development regardless the low productivity.

On the other hand, for the cost-effective areas, such as Public Admin, Energy and Manufacturing, one possible explanation might be that most of the projects in these areas have comparatively less complexity and relatively stable requirements. Also, formal public bidding institutionalization in Chinese government contributes to guarantee for the quality and efficiency of the entrusted software development companies in the recent years [18]. Generally speaking, the market competition, requirement of functionality, evolution and complexity of techniques, integration extent of hardware, and other issues influence the software development in each business area.

Programming Language (RQ6): Programming Language is the last but not least influencing factor to development effort. By comparing the coefficients of each type of language, projects using ASP costed the least effort, and then followed by Cobol, C#, C, Java, C++, and Visual Basic. In contrast to the comparison result in [15], there exist inconsistencies for Cobol and VB. Among 24 projects using Cobol, 23 of them are enhancement and from Finance or Retail & Inventory areas with relatively complex requirements. This might result in Cobol's low productivity level when compared in the whole dataset. On the contrary, for the 48 projects using VB, 87.5% are for Manufacturing area whose system functions were relatively stable, and they were all new development. Hence, the relatively high productivity could be explained by the factors other than language alone. In previous studies, specific language was seldom used to discuss the influence of language on software development effort; instead, language generations, called 2GL, 3GL, 4GL etc., have been considered by some researchers [9], [3]. However, almost all the languages presented in CSBSG are 3GL, and it is difficult to compare our result with the others that classified languages by their generations.

5 Conclusions and Future Work

A better understanding the factors influencing development effort/cost can enable software project practitioners to achieve more reasonable and realistic resource estimation and allocation solutions. As a matter of fact, many researchers tried to contribute in this direction. However, due to the lack of support of relatively large datasets, in-depth studies on the basis of real projects in software industry, particularly in China, were limited. This study analyzes the data of 999 projects from 140 software organizations in China to revisit the factors that significantly influence software development effort, and to figure out how they influence in this context.

As a result, the set of factors that are significant to Chinese software development effort are prioritized: Project Size, Duration, (maximum) Team Size, Development Type, (primary) Programming Language, and Business Area. In terms of the analysis results, we can confirm some findings from the previous related researches, and also conclude the answers to the research questions (Section 2), some of which seem to be counter-intuitive somehow.

1) The effort increased while software (project) size increased, and this dataset reveals the phenomenon of Economies of Scale.
2) More effort were needed for larger team size while other factors maintained the same.
3) Extending the deadline of projects might cause additional development effort.
4) Given the other attributes with the same values, enhancement projects consumed the most effort, while re-development required less effort than enhancement, and new development took even less than re-development.
5) Without changing the other attributes' values, projects in the business areas like Media, Finance and Retail & Inventory costed more effort than in the other sectors like Public Admin, Energy and Manufacturing, where projects were observed more productive.

6) Projects using ASP costed the least effort, which was followed by Cobol, C#, C, Java, C++, and Visual Basic in ascending order.

However, as the limitation of some missing or ignored information in the current dataset results in a difficulty in further examining the exact reasons, we only present some preliminary reason analysis at the current stage. These analyses can provide the project managers some empirical suggestions in real word project management.

For the future work, we plan to add more factors while modeling cost estimation for some type of projects, for example, focusing on one specific business area. Moreover, to construct a cost prediction model for some type of projects is also an important subject in the future research.

Acknowledgments

This work is supported by the National Natural Science Foundation of China under Grant Nos. 90718042 and 60873072; the National Hi-Tech R&D Plan of China under Grant No. 2007AA010303; the National Basic Research Program (973 program) under Grant No. 2007CB310802.

NICTA is funded by the Australian Government as represented by the Department of Broadband, Communications and the Digital Economy and the Australian Research Council through the ICT Centre of Excellence program. This work was also supported, in part, by Science Foundation Ireland grant 03/CE2/I303 1 to Lero - the Irish Software Engineering Research Centre (www.lero.ie).

References

1. Boehm, B.W., Abts, C., Chulani, S.: Software Development Cost Estimation Approaches - A Survey. Annals of Software Engineering 10(1-4), 177–205 (2000)
2. Li, M., He, M., Yang, D., Shu, F., Wang, Q.: Software Cost Estimation Method and Application. Journal of Software 18(10), 775–795 (2007)
3. Jiang, Z., Naudé, P.: An examination of the factors influencing software development effort. International Journal of Computer, Information, and Systems Sciences, and Engineering 1(3), 182–191 (2007)
4. Maxwell, K.D., Wassenhove, L.V., Dutta, S.: Software Development Productivity of European Space, Military, and Industrial Applications. IEEE Transactions on Software Engineering 22(10), 706–718 (1996)
5. Jiang, Z., Naudé, P., Comstock, C.: An investigation on the variation of software development productivity. International Journal of Computer, Information, and Systems Sciences, and Engineering 1(2), 72–81 (2007)
6. Agrawal, M., Chari, K.: Software development effort, Quality and Cycle Time: A Study of CMM Level 5 Projects. IEEE Transactions on Software Engineering 33(3), 145–156 (2007)
7. Kemerer, C.F., Slaughter, S.: Determinants of software maintenance profiles: an empirical investigation. Journal of Software Maintenance 9, 235–251 (1997)
8. Premraj, R., Shepperd, M., Kitchenham, B.A., Forselius, P.: An Empirical Analysis of Software Productivity over Time. In: IEEE METRICS 2005, p. 37 (2005)
9. ISBSG Benchmark Release 8, http://www.isbsg.org

10. Premraj, R., Twala, B., Mair, C., Forselius, P.: Productivity of Software Projects by Business Sector: An Empirical Analysis of Trends. In: 10th IEEE International Software Metrics Symposium (Late Break-in Papers) (September 2004)
11. SPR programming languages table (2003), `http://www.spr.com/`
12. Maxwell, K.D.: Applied statistics for software managers. Prentice Hall, New Jersey (2002)
13. Green, S.A.: How many subjects does it take to do a multiple regression analysis? Multivariate Behavioral Research 26, 499–510 (1991)
14. Boehm, B.W.: Software Engineering Economics. Prentice-Hall, Englewood Cliffs (1981)
15. He, M., Li, M., Wang, Q., Yang, Y., Ye, K.: An Investigation of Software Development Productivity in China. In: Wang, Q., Pfahl, D., Raffo, D.M. (eds.) ICSP 2008. LNCS, vol. 5007, pp. 381–394. Springer, Heidelberg (2008)
16. Pfleeger, S.L.: Software Cost Estimation and Sizing Methods: Issues, and Guidelines. Rand Corp. (2005)
17. Maxwell, K.D., Forselius, P.: Benchmarking Software Development Productivity. IEEE Software, 80–88 (January/February 2000)
18. He, M., Yang, Y., Wang, Q., Li, M.: Cost Estimation and Analysis for Government Contract Pricing in China. In: Wang, Q., Pfahl, D., Raffo, D.M. (eds.) ICSP 2007. LNCS, vol. 4470, pp. 134–146. Springer, Heidelberg (2007)
19. `http://www.stata.com`

Lean Management of Software Processes and Factories Using Business Process Modeling Techniques

Javier Berrocal, José García-Alonso, and Juan Manuel Murillo

Escuela Politécnica, University of Extremadura,
Av. Universidad S/N, 10071, Cáceres, Spain
{jberolm,jgaralo,juanmamu}@unex.es

Abstract. The software industry is moving towards a software factory business model, usually involving several centres collaborating on company contracts. The expected benefits of using specialized teams at lower cost locations are increased productivity and reduced costs. The tasks of project and process management have as a consequence become more complex. Managing such large structures requires more collaboration in development processes to enable rapid reaction to project needs, and support for the variety of technologies, methods, and levels of quality required by the different projects. This situation demands new practices and management support tools. This paper presents Zentipede, a tool for software process management. Its focus is on lightening, or even automating, management tasks by using Business Process Management (BPM) techniques. The tool does not force any particular practice on a company, but encourages it to model the practices which will finally be automated. Also, it supports process-to-product traceability.

Keywords: Software Process and Project Management, Distributed Software Development, Software Process Quality, Process and Project KPI.

1 Introduction

In the last few years, software development companies have changed their business strategies, objectives, and processes to adapt to new customer demands and market trends.

One of the main changes has been the adoption of agile development processes. The essence of these processes is increased communication and collaboration among developers, fostering a self-organizing culture and encouraging development tailored to customer needs [1], [9].

Another change has been the evolution of these companies towards the software factory business model. They now site their development centres (factories) at lower cost locations near their zone of action (nearshore) or even far away (offshore) [10], [11]. These factories usually specialize in specific development activities or technologies, so that the implementation of a project is distributed among different factories according to their specialities and workload. Thus, although the software factory business model increases productivity and reduces development costs [12], it has a

M. Ali Babar, M. Vierimaa, and M. Oivo (Eds.): PROFES 2010, LNCS 6156, pp. 321–335, 2010.
© Springer-Verlag Berlin Heidelberg 2010

negative impact on communication and task completion [19], [20]. So, its full benefits can only be obtained by deploying highly industrialized development processes and tools that stimulate collaboration, and by closely monitoring the workload on resources to ensure their rapid reallocation [17].

Finally, since quality certification has become one of the most important assets contributing to software companies' competitiveness [30], they are adopting models to manage the quality of their software processes [2] and even the entire life-cycle of the services they provide [3], [4]. Customers of IT products and services no longer make their project investment decisions solely on the basis of development costs and time. Today, the final quality of the product or of the process followed to develop it is equally or even more important. This trend is another key factor contributing to the increasing effort companies are putting into the optimization of management tasks.

Hence it is clear that companies' management practices need both to be streamlined and to increase in scope [8]. The use of software management tools can contribute to resolving this dilemma. Examples are the so-called software cockpits, also known as Software Project Control Centres (SPCC) [5] or Project Management Offices (PMO) [6]. They are specially designed to provide support for project managers' most important activities.

However, these tools usually do not cover all the areas and roles that are involved in a company's process management, resulting in managers using separate tools for different areas [14], [15]. This leads to duplication of effort and a loss of productivity because the same or similar data must be provided to each tool while guaranteeing the coherence of the overall system [13]. A further drawback is that these tools are not usually designed to be adapted to an organization's changing needs [7], and thus end up constituting a barrier to the evolution of its business strategies and the improvement of its processes.

Companies therefore require integrated tools which cover all the tasks and roles of the management of their software processes, projects, and factories [13], [14]. These tools should be capable of dealing with different processes and life-cycles, providing management with support for both software product development and IT services. They should also be able to adapt to any new strategies or processes that the company wants to implant. This paper presents Zentipede[1], a suite of integrated tools developed with the objective of meeting the above needs – lightening or even automating the widest possible range of management activities. It does not force any particular practice on management. Instead, it allows them to model their practices using Business Process Management Notation (BPMN). These practices are then automated by a Business Process Management System (BPMS) which delivers orders to the management tools. These tools support process, product, and process-to-product traceability.

The paper is organized as follows. Section 2 briefly describes some of the tools used to manage and control software development. Section 3 presents Zentipede, detailing its architecture and modules. Section 4 describes the results of using Zentipede. Finally, Section 5 presents some conclusions and outlines future work.

---

[1] Although the correct spelling is Centipede, a "Z" was substituted for the "C" when composing the image of the product to associate it with a sinuous centipede in the form of a Z.

2 Background and Related Work

Since management is one of the keys to the success of a software project, its optimization has long attracted the attention of companies and researchers. Some of these efforts have been devoted to producing configuration management [21] or documentation tools [16], provide support to developers and improving their collaboration and coordination.

Another trend has focused on the development of tools (SPCC [5] or PMO [6]) to provide greater control over software processes. Examples such as Rational Team Concert [23] or Artemis 7 [27] include features that facilitate the implementation of iterative and agile software processes. Other tools generate statistics about a project's status. An example is Specula [7] which includes a method to help project managers define metrics aligned with the project's objectives.

Since dealing with process improvement involves a major investment in quality assurance activities [29], many tools (such as SIMPLe [22] or MKS [28]) have been developed to help reduce this effort. These tools facilitate the quality assurance managers' tasks by implementing key good practices or generating the artefacts defined by their models.

Table 1. Functionalities covered by some tools

	Configuration management	Documentation management	Traceability	Users management	Soft. Process management	Soft. Process monitoring	Adaptation to B. Strategy	Management tasks lightened	Software Quality	Quality management
SVN	Yes	No	No	No	No	No	No	No	No	No
TWiki	No	Yes	NO	No	No	No	No	No	No	No
Rational Team C.	Yes	Yes	Process Product	Yes	Yes	Yes	No	No	No	No
Artemis 7	No	No	No	Yes	Yes	Yes	No	No	Yes	Yes
Specula	No	No	No	Yes	Yes	Yes	Yes	No	Yes	Yes
SIMPLe	No	No	No	Yes	No	No	No	No	Yes	NO
MKS	No	No	Process	Yes	Yes	Yes	No	No	Yes	Yes

Notwithstanding the utility of these tools in reducing the effort spent in each area, they still function independently, as is shown in Table 1. In particular, specific information has to be provided to each of them separately. In many cases, this information is similar or even the same, so that the result is a duplication of effort and loss of productivity [13] that could be avoided by using integrated tools. In addition, some management activities such as task allocation, project monitoring, and resource management are highly repetitive. Tools to automate as many of these management activities as possible would therefore also be greatly welcomed.

Finally, software companies and software processes are continuously evolving to cover new necessities, trends, and demands. Management tools should therefore also be capable of adapting to new strategies or processes [24]. Zentipede was born with this motivation, as well as with the aim of providing centralized monitoring of process and project status. Also, it is an open-source tool.

3 The Zentipede Approach

This section introduces Zentipede. The origin of the suite was the perceived need for integrated management tools, capable of dealing with distributed factories and various process models, and of collecting and producing statistics about project status, factory workloads, resources productivity, the typical project Key Performance Indicators (KPIs), etc. The suite was designed to adapt to any company, as well as to support any need for evolution that the company might have. Figure 1 shows the Zentipede architecture.

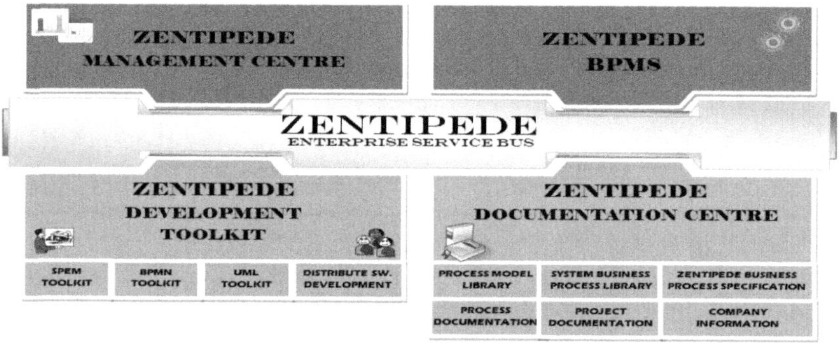

Fig. 1. Zentipede architecture

The Zentipede architecture is divided into three layers and four modules:

- *Process Layer*. The layer in charge of managing the processes and projects deployed by the company. Two modules are responsible for covering all management activities, collecting data, monitoring projects, and lightening or automating management tasks. They also implement features that allow the information stored to be browsed. This information can be browsed starting from different points of view.
- *Modeling and development layer*. The layer in charge of providing support for modeling and development tasks. The modules comprising this layer were specifically designed to provide support to distributed task groups. This layer also stores and synchronizes the company's knowledge databases.
- *Connection Layer*. The layer in charge of connecting and integrating (by means of an Enterprise Service Bus) the modules of the other two layers.

The main motivations and responsibilities of each module are the following:

- Software processes management and monitoring is ever more complex, requiring more tasks and more experienced managers. *Zentipede BPMS* has been developed with the objective of lightening or even automate some of these tasks. It supports the specification of the company's software processes using Software Process Engineering Metamodel (SPEM) and BPMN. These processes can differ depending on the applicable quality level, the management workload allocated to the project, the technology to be used, and the client's requirements. Once modeled, they are executed by a BPMS whose results are delivered as orders to the Zentipede Management Centre.

- Project managers have to know the project status to make the right decisions. This requires keeping track of the tasks being undertaken, their data and results. *Zentipede Management Centre* has been developed to facilitate this activity. For all practical purposes it behaves as a process management tool. However, tasks can be inserted manually by users, or automatically by Zentipede BPMS as a result of the execution of a software process. This module collects information on the tasks being undertaken in order to monitor the status of each project, and to link the data so as to maintain process traceability. These data are used to extract different KPIs. Also, since all the tools are integrated, they are capable of reusing this information, thus avoiding the duplication of effort.
- Software development is more complex in distributed environments due to additional problems introduced by special communications and coordination needs. *Zentipede Development Toolkit* has been developed to minimize some of these problems. In addition to a BPMN Toolkit, to model business processes, and a UML Toolkit, to model software products, some Eclipse plug-ins have been developed for the support of distributed development. As does any configuration management tool, these plug-ins facilitate synchronization among developers. But they also store each change made to the source code, linking that change with the task causing it (which is registered in the Zentipede Management Centre). In this way, one has process-to-product traceability.
- Create the projects and processes documentation is a highly collaborative activity. It requires developers working together to continuously update their status. In distributed environments, this activity is even more complex because of the coordination problems, as those stated in [19]. *Zentipede Documentation Centre* has been developed to facilitate this activity. It allows developers, regardless their location, to work together to register all the company's knowledge used by Zentipede. Examples are the processes Zentipede is following, the business processes of the systems developed, and the different artefacts generated. This data allows the company to manage all of its knowledge, facilitating evolution.

In the following, each of Zentipede's modules will be described in detail, explaining its objectives, its functionalities, and the plug-ins or tools that it contains. In addition, an example will be presented of the integrated use of all these modules.

3.1 Zentipede's Main Workflow

Figure 2 shows the usual workflow followed when these tools are used in an integrated form. It needs to be borne in mind that, despite the simple way in which the steps are presented, Zentipede is a complex tool covering a wide range of tasks. Imagine a company that wants to start developing a project with Zentipede. The steps that would normally be taken using Zentipede are the following:

1. The software processes to follow in developing the project have to be defined. To this end, the processes are modeled (if they have not already been modeled) with *SPEM Toolkit*. The information generated is stored in the *Process Model Library* to be reused in future projects.
2. Once the software processes have been modeled, they are translated internally to BPMN using *BPMN Toolkit*.
3. The new project has to be added to the *Zentipede Management Centre*. As part of this action, additional information is recorded, such as the project leader, the technology, etc.
4. The project leader defines the development teams.
5. An instance of the software process followed is deployed in *Zentipede BPMS*. As a result, the process begins scheduling the first tasks for the development teams to do. Associated with these tasks is an estimate of the effort required. The tasks are generated semi-automatically by *Zentipede BPMS*, but the effort estimate has to be provided by those responsible for each task.
6. Each team leader reserves for each of his or her team's members the number of hours to be dedicated to the project (during the next iteration, sprint, week, or evaluable time period). Team leaders can divide the tasks into subtasks and allocate them to resources through the *Zentipede Management Centre*.
7. The developers perform their assigned tasks using the tools provided in *Zentipede Development Centre*, through which they can also report results to *Zentipede Management Centre*.
8. Once results are obtained, they are interpreted by *Zentipede BPMS* so as to update the software process consistent with the project's status.

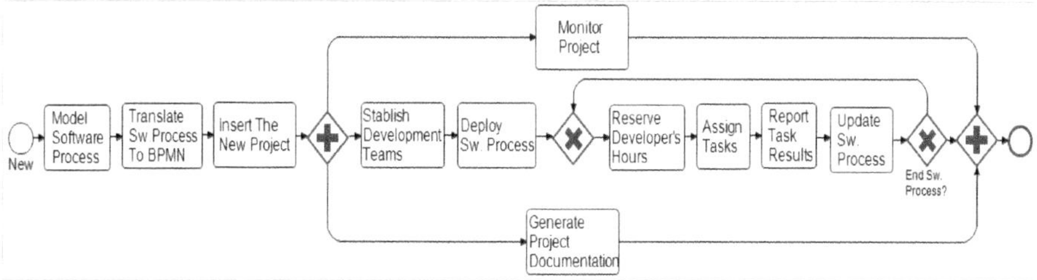

Fig. 2. Basic business processes of Zentipede

Throughout the project, *Zentipede Management Centre* generates metrics to evaluate the status of the process, the project, and the company objectives.

3.2 Zentipede BPMS

Zentipede BPMS is the module that executes software processes, lightening or even automating a wide range of management activities. The specific objectives which guided its development were:

- To supervise and advise on the work to be done to complete the software process being followed.

- To monitor the status of each process and project.
- To automate as many management activities as possible.

In order to fulfil these objectives, an engine, termed a BPMS, was needed to execute business processes. A BPMS is an engine that executes business processes, normally modeled with BPMN or BPEL, to orchestrate the tasks and interactions that are defined in them. In this case, this engine had to execute the software process followed in each project.

To develop this engine, we evaluated existing BPMSs (Apache ODE [25] and Intalio BPMS [26]). We decided to develop the Zentipede BPMS by adding features to Apache ODE to support the characteristics of software process execution and software development. Among these features, new attributes were added to the BPMN specification to include specific information on the software process, such as:

- Artefacts or models that should be generated as a result of each task.
- Modules of Zentipede that should be used to complete each task.
- Automatic or manual activities. Automatic activities are those that can be completed by Zentipede without user intervention. Manual activities are those that at least one user has to work on.

BPMN Core Elements	Attributes	BPMN Core Elements	Attributes
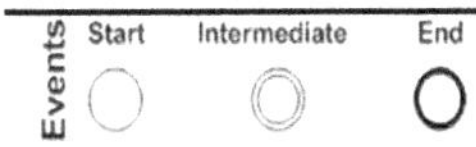	Users Roles Guidance	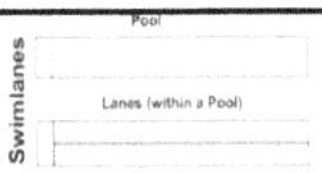	Users Roles Guidance
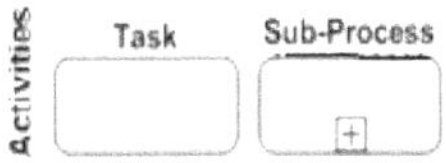	Users Roles Tools Auto/manual		Users Roles Auto/Manual Guidance
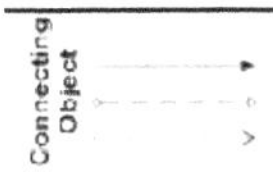	Condition		Artifacts: IN /OUT Mandatory / Optional

Fig. 3. BPMN elements and the attributes used in the BPMS

Figure 3 shows some of the attributes added to the BPMN elements. Most were identified by observing the information already modeled with SPEM, and extracting those attributes that were useful for the execution of the software process.

The following is a brief description of the main steps in the Zentipede BPMS workflow:

- When a decision has to be made as to what software process to follow, the project leader either models a new one or chooses one from among those stored in Zentipede Documentation Centre.
- A new instance of the chosen process is deployed in the BPMS.
- Using that instance, the project is monitored and, as it advances, the tasks defined in the process are scheduled.

- Automatic tasks are completed by the BPMS, reusing previously stored information (for example to update some part of the documentation, it can reuse the information already inserted in other tasks or in the artefacts that have been generated).
- Manual tasks are automatically added to Zentipede Management Centre, and the roles responsible for each task are notified that they have to be assigned to developers.

However, although some projects may initially follow the same software process, as each project advances the processes will eventually evolve differently. Therefore, software processes must be flexible enough to adapt to the status of each project.

To provide this flexibility, software processes can be modeled such that they comprise many sub-processes. Then Zentipede BPMS will execute each sub-process depending on the artefacts generated and the status of the corresponding project. For example, how some sub-processes are executed will depend on the elements and interactions between the product's business processes, the number of use cases defined in the use case diagram, or the packages and interactions between classes of the class diagram. Figure 4 shows a sub-process for a use-case driven development modeled by OpenUP, in which the number of instances created for this sub-process depends on the number of use cases modeled in the use case diagram.

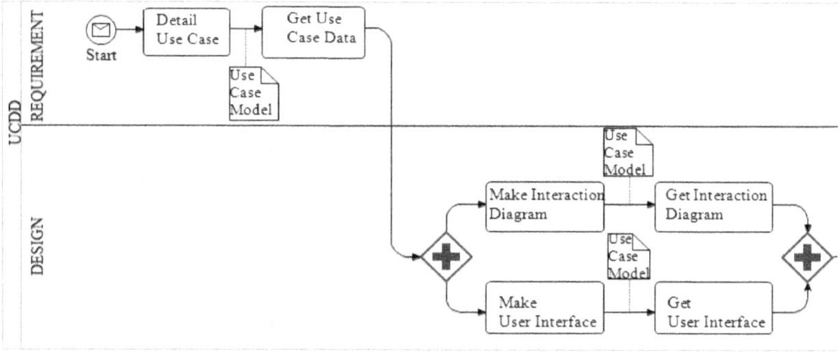

Fig. 4. A sub-process used for use-case driven development

Thus the activities defined in a software process are monitored by executing the process, leading to automating, or at least lightening, many management activities such as task assignment or progress logging. Also, the process can be modeled and executed in a way that endows it with the flexibility needed for its continuing adaptation to the progress of the project.

3.3 Zentipede Management Centre

Zentipede Management Centre is the most important module of Zentipede. It covers the basic functionality for the management of projects and processes. Its main characteristics are:

- Supporting software development distributed among different software factories.
- Providing support for the management activities of all of a software company's roles.
- Collecting data on processes, projects, and factories while they are being managed, and enabling this information to be browsed from different points of view.
- Generating statistics for project, process, and factory monitoring.

To fulfil these objectives, Zentipede Management Centre was designed as a web application with a three-tier architecture using the latest technologies. It can be deployed in the context of any organization, and accessed by any of the personnel, regardless of location.

Fig. 5. Zentipede Management Centre: (a) Snapshot; (b) KPIs

This module includes the definitions of the software company's principal roles, with each role assigned a series of responsibilities and obligations. The main functionalities implemented to cover these obligations are detailed in the following paragraphs (see also Figure 5a), but it should be borne in mind that the roles and their obligations are highly flexible, so that each company can define new roles, and assign obligations that are in accordance with the company's organizational structure.

- *Company managers.* Their activities may include managing factories (adding new factories and updating their information), projects (adding projects and assigning project leaders), or the company overall (defining policies and rules).
- *Factory managers.* They can control information on personnel, tasks performed within the factory, projects in which the factory is involved, etc.
- *Project leaders.* They can decide which software process is to be followed, divide the project into iterations, and decide what requirement are to be addressed in each iteration. In addition, they can constitute and supervise development teams.
- *Team leaders.* They control the developers comprising their team, detailing information and reserving the number of hours that each developer is to dedicate to the

project during the next iteration. Unreserved hours denote the developer's availability to collaborate in other teams or projects. Zentipede supports the possibility that a resource may have hours reserved that, for some reason or other, are eventually not used. Team leaders can also divide requirements into more specific tasks, estimate the effort required to complete them, and assign tasks to developers.

- *Developers.* They can see what tasks they have been assigned, and the details, estimates, and documents to generate for each of those tasks. Additionally, they can report the actual effort devoted to each task, and the documents that were generated.
- *Quality managers.* They can automate the generation of reports on the status of each project or factory.

Zentipede Management Centre continuously gathers large quantities of data – the phases or iterations of each project, the requirements covered in each iteration, the tasks into which the requirements were divided, the developers who worked on each task, the estimated effort for each task and the actual effort finally to it, the time reserved for each resource and the actual time used, etc. The collection of this data is transparent to the users. The information is stored in Zentipede Documentation Centre for subsequent reuse by Zentipede Management Centre. This yields a twofold benefit – first, it reduces the new information required by other tasks, and second, it enables KPIs to be automatically generated to help users monitor and evaluate the areas they are responsible for (Figure 3b).

- *Company managers* can see KPIs on costs, profits, company efficiency, and the average level of occupation of each factory.
- *Factory managers* can evaluate the productivity of the factory overall or of each employee in particular, and view the contribution of each project to the factory's workload.
- *Project leaders* can view statistics about the progress of a project, the averages of resources assigned and actually used, and gaps in the estimates.
- *Team leaders* can view metrics about the tasks undertaken or the work done by each resource.
- *Quality managers* can set up controls to evaluate the quality of processes, the efficiency of developers, or bugs in the products.

Each user can also adapt these indices to their own needs. To that end, the indices are parametrized, allowing such changes as the level of detail, the form in which the information is displayed, and the source of the data. Additionally, new indices can be inserted based on the data collected.

Finally, as the data is collected, it is immediately linked to the previously stored data to provide process traceability, allowing users to browse through the information from different points of view. For example, starting with a given project, they can view its objectives and iterations, and inquire deeper into the requirements addressed in each iteration, the tasks proposed to satisfy those requirements, the resources dedicated to each task, and the effort and dates spent on carrying it out. Starting with a given resource, they can view the projects on which they collaborated, the goals that were attained, the tasks carried out and the time spent on each, etc. Or, starting with a date, they can see the tasks and requirements carried out on or up to that date, the resources involved in them and their workload, or the status of each project.

3.4 Zentipede Development Toolkit

Zentipede Development Toolkit is a suite of tools that facilitates the creation of artefacts with information about the company or project results. The specific objectives which guided its development were:

- To provide tools to mitigate the handicaps of distributed software development.
- To facilitate the creation of artefacts with information about the company or projects.
- To collect information about the work done by each developer.

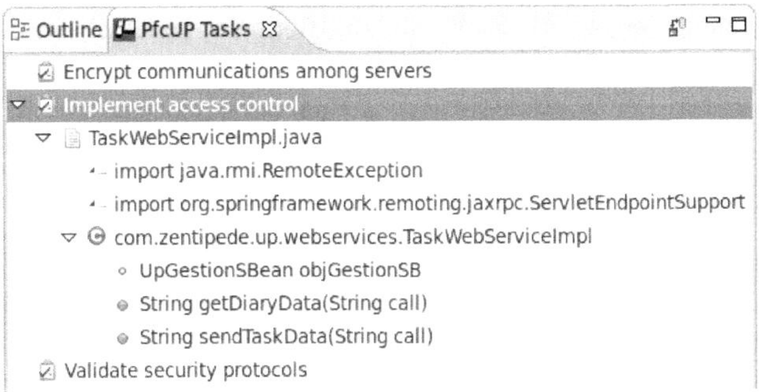

Fig. 6. Zentipede Development Toolkit

To fulfil these objectives, this module contains four subsets of tools:

- *SPEM Toolkit* is an Eclipse plug-in that allows company managers or quality managers to model the software processes that can be followed. Thus, the processes are defined and made accessible so that any user can see what they are to do in each task, why, and how to do it.
- *BPMN Toolkit* is an Eclipse plug-in that allows users to model business processes with BPMN. This tool can be used to model the business processes of the products that are being developed (with these models then forming part of the project's documentation), or to translate the software processes defined with SPEM into BPMN (these processes can then be executed by Zentipede BPMS).
- *UML Toolkit*. This subset includes Eclipse plug-in tools that facilitate the UML modeling of the artefacts required over a project's life-cycle. Developers can then access these plug-ins without having to change IDE.
- *Distributed Software Development Toolkit*. First, this subset provides tools to help developers communicate with each other. These tools are Eclipse plug-ins that allow developers to describe the doubts or problems they encounter in their assigned tasks. These doubts are automatically notified to all the personnel subscribed to the task (project leader, team leaders, and other developers). For all practical purposes, these plug-ins behave as communication tools, but they also store the communications and link them to the tasks that gave rise to them. And second, this subset includes another plug-in which facilitates developers' management activities (Figure 6). This plug-in shows each developer the tasks assigned to them in their working environment, and allows them to specify further information on each task.

It also automatically collects such information as the time spent on each task and each change made to the source code (such as which packages, classes, or lines have been modified). As this information is captured, it is immediately linked to the task that gave rise to it. With the information collected with this subset's plug-ins, the process traceability already supported by Zentipede Management Centre is enhanced with process-to-product traceability. This feature facilitates reverse engineering, allowing users to browse the information by starting with a given project, requirement, task, or resource in order to view the corresponding changes made to the source code or the doubts and problems that were encountered, and *vice versa*. It also reduces the impact of resource mobility and task reassignment by providing information on the changes already implemented in completing each task.

Finally, all the information captured or defined with these tools is stored in the module Zentipede Documentation Centre for reuse by other tools.

3.5 Zentipede Documentation Centre

Zentipede Documentation Centre is the module responsible for storing and maintaining the consistency of all the project and process data and company information. The specific objectives which guided its development were:

- To maintain libraries in which to store all the information collected.
- To manage all the software company's information and knowledge.

To fulfil these objectives, six integrated repositories were set up. They were assigned the following responsibilities:

- *Process Model Library*. This library stores the software processes that can be followed by project leaders. When a new project is started, the project leader selects the process to follow according to the project's needs and objectives, and this is executed in Zentipede BPMS to guide the management activities.
- *System Business Process Library*. This library stores the business processes of the products under development. When a new project is started, the processes can be modeled as part of the product's documentation, and as the first step to adapt the software process to the characteristics of the project.
- *Zentipede Business Process Specification*. This repository stores business processes defining the interactions between the tools of Zentipede.
- *Project Documentation*. This repository stores all the artefacts generated as a result of software process activities (use case diagram, class model, activity diagrams, etc.).
- *Process Documentation*. This repository stores information on the instances of the software processes being followed in each project. The information is stored as phases or iterations of each process, the requirements covered, the developers who worked on each requirement or task, the estimated effort needed by each task and the actual effort devoted to it, etc.
- *Company Information*. This repository stores information about the company's objectives and rules, such as business rules, objectives, or good practices.

These repositories store and maintain all the information on the processes, projects, and factories. Because all the modules are perfectly integrated, this information is used by the other modules to monitor each project or process's status, to generate indices, to lighten or automate certain tasks, and to maintain process and process-to-product traceability.

4 Validation and Evaluation of Zentipede

This suite of tools has already been tested in use in some software companies. The testing period lasted more than seven months, in which time more than ten projects were managed. Most of them were distributed over various locations, including Cáceres, Madrid, and Barcelona.

At the end of the testing period, members of those companies reported on its usefulness in managing their projects and factories. Some of the most interesting benefits that they indicated were:

- The capacity to generate indices to evaluate compliance with the company's objectives and rules.
- Constant evaluation of projects and processes, with rapid reaction to any deviations detected.
- Improvement of work coordination, including better coordination among factories and communication among distributed workers.
- Better use of manpower and increased productivity (some reports described a 25% to 50% increase in the use of manpower) due to the facility of monitoring each developer's workload. In this sense, some of the managers pointed to the value of the feature of reserving the developers' hours, and the statistics comparing the reserved hours and the actual hours used, since they had detected that some team leaders were reserving more hours than necessary to simulate that their project was advancing faster than was really the case.
- A reduction in the impact of incorporating new developers, of allocating tasks that had already started to developers, or of solving bugs, due to the use of process and process-to-product traceability.

Although, these tests were very promising, this tool is not yet in the production use because we are adding new functionalities. Once these functionalities are finished, a more scientific evaluation of the tool will be done and, then, it will be used in production.

5 Conclusions

This paper has presented Zentipede, a tool designed to cover all areas of project, process, and software factory management. For the coverage of each area, four modules were developed comprising many perfectly integrated and coordinated tools. One of the benefits of this integration is that the information inserted in one module is reused by the others. For example, the information captured during the process management can be used to create the documentation or to automatically generate quality indices. This contrast with the tools listed in Table 1, in which the similar or even the same information has to be provided to different tools for different purposes. Therefore, this integration increases the effectiveness of each module and the data consistency. In addition to this benefit, together with the process and product traceability, already provided by other tools, the modules integration allows information to be captured to achieve process-to-product traceability.

As it has been seen throughout the paper, methods and tools facilitating the software project management are required. Zentipede incorporates a module that executes software processes using BPM techniques to lighten or even automate a wide range of the management tasks. This feature has not yet been covered by the tools evaluated in Table 1.

Finally, Zentipede was designed to be adaptable to the characteristics of any environment or company, taking into account their present or planned future strategies and processes.

Acknowledgments. This work has been funded by PDT08A034, TIN2008-02985, GRU09137, PRE09156 and Fundación Valhondo Calaff.

References

1. Agile Manifesto, `http://www.agilemanifesto.org/`
2. CMMI, `http://www.sei.cmu.edu/cmmi/`
3. ITIL, `http://www.itil-officialsite.com/home/home.asp`
4. CMMI for Services, `http://www.sei.cmu.edu/cmmi/tools/svc/`
5. Münch, J., Heidrich, J.: Software Project Control Centers: Concepts and Approaches. J. Syst. and Soft. 70(1), 3–19 (2003)
6. Project Management Institute: A Guide to the Project Management Body of Knowledge (PMBOK Guide). Project Management Institute, Pennsylvania (2000)
7. Heidrich, J., Münch, J.: Goal-Oriented Setup and Usage of Custom-Tailored Software Cockpits. In: Jedlitschka, A., Salo, O. (eds.) PROFES 2008. LNCS, vol. 5089, pp. 4–18. Springer, Heidelberg (2008)
8. Jennings, T.: Planning for value. Technical report, Butler Direct Limited (2005)
9. Larman, C.: Agile & Iterative development: a manager's Guide. Addison Wesley, Boston (2005)
10. Johnson, J.R.: The Software Factory: Managing Software Development and Maintenance. John Wiley & Sons, Portland (1991)
11. Greenfield, J., Short, K., Cook, S., Kent, S.: Software Factories: Assembling Applications with Patterns, Models, Frameworks, and Tools. Wiley, Indianapolis (2004)
12. Sengupta, B., Chandra, S., Sinha, V.: A research agenda for distributed software development. In: 28th International Conference on Software Engineering, pp. 731–740. ACM, New York (2006)
13. Sinha, V., Sengupta, B., Gosal, S.: An adaptive tool integration framework to enable coordination in distributed software development. In: 2nd International Conference on Global Software Engineering, pp. 151–155. IEEE Comp. Society, Washington (2007)
14. Krishnamurthy, V.: Benefits of Tool Integration In Distributed Agile Development. AgileJournal 1 (2006)
15. Maurer, F., Dellen, B., Bendeck, F., Goldmann, S., Holz, H., Kötting, B., Schaaf, M.: Merging Project planning and Web enabled dynamic workflow technologies. IEEE Internet Computing 4, 65–74 (2000)

16. TWiki, http://twiki.org/
17. Ambler, S.W., Nizami, K.: Agile Strategies for Geographically Distributed Quality Management. AgileJournal 2 (2007)
18. Prikladnicki, R., Audy, J.L.N., Damian, D., de Oliveira, T.C.: Distributed Software Development: Practices and challenges in different business strategies of offshoring and onshoring. In: 2nd International Conference on Global Software Engineering, pp. 262–274. IEEE Computer Society, Washington (2007)
19. Nguyen, T., Wolf, T., Damian, D.: Global software development and delay: Does distance still matter? In: 3rd International Conference on Global Software Engineering, pp. 45–58. IEEE Computer Society, Washington (2008)
20. Grinter, R.E., Herbsleb, J.D., Perry, D.E.: The Geography of Coordination: Dealing with Distance in R&D Work. In: ACM SIGGROUP conference on Supporting group work, pp. 306–315. ACM, New York (1999)
21. Subversion, http://subversion.tigris.org/
22. SIMPLe, http://alturasoluciones.com
23. Rational Team Concert, http://www-01.ibm.com/software/awdtools/rtc/
24. Selby, R.W.: Analytics-Driven Dashboards Enable Leading Indicators for Requirements and Designs of Large-Scale Systems. IEEE Software 26, 41–49 (2009)
25. Apache ODE, http://ode.apache.org/
26. Intalio BPMS, http://community.intalio.com/
27. Artemis 7, http://us.aisc.com
28. MKS Integrity Suite, http://www.mks.com/
29. Kelly, G.: Barriers to adoption of the CMMI process model in small settings. In: 1st Workshop for Process Improvement in Small Settings, pp. 36–40. SEI, Pittsburgh (2006)
30. Barnes, F.: Good Business Sense Is the Key to Confronting ISO 9000. Review of Business (2000)

Improving Efficiency of Change Impact Assessment Using Graphical Requirement Specifications: An Experiment

Niklas Mellegård and Miroslaw Staron

Department of Applied IT,
Chalmers Tekniska Högskola, Göteborgs Universitet
SE-412 96 Gothenburg, Sweden
{niklas.mellegard,miroslaw.staron}@ituniv.se

Abstract. *Objective*: Graphical requirements representation is often considered needed to advance model-driven development. Dedicated modelling languages include formalisms for graphically representing requirements, and together with new methods for structuring requirements, graphical modelling promises improvements such as more efficient change management. This paper examines whether the use of a graphical notation of a requirements affects the task of assessing the impact of a proposed change to a requirements specification.
Method: The efficiency of using a graphical requirements representation was examined through an experiment – using 18 student subjects. Time, perceived confidence and accuracy were measured as dependent variables.
Result: The results showed that using a graphical representation decreased the time required and increased the perceived confidence, but the accuracy decreased. However, the statistical analysis of the results showed that only the difference in time was significant. Furthermore, there was a large difference in variance within the dependent variables between the groups.

Keywords: Requirements Engineering, Visualization, Efficiency, Experiment.

1 Introduction

Model Driven Engineering (MDE) [1] is an established software analysis and design paradigm, bringing software engineering even closer to other engineering disciplines [2, 3]. Despite the numerous advantages of the state-of-the-art modelling techniques (e.g. UML [4], DSL[1]s [5], SysML [6]) engineers still struggle to efficiently link requirements to design models for the purpose of documentation, traceability, or later change impact assessment. The traditional 'use case driven' approach rooted in Objectory [7] is well suited for capturing the functional, scenario-like requirements, whereas they are not suitable for other kinds of requirements (e.g. non-functional, pure text based). One of the domains where text-based requirements are commonplace is the automotive domain in which the requirement specifications are often used

[1] Domain-specific Language.

M. Ali Babar, M. Vierimaa, and M. Oivo (Eds.): PROFES 2010, LNCS 6156, pp. 336–350, 2010.
© Springer-Verlag Berlin Heidelberg 2010

when handshaking development between the car manufacturers and their subcontractors [8-11]. The complexity and volume of the requirement specifications are usually problematic for understanding of the specifications. The problems with understanding and incompleteness of the specification [12] may lead to quality problems with the final products or timeliness of development projects (when the quality has to be improved before the release).

In this paper, we evaluate whether using a graphical way of structuring requirements leads to improved quality of the design models during development projects. In particular, we address the following research question:

Does using a graphical representation of requirements result in more correct and more efficient change impact assessments in model-driven design?

In order to address this question we conducted an experiment with students as subjects. The objects of the experiment were inspired by the research project that we conduct together with Volvo Car Corporation (VCC) [13]. In order to control the environment we created a dedicated domain specific modelling language [14] that was integrated with the existing requirement engineering practices and tools – e.g. IBM/Rational RequisitePro. The dedicated modelling language was also chosen as we in the future work intend to investigate whether adding more informal information about requirements (as advocated by [15]) lead to improved requirement specification, thus making the requirements model as the core requirements artefact in model-driven projects. The proprietary model for structuring textural requirements at VCC was replaced in the experiment with the Requirement Abstraction Model (RAM) [16] and our implementation of RAM as a graphical Domain-Specific Language (DSL) called gRAM [14], without the loss of generality of the results[2].

The results show – with statistical significance – that using a graphical representation of the requirements hierarchy decreased the time required to assess the impact of a proposed change – in our experiment it decreased with 37%. The results also indicate, although without statistical significance, that the accuracy of the assessments may deteriorate with the use of a graphical representation.

This paper is structured as follows; Section 2 presents work related to our research. Section 3 briefly outlines the requirements specification formats. Section 4 details the experiments we conducted as well as the results, section 5 contains discussions about the result and section 6 concludes the paper.

2 Background and Related Work

The intended main contribution of the experiment reported in this paper was to evaluate what effect a graphical representation of a model. In particular, the experiment focused on the representation of requirements specification and its effect on the efficiency of assessing the impact of a proposed change. Hence, the work related to this paper concerned the evaluation of different model notations and their effect on the efficiency of using the models. Additionally, as we chose to comply with the Requirements

---

[2] The replacement was made in order to avoid biasing the generality of the study with the proprietary model for requirements structuring. RAM was found to be good enough to approximate the proprietary model.

Abstraction Model (RAM), its effectiveness was also of interest. Moreover, in the experiment we evaluated the requirements' representation by having the subjects perform tasks related to change impact assessment – as our industrial partner has expressed this as a significant challenge – work related to assessing the impact of a proposed change was also of interest.

The work presented in this paper was part of our ongoing research (outlined in [17]) within the research project ASIS, done in cooperation with Volvo Car Corporation [13]. One part of the project aimed at improving the way requirements were specified, and in particular, the extent to which requirement specification can be reused with a minimum of effort. As part of this research, a model for the requirements specification process was developed (gRAM [14]) with the intention of finding areas where Model-Driven Engineering (MDE) approaches may improve efficiency. This paper contributes to that research by examining to what extent a graphical model of the requirements affect the efficiency of assessing the impact of a change request to a specified system.

Much of the empirical studies done on modelling – in both system modelling and requirements engineering fields – have been with the focus on investigating and improving aspects of specific approaches. Maiden et al.'s CREWS experiment [18] and its replications [19] proposed and evaluated whether templates and style guidelines improve the quality of use-case descriptions. Although the replications found some contradictions, both studies provided evidence of that the use of guidelines improved the quality of the use-case descriptions. Phalp et al. [20] extended the CREWS research by comparing their approach with a leaner set of guidelines and found that it performed at least as well as the original approach. Gravino et al. [21] examined, through a controlled experiment, whether dynamic modelling and UML sequence diagrams provided an accurate account of stakeholder requirements, with the focus on evaluating whether a behavioural modelling approach improved the comprehension of software requirements. In their study, they found no evidence of any significant differences in the comprehension of system requirements by using dynamic modelling, even though the subjects perceived the use of dynamic modelling as useful, thus showing a difference between the perceived usefulness of a given method and effective advantage of using it. Our study examined the use of a graphical representation of the RAM with the traditional text based one, isolating and exploring what effect a visual representation had on the comprehension of requirements as well as traceability to design and implementation. Thus, our study examined the effect of introducing a graphical representation in an earlier phase of the development cycle.

In their paper [22] Lange and Chaudron performed a similar study to ours, in the sense that they measured correctness and the effort required to comprehend a software system. Lange and Chaudron compared four novel graphical views of a set of UML diagrams to the representation used by traditional UML modelling tools. The study found statistically significant improvements in both time and correctness (20% and 4.5% respectively) when using the alternative representation. Our study compared a graphical and a textual representation of requirements – with linking to high-level design – in order to evaluate specifically what influences the graphical representation had on the comprehension of the specification in the context of assessing the impact of a proposed change to the requirements or to some underlying software component.

There have been numerous comparisons of the efficiency of different modelling approaches, e.g. De Lucia et.al [23] comparing the comprehension of a data model represented in ER and UML diagrams, in which they found that the use of UML significantly improves comprehension. Otero and Dolado [24] examined the effect of different notation types with respect to comprehension of dynamic modelling, by comparing the use of UML and OML in a design document, and found evidence that the use of OML improved the semantic comprehension and required less time. In contrast, our study was intended not to be dependent on any particular modelling notation, but rather to evaluate the effect of graphical representation itself.

Studies to validate the effectiveness of the RAM approach have been done in e.g. [16, 25, 26] and in our paper we intended to extend these studies by investigating change impact assessment and using graphical representation. In that context, we evaluated whether adding a graphical representation for a RAM-structured requirement specification can lead to further improvements. However, we also considered time as one of the factors, thus we focused on efficiency, not only effectiveness.

In the light of the paper by Wong and Sun [27], where they examined how diagram layout affected the comprehension of the programs they represent, we have chosen to design the gRAM to as closely as possible resemble the original RAM, in order to assure that our results can be generalized to the same contexts as the RAM itself.

Noppen et al. [12] showed that creating requirement specifications was an iterative process and subject to frequent changes. Therefore, it was important that the time required to identify what changes need to be made was short. Our experiment showed that by using a graphical language the time required to assess the impact of a proposed change can be substantially reduced, which means that using the graphical language can lead to quite substantial improvements in iterative SRS development.

Lindvall [28] examined the accuracy of predicting the impact of introducing or changing a requirement prior to design and implementation by examining real data in best-of-practice projects, and found an under-prediction factor of 3.1 showing evidence of the need to improve change impact predictions. The study by Lindvall was done mainly to explore the accuracy of state-of-practice approaches to change impact assessment, and did not take the perspective of requirements representation, nor did it take traceability between requirements and high-level design into consideration, as done in our study.

Arisholm et al. [29] examined the cost effectiveness of model-driven development with UML by studying – in two consecutive controlled experiments – what impact the presence of UML models in design and implementation documentation had on the task of system maintenance, in terms of effort and correctness of performing post-release changes. They concluded that when considering only the time required making code changes, the UML documentation did help save effort but when also considering the time required to change the UML documentation accordingly, no savings were visible. They also concluded, however, that in terms of functional correctness, the use of UML documentation had a positive effect on the most complex tasks. Our evaluation examined a similar research question, but from the perspective of a graphical requirements model, and what influence the graphical representation had on the correctness and effort required to assess the impact of a change.

In the context of our research (i.e. product line oriented, large, complex embedded software systems), reuse was commonly achieved by modification of a requirements specification of a similar existing system. Additionally, it was commonplace in many business areas to manage requirements using structured text documents, thus, the effect of the representation of requirements, and their linking to design artefacts, on change impact assessment were of interest to examine.

3 Requirement Specification Format

In this section, we briefly describe the requirement specification format that was used to create the domain specific graphical notation. The requirement specification format is an established one with published evidence that this specification format is indeed improving industrial requirements engineering practice [25].

3.1 Requirements Abstraction Model

The Requirement Abstraction Model (RAM) [16] has the goal of ensuring consistency and traceability among requirements in order to increase the overall quality of requirement specifications. The RAM defines a number of abstraction levels to which each requirement is classified, and checklists to ensure that the requirements are assigned their proper level. In their original paper Gorschek and Wohlin [16] suggest, but do not limit their model to, four different abstraction levels:

- *Product*: Product level requirements have a goal-like nature, very high-level descriptions of the desired functionality of the product.
- *Feature*: Feature level requirements describe the features that fulfil the product level goals.
- *Function*: Function level requirements define which functions should be provided by the system in order to provide the features.
- *Component*: Component level requirements describe how something should be solved, i.e. bordering to design information.

RAM ensures traceability between requirements through all levels of abstraction by enforcing that, with the exception of the product level, no requirement may exist without a link to a requirement one level of abstraction higher. The rationale for this rule is that no requirement may exist unless there is a clear and unambiguous reason for its existence motivated by higher-level requirements, and conversely, high-level requirements should be traceable to the lower-level requirements that satisfy them.

3.2 gRAM – DSL for Modelling Requirements

gRAM is a Model-Driven Engineering (MDE) language with the purpose of creating an easy to use requirements management environment for directly manipulating a requirements structure, from which other documents can be automatically generated through translational semantics. The gRAM is a formalized graphical Domain Specific Language[3] (DSL) complying with the RAM, where validation rules (i.e. static semantics) built into the gRAM ensures that the model and the resulting requirement specification are syntactically correct and well formed according to the RAM.

[3] "Domain specific" refers to the horizontal domain of requirements engineering.

In addition to the traceability link RAM defines between requirements at adjacent abstraction level – which gRAM represents with an *Owns*/*Satisfies* link – gRAM also adds the *Depends-on* traceability link, which indicates that there is a dependency between two requirements within the same abstraction level.

In [14] we provide a more detailed description of gRAM, and the full set of experiment material – including a textual and a gRAM requirements specification – is available from [30].

4 Experiment Design

The experiment presented in this paper, was designed to compare the use of a requirements specification represented with the gRAM language, with a textual representation written according to RAM. The objective of the experiment was to examine whether a graphical representation of requirements (as advocated by MDE) increases the efficiency and effectiveness of assessing the impact of a change to the requirements from the perspective of system designers. This section presents the design of the experiment, which was conducted as a standard two-group design – the control group (using the textual specification) and the test group (using the gRAM specification).

4.1 Population and Sample

The subjects in this experiment were students – i.e. convenience sampling. A total of 18 subjects participated in the experiment, of which 14 were first and second year master students (i.e. in their 4th and 5th year of university studies) attending Software Engineering and Management programme, and 4 were 3rd year bachelor students (i.e. their 3rd year of education) from the same programme.

Blocking – in order to assign subjects to experiment groups – was done based on the subjects prior knowledge of UML, requirements engineering, industrial experience and experience with projects.

The population of this experiment is software designers working with implementation of software requirement specifications and systems analysts creating/maintaining these specifications. Most of the participating master students had over one year of industrial experience prior to their studies, which makes them representative for junior designers in industry.

4.2 Instrumentation

Objects

The experiment objects shown to the subjects in both groups consisted of:

- Generic description of a toy software system
- Detailed design of the toy system (a class diagram)
- Requirement specification for the toy system complying with the RAM:
    - For the control group: the textual requirements specification
    - For the test group: the graphical representation (gRAM) of the requirements

The toy system used in the experiment was a simulator of a power steering function in a car with customizable algorithm for automated power steering. The simulator was implemented in Java prior to the experiment and the requirements were traced (linked) to the software components of the simulator. The toy system was inspired by the real-world systems our partners work with, which could not be used due to confidentiality and the complexity of the systems.

The requirements specification consisted of 56 requirements, out of which 29 were at the lowest level of abstraction. The high-level logical design view – represented by a class diagram of the implemented power steering simulator – consisted of 10 classes and 15 associations.

The full set of experiment material is available from [30].

Data Collection

Five tasks were prepared and used in the experiment, and were concerned with:

- listing requirements related to some functionality or having some, by the task, defined property
- listing components in the logical view that implement a given requirement
- listing components which may be affected by a given change request

The instruments of data collection were (i) a form with the tasks and (ii) a questionnaire surveying the background of the subjects. We used a separate answer sheet for each task to collect the data, on which the subjects were asked to note the time when they began the task, write their answer and finally note the time the task was finished. We also asked the subject to note how confident they were in their answer; the 5-point Likert scale was used for that purpose.

Additionally, we conducted informal, semi-structured interviews with subjects from both groups in order to acquire qualitative data about how they perceived the experiment. The interview questions were concerned with how the subject used the material and what they found difficult.

Independent and Dependent Variables

There was only one independent variable in the experiment: the type of the requirement specification with the values – graphical (`gRAM`) and textual (`TEXT`).

The following direct dependent variables were used for each task and subject:

- *Tx_SCORE* The percentage of correctly identified requirements/ components (%) for task x
- *Tx_FP* The absolute number of falsely identified requirements / components for task x
- *Tx_TIME* The time in seconds spent on task x
- *Tx_CONF* The perceived confidence of the answer for task x (LIKERT scale 1-5)

The following variables were derived from the collected variables for each subject:

- *AVG_SCORE* The subject's average score over all tasks (percentage)
- *TOT_FP* The subject's total number of false positives for all tasks
- *TOT_TIME* The total amount of time the subject spent on the tasks

- *TOT_CONF* The sum of the subject's confidence level over all tasks
- *EFF* The efficiency of the change impact assessment process, calculated as *AVG_SCORE / TOT_TIME*

In the Analysis, We Used the Derived Variables. Hypotheses
The hypotheses posed in the study were tested at a 2-tailed confidence level of 95% ($p <= 0.05$). For each task, we posed the following null hypotheses[4]:

- $H\text{-}AS_0$: $\mu_{AVG\_SCORE\_TEXT} = \mu_{AVG\_SCORE\_gRAM}$
- $H\text{-}TF_0$: $\mu_{TOT\_FP\_TEXT} = \mu_{TOT\_FP\_gRAM}$
- $H\text{-}TT_0$: $\mu_{TOT\_TIME\_TEXT} = \mu_{TOT\_TIME\_gRAM}$
- $H\text{-}TC_0$: $\mu_{TOT\_CONF\_TEXT} = \mu_{TOT\_CONF\_gRAM}$
- $H\text{-}EF_0$: $\mu_{EFF\_TEXT} = \mu_{EFF\_gRAM}$

Each null hypothesis had a corresponding two-sided alternative hypothesis.

Analysis Methods
The collected data was analysed using both descriptive and inferential statistical methods; box plots were used to identify outliers (complemented with Little's MCAR test [31] for analysis of missing values) and extreme values, mean values and standard deviations were used to characterize the data set.

For the inferential statistics, we used Shapiro-Wilk test [32] to check whether the variables fit the normally distribution, and Mann-Whitney U-test [33] for testing the hypotheses stated in the previous section.

Validity Evaluation
The main threats to the validity of the study – as described by Wohlin et al. [34] – are analysed below.

Internal Validity – As blocking was made by us based on our experience of the subjects – all subjects were at some point students in courses taught by us – we assessed the threat to internal validity by collecting background information using a survey. After analysis we found no significant difference between the groups.

The introductory lecture was given to the two groups by different presenters, which might have affected the internal validity of the study. This threat was minimized by (i) having a common set of slides, which only differed in the presentation of the treatment for each group, and (ii) supplying the same information presented at the lecture in written format, which the subjects were allowed to study for 15 minutes before the test started.

External Validity – The main threat to the external validity is the use of student subjects, which may limit the ability to generalize the result to an industrial situation. The study was mainly done to evaluate the format of the requirements specification, and we do not make any conclusions about its applicability in an industrial situation yet. Eventhough these subjects are not completely representative of this population we could consider them the worst-case scenario sample, in the light of our previous research [35, 36].

---

[4] μ denotes the mean value for all subjects in the group.

An industrial evaluation of gRAM is planned for the future in the same way as an industrial evaluation presented in [35].

Construct Validity – The following bullets state, in our opinion, the main threats to construct validity according to Wohlin et.al. [34] and how we have avoided those threats

- *Inadequate preoperational explication of constructs.* All variables, as well as the correct answer to all experiment tasks, were clearly defined prior to the experiment.
- *Mono-method bias* and *Restricted generalizability across constructs.* We collected a number of different measurements; time, correctly given answers, false positives and the subjects perceived confidence of the given answer. By contrasting these to each other, we believe to have minimized this threat to the validity of the experiment.
- *Mono-operation bias.* The experiment was conducted only once and with one set of instruments, which poses a threat to construct validity. In order to confirm the findings in this evaluation, replication experiments, using different instrumentation is planned for the future, after an industrial case study on the applicability of this method has been done.

Conclusion Validity – The statistical power of the conclusions is quite low due to the small sample size. This threat to validity limits the strength of the conclusions drawn from the study. Rather than stating firm conclusion, we limit ourselves to *indications* and *tendencies*, and keep in mind that the results that showed no statistical significance may be due to random variation in the sample (the ρ-value is also reported for each hypothesis test). As the post-experiment interviews were, few they are not used in the result analysis. Instead, they are only used in the discussion section as evidence to support findings from the statistical analyses.

The original data set contained a number of missing data points (as reported in section 4.3 below). Due to our low sample size, we chose to impute the missing data. The imputation of the missing values was done using the Estimation-Maximization method [31] that may inflate the correlation between variables, which however, does not influence the statistical tests used in our study.

Testing of the collected data showed that several variables did not fit to the normal distribution – reported in section 4.3 below. For this reason, non-parametric tests were chosen for the inferential analyses, which further decrease the statistical power of the results but avoids the risk of violating assumptions and introducing further threats to the conclusion validity.

4.3 Analysis of Results

Normality Tests

The second column in Table 1 (Norm.(ρ)) shows the ρ-value for the Shapiro-Wilk test – a value below 0.05 indicates that the variable fits the normal distribution. The results show that none of the variables fit the normal distribution. Thus, the less powerful non-parametric Mann-Whitney U-test was used to analyse the posed hypotheses.

Missing Data and Extreme Values

The following data points were missing in the collected data: (i) one subject omitted to note the finish time on task 3; (ii) two subjects omitted to note the confidence on task 4; (iii) one subject omitted to note the finish time on task 5; (iv) one subject omitted to note the confidence on task 5; and (v) one subject did not submit the background survey at all.

Little's MCAR test could not reject that the values are missing completely at random, indicating that methods for data imputation may be used. All missing values were imputed using the Expectation-Maximization method [31].

Two outliers were found and removed from the EFF_{gRAM} variable. The removed values were excluded pair-wise in the subsequent analyses.

Descriptive Statistics

The descriptive statistics for the derived variables are shown in Table 1. The *Diff*-column in Table 1 shows the difference between the text group and the gRAM group, using the text group as baseline. The descriptive statistics indicate that the gRAM group was 37% faster than the text group (TOT_TIME). On the other hand, the results also show that the text group scores 23% better (AVG_SCORE) and produce 26% less false positives (TOT_FP) than the gRAM group. There is also an indication of a 9% higher perceived confidence level of the answers (TOT_CONF) in the gRAM group.

Table 1. Descriptive statistics

Variable	Norm. (p)	Mean	Std. Dev.	Diff	Better
AVG_SCORE_{TEXT}	0.845	49.07	12.16	-23%	Text (higher score)
AVG_SCORE_{gRAM}	0.131	40.00	17.53		
TOT_FP_{TEXT}	0.814	17.75	11.25	26%	Text (less false positives)
TOT_FP_{gRAM}	0.344	22.40	11.29		
TOT_TIME_{TEXT}	0.335	3113.00	253.49	-37%	gRAM (faster)
TOT_TIME_{gRAM}	0.192	1965.50	741.65		
TOT_CONF_{TEXT}	0.369	14.13	1.64	9%	gRAM (more confident)
TOT_CONF_{gRAM}	0.498	15.4	4.67		
EFF_{TEXT}	0.580	0.01572	0.0035	4%	gRAM (more efficient)
EFF_{gRAM}	0.153	0.01629	0.0047		

The results also show that the difference is time between the groups does not imply a higher efficiency, as the gRAM group has a lower score; the difference in the efficiency variable (EFF) is only 4%.

There is, furthermore, a large difference in the standard deviation between the groups for all variables except TOT_FP variable – Fig 1 and Fig 2 show boxplots for the TOT_TIME and EFF variables respectively. This variance within the gRAM group may indicate that the difference between the groups is not statistically significant.

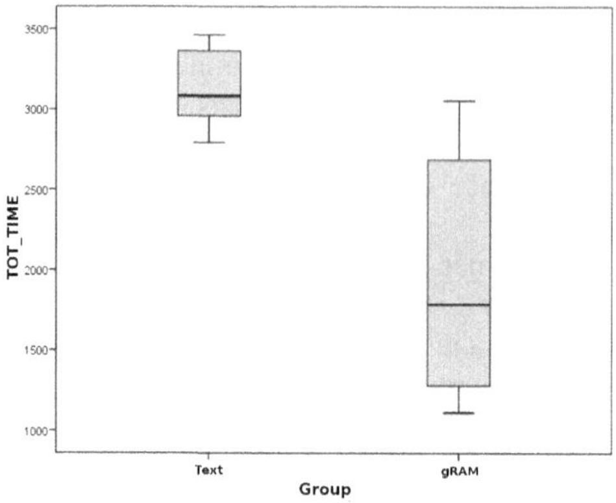

Fig. 1. TOT_TIME variable

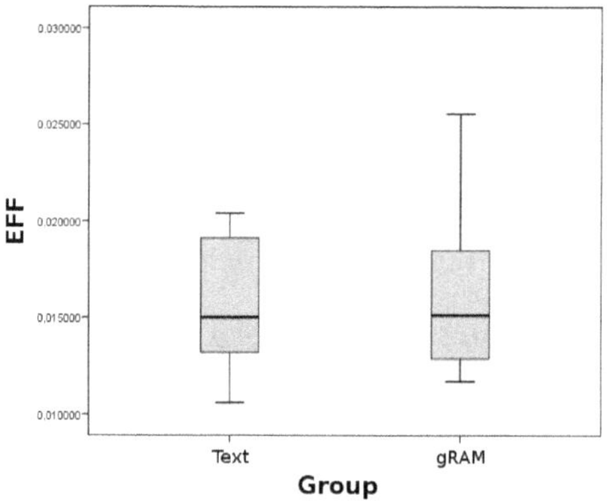

Fig. 2. EFF variable

Hypotheses Tests

The result of the hypotheses tests (Table 2) using the Mann-Whitney U-test shows that only the hypothesis $H-TT_0$ could be rejected. Fig 1 shows a box plot for the total amount of time spent on the tasks (the unit on the y-axis is seconds). The descriptive statistics show that the time required to perform a change impact assessment is in this experiment 37% shorter when using gRAM (see Table 1).

Table 2. Hypotheses tests

Hypothesis	*p*-value	MWW *U*	H_0 rejected
$H-AS_0$	0.264	27.50	No
$H-TF_0$	0.351	29.50	No
$H-TT_0$	0.002	5.00	Yes
$H-TC_0$	0.501	32.50	No
$H-EF_0$	0.834	30.00	No

Interviews

When asked how the requirement specification was used, subjects in the groups with the textual specification stated that they constructed a hierarchical structure of requirements similar to the gRAM, either mentally or on paper. Subjects from the text group stated that the model they drew was revised many times during the experiments, making them doubt whether they answered earlier tasks correctly.

Subjects in the gRAM group stated that they mainly used the graphical representation; in the interview one subject said: "*When I read the task, I had an initial idea about what the answer would be, and a quick look at the diagram confirmed it. I felt no need to read the detailed description*".

The interviews suggest that the text group, while constructing a visualization of the requirements themselves (either mentally or by drawing), read through the detailed description of the requirements more thoroughly than the gRAM group. The gRAM group seemed content with drawing their conclusions based on the graphical model, turning to the details only when in doubt. The large standard deviation in required time (`TOT_TOME`) and score (`AVG_SCORE`) within the gRAM group, however, might indicate that some subjects did read the detailed requirements description more thoroughly than others did.

5 Discussion

The results of our experiment show with statistical significance that the use of a graphical representation reduces the time required to perform the tasks. During the post-experiment interviews, subjects from the text group stated that they tried to construct visualizations of the textual document themselves, and some even stated that the structure they created was similar to the representation used in the gRAM. This suggests that there is a justification for creating such structure as part of making the specification; if it is not done, it will result in redundant work each time the text specification is used. Moreover, statements from the text group suggest that they had doubts whether the structure they created was correct, resulting in revising it during the course of the experiment, which may contribute to the extra time spent by the textual group.

On the other hand – although not statistically significant in our experiment – the textual group had higher score and fewer false positives (variables `AVG_SCORE` and `TOT_FP` in Table 1). This might be explained by interview statements from the group presented with the gRAM representation, which show that they had an initial idea of an answer and used the graphical structure to confirm it; they mainly used the detailed description when in doubt. This indicates that they put a lot of trust in the material provided, while the textual group – knowing that they created the graphical structure themselves – were more inclined to double-check their answer. This suggests that a graphical representation promotes quicker decisions, while the textual representation forces the subject to study the material more closely.

Furthermore, the statements made by the gRAM group – saying that they mainly turned to the detailed requirement description when in doubt – suggest the importance of clearly defining what information is shown in the diagram. The graphical representation might end up being misleading if in fact the detailed description is needed in order to fully understand the specification. This may explain the large variance in time (TOT_TIME) and score (AVG_SCORE) within the gRAM group – the subjects may have used the detailed requirement description to different degrees.

It should be noted that the experiment was done using student subjects, and that in a real world situation the repercussions of making a mistake would be much more severe than in our superficial case. Furthermore, only one of our five hypotheses could be confirmed with statistical significance, possibly due to the large variation in the gRAM group – which is not adequately explained by the experiment. For these reasons, we plan to do a larger experiment and include subjects from the industry in order to verify our conclusions.

6 Conclusions

Graphical modelling of requirements has been considered in several modelling languages like SysML (the notion of requirement) or UML (the notion of use case). Nevertheless, not much empirical evidence is provided whether graphical modelling of requirements improves typical requirements engineering activities like elicitation, packaging, validation or change management. In this paper we present results from an experiment performed at academia with the objective to verify whether a graphical model of requirements is better than a textual one. As a basis for the experiment, a state-of-the-art method was used – Requirements Abstraction Model – to specify the requirements in a textual form, whereas a dedicated modelling language based on the Requirements Abstraction Model was used for the graphical specification.

The results from the experiment show that the time required to assess impact of a change was substantially shorter for the graphical notation. Aspects such as accuracy of the assessment and the confidence in the result (as perceived by the subjects) were found to be within the limit of statistical error (i.e. statistically insignificant).

In our future work, we plan to replicate the study in an industrial context and to further experiment with such aspects as time required to create the requirement specification and its correctness.

Furthermore, we plan to examine the consistency among the different abstraction levels of gRAM as well as the effectiveness of mapping the requirements specification to design model – i.e. traceability correctness.

Acknowledgments

This research is partially sponsored by VINNOVA under the V-ICT program and the ASIS (Algorithms and Software for Improved Safety) project. We would also like to thank the students who participated in the experiment. Additionally, we like to thank the anonymous reviewers for their valuable comments.

References

1. Kent, S.: Model Driven Engineering. Integrated Formal Methods, 286–298 (2002)
2. France, R., Rumpe, B.: Model-driven Development of Complex Software: A Research Roadmap. In: 2007 Future of Software Engineering, pp. 37–54. IEEE Computer Society, Los Alamitos (2007)

3. Ludewig, J.: Models in software engineering – an introduction. Software and Systems Modeling 2, 5–14 (2003)
4. Object Management Group, http://www.omg.org/
5. Greenfield, J., Short, K.: Software factories: assembling applications with patterns, models, frameworks and tools. In: Companion of the 18th annual ACM SIGPLAN conference on Object-oriented programming, systems, languages, and applications, pp. 16–27. ACM, Anaheim (2003)
6. SysML - Open Source Specification Project, http://www.sysml.org/
7. Jacobson, I.: Object Oriented Software Engineering: A Use Case Driven Approach. Addison-Wesley Professional, Reading (1992)
8. Hänninen, K., Mäki-Turja, J., Nolin, M.: Present and future requirements in developing industrial embedded real-time systems - interviews with designers in the vehicle domain. In: 13th Annual IEEE International Symposium and Workshop on Engineering of Computer Based Systems, ECBS 2006, p. 9 (2006)
9. Kallenbach, R.G., Emig, R.: Automotive Electronics - What Makes It So Special? Presented at the October 1 (2004)
10. Salzmann, C., Stauner, T.: Automotive software engineering: an emerging application domain for software engineering. In: Languages for system specification: Selected contributions on UML, systemC, system Verilog, mixed-signal systems, and property specification from FDL 2003, pp. 333–347. Kluwer Academic Publishers, Dordrecht (2004)
11. Broy, M., Kruger, I., Pretschner, A., Salzmann, C.: Engineering Automotive Software. Proceedings of the IEEE 95, 356–373 (2007)
12. Noppen, J., van den Broek, P., Aksit, M.: Imperfect Requirements in Software Development. In: Sawyer, P., Paech, B., Heymans, P. (eds.) REFSQ 2007. LNCS, vol. 4542, pp. 247–261. Springer, Heidelberg (2007)
13. ASIS - Algorithms and Software for Improved Safety, http://www.ait.gu.se/english/research_groups/se_management/research_projects/ASIS_Active_Safety_Systems/
14. Mellegård, N., Staron, M.: A Domain Specific Modelling Language for Specifying and Visualizing Requirements. In: The First International Workshop on Domain Engineering, DE@CAiSE, Amsterdam (2009)
15. Winkler, S.: Information Flow Between Requirement Artifacts. Results of an Empirical Study. In: Sawyer, P., Paech, B., Heymans, P. (eds.) REFSQ 2007. LNCS, vol. 4542, pp. 232–246. Springer, Heidelberg (2007)
16. Gorschek, T., Wohlin, C.: Requirements abstraction model. Requir. Eng. 11, 79–101 (2006)
17. Mellegård, N., Staron, M.: Methodology for Requirements Engineering in Model-Based Projects for Reactive Automotive Software. In: Vitek, J. (ed.) ECOOP 2008. LNCS, vol. 5142. Springer, Heidelberg (2008)
18. Maiden, N., Minocha, S., Sutcliffe, A., Manuel, D., Ryan, M.: Co-operative scenario based approach to acquisition and validation of system requirements: how exceptions can help! Interacting with Computers 11, 645–664 (1999)
19. Cox, K., Phalp, K.: Replicating the CREWS use case authoring guidelines experiment. Empirical Software Engineering 5, 245–267 (2000)
20. Phalp, K., Vincent, J., Cox, K.: Improving the quality of use case descriptions: Empirical assessment of writing guidelines. Software Quality Journal 15, 383–399 (2007)
21. Gravino, C., Scanniello, G., Tortora, G.: An Empirical Investigation on Dynamic Modeling in Requirements Engineering. In: Czarnecki, K., Ober, I., Bruel, J.-M., Uhl, A., Völter, M. (eds.) MODELS 2008. LNCS, vol. 5301, pp. 615–629. Springer, Heidelberg (2008)

22. Lange, C., Chaudron, M.: Interactive views to improve the comprehension of UML models - An experimental validation. In: Proceedings - ICPC 2007: 15th IEEE International Conference on Program Comprehension, pp. 221–230 (2007)
23. De Lucia, A., Gravino, C., Oliveto, R., Tortora, G.: Data model comprehension an empirical comparison of ER and UML class diagrams. In: Proceedings of the 16th IEEE International Conference on Program Comprehension, ICPC, pp. 93–102 (2008)
24. Otero, M., Dolado, J.: An empirical comparison of the dynamic modeling in OML and UML. Journal of Systems and Software 77, 91–102 (2005)
25. Gorschek, T., Garre, P., Larsson, S., Wohlin, C.: Industry evaluation of the Requirements Abstraction Model. Requirements Engineering 12, 163–190 (2007)
26. Mohammad, N., Vandewoude, Y., Berbers, Y., Feldt, R.: Suitability of Requirements Abstraction Model (RAM) Requirements for High-Level System Testing. International Journal of Computer and Information Science and Engineering, 2
27. Wong, K., Sun, D.: On evaluating the layout of UML diagrams for program comprehension. Software Quality Journal 14, 233–259 (2006)
28. Lindvall, M.: Evaluating Impact Analysis - A Case Study. Empirical Software Engineering 2, 152–158 (1997)
29. Arisholm, E., Briand, L., Hove, S., Labiche, Y.: The impact of UML documentation on software maintenance: An experimental evaluation. IEEE Transactions on Software Engineering 32, 365–381 (2006)
30. gRAM Experiment Material, `http://www.ituniv.se/~miroslaw/ram-dsl_experiment/`
31. Little, R., Rubin, D.: Statistical Analysis with Missing Data. Wiley, Chichester (2002)
32. Altman, D.: Practical Statistics for Medical Research. Chapman-Hall, Boca Raton (1991)
33. Bowerman, B., O'Connell, R., Murphree, E.: Business Statistics in Practice. McGraw-Hill, New York (2008)
34. Wohlin, C., Runeson, P., Höst, M., Ohlsson, M.C., Regnell, B., Wesslèn, A.: Experimentation in Software Engineering: An Introduction. Kluwer Academic Publisher, Boston (2000)
35. Staron, M., Kuzniarz, L., Wohlin, C.: Empirical assessment of using stereotypes to improve comprehension of UML models: A set of experiments. Journal of Systems and Software 79, 727–742 (2006)
36. Staron, M.: Using Experiments in Software Engineering as an Auxiliary Tool for Teaching – A Perspective of Students' Learning Process. In: Borsler, J., Eriksson, J. (eds.) 6th Conference on Software Engineering Research and Practice, Sweden, pp. 29–38. Umeå University, Umeå (2006)

Vague Project Start Makes Project Success of Outsourced Software Development Projects Uncertain

Paula Savolainen[1,2]

[1] School of Computing
University of Eastern Finland
P.O. Box 1627
FI-70211 Kuopio, Finland
[2] Lero — The Irish Software Engineering Research Centre
University of Limerick, Ireland
paula.m.savolainen@uef.fi

Abstract. A definition of a project success includes at least three criteria: 1) meeting planning goals, 2) customer benefits, and 3) supplier benefits. This study aims to point out the importance of the definition of the project start, the project start date, and what work should be included in the project effort in order to ensure the supplier's benefits. The ambiguity of the project start risks the profitability of the project and therefore makes project success at least from supplier's point of view uncertain. Moreover, vague project start makes it more difficult to compare project management metrics, such as duration and effort, between projects. There is no clear definition for the project start either in literature or practice. Based on interviews, the definitions are provided for project start, project start date, and project start-up effort included in the project.

1 Introduction

An ever increasing part of the software development activities are bought from external suppliers. In those cases both the customer and the supplier plan to do viable business together in a way in which the supplier develops the software in a project and the customer will get the desired outcome of the project. In order to have a prosperous relationship between the customer and the supplier the projects should be as successful as possible. The definition of success includes at least three criteria: 1) meeting planning goals, 2) end-user benefits[1], and 3) contractor benefits[2] (including at least two criteria: commercial success of the project and potential for future revenues) [1]. Without understanding all three criteria of project success and their implications it is less likely to achieve a common project success.

The first project success criterion, the ability of the project to meet the planning goals, is closely related to the traditional measures of project success, namely cost, time and quality [2]. In the case of software projects it is more common to speak about scope instead of quality. The reason to adhere to time, cost and scope is understandable

[1] In this article the end-user benefits are considered to be customer benefits.

[2] In this article the term contractor is replaced with the term supplier because in software engineering standards the used term is supplier.

M. Ali Babar, M. Vierimaa, and M. Oivo (Eds.): PROFES 2010, LNCS 6156, pp. 351–365, 2010.
© Springer-Verlag Berlin Heidelberg 2010

because for example ISO/IEC 12207 standard defines a project as an endeavor with defined start and finish dates undertaken to create a product or service in accordance with specified resources and requirements [3].

The second project success criterion, the customer benefits provided by the project, can be defined by the project's impact on general corporate strategy, business operations, research and development, IS/IT development, and facilities provision and management [4]. The impact on corporate strategy can lead directly to improvement competitiveness and enhanced shareholder value. The impact of project success on IS/IT development is improved financial benefits and reduced wastage on canceled projects. These benefits cannot always be measured when the project ends because it may take some time and sometimes it may take several years before the actual customer benefits can be estimated.

The customer benefits are not the same as the project delivered in time, within the budget and according to the scope [4]. There are several examples of projects that were clearly over budget and over time, but which were clear successes. The final success of the project is more likely to be influenced by the customer's ability to select a project that has potential to provide actual benefits to the customer than any other factor. Selecting a fundamentally flawed project will ensure project failure even if the project has been completed in time, scope and budget [5].

The third project success criterion, the supplier benefits, is necessary for good long-time relationships between the supplier and the customer. It is necessary for the supplier to run a profitable business, and therefore the overall project portfolio of the supplier has to make profit. Without profitability the supplier will get out of the business and the customer will lose the benefits of a mutually advantageous partnership. The potential for the future revenues is also a very important aspect of project success from the supplier's point of view. This is emphasized by the study by Haried and Ranamurthy [6] in which it is shown that one of the main aims of the supplier is to get additional business in the future, and therefore one of the main criteria of the success of the current activities from the supplier's point of view is the outlook of future deals with the customer.

In order to gain benefits there should be a common understanding between the supplier and the customer of the project, its scope, timetable, and costs. This understanding should come into existence during negotiations between the supplier and the customer before the project is allowed to start and this understanding is usually clarified in the commercial and legally binding agreement and the project plan.

In order to gain its own benefits (commercial success of the project and potential for future revenues) the supplier should fulfill contractual obligations with respect not only to project scope but also anticipated effort and timetable. When the agreed outcome of the project will be delivered to the customer in time and effort estimation is not overrun the supplier may assume that the customer will not only gain its own benefits but also be satisfied with supplier and its performance. Thereby the project has potential to become profitable and the possibility for the future revenue will be ensured.

Especially for the supplier it is important not to overrun estimated effort and timetable. The supplier has usually many projects going on at the same time. Continually supplying the pipeline with additional business in the form of project agreements the supplier ensures its revenue stream [7]. However, the number of people, and facilities available for a project are always limited. To be able to allocate resources from one project to another the supplier should know how many and what kind of resources are needed in one project and when these resources will be relieved and be free to be moved on to other projects. If there are delays on schedule, the supplier will have challenges not only with current project but also with the other projects waiting for the same resources. Moreover, if the effort estimation will be overrun, depending on the commercial agreement, the supplier has a risk to have a non-profitable project which will engender a shadow over the whole project and it is more difficult to achieve project success and a prosperous relationship between the supplier and the customer.

When doing software projects as a business, the supplier has a need to estimate effort as realistically as possible and the conceivable delivery date is estimated using effort estimation as a basis. The eventual effort and thus costs of the project and its end date are formed under negotiations between the customer and the supplier. The project start and the eventual start date of the project are more problematic. The author's industrial background[3] and current industrial cooperation have left the definition of the project start a confusing and unclear concept.

A project start is quite important point in time for the project. The project work should start at that moment. Moreover, the project start should form the baseline for the estimation of project duration. But according to the personal experience of the author it is not clear when the actual project work has started, what is the project start, and what is the start date of the project.

For a supplier company project start-up activities are commenced when the company has got the order from the customer or the customer has indicated some other way that it will order software development project with agreed deliverables form the supplier company. During start-up phase the supplier company starts project planning using initial project plans made for a tender as a basis, forms the project team, assign responsibilities, establish procedures, install tools and controls, set up communications and makes initial contact between the team and customer [8], and [9].

When analyzing project start-up Turner has divided different projects into four types and emphasizes that start-up activities may be considerable especially in the case of software development [10]. However, in supplier companies it is common that in some projects those activities has been counted as effort to be included in the project but in other projects that work has been neglected and has been left almost totally out from the project work, although for a given project there is a certain minimum effort the project requires in the start-up phase [11].

Because practices vary from one project to another it is not so obvious and well-defined what work is included in the project work both beforehand while making effort estimation at negotiation phase and when the actual project is about to start. Without proper resources planned and reserved for project start-up activities, there is a risk that the design and plan stages are not carried out thoroughly enough which is, according to Atkinson, a common source of difficulty in projects [12].

[3] Author has worked as a Developer, Systems Analyst, and Project Manager in Tieto developing software for customers mainly in telecom and logistics sector. She has worked also in GE Healthcare R&D unit developing software product for intensive care units in European hospitals.

While it is unclear, what activities should be and are included in the project work, it is equally obscure how project start should be defined. Fangel gives two possibilities: "The formal project start may be at the beginning of the start-up process, subject to approval of the developed project plans. Alternatively, the start-up process may be partly or fully carried out before the formal project start." [13]. This means that project start and therefore also project start date can be anchored to the beginning of the start-up phase or somewhere during the start-up phase. However, an undefined project start makes the timely and controlled execution the project start-up activities more challenging and may result in unnecessary risks.

In order to achieve all three criteria of project success, the supplier should be able to provide accurate effort estimates. The creation of accurate estimates would require an agreement on the types of work included into the project. Therefore the project start-up work and the project start should be defined and agreed on by both the supplier and the customer. Such clarification would benefit both parties by creating a more truthful picture of the project and related activities and possible costs.

As long as both project start and what work is included in the project work are unclear concepts it is difficult for the supplier to measure project profitability truthfully. Moreover, basic project management metrics such effort, duration and timetable are more unsteady than normally presumed. Therefore in this article the research question is formulated as "What is 'project start' and how it is defined?". The question stems from the lack of clarity and the aim of this study is to help professionals to define project start and related issues in a way that makes project success more likely.

A literature review is presented in Section 2. Since literature review was not able contribute a definition to the project start the practitioners were interviewed to obtain a practical definition for the project start. The performed interview is presented in Section 3. The results of the analysis of interviews are presented in Section 4. In Section 5 there are a few definitions and the article is concluded in Section 6.

2 A Literature Review

Both the project start and the project start date as concepts may appear so obvious that they do not seem to have a definition at all. An exact definition is, however, important on order to achieve a common understanding. The literature review was split in three parts. Those parts are a review of the standards, a brief search of definition from common textbooks, and a search of relevant research from databases.

The first part, the analysis of standards, was restricted to the ISO and IEEE standards. Later on the review of standards was backed up with an analysis of project management standards. The first part of the search was by using the keywords "project", and "start", and "date" in various combinations. No definition was found through database searches.

After the unsuccessful keyword search the standards ISO/IEC 12207, ISO/IEC 15288, ISO/IEC 15504, ISO/IEC 16085, and ISO/IEC 16326 [3], [14], [15], [16], and [17] were analyzed. The analyzed standards do not provide a definition for project start or project start date.

The analysis of standards was extended to the most common project management standard, which is "A Guide to the Project Management Body of Knowledge" (PMBOK) and is often mentioned as "*...the sum of knowledge within the profession of* *project management.*" [18]. PMBOK describes activities to be done at the project start-up phase but doesn't describe when the project actually starts and therefore doesn't define either the project start or the project start date. PMBOK defines, however, a start date as "*A point in time associated with schedule activity's start, usually qualified by one of the following: actual, planned, estimated, scheduled, early, late, target, baseline, or current.*" Schedule activity means "*A discrete scheduled component of work performed during the course of a project.*" Start date is thereby associated with an activity, which is scheduled and performed during the course of the project. Therefore the definition of the start date doesn't give definition for the project start, which is the starting point for the whole project and its activities.

The most common standards related to software projects do not provide a useful definition. Therefore the literature review was extended to the common software engineering books like [19], [20], and [21]. Such books cover wide range of concepts and methods for software development as well as short description of project management. As their main purpose is to describe software engineering as a whole without concerning details of software projects, they don't give definitions for project start or project start date. Moreover, they do not pay any attention to the supplier's problem of resource allocation and management in a multi-project environment.

The last part of the literature review was searches performed in the scientific databases. The first database used was IEEE database. The search strings used were `((project <and> start date) <in> metadata)`, `((project <and> start time) <in> metadata)`, and `(('project start') <in> metadata)`. All those searches produced only one page of results. The abstracts of the result articles were read and the most promising article found was [9].

Egginton concentrates on two things: the handover from the sales organization to the project organization and how to achieve a rapid launch of the project [9]. For the former he presents a handover workshop as a way to ensure a smooth and complete transition of responsibility from the sales management to the project management. For the latter, the rapid launch of the project, he suggests a project kick-off meeting with participants from all major project partners. With the help of both handover workshop and kick-off meeting it is possible without dispute to contribute to the successful start of the project. It is, however, unclear if the kick-off meeting is intended to be the actual project start.

From the ACM portal the search strings were `project "start date"` (328), `project "start time"` (1 777), `project "start-date"` (328), `project "starttime"` (1 777), and `"project start"` (156). The number in parenthesis after the search string denote the number of hits. With those cases in which the number of hits was larger than 200 only the first five pages of results were subjected for closer scrutiny. With the string `"project start"` the whole list was looked at, although only those articles with a promising title and abstract were considered more closely. No definitions were found.

The Elsevier ScienceDirect database was used with the search term `"project start"`. The search was limited to the journals *International Journal of Project Management*, *European Journal of Operational Research*, *Journal of Systems and Software*, *Information and Software Technology*, *Research Policy* , *Technovation*, *Information & Management*, and *European Management Journal*. The search produced 229 hits. The hits were looked at by the title and the abstract. Only those articles that seemed most promising were looked at more closely.

Fangel discusses purpose of project start-up, planning of the project start-up, and presents tools for the project start-up procedure [8], [13].He also describes differences between project start and project start-up [13]:

> *...To me it is natural to distinguish between to* start *and to* start-up. *When you are going to drive a car, you* start *by merely turning the key, releasing the clutch, and simply drive away. You rarely give any thought to the matter of performing the kick-off.*
>
> *When you are going to run the diesel engine of a ship, you perform a* start-up *which is a process involving several activities all needed before the marine engineer can give the final 'Go'. Examples of the activities are the manning of the start-up, communication with the captain, fuel check, lubrication of bearings, starting pumps, initiation of filters, and building up sufficient air pressure.*
>
> *Such a professional start-up* process *is the basis for getting the engine going, but at the same time it gives an effective and economical operation of the engine.*
>
> *It seems to me that the difference between a project start and a project start-up is just as obvious as the difference between starting a car and starting up a ship's diesel engine.*

Using the example above he succeeds to clarify difference between project start and project start-up, but, however, he gives incomplete definition for project start and project start date, and these are already presented in Section 1.

In addition to Fangel, Turner and Cochrane [10] have analyzed the relationship between methods, goals, and start-ups. According to them, the start-up is important and may require considerable amount of effort [10]. Two other studies concentrate on efficient project start-up [22] or evaluating effectiveness of project start-ups [23]. Both studies emphasize the importance of the project start-up in order to ensure the successful completion of a project. They do not, however, commit themselves on a definition of the project start or the project start date.

In a fairly recent article it is noted that at present some projects may have unclear boundaries, e.g. the start and end dates of the project are unclear [12]. The example of a project type that has unclear boundaries is organizational change projects, which are totally different from outsourced software projects, which are contract based and should start and end sometime and provide a deliverable result. In that article the project start was not defined at all, although it was mentioned to be sometimes a fuzzy concept.

Wiley InterScience database did not provide any interesting results. The search string `project NEAR/3 start` for journals did produce 244 hits, but the results were not promising. The titles of the articles and the names of the journals made it unlikely that any of the articles would have provided the searched definition for the project start. Due to the seeming inaccuracy of the Wiley's search engine, *Information Systems Journal*, *Software Process Improvement*, and *Project Management Journal* were looked at more closely. No relevant articles were found.

SpringerLink database was searched with the string `"project start"`. The search produced 362 hits. The title of every hit was considered and the more interesting articles were opened for further analysis. If the abstract of the article did not include relevant terms, then the article was not considered any further. There were only two articles [24], and [11] that somewhat covered the project start. Neither of those articles defined the project start, but Barry et al. [11] considered the start-up important in the beginning of the project and after interruptions. This is because an organization needs time to set up the project team, train them, and allow them to become familiar with the project [11].

The literature review made it clear that there exists no common definition of the project start. A clear definition of the project start is, however, important because confusion and delays make project success less likely. The lack of definition in the literature does not mean that companies that supply projects to customers do not have a clear definition. The interview was performed in order to get a definition formulated by practitioners and the analysis of the interview is presented in the following section.

3 The Interview

The interview described in this section is a part of a larger study which consisted of two different interviews performed in four software engineering companies. The larger study aims to gain better understanding of those activities which are performed in a supplier company before the actual project has been started and which will affect the project during its life-cycle. One part of interviews concentrated on activities performed in tendering process and another part concentrated on initiation activities performed in the project start-up phase. This study concentrates on the interviews on the project start-up phase.

The project start-up phase is the phase that succeeds the sales process and precedes the actual project. Project start-up phase starts when company has got the order from the customer or the customer has indicated some other way that it will order software development project with agreed deliverables from the supplier company. The project start-up phase has been discussed in [8], [13], [10], [9], [23], and [24]. The project start-up phase and its relationship with the sales process and the actual project are depicted in Fig. 1.

Two software engineering companies where interviews were performed made software development projects to various customers. Other two companies made embedded software projects with close cooperation with industrial companies. The main characteristic of all four companies was that they delivered unique product (software or

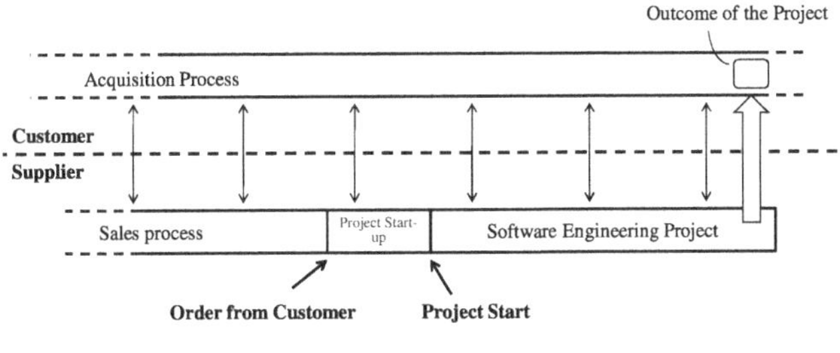

Fig. 1. The Start-up phase of a project

embedded software, or in some cases specialized hardware with embedded software) to their customers. For these companies projects are their main way of doing business.

The persons interviewed were selected by the higher management of the companies. For the project start-up interview the management were asked to select project managers or other people who are responsible for project management. The interviewed people included eleven Project Managers, one Business Unit Manager, one Team Manager, and one Engineering Manager, altogether 14 people. Summary of the project start-up interviews is presented in Table 1.

Table 1. Summary of the project start-up interviews

Company	Project focus	Persons interviewed	Position
Company A	Software	3	Project Manager Project Manager Business Unit Manager
Company B	Software	3	Project Manager Project Manager Team Manager
Company C	Embedded Software	2	Project Manager Engineering Manager
Company D	Embedded Software	6	Project Manager Project Manager Project Manager Project Manager Project Manager Project Manager

An interview instrument was developed for interviews and it consisted of main themes and a form for background data. In addition, few questions were planned to obtain definitions. The interview instrument was constructed by one researcher and validated by two other researchers. The interviews were performed as semi-structured interviews, more the forms of a discussion, using the interview instrument as a guide of discussion. Every interview was recorded and the recordings were transcribed to text. The analysis of the interviews was based on these transcribed texts.

One of the questions made for definition formulation was "When do you consider a project started?". The question and especially answers of this question turned out to be not so straightforward than it could have been supposed to be. Analysis of the various answers and results of the analysis are described in the next section.

4 Results of the Analysis

The first step of the analysis was to extract all answers of question "When do you consider a project started?" from transcript files into one manageable file keeping data traceable. Each answer was analyzed and a simplified individual definition for project

Table 2. Individual definitions of the project start

Company	Project focus	Individual definitions
Company A	Software	- There has been a kick-off meeting with the customer. - Work to achieve the goals of the project has been started. - First hours have been registered to the project.
Company B	Software	- We got the deal. - The project manager has taken over the project. - There has been a kick-off meeting with the customer.
Company C	Embedded Software	- We have got the deal. - A project number for the project has been opened.
Company D	Embedded Software	- The order has been got. - The order has come. - The project manager has been appointed. - There has been an official kick-off meeting with the customer. - There has been an internal kick-off meeting. - Someone is working on the project.

start was formulated for each interviewee. The result of this step is presented company by company in Table 2.

It can be seen that there are many quite similar definitions as "The order has been got." and "The order has come." These quite similar definitions were grouped together and altogether five groups were comprised of individual definitions. After analysis of each group one definition of project start was derived for each group. These definitions and the number of different definitions in each group are presented in Table 3.

Table 3. Definition and the number of individual definitions

Definition	Number of individual definitions
We got the order.	4
Project work has been started.	4
There has been a kick-off meeting with the customer.	3
The project manager has been appointed.	2
There has been an internal kick-off meeting.	1

The most common definitions were "We got the order" and "Project work has been started" but only one interviewee defined the project start via internal kick-off meeting. This may reflect that it is not very common to have internal kick-off meetings or that a project is considered started before an internal kick-off meeting.

It is possible to place the definitions presented in Table 3 in a time-scale. The placing represent the relative ordering of the definitions and reflects the opinion of the author of this article. The ordering of the definitions is shown in Fig. 2.

After the supplier has got the deal, it takes some time to appoint the project manager. When the project manager has been appointed, he/she will start getting familiar with the project. That time can be considered to represent the first moments when some work

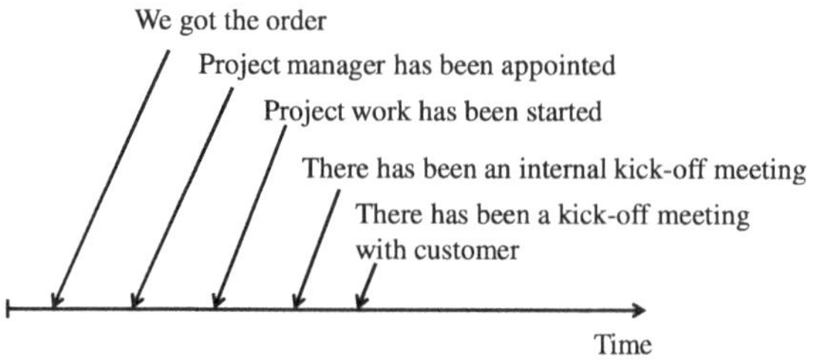

Fig. 2. The definitions of the project start in a timeline

has been done to the project. The project resources are selected by the project manager or the resources are given to the project manager. In many cases the project manager may have some influence on the decisions regarding the project team, but that influence can be very limited. After the project team has been selected it is possible to have an internal kick-off meeting. Before or after the internal kick-off meeting the members of the project team have familiarized themselves with the project. The formal project kick-off meeting requires that the supplier's project team and the customer's relevant personnel are known. Both sides should have familiarized themselves with the project and be ready for the meeting. It may, however, be the case that it will take some time before the formal project kick-off meeting can be held.

The time between the order and the kick-off meeting with the customer may be several weeks. During that time there may have been a considerable amount of effort spent in addition to the effort directly related to start-up activities. Hence, it is not easy to compare the effort, the duration, and the schedule of individual projects even inside a single company. This problem is clearly seen in Table 4 where different definitions are presented company by company. Each definition is presented once and number of interviewed persons per company is also presented.

It is quite amazing how many different meanings project start can have amongst professionals. There is no common understanding inside any company. If we look at the Company B one of the interviewees define project start as "The order has been got." and another as "There has been a kick-off meeting with the customer." If their process follows author's own experience there is a huge difference between project managers how they manage project start and project timetable, and how they manage hours spent for the project.

After collecting and analyzing the definitions the actual transcripted interviews were re-read. That made the vagueness of the project start much easier to understand. The ambiguity of the project start is described by one manager, who was not able to make up his/her mind. He/she finally conceded that the project start is a fuzzy concept and difficult to define.

> Now, we usually have a kick-off meeting with a customer. It can be considered a starting point of the project... But how it goes, when the project starts, anyway, what is pre-planning of the project then... So, yes, the kick-off meeting can be before the pre-planning, that we have agreed that we get our finger out. But we, of course, discuss it with the customer as early as possible, what have to be done, and so on. That it is a basis for the planning, case-specifically, maybe... This is such a gray area.

Table 4. Different definitions and the number of interviews for each company

Company	Project focus	Definitions	Number of interviewed persons
Company A	Software	- Project work has been started. - There has been a kick-off meeting with the customer.	3
Company B	Software	- The order has been got - The project manager has been appointed - There has been a kick-off meeting with the customer	3
Company C	Embedded Software	- The order has been got - Project work has been started	2
Company D	Embedded Software	- The order has been got - The project manager has been appointed - Project work has been started - There has been an internal kick-off meeting - There has been a kick-off meeting with the customer	6

All interviewed managers worked for companies which make various software projects to different customers. The difficulties to manage project starts and how to define the project start after delays is clearly seen from the quotation of one manager:

> I don't know... Well, I, for one, think it's when someone has started to work for the project. It's common that we have some timetable. We have offered a project, we made a tender today, the project will start 1st January 2009 and end 30th May 2009. Some time passes, we'll get the order, perhaps in the mid January, we won't update the schedule. We'll start the ball rolling, we'll get maybe one guy for the project and another maybe in the mid February. Now, we've failed the start and schedule, it doesn't matter as such, but what is actually the project start. In my opinion, it's when there is someone working for the project.

His/her answer included some further insight in addition to the definition of the project start. He/she illuminated one of the problems that are inherently present in contractual software projects. The timetable, i.e. schedule, has been outlined in a binding tender, but the order comes much later than expected. The project is already late, the schedule is presumably not updated, the resources are not available at once (it has to be remembered that the order comes much later than expected) and the project is delayed even more. The actual project start and the start date defined in the original project plan have nothing to do with each other anymore.

Ambiguity with a moving project start and the activities performed during start-up create difficulties for the supplier because the supplier has to cope not only with the already late project but with several other projects at the same time. It is likely that at least some of the other projects use the same resources than the original project. The other projects may be delayed or disrupted by the timetable changes of the original project.

The fact that the managers interviewed work for companies which operate in project business makes the managers to pay special attention to anything that incurs difficulties to the supplier. Therefore some experienced managers may select a more or less arbitrary date and present it as the start date of the project. By using such a date he/she strengthens his/her bargaining position with the customer because he/she can always refer to that date and negotiate a new schedule. That is clearly expressed by one manager who said:

> I personally write it always in the project plan. I'll try to keep it easy for me, it's quite difficult to define when the project has been started and therefore it's always written in my project plans. There can be delays for different reasons but we have to have readiness to start the project. And when we are able to show the project start date and the project has been started we are stronger to negotiate with the customer for the changes of timetable.

Differences between various definitions for the project start can be interpreted to mean that the concept of the project start was at least partly ambiguous in every company. The ambiguity is expressed in a clear way by one experienced manager who said:

> *My strong opinion* is that it is when project manager is appointed. The order has come, is forwarded to project manager, and that's it.

The emphasis is used in the quotation in order to point out that the definition provided by the interviewee is his/her personal opinion, not a fact nor a company level definition.

To summarize the results of the analysis of the interviews we can conclude that the definition of the project start has obviously been accepted to be very difficult to create. Moreover, it is an ambiguous issue and the definition of the project start date is at least partly arbitrary and may have no real connection to the real start of the project. In the world of contract based — or outsourced — software projects the relationship between the project start and the project start date written into the schedule is not always a reality. The ambiguity of the project start definition may make it difficult for software companies to define and show if a project has been profitable or not. If a part of the project work has been done without including that work in the official project, then that work has been done outside the official agreement and the situation is not tenable considering project success and a prosperous long-time partnership.

In order to make the situation clearer and both the customer benefits and the supplier benefits easier to achieve the relationship between project start and the project start date should be clarified and the term defined. In the following section such definitions are proposed and the some impacts of the current ambiguous situation discussed.

5 Definitions

It seems to be the case that the state of the practice is as fuzzy as the almost non-existent literature definition. The start date of the project has to be defined somehow, but every project manager seems to have his/her own definition for the project start and therefore he/she has his/her own definition also for the start date of the project. This type of ambiguity may result in a situation in which the supplier performs work that is necessary for the project but not included in the agreement.

This kind of situation is not beneficial for the supplier because there is a risk to lose not only the profitability of one project but also the profitability of other projects if

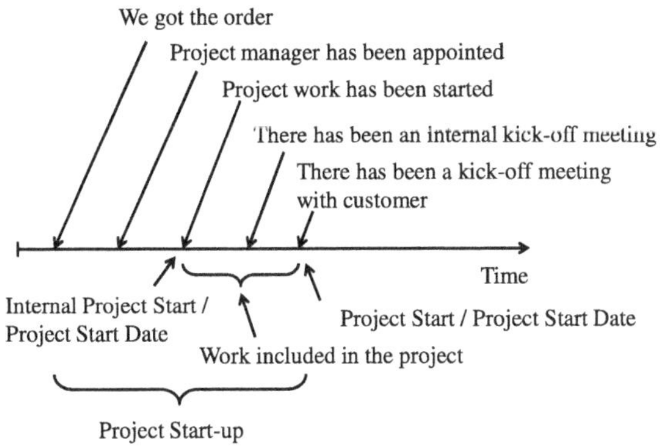

Fig. 3. The definitions of the project start and other relevant times

there are many project managers who may act alike. Therefore the project start, project start date and the work included in a project work should be defined. These definitions were made by the author, and the definitions and their relationships are presented in the Fig. 3.

The most obvious moment for having the project start is the day when the supplier and the customer have the project kick-off meeting. This moment is defined also as the project start date. The customer may expect the supplier to have the project team up and running immediately after that meeting. The project start-up activities that are required should be performed before the project start.

For the supplier the project start-up activities are a necessary part of the project [11][24][10] and actually a part of the project effort. The start-up activities should be included in the project work from moment when the project work has been started (internal project start / project start date) to moment when the kick-off meeting has been performed with the customer. In that span a remarkable amount of work has been done and that effort should be included into the project despite the fact that the work is invisible to the customer.

6 Conclusion

When discussing successful software development project, we should consider all three success criteria, which are: 1) time, cost, and scope, 2) customer benefits, and 3) supplier benefits. In order to achieve those criteria and create a prosperous relationship between the customer and the supplier there has to be a common understanding of several issues. One of the issues is the definition of the project start and the role of project start-up activities discussed in [10], and [24].

Although the amount of effort spent in the start-up activities may be remarkable — at least there is a minimum amount of effort that a project start-up requires [11] — the relationship between those activities and the project start has not been clearly defined in literature. The relationship is vague in practice also and an interview of practitioners provided five different definitions, all of which have a clearly different meaning considering the project start and the type of work that belongs to a project.

Without proper understanding which start-up activities are needed, which start-up activities are included in project work, when project starts, and what is actual start date of the project, there is a risk that proper planning and design are not carried out thoroughly enough, effort estimations made before and after project start are faulty, project planned delivery date has been missed before project start, and overall resource usage planning of the company becomes more challenging. All these difficulties minimize possibility to achieve successful project from supplier's point of view: to have commercial success of the project and potential for future revenue. Moreover, basic project management metrics such effort, duration and timetable are misleading from the beginning the project and comparing different projects is unreliable.

The understanding may be based on the definition proposed in this article. The definition is that the project start and also the project start date is the moment when the supplier and the customer have a kick-off meeting, but the internal project start / project start date is the moment when the supplier performs the first project start-up efforts. The project work that should be agreed includes the start-up effort required by the project. The customer and the supplier should agree on the inclusion of the start-up effort to the official agreement.

Although the reported study is based on a fairly limited number of interviews its results can be considered valid because similar problematic have been reported earlier [24]. The actual usability of the proposed definition in the business environment and the detailed steps present in the start-up phase are left for further research.

Acknowledgment

This research was funded by the Finnish Funding Agency for Technology and Innovation (Tekes) with the grant 70011/08, and supported in part by Science Foundation Ireland grant 03/CE2/I303_1 to Lero—The Irish Software Engineering Research Centre.

References

1. Dvir, D., Raz, T., Shenhar, A.J.: An empirical analysis of the relationship between project planning and project success. International Journal of Project Management 21, 89–95 (2003)
2. Atkinson, R.: Project management: cost, time and quality, two best guesses and a phenomenon, it's time to accept other success criteria. International Journal of Project Management 17, 337–342 (1999)
3. ISO/IEC, ed.: ISO/IEC 12207-2008: Systems and software engineering — Software life cycle processes. ISO/IEC, Geneva, Switzerland (2008)
4. Cooke-Davies, T.: The "real" success factors on projects. International Journal of Project Management 20, 185–190 (2002)
5. Munns, A.K., Bjeirmi, B.F.: The role of project management in achieving project success. International Journal of Project Management 14, 81–87 (1996)
6. Haried, P., Ramamurthy, K.: Evaluating the success in international sourcing of information technology projects: The need for a relational client-vendor approach. Project Management Journal 40, 56–71 (2009)
7. Cooper, M.J., Budd, C.S.: Tying the pieces together: A normative framework for integrating sales and project operations. Industrial Marketing Management 36, 173–182 (2007)

8. Fangel, M.: Planning project start-up. International Journal of Project Management 2, 242–245 (1984)
9. Egginton, B.: The project start-up process — getting it to work better. Engineering Management Journal 6, 88–92 (1996)
10. Turner, J.R., Cochrane, R.A.: Goals-and-methods matrix: coping with projects with ill defined goals and/or methods of achieving them. International Journal of Project Management 11, 93–102 (1993)
11. Barry, E.J., Mukhopadhyay, T., Slaughter, S.A.: Software project duration and effort: An empirical study. Information Technology and Management 3, 113–136 (2002)
12. Atkinson, R., Crawford, L., Ward, S.: Fundamental uncertainties in projects and the scope of project management. International Journal of Project Management 24, 687–698 (2006)
13. Fangel, M.: To start or to start-up?: That is the key question of project initiation. International Journal of Project Management 9, 5–9 (1991)
14. ISO/IEC, ed.: ISO/IEC 15288–2008: Systems and software engineering — System life cycle processes. ISO/IEC, Geneva, Switzerland (2008)
15. ISO/IEC, ed.: ISO/IEC 15504: Information Technology — Process Assessment. ISO/IEC, Geneva, Switzerland (2004)
16. ISO/IEC, ed.: ISO/IEC 16085: Systems and software engineering — Life cycle processes — Risk management. ISO/IEC, Geneva, Switzerland (2006)
17. ISO/IEC, ed.: ISO/IEC 16326: Systems and software engineering — Life cycle processes — Project management. ISO/IEC, Geneva, Switzerland, Final Draft (2009)
18. Project Management Institute, ed.: A Guide to the Project Management Body of Knowledge, 3rd edn. Project Management Institute, Pennsylvania, USA (2004), ANSI/PMI 99-001-2004
19. Sommerville, I.: Software Engineering, 8th edn. Pearson Education Limited, London (2007)
20. Pressman, R.S.: Software Engineering: A Practitioner's Approach, 6th edn. McGraw-Hill, New York (2005)
21. Royce, W.: Software project management: a unified framework. Addison-Wesley Longman, Inc., Amsterdam (1998)
22. Torp, O.: Efficient project start-up (2003), http://www.concept.ntnu.no/attachments/058_2004_johanesen_nordnett_efficientprojectstart_up_torp.pdf, Unpublished paper (accessed January 4, 2010)
23. Halman, J.I.M., Burger, G.T.N.: Evaluating effectiveness of project start-ups: an exploratory study. International Journal of Project Management 20, 81–89 (2002)
24. Haapio, T., Ahonen, J.J.: A case study on the success of introducing general non-construction activities for project management and planning improvement. In: Münch, J., Vierimaa, M. (eds.) PROFES 2006. LNCS, vol. 4034, pp. 151–165. Springer, Heidelberg (2006)

The Rosetta Stone Methodology – A Benefits Driven Approach to Software Process Improvement

Fionbarr McLoughlin and Ita Richardson

Lero – The Irish Software Engineering Research Centre
University of Limerick, Limerick, Ireland

Abstract. In response to the lack of a business-focused approach to software process improvement (SPI), the Rosetta Stone objective-driven SPI Methodology (RSM) has been developed which allows organizations to undertake SPI based on business-driven objectives using proven SPI methodologies. To demonstrate usefulness and practicality, the Rosetta Stone IGSI-ISM to CMMI Instance mapping (RS-ICMMI) is developed using a generic set of business objectives which are mapped to the CMMI (Staged) model using a modified version of GQM. This methodology and the RS-ICMMI instance have been validated by experts.

1 Introduction

In companies, a significant amount of capital expenditure and operating expenses are spent on Information and Communications Technology (ICT). In fact, according to the Organization for Economic Co-Operation and Development (OECD) [1], total worldwide spending on ICT was expected to reach $2.964 trillion in 2005 (the most recent OECD estimates). Therefore, it is important that the ICT maturing process continues to evolve. From a Software Process Improvement (SPI) perspective, there are several competing and, in some cases, complementary standards such as the Software Engineering Institute's CMMI for Development version 1.2 [2]; the International Standards Organization's (ISO) ISO15504 [3], formerly known as SPICE; the Trillium Model [4], developed originally in 1991 by Bell Canada; the ISO's 9000-3 standard [5] and the ISO 9001:2000 standard [6], a process-driven approach to define, establish and maintain software quality within an organization that will allow organizations to meet their business objectives [7].

Quite a deal of literature supports the hypothesis that implementation of the various SPI methodologies will result in benefits to organizations. However, they do so from an IT perspective. There are few, if any, methodologies which approach systems improvement from a business goals and objectives perspective. Our research has demonstrated that these benefits come about *as a result* of implementation of SPI which is IT-centric. In other words, ICT drives the business benefits. The Rosetta Stone Methodology[1], developed and evaluated as part of our research and presented in this paper,

---

[1] The Rosetta Stone is an Egyptian stele found by the French in 1799 with three translations of a single passage in Hieroglyphics, Demotic, and classical Greek. It allowed scholars to translate between these three languages. The analogy is that the Rosetta Stone Methodology will allow the translation between business objectives and SPI methodologies.

M. Ali Babar, M. Vierimaa, and M. Oivo (Eds.): PROFES 2010, LNCS 6156, pp. 366–379, 2010.
© Springer-Verlag Berlin Heidelberg 2010

consists of a methodology which allows businesses to undertake business- and organizational-driven goals and objectives.

Section 2 of this paper describes the reported benefits of implementing software process improvement, and our research method is described in section 3. In section 4, we present the development of the Rosetta Stone Methodology, its constituent elements and a specific implementation. This is followed by a discussion and conclusion in sections 5 and 6.

2 Benefits of SPI

Software and systems development methodologies have evolved to enable the development of ever larger and more complex solutions to real-world problems. However, there are concerns and while advances have been made there are still quite a few horror stories reported [8]. To get to where we are now has resulted from the gradual evolution of development processes. This evolution includes, but is not limited to, solutions such as software inspections [9], structured programming [10], software process improvement techniques and project management methodologies. We are cognisant of the work of Solon and Statz [11] and Zahran [12] when they discuss the difficulties of using benchmark SPI benefits in making business cases for the implementation of SPI. While at a high level benefits are categorized consistently in macro terms such as Return On Investment (ROI), Quality, Defect Density, and Reduced Cycle Times, upon more detailed review results are not normalized nor is there consistency in how benefits are defined. An additional problem is that much of the literature deals with the results of SPI from individual organizations. Also, there are benefits which, while of interest to the community as a whole, are mentioned in only a small minority of research reports.

We now present an overview of the reported benefits resulting from the implementation of SPI. Our intention here is not to provide an exhaustive review of all the reported benefits of SPI but merely to demonstrate that there is considerable evidence to support the view that SPI is beneficial to organizations.

2.1 Reported Benefits of SPI

Return On Investment (ROI) reviews often feature large companies. Humphrey et al. [13] described the Software Process Improvement initiative at Hughes Aircraft where, during a 4 year period (1987-1990) they progressed to CMM Level 3. From an ROI perspective, the assessments cost Hughes Aircraft \$45,000 and a further \$400,000 over the two-year program of improvements. Hughes estimated savings to be about \$2 million. The effects of a CMM-based SPI program at Software Systems Laboratory (SSL) within Raytheon Inc. are described in [14], [15]. Over 5 years this program cost \$5million, and the organisation progressed from Level 1 to Level 3, and was working towards a Level 4 assessment. ROI had increased by a factor of 7.7 based on a sample of six projects. Boeing STS, a division of Boeing Inc. that supports space transportation programs for the Department of Defense and NASA, achieved a rating of CMM Level 5 in July 1996. Yamamura and Wigle [16] present an analysis of cost-to-benefit ratios citing a reduction in rework effort by 31% due to formal inspection alone - this translated into a 7.7:1 ROI. In reporting on the progression of the Oklahoma City Air Logistics Center (OC-ALC) from CMM Level 1 to CMM Level 4, Butler and Lipke [17] reported that, for an investment of $6 million, the OC-ALC calculated a reduction in cost of $50.5 million – an 8.4:1 ROI. To further support the argument that ROI increases as a result of implementation of CMMI, the SEI [18] reported an increased ROI of between 2:1 and 27.7:1%, with a median increase in ROI of 4.7:1, based on 16 separate data points. In addition to the individual reports outlined above, both El Emam and Briand [19] and Krasner [20] report summary evidence of the benefits of SPI.

There are many studies which demonstrate that productivity increases as a result of software process improvement. Brodman and Johnson [21], [22], [23] investigated the effect of improving process capability in 33 companies who were at various levels of CMM maturity. They demonstrate increases in productivity ranging from 6.4% to 100%. A study of four projects was undertaken by Software Productivity Research Inc. of the benefits of SPI within Oklahoma City Air Logistics Center (OC-ALC) [24]. This determined that there was a 10 times increase in productivity from the baseline project to their most recent project (while OC-ALC was at CMM Level 2, working its way to Level 4). Dion [14], [15] also reported Productivity increases of a factor of 2.3 in a 5 year time period as a result of implementing CMM. Also reporting productivity increases as a result of implementation of CMM are Herbsleb et al.[25], [26]. Their report shows a productivity increase of between 9% and 67% over a wide range of maturity levels after implementing CMM, with the median increase being 35%.

Goldenson and Gibson [27] detail some preliminary results from the application of CMMI process improvement. In particular, they quoted a 30% increase in Productivity as a result of implementation of CMMI. In a follow-up to the initial 2003 report, the SEI [28] attributed productivity increases as a result of implementation of CMMI of between 9% and 255%, with a median value of 62%. Garmus and Iwanicki [29] report productivity increases of 132% (based on Function Point/Effort Month), and an effort reduction by 50%. NASA's (National Aeronautics and Space Administration) SEL (Software Engineering Laboratory) spent 10 years undertaking an SPI initiative at their Goddard Space Flight Center. Reporting on the SEL in 1994, Krasner, Pyles et al. [30] report that predicted costs were always within 10% of actual costs; only one deadline was missed in 10 years; maintenance cost of code was half that at other IBM software facilities; defects of 0.01 per thousand lines of source code (KSLOC); and an increased error detection rate of 95%. Krasner [31] further reported a reduction in error rates of 75% between 1985 and 1993, a reduction of software development costs by 55%, and an increase of reuse by 300%. He also notes that costs have become more predictable. Yamamura and Wigle [16], in their report on their implementation of CMM Level 5, report that their processes were finding 89% of the defects – thus leaving 11% still baked in. After implementing SPI, virtually 100% of all defects are found. Putnam and Myers [32] reported that quality improvements (by defect ratio) fell from just over 0.1 defects per 1 KSLOC to 0 defects per KSLOC.

The SEI [18], based on 20 separate data points, has attributed quality increases of between 7 and 132%, with a median of 50% to the successful implementation of CMMI. From a defect perspective, McLoone and Rohde [33] found a significant reduction in the hours/KSLOC metric and another reduction in the dollars/KSLOC cost while Garmus and Iwanicki [29] report a reduction in defect density of 75%, all through CMMI implementation. Liu [34] reports significant improvements as a result of Motorola's implementation of CMMI Level 5 in their sites in China. Between 2003 and 2006, Cost of Quality was reduced from approximately 35% to 25%, fewer defects were inserted into code and the faults per line of code was reduced by 13.01% from its pre-CMMI Level 5 level. Studies analysed demonstrate that as organizations implement more quality-oriented processes, the quality of code improves. Additionally, quality increases as process capability maturity levels increase. We also note that it becomes more difficult, and therefore more costly, to increase quality between higher maturity levels.

There is a note of caution, however, associated with these reported results. While there appears to be clear evidence of a correlation between increased ROI and implementation of various SPI initiatives, there also seems to be a trade-off between ROI and Quality, which would seem natural. In the case of SPI programs like CMM and CMMI, the higher an organization progresses up the maturity ladder, the more quality processes are put in place and therefore there is a tendency for quality to increase but, at the same time, ROI decreases [35]. As Fayad and Laitinen [36] note, "moving to levels 4 and 5 sounds worthwhile but there is little empirical evidence to support the move." In addition, while there is consistent evidence of increases in productivity coinciding with the implementation of CMM/CMMI, there is also evidence to suggest that the rate of increase in productivity is not uniformly higher as successive CMM/CMMI levels are implemented. In addition, some research suggests that at least part of the productivity increases relates to technological innovation as a result of process improvement.

2.2 SPI Challenges

There are several challenges associated with the interpretation and use of the research we have reported in the previous sections. Firstly, there is a lack of uniformity in the definition and interpretation of the metrics/indicators used as evidence of the benefits of SPI. Different researchers and practitioners use the same metric to mean different things. Secondly, for various reasons, not all companies, even when using standard industry definitions for metrics, use the same metrics in their studies. The effect of this is that, while there may be quite a lot of research, it is sometimes difficult to find like-metrics upon which to base comparisons. Thirdly, companies may be reluctant to divulge information for commercial reasons, particularly if the results of their SPI effort paint them in a worse light than their peers. Therefore, it is difficult to find studies which report negatively on process improvements.

However, to say that SPI in itself is the silver bullet for the software development process would be less than disingenuous. Nothing in life is free and SPI is no exception to this rule. Various criticisms such as high cost, rigidity in approach, and the increased administrative overhead associated with SPI have all been levelled at SPI – or more particularly at SPI models such as CMMI or ISO15504 [37], [38]. These have been legitimate criticisms. However, it is up to individual organizations to balance the increased costs of assessment and accreditation, the increased size and overhead associated with the SPI model, and any issues arising from rigidity in application of the model with the benefits to the organization as a whole.

In summary, there is a lot of evidence in the literature to show that there are definite benefits to be realized from implementing SPI. However, we have noted little evidence to show that implementation of particular process improvements have a particular effect on the business requirement.

2.3 Bridging the Gap between SPI and the Business

As noted in section 1, there are several SPI methodologies currently available for organizations to use in order to improve their software processes. These methodologies are software centric and are often not tightly linked to an organization's business goals and objectives. In fact, Debou and Kuntzmann-Combelles [39] contend that the major bottleneck to the success of SPI initiatives is the lack of business orientation in how the program is run. Specifically with regard to CMMI, Liu et al. [40] state that there exists a disconnect between business goals and maturity levels. The RSM bridges these gaps by adding two weapons to the practitioner's arsenal. Firstly, it provides a generic methodology, based on a modified version of GQM [41], [42], which can be used to couple a generic benefits model to an arbitrary SPI. Secondly, and perhaps more importantly from a practitioner's perspective, it provides an implementation of the RSM using a for-profit benefits model tied to an industry-standard SPI methodology which has been validated by industry peers and modified based on their feedback.

3 Research Methodology

The research commenced with a literature review and initial interviews with academics and industry personnel. No approach was identified which supported businesses in deciding which software processes to improve to gain specific business benefits. Therefore, the purpose of our research is to create an objectives-driven approach whose use should allow this. It is expected to save organizations both time and resources by allowing them to focus only on those process areas which have a direct bearing on the business objectives they are trying to achieve.

The first step was to create a generic methodology, the Rosetta Stone Methodology (RSM). This was done by creating a meta-model of all the elements involved in an SPI implementation (see LHS of Fig. 1). After this, a step-by-step approach was developed which guides practitioners in using an SPI methodology and benefits model to define a mapping between business-focused benefits and individual SPI process areas. In essence, this process allows practitioners to substitute the meta-model with a concrete implementation instance of the model (see RHS of Fig. 1). This mapping is then used as the basis to answer various questions regarding which process areas should be implemented to achieve specific business benefits and in what particular order.

To demonstrate the implementation of the RSM in a specific instance, we investigated available return on investment models which did not deal exclusively with software process improvement, but with which existing SPI models could be combined. We chose to work with the IGSI-ISM Benefits Model [43] and CMMI Version 1.2 [2]. This is done as follows:

1. Determine which benefits model and which SPI model which is to be used;
2. Define the mapping (relationships) between objectives/benefits and software processes;
3. Answer the questions that are relevant to the individual organization.

The initial methodology, meta-model and implementation instance were developed as described and were then reviewed by a small group of peers for validity. For triangulation purposes, they were validated through a Delphi review of 17 people with an average work experience in the software industry of 19 years along with an average of 11 years of SPI experience. Additionally, to validate the implementation instance, a group of experts was interviewed about each relationship within the RS-ICMMI model. Out of a pool of ten experts, two experts were randomly selected to review a set of IGSI-ISM Benefit/CMMI Level 2 combinations. They discussed whether they agreed with the relationship presented and where they had seen these relationships work in practice. This process was repeated until all combinations had been reviewed. In some cases, the RS-ICMMI was modified as a result of these interviews.

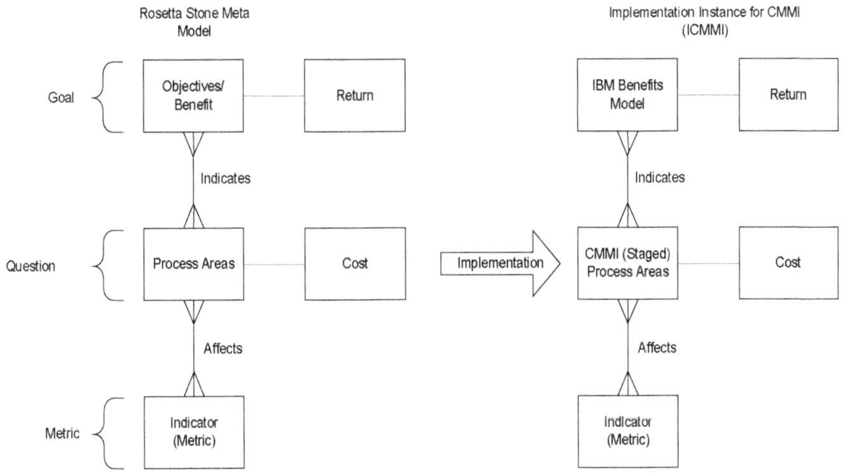

Fig. 1. Rosetta Stone objective-driven software process improvement Model (RSM)

4 Rosetta Stone Methodology

While there are many reported benefits from SPI projects, our observation is that the SPI agenda has been undertaken to improve particular processes for the process-sake, rather than organizational benefits as the primary objective. This is typically not the way the commercial world works. Therefore, to achieve a business-oriented focus, the outcome from our research will allow organizations to achieve organization-specific objectives through improving their software process.

In the first instance we have developed the Rosetta Stone Meta Model. The meta-model is, in essence, an entity-relationship model which relates together all the major elements within any SPI initiative – business objectives desired, returns associated with achieving the business benefits, process areas, costs of implementing the process areas, and the metrics/indicators to determine progress/regression towards the objectives (see LHS of Fig. 1). The Rosetta Stone Methodology (RSM) consists of using the Rosetta Stone Meta Model to create a concrete instance of the meta model. The main benefits of using this methodology are that users are able to:

- Achieve specific business objectives by targeting particular software processes to improve in order to achieve business benefits
- Understand what benefits may be derived from the improvement of which particular software process
- Given a set of existing metrics and values, determine what processes may be more readily and quickly implemented than others.

4.1 Objectives, Process Areas, and Indicators

The most important element in RSM is the *set of business objectives* or *benefits* which an organization wishes to achieve. If possible, these should be hierarchical so that the achievement of one should lead to the achievement of others. For example, if on-time delivery of projects is achieved (one possible business objective) then this should result in better customer satisfaction (another possible business objective). Each benefit should have some form of *return* associated with it – some way of determining, frequently quantifiable but sometimes qualitative, the value of the benefit. Returns are meaningful to the business and, as such, are typically not SPI-type metrics such as defects/KSLOC or defects/function point – unless, of course, the business is primarily focused on software development. For example, if productivity were the objective, it might be possible to say that, for an x% increase in productivity, there should be an increase in profits of y%. For each objective, there is at least one *indicator* - a set of metric(s) that are an indication that a particular benefit has occurred. In other words, a set of indicators that can prove (or disprove) that progress is being made towards a specific benefit – a way to measure a benefit. *Process areas* are those processes which are being improved during the SPI program, and would include, for example requirements management, risk management and project planning. Each process area has a *cost* associated with it – costs associated with implementing the improvement.

In order to make a concrete instance of the model, the practitioner must first choose which objectives are most relevant to their business and then choose which SPI model is most appropriate for their organization. These two entities then drive the choice of costs, returns, and indicators. In addition, it is important to define the relationships between the objectives/benefits model and the software processes. This can be done using specific instances of the model.

4.2 Return, Costs and ROI

For the majority of organizations, where profit is a primary goal, benefits should ultimately lead to a monetary impact on the organization. One of the main advantages of RSM is that it is now possible to tie software process improvements to specific benefits due to the fact that the benefits defined in RSM are very granular. It must be recognized, however, that in some cases it is difficult to measure the monetary value of a benefit – for example, how can a dollar value be put on increased team morale? In the case of RSM, the return on the SPI is compared to the cost of improving the specific software process. Great care must be taken, therefore, to not only capture the monetary equivalents that accrue from the benefits of process improvement but also the cost of implementation.

5 Rosetta Stone Methodology: CMMI Implementation Instance

We demonstrate the implementation of the RSM through mapping the CMMI (staged) model to a benefits model developed by IBM Global Services, the IGSI-ISM Benefits Model [43]. The implementation of this instance is illustrated in the RHS of Fig. 1 and the final output is the RS-ICMMI.

The IGSI-ISM model (see Fig. 2) shows the relationships between the various benefits which culminate in the ultimate benefit for the organisation – *increased revenues/profits*. This benefit can be achieved through relationships between 21 separate identifiable benefit areas. These include benefits such as lower time-to-market, better risk management and competitive proposals. In addition, the model is a hierarchy of benefits – higher level benefits are derived from elements that are lower in the benefit tree. For example, *better product quality* leads to *increased productivity*. Similarly, *increasing the understanding of customer needs* leads to *setting right customer expectations,* thus to *improved predictability* and to *more competitive proposals*. Both *increased productivity* and *more competitive proposals* lead to an *improved image* which feeds directly to *increased revenues/profits*.

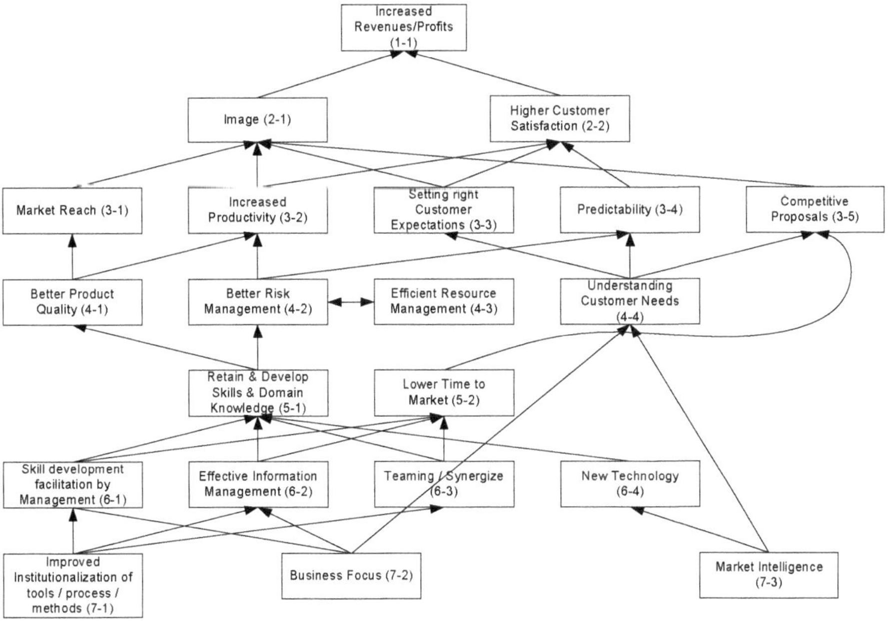

Fig. 2. IGSI-ISM Benefits Model

The RSM requires us to map the IGSI-ISM Benefits model to the software processes whose improvements will provide these benefits. To do this, each the generic goal, specific goal and specific practice of each CMMI process area was reviewed, determining which ones have particular relevance to the IGSI-ISM benefit model. To define the mapping between objectives/benefits and software processes, a modified approach to Basili's Goal-Question-Metric approach [41], [41] is used. A *reverse mapping* between process areas (Questions) and business objectives (Goals) is created by asking what process areas (Questions) impact what business objectives (Goal). In effect, the reverse lookup asks "What objectives does this process area fulfil?"

We note here that not all benefits are equal and the RSM differentiates between primary and secondary benefits. A *primary* benefit of a process area is one that is brought about as a direct result of implementation of that process area where the cause and effect relationship between the process area implementation and the benefit is very strong. *Secondary* benefits are those benefits which are not primary benefits and include *derived* benefits. A *derived* benefit is a benefit which is a hierarchical ancestor of either a primary or secondary benefit. As we shall see later, the benefit classification is used to determine the recommended order of process areas to be implemented.

5.1 Examples of CMMI Level 2 Process Area to Benefit Mappings

Requirements Management. The Requirements Management (REQM) process area contains 1 Specific Goal (SG) which in turn consists of 5 Specific Practices (SP). The goal is that "requirements are managed and inconsistencies with project plans and work products are indentified", maintaining a current approved set of requirements over the life of the project. REQM requires the implementation of the obtaining of an understanding of requirements (SP 1.1-1), the obtaining of a commitment to requirements (SP 1.2-2), the management of requirements (SP 1.3-1), and the identification of inconsistencies between project work and requirements.

Based on the specifications of the REQM as defined by the SEI, the following are the expected primary benefits of implementing REQM:

- *Better Risk Management*: By managing requirements and identifying inconsistencies, we are better able to identify alternative strategies and avoid building software that isn't part of a customer's requirements.
- *Understanding Customer Needs*: Proper management of requirements forces us to consistently review those requirements and thus focus on understanding customer needs. By indentifying inconsistencies between requirements, plans, and work products we are constantly ensuring that the customer's needs are always foremost.
- *Lower Time to Market*: by identifying inconsistencies up front, we will spend less time working on items that are not required by customers or that are inconsistent with customers' needs and expectations. As a result, less time will be spent on rework, thus saving resources and reducing time to market.

Configuration Management. The purpose of Configuration Management (CM) is to establish and maintain the integrity of work products using configuration identification, configuration control, configuration status accounting, and configuration audits

[44], [45]. CM consists of 3 SGs – SG1 (the establishment of baselines), SG2 (the tracking and control of changes), and SG3 (the establishment of integrity). In software projects it is absolutely essential that all artefacts are correctly baselined and tracked. Without this baselining and tracking, there is no guarantee that code, requirements or any other project artifact will be consistent with each other, thus increasing risk and reducing quality. In fact, the opposite is true, effective configuration management is essential for increasing quality and reducing risk. In addition, as [28] note, "configuration management, and in particular version control, plays a role in supporting to work of teams" and that "software configuration management serves as a mechanism for communication, change management and reproducibility."

Configuration management allows projects to properly track the various parts that make up their products. By instituting CM, multiple teams will be able to edit/modify code without stepping over each others' toes. In addition, CM allows project teams to map changes back to specific issues or requirements, this increasing product quality and managing risk. Therefore in the RS-CMMI, CM results in the primary benefits: *Better Quality Product, Better Risk Management, Teaming / Synergize.*

5.2 Achieving Specific Business Objectives

In the exemplar we have demonstrated that organisations may (normally) require increased revenues/profits, and are not particularly interested in which software process improvement methodology or software process area is used to deliver the business benefits. The process to determine which process areas to execute in order to achieve specific business benefits is as follows:

1. Determine which of the IGSI-ISM objectives that we wish to achieve. This is normally determined from outside the software process improvement group, possibly from either external clients or senior management. We will use *lower time-to-market* as the objective in this example.
2. Using the IGSI-ISM model (Fig. 2), determine which other objectives, if any, contribute to achieving our primary objective. We observe that *skill development facilitation by management, effective information management, teaming/synergize, improved institutionalization of tools/process/methods* and *business focus* all contribute to *lower time-to-market.*
3. Using the implementation mapping developed during the creation of the implementation instance of the RSM methodology, establish which process areas contribute to both the primary and secondary objectives of the selected business benefits. For illustrative purposes we will use *lower time-to-market* (node 5-2 in Fig. 2) as the example benefit we wish to achieve and have provided a reduced version of the RS-ICMMI mapping in Table 1 which contains only those process areas which have *lower time-to-market* as either a primary or secondary benefit.
4. Rank the PAs in order of relevance and implementation. There are quite a few PAs which have an effect on lower time-to-market. Most organizations have finite resources and therefore will need to prioritise their implementation. There are many different ways to rank them. More consideration should be given to those PAs that *primarily* satisfy a particularly objective. In the case of lower time-to-market, we would implement Process and Product Quality Assurance (PPQA) before implementing Configuration Management (CM) as PPQA primarily satisfies lower time-to-market while CM only secondarily satisfies lower time-to-market (see Table 1).

> Additionally, we should observe the software process model we are using. Although within RS-ICMMI both Requirements Management (RM) and Requirements Development (RD) directly satisfy *lower time-to-market*, as, within the CMMI staged model, RM is a Level 2 PA, it should be undertaken before RD. Using these principles, the first three process areas that we propose implementing to *lower time-to-market* from the Level 2 Process Areas would be Requirements Management, Supplier Agreement Management, Measurement and Analysis and Process and Product Quality Assurance. Configuration Management would not be implemented until later as lower-time-time market is only a secondary benefit. By ordering implementation based on relevance, as above, we ensure that those process areas are implemented which have most impact on the business objective. As a result, we implement those process areas up front which provide biggest bang for the buck for the business objective desired.

We must recognize, however, that this proposed methodology is not without its limitations. From a practical perspective, while both the methodology and the RS-ICMMI implementation instance have been reviewed at length by practitioners, it has not yet

Table 1. Example Objective - Lower Time to Market

Staged Level	Process Area	Expected Primary IGSI ROI Benefits	Expected Secondary IGSI ROI Benefits
2 - Managed	Requirements Management	4-2, 4-4, 5-2	7-3, 5-1, 4-3, 3-4, 3-5, 2-1, 2-2, 1-1
	Supplier Agreement Management	5-2, 4-1, 4-2, 3-4	3-1, 3-2, 3-3, 3-4, 2-1, 2-2, 1-1
	Measurement and Analysis	5-2, 4-1, 4-2, 3-4	3-1, 3-2, 3-3, 3-4, 2-1, 2-2, 1-1
	Process and Product Quality Assurance	7-1, 5-2, 4-1, 4-2, 3-4	6-1, 6-2, 6-3, 5-1, 5-2, 4-3, 4-4, 3-1, 3-2, 3-3, 3-4, 3-5, 2-1, 2-2, 1-1
	Configuration Management	6-3, 4-2, 4-1	5-1, 5-2, 4-3, 4-4, 3-1, 3-2, 3-3, 3-4, 3-5, 2-1, 2-2, 1-1
3 - Defined	Requirements Development	5-2, 4-1, 4-2, 4-4,	4-3, 3-1, 3-2, 3-3, 3-4, 3-5, 2-1, 2-2, 1-1
	Organizational Process Focus	7-1, 7-2, 7-3	6-1, 6-2, 6-3, 6-4, 5-1, 5-2, 4-1, 4-2, 4-3, 4-4, 3-1, 3-2, 3-3, 3-4, 3-5, 2-1, 2-2, 1-1
	Organizational Process Definition	7-1, 6-2	6-1, 6-3, 5-1, 5-2, 4-1, 4-2, 4-3, 4-4, 3-1, 3-2, 3-3, 3-4, 3-5, 2-1, 2-2, 1-1
	Organizational Training	6-1, 6-3	5-1, 5-2, 4-1, 4-2, 4-3, 4-4, 3-1, 3-2, 3-3, 3-4, 3-5, 2-1, 2-2, 1-1
	Integrated Project Management	6-3, 4-1, 4-2, 4-3, 4-4	5-1, 5-2, 3-1, 3-2, 3-3, 3-4, 3-5, 2-1, 2-2, 1-1
	Integrated Project Management for IPPD	6-3, 4-1, 4-2, 4-3, 4-4	5-1, 5-2, 3-1, 3-2, 3-3, 3-4, 3-5, 2-1, 2-2, 1-1
	Integrated Teaming	6-3, 6-2, 4-1, 4-3, 4-2, 4-4	5-1, 5-2, 3-1, 3-2, 3-3, 3-4, 3-5, 2-1, 2-2, 1-1
	Integrated Supplier Management	7-2, 7-3, 6-3, 6-4, 5-2, 4-1, 4-2, 3-4	5-1, 5-2, 4-3, 3-1, 3-2, 3-3, 3-5, 2-1, 2-2, 1-1
	Organizational Environment for Integration	7-1, 7-2, 6-2, 6-3, 5-2	6-1, 6-2, 6-4, 5-1, 5-2, 4-1, 4-2, 4-3, 4-4, 3-1, 3-2, 3-3, 3-4, 3-5, 2-1, 2-2, 1-1
4 - Quantitatively Managed	Organizational Process Performance	7-1, 7-2, 7-3, 6-2	6-1, 6-3, 5-1, 5-2, 4-1, 4-2, 4-3, 4-4, 3-1, 3-2, 3-3, 3-4, 3-5, 2-1, 2-2, 1-1
	Quantitative Project Management	5-2, 4-1, 4-2, 4-3	4-3, 4-4, 2-1, 3-3, 3-4, 3-5, 2-1, 2-2, 1-1
5 - Optimizing	Organizational Innovation and Deployment	7-1, 7-2, 7-3	6-1, 6-2, 6-3, 6-4, 5-1, 5-2, 4-1, 4-2, 4-3, 4-4, 3-1, 3-2, 3-3, 3-4, 3-5, 2-1, 2-2, 1-1
	Causal Analysis and Resolution	7-1, 6-2, 5-2, 4-1, 4-2, 4-3	6-1, 6-3, 5-1, 4-4, 3-1, 3-2, 3-3, 3-4, 3-5, 2-1, 3, 1-1

been actually put into practice. Another challenge is that this research has taken place over several years and one of the challenges is to keep the RS-ICMMI model up to date with the latest version of CMMI. Finally, while the IGSI-ISM Benefits model is a good generic business objectives model there are many organizations out there which do not follow a for-profit business model such as represented by the IGSI-ISM model. Further research may be appropriate to bring in other types of benefits model.

6 Conclusion

The purpose of this research was to develop a generic methodology that allows organizations to achieve specific business-focused objectives by implementing various existing and proven SPIs. While a business-driven approach to SPI is research-worthy in itself, in order for such a model to be successful in the real world it should be flexible enough to be able to support the sometimes vastly different organizational objectives of various types of business – government organizations, non-government organizations (NGOs), the military, and for-profit commercial companies to name but a few. Not only should it be flexible enough to support these various organization types, but it should also be customizable so that individual organizations are able to customize benefit models. In addition, as an enormous amount of effort has been spent on SPI and SPI research, any proposed model should leverage existing work as much as possible. In order to meet these objectives the Rosetta Stone methodology was developed. It is a generic benefits-driven methodology which, in its essence, allows practitioners to map from a benefits model which is appropriate to an organization to a proven SPI methodology. In addition, is it fully customizable and allows organizations to make adjustments to the model where they feel it appropriate.

This research has brought together business focus and SPI. Two business-focused SPI models are presented – the RSM meta-model which maps from arbitrary benefits models to arbitrary SPI models and the RS-CMMI model which maps from the IGSI-ISM benefits model to the CMMI (Staged) model. We are currently evaluating both models through case study research with software process practitioners.

Acknowledgement

This research was supported by the Science Foundation Ireland funded projects, Global Software Development in Small to Medium Sized Enterprises (GSD for SMEs) grant number 03/IN3/1408C and B4-Step grant number 02/IN.1/108 within Lero - the Irish Software Engineering Research Centre (http://www.lero.ie).

References

1. Organization for Economic Co-Operation and Development: OECD Information Technology Outlook, 2006. OECD (2006)
2. Software Engineering Institute: CMMI for Development Version 1.2. SEI (2006)
3. International Standards Organization: ISO/IEC 15504-2:2003 Information technology - Process assessment - Part 2: Performing an assessment (2003)

4. Coallier, F.: Trillium Reference Manual (1994)
5. International Standards Organization: ISO 9000-3. International Standards Organization (1994)
6. International Standards Organization: ISO 9001:2000. International Standards Organization (2000)
7. Hailey, V.A.: ISO 9001: A Tool for Systematic Software Process Improvement. In: Hunter, R., Thayer, R.H. (eds.) Software Process Improvement, pp. 291–309. IEEE Computer Society, Los Alamitos (2001)
8. Standish Group: The Chaos Report. The Standish Group (2009)
9. Fagan, M.E.: Design and Code inspections to reduce errors in program development. IBM Systems Journal 15, 182–211 (1976)
10. Dijkstra, E.: Go to statement considered harmful. Classics in Software Engineering, pp. 27–33. Yourdon Press (1979)
11. Solon Jr., R., Statz, J.: Benchmarking the ROI for Software Process Improvement (SPI). Software Tech. News 5, 6–11 (2002)
12. Zahran, S.: Business and Cost Justification of Software Process Improvement - "ROI from SPI". In: International Software Process Association Conference, Brighton, England (1996)
13. Humphrey, W.S., Snyder, T.R., Willis, D.R.: Software Process Improvement at Hughes Aircraft. IEEE Software 8, 11–23 (1991)
14. Dion, R.: Elements of a Process-Improvement Program. IEEE Software 9, 83–85 (1992)
15. Dion, R.: Process Improvement and the Corporate Balance Sheet. IEEE Software 10, 28–35 (1993)
16. Yamamura, G., Wigle, G.B.: SEI CMM Level 5: For the Right Reasons. CrossTalk - The Journal of Defense Software Engineering (1997)
17. Butler, K.L., Lipke, W.: Software Process Achievement at Tinker Air force Base, Oklahma. Software Engineering Institute, 58 (2000)
18. Software Engineering Institute: CMMI Performance Results - 2005, vol. 2008 (2005)
19. El Emam, K., Briand, L.: Cost and Benefits of Software Process Improvement. Fraunhofer IESE, 27 (1997)
20. Krasner, H.: Accumulating the body of Evidence for the Payoff of Software Process Improvement. In: Hunter, R., Thayer, R.H. (eds.) Software Process Improvement, pp. 519–539. IEEE, Los Alamitos (2001)
21. Brodman, J.G., Johnson, D.L.: Return on Investment (ROI) from Software Process Improvement as Measured by US Industry. Software Process: Improvement and Practice 1, 35–47 (1995)
22. Brodman, J.G., Johnson, D.L.: Return on Investment from Software Process Improvement as Measured by U.S. Industry. CrossTalk - The Journal of Defense Software Engineering (1996)
23. Brodman, J.G., Johnson, D.L.: Realities and Rewards of Software Process Improvement. IEEE Software 13, 99–101 (1996)
24. Butler, K.L.: The Economic Benefits of Software Process Improvement. CrossTalk - The Journal of Defense Software Engineering 1995 (1995)
25. Herbsleb, J., Carleton, A., Rozum, J., Siegel, J., Zubrow, D.: Benefits of CMM-Based Software Process Improvement: Initial Results. Software Engineering Institute, Carnegie-Mellon University (1994)
26. Herbsleb, J., Carleton, A., Rozum, J., Siegel, J., Zubrow, D.: Benefits of CMM-Based Software Process Improvement: Executive Summary of Results. Software Engineering Institute, 16 (1994)

27. Goldenson, D.R., Gibson, D.L.: Demonstrating the Impact and Benefits of CMMI®:An Update and Preliminary Results. The Software Engineering Institute, 55 (2003)
28. Burzcuk, S.P., Appleton, B.: Software Configuration Management Patterns: Effective Teamwork, Practical Integration. Addison Wesley, Reading (2002)
29. Garmus, D., Iwanicki, S.: Improved Performance Should Be Expected from Process Improvement. Software Tech. News 10, 14–17 (2007)
30. Krasner, H., Pyles, J., Wohlwend, H.: A Case History of the Space Shuttle Onboard Systems Project (1994)
31. Krasner, H.: A Case History of Process Improvements at the NASA Software Engineering Laboratory (1995)
32. Putnam, L.H., Myers, W.: How Solved is the Cost Estimation Problem. IEEE Software 14, 105–107 (1997)
33. McLoone, P.J., Rohde, S.L.: Performance Outcomes of CMMI-Based Process Improvements. Software Tech. News 10, 5–9 (2007)
34. Liu, A.Q.: Motorola Software Group's China Center: Value Added by CMMI. Software Tech. News 10, 18–23 (2007)
35. O'Neill, D.: Determining Return on Investment Using Software Inspections. CrossTalk - The Journal of Defense Software Engineering (2003)
36. Fayad, M.E., Laitinen, M.: Process Assessment Considered Wasteful. Communications of the ACM 40, 125–128 (1997)
37. Jones, C.: The economics of software process improvement. IEEE Computer 29, 95–97 (1996)
38. Reifer, D.: The CMMI: it's formidable. The Journal of Systems and Software 50, 97–98 (2000)
39. Debou, C., Kuntzmann-Combelles, A.: Linking Software Process Improvement to Business Strategies: Experiences from Industry. Software Process: Improvement and Practice 5, 55–64 (2000)
40. Liu, X.F., Sun, Y., Kane, G., Kyoya, Y., Noguchi, K.: Business-oriented Software Process Improvement Based on CMM using QFD. Software Process Improvement and Practice 11, 573–589 (2006)
41. Basili, V.: Software Modeling and Measurement: The Goal/Question/Metric Paradigm. University of Maryland (1992)
42. Basili, V., Caldiera, G., Rombach, H.D.: The Goal Question Metric Approach. In: Marciniak, J.J. (ed.) Encyclopedia of Software Engineering, vol. 1. John Wiley & Sons Inc., Chichester (1994)
43. Goyal, A., Kanungo, S., Muthu, V., Jayadevan, S.: ROI for SPI: Lessons from Initiatives at IBM Global Services India. In: SEPG 2001 (2001)
44. Chrissis, M.B., Konrad, M., Shrum, S.: CMMI: Guidelines for Process Integration and Product Improvement. Addison-Wesley, Boston (2003)
45. Software Engineering Institute: CMMI for Software Engineering, Version 1.1, Staged Representation (CMMI-SW, V1.1, Staged) - CMU/SEI-2002-TR-029 (2002)

Defining and Monitoring Strategically Aligned Software Improvement Goals

Andrea Oliveira Soares Barreto and Ana Regina Rocha

COPPE/UFRJ, Universidade Federal do Rio de Janeiro
Caixa Postal 68511, CEP 21945-970, Rio de Janeiro, Brazil
{ansoares,darocha}@cos.ufrj.br

Abstract. Software engineers are always aiming at improving software processes and products. However, the adoption of these improvements on software organizations must be aligned to their strategic goals. Otherwise, these improvements may not improve the organization. However, to guarantee this alignment can be complex, since improvement initiatives would have to be planned and monitored considering aspects starting from strategic level and going all the way to the organization daily operations. Thus, this work presents an approach to define and monitor software improvement goals, which are decompositions of strategic goals and are related to software products or processes. Our approach comprises strategic, tactical and operational planning activities, always aiming at strategic alignment. As important tools to monitor the goals defined, software measurement and statistical process control are also considered. An infrastructure to monitor the goals is described, and also an experience of use of the approach at a Brazilian software development organization.

Keywords: Software Improvement Goal, Strategic Planning, Software Process.

1 Introduction

The increase of demand for high quality software products has forced organizations to find out alternatives to improve their products, including the improvement of their software processes. However, the search for better software processes and products without aligning them to business goals can be insufficient. Software process improvement initiatives have to be consistent with business goals of an organization and also with its business strategy [1].

Although the literature highlights the need for strategic alignment in software process improvement [2], [3], [4], [5], [6], achieving this alignment may be difficult. Even existent software reference models, such as CMMI-DEV [5], do not provide proper guidance on how organizations should define their processes based on their strategic priorities. As a result, although the practices suggested by the models may be successfully deployed in an organization, there is no guarantee that they will satisfy business goals [2]. Moreover, translating business goals into actions and more specific plans that can be enacted in projects can be difficult, mainly when there is no specification of the steps to be followed.

M. Ali Babar, M. Vierimaa, and M. Oivo (Eds.): PROFES 2010, LNCS 6156, pp. 380–394, 2010.
© Springer-Verlag Berlin Heidelberg 2010

In this context, we define a software improvement goal as a decomposition of a business goal (i.e., it is strategically aligned) which is related to software products or processes and that can guide software process improvement.

One of the ways an organization can control its processes is through the use of statistical process control – SPC. Applying SPC means using statistical methods to analyze processes and provide subsidies for its improvement [5]. Moreover, SPC practices are required by maturity models, like the CMMI-DEV, to achieve their higher maturity levels. Although SPC can be seen as a practice usually performed only by more mature organizations, it can be a powerful tool to determine whether goals are being achieved or not. However, if SPC is adopted in an organization without taking business goals into account, it is possible that the initiative does not satisfy or even conflict with them. In this context, planning software process improvement initiatives that are strategically aligned can be even harder.

Software improvement goals must be measurable, making it possible to frequently check their achievement. If monitoring is not continuous, even if goals are strategically aligned, the effort to define suitable goals can be less beneficial, since it will not be possible to determine if they tend to be achieved. Nowadays, organizations have realized that monitoring and continuously analyzing business performance is crucial to achieve operational excellence, and to better align daily operations with long-term business strategies [7].

In this context, we present an approach that aims to define and monitor software improvement goals promoting their alignment with business goals. Our approach defines a method to support strategic planning activities, tactical planning activities related to software, considering software improvement goals, SPC and software measurement planning, and also project planning activities related to the defined goals. Our approach also defines an infrastructure to monitor the defined goals.

This paper is divided into six sections, including this introduction. Section 2 presents some background concepts and related work on strategic planning and software improvement goals. In Section 3 we present the proposed method to define software improvement goals and Section 4 describes the infrastructure to monitor the defined goals. Section 5 presents the experience of defining software improvement goals at a Brazilian software development organization. Finally, Section 6 presents some conclusions and future work.

2 Strategic Planning and Software Improvement Goals

According to Mintzberg et al. [8], strategic planning can be seen as the definition of goals, investments and plans based on the analysis of strengths, weaknesses, opportunities and threats related to the organization. Each organization can be analyzed in three different levels [9]:

- *Strategic or Top level*: the highest level of the organization, responsible for identifying the business goals and performing strategic planning. This level aims at long term goals.

- *Tactical or Middle level*: the intermediate level responsible for linking the strategic and operational levels, defining tactical goals and performing tactical planning. This level aims at medium term goals.
- *Operational or Low level*: is the basis of the organization and is related to the actual accomplishment of tasks. In this level, operational planning is performed to define the tasks to be done. This level aims at short term goals.

To accomplish strategic planning, one of the possible approaches is to use BSC - Balanced Score Card [10], a framework for describing strategy and managing its execution, linking goals, actions and indicators. BSC recommends an analysis based on performance indicators using four perspectives: (i) Financial; (ii) Customer; (iii) Internal Business Process; and (iv) Learning and Growth.

Aiming at aligning the efforts related to support business goals applied to the context of information technology (IT), COBIT - Control Objectives for Information Technology [11] was proposed. COBIT describes a set of generic business goals and a set of generic IT goals linked to business goals. Although COBIT is a synthesis of good practices about management, measurement and control of business and IT goals, it does not address specifically the software improvement.

Some researchers have investigated how to support and improve strategic planning. Huang [12] presents an integrated approach for the BSC and a knowledge-based system to support strategic planning. In [13] the MECIMPLAN is presented as a methodology to support strategic planning using agents to generate a list of the most possible scenarios, considering some events and their influence and probability.

To achieve what was established by strategic planning we have to implement the strategies at lower levels of the organization. This requires breaking down strategic planning into tactical planning that can be understood and enacted by the middle level [9]. In software organizations, some tactical goals can be related to software while others can be related to other issues like marketing, training and so on. The tactical goals that are related to software usually indicate the organization desires to improve its software processes and products. Thus, in this work, we are considering the tactical goals related to software as the software improvement goals.

Although tactical planning addresses strategic planning translation to the middle level, the actions defined on the tactical level aim at medium term goals. These actions still have to be more detailed to allow their execution on the operational level, which is the operational planning purpose. Sometimes, projects are utilized as a mean to achieve strategic plan of an organization [14]. Specifically in software organizations, operational level is frequently arranged in software projects. Therefore, operational planning usually becomes project planning.

In project planning, one of the first steps is to define project goals. Projects may have a wide variety of goals. They can also include cost, schedule, and quality requirements [14]. Project goals, as operational goals, provide the basis for measuring the progress toward meeting strategic goals [15].

In addition to identify the strategic, tactical and operational goals, it is important to plan how to monitor and control the defined goals. The measurement of a goal is a way to check whether it has been achieved or not [15]. In software organizations, the control of the goals depends on software measures. Thus, these organizations also need to plan how to measure their software processes and products.

An approach for software measurement is Goal Question Metric – GQM [16], which proposes to plan the measurement based on measurement goals. A variant of GQM is the Goal-Question-(Indicator)-Measure - GQ(I)M [17], a measurement method to guide the identification and definition of software measures to support business goals of the organization. This method defines ten steps to explicitly align software measures to business goals. Another software measurement approach is the GQM^{+} Strategies that provides mechanisms for explicitly linking software measurement goals, to higher-level goals for the software organization [18]. These software measurement approaches focus on measurement and they do not intend to guide the execution of strategic planning activities.

Monitoring and controlling the processes is crucial. However it can be difficult to effectively monitor process data, analyze current status, detect and diagnose process anomalies, or take appropriate actions to control the processes [19]. As mentioned earlier, SPC can be used as a mean to monitor software processes. However, SPC may bring some extra complexity to the context of strategically aligned software improvements, since some extra steps need to be performed in this case.

One of the possible ways to continuously monitor processes is to use agents. An agent is anything that can be viewed as perceiving its environment through sensors and acting upon that environment through effectors [20]. Huang et al. [7] propose an agent based system to support business performance monitoring and analysis. An agent based architecture to business performance monitoring is presented in [21].

Although there are several works that deal with strategic planning, goals monitoring, measurement planning and SPC, these works usually do not address these issues together. We believe that an integrated approach that deals with the definition of strategic, tactical and project goals, considering SPC and software measurement, also supporting the monitoring of the defined goals would be of great value for organizations aiming at addressing these questions.

3 Defining Strategically Aligned Software Improvement Goals

Before the definition of software improvement goals, an organization needs to perform its strategic planning, which will provide guidelines to define these goals in a way that they are aligned with business goals. Our approach defines a method that describes steps to plan and monitor the strategic, tactical and operational levels. The method starts on the strategic level, as shown in Fig. 1.

The characterization of the organization is necessary as a guide for the beginning of strategic planning, outlining the expected time period to perceive planning results, and defining the perspectives of the organization to be considered. In this step, the scope of planning and the intervals of short, medium and long term adopted for the organization, considering its specific characteristics are specified.

To make it easier to establish the right focus on critical areas of the organization, some perspectives which focus on specific issues and are interrelated can be defined, making it possible to address each critical area in a balanced way. In our method, the characterization of the organization includes the definition of important perspectives for the organization. As an example, organizations can use the perspectives suggested by BSC.

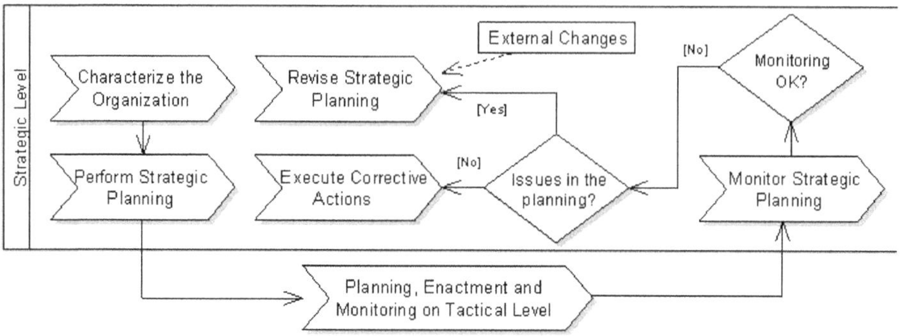

Fig. 1. Context of definition, monitoring and review strategic planning

The next step is to perform strategic planning followed by tactical and operational planning. In the following sections we describe our method considering each level, i.e. strategic, tactical and operational (project). Throughout the description, some examples based on real situations are presented.

3.1 Strategic Planning

In our approach, strategic planning is performed by eight steps, as Fig. 2 illustrates. The first step is the definition of the mission and the vision of the organization, which will guide the definition of strategic goals. The mission of an organization represents its overall purpose and the vision describes what it would like to be, considering a determined time period [9]. After that, the strategic goals and their indicators must be defined. To make it possible to focus on critical areas of the organization, each strategic goal must be related to one perspective, among those that were specifically defined for the organization. To assure balanced perspectives, there must be at least one strategic goal for each perspective defined to the organization.

The definition of a strategic goal must describe the following information: (i) Action: desired action, such as: increase, decrease, improve, maintain; (ii) Action target: what must be affected by the action, for example: revenue, client satisfaction, quality; (iii) Perspective: perspective to analyze the goal, such as financial. Table 1 shows some examples of strategic goals.

In addition to identify the strategic goals, it is important to plan how to continuously monitor them. Therefore, indicators must be identified and related to each strategic goal defined. To promote pro-active monitoring, the description of the indicators specifies the target in three ranges of values: (i) Acceptable range: values are considered within the target and there is no risk of deviation around; (ii) Risk range: values are considered within the target, however, they indicate some risk of deviation around (potential deviation); and (iii) Unacceptable range: values are considered out of the target, pointing a real deviation.

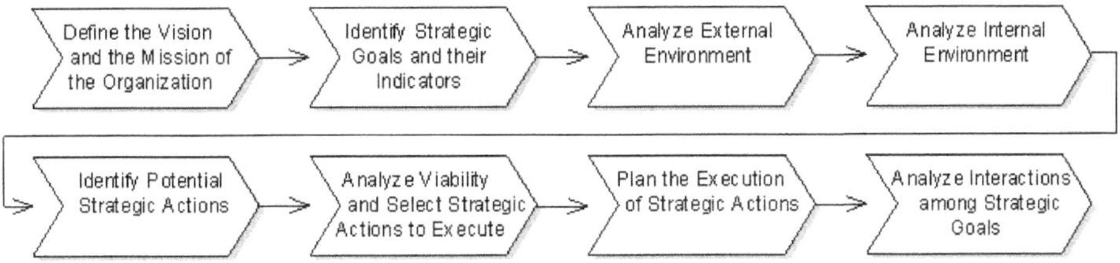

Fig. 2. Strategic planning steps

Depending on the defined indicator, it can be necessary to specify three targets considering the expected results in the short, medium and long term. These targets can be specified in an ad-hoc way, based on historical data or using simulation to identify possible values. A high maturity organization (i.e. the one that performs the practices required by higher levels of maturity models, like the CMMI-DEV) must specify these targets based on knowledge about its processes, acquired using SPC.

Table 1. Examples of strategic goals

Strategic Goals		
Action	**Action Target**	**Perspective**
Increase	Revenue	Financial
Increase	Client satisfaction	Client

To facilitate the achievement of strategic goals, it is important to analyze the internal and the external environments of the organization, identifying forces that can contribute or threaten their achievement. The analysis of external environment includes identifying factors or tendencies which are external to the organization and could represent threats or opportunities. Moreover, it is necessary to analyze possible impacts related to each factor: an impact can be positive, identifying an opportunity, or negative, identifying a threat. The analysis of internal environment includes an evaluation of its strengths and weaknesses based on the defined strategic goals.

Strategic goals aim at long term results. Thus it is necessary to decompose them into strategic actions that when executed, make it easier to achieve the strategic goals defined. Strategic actions must aim at achieving strategic goals increasing the opportunities and strengths identified and addressing the threats and weaknesses perceived in external and internal environments analysis. Potential strategic actions should be identified with the participation of professionals from the tactical level. The definition of a strategic action must describe the action, the expected value, the target of the action and the expected contribution for the related strategic goal. This definition must determine if the strategic action is related to software. Table 2 shows examples of these actions.

Table 2. Examples of strategic actions

Strategic Goal:		Improve client satisfaction		
Strategic Actions			**Contribution**	**Software Related**
Decrease	20%	Software products price	40%	Yes
Improve	-	Software products quality	30%	Yes
Decrease	15%	Time to market	20%	Yes
Improve	-	Client attendance	10%	No

After the identification of the strategic actions, it is necessary to analyze their viability and select those that will be executed. For each strategic action selected, it must be defined: (i) Its priority; (ii) Responsible: responsible for executing the action (tactical level); (iii) Resources: financial resources available for executing the action; (iv) Indicator: indicator related to the action monitoring.

To complete strategic planning, it is important to analyze the strategic goals defined, the strategic actions and the indicators to identify and document possible interactions among them. Each interaction among any goals defined in our method can be classified as a qualitative and direct interdependence, a qualitative and inverse interdependence or a quantitative interdependence.

3.2 Tactical Planning Aligned to Strategic Planning

In strategic planning, strategic actions are planned and the responsibility for their implementation is assigned to some professionals. In tactical level, on the other hand, these professionals perform tactical planning to execute the assigned strategic actions. Tactical planning guides operational planning. It can be monitored through the use of operational level execution and monitoring data. If any deviation is detected, an analysis must be performed to determine if it is necessary to execute corrective actions or if tactical planning has to be revised.

Tactical planning starts with the decomposition of the strategic actions into tactical goals. Fig. 3 shows the steps for tactical planning. Since the focus of this work is on software organizations, the method proposed by us details only the tactical goals that are related to software products or processes, what we name software improvement goals, as mentioned earlier. However, to allow adequate monitoring of strategic goals, it is also recommended to identify tactical goals not related to software and their monitoring indicators. A tactical goal not related to software is described as the action, the action target, the expected value, the expected contribution to the related strategic action, and the interactions with other goals.

Strategic actions related to software must be decomposed into software improvement goals. To make it easier to monitor software improvement goals and to allow a better visibility of the results, we propose the definition of medium term software improvement goals (from now on, MTSIG) and short term software improvement goals (from now on, STSIG). Each MTSIG has to be decomposed into STSIGs, which indicate nearer milestones in the way to achieve the MTSIG. From time to time, tactical planning needs have to be updated, and in these occasions, MTSIG could become STSIG. To illustrate, an organization could have as a MTSIG to adopt CMMI Level 3 practices, while adopting CMMI Level 2 practices could be one of its STSIG.

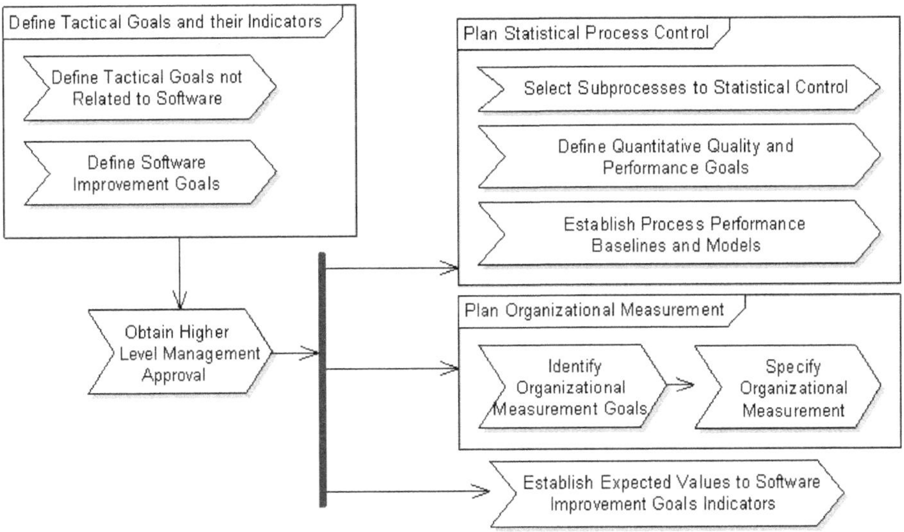

Fig. 3. Tactical planning steps

The definition of software improvement goals describes: the action, the expected value, the action target, the expected contribution to the strategic action related (if it is a MTSIG) or to the MTSIG (if it is a STSIG). The interactions with other goals are also described. Table 3 exemplifies two MTSIG. To allow the monitoring of the defined software improvement goals, indicators related to each goal are defined in the same way as the indicators related to strategic goals.

Table 3. Examples of medium term software improvement goals

Strategic Action:	Improve software products quality		
Medium Term Software Improvement Goals			
Action	**Value**	**Action Target**	**Contribution**
Deploy	-	CMMI level 3	40%
Decrease	10%	Defect density	60%

The definition of software improvement goals (considering MTSIG and STSIG) may involve important decisions to the organizations, which may need the approval from higher level management. Therefore, once the goals are defined it may be necessary to present them to higher level management to guarantee their approval and commitment. This step could be unnecessary, depending on the relationship among the different levels of the organizations, considering the autonomy of the tactical level and the participation of higher level management throughout the definition phase.

Once their software improvement goals are defined, an organization needs to plan SPC of its processes (if it is a requirement) and also plan the measurement initiative of the organization. Our method applies to organizations that want to statistically control its processes as well to the ones that want to use less formal ways of control, since it optionally supports software SPC planning as part of tactical planning.

SPC requires time and adds costs to the organization and, therefore, does not need to be applied to all software processes of the organization. Thus, this step starts with the selection of the subprocesses that are going to be statistically controlled. This selection must be based on the software improvement goals defined. Based on the selected subprocesses, it is necessary to identify the quantitative quality and performance goals of the organization and analyze the behavior of these subprocesses, considering these goals and also measurement data from the enactment of the subprocesses. This knowledge must be stored through the establishment of process performance baselines, that characterize real results previously obtained through the enactment of the processes, describing their expected behavior. It is also possible to define process performance models, which relate statistically controlled process attributes to try to forecast the process behavior.

Regardless of the adoption of SPC by the organization, the monitoring of each of the defined goals is strongly related to measurement data from projects and from the organization itself. However, if SPC is used, software measurement becomes even more critical. Therefore, organizational measurement planning is part of tactical planning, and is performed in parallel with SPC planning (if applicable).

The measurement planning step consists of identifying measurement goals from the short term software improvement goals and from the quantitative quality and performance goals, if available. Afterwards, it is necessary to specify organizational measurement, identifying and describing measures from the goals. Literature presents some approaches to derive measures from goals, such as GQM [16].

The monitoring of software improvement goals is done through the analysis of the indicators related to these goals, as described earlier. However, the expected values for these indicators have to be defined or updated in the last step of tactical planning, since SPC and measurement on the organization could influence these values. Thus, to complete tactical planning related to software, it is necessary to establish expected values to the indicators related to the software improvement goals.

3.3 Project Planning Aligned to Tactical Planning

On the operational level of software organizations, tactical planning guides the planning and execution of each software project. Each project is monitored, and if any deviation is detected, an analysis is done to determine if it is necessary to run corrective actions or if project planning has to be revised.

Our approach to project planning focuses on project goals, SPC and measurement as shown in Fig. 4. Therefore, the several other steps usually required to plan a project are not considered.

Each project has its unique characteristics that must be addressed. Thus, project planning begins characterizing the project. This step defines, among other kinds of information, the expected contribution of the project to the tactical goals, considering each project being run. This information is important to determine the achievement of tactical and strategic goals.

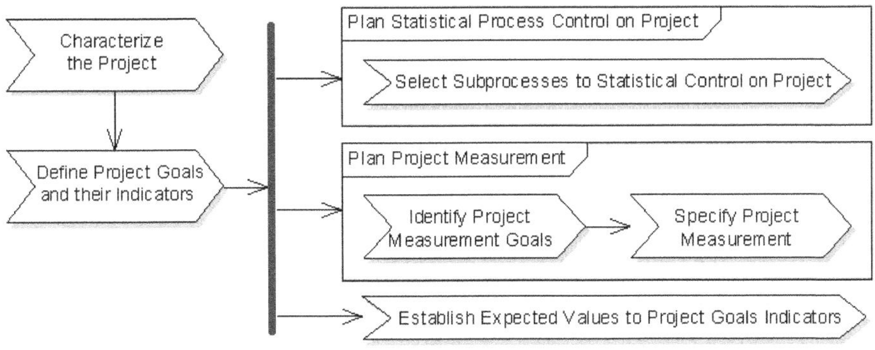

Fig. 4. Project planning steps

Once the project is characterized, it is necessary to define its goals, which are initially selected from short term software improvement goals (STSIG) and from quantitative quality and performance goals (if SPC was selected during tactical planning) that apply to the project. To assure project alignment to tactical planning, and therefore to strategic planning, it is common to consider all STSIG and quantitative quality and performance goals (if available) as project goals. If on very specific situations some of these goals do not apply to the project, it is necessary to document and justify this situation. An example of this situation is when the organization has some projects related to a specific software product and there is a STSIG which specifies the maximum response time for this product. This STSIG is not applicable to a project that is not related to this product.

Project goals definition also considers the needs of projects, their characteristics and constraints, as well as customer requirements. Thus, the analysis of these project specific kinds of information can lead to new project goals, regardless of the software improvement goals. Therefore, it is possible to assure that projects are going to implement the software improvement goals, but projects are not constrained by them. Each new project goal has to describe the action, the expected value, the action target, and the interactions with other project goals.

If the organization has adopted SPC and planned it on the tactical level, each project needs to plan how to statistically control processes throughout its enactment. SPC planning on a project consists of selecting subprocesses that will be statistically controlled on the project, based on quantitative quality and performance goals. This selection must be based on the subprocesses selected for SPC during tactical planning.

Regardless of the adoption of SPC by the project, the monitoring of each project goal is performed through measurement. Therefore, measurement planning of the project is part of project planning, and is performed in parallel with SPC planning (if applicable). The measurement planning step consists of identifying measurement goals from the project goals, identifying measures related to measurement goals, planning how to collect and analyze each measure, based on the measurement planning performed on tactical level.

To complete project planning, it is necessary to define or update the expected values for the indicators related to the project goals. At this point it is important to check the consistency among these expected values and the quantitative quality and performance goals considered on the project.

4 An Infrastructure to Monitor Software Improvement Goals

Throughout the enactment of projects, project goals must be continuously monitored aiming at detecting real or potential deviations. This information is also used to monitor goals that were defined on tactical and strategic levels. However, to continuously monitor the three levels at the same time can be very hard.

To support monitoring activities, our approach suggests an infrastructure to continuously and proactively monitor the defined goals. This infrastructure is based on agents and is capable of monitoring goals, searching for deviations and alerting whenever a real or potential deviation is detected. To do so, we have defined two agents: Indicators Update Agent and Deviation Detection and Notification Agent, as depicted in Fig. 5 and Fig. 6.

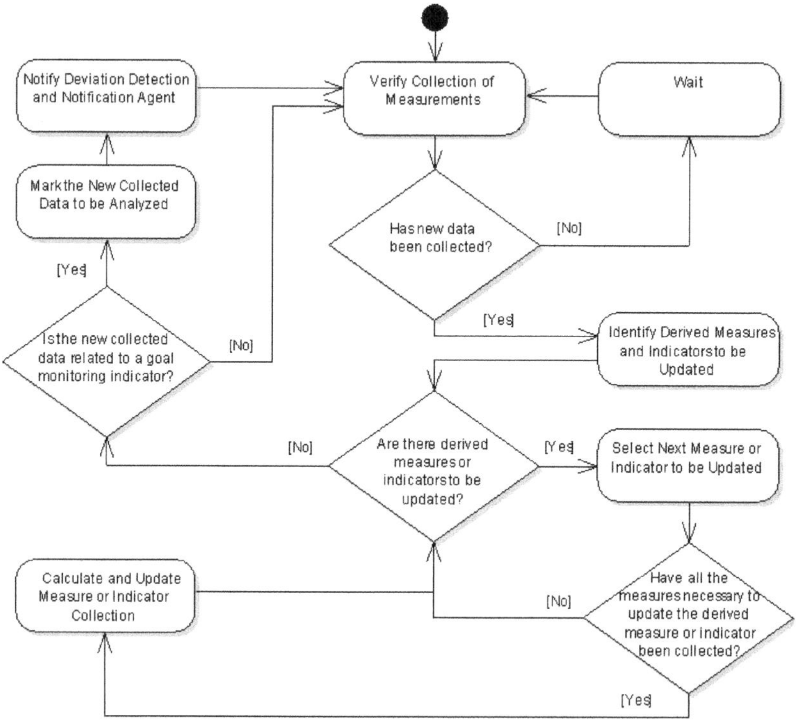

Fig. 5. Steps of the Indicators Update Agent

The monitoring of the goals defined on each level happens through the monitoring of the actual values of the indicators related to the goals. However, indicators are often measures derived from other ones. Thus, to be able to get an online updated monitoring of these indicators, it is necessary to continuously monitor the collection of new measures, to analyze if any indicator has to be updated (recalculated), and update it, if necessary. Likewise, the analysis and detection of deviations are accomplished through the collection of measures that are part of indicators related to goals. Thus, goals' monitoring begins by monitoring each measure collected.

The Indicators Update Agent is responsible for assessing the need to update indicators whenever new measurement data is collected, and then update them. Fig. 5 shows the steps performed by the Indicators Update Agent. The Deviation Detection and Notification Agent is responsible for analyzing each measure collection that affects indicators related to the defined goals, checking the occurrence of deviation and, whenever a deviation is detected, notifying the occurrence through an alert. The deviation checking consists of analyzing the data collected to compare it with the three ranges of values defined for the indicator (as defined in Section 3.1). If data is out of the acceptable range, a real or potential deviation occurred. The main steps performed by the Deviation Detection and Notification Agent are shown in Fig. 6. These agents and the related infrastructure are currently being implemented and will be fully functional in the near future. Once implementation is complete, we will be able to use them in real situations and properly evaluate their behavior.

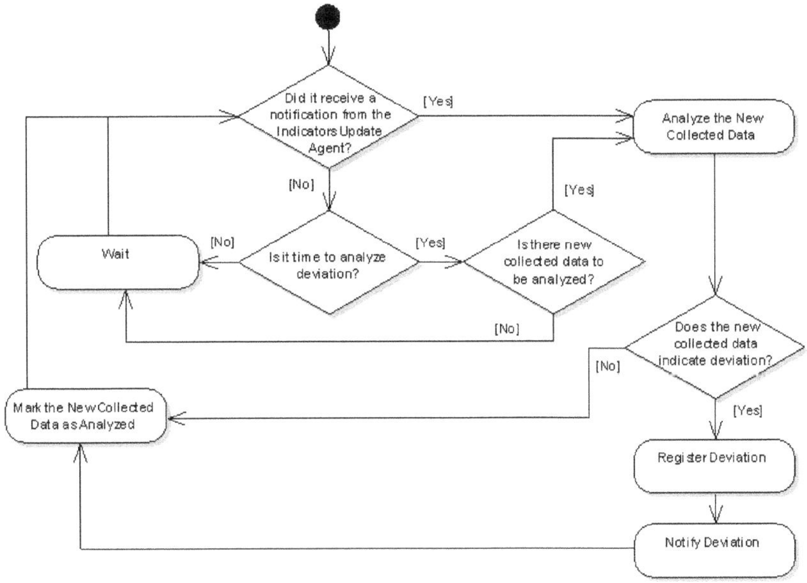

Fig. 6. Steps of the Deviation Detection and Notification Agent

5 Defining Software Improvement Goals at a Brazilian Software Development Organization

COPPE/UFRJ is one of the most important Software Engineering research and consulting centers in Brazil, located at Rio de Janeiro. Its Software Engineering initiatives are supported by the Software Engineering Laboratory – LENS (the acronym in

Portuguese), which develops software products aiming to aid these initiatives [22]. As a software organization, this laboratory was successfully appraised in accordance with the level E of MR-MPS model [3], a Brazilian reference model for software process improvement, compatible with CMMI-DEV [5]. Recently, our approach was used by LENS to accomplish its strategic and tactical planning.

We believe this experience was a great opportunity to evaluate parts of our approach. Subjects were all master or PhD students or professionals, but all of them were also working on industry initiatives. The group of subjects consisted of fourteen people and involved professionals that had never took part on strategic planning activities before as well as professionals that had already participated in different strategic planning efforts. The strategic and tactical level professionals accomplished some meetings at which each strategic planning step proposed by our approach was enacted. During this planning, five strategic goals, eight external factors, three strengths and two weaknesses were identified. Based on the external and internal analysis, eighteen strategic actions were planned. One of the defined strategic goals was "Achieve the level A of MR-MPS" model and one related strategic action defined was "Deploy new software processes required by the level A".

After performing strategic planning, as suggested by our method, we have performed tactical planning activities. It is important to mention that strategic level professionals also participated in this planning. The strategic actions which were related to software were decomposed into software improvement goals. However, we have observed that before planning statistical process control, it was necessary to address some specific issues identified throughout the strategic and tactical planning. Thus, the tactical planning was temporarily suspended and some action plans were defined to address these issues. It was interesting to realize that throughout strategic planning it was possible to identify issues that could threaten the achievement of the defined goals. Thus, before finishing this planning, strategic level professionals took some important decisions in order to address these issues and notified them to all organization.

To complete the study, a brief survey about the proposed approach was sent to all subjects of the study. We have reached 86% of answer rate. Subjects were asked about some aspects of our approach, such as: the expected benefits from the enactment of the strategic planning performed, the adequacy of the method used and the adequacy of the sequence of steps. The survey showed that the professionals expected good benefits from the enactment of the strategic planning accomplished. In regard of the proposed method, considering the opinion of the subjects, there is some indication that the sequence of steps is adequate. According to the subjects, the use of a method that guides the steps that need to be followed and the information that has to be provided, considering the specific context of a software organization, made it easier to accomplish strategic and tactical planning and guided the debate, avoiding waste of time. Some improvements to our approach were identified and they were already analyzed and deployed.

6 Conclusions

Software process improvement initiatives need to be aligned with the business goals of the organization. If these initiatives are performed in an organization without taking business goals into account, it is possible that the initiatives do not satisfy or even conflict with them.

In this paper we present an approach to define and monitor software improvement goals promoting strategic alignment. Our approach supports strategic, tactical and operational planning activities focusing on software processes and products. Measurement planning and statistical process control are addressed too. A method for strategic, tactical and operational planning is described and an infrastructure to support the monitoring of the defined goals across the three levels is presented.

Our method was partially used on a real context and brought several good results, guiding the strategic and tactical planning, promoting the software improvement alignment and avoiding waste of time. There is some expectative that the aspects addressed by our approach can help software organizations to achieve the expected software improvement benefits.

We intend to use our approach on other real contexts soon. We are also developing the infrastructure to continuously monitor the goals defined in the strategic, tactical and operational levels. We also intend to develop a tool to support the use of the method to make it easier to use the approach in others situations. Currently, we are performing a survey to characterize similarities among software projects. We believe this characterization will make it possible to compare similar deviation scenarios. Based on previous deviations, our infrastructure can monitor the project goals, recommend adequate actions to address detected deviations and propagate it to the upper levels.

References

1. Conradi, R., Fuggetta, A.: Improving Software Process Improvement. IEEE Software 19(4), 92–99 (2002)
2. Becker, A., Prikladnicki, R., Audy, J.: Strategic Alignment of Software Process Improvement Programs Using QFD. In: 1st International Workshop on Business Impact of Process Improvements, Leipzig, Germany, pp. 9–14 (2008)
3. SOFTEX: MPS.BR Official Web site (hosted by Association for Promoting the Brazilian Software Excellence - SOFTEX), `http://www.softex.br/mpsbr/_home/default.asp`
4. Rocha, A., Montoni, M., Santos, G., Oliveira, K., Natali, A., Mian, P., Conte, T., Mafra, S., Barreto, A., Albuquerque, A., Figueiredo, S., Soares, A., Bianchi, F., Cabral, R., Neto, A.: Success Factors and Difficulties in Software Process Deployment Experiences based on CMMI and MR-MPS.BR. In: 8th International Workshop on Learning Software Organizations, Rio de Janeiro, Brasil, pp. 77–87 (2006)
5. Chrissis, M.B., Konrad, M., Shrum, S.: CMMI: Guidelines for Process Integration and Product Improvement, 2nd edn. Addison-Wesley, Nova York (2006)
6. Dyba, T.: An Empirical Investigation of the Key Factors for Success in Software Process Improvement. IEEE Transactions on Software Engineering 31(5), 410–424 (2005)
7. Huang, P., Lei, H., Lim, L.: Real Time Business Performance Monitoring and Analysis Using Metric Network. In: IEEE International Conference on e-Business Engineering, Shanghai, China, pp. 442–449 (2006)
8. Mintzberg, H., Ahlstrand, B., Lampel, J.: Safári De Estratégia: Um Roteiro Pela Selva Do Planejamento Estratégico. Bookman, Porto Alegre (2000)

9. Chiavenato, I.: Administração: Teoria, Processo e Prática, 3rd edn. Makronbooks, São Paulo (2000)
10. Kaplan, R., Norton, D.P.: The Balanced Scorecard Translating Strategy Into Action. Havard Business School Press, Boston (1996)
11. IT Governance Institute: Control Objectives for Information and Related Technology, 4.1th edn., http://www.itgi.org
12. Huang, H.: Designing a knowledge-based system for strategic planning: A balanced scorecard perspective. Expert Systems with Applications 36, 209–218 (2009)
13. Castillo, J., Ossowski, S., Pastor, L.: The 'MECIMPLAN' approach to Agent-based Strategic Planning. In: International Conference on Web Intelligence and Intelligent Agent Technology, Hong Kong, China, pp. 540–543 (2006)
14. Project Management Institute: PMBOK - A Guide to the Project Management Body of Knowledge, 3rd edn., Newtown Square (2004)
15. Markovic, I., Kowalkiewicz, M.: Linking Business Goals to Process Models in Semantic Business Process Modeling. In: 12th International IEEE Enterprise Distributed Object Computing Conference, Munich, Germany, pp. 332–338 (2008)
16. Basili, V., Caldiera, G., Rombach, H.: Goal Question Metric Paradigm. Encyclopedia of Software Engineering 1, 528–532 (1994)
17. Park, R.E., Goethert, W.B., Florac, W.A.: Goal-Driven Software Measurement — A Guidebook. CMU/SEI-96-HB-002, Carnegie Mellon University (1996)
18. Basili, V., Heidrich, J., Lindvall, M., Münch, J.: GQM^+ Strategies - Aligning Business Strategies with Software Measurement. In: 1st International Symposium on Empirical Software Engineering and Measurement, Madrid, Spain, pp. 488–490 (2007)
19. Uraikul, V., Chan, C.W., Tontiwachwuthikul, P.: Artificial Intelligence for Monitoring and Supervisory Control of Process Systems. Engineering Applications of Artificial Intelligence 20(2), 115–131 (2007)
20. Russell, S., Norvig, P.: Artificial Intelligence: A Modern Approach, 2nd edn. Prentice Hall, Englewood Cliffs (2003)
21. Thomas, M., Redmond, R., Yoon, V., Singh, R.: A Semantic Approach to Monitor Business Process Performance. Communications of the ACM 48(12), 55–59 (2005)
22. Montoni, M., Santos, G., Rocha, A., Weber, K., Araújo, E.: MPS Model and TABA Workstation: Implementing Software Process Improvement Initiatives in Small Settings. In: 5th International Workshop on Software Quality, Minneapolis, USA, pp. 4–9 (2007)

A Strategy for Painless Harmonization of Quality Standards: A Real Case

Maria Teresa Baldassarre[1], Danilo Caivano[1], Francisco J. Pino[2], Mario Piattini[3], and Giuseppe Visaggio[1]

[1] Department of Informatics, University of Bari, SER&Practices SPINOFF
Via E. Orabona 4, 70126, Bari, Italy
{baldassarre,caivano,visaggio}@di.uniba.it
[2] IDIS Research Group University of Cauca,
Calle 5 # 4 – 70 Popayán, Colombia
fjpino@unicauca.edu.co
[3] University of Castilla-La Mancha,
Paseo de la Universidad, 4, 13071, Ciudad Real, Spain
Mario.Piattini@uclm.es

Abstract. Globalization, is pushing companies towards continuous improvement. Quality frameworks addressing SPI practices are classifiable in ones describing: "what" should be done (ISO9001,CMMI); "how" it should be done (Six Sigma, GQM). When organizations adopt improvement initiatives, many models may be implied, each leveraging best practices for addressing improvement challenges. This may generate confusion, extra effort and cost, as well as increase the risk of inefficiencies and redundancies. So, it is important to harmonize quality frameworks, i.e. identify intersections and overlapping parts and create a multi-model improvement solution. Our aim is to propose a Harmonization Process supporting organizations interested in introducing/improving SPI practices. We present: a *what/what* combination of ISO9001 and CMMI-DEVv.1.2 models in the direction from ISO-CMMI; and detail the *what/how* perspective by showing how GQM is used to define operational goals that address ISO9001 statements, reusable in CMMI appraisals. The harmonization process has been applied to a SME certified ISO9001:2000.

Keywords: Harmonization, Mapping, SPI, Multi-model Process Improvement, GQM, CMMI-DEV, ISO9001.

1 Introduction

The increasing rate of globalization, following to the competition of international markets, is pushing companies towards continuous innovation and improvement of processes and products. This asks for methods and approaches able to manage business processes, as well as processes for measuring and controlling quality.

As so, quality management and SPI in general become of strategic importance not only as internal factor for improvement, but also as success factor once a company decides to overlook the global market and interacts with contractors, suppliers and

M. Ali Babar, M. Vierimaa, and M. Oivo (Eds.): PROFES 2010, LNCS 6156, pp. 395–408, 2010.
© Springer-Verlag Berlin Heidelberg 2010

customers. In this scenario, SPI efforts are motivated by the need for achieving competitiveness advantage related to aspects like customer satisfaction, business profitability, market share, product and service quality, cost reduction and so on. Furthermore, the need for standardized quality management systems is important in a market where, from a few years this way, a lot of attention is being paid to the quality of products and services offered.

Literature offers numerous reference models, standards, best practices, technologies for addressing software process improvement practices. In general we can classify the frameworks into two groups: the ones that describe *what* should be done, like for example ISO 9001 [1] and CMMI [2], and the ones that describe *how* it should be done, just to cite a few: Six Sigma, Team Software Process [3], PMBOK [4], GQM [5], [6]. All offer unique features and address particular problems. In some cases they are discipline-oriented, others relate to the enterprise as a whole. When organizations decide to adopt improvement initiatives related to different organizational functions and different hierarchical levels, many models may be implied, each leveraging the best practices provided in order to address the improvement challenges in the best of ways. However, this may at the same time generate confusion and overlapping activities as well as extra effort and cost. This risks to generate a series of inefficiencies and redundancies that end up leading to losses rather than effective process improvement. Consequently, it is important to move towards a harmonization of quality frameworks in order to identify intersections and overlapping parts and create a multi model improvement solution.

A recent study [10] has pointed out that more and more product development organizations are tending towards multi-certifications with specific attention to ISO 9001, CMM and ITIL technology standards respectively. In Europe interest in multi-certifications has increased especially because in some sectors and in calls for bids, on behalf of government institutions and public administrations, they are compulsory and are explicitly requested. Our work focuses on ISO and CMMI. Although the two constellations have been developed independently and have different purposes they have intersections and connections with each other. In this sense our contribution is twofold:

- investigate to what extent the practices described in the CMMI-DEV and ISO 9001 models are related (i.e. what/what relation);
- how a certified organization implements its quality model by using a GQM-based approach (i.e. what/how relation).

Our Harmonization Process, presented in this work analyzes both these aspects, as well as applies them to real industrial data of an enterprise certified ISO 9001:2000.

More precisely, our aim in this work is to propose a harmonization process that supports organizations interested in introducing or improving their practices for quality management and software development. In this sense and considering that mapping is one of the most widely used specific strategies for the harmonization of models [11], we present a *what/what* combination of ISO 9001 and CMMI-DEV v.1.2 models, in the direction from ISO to CMMI, as well as an application of the comparison to an Italian SME providing detail on the what/how perspective by combining ISO 9001 & GQM, i.e. how measurement goals are defined to operationally address ISO statements in order to be possibly reused in a CMMI appraisal.

The rest of the paper is organized as follows: Section 2 provides a quick overview of the frameworks considered (ISO 9001:2000, CMMI DEV v.1.2, GQM) and then presents the related works from other research works. Section 3 outlines the Harmonization Process which is described with respect to the comparison and application sub-processes. Each step of the process is described with respect to the outcomes of an application to a real case. Finally conclusions are drawn.

2 Background

In this section, we first of all outline a general view of ISO 9001:2000 and CMMI DEV v.1.2 and then we present the related works from other research.

2.1 ISO 9001:2000 and CMMI v.1.2 Overview

Next will provide some general and synthetic information to the reader on the three quality models that we have considered in our work.

ISO 9001:2000

ISO 9001:2000 is an international standard that gives requirements for an organization's Quality Management System ("QMS"). It is part of a family of standards published by the International Organisation for Standardisation ("ISO") often referred to collectively as the "ISO 9000 series". A process model based on the QMS is shown in figure 1. The objective of ISO 9001:2000 is to provide a set of requirements that, if effectively implemented, will provide the organization with confidence that they can provide goods and services that: meet needs and expectations and comply with applicable regulations. The requirements cover a wide range of topics, including supplier's top management commitment to quality, its customer focus, adequacy of its resources, employee competence, process management, quality planning, product design, review of incoming orders, purchasing, monitoring and measurement of its processes and products, calibration of measuring equipment, processes to resolve customer complaints, corrective/preventive actions and a requirement to drive continual improvement of the QMS.

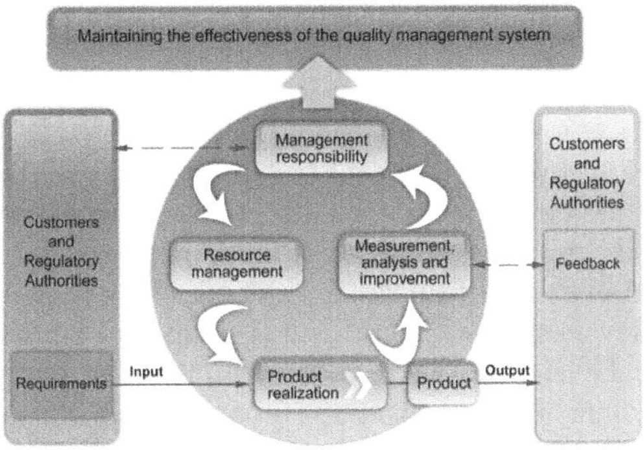

Fig. 1. Model of a process based QMS

CMMI

Capability Maturity Model Integration (CMMI) is a process improvement approach that provides organizations with the essential elements of effective processes that ultimately improve their performance. Developed by a group of experts from industry, government, and the Software Engineering Institute (SEI) at Carnegie Mellon University, CMMI models provide guidance for developing or improving processes that meet the business goals of an organization. It can be used to guide process improvement across a project, a division, or an entire organization [12]. An organization cannot be certified in CMMI; instead, an organization is appraised. Appraisals are typically conducted for one or more of the following reasons: to determine how well the organization's processes compare to CMMI best practices, and to identify areas where improvement can be made; to inform external customers and suppliers of how well the organization's processes compare to CMMI best practices; to meet the contractual requirements of one or more customers.

Level	*Continuous Representation Capability Levels*	*Staged Representation Maturity Levels*
Level 0	Incomplete	N/A
Level 1	Performed	Initial
Level 2	Managed	Managed
Level 3	Defined	Defined
Level 4	Quantitatively Managed	Quantitatively Managed
Level 5	Optimizing	Optimizing

Fig. 2. Comparison of Continuous and Staged Representation Levels

Depending on the type of appraisal, the organization can be awarded a maturity level (Staged Representation) rating (1-5) or a capability level achievement profile (Continuous Representation). Figure 2 summarizes both representations in levels.

Goal Question Metrics (GQM)

The main idea behind GQM is that measurement should be goal-oriented and based on context characterization.

According to [5], [25], the measurement model has three levels (figure 3):

- Conceptual Level (GOAL): a goal is defined for a specific purpose based on the needs of the organization, for a variety of reasons, with respect to various quality models, from various points of view, in a particular environment.
- Operational Level (QUESTION): a set of questions is used to characterize the way the achievement of a specific goal is going to be performed.
- Quantitative Level (METRIC): a set of collectable data is associated with every question in order to quantitatively answer them.

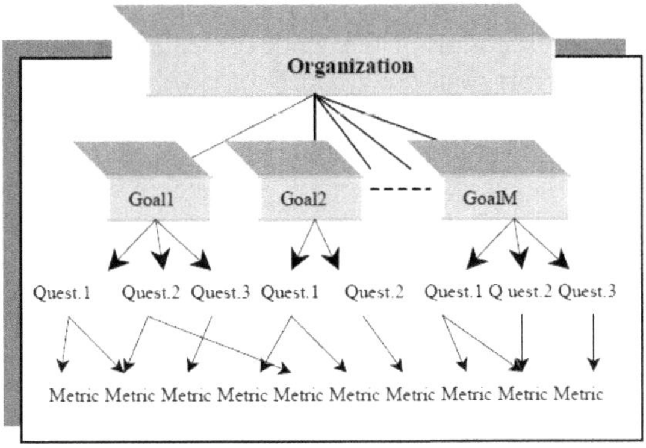

Fig. 3. Goal Question Metrics Structure

In the interpretation phase, measurements are used to answer the questions and to conclude whether or not the goal is achieved. Thus, GQM uses a top-down approach to define metrics and a bottom-up approach for analysis and interpretation of measurement data. GQM defines a dynamic quality model on which basing an effective measurement program. Quality goals reflect the business strategy and GQM is used to identify and refine goals based on the characteristics of software processes, products and quality perspectives of interest.

2.2 Related Works

Although the number of related works on the harmonization of multiple models is small, in the last 4 years there is within the software engineering community an ever-increasing interest in defining solutions for this type of environments. This is evidenced by the initiatives and projects performed or being carried out, such as: PrIME project [16], ARMONÍAS project [17], Enterprise SPICE [18]. Furthermore, some experiences reported in literature involve comparisons and mapping between different versions of CMMI and other processes models, including ISO 9001. Among these, some relate to what/what combinations such as CMMI & ISO; more precisely:

- A mapping between two models is described in [19].
- In [7] a proposal that integrates the content of these two models is introduced.
- A proposal for transiting from ISO 9001 to SW-CMM is defined in [8]
- In [9] a comparison and a correspondence between ISO 9001 and SW-CMM are shown.
- In [20] an recent comparative analysis of the CMMI DEV v.1.2 and the ISO 9000 family is discussed.
- An ontology for the integration of these quality standards for collaborative projects is show in [21].
- Some works that involve relationships, comparisons and mapping between different versions of CMM(I) and SPICE (ISO/IEC 15504) can be found in [15], [22], [23], [24].

However, in all these comparisons none of the studies refer to the latest versions of these models (with the exception of the work presented in [20]); none describe the specific process used to carry out the comparison and/or mapping. Consequently the approach is not replicable from others. They are all theoretical works and none have been applied to real enterprise data. Furthermore, no insight is given on the what/how perspective. None of the studies adopt or indicate a strategy used for defining the measurement goals with the aim of harmonizing the models. The contribution of the proposal described in this paper consists in taking into account and addressing the issues above in order to provide organizations a specific stepwise strategy for harmonizing quality standards.

3 Harmonization Process

Any organization that have a software process improvement (SPI) strategy follow it as a means for assessing and assuring quality. They will most likely have their business, organizational and production processes formalized in some way. The processes can be formally defined and conform to some kind of SPI framework (CMMI; ISO, TQM, SPIQ, etc.) [13], or can be informally defined based on the previous history and experience of the organization. Independently of the framework adopted, the description of the processes contain details on the: activities, procedures, products produced, relations with other activities, tools and technologies used to execute them; the quality model (i.e. goals, metrics and interpretations) defined to assess the achievement of desired quality levels. In this sense, the quality model must be structured so that its goals (G_i) relate to specific process model grains (P_j) specified by the SPI framework referred to (eg. Process areas for CMMI, statements for ISO 9001, etc.), forming a matrix [GxP] (Table 1) where each crossing (G_i, P_j) means that the goal G_i measures that process grain P_j.[5].

Table 1. Goal x Process Model matrix

GOALS	Process Grain				
	P_1	P_2	P_j	...	P_n
G_1	X				
G_2		X			
G_i			X		X
...					
G_k	X		X		

In this scenario it is reasonable that an organization with an organized SPI strategy may to want to or have to conform to other frameworks due to explicit requests on behalf of contractors, public administrations or restrictions in bids. For simplicity, let us define the process model of the current SPI framework $P_{Current}$, and the process model of the new SPI framework the organization wants to conform to as P_{Target}. An interesting question is therefore: How can an organization painlessly shift from $P_{Current}$ to P_{Target} and reuse as much possible of the information produced in $P_{Current}$? Given an SPI framework (eg. ISO or CMMI), how can an organization operationally define a quality model (i.e. measurement goals and interpretation models) for it?

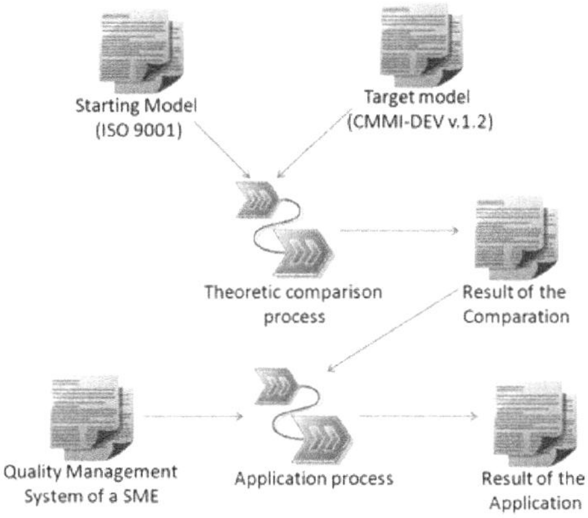

Fig. 4. Harmonization Process

To answer these two questions we have defined a Harmonization Process made up of two sub-processes: a comparison process and an application process. The process is general and can be instantiated to any couple of SPI frameworks ($P_{Current,}$ P_{Target}). In this specific work, we have considered $P_{Current}$: ISO 9001:2000 and P_{Target}: CMMI-Dev A general representation is given in Figure 4. This section will primarily focus on the application sub-process, as the comparison one has been described more in detail in a previous work [14]. In the next two sections we will provide a description of the two processes, with more detail on the application process.

3.1 Comparison Sub-Process

The Comparison Sub-Process is the first part of the harmonization of any two SPI frameworks. This activity followed the process for mapping described in [15]. In this specific case, the comparison process considers the ISO 9001:2000 standard as starting point, i.e. supposing that an enterprise is currently certified ISO 9001, and sees CMMI v1.2 as the target one. The outcome of this sub-process is a document that maps the two models and points out the relations between them, i.e. in this specific case, the extent to which ISO satisfies CMMI requirements and whether there are any overlapping areas that possibly allow to reuse information and data collected in the ISO certification to assess any of the CMMI levels, allowing for a quantitative analysis (*what/what* comparison). The mapping is tracked on a spreadsheet having the ISO statements as rows and CMMI Process Areas with detailed Practices as columns. The overlapping areas are filled with colour. An extract related to the ISO statement "4. Quality Management System" and CMMI process area "Organizational Process Definition + IPPD" is shown in Figure 5. The mapping criteria was iterated for each statement, one at a time, with respect to every process area.

This sub-process steps have been completely described in more detail in a previous work by the authors [14]. For completeness sake we have however provided a brief description to give the reader a general picture of the approach and better understand the application sub-process. The approach is general and stepwise. So if the SPI standards change, the instantiations change, but the approach remains the same.

The outcome of the mapping is a document (Result of Comparison) that specifies the correlations between the two models traced on the spreadsheet, i.e. the intersections of the ISO 9001 statements with the specific practices of CMMI process areas together with their degree of relation. . The degree of relationship indicates the extent to which an ISO 9001 statement supports, or has any connection with, a Process area of CMMI. This expresses a one-to-one relationship. In order to express the degree of relationship between an ISO 9001 statement and a CMMI Process area, we have defined a discrete scale (scale of comparison) when each of the elements of the scale has been associated with a set of numeric values which are described in terms of percentage. This scale is made up of the following elements: Strongly related (86% to 100%), Largely related (51% to 85%), Partially related (16% to 50%), Weakly related (1% to 15%) and Non-related (0%). The numeric values can be found by dividing the number of specific practices (from a Process area of CMMI) that are related to shall statements (from ISO 9001) by the total number of specific practices defined in that Process area. For this work, it is important to highlight that this numeric value is only indicative of the extent to which a process area of CMMI is addressed by means of the statements of ISO 9001. The degree of relationship is hence expressed only through the discrete scale. So, the blue indicate correlations/intersections between the areas. For each area, a degree of relation is quantified.

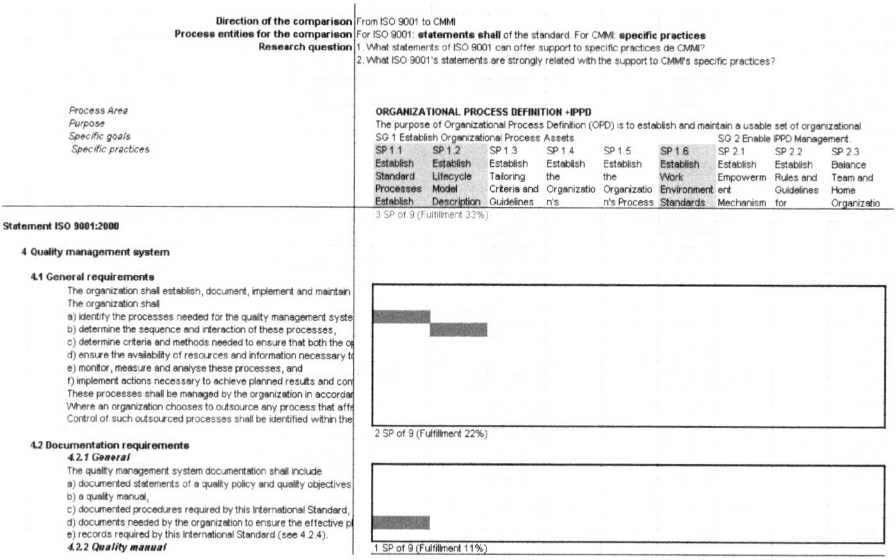

Fig. 5. Extract of results for the comparison sub-process

3.2 Application Sub-Process

If the comparison sub-process points out the overlapping common areas between the two SPI frameworks, and therefore provides a what/what perspective, instantiated in this case on ISO 9001 and CMMI, the application sub-process applies the comparison results to a specific organization's Quality Management System (QMS).

Indeed, if an organization certified, lets say ISO 9001 intends addressing CMMI, it would be worth investigating what part of the data and information collected with the ISO standard could be reused for a CMMI appraisal. This is done by formalizing a GQM-based quality model and then, according to the overlapping areas, reusing the data/information related to the intersections. More precisely, this part of the process defines how to structure a quality model, through operational goals, based on the mapping results and in accordance to the organization's QMS, and provides a what/how perspective by tracing ISO 9001:2000 with GQM.

The steps of the application sub-process are represented in figure 6.

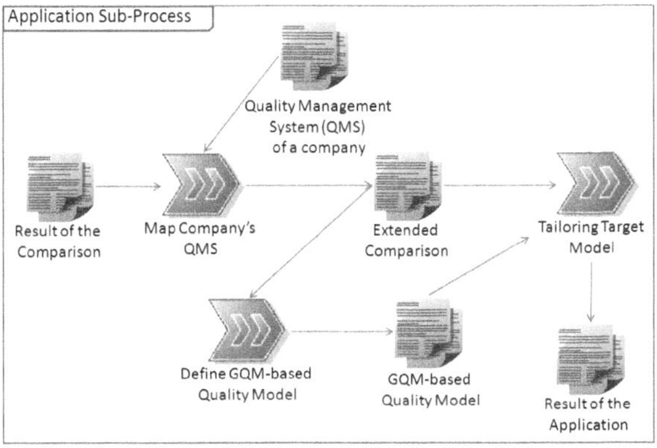

Fig. 6. Application Sub-Process

In the following, we will describe each of the three steps that make up the sub-process and provide evidence on their application to the data of an Italian SME. The company involved in the application operates in the ICT sector that for privacy reasons will be referred to as SME. It is certified ISO 9001:2000, other than having other certifications of the ISO family. The company allowed us to access their entire QMS which is structured conformingly to the chapters of the standard. For the case study, we simulated their intention to certify their processes according to CMMI levels.

Map Company's QMS

This step starts from the outcome of the comparison sub-process, i.e. the theoretical mapping of the two frameworks. Moreover, it consists in extracting the relevant documents from the QMS, based on the relations pointed out in the general comparison, in order to identify the specific documents, procedures, guidelines, templates and operational instructions that can be used in the future CMMI-DEV quality model.

The result of this step is an extension of the comparison (Extended Comparison), which not only contains the mapping of the two SPI frameworks, ISO 9001 and CMMI, but with respect to each relation identified, it also explicitly specifies the documents of the QMS. An example is shown in figure 7.

The two columns added are: *SME's QMS*, which contains the references to the paragraphs of the QMS, and *SME's Procedures*, which refers to the procedures, through links. This was done for each ISO statement having relations with a CMMI process area. This step is important because the references can be reused when the SME decides to shift to the target SPI framework, i.e. CMMI, and must define the target quality model. The question this step answers is: "How are the ISO 9001 statements, which are mapped with CMMI specific practices, traced in the SME's Quality Manual and other procedures?"

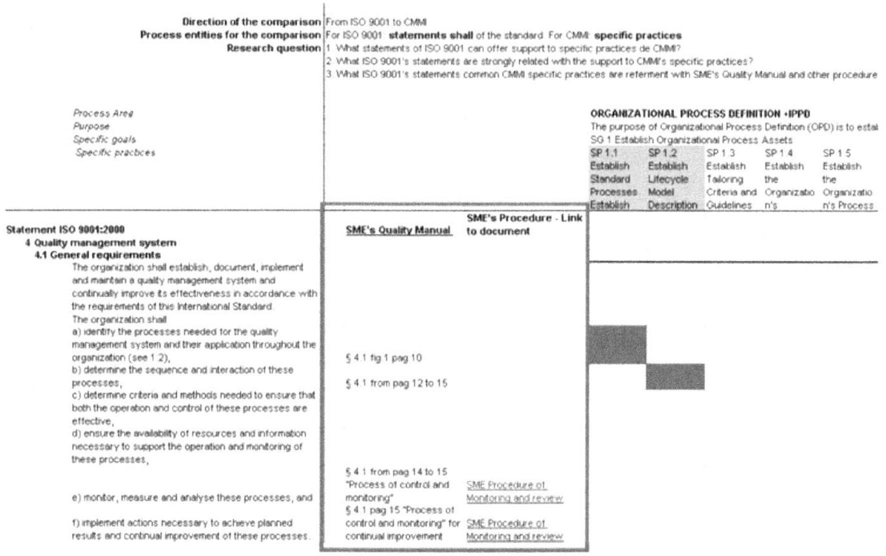

Fig. 7. Extended Comparison

Define GQM-Based Quality Model

The second step of the sub-process consists in defining a quality model. This is done by adopting a GQM-based approach [5], [25], according to the output of the previous step. Moreover, analyze the QMS documentation traced in the extended comparison, in depth, and define measurement goals based on the mapped areas. As so, the quality model produced allows to quantitatively measure the organization's processes with respect to the mapped areas.

This step provides insight on the what/how perspective mentioned in the previous sections, in that it shows how to operatively produce a quality model by instantiating ISO 9001 statements (what to do) through measurement goals (how to do it).

The result of this step is a matrix like the one in table 1, where the process $P_{Current}$ is ISO 9001, and the process grains are the ISO statements, while the Goals are the GQM measurement goals related to each statement. In Table 2 we show an example of a measurement goal, with questions and metrics defined for the ISO Shall Statement n.4.1. In our real case study, the procedure was iterated for each statement of the framework to obtain a complete quality model for all the ISO statements. The question this step answers is: "Given an ISO Statement, how can the related SME's QMS and Procedures be measured through operational GQM goals?"

This information is then used to evaluate the degree of coverage of the CMMI practices with respect to each "shall statement".

Table 2. Goal for ISO Shall Statement 4.1

Statement ISO 9000:2001		4.1 General requirements a) identify the processes needed for the quality management system and their application throughout the organization
		Goal 1
Object of study		Management Manual (Quality management system)
Purpose		Evaluate
Quality Focus		defined processes' correctness
Point of view		Management
Context		Italian SME
Question	*Metric*	*Description*
Q1.1	M1.1.1	List of processes expected for the quality management system
Q1.2	M1.2.1	List of processes for the quality management system really runned
Q1.3	M1.3.1	Level of adhesion of defined processes to the standard normative
Q1.4	M1.4.1	Level of completeness of defined processes for the quality management system
Q1.5	M1.5.1	Level expected of adhesion of defined processes to the standard normative
Q1.6	M1.6.1	Level expected of defined processes for quality management system

Tailoring Towards the Target Model

The last step of the sub-process collects the results of the previous steps and organizes them according to the practices of CMMI-DEV. It consists in identifying to what extent the CMMI-DEV process areas are covered by the ISO statements, based on the measurement goals (GQM-Based QM) defined in the previous step and the mapping applied to the SME (Extended Comparison). Given a Process Area (eg. Organizational Process Definition + IPPD), the goals that relate to that process area are identified. These goals are extracted from the previous step based on the mapping results with the ISO Statements. Next, a similar activity is done with respect to the work products and sub-practices of the process area considered. In other words, for each work product and sub-practice, we evaluate their degree of coverage with respect to the SME's QMS. Figure 8 reports the result of the step with respect to the Organizational Process Definition + IPPD process area. For each Specific Practice, the goals of the ISO quality model that can be reused in CMMI assessment are specified; for each work product and sub-practice the coverage is highlighted in color, together with a specification of the document in the SME's QMS.

In this way, we assure that the migration towards the target model (P_{target}), CMMI, reuses as much as possible of what is already defined in the current model ($P_{current}$). This time the step produces a matrix like the one in table 1, where the process grains are the specific practices of the CMMI Process Areas and the goals are the GQM-based measurement goals reused from the quality model defined in the previous step. The matrix of the target model is obtained as follows: $[G \times P_{target}] = [G \times P_{current}] \times [P_{current} \times P_{target}]$, where $[G \times P_{current}]$ is the set of goals for each ISO statement, and $[P_{current} \times P_{target}]$ is the mapping between ISO and CMMI. In our application, the completeness of the target model matrix indicates the degree of coverage of the CMMI-DEV with respect to ISO. Although, the matrix is not complete for the areas that are not mapped and for those that are not related, it assures that the existing quality model is reused as much as possible.

ORGANIZATIONAL PROCESS DEFINITION +IPPD

The purpose of Organizational Process Definition (OPD) is to establish and maintain a usable se

SG 1 Establish Organizational Process Assets

	SP 1.1 Establish Standard Processes Establish and maintain the organization's set of standard processes.		SP 1.2 Establish Lifecycle Model Descriptions Establish and maintain descriptions of the lifecycle models approved for use in the organization.		SP 1.3 Establish Tailoring Criteria and Guidelines
	Work Product 1. Organization's set of standard processes	Subpractice 1. Decompose each standard process into constituent	Work Product 1. Descriptions of lifecycle models	Subpractice 1. Select lifecycle models based on the needs of projects and the	
Statement	4.1 a) Goal 1 4.2.1 d) Goal 7 4.2.2 b) Goal 8 5.3 a) Goal 2 5.3 e) Goal 4 7.1 the Goal 1 7.1 Planning Goal 2		4.1 b) Goal 2		
Work Product	1. Organization's	$ 4.1 fig 1pag 10	1. Descriptions of lif	CASQPRG	
Subpractice	1. Decompose each 2. Specify the critica 3. Specify the relatic 4. Ensure that the o 5. Ensure that the o 6. Ensure that there 7. Document the or 8. Conduct peer rev 9. Revise the organi	§ 4.2.1 fig. 2 pag. 16 $4.1 fig.1 pag 10 $4.1 fig.1 pag 10 $4.1 fig.1 pag 10 CASQMOR CASQMOR	1. Select lifecycle mc 2. Document the de 3. Conduct peer rev 4. Revise the descri	 CASQPRG CASQPRG	

Fig. 8. Coverage of CMMI Process Area from ISO Statements

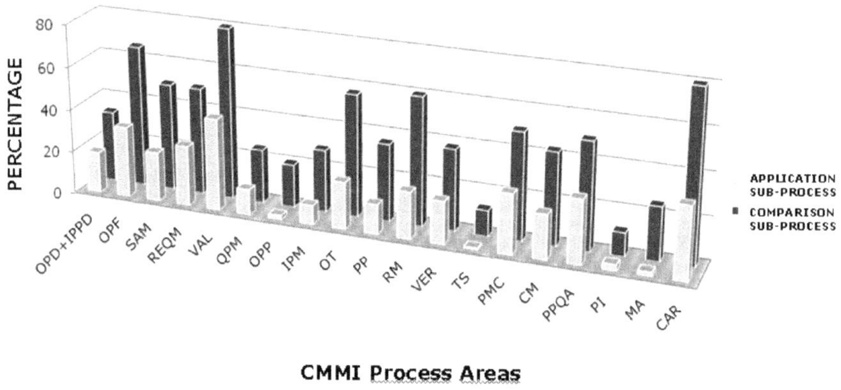

Fig. 9. Degree of Coverage of CMMI Process Areas

For space reasons we are not able to show the results of every single process area. We have provided a general picture, i.e. the overall results of the application process to the Italian SME, shown in Figure 9. The results are shown with respect to the comparison sub-process, which represents the theoretical mapping of the two SPI frameworks; and the application sub-process, where the comparison was applied to the QMS of a real enterprise.

As it can be seen, the percentages related to the Process Areas in the application sub-process are lower than the ones defined in the comparison one. This was predictable because the application not only considers the theoretic comparison but also how it is actually accomplished within the enterprise. These results relate to the QMS of the Italian SME considered, and therefore represent a first application of the harmonization process in the direction from ISO to CMMI.

4 Conclusions

In this paper we have presented a harmonization process of two SPI frameworks: ISO 9001:2000 and CMMI-DEV v1.2, by mapping the models and identifying overlapping areas in the direction from ISO to CMMI. Furthermore the general results of the mapping have been applied and instantiated to a real case, i.e. a QMS of an enterprise. This has also provided some insight on the differences between the theoretical comparison, carried out based on the documentation available from the SPI institutions, and the application sub-process in which the instantiated documentation to the real QMS has been considered.

Such harmonization can help an organization to: (i) understand both the differentiating and the overlapping features of the improvement models, and (ii) determine and understand which of these improvement models can support the organization's mission. Carry out cost/benefit analysis before transiting to a new quality standard.

The application of the harmonization process to the QMS of an ISO 9001 certified company QMS represents a first validation. Indeed, the relations pointed out by the mapping of the two frameworks are the starting point for applying the harmonization and identify the existing data of the organization that can be reused for appraising CMMI levels.

For what concerns the theoretical comparison, this work is limited to the viewpoint from ISO to CMMI, and therefore represents only half of the complete picture. Moreover, the application process data relates to a small enterprise so, this may also be the reason for such differences for the degree of coverage between the application and theoretical sub processes. As so, other applications will be necessary with refer to various types of certified organizations of various dimensions.

Currently we have applied the application process to a large enterprise, we are analyzing the data. We expect, for example, that in the large enterprise the comparison and application sub-processes have similar coverage percentages.

References

1. ISO, ISO 9001:2000. Quality management systems-Requirements. International Organization for Standardization: Geneva (2000)
2. SEI, CMMI for Develpment, Version 1.2. Technical Report CMU/SEI-2006-TR-008. Software Engineering Institute (SEI): Pittsburgh (2006)
3. Humphrey, W.S.: TSP(SM): Coaching Development Teams. Addison Wesley, Reading (2006)
4. Project Management Institute.: A Guide to the Project Management Body of Knowledge. Pmbok Guide, 4th edn. (2009) ISBN: 978-1933890517
5. Ardimento, P., Baldassarre, M.T., Caivano, D., Visaggio, G.: Multiview framework for goal oriented measurement plan design. In: Bomarius, F., Iida, H. (eds.) PROFES 2004. LNCS, vol. 3009, pp. 159–173. Springer, Heidelberg (2004)

6. Basili, V.R., Caldiera, G., Rombach, H.D.: Goal Question Metric Paradigm. Encyclopedia of Software Engineering, vol. 1, pp. 528–532. John Wiley & Sons, Chichester (1994)
7. Yoo, C., Yoon, J., Lee, B., Lee, C., Lee, J., Hyun, S., Wu, C.: A unified model for the implementation of both ISO 9001:2000 and CMMI by ISO-certified organizations. Journal of Systems and Software 79(7), 954–961 (2006)
8. Jalote, P.: CMM in Practice: Processes for Executing Projects. Addison-Wesley, Reading (1999)
9. Paulk, M.C.: A Comparison of ISO 9001 and the capability maturity model for software (CMU/SEI-94-TR-12). Software Engineering Institute (1994)
10. Violino, B.: Frameworks Boost Business Efficiency. Optimize Magazine 4(3), 68–70 (2005)
11. SEI: Process Improvement in Multimodel Environments (PrIME Project) (2008), http://www.sei.cmu.edu/prime/primedesc.html
12. Godfrey, S.: What is CMMI? NASA presentation (December 2008), http://software.gsfc.nasa.gov/docs/What%20is%20CMMI.ppt
13. Halvorsen, C.P., Conradi, R.: A Taxonomy to Compare SPI Frameworks. In: Ambriola, V. (ed.) EWSPT 2001. LNCS, vol. 2077, pp. 217–235. Springer, Heidelberg (2001)
14. Baldassarre, M.T., Caivano., D., Pino, F.J., Piattini, M., Visaggio, G.: A strategy to harmonize ISO/IEC 9001:2000 and CMMI-DEV. In: Proc.of the 4th Int.Workshop on Software Quality and Maintainability, Madrid, Spain (to appear, March 2010)
15. Pino, F., Baldassarre, M.T., Piattini, M., Visaggio, G.: Harmonizing maturity levels from CMMI-DEV and ISO/IEC 15504. Software Process: Improvement and Practice 10.1002/spip.437 (online) (September 2009)
16. Siviy, J., Kirwan, P., Marino, L., Morley, J.: The Value of Harmonization Multiple Improvement Technologies: A Process Improvement Professional's View. Software Engineering Institute, Carnegie Mellon (2008)
17. ARMONÍAS: A Process for Driving Multi-models Harmonization, ARMONÍAS Project (2009), http://alarcos.esi.uclm.es/armonias/
18. SPICE. Enterprise SPICE. An enterprise integrated standards-base model (2008), http://www.enterprisespice.com/
19. Mutafelija, B., Stromber, H.: ISO 9001:2000-CMMI V1.1 Mappings. Software Engineering Institute - SEI, 1–31 (2003)
20. Kitson, D.H., Vickroy, R., Walz, J., Wynn, D.: An Initial Comparative Analysis of the CMMI Version 1.2 Development Constellation and the ISO 9000 Family. SEI (2009)
21. Ferchichi, A., Bigand, M., Lefebvre, H.: An Ontology for Quality Standards Integration in Software Collaborative Projects. In: 1st International Workshop on Model Driven Interoperability for Sustainable Information Systems (MDISIS 2008), France (2008)
22. Lepasaar, M., Mäkinen, T., Varkoi, T.: Structural comparison of SPICE and continuous CMMI. In: SPICE 2002, Venicia, Italia, pp. 223–234 (2002)
23. Wangenheim, C.G., Thiry, M.: Analysing the Integration of ISO/IEC 15504 and CMMI-SE/SW. Technical Report LPQS001.05E, UNIVALI: Sao José/SC, Brazil, p. 28 (2008)
24. Rout, T., Tuffley, A.: Harmonizing ISO/IEC 15504 and CMMI. Software Process: Improvement and Practice 12(4), 361–371 (2007)
25. Basili, V.R., Caldiera, G., Rombach, H.D.: Goal Question Metric Paradigm. Encyclopedia of Software Engineering, vol. 1, pp. 528–532. John Wiley & Sons, Chichester (1994)

Author Index

GPSR Compliance

The European Union's (EU) General Product Safety Regulation (GPSR) is a set of rules that requires consumer products to be safe and our obligations to ensure this.

If you have any concerns about our products, you can contact us on ProductSafety@springernature.com

In case Publisher is established outside the EU, the EU authorized representative is:

Springer Nature Customer Service Center GmbH
Europaplatz 3
69115 Heidelberg, Germany

Batch number: 10682617

Printed by Printforce, the Netherlands